Canada's Residential Schools:
# The Legacy

The Final Report of the
Truth and Reconciliation
Commission of Canada

Volume 5

Truth and
Reconciliation
Commission of Canada

# Canada's Residential Schools

Volume 5

# Canada's Residential Schools:
## The Legacy

The Final Report of the
Truth and Reconciliation
Commission of Canada

Volume 5

2015

Truth and Reconciliation Commission of Canada

Website: www.trc.ca


An index to this volume of the final report is available online. Please visit http://nctr.ca/trc_reports.php


Library and Archives Canada Cataloguing in Publication
Truth and Reconciliation Commission of Canada
[Canada's residential schools]
     Canada's residential schools : the final report of the Truth and Reconciliation Commission of Canada.

(McGill-Queen's Native and northern series ; 80–86)
Includes bibliographical references and index.
Contents: v. 1. The history. Part 1, origins to 1939 — The history. Part 2, 1939 to 2000 — v. 2. The Inuit and
     northern experience — v. 3. The Métis experience — v. 4. The missing children and unmarked burials
     report — v. 5. The legacy — v. 6. Reconciliation

E96.5.T78 2016          971.004'97          C2015-905971-2
                                            C2015-905972-0

# Contents

# Canada's Residential Schools

Volume 5

# Introduction

The closing of residential schools did not bring their story to an end. The legacy of the schools continues to this day. It is reflected in the significant educational, income, and health disparities between Aboriginal people and other Canadians—disparities that condemn many Aboriginal people to shorter, poorer, and more troubled lives. The legacy is also reflected in the intense racism some people harbour against Aboriginal people and the systemic and other forms of discrimination Aboriginal people regularly experience in Canada. Over a century of cultural genocide has left most Aboriginal languages on the verge of extinction. The disproportionate apprehension of Aboriginal children by child welfare agencies and the disproportionate imprisonment and victimization of Aboriginal people are all part of the legacy of the way that Aboriginal children were treated in residential schools.

Many students were permanently damaged by residential schools. Separated from their parents, they grew up knowing neither respect nor affection. A school system that mocked and suppressed their families' cultures and traditions destroyed their sense of self-worth. Poorly trained teachers working with an irrelevant curriculum left students feeling branded as failures. Children who had been bullied and abused carried a burden of shame and anger for the rest of their lives. Overwhelmed by this legacy, many succumbed to despair and depression. Countless lives were lost to alcohol and drugs. Families were destroyed, children were displaced by the child welfare system.

The Survivors are not the only ones whose lives have been disrupted and scarred by the residential schools. The legacy has also profoundly affected their partners, their children, their grandchildren, their extended families, and their communities. Children who were abused in the schools sometimes went on to abuse others. Some students developed addictions as a means of coping. Students who were treated and punished as prisoners in the schools sometimes graduated to real prisons.

These impacts cannot be attributed solely to residential schooling. But they are clearly linked to the Aboriginal policies of the federal government over the last 150 years. Residential schooling, which sought to remake each new generation of Aboriginal children, was both central to and an emblematic element of those policies.

The beliefs and attitudes that were used to justify the establishment of residential schools are not things of the past: they continue to animate much of what passes for Aboriginal policy today. Reconciliation will require more than pious words about the shortcomings of those who preceded us. It obliges us to both recognize the ways in which the legacy of residential schools continues to disfigure Canadian life and to abandon policies and approaches that currently serve to extend that hurtful legacy.

This volume examines the legacy of Canada's policy of assimilation and the residential schools it created in five specific areas: child welfare, education, language and culture, health, and justice.

## Child welfare

The federal government and the churches believed that Aboriginal parenting, language, and culture were harmful to Aboriginal children. Consequently, a central objective of the residential schools was to separate Aboriginal children from their parents and communities to "civilize" and Christianize them. For generations, children were cut off from their families. At the height of the system in 1953, over 11,000 Aboriginal children were in residential schools.[1] The schools were in many ways more a child welfare system than an educational one. A survey in 1953 suggested that 4,313 of those students were thought to be suffering from "neglect" at home.[2] From the 1940s onwards, residential schools increasingly served as orphanages and child welfare facilities. By 1960, the federal government estimated that 50% of the children in residential schools were there for child-protection reasons.[3]

The schools were intended to sever the link between Aboriginal children and parents. They did this work only too well. Family connections were permanently broken. Children exposed to strict and regimented discipline in the schools not only lost their connections to parents, but also found it difficult to become loving parents.

Child welfare agencies across Canada removed thousands of Aboriginal children from their families and communities and placed them in non-Aboriginal homes with little consideration of the need to preserve their culture and identity. Children were placed in homes in different parts of the country, in the United States, and even overseas. The mass adoptions continued between 1960 and 1990.[4]

Aboriginal children are still being separated from their families and communities and placed in the care of child welfare agencies. Like the schools, child welfare agencies are underfunded, often culturally inappropriate, and, far too often, put Aboriginal children in unsafe situations. The child welfare system is the residential school system of our day.

# Education

The residential school system failed as an educational system. Those who administered the system and many of its teachers assumed that Aboriginal children were unfit for anything more than a rudimentary elementary or vocational education. The focus on elementary level and religious training amounted to a self-fulfilling prophecy. Most students left residential schools unprepared to succeed either in the market economy or to pursue more traditional activities such as hunting and fishing. The educational impact of the government's policy of assimilation was pervasive. Both Aboriginal and non-Aboriginal children attending public schools received the same message about Aboriginal inferiority as students in residential schools. This helps explain why even those Aboriginal children who did not attend a residential school grew up with the same sense of humiliation and low self-esteem, and why so many Canadians have such a low opinion of Aboriginal people.

One of the most far-reaching and devastating legacies of residential schools has been their impact on the educational and economic success of Aboriginal people. The lack of role models and mentors, insufficient funds for the schools, inadequate teachers, and unsuitable curricula taught in a foreign language all contributed to dismal success rates. The Truth and Reconciliation Commission of Canada has heard many examples of students who attended residential school for eight or more years, but left with nothing more than Grade Three achievement, and sometimes without even the ability to read. According to Indian Affairs annual reports, in the 1950s only half of each year's enrolment made it to Grade Six.[5]

Poor educational achievement has led to the chronic unemployment or underemployment, poverty, poor housing, substance abuse, family violence, and ill health that many former students of the schools have suffered as adults.

Governmental failure to meet the educational needs of Aboriginal children continues to the present day. Government funding is both inadequate and inequitably distributed. Educational achievement rates continue to be poor. While secondary school graduation rates for all Aboriginal people have improved since the closure of the schools, considerable gaps remain with the non-Aboriginal population.

Lower educational attainment for the children of Survivors has severely limited their employment and earning potential, just as it did for their parents. Aboriginal people on average have much lower incomes and are more likely to experience unemployment, and are more likely to collect employment insurance and social assistance benefits than non-Aboriginal people in Canada.[6]

The income gap is pervasive: non-Aboriginal Canadians earn more than Aboriginal workers no matter whether they work on reserves, off reserves, in urban, rural, or remote locations.[7] The rate of poverty for Aboriginal children is disturbingly high—40%, compared to 17% for all children in Canada.[8] Overcoming this legacy will require

Aboriginal education systems that meet the needs of Aboriginal students and respect Aboriginal parents, families, and cultures.

## Language and culture

In a study of the impact of residential schools, the Assembly of First Nations noted in 1994 that

> language is necessary to define and maintain a world view. For this reason, some First Nation Elders to this day will say that knowing or learning the native language is basic to any deep understanding of a First Nation way of life, to being a First Nation person. For them, a First Nation world is quite simply not possible without its own language. For them, the impact of residential school silencing their language is equivalent to a residential school silencing their world.[9]

Residential schools were a systematic, government-sponsored attempt to destroy Aboriginal cultures and languages and to assimilate Aboriginal peoples so that they no longer existed as distinct peoples. English—and to a far lesser degree French— were the only languages of instruction allowed in most residential schools.

Students were punished—often severely—for speaking their own languages. Conrad Burns, whose father attended the Prince Albert school, named this policy for what it was: "It was a cultural genocide. People were beaten for their language, people were beaten because ... they followed their own ways."[10]

The damage affected future generations, as former students found themselves unable or unwilling to teach their own children Aboriginal languages and cultural ways. As a result many of the almost ninety surviving Aboriginal languages in Canada are under serious threat. The United Nations Educational, Scientific and Cultural Organization (UNESCO) has found that 70% of Canada's Aboriginal languages are endangered.[11] In the 2011 census, 14.5% of the Aboriginal population reported that their first language learned was an Aboriginal language.[12] In the previous 2006 census, 18% of those who identified as Aboriginal had reported an Aboriginal language as their first language learned, and, a decade earlier, in the 1996 census, the figure was 26%. If the preservation of Aboriginal languages does not become a priority both for governments and for Aboriginal communities, then what the residential schools failed to accomplish will come about through a process of systematic neglect.

## Health

Residential schools endangered the health and well-being of the children who attended them. Many students succumbed to infectious disease—particularly tuberculosis—at rates far in excess of non-Aboriginal children.[13] Children who had been poorly fed and raised in the unsanitary conditions that characterized most residential schools were susceptible to a variety of health problems as adults. Many would later succumb to tuberculosis that they contracted in the schools.[14]

Sexual and physical abuse, as well as separation from families and communities, caused lasting trauma for many others. In many cases, former students could find no alternatives to self-harm.[15] The effects of this trauma were often passed on to the children of residential school Survivors and sometimes to their grandchildren.

The overall suicide rate among First Nation communities is about twice that of the total Canadian population. For Inuit, the rate is still higher: six to eleven times the rate for the general population. Aboriginal youth between the ages of ten and twenty-nine who are living on reserves are five to six times more likely to die by suicide than non-Aboriginal youth.[16]

Health disparities of such magnitude have social roots. They are stark evidence of federal policies that separated Aboriginal people from their traditional lands and livelihoods, confining them to cramped and inadequate housing on reserves that lacked the basic sanitary services. It was from these communities that residential school students were recruited and to them, their health further weakened, that they returned. A comprehensive health care strategy that recognizes the value of traditional healing practices is desperately needed to help close these gaps in health outcomes.

## Justice

Residential schools inflicted profound injustices on Aboriginal people. Aboriginal parents were forced, often under pressure from the police, to give up their children to the schools. Children were taken far from their communities to live in frightening custodial institutions that felt like prisons. The children who attended residential schools were treated as if they were offenders and were at risk of being physically and sexually abused.

The Canadian legal system failed to provide justice to Survivors who were abused. When, in the late 1980s, that system eventually did begin to respond to the abuse, it did so inadequately and in a way that often re-victimized the Survivors. The Commission has been able to identify fewer than fifty convictions stemming from abuse at residential schools, a small fraction of the more than 38,000 claims of sexual and serious physical abuse that were submitted to the independent adjudication process that was established to assess and compensate residential school abuse claims.[17]

In many ways, the residential school experience lies at the root of the current over-incarceration of Aboriginal people. Traumatized by their school experiences, many succumbed to addictions and found themselves among the disproportionate number of Aboriginal people who come into conflict with the law.

Once Aboriginal persons are arrested, prosecuted, and convicted, they are more likely to be sentenced to prison than non-Aboriginal people. In 2011, Aboriginal people made up 4% of the Canadian population, yet they accounted for 28% of admissions to sentenced custody.[18] Of those admitted into provincial and territorial custody in 2011–12, Aboriginal females accounted for 43%, compared to 27% for Aboriginal males.[19] And in the same year, 49% of girls below the age of eighteen admitted to custody were Aboriginal, compared to 36% of males.[20]

There is a troubling link between the substance abuse that has plagued many residential school Survivors and the overincarceration of Aboriginal people. Fetal alcohol spectrum disorder (FASD) is a permanent brain injury caused when a woman's consumption of alcohol during pregnancy affects her fetus.[21] The disabilities associated with FASD include memory impairments, problems with judgment and abstract reasoning, and poor adaptive functioning.[22] Studies from Canada and the United States suggest that 15% to 20% of prisoners have FASD. A recent Canadian study found that offenders with FASD had much higher rates of criminal involvement than those without FASD, including more juvenile and adult convictions.[23] Diagnosing FASD can be a long and costly process and the lack of a confirmed diagnosis can result in the unjust imprisonment of Aboriginal people who are living with a disability. In this way, the traumas of residential school are quite literally passed down from one generation to another.[24]

As well as being more likely to be involved as offenders with the justice system, Aboriginal people are 58% more likely than non-Aboriginal people to be the victims of crime.[25] Aboriginal women report being victimized by violent crime at a rate almost three times higher than non-Aboriginal women—13% of Aboriginal women reported being victimized by violent crime in 2009.[26] The most disturbing aspect of this victimization is the extraordinary number of Aboriginal women and girls who have been murdered or are reported as missing. A 2014 RCMP report found that, between 1980 and 2012, 1,017 Aboriginal women and girls were killed and 164 were missing. Of these, 225 these cases remain unsolved.[27]

## Conclusion

The Commission is convinced that genuine reconciliation will not be possible until the broad legacy of the schools is both understood and addressed. Canada has acknowledged some aspects of the ongoing legacy and harms of residential schools; the Supreme Court has recognized that the legacy of residential schools should be considered when sentencing Aboriginal offenders. While these have been important measures, they have not been sufficient to address the grossly disproportionate imprisonment of Aboriginal people, which continues to grow, in part, because of a lack of adequate funding and support for culturally appropriate alternatives to imprisonment. There has been an increase in Aboriginal child welfare agencies, but the disproportionate apprehension of Aboriginal children continues to increase because of a lack of adequate funding for culturally appropriate supports that would allow children to remain safely with their families.

Many of the individual and collective harms have not yet been addressed, even after the negotiated out-of-court settlement of the residential school litigation in 2006, and Canada's apology in 2008. In fact, some of the damages done by residential schools to Aboriginal families, languages, education, and health may be perpetuated and even worsened as a result of current governmental policies. New policies may be based on a lack of understanding of Aboriginal people similar to that which motivated the schools. For example, child welfare and health policies may fail to take into account the importance of community in raising children. We must learn from the failure of the schools to ensure that the mistakes of the past are not repeated in the future.

Understanding and redressing the legacy of residential schools will benefit all Canadians. Governments in Canada spend billions of dollars each year responding to the symptoms of the intergenerational trauma of residential schools. Much of this money is spent on crisis interventions related to child welfare, family violence, ill health, and crime. Despite genuine reform efforts, the dramatic overrepresentation of Aboriginal children in foster care, and among the sick, the injured, and the imprisoned continues to grow. Only a real commitment to reconciliation and change will reverse the trends and lay the foundation for a truly just and equitable nation.

*　*　*

The following chapters include Calls to Action as developed by the Truth and Reconciliation Commission. The Calls to Action in this volume are numbered according to the order in which they appear in *Honouring the Truth, Reconciling for the Future: Summary of the Final Report of the Truth and Reconciliation Commission of Canada*. Also see the Calls to Action in this volume.

# CHAPTER 1

# Child welfare: A system in crisis

## Introduction

Residential schools were an early manifestation of a child welfare policy of child removal that continues to this day. Since government and the churches believed that Aboriginal parents were inferior when it came to raising children, and could not be relied upon to raise them to be "proper" Canadians, a central objective of the residential schools was to separate Aboriginal children from their parents and communities to "civilize" and Christianize them.

For generations, children were cut off from their families. At the height of the system in 1953, just over 11,000 Aboriginal children were in residential schools.[1] A 1953 survey suggested that 4,313 of them were thought to be suffering from "neglect" at home.

The end of the residential school system did not mean that Aboriginal children were no longer forcibly separated from their families. Child welfare services carried on where the residential schools left off. More Aboriginal children are removed from their families today than attended residential schools in any one year. Following the inquiry into the death of an Aboriginal girl in Manitoba, the Honourable Ted Hughes concluded that the overrepresentation of Aboriginal children in care in Canada is "unconscionable" and "a national embarrassment."[2]

Why are so many Aboriginal children taken into care? Poverty, family violence, sexual violence, and substance abuse—conditions that are part of the sad legacy of residential schools—certainly play a role. The connection between residential schools and the present-day crisis of the overrepresentation of Aboriginal children in the child welfare system was painfully obvious to many Survivors who shared their statements with the Commission. Kay Adams explained that "all these years of growing up in the dorm I didn't go home to my family. I wasn't taught how to love. I wasn't taught how to be a family. I knew none of that."[3]

Tim McNeil felt the impact of residential schools when his children were older: "I was a good parent until my kids turned thirteen, and when my kids turned thirteen then I started parenting them the way that I was when I was in school. So suddenly my love was gone, my affection was gone, my time was gone. I started treating them the way I was treated in the dorm. And that was with strict rules, strict discipline, you had to follow a certain order, there was no love, there was no affection."[4] These Survivors suffered in residential schools. Their children suffered because of their suffering.

The perception that separation from their families is in the best interests of Aboriginal children may still be influenced by assumptions about the inferiority of Aboriginal parenting. These assumptions seem to be reflected in funding for child welfare services. Federal funding of on-reserve child welfare has been the subject of prolonged litigation before the Canadian Human Rights Commission and the Federal Courts since 2007. Aboriginal groups have long argued that not only is the amount of funding inequitable, but also the funding structure shows a preference for taking Aboriginal children into care rather than providing supports that would allow them to remain safely with their parents.[5]

At five years old, Daniel Big George and his four-year-old sister were taken to a residential school. He did not see his family for over two years. Reflecting on today's child welfare system, Big George observed, "they're utilizing the [Children's Aid Society] as how the residential school system was run."[6] At Commission hearings in Inuvik, Chief Norma Kassi agreed: "the doors are closed at the Residential Schools but the foster homes are still existing and our children are still being taken away."[7]

## More than a century of taking Aboriginal children from their families

For many years the assimilation of all Aboriginal people was government policy, and residential schools were one of the tools used to implement that policy. At the same time, protecting Aboriginal children from their parents was often the stated reason for forcibly removing children from their homes. Aboriginal parenting was considered inferior, a prejudice that clearly shows in documents throughout the long history of residential schools.

In his 1879 report on residential schools, Nicholas Flood Davin wrote that "the children should be kept constantly within the circle of civilized conditions."[8] A few years later, in 1883, according to Indian Commissioner Edgar Dewdney, residential schools were preferable to day schools for producing workers:

> [It is] difficult to make day schools on reserves a success, because the influence of home associations is stronger than that of the school, and so long as such a state of things exists I fear that the inherited aversion to labour can never be successfully met. By the children being separated from their parents and property and regularly instructed not only in the rudiments of English language, but also in trades and agriculture, so that what is taught may not be readily forgotten, I

can but assure myself that a great end will be attained for the permanent and lasting benefit of the Indian.[9]

Over two decades later, in 1915, the principal of the Kuper Island school in British Columbia wrote that the "only way" to educate Aboriginal children "is to bring them to an industrial school, where they are completely under the control of their teachers, and separated from the evil influences of most of their homes."[10]

These architects and administrators of the residential school system believed that Aboriginal children would be much better off away from their parents. Residential schools were often deliberately built at a distance from reserves to discourage Aboriginal parents from even visiting their children.[11]

## Prejudice is embedded in policy

Compulsory schooling and school attendance has been in place in Canada since the 1870s. However, compulsory attendance laws provided that, for non-Aboriginal children, school attendance was not mandatory if the school was not conveniently close to the child. Non-Aboriginal children were not required to attend schools where they could not return to their families each day.[12]

In 1894, the *Indian Act* was amended to authorize the government "to secure the compulsory attendance of children at school."[13] Government officials had already noted the necessity for family ties to be "severed during the school term."[14] The *Regulations Relating to the Education of Indian Children* granted Indian agents and justices of the peace the power to authorize the apprehension and placement of Aboriginal children in industrial or boarding schools, if they were satisfied that their parents or guardians were "unfit or unwilling to provide for the child's education."[15] Indian agents were authorized to appoint truant officers with "police powers." A year later, the acting superintendent general of Indian Affairs asked the Department of Justice to develop a standard warrant for the removal of Aboriginal children from their families where "adequate provision is not being and will not be made for the care, or education or the education and care of the said [child]."[16]

Twenty years later, in 1914, an Indian Affairs circular was reminding Indian agents that the government had the power to place children "who are not being properly cared for or educated" in residential schools. Agents were told that "orphan children and children neglected by their parents should have the preference."[17] Thus, apprehending Aboriginal children, for assimilation purposes or in response to perceived neglect, became routine over a hundred years ago.

## The 1940s and 1950s

Support for residential schools had decreased by the Second World War, and the federal government started closing residential schools in some parts of the country. However, in 1943, senior civil servant R. A. Hoey warned that places in residential schools would still be necessary for "orphans and children from disrupted homes."[18] With fewer places available, the emerging cadre of professional child welfare workers were to give priority to admitting children considered to be neglected.

In 1947, the Canadian Welfare Council and the Canadian Association of Social Workers collaborated on a report to a Special Joint Committee of the Senate and the House of Commons that was examining the *Indian Act*. The two organizations argued for the assimilation of Aboriginal peoples to ensure "not only their admission to full citizenship, but the right and opportunity for them to participate freely with other citizens in all community affairs."[19] The authors noted disparities in the education, health, and welfare services provided to Aboriginal people. They recommended immediate reforms to address the gaps. One of their recommendations was to investigate extending provincial education, health, and welfare services to reserves.

The provinces and territories assumed responsibility for child welfare services on reserves in the 1950s, facilitated by amendments to the *Indian Act* in 1951 that allowed all provincial laws of general applications to apply on reserve.[20] At first, the provinces and territories provided only emergency on-reserve services. With more federal funding, services expanded to receiving and assessing child protection reports, family services, guardianship of children in care, and adoption.[21] Funding mechanisms encouraged the removal of children from their homes because, while the federal government was willing to pay for child-in-care costs, there was considerable resistance by both federal and provincial governments to support preventive services.[22]

Even as some residential schools shut down, provincial child welfare authorities began to apprehend increasing numbers of Aboriginal children. Many were eventually given up for adoption, often to non-Aboriginal families.

## The "Sixties Scoop"

The provincial social workers assigned to reserves assessed child safety and welfare by mainstream cultural standards. They received little or no training in Aboriginal culture. They were not trained to recognize problems rooted in generations of trauma related to the residential schools. Instead, they passed judgment on what they considered bad or neglectful parenting. As a result, beginning in the 1960s, provincial child welfare workers removed thousands of children from Aboriginal communities. It has been called the "Sixties Scoop."[23]

Aboriginal children were placed in non-Aboriginal homes across Canada, in the United States, and even overseas, with no attempt to preserve their culture and identity. The mass adoptions continued between 1960 and 1990.[24]

The Sixties Scoop children suffered much the same effects as children who were placed in residential schools. Aboriginal children adopted or placed with white foster parents were sometimes abused. They suffered from identity confusion, low self-esteem, addictions, lower levels of educational achievement, and unemployment.[25] They sometimes experienced disparagement and almost always suffered from dislocation and denial of their Aboriginal identity.

## Canada ignores recommendations to support Aboriginal parents

Meanwhile, as Aboriginal children continued to be placed in residential schools and the mass adoptions of the Sixties Scoop were under way, some officials within Canada's Department of Indian Affairs, as well as outside experts, were recommending the better solution of providing supports for parents.

In 1965, J. R. Tully, superintendent of the Blood Indian Agency, wrote, "the main reason for the majority of younger children being in Residential School here is because their parents just cannot afford to properly feed and clothe them for part of the school year."[26] He suggested that it was not efficient to house a child in residential school for ten months per year when the parents had economic problems for only four months. In the absence of "welfare assistance" for the parents, however, he concluded that there was no practical alternative to placing children in residential schools.

A confidential 1966 report by the Department of Indian Affairs estimated that 75% of the children in residential schools were "from homes which by reasons of overcrowding and parental neglect or indifference are considered unfit for school children." Return to the reserve was considered undesirable because "the security that the child finds in the school is shaken on his return to the reserve."[27] The report noted that the substantial funds required for residential schooling might have been more usefully put towards "improving the home and training the parents" to increase "self support."[28] The report did not result in a policy change, and the money continued to go to the schools.

In 1967, George Caldwell, a child care specialist with the Canadian Welfare Council, investigated and reported to the federal government on placements in nine Saskatchewan residential schools. Caldwell noted that family welfare needs appeared to be the main reason for placing 60% of the children. Although "neglect" was frequently cited, Caldwell observed a "serious absence of recorded data on the child and the reason for admission is open to question because of this lack of information."[29] He recommended that services to assist Aboriginal families should "not be restricted to the narrow definition of investigating allegations or evidence of neglect of children, but recognition should be given to prevention of family deterioration, and professional services given to strengthen and maintain family life."[30]

Caldwell, like the authors of the 1966 Indian Affairs report, believed that support for families would be a better and less drastic alternative to apprehending children or placing them in residential school. Caldwell's humane and sensible recommendations were also not adopted.

## Apprehension put children in triple jeopardy

In a 1983 report for the Canadian Council on Social Development, Patrick Johnston wrote that the child welfare system placed Aboriginal children in "triple jeopardy," removed from parents, extended family, and culture:

> The effects of apprehension on an individual Native child will often be much more traumatic than for his non-Native counterpart. Frequently, when the Native child is taken from his parents, he is also removed from a tightly knit community of extended family members and neighbours, who may have provided some support. In addition, he is removed from a unique, distinctive and familiar culture.[31]

As the Commission heard from some Sixties Scoop Survivors, the child welfare system continued a multigenerational cycle of displacement and alienation. Many children lost contact with both their families and their Aboriginal identity forever.

In a 1985 Manitoba public inquiry report, Associate Chief Judge Edwin Kimelman decried the systematic placement of thousands of Aboriginal children in white homes outside Manitoba and described the practice as "cultural genocide," which had "taken place in a systematic, routine manner."[32] Judge Kimelman continued,

> An abysmal lack of sensitivity to children and families was revealed. Families approached agencies for help and found that what was described as being in the child's "best interest" resulted in their families being torn asunder and siblings separated. Social workers grappled with cultural patterns far different than their own with no preparation and no opportunity to gain understanding.[33]

## Survivors tell their stories

The residential schools failed to protect Aboriginal children from abuse, but so did many child welfare agencies. The Commission heard from many Survivors of both residential schools and the Sixties Scoop.

A Sixties Scoop Survivor placed with a white family was told that her parents were "the drunken Indians on Main Street." Her foster father sexually abused her and her brothers, and her brothers also sexually abused her.[34]

Tara Picard, whose birth name was Rhonda Eagles, was adopted into a white family and "was basically told that the First Nations people were really horrible people, and not to be that way." She "turned into white, being white, more white than anything."[35]

At the age of three, Marci Shapiro was taken from her mother, who had attended residential school, and adopted into a Montréal family: "There was a huge movement in the seventies, where they took children from Manitoba and put them into Montréal Jewish Family Services." Many of those adoptees "are drug addicts. They've had children; their children go into care. It's like the whole cycle's been perpetuated and it continues."[36] She is committed to working with her community to help break the cycle.

One former student of the Christie Residential School in British Columbia was also placed in a number of foster homes. She was abused at the school and by her stepfather at home. She remarked, "That's why I'm so against apprehension of our Aboriginal children. They should stay with the parents.... Don't be like us, without our parents, that we never grew up with, we never really got to know."[37]

Another woman who made a statement to the Commission in Alberta was placed in a foster home with three other children. She explained,

> In that foster home there was a pedophile, and I don't [know] what was happening to anybody else, but I became his target. The mother used to always send me to do errands with him. And so every time, he would make me do things to him and then he would give me candy. Also, in that home there was no hugging of us foster kids or anything like that. And I carried a great guilt for many, many years, because sometimes I didn't want to resist it, I just ... But I knew it was very bad.[38]

One foster child told the Commission of the abuse she suffered in her foster home. Her Aboriginal identity was constantly disparaged and she was "singled out" because she was "not as white as the others": "[They were] adamant about Aboriginal culture being less than human, living as dirty bush people, eating rats. It made me not want to be one of those people. And for years, I didn't know how to be proud of who I was because I didn't know who I was."

This person has now reconnected with her culture and made a great effort to attend one of the Commission's gatherings. Her mother, who attended residential schools, "was led to believe that her mother and her sisters were heathens, living in the bush ... because that's what the church had told her."[39] However, her mother and her own daughters remain estranged from their family, their community, and their culture.

Joanne Nimik, the daughter of two residential school Survivors, was apprehended at age four and adopted by a white family. Until she reconnected with her birth mother, she had "limited exposure to Aboriginal culture." She had difficulties growing up, and when she was eighteen she "went into the bad crowd and started partying and drinking and drugging." Only recently has she realized how much residential schools affected her life. With the help of her family and Aboriginal traditions, she is determined to "break the cycle"[40] in which generations of families are involved with the child welfare system.

Class actions before courts across the country are seeking accountability and compensation from the federal government for the Sixties Scoop.[41] The federal government is vigorously fighting these suits. In December 2014, an Ontario court dismissed the federal government's attempt to have the Ontario-based class action thrown out. In allowing the class action to continue to the next stage, the Court observed that "it is difficult to see a specific interest that could be of more importance to aboriginal peoples than each person's essential connection to their aboriginal heritage."[42]

## Delivery of Aboriginal child welfare services

A patchwork of three hundred provincial and territorial child welfare agencies, operating in thirteen different jurisdictions, deliver Aboriginal child welfare services in Canada. The provinces and territories have jurisdiction over child welfare within their borders, including almost all services provided off reserve. The federal government is responsible for funding child welfare services on reserves.

Through its First Nations Child and Family Services Program, Canada has committed to funding child welfare services on reserves that are culturally appropriate, comply with provincial legislation and standards, and are reasonably comparable with services provided off reserves in similar circumstances.[43] As this section will demonstrate, that commitment is not being honoured.

The Canadian First Nations child welfare system is a complex array of governance models: the delegated model, the integrated model, band bylaws, and bilateral and tripartite agreements.

### Delegated model

Delegated delivery is the most common governance model. Provincial governments delegate responsibility for the delivery of child welfare services to Aboriginal child and family services agencies.[44] These agencies are required to conform to provincial/territorial laws as a condition for funding.

Ontario's child welfare system is governed by a unique delegation arrangement because of an *Indian Welfare Agreement* that was signed between the Province of Ontario and Aboriginal Affairs and Northern Development Canada (then named Department of Indian Affairs) in 1965. The agreement was negotiated without input from First Nations and provides for the federal government to reimburse Ontario for 93% of the cost of providing child welfare services on reserves in Ontario.

## Integrated model

A smaller number of agencies operate under the integrated model in which the Aboriginal community and the provincial government share governance responsibilities. Manitoba provides the best example of the integrated model in action. Four regional authorities operate the province's child welfare agencies: the General Authority, Métis Authority, First Nations of Northern Manitoba Authority, and First Nations of Southern Manitoba Authority. This system, first implemented in 2000, developed as a result of recommendations made by the Manitoba Aboriginal Justice Inquiry in 1991. The Province of Manitoba, the Manitoba Metis Federation, the Assembly of Manitoba Chiefs, and Manitoba Keewatinook Ininew Okimowin jointly developed the model.[45]

Each regional authority has the right to direct its child and family services agencies, and the Manitoba government is responsible for determining policies and standards, monitoring compliance, and funding.[46] Each authority is mandated to provide services anywhere in the province.[47] As a result, Manitoba is the only province where Aboriginal child welfare agencies provide mandated services both on and off reserve, and First Nations, Inuit, and Métis children and families have access to culturally appropriate services no matter where they live in Manitoba.[48] There are sixteen First Nations child welfare agencies in Manitoba, including the Child and Family All Nations Coordinated Response Network. The network is located in Winnipeg, which has one of the largest urban Aboriginal populations in Canada. It is the only Aboriginal agency in Canada to serve both Aboriginal and non-Aboriginal families in a major metropolitan area.[49]

The General Authority provides services to about 18% of Manitoba's child welfare clients, but about 82% of children in care receive services from a First Nation or Métis authority. This reflects the dramatic overrepresentation of Aboriginal children in care.[50]

## Self-governance: Band bylaw and tripartite agreements

Two First Nations have developed self-government systems that afford greater control over child welfare services. The Spallumcheen First Nation in British Columbia signed an agreement with Canada in 1981 acknowledging the nation's jurisdictional control over child welfare services. This First Nation operates under band bylaws rather than provincial laws and standards.[51] The Nisga'a Lisims First Nation signed a treaty in 1999 that confirms the nation's right to "make laws with respect to children and family services on Nisga'a lands." Those laws must be consistent with provincial standards. It operates under a tripartite agreement.[52]

## Recent developments in governance

Although Aboriginal child welfare systems governed by delegated and integrated models apply the same child welfare legislation as their non-Aboriginal counterparts, there have been significant reforms to child welfare laws across the country since the 1960s.

Today, most child welfare laws include special considerations for Aboriginal children, families, and communities. Measures include the requirement to notify Aboriginal bands of court hearings involving Aboriginal children; Aboriginal engagement in service design and delivery; consultation with Aboriginal representatives in cases involving Aboriginal children; and priority status for kinship care.[53]

Ontario legislation requires that culturally appropriate services be made available for Aboriginal children. The government may exempt First Nations child welfare authorities from any provision in the *Child and Family Services Act*. Five First Nations agencies in Ontario have agreements with the provincial government that exempt them from applying specific aspects of the child welfare legislation.[54]

Some provinces have implemented Aboriginal-specific practice standards. In British Columbia, the Aboriginal Operational and Practice Standards manual prioritizes child placement within Aboriginal communities and involvement of families and communities in intervention plans. It also promotes access to cultural ceremonies and information on Aboriginal heritage.[55] In New Brunswick, the *MicMac and Maliseet First Nations Services Standards Manual* introduced culturally based standards in 1993.[56] The Federation of Saskatchewan Indian Nations has gone further. Its *Indian Child Welfare and Family Support Act* exists alongside provincial legislation and includes standards recognized by the province as equivalent to ministerial policies, practices, and standards.[57]

## Jurisdictional disputes and litigation

Jurisdictional responsibility for child welfare is intensely contested, with both the federal government and provincial and territorial governments essentially trying to shift the responsibility for Aboriginal child services to the other level of government. The federal government maintains that child and family services are solely within the jurisdiction of the provinces and territories. To the extent that it provides funding for such services on reserves, it does so merely at its own discretion. Canada maintains that any obligation it may have ends at the borders of reserves. The provinces maintain that the federal government has constitutional responsibility for "Indians" and argue that the federal government has offloaded responsibility to the provinces to provide services to an increasingly urban, non-reserve population.[58] The result is that there are often disputes over which level of government or department is responsible for paying costs.

A 2005 survey of twelve First Nations child welfare agencies found that collectively, the agencies had experienced 393 jurisdictional disputes within the previous year. Each dispute required an average of 54.25 person hours to resolve, with some disputes taking up to 200 hours of staff time to sort out. The most frequent disputes were between the federal government's own departments (36%), between two provincial departments (27%), and between federal and provincial governments (14%).[59]

## Funding formulas

### Directive 20-1: "We had all the incentives wrong"

Beginning in 1988, most First Nations child and family service agencies received funding through a federal policy called "Directive 20-1." First Nations had little input in creating it. Until 2007–08, Directive 20-1 applied in all jurisdictions except Ontario.[60]

Directive 20-1 has two funding streams. "Operations" funds are intended to cover the cost of running a child welfare agency, including costs such as salaries and rent. Operations funding is based on the size of the child population the agency serves. "Maintenance" funds are intended to cover the full cost of maintaining children in care outside of their family homes.[61]

Directive 20-1 does not cover other types of services. Notably, it does not cover preventive services to support families. Not surprisingly, Directive 20-1 has come under fire. An evaluation by the Department of Indian and Northern Affairs Canada concluded that "the program's funding formula, Directive 20-1, has likely been a factor in increases in the number of children in care and program expenditures because it has had the effect of steering agencies towards in-care options—foster care, group homes and institutional care because only these agency costs are fully reimbursed."[62]

Failure to provide supports to families that would assist them to maintain custody of their children could very well be a violation of international law. The *Convention on the Rights of the Child* requires states to provide assistance to ensure that the integrity of Indigenous families and communities is protected.[63] Directive 20-1 does not do so. Canadian officials are well aware of this. In 2011, Michael Wernick, then the deputy minister for the Department of Indian and Northern Affairs, pointed out the flaws to the Standing Committee on Public Accounts:

> What I think we identified, with the help of the work from the Auditor General, was that we had the incentives all wrong.... We didn't really have a funding formula that provided a lot of resources for prevention. In many cases, early intervention and prevention with the families in the communities means that the kids can be protected from harm and risk without having to be taken out of the home and put into care. So children in care is sort of a flawed measure as well for what we're trying to get at.[64]

## The Enhanced Prevention Focused Approach

Canada responded to criticism of Directive 20-1 with a new funding formula called the "Enhanced Prevention Focused Approach." Operations and maintenance funding streams still exist, but there is now a third stream for prevention services with the goal of reducing out-of-home placements. In a further improvement over Directive 20-1, the Enhanced Prevention Focused Approach does not require block funding. Agencies have the flexibility to shift funds between streams to meet the needs of the community.[65]

The new funding formula is being rolled out based on tripartite agreements between Canada, the provinces, and First Nations child and family services agencies. Tripartite framework agreements based on the Enhanced Prevention Focused Approach have been negotiated in Alberta, Manitoba, Nova Scotia, Prince Edward Island, Québec, and Saskatchewan.[66] They have led to significantly increased funding.[67] Canada plans to negotiate agreements in all jurisdictions. In the meantime, Directive 20-1 continues to be applied in the remaining provinces despite its serious acknowledged flaws.

## Shifting money between streams: A shell game

Funding for prevention services is certainly a welcome development, but the new formula is already raising concerns.

Maintenance funding is based on the actual costs of maintaining children in care from the year prior. Agencies dealing with an increase in the number of children in care then face deficits that must be covered by shifting resources from prevention and operations. The resulting lack of predictability makes it difficult for agencies to develop and sustain prevention programs.

As with Directive 20-1, operations funding continues to be based on the assumption that 6% of on-reserve children are in care (with the exception of Manitoba, which assumes 7%).[68] Agencies with a higher number of children in care will have fewer resources for operations and may have to cut prevention services to cover the shortfall. The auditor general expressed concern about this aspect of the new funding formula:

> The new formula does not address the inequities of the existing formula. It still assumes that a fixed percentage of First Nations children and families need child welfare services. Agencies with more than 6% of their children in care will continue to be hard-pressed to provide protection services while developing family enhancement services. In our view, the funding formula should be more than a means of distributing the program's budget; it should take into account the varying needs of First Nations children and communities.[69]

The Standing Committee on Public Accounts agreed, noting that "the result of this approach is that communities that need funding the most, that is, where more than 6% of the children are in care, will continue to be underfunded and will not be able to provide their children the services they need."[70]

## Shifting money between program areas: Another shell game

Since 1996, the Department of Indian Affairs and Northern Development (which became the Department of Aboriginal Affairs and Northern Development in 2011) has capped annual department funding increases at 2%. But funding for the First Nations Child and Family Services Program budget has increased significantly, more than doubling from $193 million in 1997 to $450 million in 2007. These increases were funded by transferring money from other program areas, such as community infrastructure and housing.[71]

Starving community infrastructure and housing of funds is self-defeating and unsustainable. Neglected community infrastructure and poor housing conditions contribute to the growing number of child welfare cases that are causing the financial pressures on the system in the first place.

## Will it work?

Shifting the money around would not be as serious a problem if the new funding approach could achieve the goals of preventing family violence, protecting children, and reducing the overrepresentation of Aboriginal children in care. It is still early days for the Enhanced Prevention Focused Approach, but the results of several formal evaluations conducted for the Department of Aboriginal Affairs have been, at best, mixed.

A 2010 evaluation by Indian Affairs and Northern Development Canada found that "the research is inconclusive regarding the extent to which prevention programming has been effective to date." The number of First Nations children in care increased after the new model was introduced. The average number of days in care also went up, though there were wide variations between agencies. A small number of agencies had increased prevention spending and also reduced the numbers of children in care, but the evaluation was unable to determine whether this was a direct result of prevention activities.[72]

Based on evaluations, in 2012 Aboriginal Affairs identified a series of issues undermining the effectiveness of the Enhanced Prevention Focused Approach: complex medical needs, the high cost of institutional care, an increase in older children coming into care, housing shortages and overcrowding, shortages of Aboriginal foster parents, lack of program supports for parents with addiction or mental health problems, and poverty.[73] Aboriginal Affairs noted that "agencies report that some families are unable to meet their basic needs (food, fuel for heating, transportation to medical appointments, etc.) and find themselves unable to care for their children."[74]

Because the most significant driver of high child welfare rates in Aboriginal communities is "neglect" that is actually tied to poverty, there are limits to how successful the new formula can be. The Enhanced Prevention Focused Approach does not put more money into the hands of Aboriginal families, provide them with safe housing, or put food on their tables.

Formulas for funding aside, the auditors general of Canada and British Columbia have concluded that Aboriginal child welfare agencies do not receive adequate funding to ensure equitable access to a level and quality of services comparable with those provided to other children.[75] The Government of Canada, in meaningful consultation with Aboriginal communities, should undertake immediate measures to ensure that Aboriginal child and family service agencies are provided with adequate and sustainable resources to ensure culturally based services regardless of their place of residence. Funding arrangements should ensure that Aboriginal agencies and communities have adequate resources to strengthen families so as to minimize the need for drastic interventions that take Aboriginal children away from their families.

## Human rights complaint

There are several examples of the highly charged legal atmosphere surrounding services to Aboriginal children and families. In 2007, the Assembly of First Nations and the First Nations Child & Family Caring Society of Canada[76] filed a complaint with the Canadian Human Rights Commission under the *Canadian Human Rights Act*, alleging that Canada's failure to ensure equitable and culturally based child and family services for First Nations amounted to discrimination on the basis of race and national ethnic origin.[77]

Canada disputed the Canadian Human Rights Tribunal's jurisdiction to review the complaint and spent more than $3 million on legal proceedings aimed at getting the case dismissed.[78] Canada argued that a discrimination analysis should not be based on comparing federal levels of funding to those of the provinces and territories. If accepted, that argument would render the concept of discrimination meaningless with respect to Aboriginal peoples. The federal government could, with impunity, deny Aboriginal peoples the quality of services enjoyed by all other groups in Canada simply by saying that there is no basis for comparison.

In 2011, the tribunal accepted Canada's arguments and dismissed the human rights complaint, ruling that the Canadian human rights regime "does not allow a comparison to be made between two different service providers with two different service recipients. Federal funding goes to on-reserve First Nations children for child welfare. Provincial funding goes to all children who live off reserve. These constitute separate and distinct service providers with separate service recipients. The two cannot be compared."[79]

On judicial review, the Federal Court and the Federal Court of Appeal soundly rejected this restrictive approach as unreasonable.[80] The Federal Court of Appeal ordered the Canadian Human Rights Tribunal to hear the case.[81] In concluding that the tribunal's decision to dismiss the case was unreasonable, the court emphasized that "discrimination is a broad, fact-based inquiry" that requires "going behind the façade of similarities and differences" and "taking full account of social, political, economic and historical factors concerning the group."[82]

The Canadian Human Rights Tribunal has been hearing evidence sporadically since February 2013, although a lengthy adjournment was required when Canada disclosed an additional 50,000 pages of documents. The hearing was completed in October 2014. At the time of writing, it is anticipated that the tribunal will publish its decision in 2015.

The litigation in this case has been particularly prolonged. The federal government's aggressive approach aligns awkwardly with its recognition and apology regarding the ongoing legacy of residential schools in child welfare cases.

## Jordan's Principle

The repercussions of these disputes over jurisdiction can be serious. Aboriginal children pay the highest price, especially children with complex developmental, mental health, and physical health issues.[83]

Jordan River Anderson was a member of the Norway House First Nation in Manitoba. He was born with complex medical needs. Jordan remained in hospital two years longer than medically necessary while the provincial and federal governments fought over who would pay for his at-home care. Before the two governments could come to an agreement, Jordan died, at age five, never having spent a day in a family home.[84]

In theory, situations such as Jordan's should not arise again. On December 12, 2007, the House of Commons unanimously supported a private member's motion (M-296) stating that "the government should immediately adopt a child-first principle, based on Jordan's Principle, to resolve jurisdictional disputes involving the care of First Nations children."[85] According to Jordan's Principle, the government department that is first contacted for a service readily available off reserve must pay for it while it is pursuing reimbursement for the expenses.[86]

Jordan's Principle was not passed as legislation. It is merely a statement by Parliament.[87] The Canadian Paediatric Society noted in 2011 that not one province or territory had implemented a child-first approach to resolving jurisdictional disputes over services provided to First Nations children and youth.[88] Jurisdictional disputes continue to delay Aboriginal children and families' access to services.

3) We call upon all levels of government to fully implement Jordan's Principle.

## Jeremy's case

An Aboriginal family from Pictou Landing, Nova Scotia, went to court in 2013 seeking to enforce Jordan's Principle so that a disabled child would receive the supports he required to remain in the family home and avoid institutionalization.[89] Both levels of government took the position that the child was not entitled to the supports his family had requested. Since both governments denied entitlement, they both took the position that in fact there was no jurisdictional dispute and Jordan's Principle did not apply. The Federal Court concluded that both levels of government were wrong and that the child was entitled to the services. The court ordered Canada to pay the necessary costs.

The costs for one child had consumed 80% of the six-hundred-member band's budget for personal and home care services. The judge stressed that "Parliament has unanimously endorsed Jordan's Principle and the government, while not bound by the House of Commons resolution, has undertaken to implement this important principle."[90] The judge also noted that the only other option for Jeremy would be institutionalization and separation from his mother and his community. His mother is the only person who, at least at times, can understand and communicate with him.

# First Nations child and family services agencies

In the early 1980s, Indian Affairs and Northern Development Canada (as it was then called) began approving the establishment of First Nations child and family service agencies on reserves on a case-by-case basis. The first were established in Alberta, Manitoba, and Nova Scotia. Canada now provides funding to 106 Aboriginally con- trolled agencies. In 2010–11, 9,242 Aboriginal children were outside of the parental home and in the care of First Nation child and family service agencies, which rep- resents 5.6% of on-reserve children.[91]

A few larger Canadian cities (such as Toronto and Vancouver) also have First Nation child and family service agencies.[92] There are none in the territories, where the same agencies that serve all children provide services to Aboriginal children. In Yukon, Canada provides funding for these services to the territorial government. The funding arrangement is slightly different in the Northwest Territories and Nunavut, where there are territorial transfer agreements with the federal government.

Canada rejected First Nation demands to operate services in accordance with tra- ditional laws and traditional justice systems. By contrast, in the United States, tribal courts have played an important role in the child welfare system since 1978.[93]

## Persistent problems

The discouraging news is that, despite the expansion of First Nations child and family services agencies, the overrepresentation of Aboriginal children in care contin- ues. Sometimes, the emphasis has seemed to be on simply creating more First Nations agencies.

There is a lack of vision for a system that can truly serve Aboriginal peoples. The BC Representative for Children and Youth has had some harsh words on the subject for the parties involved in child welfare in that province: "There is no clear direction as to how the Aboriginal child welfare system will be improved; there is no observable logic between how the current Aboriginal governance and service structure initiatives will improve services and there is no monitoring of the impact of the various initiatives undertaken to date."[94]

It is also troubling that the ability of First Nations child and family services agen- cies to develop culturally appropriate services has been constrained by inadequate funding. Of twelve First Nations agencies surveyed in 2005, 83.4% reported that they did not receive enough funds to ensure culturally appropriate services.[95] This hinders their capacity to provide effective services and contributes to the continuing overrep- resentation of Aboriginal children in care.

# Overrepresentation of Aboriginal children in care

## The data picture is far from complete

Data on Aboriginal children in child welfare care is not collected in a uniform and accessible manner across the country. Each province and territory has its own child welfare system, with different definitions of terms such as *child in care* and different methods for collecting information. Some data collection systems allow for comparison between Aboriginal and non-Aboriginal children but others do not. In terms of the reasons for investigations, the grounds for interventions, and the characteristics of children and families who are investigated, the picture across the country is far from complete.

Children may be placed in foster care, in group homes or residential facilities, or with relatives (often called kinship arrangements). However, whether a child welfare agency defines the child as being in care depends on factors such as the type of placement, whether it is formal or informal, and whether it is permanent or temporary. Direct comparisons are difficult, making national statistics ambiguous. Thus, it is a challenge to compile reliable statistics about the number of Aboriginal children in care at any given time.

## Alarming findings from recent research

The Public Health Agency of Canada, a federal agency designed to promote health and apply research to health problems, has partnered with some of Canada's leading child welfare researchers to develop the Canadian Incidence Study of Reported Child Abuse and Neglect. The study is developing information about the incidence of child welfare investigations in Canada, the numbers of children in care, the reasons for child welfare agency involvement with families, and the types of family stressors that can lead to child maltreatment.[96] So far, the study has analyzed data collected from selected child welfare agencies across the country in 1998, 2003, and 2008.[97]

In 2011, for the first time, the study published a First Nations Component, based on data collected in 2008.[98] The First Nations Component is a result of a partnership between the study's research team and the First Nations Component advisory committee, which includes representatives from national and provincial First Nations child welfare organizations.[99] It includes data from 89 provincial/territorial agencies, 22 First Nations and urban Aboriginal agencies, and 1 Métis agency (on a pilot basis).[100]

The authors of the 2011 First Nations Component of the Canadian Incidence Study of Reported Child Abuse and Neglect note that First Nations child welfare agencies vary enormously. Added to resource limitations, this made it impossible for the researchers to identify a sample of First Nations agencies that could reliably represent all such agencies. Thus, the study findings cannot be generalized and can only be said to apply to children living in the geographic areas served by the sampled agencies.[101]

Nevertheless, the findings point to vast overrepresentation of Aboriginal children in care. The study found that investigations involving Aboriginal children resulted in formal child welfare placements, including foster care, group home, and residential secure treatment (but excluding informal kinship care) at 12.4 times the rate for investigations involving non-Aboriginal children.[102] Placements into informal kinship care occurred at 11.4 times the rate for non-Aboriginal children. Overrepresentation in the latter category may not be entirely negative if it indicates that child welfare agencies were increasingly respecting the informal kinships structures in Aboriginal communities. Nevertheless, the number of Aboriginal children in formal care placement was found to be grossly disproportionate.

Statistics Canada's 2013 National Household Survey provides some further insight. The survey found that 14,225 Aboriginal children under the age of 14 were in foster care, representing 3.6% of all Aboriginal children under the age of 14. To put that in perspective, at the height of the residential school era, 10,112 students were in those schools.[103] Only 15,345 non-Aboriginal children were in foster care, representing 0.3% of non-Aboriginal children.[104] Figures from the 2011 Canada Household Survey show that, although Aboriginal people make up only 4.8% of Canada's population, Aboriginal children represent almost half (48.1%) of all children aged 14 and younger in foster care in Canada.[105]

The percentages vary considerably across the country, but Aboriginal children in care are grossly overrepresented in all the jurisdictions for which data is available. Table 1.1 shows stark differences in Ontario, Manitoba, Saskatchewan, Alberta, and British Columbia:[106]

**Table 1.1**
Aboriginal children in care vs. their proportion of provincial child populations

| Province | Aboriginal children as a % of the total child population | Aboriginal children as a % of children in care |
|---|---|---|
| Nova Scotia | 6 | 16 |
| Québec | 2 | 10 |
| Ontario | 3 | 21 |
| Manitoba | 23 | 85 |
| Saskatchewan | 25 | 80 |
| Alberta | 9 | 59 |
| British Columbia | 8 | 52 |

Source: Extracted from Sinha et al., *Kiskisik Awasisak: Remember the Children: Understanding the Overrepresentation of First Nations Children in the Child Welfare System*, 5.

NB: Data for New Brunswick and Canadian territories were not publicly available. Data collection protocols vary from province to province

Among these provinces, Ontario's rate of overrepresentation is the most dispro-portionate, with seven times as many Aboriginal children in care as their proportion of the population. Statistics are not available for the territories, but the ratios could be even higher than those for the western provinces given that the North has more recent experience with residential schools.

## International criticism

International law recognizes that children require special care in order to ensure that they enjoy fundamental human rights and dignity. The preamble of the United Nations *Convention on the Rights of the Child* states that to ensure that a child has the opportunity for "the full and harmonious development of his or her personality, [he or she] should grow up in a family environment, in an atmosphere of happiness, love and understanding." In safe and secure homes, children can be "brought up in the spirit of the ideas proclaimed in the Charter of the United Nations, and in particular in the spirit of peace, dignity, tolerance, freedom, equality and solidarity."

Concern for the "best interests of the child" is a central feature of the *Convention on the Rights of Child* and, in particular, must guide decisions about child welfare. In *Commentary 11*, the United Nations Committee on the Rights of the Child considered the application of international children's rights to Indigenous peoples, and stated clearly that it is in the best interests of children to be raised in a setting that respects their ethnic, religious, cultural, and linguistic background.[107] Indigenous children have the right to the preservation of their identity, including their nationality, name, and family relations. Where a child is illegally deprived of some or all of the elements of their identity, states must provide assistance to re-establish that identity.[108] Parents, extended families, and communities have rights, responsibilities, and duties when it comes to raising children, and the Convention requires states to provide assistance to ensure that the integrity of Indigenous families and communities are protected. The best interests of the child are the paramount consideration in any alternative care placement of Indigenous children.[109]

These international law principles are also firmly entrenched in the *Declaration on the Rights of Indigenous Peoples*. The declaration prohibits the forcible removal of Indigenous children to other groups.[110] Indigenous peoples also have the right to identity and to the preservation of their language and culture.[111] These rights are threatened by child welfare decisions that remove children from their families and communities without due consideration being given to those issues.

The overrepresentation of Aboriginal children in Canada's child welfare sys-tem has not gone unnoticed in the international community. In 2006, the United Nations Committee on Economic, Social and Cultural Rights noted "with concern that low-income families, single-mother-led families and Aboriginal and African Canadian families are overrepresented in families whose children are relinquished to foster care. The committee is also concerned that women continue to be forced to relinquish their children into foster care because of inadequate housing."[112] The committee recommended that, "in accordance with the provisions of article 10 of the covenant on the protection of families, the federal, provincial and territorial governments undertake all necessary measures including through financial support, where necessary, to avoid such relinquishment."[113]

In 2012, the UN Committee on the Rights of the Child cited the frequent removal of children from families as a "first resort" in Canada in cases of neglect, financial hardship, or disability, and decried the frequency with which Aboriginal children were placed outside their communities.[114] Noting that Canada had also failed to act on the federal auditor general's findings of inequitable child welfare funding, the committee concluded that "urgent measures" were needed to address the discriminatory overrepresentation of Aboriginal children in out-of-home care.[115]

The UN committee also urged Canada to "intensify its efforts to render appropriate assistance to parents and legal guardians in the performance of their child-rearing responsibilities with timely responses at the local level, including services to parents who need counselling in child-rearing, and, in the case of Aboriginal ... populations, culturally appropriate services to enable them to fulfil their parental role."[116] The committee called on Canada to "take immediate steps to ensure that in law and practice, Aboriginal children have full access to all government services and receive resources without discrimination."[117] There appears to have been little sense of urgency within the Government of Canada to respond to these repeated calls to take action.

## Why are so many Aboriginal children in care? The links to residential schools

The research literature and Survivors' statements to the Commission suggest that the legacy of residential schools is a significant factor in the overrepresentation of Aboriginal children in the child welfare system. According to a Saskatchewan study, there is strong evidence that "the residential school period [was] the beginning of an intergenerational cycle of neglect and abuse. This cycle is seen as one very important contributor to the significant over-representation of First Nations and Métis children and families in child welfare systems in the country today."[118]

In *Kiskisik Awasisak: Remember the Children*, the authors discuss the link between overrepresentation and the residential schools and mass removals:

Though [the 2008 data] cannot establish how many caregivers of investigated First Nations children may have experienced direct or intergenerational effects of the Sixties Scoop or residential schools, the data presented here cannot be properly interpreted without recognition of the ongoing implications of the historic pattern of mass removal of First Nations children from their homes and communities.[119]

In a 2002–03 survey by the First Nations Centre, 71.5% of residential school Survivors reported that they had witnessed the abuse of others and had experienced abuse themselves in the schools.[120] In the same survey, 43% of intergenerational Survivors believed that they were affected by their parents' experience at residential schools, and 73.4% reported that their parents were affected by their grandparents' experience at residential schools.[121]

At the Commission's request, the Indian Residential Schools Adjudication Secretariat analyzed information from claims submitted through the Independent Assessment Process (IAP) by Survivors of abuse at residential schools.[122] In a random sample of 203 files, claimants had a range of lasting effects of abuse:

- Depression or low self-esteem: 94%
- Relationship problems: 90%
- Parenting problems: 42% (more women than men)[123]
- Substance abuse: 78% (more men than women)
- Sexual issues: 65% (more women than men)[124]

One-third (33%) of the claimants reported having an encounter with the criminal justice system (40% of males and 24% of females).[125] This is significant because a parent who has been charged with a crime or has been the victim of a crime may be particularly vulnerable to child welfare investigations and apprehensions.

A majority of the IAP claimants in the sample had received some type of treatment, but 40% reported that they had none. Of those who sought one or more types of treatment, 32% received mental health therapy, 29% received alcohol treatment, 24% took part in traditional healing, and 12% received drug treatment.[126]

## No opportunity to learn to be parents

Residential school Survivors carry a heavy burden that profoundly influences their relationships and their ability to provide secure and safe homes for their families. The Royal Commission on Aboriginal Peoples concluded that the lack of opportunity to acquire parenting skills is one of the factors that contributed to the grossly dispropor-tionate incidence of violence and child apprehension in Aboriginal families.[127]

Many former residential school students who spoke to the Commission acknowledged the mistakes they made as parents and feel guilt for passing their trauma on to their own children. Alma Scott of Winnipeg was raped by fellow students and sexually abused by a headmaster at a residential school. Her experience at residential school had lasting impacts. She explained,

> [As] a direct result of those residential schools, I was a dysfunctional mother.... I spent twenty years of my life stuck in a bottle in an addiction where I didn't want to feel any emotions, and so I numbed out with drugs and with alcohol.... That's how I raised my children, that's what my children saw, and that's what I saw.[128]

The intergenerational impact of the residential school experience has left some families without strong role models for parenting. An investment in culturally appropriate programs in Aboriginal communities has the potential to improve parenting skills and enable more children to grow up safely in their own families and communities.

5) We call upon the federal, provincial, territorial, and Aboriginal governments to develop culturally appropriate parenting programs for Aboriginal families.

## Disproportionate numbers of investigations, disproportionate findings of "neglect"

In an analysis of the data gathered for the First Nations Component of the Canadian Incidence Study of Reported Child Abuse and Neglect, the authors of *Kiskisik Awasisak* confirmed that Aboriginal children in the geographic areas studied were significantly overrepresented as subjects of child maltreatment investigations. In the geographic areas served by the agencies sampled for this study, the rate of investigations of First Nations children was 4.2 times the rate of non-Aboriginal investigations.[129] The study also found that allegations were more likely to be "substantiated" in cases involving Aboriginal children. This was so in all categories of maltreatment, but the difference was most extreme for "neglect" investigations.[130] The investigations substantiated the allegations of neglect at eight times the rate for the non-Aboriginal population.[131]

In a further analysis of the First Nation Component data, Aboriginal families were found to have been investigated for neglect at six times the rate for non-Aboriginal families. The authors concluded that child welfare caseworkers were more likely to "substantiate" concerns about neglect when investigating Aboriginal families, even when compared to non-Aboriginal families experiencing the same kinds of risk factors (such as poverty, housing instability, domestic violence, etc.).[132] For example, they noted that a finding of substance abuse almost always resulted in a finding of neglect in the case of Aboriginal parents, but this was not so when the parents were non-Aboriginal. Concerns about housing were also more likely to substantiate findings of neglect involving non-Aboriginal children. This may reflect implicit assumptions that poor housing is more "normal" for Aboriginal families.

In a report for the Child and Youth Services Review, the authors concluded that "ethno-racial bias on the part of investigating workers" could not be excluded as a cause of the increased tendency to find neglect in investigations of Aboriginal children.[133] The authors stressed that findings of neglect account for much of the over-representation of Aboriginal children in the child welfare system.[134] This suggests that today, as in the residential school era, Aboriginal children are often taken away from their parents because of assumptions that they will be neglected.

## No clear standards for findings of neglect

Very little is known about how child protection workers identify cases of neglect.[135] In an analysis of supervisory neglect cases from the 2008 Canadian Incidence Study of Reported Child Abuse and Neglect, the researchers found that only 2% of cases resulted in injuries. They observed that "in the absence of visible signs of harm and established standards for adequate supervision of children, a question emerges on … the extent to which those take into account a variety of specific circumstances or cultural and social class differences and norms affecting 'acceptable' patterns of child care."[136] Moreover, "differences in family practices, in particular cultural difference, rather than clear evidence of harm or potential harm, may be driving some child welfare investigations."[137] The authors point out that providing family supports and prevention services may be a better response to supervisory concerns.[138] As noted earlier, however, similar recommendations have largely gone unheeded to date.

Social workers and others who conduct child welfare investigations need education and training about the history and impacts of residential schools. They should also be trained to assess the potential within Aboriginal communities and families to provide more appropriate solutions to family healing.

## Poverty and other risk factors

An analysis of the First Nations Component of the Canadian Incidence Study of Reported Child Abuse and Neglect confirms that poverty and social stressors are major factors in child welfare investigations involving Aboriginal families. Aboriginal parents were more likely to experience a host of serious risk factors, including domestic violence, alcohol abuse, lack of social supports, drug or solvent abuse, and a history of living in foster care or group homes.[139]

In cases of maltreatment investigations, poverty was much more prevalent in Aboriginal families. They were more likely to rely on income supports such as social assistance (49%) than non-Aboriginal parents (26%).[140] The researchers suggest that the high rate of Aboriginal child welfare investigations reflect "challenges linked with poverty."[141] It follows that reducing social assistance to Aboriginal parents may increase child welfare apprehensions. The direct connection between Aboriginal poverty and high child welfare apprehensions has been known for half a century. Yet Aboriginal children are still being taken away from their parents because their parents are poor.

First Nations represent ninety-six of the one hundred most disadvantaged communities in Canada.[142] Reserve communities have very limited emergency housing, food security, wellness and addictions services, supports for families, and recreation services. More research is needed, but the evidence suggests that the disproportionate number of Aboriginal children taken from their parents for "neglect" is tied to poor funding for their schools and health care services as well as other factors related to the legacy of residential schools.

True neglect is undoubtedly a threat to a child's health and well-being. However, the Commission is deeply concerned that the concept of neglect may be used to target Aboriginal families for child apprehensions. To eliminate any systemic discrimination and unconscious bias as a legacy of residential schools, it is clear that neglect investigations and outcomes should be assessed and monitored based on clear evaluation criteria.

For over a hundred years, Canadian law has, in various ways, continued to authorize government officials to take Aboriginal children away from their parents. The federal government funds child welfare services on reserves, but provincial laws are generally applied. Provincial and territorial child welfare laws continue to allow officials to apprehend Aboriginal children who are deemed to need protection. Parental rights can be curtailed or even ended if a judge determines that it is in the best interests of the children.[143]

Withdrawal from the child welfare field is not possible. That would leave many Aboriginal children vulnerable. However, without action to reduce the number of Aboriginal children taken from their families, the child welfare system itself will take the place of residential schools in doing damage to them. As adults, the children taken into care in the years to come will place high demands on social assistance and the health and justice systems. They will struggle economically and socially. They may pass damage on to their own children.

1) We call upon the federal, provincial, territorial, and Aboriginal governments to commit to reducing the number of Aboriginal children in care by:

  i. Monitoring and assessing neglect investigations.

ii.  Providing adequate resources to enable Aboriginal communities and child welfare organizations to keep Aboriginal families together where it is safe to do so, and to keep children in culturally appropriate environments, regardless of where they reside.

iii. Ensuring that social workers and others who conduct child welfare investigations are properly educated and trained about the history and impacts of residential schools.

iv.  Ensuring that social workers and others who conduct child welfare investigations are properly educated and trained about the potential for Aboriginal communities and families to provide more appropriate solutions to family healing.

v.   Requiring that all child welfare decision makers consider the impact of the residential school experience on children and their caregivers.

2)  We call upon the federal government, in collaboration with the provinces and territories, to prepare and publish annual reports on the number of Aboriginal children (First Nations, Inuit, and Métis) who are in care, compared with non-Aboriginal children, as well as the reasons for apprehension, the total spending on preventive and care services by child welfare agencies, and the effectiveness of various interventions.

## Deaths of Aboriginal children in care

It is very difficult to get a clear picture of Aboriginal child welfare across the country, but information about deaths of Aboriginal children in care is even more fragmentary. Where province-specific statistics are available, they are very troubling. In some parts of the country, Aboriginal children who come into contact with child welfare authorities are more likely to die than their non-Aboriginal counterparts.

In January 2014, the *Edmonton Journal* published a series of articles about deaths in Alberta's child welfare system. Alberta had never publicly reported on deaths of children in care. The newspaper's investigation revealed that Aboriginal children accounted for 78% of children who died in foster care between 1999 and 2013.[144] Aboriginal children are a small minority but represent 59% of children in care in Alberta. Yet the number of Aboriginal child deaths in care is even more disproportionate than the number of them in care in the first place. Of the seventy-four Aboriginal child deaths recorded in foster care, thirteen were due to accidents, twelve committed suicide, and ten were the victims of homicide.[145]

Forty-five of these Aboriginal children died while in the care of a provincial child welfare agency and twenty-nine died in the care of an on-reserve First Nations child and family service agency. Since First Nations agencies care for only a fraction of the children (27% in 2012–13) Aboriginal children are much more likely to die if they are in care on reserve. According to reporter Darcy Henton, this statistic "starkly highlights the federal/provincial funding disparity that gives off-reserve aboriginal children more services and more support."[146]

In the outcry following the *Edmonton Journal*'s revelations, the Alberta Centre for Child, Family and Community Research obtained more information about child welfare deaths from the provincial government. Their analysis showed that "Aboriginal children were much more likely than non-Aboriginal children to enter the intervention system, and had higher rates of mortality than non-Aboriginal children once they were in the system."[147]

By contrast, in British Columbia, a review covering the period between 1997 and 2005 found that Aboriginal children and youth represented 34% of children in care and 36% of the deaths.[148] While this roughly equal figure is not cause to celebrate, it illustrates that it is difficult to generalize about the scope of the problem across the country.

In Ontario, under a joint directive from the Coroner's Office and the Ministry of Children and Youth Services, children's aid societies report child deaths when the child or family was involved with child welfare in the year prior to the death. There are approximately one hundred such deaths in Ontario each year, representing about 8% of all child deaths in Ontario.[149] The Coroner's Office's Paediatric Death Review Committee chooses a subset of these cases for more extensive review, generally excluding cases in which the death was due to expected or uncomplicated natural causes. In 2012, 29% of the reviewed cases involved Aboriginal children.[150] (Twenty-one per cent of children in care in Ontario are Aboriginal.)[151] The committee found that in many of the Aboriginal cases, there were issues related to the child welfare agency's capacity to meet ministry requirements. A strained relationship between child welfare agencies and local First Nations communities was also identified as a problem.[152]

Death is only the most extreme example of harm coming to a child. This sample of experiences from different provinces strongly suggests that Aboriginal children in care specifically, disproportionately, and on a widespread basis throughout the country, continue to be deprived of services they require and protections they deserve.

## The death of Phoenix Sinclair

Phoenix Sinclair was a healthy baby girl born to Aboriginal teenage parents in Manitoba. Both parents had troubled pasts, and because of their own history as foster children, they intensely mistrusted the child welfare system. Phoenix was taken into care twice during her five years of life. She was twice returned to her family, with little support, on either occasion. The caseworkers assigned to her changed frequently. They had little face-to-face contact with the family or with Phoenix herself.

At least thirteen times, Winnipeg Child and Family Services received notices of concern about Phoenix's safety and well-being. In 2005, three months after the last notice, her mother and her mother's partner killed her. Her death went undiscovered for nine months.[153]

A commission of inquiry examined Phoenix's life, the services she received through Winnipeg Child and Family Services, and Manitoba's child welfare system generally. Former Saskatchewan judge Ted Hughes led the inquiry. He found that child welfare workers lacked awareness of the reasons families came into contact with the child welfare system and the steps caseworkers should take to support them. In Phoenix's case, caseworkers repeatedly closed her file, with minimal investigation, because they concluded that Phoenix was not in danger in the short-term. They failed to consider her long-term risk.[154]

Reporting on the inquiry in 2014, Justice Hughes noted that new practices had been put in place in recent years to identify families that needed help earlier, to assess a family's needs and strengths, and to provide services to enable them to keep their children safely at home. However, Justice Hughes also found that many of the services and supports families needed were still missing.[155] He endorsed a "prevention" approach that provides essential services to all children, accessible without the need to come into contact with a child welfare agency first.[156] This approach would draw on many resources within Aboriginal communities and support parents and families in a culturally appropriate way. Social workers would need better training in this scenario, including education on the legacy of residential schools.

Justice Hughes pointed out that the child welfare system alone cannot solve the child welfare problem. Nor can it address the fact that over 80% of children in care in Manitoba are Aboriginal, which he called a "national embarrassment." He wrote that Aboriginal children are overrepresented in the child welfare system because they live in "far worse circumstances than other children," for reasons that are "rooted in the legacy of colonization and residential schools, the conditions on reserves, cultural dislocation and loss of identity."[157] Observing that the child welfare system was doing a poor job of connecting families with the supports that are available to them, Justice Hughes acknowledged that the system could do little to alleviate poverty or the underlying causes of substance abuse, family violence, and sexual abuse.

Justice Hughes called for a collaborative approach: "Working with parents and harnessing the collective resources of child welfare and other provincial government departments, other levels of government, and the province's many community-based organizations, can make a difference to vulnerable families."[158] Central to such a collaboration would be the inclusion of Aboriginal governments, communities and community organizations, and families.

Following Phoenix Sinclair's death, the Manitoba Office of the Children's Advocate conducted a "child death review" of the deaths of all children, from January 2004 to May 2006, who were in receipt of child welfare services within one year of their death. Of the 145 deaths in the period, 99 files were available for review. The review concluded that no child died as a direct result of a breakdown in the provision of child welfare services, but there was a "pattern of difficulties that may have led to the death of the child." Many cases revealed a lack of appropriate community services, or if services did exist, they were difficult to access or coordinate.[159] Of the child deaths included in the study, 76% were Aboriginal or Métis [sic] and 24% were non-Aboriginal. The authors point out that "these figures closely follow the breakdown of children involved in the child welfare system, but given the fact that Aboriginal people comprise 14% of the total population, it appears that Aboriginal, including Métis children, are overrepresented in both the child welfare system and the deaths of children in general." Deaths by suicide appeared to be driving the higher mortality rates for Aboriginal children.[160] Eleven of the twelve suicides included in the study were Aboriginal children. Half of these deaths occurred while the children were in foster care.[161]

Deaths at the hands of others occurred with terrible frequency. Eighteen of the ninety-nine deaths reviewed were homicides. Aboriginal children accounted for fourteen of those deaths. Seven of the eighteen homicides involved children who, like Phoenix, were under the age of five. All of them were killed by a parent or caregiver, whether Aboriginal or non-Aboriginal. The killers of the older children were generally people outside the child's family. The review noted that "the majority of these children were living in homes with a very high level of risk to the children, but none had received a formal risk and/or safety assessment conducted when they first came into contact with a child welfare agency or when they were moved or returned to their family."[162] Authorities most often reported high-risk children as "absent without leave" when they went missing.[163]

## The Inuit experience with child welfare

Almost 60,000 Inuit people live in Canada.[164] Inuit also live throughout the circumpolar Arctic region, including parts of the United States (Alaska), Russia, and Denmark

(Greenland). Three-quarters of Canadian Inuit live in the traditional homeland known as Inuit Nunangat. Inuit Nunangat consists of four regions: Nunatsiavut in Newfoundland and Labrador, Nunavik in Northern Québec, Nunavut Territory, and Inuvialuit in the Northwest Territories. The Inuit have traditionally occupied these areas, but the regions are not fully autonomous self-governing entities. Of the approximately 16,000 Inuit people who live outside Inuit Nunangat, 37.5% live in large urban centres such as Ottawa and Montréal. The Inuit population is one of the youngest and fastest growing in Canada. About 40% of Inuit in Nunavik and Nunavut are under the age of 15.[165]

After the federal government forced Inuit people to move off the land and into permanent settlements in the 1950s, Inuit communities made significant attempts to regain self-determination and follow *Inuit Qaujimajatuqangit* (Inuit traditional knowledge). Traditional knowledge is grounded in principles for living a good life, including working for the common good, respecting all living things, maintaining harmony and balance, and planning and preparing for the future.[166]

Inuit communities are not organized by reserve or band systems like First Nations communities. Instead, they work within municipal and legislative models. The relatively new territory of Nunavut has the largest Inuit population and has incorporated Inuit traditional knowledge into all aspects of its formal governance, management, and operational structures. This has both successes and limitations.[167] Each Inuit region of Inuit Nunangat has gained increased control of the administration of social services, including child and family services. All regions struggle to build capacity to deliver these services, including the particular challenge of developing child welfare services that are culturally appropriate and take into account traditional Inuit practices of childrearing.[168]

## Traditional Inuit parenting

Traditional Inuit parenting is based on kinship relationships and cultural and spiritual beliefs. Inuit believe that a newborn named after a deceased relative takes possession of that relative's soul or spirit, and this is reflected in the parents' relationship with the child.[169] According to the national Inuit women's association, Pauktuutit, it "would not be considered appropriate ... to tell a child what to do, as this would be the equivalent of ordering an elder or another adult about, thus violating an important social rule in Inuit culture."[170]

Ignorance of this aspect of Inuit culture caused many non-Aboriginal people, including residential school administrators and child welfare officials, to make culturally biased judgments. They often saw Inuit parents as extremely permissive and indifferent to discipline.[171] At the residential schools, in contrast, teachers attempted to control a child's behaviour through corporal punishment and other harsh disciplinary measures distasteful to Inuit parents.

## Inuit custom adoption

In Inuit custom adoptions, the children have knowledge of and access to their birth parents. Traditionally, Inuit grandparents were integral in helping to raise their grandchildren, as well as orphaned or neglected children, through custom adoption. Inuit researcher Heather Ochalski points out that, traditionally, "many grandparents adopted their biological grandchildren. They often took orphaned children in as their own and called them *panik* (daughter) or *irnik* (son) ... Sometimes they took them in briefly to help the biological parents that were nearly starving and returned them to their parents when they were back on their feet."[172]

Residential schools and child welfare apprehensions eroded custom adoption practices, along with many other values and traditions of Inuit culture. Because they found Inuit names difficult to pronounce and spell, non-Aboriginal officials changed names to accord with Christian traditions. They imposed the European tradition of naming women and girls after the male head of the household, which devalued traditional kinship ties and imposed unfamiliar belief that females were inferior. From the 1940s to the early 1970s, the federal government assigned numbered disks as a naming system for Inuit, or "Eskimos" as the government and others called them. Despite the pressures, many Inuit continued to name their children after their ancestors and maintain traditional beliefs about naming practices.[173]

## Inuit communities get residential schools

The residential school system was fully operational in the rest of Canada by the time the federal government extended it to the Eastern Arctic in 1955. Until then, the government had largely ignored the Inuit.

The Inuit began moving closer to trading posts and trapping non-traditional animals to benefit from the fur trade, but poverty and the loss of a way of life was too often the result.[174] American officials witnessed these tragedies from their vantage point along the Distant Early Warning (DEW) Line sites spread across the Arctic Inuit homeland. The international criticism that followed prompted the Canadian government to establish residential schools for Inuit children on so-called humanitarian grounds.[175]

The *Indian Act* was amended in 1951 to state that "the race of aborigines commonly referred to as Eskimos" was not entitled to the legal rights and benefits defined for

Indians. This legal status did not protect Inuit children from being forced to attend residential schools.[176]

Most Inuit parents did not want this compulsory school system and tried to prevent their children from attending or returning to the residential schools and day schools. Researcher David King reports that the Family Allowance program, introduced in 1944 for families with children aged sixteen and under, encouraged school attendance. The government did not have an official policy of denying Family Allowance payments to families who refused to send their children to residential school, but it was federal policy to withhold these payments if students were not attending either residential or day school.[177]

There was a significant increase in the number of Inuit students attending day and residential schools between 1956 and 1963. During that time, attendance rose from 201 to 1,173 in the Eastern Arctic. In the Western Arctic, attendance rose from 1,755 to 3,341.[178]

As at the residential schools in the South, students were separated from their cultural practices and teachings. Inuit Elders were not allowed to be part of the education system in their traditional role as cultural teachers. Inuit children attending residential schools were expected to behave like *Qallunaat* (white people) in their communication, dress, and eating habits. The traditional diet was considered unhealthy because meat and fish were eaten raw. Inuit children were stripped of their Inuit name, family, language, and culture, and subjected to verbal, psychological, physical, and sexual abuse.[179]

Without their cultural teachings, Inuit children who attended the residential schools lacked the knowledge and tools to raise their own children in traditional ways. The cumulative effect of these experiences continues to affect Inuit communities and families, and it is within this context that contemporary Canadian Inuit child welfare issues must be addressed.

## From residential schools to child welfare in Inuit communities

The systemic abuse and breakdown of the culture and traditions that supported the health and well-being of Inuit families had far-reaching effects in Inuit Nunangat, profoundly changing family relationships. Anthropologist Nelson Graburn wrote that the vast majority of historical descriptions "bear little evidence of any kind of child abuse among the [Inuit] peoples."[180] But the residential schools deprived Inuit children of the opportunity to learn how to parent in traditional ways and left many students with the lifelong effects of trauma.

When residential school Survivors became parents, some modelled the harsh discipline and abusive punishments they had been subjected to as children. Today's

Inuit children, like First Nations and Métis children in other regions of the country, now bear the burden of the intergenerational trauma of the residential school era. Physical and emotional abuse suffered during childhood, loss of culture, overcrowded housing, and widespread drug and alcohol addiction all contribute to the prevalence of child abuse.[181]

Conditions for too many Inuit children include low educational outcomes, poverty, food insecurity, exposure to communicable diseases, poor health, family violence, intergenerational trauma, the loss of coping strategies, and epidemic suicide rates.[182]

In many Inuit communities, healthy food is very expensive. A single char sells for $99.53; a head of lettuce for more than $28; and four tomatoes for $8.20.[183]

Isolation, addictions, and a lack of resources and services can make it very difficult for Inuit parents to provide safe and healthy environments for their children, which increases the prospects of child welfare apprehension. The child welfare system in Inuit Nunangat is unable to deal with these challenges effectively.

Since the Inuit homeland is spread out over several territories and provinces, child welfare services depend largely on where an Inuit family lives. There are no Inuit-specific (or even Aboriginal-specific) child protection agencies in the North, although most of the child welfare laws include requirements to take the particular needs of Aboriginal children into account. Unlike the southern regions, child welfare services tend not to be specialized. Instead, child protection is often simply one of many responsibilities of local health and social service centres that must also deliver other types of supports and programs. For example, in addition to child and family services, social workers often also provide services to the elderly and people with disabilities.[184]

## Northwest Territories

In the Northwest Territories (NWT), the Department of Health and Social Services is responsible for the delivery of child and family services, including providing for the protection and well-being of children and youth through setting standards and ensuring compliance with policy and legislation. These services are currently delivered through six regional health and social services authorities and the Tlicho Community Services Agency (established under the Tlicho Land Claims and Self-Government Agreement). There are approximately seventy-five frontline workers and supervisors assigned to child protection duties across the Northwest Territories.

In an effort to improve service delivery, effective April 1, 2016, a new Northwest Territories Health and Social Services Authority will be established, which will replace the six existing regional authorities and work with the Tlicho Community Services Agency. Regional advisory councils will provide leadership and guidance to local program delivery to ensure that services remain culturally responsive. In the future,

Aboriginal governments in the NWT may choose to exercise jurisdiction over child and family services.[185]

Child welfare legislation requires that the child's cultural, linguistic, and spiritual or religious upbringing be considered. In addition, the child's Aboriginal community must be notified of any application for a child protection court order. There is also a provision for Aboriginal community councils and Aboriginal non-profits to form child and family services committees. These committees can participate in case planning for Aboriginal children and families. The *Aboriginal Custom Adoption Recognition Act* allows for the privately arranged adoption of children in a manner that respects cultural traditions.[186]

The rate of child welfare investigations is very high. The 2003 Canadian Incidence Study of Reported Child Abuse and Neglect found a rate of 141.48 child maltreatment investigations per 1,000 children.[187] Although this was not further broken down by Aboriginal identity, it is safe to assume that Inuit children would be deeply affected given that more than half of the population of the Northwest Territories is Aboriginal.[188] By comparison, the investigation rate for all of Canada was only 38.33 per 1,000.[189] In general, the Northwest Territories mirrored other trends identified in the Canadian Incidence Study of Reported Child Abuse and Neglect, with the top three categories of substantiated child maltreatment being neglect, exposure to domestic violence, and physical abuse. However, the rate of neglect investigations in the Northwest Territories was very high: 51% as compared with the national rate of 30%.[190]

## Nunavut

In Nunavut, where Inuit represent the large majority of the permanent population, there are no distinct Aboriginal or Inuit child welfare agencies. However, the territorial government has made a commitment to integrate Inuit social values into all programs and services. The Department of Health and Social Services is responsible for the delivery of all health and social services, including child welfare services. Community social workers provide a range of programs in addition to child protection, including early intervention and support to families, adoption services, and family violence prevention.[191] As in the Northwest Territories, Aboriginal community councils and non-profits can form child and family services committees to participate in case planning for Aboriginal children and families. As with many territorial government laws and policies modelled on those in the Northwest Territories when Nunavut was created in 1999, Nunavut also has an *Aboriginal Custom Adoption Recognition Act*, which allows for private adoptions of Inuit children in a manner that respects cultural traditions.[192]

There are no treatment facilities for mental health problems or addictions in Nunavut.[193] Individuals who need such services must travel to facilities in Saskatchewan, Alberta, or Ontario.

Lack of services within Nunavut has also posed a serious challenge for child protection. A recent social services review concluded that there is a perception that too many Inuit children have been placed outside the territory, leading to distrust of the system and a concern by Inuit that their cultures and values are not being respected.[194]

## Newfoundland and Labrador

In Newfoundland and Labrador, there are no delegated Aboriginal child and family service agencies. Aboriginal families receive child welfare services from the regional health authorities. The Labrador-Grenfell Regional Health Authority serves Inuit families.[195] The province's child welfare legislation recognizes the importance of respecting and preserving the cultural heritage of children, as well as the responsibility of the community and the extended family to support the safety, health, and well-being of children. Social workers use these cultural concepts in case planning for Aboriginal children. To enhance child and family service delivery in Aboriginal communities, the health authorities employ community members as community services workers. They assist social workers in providing culturally appropriate supports to Aboriginal families.[196]

## Nunavik

In Nunavik, Northern Québec, the Nunavik Regional Board of Health and Social Services is responsible for providing child protection services for Inuit families. The board covers two regions: Ungava Bay and Hudson Bay. Each region has a health centre that is responsible for health services, social services, a child and youth protection centre, a short-term hospital, a long-term residential care centre, and a rehabilitation centre for troubled youth. A board of directors oversees the regional board, and includes representation from each of the communities, the two local health centres and the Kativik Regional Government.[197] A director of youth protection reports to each of the health centres. These directors are responsible for applying child welfare legislation, recruiting foster families, and acting as provincial director for the purposes of the *Youth Criminal Justice Act*.[198] Clearly, child protection is only one of many significant tasks.

Inuit custom adoptions are not only permitted, but are frequent in Nunavik. One-quarter of the children born between 2000 and 2004 have been adopted.[199] However, concerns have been raised about the process of custom adoption in Nunavik. There are reports of some families forcing mothers to give up children for adoption. Some adoptions have proceeded in circumstances in which the adoptive family is known to be inadequate. If difficulties arise, the child may end up being adopted repeatedly.[200]

Following complaints about inadequate child welfare services in Nunavik, Québec's Commission des droits de la personne et des droits de la jeunesse launched an investigation. The commission's report, released in 2007, found that Inuit families in Nunavik are facing intense stressors and change, and that the child protection services are not meeting the challenge. The commission described the organizations as operating "in continual crisis mode."[201] There are not enough staff members and social workers to cover the vast geography and remote locations of Nunavik.[202] The lack of frontline social services and of preventive programs for children under eighteen is a deficiency that significantly undermines the effectiveness of child protection in Nunavik.

The commission concluded that the fundamental rights of children and young people in Nunavik had been infringed, "in particular the right to personal inviolability, to the safeguard of their dignity, and to the protection, security and attention that their parents or the persons acting in their stead are capable of providing."[203] Slight improvements were reported in 2010, but the commission said the Nunavik system remained fragile and precarious.[204]

## Gaps in services throughout the Inuit homeland

Regardless of where an Inuit family lives, they are likely to experience gaps in services, high numbers of child protection cases, difficulties with custom adoption and foster care, tensions between Inuit cultural values and the mandates and approaches of the agencies serving them, and inadequate prevention services.[205]

The shortage of social service workers is a significant problem. For example, the auditor general has found that in Nunavut, one-third of its community social service workers positions were unfilled. The Department of Health and Social Services was not meeting its key responsibilities for the protection and well-being of children, youth, and their families. Safety checks of foster and adoptive homes were not done routinely, nor were complete annual compliance reviews of child protection files being completed. These failures to meet legislative requirements placed children at risk. The department could not accurately track the status of children in care or understand their changing needs.[206] The government of Nunavut took these criticisms seriously and is taking steps to implement the auditor general's recommendations.[207]

Social workers who serve Inuit communities need more than simply an academic degree. They must understand the cultural needs and traditional practices of the communities in which they work. However, the Nunavut Law Review Commission (*Maligarnit Qimirrujiit*) reported that it is challenging for the social service system to deal with the custom adoption practice.[208] Nunavut continues to try to raise awareness and understanding of the Inuit way of life among those who make policies and work in child welfare. According to a report published by the National Aboriginal Health Organization, "traditional Inuit practices, such as custom adoption, [are] essential to improving family and child security. Formal support for kinship relationships and extended family and community responsibility for children can create healthy family environments for all Inuit children."[209]

Urban Inuit families and children also have difficulty accessing culturally appropriate services, with only a handful of agencies in the South offering programs for Inuit children and families. Promising approaches to adapting traditional practices to life in the city can be found at the Ottawa Inuit Children's Centre, Ottawa's Tungasuvvingat Inuit (a counselling and resource centre), the Manitoba Urban Inuit Association (providing culturally relevant services and helping Inuit peoples with the transition from the North to urban settings), and the Association of Montreal Inuit (a community organization for Inuit peoples). These non-profit organizations are working with Inuit families and child welfare agencies, providing cultural linkages, and promoting safe environments for healthy child development and family stability.

## The Métis experience with child welfare

Métis histories and experiences differ from those of other Aboriginal peoples in Canada in terms of their territories, relationship to the land, political institutions, and legal status. The Métis emerged as a distinct nation in the eighteenth and nineteenth centuries, and their historic homeland includes Manitoba, Saskatchewan, Alberta, and parts of Ontario, British Columbia, the Northwest Territories, and the northern United States.[210]

The Métis population in Canada is growing and increased by 16.3% between 2006 and 2011. The Métis now account for an estimated 32.3% of the total Aboriginal population and 1.4% of the Canadian population. Michif is the Métis language, spoken by an estimated 940 Métis in Canada. Many Métis people also speak Cree or other First Nation languages as well as French and/or English.[211]

Métis are defined through their identification with ancestors who lived in the historic Métis nation, and through their way of life, culture, language, and relationship to the land, rather than solely by bloodlines.[212] The Métis National Council says that a Métis is "a person who self-identifies as Métis, is distinct from other Aboriginal peoples, is of historic Métis Nation Ancestry, and who is accepted by the Métis Nation."[213]

Métis peoples have diverse cultural practices and different traditions of childrearing, which evolved from a variety of First Nation and European influences. However, Métis identity is intrinsically linked with and influenced by the extended family, which is the basic unit of Métis society. The residential schools challenged these familial connections, with far-reaching consequences.

## Fighting to be heard: Métis children in residential school

Originally, the federal government mandated residential schools to admit "Indian" children exclusively, although many Métis children attended these institutions unofficially. In 1913, the government policy to exclude Métis children from residential schools was reversed. As reported by the Royal Commission on Aboriginal Peoples, "they registered children from every Aboriginal culture—Indian, Inuit, and Métis children too—though the federal government assumed no constitutional responsibility for Métis people. While Métis children would be invisible, rarely mentioned in the records, they were nevertheless there and were treated the same as all the children were."[214]

Rates of admittance and attendance of Métis students ranged widely across geographical locations, communities, and even within families. At some schools, such as St. Paul de Métis in Alberta, Métis children were in the majority.[215] Before the Commission began gathering statements from Survivors, Tricia Logan was one of the only researchers to collect stories, memories, and oral histories from Métis Survivors of residential schools. Survivors frequently told her of their experiences as outsiders in "Indian schools."[216]

The more "Indian" a Métis child appeared, the more likely that he or she would be forced into a residential school. As a report for the Aboriginal Healing Foundation described it, "the closer the government thought the Métis were to First Nation communities, in a geographical or societal sense, the lower class of person they were thought to be. This lower class had priority over other Métis when being considered for admission to residential schools to ensure that the *outcasts and menaces* of society, living like Indians, were civilized."[217] School admittance was thus based on the perceived inferiority of children who presented as "Aboriginal" and were therefore in greater need of intervention.

With only a half-day of instruction at many schools, it was not unheard of for Métis children to attend schools for a decade or more yet receive nothing more than a Grade Two education.[218] As the Métis Nation of Alberta has observed, "There has been some documentation to suggest that the churches considered Métis to be half-white and therefore they were already half-civilized. This apparently justified offering less education to Métis students. Their labour went to financially support the school since much of what was produced in the farm programs was sold to business interests to support the schools and not used to feed the children."[219]

The intergenerational impacts of Métis experiences in residential and day schools include the loss of parenting skills, the inability to express feelings, and the loss of language and culture. Elmer Ghostkeeper, a Métis Elder from Alberta has eloquently expressed the impact of the residential school experience:

> Love is the greatest emotion in Métis families and this love for each other was greatly impacted by residential schools. Our ways of being as families were also affected. Our family life included fishing, hunting, and family activities such as learning language, berry picking, social time, baby caring traditions, and rites of passage. Our children were enslaved through the residential school system and lost those connections to our culture. [220]

Métis Elder Deborah Dyck recounted her story of attending Cranberry Portage school in Manitoba as a day student. Both of her parents taught at the school and tried to show kindness in the harsh environment. She recalled that "the residential setting was totally different than what Native kids were used to, it didn't have the aunty relationships.... As a people, the Métis had to be so resilient and ever chang-ing to live with an environment that was ever changing and moving. We were made stronger by this."[221]

Métis cultural consultant Tom McCallum, who attended residential school in Saskatchewan, reflected on parenting and residential schools:

> The most important thing is to keep children in touch with their family. They need to understand where they come from and experience love—they need love! Healthy, beautiful, love-filled family interactions were destroyed or attacked in the child welfare/residential school experience.... All parents sang to their chil-dren. Each child had a special song that was their song.... I'd walk into the house and my mom would be there and would start singing my song to me. She did this even when I was older. That's how we got nicknames.... They would always come from your song. We never called each other by our given names.[222]

The loss of culture and family relationships continues to reverberate, and poses challenges for today's child welfare system.

## Métis children and child welfare

Richard Cardinal was seventeen years old when he hanged himself in 1984. From the age of four until his death, this Métis boy lived in twenty-eight different child welfare placements across Alberta, including sixteen foster homes and twelve group homes, shelters, and locked facilities.[223] His diary documents his experience and his deep longing to be reunited with his family: "I kept telling myself that this was all a bad dream that I would wake up soon with Charlie and Linda and the rest of my family in our home in Fort Chipewyan but in reality I knew that I wouldn't wake and that this was real and not just a bad dream." [224] His tragic story brought public attention to the experience of many Aboriginal children in foster care.

Researcher Deborah Canada found that the Sixties Scoop had a profound impact on Métis in Manitoba, where "between 1971 and 1981, 70% to 80% of Manitoba's First Nation and Métis adoptions were made into non-Native homes."[225] Robert Doucette was a Sixties Scoop child. He recalled being told that his *mooshum* (grandfather), who attended residential school, was "quite mad" when Doucette was taken away at only four months old. His mooshum "was throwing rocks at the car and swearing at them in all the languages that he knew he could speak, Michif, Cree, Dene, French and English. I think he probably swore at them in each language, but he was powerless to stop them."

Doucette was adopted into a family with five other Métis foster children. His foster father had to fight with the school in Prince Albert to allow him to use his birth name of Doucette. He faced much racism in Prince Albert. Despite being an excellent hockey player who was offered a tryout with a Junior A team, he turned to individual sports like track and field where he had more control over how he was treated. Doucette recalled how he was "a brown white guy" until he began to study his culture as an adult. His sister in his foster home was not as lucky and took her own life while in a penitentiary in Kingston, Ontario. He recalled "how sad" it was that her birth father only saw his daughter when she was born and when she was buried.

Doucette told the Commission, "We have to deal with our own internal racism amongst ourselves, because there are a lot of people from the Sixties Scoop that are trying to make their way back, that are being abused by our own people, because they just don't want to believe that they are who they say they are."[226]

As is the case with the number of Métis children in child welfare, the number of Métis children adopted out in the Sixties Scoop can only be estimated. Reliable numbers are not available because Métis identity is inconsistently recorded. Métis children may not self-identify or even be aware of their Métis heritage. A lack of knowledge and training leads some social workers to misidentify Métis children as Aboriginal. Estimates of the number of Métis children in care are likely conservative and researchers are often unable to track the progress and outcomes of Métis children involved with child and family services.[227]

The First Nations Component of the Canadian Incidence Study of Reported Child Abuse and Neglect was not able to generate separate estimates of Métis child maltreatment investigations because there were not enough investigations of Métis children in the data to be statistically reliable.[228] Data is likewise scarce provincially. In British Columbia, the Ministry of Children and Family Development reported that of the 4,642 Aboriginal children in care in 2009, just over 650 (14%) were identified as Métis.[229] The provincial auditor in Manitoba reported an increase in the number of Métis children in care between the fiscal year 2009–10 and 2010–11, from 797 to 908.[230] But this appears to be the extent of concrete information. Clearly, there is a gaping hole in terms of knowledge about the experience of Métis children and child welfare; accurate and up-to-date research is vitally needed.

## Jurisdiction for providing services to Métis children

Without information, the distinct needs of Métis families cannot be met. A pan-Aboriginal approach is not appropriate. A Métis child's identity development "can be compromised in cross-cultural care if they are immersed in the dominant culture."[231] Métis peoples have traditional concepts of connectedness and kinship relationships that can form the basis for positive and effective child welfare interventions. Culturally appropriate supports from extended family can permit children to remain in their homes and communities.[232]

The development of Métis-specific child welfare institutions is in its infancy. The federal government does not provide funding for these services, taking the position that it is not responsible for Métis peoples, or indeed for any Aboriginal peoples who do not live on reserves. The government fought for twelve years to stop litigation aimed at obtaining a legal ruling on federal jurisdictional obligations with respect to Métis and "non-status Indians." In April 2014, the Federal Court of Appeal ruled in *Daniels v. Canada* that Métis are included as "Indians" within the meaning of the *Constitution Act, 1867*, which would mean that the federal government does indeed bear responsibility for Métis peoples.[233] The Federal Court of Appeal dismissed a lower court's finding that "non-status Indians" also fall within federal jurisdiction.[234] Both sides have appealed to the Supreme Court. It is anticipated that the Supreme Court will hear the case in 2015.[235] In the meantime, Métis children rely upon provincial child welfare agencies that, for the most part, are not designed to meet their unique needs.

There are some exceptions. The most developed Métis child welfare system is in Manitoba, where the first Métis child and family service agency in Canada was opened in 2000 as a result of an agreement between the province and the Manitoba Metis Federation.[236] Today, Métis peoples in Manitoba requiring child and family services receive culturally appropriate services from the Métis Child and Family Services Authority, delivered by the Métis Child, Family and Community Services and the Michif Child and Family Services Agency. The creation of this Métis-specific child welfare authority may lead to the more accurate identification of Métis children in care over time.

In Alberta, the province funds municipalities as well as Métis settlements for Métis child welfare services,[237] such as the Metis Child and Family Services Society in Edmonton and the Métis Calgary Family Services Society. In British Columbia, five Métis child and family service agencies deliver services while a non-profit organization, the Métis Commission for Children and Families, consults with the provincial government.[238]

Little progress has been made in Ontario, but the Métis Nation of Ontario has made recommendations to the provincial government to better adapt child welfare laws to the needs of its community. The Nation has recommended amendments to the *Child and Family Services Act* to allow for Métis-run child and family services. It has also suggested changes to the collection of data to identify Métis children in care, and better training for social workers to work effectively and respectfully with Métis families. As of spring 2015, these recommendations have not been implemented.[239]

Inequitable access to the kinds of health and healing services that can prevent the need for child welfare interventions further undermines the effectiveness of child welfare services. Health disparities, high unemployment, inadequate housing, and educational issues need to be addressed to ensure that Métis children have the best chance for a happy and healthy life.[240]

Métis Elder Leanne Laberge from British Columbia stressed the importance of taking every opportunity to take the Métis spirit into spaces where Métis people need to be represented.[241] In spite of the geographical differences of Métis peoples in Canada, Métis peoples are an extended family. In upholding the extended family, the role of Métis women will be critical, since "women are the teachers" who keep family information, stories, inspire the work ethic, and "look after the spiritual needs and knowledge of the family."[242]

Métis who were involved with residential schools or the child welfare system will need supports to ensure that they can reconnect with their traditions and "to recover what has been stolen in terms of their family stories, their cultural identity, and their ancestral pride."[243] It is not only the children taken who require such supports—the parents, extended families, and communities have also suffered.

The Government of Canada should not let unresolved jurisdictional disputes stand in the way accepting its responsibilities. Helping Métis people reconnect with their ancestral ties "means helping families to find and reconnect with those who have been taken, those lost in the foster care system, those taken to Europe by adoption, those lying in unmarked graves away from home."[244]

## Addressing the child welfare crisis

Child welfare institutions in Canada are failing First Nations, Métis, and Inuit children. All of these groups are being disproportionately investigated and then placed in child welfare care. Many of the conditions that result in disproportionate Aboriginal involvement in the child welfare system are related to the intractable legacies of residential schools including poverty, addictions, and domestic and sexual violence.

Mary Anne Clarke was married to a residential school Survivor. She told the Commission that she worries that child and family services are

> carrying on some of the same tragedies that kids[went]through [in]the residential schools. I'm a [Child and Family Services] worker myself, and I know what it's like to be in a position to apprehend children. But there's got to be a better way than having the community decimated by it. There's got to be a way to keep, strengthen the community, putting the supports and services that they need so that they don't get removed from the community.

She suggests that we move away from "band-aid solutions" and learn from the experience of the residential schools:

> If anything that the school situation has taught us, it's to listen. And I think we need to do the same for the ones who are victims of [Child and Family Services]. And I say victims. I know [Child and Family Services] has helped some people, I'm not saying that, but there's a lot of victims out there, too. And the system is not adequate. And if we listen to the people who have been affected, I do believe we find our answers.[245]

Child apprehension is not a step that child welfare officials take lightly. Yet, for most agencies, it is the only means they have to be funded for providing services. More resources devoted to a wide range of services could help prevent the need for critical interventions. As residential school Survivor Shirley Morris told the Commission, "You look at all these kind of problems and you see even some of our child services like an extension of the residential school system. How they're taking our children away instead of working with the parents and offering them help, and maybe even respite care. Because of the stress, they never learned to be parents, especially when they're having kids [at] sixteen, seventeen, eighteen. They don't know how to look after kids."[246]

Important steps have been taken to shift control over Aboriginal child welfare to Aboriginal peoples. But without the necessary funding and tools, Aboriginal child welfare agencies have been unable to significantly reduce the number of children in out-of-home care. More Aboriginal children continue to be placed in foster care each year than attended residential school in any one year. This is the most compelling evidence of the harmful and continuing legacy of residential schools.

The governments of Canada will need to address Aboriginal child poverty, including matters of housing, water, sanitation, food security, family violence, addictions, and education inequities and outcomes. Child welfare reform is essential, and the crisis of Aboriginal overrepresentation in child welfare cannot be addressed without interventions that also target its contributing causes.

## Lessons from the US *Indian Child Welfare Act*

The United States experienced a similar crisis of dramatic overrepresentation of Aboriginal children in care. Congress enacted the *Indian Child Welfare Act* in 1978 in response. Four years of hearings confirmed that "many state and county social service agencies and workers, with the approval and backing of many state courts and some federal Bureau of Indian Affairs officials, had engaged in the systematic, automatic, and across-the-board removal of Indian children from Indian families and into non-Indian families and communities."[247] Between 25% and 35% of all Indigenous children were removed from their families. About 90% were placed in non-Indigenous homes.[248]

Professor Lorie M. Graham wrote that the legislative studies and hearings leading to the passage of the Act "revealed how deeply ingrained the assimilative attitudes of the past had become in our society. The cultural values and social norms of Native American families—particularly indigenous child-rearing practices—were viewed institutionally as the antithesis of a modern-day 'civilized' society."[249] Professor Graham explained how the Act attempted to counter those attitudes and affirm the legitimacy and the importance of Indigenous families. She recognized that "no law could dictate a change in the attitudes of social workers, educators and judges regarding indigenous culture." However, a law could "minimize the effects of those lingering attitudes by setting minimum standards and procedures for the future placement of Native American children outside the home."[250]

The American law now in force governs any custody proceeding involving the termination of parental rights, the implementation of foster care, or the adoption of a Native American child. Tribal courts have exclusive jurisdiction over custody proceedings involving Native American children living on a reservation. Tribal courts also have concurrent and presumptive jurisdiction over child custody cases where the child lives outside of a reservation.[251]

Where a state court has jurisdiction over a case involving an Indigenous child, the Act provides for minimum procedural guarantees, including notice to both the parents and the Indian tribe if a state agency is petitioning for foster care or the termination of parent rights. Parents have the right to court-appointed counsel. State agencies have to prove "beyond a reasonable doubt ... that the continued custody of the child by the parent or Indian custodian is likely to result in serious emotional or physical damage to the child," which is a higher standard than that applied in custody proceedings involving non-Indigenous children.[252] The state agency must also call the testimony of "qualified expert witnesses" before parental rights can be terminated. To be qualified, the expert must have "particularized knowledge regarding Indian culture."[253]

If the court orders a placement, it must give preference to the Indian child's extended family or, failing that, another tribal community placement.[254] Child welfare agencies must prove that "active efforts" have been made to prevent the breakup of the family before a court can order foster care or termination of parental rights.[255]

The system in the United States is far from perfect. Critics have argued that state courts have simply used creative legal arguments to get around the provisions of the Act.[256] In 2013, three families and two tribes, the Oglala Sioux and the Rosebud Sioux, filed a class action lawsuit alleging that the State of Minnesota had repeatedly removed children from their homes without due process.[257] As in Canada, high rates of poverty, unemployment, crime, and substance use have contributed to the apprehension of Indigenous children, and even a reformed child welfare system can do little to alleviate these problems.[258]

Nonetheless, after thirty years, the *Indian Child Welfare Act* has achieved a number of positive results, including greater tribal authority over the placement of Indigenous children as well as the expansion of family preservation programs. Indigenous children are still removed from their homes in disproportionately high numbers, but the rate of overrepresentation has decreased. The rate of placement with non-Indigenous caregivers has also decreased.[259]

A number of Canadian jurisdictions have similar presumptions built into their legislation, such as the need to respect the integrity of Aboriginal families, the importance of cultural continuity, and the benefits of kinship care. However, the American model has one key difference: it places judicial control over child welfare in the hands of tribal courts.

To begin to address the national Aboriginal child welfare crisis, reform is essential. A key part of that reform is greater consistency in the regulatory framework that guides the work of child welfare authorities. That framework must acknowledge the central role of Aboriginal agencies in decision making about child welfare matters. As Aboriginal justice systems evolve, they too will come to play a part in determining child apprehension and custody matters. Establishing national standards is the first step towards developing greater consistency in decision making and ensuring that overrepresentation is reduced and that culturally appropriate placements become the norm.

4) We call upon the federal government to enact Aboriginal child welfare legislation that establishes national standards for Aboriginal child apprehension and custody cases and includes principles that:

  i. Affirm the right of Aboriginal governments to establish and maintain their own child welfare agencies.

  ii. Require all child welfare agencies and courts to take into account in their decision making the residential school legacy.

  iii. Establish, as an important priority, a requirement that placements of Aboriginal children into temporary and permanent care be culturally appropriate.

## The Touchstones of Hope approach to child welfare reform

In October 2005, Cindy Blackstock and colleagues presented a report titled *Reconciliation in Child Welfare: Touchstones of Hope for Indigenous Children, Youth and Families* to an audience at Reconciliation: Looking Back, Reaching Forward—Indigenous Peoples and Child Welfare, a conference held in Niagara Falls, Ontario. The report provides some helpful guidelines to consider in approaching child welfare reform:

- Recognize the past, and current, multigenerational and multidimensional impacts of colonization on Indigenous children, youth, and families;

- Honour those who suffered the loss of their family relationships and identities as a consequence of child welfare decisions, and those who have kept family relationships strong despite all odds;

- Respect those who have worked, and continue to work, to build and develop culturally based services and policies;

- Affirm that all Indigenous children and youth have the right to family (nuclear and extended), safety, and well-being, and to be able to identify with, and thrive as, a member of their culture of origin.

Further, it is expected that the path to reconciliation in child welfare will

- Acknowledge the mistakes of the past, and establish a child welfare profession based on non-discriminatory values, social justice, and fundamental human rights;

- Set a foundation of open communication that affirms and supports Indigenous families and communities as the best caregivers for Indigenous children and youth;
- Respect the intrinsic right of Indigenous children, youth, and families to define their own cultural identity;
- Improve the quality of, and access to, services for all children, youth, and families to free the potential of each person;
- Build a united and mutually respectful system of child welfare capable of responding to the needs of all children and youth;
- Strengthen the ability of the child welfare profession to learn, ensuring past mistakes do not become tomorrow's destiny.[260]

The document sets out five principles (self-determination, holistic response, respect for culture and language, structural interventions, and non-discrimination), framed within a four-phase process of reconciliation (truth telling, acknowledging, restoring, and relating). It includes tools to assist Aboriginal communities to clearly document their vision of healthy children and families and to work with Aboriginal and non-Aboriginal community members, professionals, and other stakeholders to implement the measures needed to achieve that vision. Touchstones of Hope seeks to stimulate a process for community-specific, community-driven plans for child safety. However, communities must have the resources and powers necessary to implement their own creative community solutions to the child welfare crisis.[261]

An independent evaluation of the implementation of the Touchstones of Hope principles in Northern British Columbia suggests that it has been very effective in shifting the relationship between First Nations and mainstream child welfare providers to one based on a shared vision and a commitment to better support First Nation families.[262]

## Promising program innovations

A number of promising and innovative Canadian programs have been developed. They are subject to Aboriginal control and inspired by First Nations wisdom and practices.

### Nishwnawbe-Aski's Talking Together Program

Nishnawbe-Aski Legal Services in Thunder Bay, Ontario, launched the Talking Together Program (TTP) in 2001 as an alternative to court proceedings in child protection matters. Talking circles bring together families, social service workers, and Elders to explore creative solutions in a non-judgmental environment. Their solutions are then implemented as the plan of care for the child.

The participation of families and community members is the cornerstone of the program. Rather than the usual, often ineffective addiction and anger management treatment options, TTP allows for more innovative solutions for the care of children.

In 2005, 135 children remained in their home communities following involvement with TTP. The next year even more, 218, remained in their community.[263] In some areas, TTP has been so effective that it has evolved into a prevention program rather than a crisis intervention service. This means the program is able to address concerns early so that child protection services do not have to become involved.

## Manitoba's Meenoostahtan Minisiwin
## First Nations Family Justice Program

The Meenoostahtan Minisiwin First Nations Family Justice Program in Manitoba was developed by a mandated Aboriginal child protection agency. The program brings families, community members, and service providers together to achieve long-term protection of children by getting at the roots of the family's concerns. The process is based on Aboriginal traditions of peacemaking, and all participants must be fully informed volunteers. Since 2000, the program has served approximately two hundred families each year.

A 2004 evaluation indicated very high levels of participant satisfaction. Participants said that their voices were heard, there was positive and open communication, and it was a safe and comfortable environment for families. The evaluation found that "95% of referring agents stated that the program was valuable to their First Nation community."[264]

## Aboriginal Legal Service of Toronto's Giiwedin Anang Council

This talking circle program involves volunteers from Toronto's Aboriginal community, including an Elder and an auntie for each talking circle. The talking circle may also include a representative from the child's community. The program provides a safe and culturally relevant place for families, children, and child welfare officials to come together to develop a plan that will meet the needs of the child.

Talking circles can take place before or after apprehension. After apprehension, the program requires the consent of at least one parent as well as Native Child and Family Services of Toronto, the mandated child protection agency for Aboriginal families in Toronto. Children over twelve years of age may participate in the talking circle. An auntie from the council will also meet with the child and represent the child's interests in the circle.

A council hearing cannot usurp the role of the courts in determining the best interests of the child. However, a council hearing may arrive at a plan for the child more quickly, and with greater participation from the parties.

Rene Timleck has acted as an auntie in the council. At one time, her own children were taken into care by the Children's Aid Society. Her own experiences help her "understand the fear the parents feel in their dealings with Native Child and Family Services," which has "the power to take or keep their children away." She also understands "the responsibility that the agency's workers feel in keeping the children safe."[265] Timleck described the circle as "a process that helps to heal families while protecting children." She continued,

> Much is revealed in a day-long hearing. Everyone involved comes closer to the truth than when they are in a courtroom. There is less chance of losing sight of the real issues in the Council process. In court proceedings, it is often how knowledgeable the lawyers are and who presents their case the most eloquently, rather than the real issues at hand—whether it be criminal or family proceedings. The council process allows for the problem to be dealt with on a more personal level, with the people involved being a part of the process. I believe that such councils could be a very effective tool in assisting people of any culture and, therefore, in all society.[266]

Timleck believes that the collective plans formulated in the circles can "allow for more people to be involved in the safekeeping of children in their communities.... With the Council, decisions are made by a collective, so the onus of responsibility is spread out amongst several people" rather than placed on a single judge.[267]

Another recent innovative approach to child protection cases is one that has been used with Indigenous families in Australia called the Signs of Safety approach.[268] Signs of Safety is a child protection model that focuses on partnerships with parents and children to stabilize and strengthen families. Some Aboriginal agencies in Manitoba have started studying this approach to whether it might be useful in a Manitoba context.

A move toward more community participation in child welfare matters and programs that draw on Aboriginal traditions and wisdom is encouraging. However, although Aboriginal programs may be better able to draw on kinship and community resources than court-based child welfare proceedings, it is important to recognize that most Aboriginal communities have limited resources. Such programs are resource intensive and require stable funding. Like all programs involving children, they should also be carefully evaluated.

Community programs are important and inspiring, but the ultimate solution to the child welfare crisis must lie in better child welfare decision making and culturally appropriate support of families, together with broader reform to address poverty, addiction, mental health, and family violence issues, which are themselves part of the legacy of residential schools.

## Conclusion

The legacy of Canada's colonial past, including the residential school system, cannot be simply willed to an end. We must ensure that Aboriginal parents, families, and communities have the resources they need to overcome the trauma of how they have been treated in residential schools and in broader society. The story of Canada's child welfare institutions and Aboriginal peoples suggest that the lessons of the residential schools have not yet been learned. A renewed approach to child welfare, based upon the *Touchstone of Hope* principles of self-determination, holistic response, respect for culture and language, structural interventions, and non-discrimination, can be a starting point to reversing the harmful legacy of the residential schools upon Aboriginal children and bringing about reconciliation.

Recognizing and prioritizing actions to redress the present and growing crisis of Aboriginal overrepresentation in the Canadian child welfare system will be a test of the political will and courage of the parties to the residential schools settlement agreement, and ultimately all Canadians.

# The failure to educate

The darkness of ignorance is in me, from the residential
school experience.

*—Howard Stacy Jones, former Kuper Island student*[1]

## Introduction

Given all the damage caused by the residential schools—the physical and mental abuse, the loss of culture and language, the forced separation of families—it is a bitter irony that one of the schools' greatest failings was the very quality of the schooling they provided.

Many principals and teachers had low expectations of their students. Wikwemikong, Ontario, principal R. Baudin wrote in 1883, "What we may reasonably expect from the generality of children, is certainly not to make great scholars of them. Good and moral as they may be, they lack great mental capacity." He did not think it wise to expect them to "be equal in every respect to their white brethren."[2] In preparing a 1928 report on the Anglican school at Onion Lake, a Saskatchewan government school inspector expressed his belief that "in arithmetic abstract ideas develop slowly in the Indian child."[3] Some thought it was a risky matter to give the students too much education. Mount Elgin principal S. R. McVitty wrote in 1928, "classroom work is an important part of our training, but not by any means the most important." He added, "In the case of the Indian 'a little learning is a dangerous thing.'"[4]

Given these attitudes it is not surprising to discover that the schools failed as educational institutions. Many Aboriginal students who attended residential schools were so ill-served there that they later struggled to succeed, either in furthering their education, or in the market economy, or in more traditional activities such as hunting and fishing. They were, as the Survivor John Tootoosis famously observed, "left hanging" between two worlds.[5]

Theirs is a story of marginalization and lost opportunity. The residential schools graduated few role models and mentors. The poor-quality education led people into chronic unemployment or underemployment. Beyond that, it led to levels of poverty, poor housing, substance abuse, family violence, and ill health. Although educational success rates are slowly improving, the fact remains that Aboriginal people still have lower educational and economic achievements than other Canadians. This is the legacy of residential schools.[6]

Non-Aboriginal Canadians have also been disadvantaged by educational systems that taught them that Aboriginal people were 'heathens' or 'savages.' Even today, those same systems routinely neglect the history and experiences of Aboriginal Canadians altogether.

This chapter is grounded in the understanding that education is a fundamental human and Aboriginal right, guaranteed in Treaties, international law, and the *Canadian Charter of Rights and Freedoms*. In particular, the *United Nations Declaration on the Rights of Indigenous Peoples* states that "Indigenous peoples have the right to establish and control their educational systems and institutions providing education in their own languages, in a manner appropriate to their cultural methods of teaching and learning."[7] These rights, however, have never been fully honoured.

The first part of this chapter examines the educational and income gaps that separate Aboriginal people and other Canadians and identifies the links between these outcomes and the residential school system. The second part of the chapter outlines the current crisis in Aboriginal education and how it continues the patterns of chronic underfunding and misunderstanding of Aboriginal people that characterized the residential schools. The third part of this chapter will focus on the recent history of Aboriginal educational reform. It will review how numerous task forces and parliamentary committees have recognized that the educational system is failing Aboriginal children and that the underfunding of First Nations schools on reserves is particularly acute. It will then examine how the federal government responded to these widespread calls for reform. The last part of this chapter will discuss a number of reform strategies for Aboriginal education that build on existing successes, and can ensure that the mistakes of the residential school era are not repeated.

## The long reach of the residential schools: Educational and income gaps

Canada's residential schools provided little education. Because successive governments considered Aboriginal people inferior, the schools offered only the most rudimentary education. As a result, generations of Aboriginal people ended up in the bottom ranks of Canadian society.

## A history of inadequate education

As educational institutions, residential schools were failures, and regularly judged as such. In 1923, former Regina industrial school principal R. B. Heron delivered a paper to a meeting of the Regina Presbytery of the Presbyterian Church that was highly critical of the residential school system. He said that parents generally were anxious to have their children educated, but they complained that their children "are not kept regularly in the class-room; that they are kept out at work that produces revenue for the School; that when they return to the Reserves they have not enough education to enable them to transact ordinary business—scarcely enough to enable them to write a legible letter."[8] The schools' success rate did not improve. From 1940–41 to 1959–60, 41.3% of each year's residential school Grade One enrolment was not promoted to Grade Two.[9] Just over half of those who were in Grade Two would get to Grade Six.[10]

Much of what went on in the classroom was simply repetitious drill. A 1915 report on the Roman Catholic school on the Blood Reserve in Alberta noted, "The children's work was merely memory work and did not appear to be developing any deductive power, altogether too parrot like and lacking expression."[11] A 1932 inspector's report from the Grayson, Saskatchewan, school suggests there had been little change: "The teaching as I saw it today was merely a question of memorizing and repeating a mass of, to the children, 'meaningless' facts."[12]

In the minds of some principals, religious training was the most valuable training the schools provided. In 1903, Brandon, Manitoba, principal T. Ferrier wrote that "while it is very important that the Indian child should be educated, it is of more importance that he should build up a good clean character." Such a heavy emphasis was required, in Ferrier's opinion, to "counteract the evil tendencies of the Indian nature."[13] The staff handbook for the Presbyterian school in Kenora in the 1940s stated it was expected that, upon leaving the school, most students would "return to the Indian Reserves from which they had come." Given this future, staff members were told that "the best preparation we can give them is to teach them the Christian way of life."[14]

Before the Second World War, many schools followed a system that saw the children doing farm and domestic work for half of each day. This work schedule significantly limited their classroom and study time.

When the students were in school, the classrooms were often severely overcrowded. At the Qu'Appelle school in 1911, Sister McGurk had seventy-five girls in her junior classroom. The inspector of Roman Catholic schools reported to Ottawa that this was an "almost impossible" situation.[15] In 1915, two teachers were responsible for 120 students at the Coqualeetza Institute in Chilliwack, British Columbia.[16] In 1928, there were sixty students in the junior classroom at the Port Alberni, British Columbia, school.[17]

The Indian Affairs schools branch maintained that the principals and the staff were "appointed by the church authorities, subject to the approval of the Department as to qualifications."[18] In reality, the churches hired staff and the government then automatically approved their selections.[19] The churches placed a greater priority on religious commitment than on teaching ability.[20] Because the pay was so low, many of the teachers lacked any qualification to teach.[21] In 1908, Indian Affairs inspector F. H. Paget reported that, at the Battleford school, "frequent changes in the staff at this school has not been to its advantage." The problem lay not with the principal, but with the fact that "more profitable employment is available in the District and, furthermore, the salaries paid are not as high as are paid in other public institutions."[22] When a British Columbia Indian agent recommended that schools be required to hire only qualified staff, he was told by his superior, British Columbia Indian Superintendent A. W. Vowell, that such a requirement would result in the churches' applying for "larger grants." And, as Vowell understood it, Indian Affairs "is not at present disposed to entertain requests for increased grants to Indian boarding and industrial schools."[23] In 1955, 55 (23%) of the 241 teachers in residential schools directly employed by Indian Affairs had no teacher's certificate.[24] In 1969, Indian Affairs reported it was still paying its teachers less than they could make in provincial schools. "As a result, there are about the same number of unqualified teachers, some 140, in federal schools [residential and non-residential] now, as ten years ago."[25]

Since the 1920s, Indian Affairs required residential schools to adopt provincial curricula.[26] The department also asked provincial governments to have their school inspectors inspect Indian Affairs schools.[27] The wisdom of this practice had been questioned during the hearings of the Special Joint Committee of the Senate and House of Commons inquiry into the *Indian Act* in the 1940s. Andrew Moore, a secondary school inspector for the Province of Manitoba, told the committee members that Indian Affairs took full responsibility for all aspects of First Nations education, including curriculum.[28] He said provincial education departments, including the one he worked for, were "not organized or not interested in Indian schools."[29]

The decision to leave curriculum to provincial education departments meant that Aboriginal students were subjected to an education that demeaned their history, ignored their current situation, and did not even recognize them or their families as citizens. This was one of the reasons for the growing Aboriginal hostility to the Indian Affairs integration policy. An examination of the treatment of Aboriginal people in provincially approved textbooks reveals a serious and deep-rooted problem. In response to a 1956 recommendation that textbooks be developed that were relevant to Aboriginal students, Indian Affairs official R. F. Davey commented, "The preparation of school texts is an extremely difficult matter." It was his opinion that "there are other needs which can be met more easily and should be undertaken first."[30] In the following years, assessments of public-school textbooks showed that they continued to perpetuate racist stereotypes of Aboriginal people.[31] A 1968 survey pointed out that in some books, the word *squaw* was being used to describe Aboriginal women, and the word *redskins* used to describe Aboriginal people.[32]

Despite the many challenges they faced, some of the children of the residential schools were able to enjoy subsequent success, sometimes as teachers or mission-aries themselves. However, many left the schools without adequate skills and with an aversion to education. Myrna Kaminawaish went to the Fort Alexander residential school. She remarked, "Learning became very hard for me because I associated learn-ing with being beat or, you know. So learning was very terrifying for me."[33] As a result, she attained only a Grade-Three education.

Paul Kaludjau attended school in Chesterfield Inlet on the Hudson Bay coast. He recalled how his father used to call him and his fellow students "educated bums" because, as he said,

> I knew nothing about survival on the land, because everybody was dependent on harvesting from the land and everything else. And during that time when we went to school, when we learned how to speak English, it labeled us as a little bit separate from the family now, because we knew something they didn't know in the speaking of the language.... You weren't close to the community anymore because you were not a skilled hunter anymore.[34]

As with many of the residential school students, Kaludjau's experience only strengthened his commitment to his family's ways of living: "I tried really hard to become that skillful hunter after that, and because someone was labeling you as a not very skillful hunter because of your education. But for me, that made me more aggres-sive in trying to make sure that I lived up to their expectations, and it helped me more to become stronger myself."

Walter Russell Jones attended the Port Alberni residential school. He recalled a stu-dent there asking,

> "Can I go to grade 12?" And that supervisor said, "You don't need to go that far," he says. He says, "Your people are never going to get education to be a profes-sional worker, and it doesn't matter what lawyer, or doctor, or electrician, or any-thing, that a person has to go to school for." He says, "You're going to be working jobs that the white man don't want to do."[35]

Too often the residential school system is regarded as a relic of the past. However, the last residential school closed in the mid-1990s. Forty-seven per cent of on-reserve residents between the ages of fifty and fifty-nine attended residential schools.[36] The Northern territories have the largest proportion of children whose parents attended residential schools (38%).[37]

## A legacy of abuse

In 1895, when commenting on the physical abuse of students by the staff of the Red Deer school, Indian agent D. L. Clink noted the disciplinary measures used by one teacher "would not be tolerated in a white school for a single day in any part of Canada."[38] In the coming years, others would comment on the excessive discipline employed in the schools.[39] Despite this, Indian Affairs failed to develop and implement comprehensive and consistent directives, and to monitor for effective and appropriate discipline. By so doing, it sent the message that there were no real limits or consequences to what could be done to Aboriginal children within the walls of a residential school.

In their mission to 'civilize' and Christianize, the school staff relied on corporal punishment to discipline their students. That punishment often crossed the line into physical abuse. Although it is employed much less frequently now, corporal punishment is still legally permissible in schools and elsewhere under Canadian law. Section 43 of the *Criminal Code* reads, "Every schoolteacher, parent or person standing in the place of a parent is justified in using force by way of correction toward a pupil or child, as the case may be, who is under his care, if the force does not exceed what is reasonable under the circumstances." The Commission believes that corporal punishment is a relic of a discredited past and has no place in Canadian schools or homes.

6) We call upon the Government of Canada to repeal section 43 of the *Criminal Code of Canada*.

The abuse that characterized life at the schools was not conducive to learning anything other than fear and self-hatred. Patricia Brooks recalled that at the Shubenacadie, Nova Scotia, residential school, "the way the teachers spoke to us every day, that we weren't even native, we were just like, they were talking about somebody else; so you'd just kind of disassociated yourself from the fact that the native people, it was you. But they never said anything encouraging about native people."[40] Thus, many students left the school filled with self-loathing and loathing of their own family and community. They also often left with a profound distrust of education.

## Successes and failures

Most students left residential schools as soon as they could. A 2010 study of Aboriginal parents and children living off reserve found that among those who did not complete high school, 36% had attended residential school, while 28% had not.[41] Only 7% of the parents who attended residential school obtained a university degree, compared to 10% for those Aboriginal parents who had never attended these institutions.[42]

These findings are consistent with findings of a random sample of 203 files pulled from the Independent Assessment Process (IAP), a dispute resolution process that is available to those who suffered sexual or severe physical abuse at residential school. Twenty-three per cent of the claimants in the sample did not identify any specific level of school completion, suggesting a low level of achievement. Of those reporting a level of educational attainment, 13% said they attained less than a Grade-Seven education, 28% attained Grade Seven to Nine, 28% completed Grade Ten to Twelve, and 11% received a GED (a high school equivalency diploma).[43] According to the 2011 National Household Survey, among Aboriginal people aged 25 to 64, 28.9% had "no certificate, diploma or degree," while the proportion for non-Aboriginal people in the same age group was 12.1%.[44] The residential school Survivors in the IAP sample appear to have completed high school at a much lower rate than the national averages for both Aboriginal and non-Aboriginal people generally.

Only 20% of the former residential school students captured by the IAP study had completed a college certificate/diploma or university degree. This level of post-secondary education is far below the educational attainment amongst Aboriginal people generally (48.4%) and even further below the non-Aboriginal population (64.7%).[45]

Some students, however, were able to succeed despite their negative experiences at residential school. Violet Rupp failed Grade Nine at the Assiniboia residential school after she had been sexually assaulted by a staff member. She explained to the Commission,

> I always had to watch my back 'cause I'd see him once in awhile and he'd be look, staring at me, you know, just be avoiding him all over the place, all over the residence. I was scared to meet him in the hallways; I was scared to go out, out of my dorm. I was scared that, you know, he might try to do something worse; but I didn't tell anyone because I felt ashamed and I was afraid. And I was afraid that nobody would believe me.... But after that though I, I had that determination to be strong and just to continue. I wanted to prove myself that I can, I can succeed even though, you know, I was violated. And I went on, went on. I went to university. I have, I went on and got married, I have four children. And it seems to me I'm always, you know, making my sure my girls are, you know, are ok. I'm always phoning them, asking them if they're ok. So I just, you know went, went to school and got my Bachelor of Education degrees, my two Master's degrees; I never gave up.[46]

Esther Lachinette-Diabo became a teacher after attending the Spanish residential school. She noted,

> I'm thankful that I was in there, in the school, in that system because I did become educated.... The boarding school used to have public speaking contests, and so I aspired to become a public speaker. I've learned to speak English really,

really well, and I learned to speak loud and clear. So, I think that part that I did receive an education. But as far as family connections, that was all lost.[47]

## The income gap

The failures of the residential school system had an impact well beyond the childhood of the students. It adversely affected the kinds of jobs and earnings they could obtain as adults. Darryl Siah, attended residential school in Mission, BC. He was homeless when he provided the Commission with his statement in May 2011. He told the Commission how he valued education but became uncomfortable with it as a result of his experiences at residential schools:

> And as long as you ... do your homework and stuff, and you'll get a real good education, and ... make something out of yourself. You'll be a lawyer or a doctor, or nurse, or you name it, you can do it if you always go right through the whole school, right. Now, I probably could have been something, too, if I went all the way. I didn't want to. I didn't feel comfortable being there.[48]

In the sample of IAP claimants, 55% reported working as "physical labourers," followed by 56% who identified as "casual workers."[49] The IAP statistics reflect a far greater reliance on "lower-skilled" labour than the Canadian labour market as a whole. According to the 2011 National Household Survey, only 11% of Canadian workers are employed in jobs that do not require secondary school completion or higher.[50]

The residential school litigation and subsequent settlement did little to address these aspects of the residential school legacy. The Common Experience Payments went to individuals, not communities. Although there was a promise that any residual amounts could later be allocated to educational purposes, the settlement has done little to overcome the educational barriers that the children and grandchildren of residential school Survivors still face. Their lives have also been impacted by the poor education experienced by their parents and the resulting high levels of poverty and family breakdown. As a result, poor educational attainment, low rates of employment, and high rates of poverty persist as the continuing legacies of residential schools for this next generation.

It should be noted that while successful IAP applicants have been awarded on average $115,000, this is compensation for the sexual and serious physical abuse they endured. It is not compensation for the poor education they received and its related loss of economic opportunity.

## The intergenerational impact

The barriers that residential school Survivors faced after leaving school have had serious repercussions for their children. Factors such as parents' educational levels and household income are powerful predictors of the school success of their children.[51]

While there are few studies that focus specifically on the children of residential school Survivors, some data is starting to be gathered. One study found that on-reserve First Nations youth aged twelve to seventeen are more likely to report having learning problems at school and having had to repeat a grade if one or both of their parents attended residential school.[52]

Another study found that Aboriginal children living off reserve whose parents attended residential school are less likely to be doing well at school, compared to Aboriginal children whose parents did not attend these institutions.[53] In addition, former residential school students are less likely to have incomes in the highest 20%, and are more likely to report experiencing food insecurity. All three of these factors— parental residential school experience, household income level, and food security— combine to impede success in school for their children.[54]

The study also found that students who spoke an Aboriginal language at school were more likely to be doing well in school, a further indication that the denial of language rights at residential schools contributed to difficulty in school for the children of Survivors.[55]

While secondary and post-secondary graduation rates for Aboriginal people have improved since the closure of the schools, considerable gaps remain when compared to the non-Aboriginal population. The 2012 Aboriginal Peoples Survey showed that 72% of First Nations people living off reserve, 42% of Inuit, and 77% of Métis aged 18 to 44 had a high school diploma or equivalent. These figures are similar to those from the 2006 Aboriginal Peoples Survey. In comparison, the 2011 National Household Survey revealed that 89% of the non-Aboriginal population had at least a high school diploma.[56]

The result is that access to post-secondary education is not an option for the majority of Inuit young people or for First Nations youth living on reserve.[57] In 2006, only 2.9% of First Nations people living on reserve had completed a university education, compared to 18.1% of the general Canadian population.[58] The federal auditor general commented, "In 2004, we noted that at existing rates, it would take 28 years for First Nations communities to reach the national average. More recent trends suggest that the time needed may be still longer."[59] Given the youthful demographics of Aboriginal communities, there is an urgent need for change.

According to the 2012 Aboriginal Peoples Survey, 43% of off-reserve First Nations people, 26% of Inuit, and 47% of Métis aged 18 to 44 had post-secondary credentials (i.e., a certificate, diploma, or degree above the high school level). According to the National Household Survey, the corresponding figure for the non-Aboriginal population in 2011 was 64%.[60]

Most of the gains in high school completion rates have been led by Aboriginal women.[61] Completion rates at the secondary level are higher for Aboriginal women than for Aboriginal men, although they are still below the Canadian average.[62] Again, it is young Aboriginal women who are driving most of the increases in Aboriginal post-secondary attendance.[63] More research is needed to explain the achievement gaps between Aboriginal men and women.

The connection between residential schools and lower than average educational and economic attainments is particularly evident in data that shows that residential school Survivors have less income than other Aboriginal people, and that their children have more difficulty in school.

Aboriginal people have a lower median after-tax income; are more likely to experience unemployment; and are more likely to collect employment insurance and social assistance.[64] In 2010, the employment participation rate for Aboriginal workers was 75% compared with 86.7% for their non-Aboriginal counterparts. This 11.7 percentage-point gap reflects an increase in the disparity between Aboriginal and non-Aboriginal workers over the course of the economic downturn that began in 2008.[65] These statistics cover all Aboriginal groups, with their own variations.

Aboriginal people also have earnings well below their non-Aboriginal counterparts. The median income for Aboriginal peoples in 2006 was 30% lower than the median income for non-Aboriginal workers ($18,962 vs. $27,097).[66] Earnings are highly influenced by educational attainment. Aboriginal adults aged 18 to 44 who have finished high school are more likely to be employed than those who did not have a diploma. Among off-reserve First Nations people, 72% who finished high school were employed, while only 47% of those who did not finish had jobs. Among Inuit, 71% who completed high school were employed, while 44% of those who did not finish had jobs. For Métis, the figures were 80% versus 61%. While men in the general population usually have higher rates of employment than women, this was not the case among First Nations people living off reserve, Inuit, and Métis who had completed high school. For all three groups, female completers were as likely to be employed as their male counterparts. In terms of earnings, among First Nations people living off reserve and Métis, the median employment income ranges for completers were $10,000 higher than for leavers. Among Inuit, the difference in median employment income between completers and leavers was $20,000.[67]

The income gap between Aboriginal and non-Aboriginal people closes almost completely when Aboriginal people attain a university diploma, which, as noted above, they do at a far lower rate.[68]

Not surprisingly, the child poverty rate for Aboriginal children is very high—40%, compared to 17% for all children in Canada.[69] These statistics cannot be explained away simply on the basis that many Aboriginal people live in rural communities. These children are living with the economic and educational legacy of the residential schools.

Aboriginal Canadians earn less than non-Aboriginal workers regardless of whether they work on or off reserve, in urban, rural, or remote locations.[70] The proportion of Aboriginal adults living below the poverty line[71] is also much higher than those of non-Aboriginal adults, with differences ranging from 7.8% for adult men aged 65 or older, to 22.5% for adult women aged 65 or more. The depth of poverty is also much greater, with Aboriginal people having an average income that's further below the poverty line on average than that of non-Aboriginal adults.[72]

Even with the opportunities that flow from Aboriginal rights settlements, many Aboriginal adults are not fully able to take advantage of those benefits. For example, with land-rights negotiations finalized in the four northern Inuit regions, residents are increasingly looking for opportunities to work within government to implement these final agreements. The Government of Nunavut has stated a goal of hiring beneficiaries of the Nunavut Land Claim Agreement (Inuit peoples) to match their proportion of the total Nunavut population. However, while in 2007, Inuit made up 85% of the Nunavut population, they comprised only 50% of the total public service workforce with the majority of those (92%) employed in administrative support positions. The majority of the higher paying positions were filled by non-Inuit workers.[73] Former Justice Thomas Berger, in his 2006 evaluation report on the implementation of the Nunavut Land Claims Agreement, noted that Inuit employment in the government of Nunavut was "achieved early on, and has not been improved upon for the simple reason that only a few Inuit are qualified for the executive, management and professional positions that make up the middle and upper echelons of the public service."[74]

Low education rates have an ongoing impact on the economic well-being of the North in general because of the social consequences associated with high unemployment, greater numbers of young people caught in the justice system, and more health-related issues linked to poverty.[75]

Aboriginal people also experience the feminization of poverty. Despite the fact that Aboriginal women are more likely to complete high school and attend post-secondary school, they report lower median household after-tax income than Aboriginal men.[76] Aboriginal women over the age of 65 are much more likely to live in poverty than Aboriginal men in the same age group (53.4% vs. 37.4%).[77] The unemployment rate for Aboriginal women was almost double that of non-Aboriginal women in 2006 (13.5% vs. 6.4%).[78] These markers all suggest a population suffering significant inequality and social exclusion.

# The Treaties

Aboriginal peoples have always expressed a commitment to education for their children. Such hopes are reflected in the language of the early Treaties. For example, Treaties 1 and 2 included a commitment by "Her Majesty" to "maintain a school in each reserve hereby made, whenever the Indians of the reserve shall desire it." Treaty 6 reads as follows: "Her Majesty agrees to maintain schools for instruction in such reserves hereby made, as to her Government of the Dominion of Canada may seem advisable, whenever the Indians of the reserve shall desire it." Other Treaties, such as Treaty 10, protected the right to education by way of agreements to pay teachers' salaries. Thus, access to education was an essential element of the early Treaties, capturing a desire by First Nations to foster the capacity to adapt to the changing world.[79]

Although the federal government does provide basic educational funding for First Nations communities, promises made in the Treaties have never been fully kept.[80] Without control over their own education, the educational system has more often than not been alien to Aboriginal people, both within the residential school system, and in the public system.

# International rights to education

The right to education is recognized in a number of international human rights documents, including the *International Covenant on Economic, Social and Cultural Rights* (article 13), the *Convention on the Rights of the Child* (articles 28 and 29), and the *United Nations Declaration on the Rights of Indigenous Peoples* (article 14). The right to fair wages, equal remuneration for work of equal value, social security, and an adequate standard of living are listed in the *International Covenant on Economic, Social and Cultural Rights* (see articles 6 to 11) and are also guaranteed in the *United Nations Declaration on the Rights of Indigenous Peoples* (article 17). The *International Covenant on Economic, Social and Cultural Rights* (articles 6 and 7) provides for the right to work, the opportunity to earn a living, and the right to just and favourable work conditions.

Fulfilling the promise of the *UN Declaration on the Rights of Indigenous Peoples* will be key to overcoming the legacy of the residential schools. The "expert mechanism" established by the UN to provide advice on the *Declaration on the Rights of Indigenous Peoples* observed that Indigenous peoples have been subjected to monolithic mainstream education systems that eroded traditional ways of life and languages, imposed foreign belief systems, and institutionalized discriminatory attitudes. In the face of these violations, "it is the responsibility of States to address and undo past wrongs to reform mainstream education systems."[81] Not only has a right to education been recognized in international law, but so has the right to correction of the wrongs that result when that right has been breached.

The right to education is connected to the fulfillment of other basic human rights. In a commentary on the *Convention on the Rights of the Child*, the Committee on the Rights of the Child observed,

> Quality education enables indigenous children to exercise and enjoy economic, social and cultural rights for their personal benefit as well as for the benefit of their community. Furthermore, it strengthens children's ability to exercise their civil rights in order to influence political policy processes for improved protection of human rights. Thus, the implementation of the right to education of indigenous children is an essential means of achieving individual empowerment and self-determination of indigenous peoples.[82]

In 2009, the employment rate for Aboriginal youth was 45.1%, compared to 55.6% for their non-Aboriginal counterparts. The employment gap is growing despite increased educational attainment for Aboriginal peoples.[83]

A number of residential school Survivors have put a human face on these trends in educational and income inequality. Laverne Victor attended the Kamloops, British Columbia, school. She explained,

> I didn't do well in school. I didn't like school. And nobody knew why, and I couldn't, nobody would listen to me or understand me, so I just kept it all to myself, and that's probably when I started blocking everything. It was at the age of nine and ten was when I started blocking everything out of my, my mind, because nobody would, nobody would believe me, and nobody would listen to me.

Beyond her own experiences, Victor fears for her children:

> They don't feel like they fit and belong, but the, they need the better education, so they need to go to the public schools. I've been stressing, they're ... trying to bring our, our native culture into the schools, but something I've noticed is that they're only bringing it into the schools for the natives. It's not for the non-natives to learn.

She stressed that all people need to learn about Aboriginal languages and cultures and that "everybody needs to be taught who we are, why we do what we do, and that natives are not just a bunch of drunken Indian bums that live on welfare."[84]

## Australia's "Close the Gap" commitments

In the wake of its apology in 2008 to Indigenous people for its assimilationist policies, Australia committed to closing the educational and employment gaps between its Indigenous and non-Indigenous populations. Australia's commitments include

- ensuring access to early childhood education for all Indigenous four-year-olds in remote communities by 2013;

- halving the gap in reading, writing, and numeracy achievements for children by 2018;

- halving the gap for Indigenous students aged twenty to twenty-four in Year 12 attainment or equivalent attainment rates by 2020; and

- halving the gap in employment outcomes between Indigenous and other Australians by 2018.[85]

In a detailed report in 2015 on closing the gap, the Australian prime minister acknowledged that most of these targets would not be met. However, access to early childhood education has improved, with 85% of Indigenous four-year-olds in remote communities enrolled. Nationally, the proportion of Indigenous twenty- to twenty-four-year-olds who had achieved Year 12 or equivalent increased from 45.4% in 2008 to 58.5% in 2012–13.[86] In the Commission's view, failure that is both measureable and public is far preferable to governmental silence. It is especially striking that Australia has made progress on a commitment to early childhood education for four-year-old Aboriginal children while Canada has made no similar commitment. Current proposals for First Nations educational reform in Canada only address education from six years of age, despite widespread evidence of the importance and benefits of early childhood education.

7) We call upon the federal government to develop with Aboriginal groups a joint strategy to eliminate educational and employment gaps between Aboriginal and non-Aboriginal Canadians.

## Aboriginal education in crisis

Aboriginal education in Canada is a complicated mix of policies and funding models from various levels of government, Aboriginal and non-Aboriginal. The federal government funds schools on reserve, with the actual operation of those schools often delegated to the local First Nation. Aboriginal children who live off reserve are educated through the provincial or territorial school systems.

Finally, there are some educational systems completely run and managed by First Nations through self-government and other types of tripartite agreements. The jurisdictional complexities in these different education systems create challenges for effective reform.

## Integration or assimilation

By 1945, the Indian Affairs residential school system, having been starved for funding for fifteen years, was on the verge of collapse.[87] Not only was the existing Indian Affairs education system lacking money and resources, but there were also no school facilities of any sort for 42% of the school-aged First Nations children.[88] Having concluded that it was far too expensive to provide residential schooling to these students, Indian Affairs began to look for alternatives. One was to expand the number of Indian Affairs day schools. From 1945–46 to 1954–55, the number of First Nations students in Indian Affairs day schools increased from 9,532 to 17,947.[89] In 1949, the Special Joint Committee of the Senate and House of Commons Appointed to Examine and Consider the *Indian Act* recommended "that wherever and whenever possible Indian children should be educated in association with other children."[90] In 1951, the *Indian Act* was amended to allow the federal government to enter into agreements with provincial governments and school boards to have First Nations students educated in provincially run public schools.[91] By 1960, the number of students attending such schools (9,479) was roughly equal to the number living in residential schools (9,471).[92] The transfer of First Nations students into the public school system was described as "integration." By then, the overall policy goal was to restrict the education being given in Indian Affairs schools to the lower grades. Therefore, it was expected that during the course of their schooling, at least half of the students then in Indian Affairs schools would transfer to a 'non-Indian' school.[93]

The integration policy was opposed by some of the church organizations. Roman Catholic church officials argued that residential schooling was preferable for three reasons:

1. Teachers in public schools were not prepared to deal with Aboriginal students.

2. Students in public schools often expressed racist attitudes towards Aboriginal students.

3. Aboriginal students felt acute embarrassment over their impoverished conditions, particularly in terms of the quality of the clothing they wore and the food they ate.[94]

These were all issues that students and parents raised as well.[95] Annie Wesley told the Commission about the time she spent in residential school in Kenora:

> The results were devastating. Many quit school all together. I was sent to an
> all girls' residential school in Pembroke, Ontario, and I ended up alone again,
> because the other native students were so lonely they went home. At the white

school, we were not welcome by the other students. We were outcasts in this white residential school. [96]

Dorothy Ross recalled being called "squaws, a dirty Indian" in the public school she attended in Sioux Lookout, Ontario.[97] Shirley Leon told the Commission,

I was one of the first students from the Okanagan band that was integrated in the 1950s, into the public schools … We had horrific experiences because we were the savages, we were taunted. Our hair was pulled, our clothing torn, and we hid wherever we could, and didn't want to go to school. So, those kinds of stories are, are just as traumatic as what happened at residential school.

Leon told the Commission that "when we took social studies, it was 'the damned Indians, the drunken Indian, the savages,' and it's no wonder we skipped school, we dropped out of school, and didn't want to be there."[98] She subsequently obtained her high school equivalency in the same year that one of her daughter's graduated from high school.

The abdication of federal responsibility for providing a proper education system and the necessary funding can only be viewed as a continuation of the government's long-term policy of assimilation. The First Nations Education Council, Nishnawbe Aski Nation, and the Federation of Saskatchewan Indian Nations take the position that "the fully documented chronic underfunding of our education system is among the many strategies or tactics currently being used to force our integration into the provincial system which is better funded than the First Nations system."[99] Not only are provincial schools better funded by the provincial governments that established and oversee them, but the federal government also funds them at a much higher per-student rate than they do on-reserve schools. Underfunding of on-reserve schools has meant that all too often First Nations children, as they did with residential schools, have to leave their families and communities to attend schools far away. It is difficult for the Commission to accept that such an approach, including separation from family and community and eventual assimilation into non-Aboriginal society, can honestly be seen to be in the best interest of Aboriginal children.

Today, 40% of students living on reserve attend schools that fall under provincial jurisdiction (particularly those pursuing a high school education).[100] Provincial and territorial schools are the only option for Métis students, for other Indigenous children without recognized status, and for those First Nations children who do not live on reserves. Their educational outcomes are not significantly better than those who attend First Nation schools on reserve.[101] The Royal Commission on Aboriginal Peoples (RCAP) observed that the highest drop-out rate for Aboriginal students came as they entered high school, often away from their home communities, and when they may have their "first direct experience with the attitudes of the mainstream society," including "racist attitudes and behaviour."[102] RCAP recommended innovative approaches that could facilitate distance learning and keep children in their home communities.

## Educating First Nations children on reserves

As the Senate Standing Committee on Aboriginal Peoples noted in 2011, "First Nations education is in crisis."[103] In some reserve communities, First Nations children do not even have an actual school building.[104]

There are approximately 72,000 students attending 518 First Nation schools.[105] Despite those numbers, many children must still leave their homes and families behind if they wish to obtain an education, particularly at the high school level. As was the case with many residential school students, some First Nations students do not return home from provincial schools. In Ontario, an inquest has been called to examine the deaths of seven First Nations students who died between 2000 and 2011 while boarding in Thunder Bay to attend high school.[106]

In 1969, Indian Affairs Minister Jean Chrétien introduced a white paper proposing an end to the *Indian Act* and an end to the special legal relationship between Aboriginal peoples and the Canadian state. He proposed it as an exercise in equality. However, Aboriginal leaders quickly rejected the document as an abrogation of their Treaty rights. The federal government withdrew the white paper and proclaimed its commitment to the concept of "Indian Control of Indian Education."[107]

However, the interpretation of 'Indian control' put forward by the Government of Canada bore little resemblance to the vision held by First Nations people. The government's version of Indian control meant the devolution of federal education programs to First Nations, without the benefit of adequate funding or statutory authority.[108] Indeed, when devolution began, it was designed to occur without any additional expense. This meant that schools, which were already substandard compared to provincial norms, were handed over to the First Nation bands to run, without giving the bands the means to operate them effectively. Authors Jerry Paquette and Gérald Fallon wrote,

> thrust into the world with *no* program or administrative infrastructure whatsoever, and no resources to create such infrastructure ... these communities found themselves completely alone and bereft of any means to develop the capacity to administer their schools coherently—much less in a way that would adapt provincial curricula to ensure "cultural continuity and development."[109]

Thus, devolution delivered nothing more than the illusion of control.

The Aboriginal scholar Andrea Bear Nicholas notes that local decisions are heavily constrained by the party holding the purse strings—the federal department of

Aboriginal Affairs and Northern Development. Most band-operated schools are forced to accept provincial curricula and assessment standards, teacher certification, and—with the exception of Québec and parts of the North—the use of English as the language of instruction.[110] As a result, the curriculum for the majority of First Nation schools is virtually identical to that found in the provincial and territorial schools.[111] Consequently, the current situation is not significantly different from the residential school era, when Aboriginal communities had no say in the content and language of their children's schooling.

As Verna Kirkness points out, the current system bears no relationship to traditional modes of teaching that taught

> knowledge necessary for daily living. Boys and girls were taught at an early age to observe and utilize, to cope with and respect their environment. Independence and self-reliance were valued concepts handed down to the young. Through observation and practice, children learned the art of hunting, trapping, fishing, farming, food gathering, child rearing, building shelters. They learned whatever their particular environment offered through experiential learning.[112]

The funding of First Nations schools was inadequate from the start. The formula under which they were funded was last updated in 1996, and does not take into account the range of basic and contemporary education components needed to deliver a quality education in the twenty-first century, such as information and communication technologies, sports and recreation, language proficiency, school operating costs, student data management systems, and library services.[113] Worse still, after 1996, funding increases for First Nation education were capped at 2% for nearly a decade.[114] The original 2% annual increase was initially put in place as an assurance that Aboriginal funding would be guaranteed 2% increases even while other government departments were being cut back drastically. However the 2% cap was retained even when increased spending in other government departments was permitted. In recent years, the modest growth in funding has been insufficient to keep pace with rising costs and the significant increases in the Aboriginal student population.[115]

There is a lack of information and transparency on the funding inequities that exist between federally and provincially funded schools. Even though Aboriginal Affairs has committed to funding a First Nation education system that is comparable to the provincial schools, an internal audit found that the department does not collect the information required to confirm whether or not this goal is being met. The collection of accurate, consistent, relevant, and accessible information is important if we are to measure and close gaps between Aboriginal and non-Aboriginal peoples that are in part a legacy of the residential schools.

A 2012 evaluation (commissioned by the federal government) found that Saskatchewan stood out as a province in which the provincial school boards receive significantly more funding per student (the actual difference was not identified in the report). In the other regions, evaluators with Aboriginal Affairs determined there was either no difference in funding, or that First Nation schools appeared to receive more than non-Aboriginal public schools.[116]

However, the Aboriginal Affairs consultants delved deeper, examining the funding provided to provincial school boards with fewer than 1,000 students—which are more directly comparable to First Nation schools. This comparison revealed a marked inequity in funding. For example, in Ontario, the smaller school boards receive approximately $17,000 per student, while First Nations schools receive under $10,000. In Québec, smaller school boards receive approximately $12,000 per student, while First Nation schools receive approximately $8,000. Manitoba was the only province in which funding per student for First Nations schools exceeded the funding per student for small provincial school boards.[117]

In *Canada v. Mohawks of the Bay of Quinte First Nation*, Ontario's First Nations argue that the funding policies discriminate against larger First Nations because they receive considerably less per capita than smaller First Nations.[118] The view of the Commission is that funding should be measured equitably, with comparably sized and located provincial schools.

The underfunding of schools on reserve violates legal Treaty obligations and continues the legacy of discriminatory neglect and underfunding seen in the residential schools. Even the funding that is available is unstable and short term, with First Nations schools having to re-apply with each funding cycle.[119] This makes long-term planning next to impossible.

## Capital costs

Funding shortfalls extend to capital expenditures for First Nations school buildings as well. There are at least one hundred schools that are in such poor condition that they are considered unsafe, with no plan in place to either repair or replace them.[120] For example, the school in North Caribou Lake in Northern Ontario is plagued by black mould. The outside walls of the building are so weak that they move when pushed. Large-scale repairs are necessary but are not possible with the funds provided by Aboriginal Affairs.[121]

The Office of the Parliamentary Budget Officer noted that, in 2009–10, capital expenditures were "under-funded by about $169 million in the best case, and $189 million in the worst-case scenario."[122]

## First Nations children attending provincial schools

Provincial education systems are built around a school board structure (often called second-level structures). School boards determine the number, size, and location of schools. They build, equip, maintain, supervise, and furnish schools and provide student transportation. These boards provide education programs, such as special education, prepare annual budgets, hire teachers and other staff, and organize professional development. The boards ensure schools abide by the standards established in provincial education laws. By comparison, First Nations educational organizations operate in relative isolation.[123]

Provincial schools are also governed by their ministries of education. These ministries set education policy, determine school curricula, approve texts, establish student standards, determine teacher qualifications, and set classroom size, as well as invest in research and analysis to measure the achievement of students.

Most First Nations do not have a comparable level of governance, although there are examples of First Nations working together to form education authorities and regional management organizations. There are positive examples emerging in Saskatchewan, with tribal councils establishing "second-level" services and regional management organizations.[124] In Québec, the Cree School Board was established under the 1975 James Bay and Northern Quebec Agreement.[125] Cree language and culture are at the basis of the curriculum, which is designed and controlled by the Cree—including setting a Cree school calendar that allows Cree youth to participate in traditional hunting and fishing. It provides education services to primary, secondary, and post-secondary students.[126] But even with a modern agreement, the Cree School Board has had difficulty with funding and the board had to go to court to ensure that it was an equal participant in establishing the funding formula that would apply to their own schools.[127]

There are also examples of First Nations political organizations working to provide similar supports in some areas.[128] But none have the capacity, or the mandate or, most importantly, the funding to match even a tiny portion of what a provincial or territorial ministry of education has.[129]

The education inequity continues when Aboriginal parents send their children to provincially run schools. First Nations are obliged to pay fees to school boards so that their children can attend public schools. The First Nations then receive money from the federal government to cover those fees. However, Ottawa does not take into account any increases in provincial student fees so the First Nations often have to pay the difference. Table 2.1 demonstrates the gap between federal funding and the rates that the band has to pay to send student to local school boards.

Table 2.1. Tuition fees for Timiskaming First Nation students vs. federal funding, 2010

| School Board | Provincial tuition fees charged for First Nation students attending provincial schools | | Band school rates paid by Aboriginal Affairs | |
|---|---|---|---|---|
| School Board | Elementary | Secondary | Elementary | Secondary |
| Northeastern Catholic School District of Ontario | $12,796 | N/A | $4,951 | N/A |
| District Ontario North East | $11,584 | $12,552 | $4,951 | $5,579 |
| Conseil catholique Grandes-Rivières Ontario | $12,280 | $14,528 | $4,951 | $5,579 |

Source: FNEC, NAN, and FSIN, *Report on Priority Actions in View of Improving First Nations Education,* 42.

As the table demonstrates, the Timiskaming First Nation must pay between $11,584 to $12,796 for each child they send off reserve to attend a provincial public or Catholic elementary school. Yet they receive less than half that amount from Aboriginal Affairs (just $4,951) for the funding of each student's education.

First Nations struggle to ensure their children receive even an adequate education. They do so "with tenuous authority and without any specific funding to enable their systems to provide second-and-third level services comparable to those offered by provincial/territorial systems."[130]

The Senate Standing Committee on Aboriginal Peoples found that the absence of adequate funding supports is "among the key factors that contribute to the unacceptable gap in educational attainment rates between First Nations students and their Canadian counterparts; a gap that is unlikely to substantially improve unless this educational infrastructure deficit is addressed."[131]

8) We call upon the federal government to eliminate the discrepancy in federal education funding for First Nations children being educated on reserves and those First Nations children being educated off reserves.

9) We call upon the federal government to prepare and publish annual reports comparing funding for the education of First Nations children on and off reserves, as well as educational and income attainments of Aboriginal peoples in Canada compared with non-Aboriginal people.

# Meeting learning needs of Aboriginal students

Aboriginal students in many cases have diverse and unique needs that mean simply providing identical funding to a provincial school system is not sufficient. The need for the schools to teach Aboriginal language and culture is one example of such needs. Hundreds of Survivors have told the Commission that the incorporation of Aboriginal culture and language into the life of First Nation schools and communities is essential to overcoming the impact of the residential schools.

Provincial education systems must better accommodate Aboriginal children especially given the growth of urban Aboriginal populations. A 2013 study by the education advocacy group People for Education indicates that, while over 90% of schools in Ontario have Aboriginal students, and while 82% of Aboriginal children in Ontario attend provincial schools, "51% of elementary schools and 41% of secondary schools offer no Aboriginal education programs or opportunities, such as professional development or cultural support programs."[132] Native studies scholar Leroy Little Bear notes that language, songs, stories, and ceremonies are the repositories of knowledge. He states that "knowledge, from an Indigenous perspective, is the relationships one has to 'all my relations,'" which he says includes "everything in creation."[133] These elements are generally not evident in the provincial and territorial education systems. In spite of efforts to be more inclusive of Aboriginal learners, public schools are not Aboriginal places of learning.

Although efforts are being made, such as the development of the Common Curriculum Framework for Aboriginal Language and Culture Programs in the western provinces,[134] in general provincial, federal, and territorial governments have not committed the necessary resources to accomplish the task.[135]

The Canadian Heritage department's Task Force on Aboriginal Languages and Culture has identified immersion and bilingual programming as the preferred method for providing language education. But it noted in 2005 that very few such programs are available to First Nations, Inuit, or Métis students due to lack of support from school boards or other educational authorities, limited funding, and lack of teachers and materials.[136]

Elementary schools with higher proportions of Aboriginal students are also half as likely to have specialist physical education, health, or music teachers. Studies show that 59% of First Nations and Métis high school students are in applied courses (as opposed to academic courses) compared to a 30% provincial average.[137] In other words, the legacy of low expectations for Aboriginal children manifested in the residential school era continues today.

Ontario has taken steps to improve the educational experience of Aboriginal students, to work with Aboriginal leaders and organizations to improve education outcomes for Aboriginal students, and to develop curriculum that more accurately reflects Aboriginal issues and history.[138] Support documents have been developed for teaching seven Aboriginal languages, and Aboriginal language courses are available as an alternative to French as a second language. Curriculum policy documents have been developed for teaching Native studies in Grades Nine through Twelve. [139]

The province has established a baseline from the 2011–12 year from which it will be able to more accurately measure whether outcomes for Aboriginal students improve.[140] The baseline shows that First Nation, Métis, and Inuit students are not achieving at the same level as all Ontario students. For example, Grade Three and Six reading scores show gaps ranging from 5 to 33 percentage points between the numbers of First Nation, Métis, and Inuit students and the numbers of English- and French-language students achieving at or above the provincial standard; Grade Three and Six writing scores show gaps ranging from 8 to 35 percentage points; Grade Three and Six mathematics scores show First Nation, Métis, and Inuit student results ranging from 6 to 51 percentage points below all English- and French-language student results; Grade Nine mathematics results indicate a gap of up to 19 percentage points. The percentage of First Nation, Métis, and Inuit students accumulating 8 or more credits in their Grade Nine year ranges from 10 to 24 percentage points below the provincial average.[141]

This baseline data is critical for measuring successes and failures as Ontario continues to work with Aboriginal communities to improve the quality of education provided to Aboriginal students in the provincial schools and serves as a good model for other provinces and territories.

## Early childhood education

The Royal Commission on Aboriginal Peoples stressed the importance of early childhood education, stating that "Aboriginal parents and educators consistently press for holistic programs that address the physical, intellectual, social, emotional, and spiritual development of children." The report went on to say, "This priority should guide the design and operation of all early childhood programs."[142] It also noted that early childhood programs were excellent vehicles for parental involvement and for use of Aboriginal languages, and recommended that they should be delivered in a way that maximizes Aboriginal control and parental involvement.[143]

Despite some increases in funding and availability of childcare spaces after the RCAP recommendations, Aboriginal families continue to suffer from a general lack of early childhood education. Based on 2011 data, the Assembly of First Nations (AFN) reported that 78% of children aged 0 to 5 do not have access to licensed day care.[144]

RCAP also emphasized that parents play a key role in preparing their children to participate in two worlds.[145] The Royal Commission recommended that all schools serving Aboriginal children should adopt policies that welcome the involvement of Aboriginal parents, Elders, and families in the life of the school.[146] It recognized that this would require not only Aboriginal control of schools where possible, but also that provincial and territorial governments work more closely with Aboriginal people to develop "innovative curricula that reflect Aboriginal cultures and community realities,"[147] which would also encourage the teaching and preservation of Aboriginal languages.[148]

Since 1995, Health Canada has run the Aboriginal Head Start program, claiming to support over 9,000 children in 300 different programs in First Nations communities on reserve.[149] However a 2012 evaluation done for the Public Health Agency of Canada reported that there were only 4,640 spaces for children aged 0 to 6 in these programs. Furthermore, there are almost 48,000 Aboriginal children aged 3 to 5 living off reserve. The report noted this vast underservicing despite the higher needs of Aboriginal children who

- are overrepresented in the child welfare system;
- experience higher levels of moderate and severe food insecurity (33%) than non-Aboriginal populations (9%);
- are twice as likely to experience poverty as the general Canadian population; and
- are two to three times more likely than non-Aboriginal Canadians to be raised by young, single parents.

The evaluation also reported that it found "no evidence of systematic coordination between the Public Health Agency and other federal departments delivering similar programs, namely Aboriginal Affairs and Northern Development Canada, as well as Human Resources and Skills Development Canada."[150]

Although some provinces are moving towards full-day kindergarten for five- and even four-year-olds, others are not. In provinces and territories such as Alberta, Saskatchewan, and the Northwest Territories that leave such decisions to individual school divisions, it seems unlikely that full-day programs will be extended to school districts with high Aboriginal populations.[151] Given the young demographics of First Nations communities, it is particularly disappointing that neither the federal government's 2013 *Blueprint for Legislation* nor its proposed *First Nations Education Act* featured a commitment to early childhood education.

12) We call upon the federal, provincial, territorial, and Aboriginal governments to develop culturally appropriate early childhood education programs for Aboriginal families.

## Special education

Federal funding for special education is particularly problematic when compared with provincial schools. Aboriginal Affairs consultants were told of a number of examples in which on-reserve students who are ineligible for "High-Cost Special Education" support through Aboriginal Affairs criteria on reserve would be qualified if they lived in the adjacent provincial school district.[152]

The Mississaugas of the New Credit First Nation are pursuing a human rights complaint arguing that Canada's special education funding discriminates against First Nations. The Mississaugas lodged the complaint when Aboriginal Affairs refused to pay for the special education supports required by two children with Down's syndrome. Because of their special needs, the two children must attend a provincial school, as the services they require are not available on reserve. The provincial school charges a fee of over $80,000 per year for the education supports these students require. Canada has refused to cover the cost, saying that the First Nation should pay for the costs out of their existing special needs budget. However, the Mississaugas entire budget for all its students with special needs is $165,000 per year, and these funds are already allocated for other children with different types of special needs. The complaint argues that First Nations children are not guaranteed the same level of special education services as non-First Nations children.[153] This complaint is currently being reviewed by the Canadian Human Rights Commission.

This and other similar cases fit into a growing and very disturbing pattern of Aboriginal people having to take the government to court to argue for a basic Aboriginal right to equal education. Unfortunately, Aboriginal children and communities often pay the price for the delay.

## Post-secondary education

Post-secondary education should be seen as an opportunity to increase the supply of skilled Aboriginal personnel needed by Aboriginal communities to develop and manage their own institutions. Increased access to post-secondary education is essential if the income and employment gap between Aboriginal people and other Canadians is to be closed. However, post-secondary education for Aboriginal learners is inadequate and inaccessible for many. From 1876 until 1927, the federal minister of

Indian Affairs had the right to strip First Nations individuals of their *Indian Act* status if they were

> admitted to the Degree of Doctor of Medicine, or to any other degree by any University of Learning, or who may be admitted in any Province of the Dominion to practice law either as an Advocate or as a Barrister or Counsellor or Solicitor or Attorney or to be a Notary Public, or who may enter Holy Orders or who may be licensed by any denomination of Christians as a Minister of the Gospel.[154]

Access to post-secondary education remains problematic. Only 8.7% of First Nations people, 5.1% of Inuit, and 11.7% of Métis have a university degree, according to the 2011 census.[155] Yet, as noted earlier in this chapter, where Aboriginal students have the opportunity to complete a university education, the income gap with non-Aboriginal Canadians virtually disappears.

Some of the Survivors who spoke to the Commission recounted difficulty in obtaining a higher education. Jennie Thomas attended the Kuper Island, British Columbia, school and went on to graduate from the University of Victoria with a bachelor of social work and child welfare specialization. She explained,

> I was pretty much the only native woman in the class with the class of young, white girls that just got out of high school by the looks of it, and it was, that's who were, that's who my peers were or my cohorts. So, all through my academic life at, you know, I was definitely the older woman in the class, the only native in the class. So, that really took some getting used to. But I've always known that I was gonna, if I started something, I was gonna finish it. So a lot of my experiences have, have—whether I like it or not—are based on my experience as a child at Kuper Island Residential School.[156]

Velma Jackson attended residential school in Saddle Lake, Alberta. She used the settlement money from her Common Experience Payment to study at university:

> I applied to Frog Lake band for them to pay for my education, and they said, "Oh, no, you have no money, your money ran out." He said, "You've exhausted all your resources," is what I was told. So out of the $13,000 I got, most of it went to educating myself, to try and get a Cree language instructor diploma. So, I spent most of my, my money on that.[157]

If access to post-secondary education is to be improved, clearly increasing secondary school completion rates is an important step. But even for those who qualify for a university program, there are significant obstacles.

The First Nations Education Council estimated in 2007 that there was a backlog of over 10,000 First Nations students waiting for post-secondary funding, with more than $200 million required to erase that backlog and meet current demands.[158]

There are no universities in the Northwest Territories, Nunavut, or Yukon. This poses a serious barrier to Inuit and other Northern Indigenous peoples trying to obtain a degree.[159] Southern universities and colleges are poorly equipped to provide the cultural and language instruction that northern students need if they wish to work within their communities. This helps explain why the Inuit and Northern First Nations have lower rates of post-secondary education than southern First Nations and Métis peoples. There are, however, some promising developments. For example, the First Nations University of Canada, the Saskatchewan Indian Institute of Technologies, and the Saskatchewan Indian Cultural College are important institutions that support the language, culture, history, and education of some First Nations.[160] Thomas Chase, of Royal Roads University, told the Senate Committee on Social Affairs, Science and Technology that the First Nations University of Canada played a critical role because it was a "safe place for people who are coming in from tiny, Northern Aboriginal communities that may have only 100, 200 or 300 people ... To be in an institution that is built around their culture, in which they see similar faces—the artwork, even the cuisine in the cafeteria reflects their own ways of life—is an important way to ensure that they complete their post-secondary education." The Senate Committee noted that there is evidence that Indigenous institutions have a higher graduation rate than non-targeted institutions.[161]

As of 2007, there were approximately ten thousand students attending forty-five Aboriginal post-secondary institutions.[162] Many of these institutions are technical campuses, such as the Ogwehoweh Skills and Trades Training Centre in Ohsweken, Ontario, which offers welding, automotive, and construction training, or Yellowquill College in Winnipeg, which offers diplomas in Aboriginal business management or a certificate in community health.[163] However, most such institutes do not offer degree programs. Many of their certificates and diplomas are not recognized by universities. Many of these institutions also suffer from significant underfunding, receiving only 56% of the necessary operating costs through Canada's Indian Studies Support Program.[164] Further, the Indian Studies Support Program provides project funding only, not day-to-day operational funding. As Aboriginal institutions do not have access, generally speaking, to provincial funding available to other colleges and universities, they must find alternative funding sources.[165]

11) We call upon the federal government to provide adequate funding to end the backlog of First Nations students seeking a post-secondary education.

## Métis education

Even though Canada's Métis people have equal protection under section 35 of the Constitution, jurisdictional disputes between the federal and provincial governments continue to be a major obstacle in ensuring that the Métis have control over the education of their young people.[166] A recent ruling of the Federal Court of Appeal in *Daniels v. Canada* declared that Métis are included as 'Indians' within the meaning of the *Constitution Act, 1867*, which may well mean recognition that Métis are entitled to many of the same rights as other Aboriginal peoples in Canada. The Supreme Court agreed to hear this case in November 2014; as of July 2015, the case is still before the court.

At present, though, Métis children are largely educated in public or Catholic school systems in which school boards are not specifically held accountable for the unique educational needs of Métis children.[167]

The Métis national organization, the Métis National Council, recommended the following measures to address the shortcomings in Métis education:

- Establishment of an integrated Métis early childhood system that is funded at a level that will provide administrative capacity, maximize benefits for Métis children and families, and promote Métis language, culture, responsibilities, and values.

- Establishment of Métis provincial education commissions accountable to the Métis National Council to work with provincial education authorities, including school boards, to develop Métis curricula and establish a Métis Education Active Measures Program to improve the quality of education and to improve educational outcomes.[168]

The Truth and Reconciliation Commission endorses these directions advocated by the Métis National Council.

## Inuit education

Unlike the system for First Nation students living on reserve, most Inuit education is delivered through public school systems. Education in the Inuit Nunangat (Inuit homeland) is managed by four public systems operating across two provinces and two territories. Although developing a single education system in Inuit Nunangat would not be appropriate given regional, historical, and jurisdictional differences, Inuit leaders in all the regions have united in a call for an education system that cultivates their languages and reflects the Inuit worldview, culture, and history.[169]

Only 42% of Inuit have a high school diploma or equivalent.[170] Mary Simon, the chairperson of the National Committee on Inuit Education and former head of the national Inuit organization Inuit Tapiriit Kanatami, described the Inuit educational system as "the greatest social policy challenge of our time."[171]

In 2008, the Inuit Tapiriit Kanatami hosted the first National Summit on Inuit Education. The summit resulted in the establishment of a National Committee on Inuit Education, tasked with developing a national strategy for Inuit education. The committee produced a national strategy in 2011 with ten core recommendations designed to provide support for children to stay in school.

1. Mobilize parents

2. Develop leaders in Inuit education

3. Increase the number of bilingual educators and programs

4. Invest in the early years

5. Strengthen Kindergarten to Grade Twelve by investing in Inuit-centred curriculum and language resources

6. Improve services to students who require additional support

7. Increase success in post-secondary education

8. Establish a university in Inuit Nunangat

9. Establish a standardized Inuit language writing system

10. Measure and assessing success[172]

One of the greatest problems is the lack of supports both within and outside the education system. Inuit educators have long recognized that it is important to begin working with children as early as possible, but the North lacks quality daycare and pre-school spaces.[173] The Inuit Nunangat also lacks services for those children with additional barriers to learning. For example, most schools do not have the resources to work with children with behavioural or mental health problems. Schools lack literacy and math programs, breakfast programs, or alternative discipline programs. A disproportionately high number of parents in the North (where residential schools were among the last to close in the country) are Survivors or intergenerational Survivors. Services to support struggling parents are also lacking, such as drug and alcohol programs and mental health counselling.

The National Committee on Inuit Education identified some of the goals that Inuit peoples share when it comes to education:

• Inuit want education to be delivered by Inuit educators, through quality bilingual programs based on Inuit-centred curriculum.

- The education system should inspire young Inuit to stay in school longer and advance the process of restoring confidence lost during the residential school experience.

Success will mean equipping young Inuit with the skills and knowledge they need to contribute to, and benefit from, the emerging economic and civic opportunities in Canada's northern regions.[174]

# Canada attempts education reform

For far too long, the education provisions of the *Indian Act* served as the only statutory basis for First Nations schools. These same provisions were key in the establishment of the residential schools. A new legislative approach to education is required, one that ensures adequate funding and true local control.

## Three reports recommending reform

There is no shortage of good advice when it comes to finding reforms that could improve Aboriginal education. In 2011–12, three different reports were released on First Nations education; all of them made credible recommendations. All agreed on two core points: that sustainable funding and greater Aboriginal control of education are both absolutely necessary.

The first report, in 2011, was published by the Senate Standing Committee on Aboriginal Peoples. The committee held twenty-eight public meetings, heard from over ninety witnesses, visited schools, and convened a round table of education practitioners.[175] The committee put its conclusions bluntly:

> Currently, every First Nation community is left on their own to try to develop and deliver a range of educational services to their students. First Nations schools operate without any statutory recognition and authority to do so. Federal policy to guide efforts in this regard is, at best, ad hoc and piecemeal. The department requires First Nations to educate their students at levels comparable to provincial and territorial jurisdictions, and yet provides them no meaningful supports by which to do so.[176]

The standing committee's key recommendation was a call for the formalization of an Aboriginal education system in legislation, to be developed in consultation with First Nations people. Such legislation would explicitly recognize the authority of First Nations for on-reserve elementary and secondary education and establish First Nations–controlled second- and third-level education structures (similar to provincial school boards and ministries of education).[177]

The committee also recommended that education funding address factors such as demographics, remoteness, and the need for language preservation and revitalization programs.[178] The principle underlying all the recommendations was that the federal government's role should be to enable First Nations to create and adopt viable education systems "while acknowledging that primary responsibility for education rests with First Nations."[179]

The second report in 2011 was released by a national panel that was launched jointly by the national chief of the Assembly of First Nations, and the federal minister of Aboriginal affairs.[180] Like the Senate committee, the National Panel on First Nation Elementary and Secondary Education for Students on Reserve recommended the creation of a statute that would set out rights and responsibilities for Aboriginal education. The panel argued that any education statute must enshrine every First Nations child's right to their culture, language, and identity, regardless of whether they attend a First Nations or provincial school. The panel recommended that the proposed legislation include operational and capital statutory funding that would be needs-based, predictable, sustainable, and used specifically for education purposes. The panel also suggested that additional funding be allocated to provincial schools for the direct benefit of First Nations students enrolled in them.[181] It recommended that a clause be included in the statute ensuring that the legislation did not derogate from Treaty or other Aboriginal rights.[182]

Like the Senate committee, the National Panel emphasized the need for second- and third-level education structures and supports while maintaining First Nation control of First Nation education. The panel made a specific recommendation for the "third tier": a National Commission for First Nation Education, which would be created prior to the legislation and would oversee its development.

The second tier would be made up of First Nation Education Organizations, which would fulfill the role now filled by school boards in provincial systems and allow for economies of scale to support the delivery of quality education to First Nation learners.[183]

At the same time as the National Panel began its work, three First Nations organizations launched their own review. The First Nations Education Council (FNEC) (Québec), Nishnawbe Aski Nation (NAN) (Northern Ontario), and the Federation of Saskatchewan Indian Nations (FSIN) came together out of concern that the National Panel's work might not properly respect Treaty rights or recognize international law.[184] In their own 2011 report, titled *Report on Priority Actions in View of Improving First Nations Education*, the three organizations were less supportive of a legislative approach. They warned that the development of any legislation could only be done with the consent of Aboriginal peoples. They emphasized that Canada has a constitutional obligation to ensure that First Nations peoples have access to educational services of at least equivalent quality to those provided in the public school system. At a minimum, they emphasized, this will require a significant infusion of money.[185] They also advocated for greater transparency and accountability to First Nations communities by all parties delivering education—First Nations, provincial schools, and the federal government.

While not in complete agreement, a consistent and significant thread connected all three reports—the need for a complete restructuring based on principles of self-government, a culturally relevant curriculum, stable funding, and honouring of the treaties. Aboriginal peoples themselves must lead and control the process of change.

The Senate Committee and the National Panel reports both recommended the creation of a *First Nations Education Act*. The National Panel called for the federal government and First Nations to co-create a child-centred *First Nation Education Act*. The Act would not only recognize First Nations legislative jurisdiction but also empower First Nations to enact laws for the management and administration of First Nations schools. They agreed that the Act would not abrogate or derogate existing Aboriginal or Treaty rights. While establishing clear governance objectives, responsibilities and accountability, policies and procedures, and while defining the responsibilities and powers of the various components of a First Nation education system, the Act would have to acknowledge the rights of the child to a quality education regardless of whether they are enrolled in a First Nations or provincial/territorial school system. Although developed for First Nations on-reserve education, the principles developed by the National Panel could also apply with appropriate modification to off-reserve, Inuit, and Métis populations. Aboriginal-controlled education today is widely regarded as the best tool to counter the historical use of education in residential schools as a means to assimilate and demean Aboriginal peoples.

## Canada's proposed *First Nations Education Act*

Canada's initial response to these reports was heavy-handed and reminiscent of some of the same attitudes towards Aboriginal people that inspired residential schools. In December 2012, Aboriginal Affairs began a consultation process for the establishment of a *First Nations Education Act*. After a series of meetings across the country with some First Nation leadership, education practitioners, and community members, and after organizing an online survey, Canada released its *Blueprint for Legislation* on July 12, 2013.[186] The proposal included a few different models that First Nations could choose from:

- Community-operated schools
- Delegation to a First Nation Education Authority (an amalgamation of schools, like a school board)

- Agreements with a provincial school board to: (a) operate the First Nation school on reserve; or (b) allow students who live on reserve to attend provincial off-reserve schools [187]

The *Blueprint* was a far cry from the joint development process advocated by the National Panel on Education and the Senate Standing Committee.

It provided no commitment to ensuring K–12 services would be available within a community. Rather, if a First Nation school offered education up to a certain grade, the legislation would require that school to have a transition plan for students moving into a provincial school.[188] The *Blueprint* did not address early childhood education, such as Junior Kindergarten, despite the widely recognized importance of its potential to help redress the Aboriginal child welfare crisis. While the *Blueprint* acknowledged Treaty rights, it made no specific commitment to ensure that Canada would meet its obligations under international law or preserve existing education rights found in the Treaties.

The federal government's *Blueprint* approach sent the message that it knew better than First Nations what was best for their children. This attitude was so reminiscent of the residential school era that it triggered substantial resistance from First Nations.

In October 2013 the government followed its *Blueprint* with its proposed *First Nations Education Act*. Under this proposed legislation, First Nation schools would have requirements for curriculum and graduation, student assessment and reporting, safety, daily operations, teaching supports, materials and equipment, compliance and enforcement, finance and accounting, human resources, and information technology. The Act would have legislated attendance requirements similar to provincial requirements, with all students between the ages of six and sixteen required to be registered in and attending school. Each school would be required to file an annual "student success plan."[189]

While it might be difficult to argue with such standards, there was nothing in the Act that addressed the financial ability of First Nation schools to meet or enforce such requirements. It provided no guarantee of increased or stable funding of First Nations schools. There was no assurance of equity in the distribution of resources to educate First Nations children in First Nations schools or in provincial or private schools. It also provided a mandatory structure where First Nations must have both a "Director of Education"[190] and a "school inspector."[191] This was a one-size-fits-all approach that failed to recognize the diversity of First Nations.

The *First Nations Education Act* contemplated paternalistic and punitive actions whereby the minister of Aboriginal Affairs and Northern Development could essentially take over First Nations schools for non-compliance with provisions in the Act. Special administrators could be appointed by the minister for open-ended periods of time and against the wishes of the First Nation affected.[192] The minister of Aboriginal

Affairs would also have unfettered discretion in creating regulations regarding reporting, human resources, and schooling requirements, including all matters required under the Act.[193] Such an approach did not renounce the colonial legacy of the residential schools: it continued them.

The Government of Canada defended the proposed legislation, saying that its goal was to provide better education outcomes for First Nation students.[194] But that goal is the same one that the government has consistently failed to meet for many years. Given the legacy of residential schools and the history of Aboriginal education, First Nations had little reason to trust that Canada would now fund First Nations education in a sustainable and appropriate way on the basis of policy alone, and without the corresponding force of law.

Furthermore, neither the *Blueprint* nor the proposed *First Nations Education Act* made any commitment to language revitalization or culturally tailored education. Instead, there was a mention that the curriculum may include instruction in Aboriginal culture and languages, and that there would have to be consultation with community committees on such matters.

The Commission has heard from thousands of Survivors about the loss of Aboriginal languages and culture in the residential schools, about their struggles to reconnect in later years with their languages and traditions, and about the great healing and redemptive value that such connections have had for them and their families. The frequency and conviction of these statements from Survivors and many of their descendants across all Indigenous communities within Canada make it abundantly clear that Aboriginal languages and cultures deserve much better treatment than what was contemplated in the proposed *First Nations Education Act*.

The Government of Canada's proposed *First Nations Education Act*, fit into the disturbing pattern of matters getting worse, not better, since the settlement of the residential school litigation and Canada's apology. The UN special rapporteur on the rights of Indigenous peoples, James Anaya, observed in October 2013,

> I urge the Government not to rush forward with this legislation, but to re-initiate discussions with aboriginal leaders to develop a process, and ultimately a bill, that addresses aboriginal concerns and incorporates aboriginal viewpoints on this fundamental issue. An equally important measure for improving educational outcomes, and one that could be implemented relatively quickly, is to ensure that funding delivered to aboriginal authorities for education per student is at least equivalent to that available in the provincial educational systems.[195]

## The *First Nations Control of First Nations Education Act*

Matters improved somewhat with an announcement in February 2014 of an agreement between the Government of Canada and the Assembly of First Nations on a partnership to develop the *First Nations Control of First Nations Education Act*. This act differed significantly from the *First Nations Education Act* in that it did promise sustainable funding and instruction in Aboriginal culture and languages. The agreement accepted the case for change and reform as made by the three reports examined earlier in this chapter.

The bill would establish minimum education standards on reserve, consistent with provincial standards off reserve. For example, the legislation would require that First Nation schools teach a core curriculum that meets or exceeds provincial standards, that students meet minimum attendance requirements, that teachers are properly certified, and that First Nation schools award widely recognized diplomas or degrees.[196]

The agreement's commitments to sustainable funding was accompanied by allocations in the federal budget of February 2014 of over $2 billion in new funding to reserve schools. It promised to replace the long-standing 2% cap on annual increases with a 4.5% annual increase and $1.25 billion in new core funding from 2016–17 to 2018–19. In addition, $500 million over seven years was committed to improving school infrastructure, and $160 million over four years to an enhanced education fund.[197]

However, a number of Aboriginal leaders questioned the new act. They felt that it could threaten Treaty obligations and erode Aboriginal rights. Consequently, in May of 2014, at a meeting of the Assembly of First Nations, Aboriginal leaders voted to reject the proposed legislation. National Chief Shawn A-in-chut Atleo subsequently resigned and the Government of Canada announced that it was putting the legislation on hold.

This disagreement underscores the seriousness of this issue to Aboriginal leaders, and it highlights just how much work remains to be done. This particular disagreement is also a reminder of the deep levels of distrust that have built up over the years.

In this instance, history is not helpful. The legacy of the residential schools and the years of underfunded education have given many Aboriginal parents and leaders considerable opportunity to question the commitment and sincerity of any and all government proposals.

The tainted legacy of the *Indian Act* that forced Aboriginal parents to send their children to residential schools must be fully and finally set aside. The Government of Canada must end its pattern of underfunded and culturally and linguistically inappropriate Aboriginal education, which began with the residential schools.

The Commission is well aware how much work remains to be done. The process of consultation is essential. Any legislation and its accompanying proposals for funding must recognize that the contemporary needs of Aboriginal children, for at least the short and mid-term, are greater than for children in the general population, in large part because of the legacy of the government's own policies of assimilation.

Even without the legacy of residential schools, the challenges of providing quality education for remote, diverse, and small communities are immense. The federal government must, as the Assembly of First Nations itself recognized, work in partnership not only with the AFN but also with individual Aboriginal communities to ensure that the mistakes of the residential school era, as well as the more recent mistakes of the heavy-handed 2013 *Blueprint* and proposed *First Nations Education Act* are not repeated.

10) We call upon the federal government to draft new Aboriginal education legislation with the full participation and informed consent of Aboriginal peoples. The new legislation would include a commitment to sufficient funding and would incorporate the following principles:

   i. Providing sufficient funding to close identified educational achievement gaps within one generation.

   ii. Improving education attainment levels and success rates.

   iii. Developing culturally appropriate curricula.

   iv. Protecting the right to Aboriginal languages, including the teaching of Aboriginal languages as credit courses.

   v. Enabling parental and community responsibility, control, and accountability, similar to what parents enjoy in public school systems.

   vi. Enabling parents to fully participate in the education of their children.

   vii. Respecting and honouring Treaty relationships.

## Overcoming the education legacy of residential schools

### Supportive governance structures

Both the National Panel and the Standing Senate Committee recognized the need for additional governance structures to support Aboriginal education. The National Panel recommended the establishment of an independent National Commission for First Nations Education. The commission would replace the current role played by the federal Department of Aboriginal Affairs and Northern Development. It would be responsible for developing and implementing education goals, national curricula, standards and testing criteria, education policies, and funding allocation policies, much like provincial ministries of education. The commission would set standards for culturally appropriate education as well as professional standards for teachers and principals. Additionally, the commission would develop performance measurement and accountability. The National Panel also recommended the development of regional First Nation Education Organizations to facilitate the establishment of education services.

The February 2014 agreement between the federal government and the Assembly of First Nations made no mention of structures that may be necessary to support reserve schools, especially in remote and small communities.

### Funding

The proposed *First Nations Control of First Nations Education Act* included a commitment that "the Government of Canada will provide First Nations education systems with a stable, predictable and sustainable funding model for First Nations education."[198] This was an important step forward, but it remains to be seen whether agreement can be reached on legal measures to make this commitment real. Too many programs that are necessary to redress the legacy of residential schools are vulnerable to the vagaries of governmental funding. The federal government has in many different contexts been attracted to a formal equality approach that fails to recognize the distinct and higher needs of Aboriginal students stemming in part from the legacy of residential schools and compounded by the isolation and high operating costs in so many remote Indigenous communities.

## Aboriginal control of Aboriginal education

There have been some important recent developments that show the promise and the potential of Aboriginal self-determination in designing and developing education programs and systems.

### New governance models

Across the North, Inuit education is on the cusp of significant transformation with some of the most promising models for self-governing education coming out of Northern communities. The Kativik School Board (established by the 1975 James Bay and Northern Quebec Agreement in Nunavik) has exclusive education jurisdiction in fourteen Inuit villages.[199] In addition to educating children, the board runs a training program for Inuit teachers, an upgrading program for non-Inuit teachers, adult education, and a research department.[200] The board also arranges and supervises post-secondary education for students studying in the South. The board designs its own curriculum, determines its own school calendar and languages of instruction, and trains its own teachers.

When Nunavut was founded in 1999, it passed education and language laws to protect the right to a culturally relevant curriculum. The *Consolidation of Inuit Languages Protection Act* guarantees the right to Inuit language instruction in Nunavut's school system.[201] Nunavut's *Education Act* establishes a right to a bilingual education with the Inuit language, and makes Inuit knowledge the foundation of the education system.[202] Teaching Aboriginal languages in schools is one of the best ways to ensure respect and interest in culturally appropriate learning.

In 2006 in Labrador, the Nunatsiavut land claims settlement set the stage for the Nunatsiavut government's gradual takeover of the delivery of education.[203] Several promising practices have included parents as contributors and collaborators in curriculum-based Inuit camps, heritage fairs, and breakfast programs. This is a significant break from the practices of the residential schools. In the Northwest Territories, Inuit educators and Elders have developed some specialized curricula.[204]

However, these significant changes have not come without obstacles. Some regions have a greater capacity to develop the necessary resources than others. A shortage of bilingual educators is one of the greatest barriers to expanding bilingual education in Inuit schools.[205] There is also a lack of teaching and reading materials in Inuit languages.

## Place-based learning

Based on the reports of the Aboriginal Learning Knowledge Centre (created by the Canadian Council on Learning) and the National Committee on Inuit Education, there is a need to recognize and strengthen place-based learning within classrooms that serve Aboriginal students.[206]

Place-based education is a philosophy that anchors the student's lessons in the cultures, the land, the history, and the stories of their communities. These connections are emphasized in every subject from the study of language to mathematics to social studies and science.

Such an approach allows Elders to play a role in Aboriginal education. Academically qualified teachers can work with Elders and other Aboriginal instructors to find culturally enriched ways to meet the standardized learning outcomes.

Marie Battiste is a Mi'kmaq scholar and director of the Aboriginal Education Research Centre at the University of Saskatchewan. She notes that reconciling First

Nation peoples to their own knowledge "should be a restorative feature of educa-tion for the future of First Nations."[207] Place-based learning can also be a source for all forms of Indigenous knowledge, including Indigenous science, which Professor Battiste describes as "a dynamic, living process watching, listening, connecting, responding and renewing. Indigenous science embodies a holistic view of the world in which all human, animal, and plant life are perceived as being connected, related and interdependent."[208]

Leroy Little Bear notes that "it is not enough to only know about places, its history or narrative, but a learner must experience them both physically and emotionally, achieved through rituals, and visitations."[209] In the view of the Commission, rooting learning in a local context is an important step towards effective education.

## Negotiated agreements

A growing number of self-government agreements negotiated between First Nations and federal and provincial governments contain education jurisdiction com-ponents, including Sechelt (1986), Nisga'a (2000), Tlicho (2005), Tsawwassen (2009), Maa-nulth First Nations (2011), and the Yale First Nation (2013). However, many First Nations with such self-government agreements have chosen not to exercise that juris-diction because of the lack of support for the elements of a system of education.[210]

The other emerging trend has been towards the negotiation of tripartite agree-ments. In 1998, eleven Mi'kmaq First Nations concluded the first tripartite agreement providing for the transfer of education to local control.[211] Under the agreement, the education sections of the *Indian Act*—provisions that once forced Aboriginal parents to send their children to residential school—cease to apply to the participating com-munities. The agreement also provides that First Nation laws regarding education on reserves prevail over provincial education laws. The Mi'kmaq schools under this agreement have been pioneers in programs designed to preserve and draw on the wisdom of the Mi'kmaq language and have become important cultural centres for the whole community.[212]

In 2006 the Government of Canada, British Columbia, and the First Nations Education Steering Committee signed the Education Jurisdiction Framework Agreement, which put in place a process to transfer jurisdiction over on-reserve education to participating First Nations in British Columbia.[213] The *First Nations Jurisdiction over Education in British Columbia Act* gives effect to the framework agreement.[214]

Those First Nations in British Columbia that wish to participate can negotiate individual education agreements that transfer education authority to the partici-pating and/or self-governing First Nations. Once a jurisdiction agreement has been ratified, participating First Nations assume responsibility for providing educational services from Kindergarten to Grade Twelve on reserves. The agreement also established a First Nations Education Authority to support First Nations in exercising education jurisdiction in three key areas: teacher certification, school certification, and the establishment of curriculum and examination standards. First Nations can co-manage educational services with the Authority, or delegate their jurisdiction entirely to the Authority.[215]

Apart from these approaches, other tripartite agreements have been negotiated in four provinces (Manitoba, New Brunswick, Alberta, and Prince Edward Island) and there is a sub-regional agreement with the Saskatoon Tribal Council.[216] Canada states that the seven tripartite education agreements (which include the BC and Nova Scotia agreements referred to above) cover "58% of eligible First Nation communities."[217] However, unlike the agreements concluded in BC and Nova Scotia, the agreements negotiated through the Education Partnership Program are not legally binding and do not involve a transfer of jurisdiction. Instead, the agreements are focused on promoting collaborative relationships between the parties and committing to developing strategies to improve educational outcomes for First Nations students who attend both band-operated schools and provincial schools.[218]

There are also promising examples of Aboriginal peoples working within the public education systems to better meet the needs of Aboriginal students. The Mi'kmaq Kina'matnewey (Nova Scotia) and the Ahkwesahsne Mohawk Board of Education (Ontario) have established agreements that require the public education system to be more reflective of Aboriginal culture, values, and language.[219]

In 1999, the First Nation Education Steering Committee (BC) engaged Canada, the province, and the BC Teachers' Federation in discussions aimed at improving school success for Aboriginal learners. The memorandum of understanding that was eventually signed in BC set the foundation for the creation of local enhancement agreements requiring public schools to provide strong programs on the culture of local Aboriginal peoples.[220]

These developments are promising, but there is also reason to be cautious. The Senate Standing Committee on Aboriginal Peoples observed that while these partnership agreements have some benefits, witnesses who testified before the committee argued they are not a lasting solution to the education challenges facing First Nations. Legislation developed in genuine partnership with First Nations to ensure Aboriginal control over education and adequate funding for the great challenges left by residential schools is still necessary.[221]

Meanwhile, as in other legacy areas such as child welfare and health, these education developments are taking place on a piecemeal basis, agreement by agreement across the country. Aboriginal peoples have neither the resources nor the time required to negotiate and renegotiate such temporary agreements. Significant and durable change, which honours the Treaties and Aboriginal peoples' rights to self-determination, must happen much more quickly to ensure that today's children are not left behind.

## Non-Aboriginal students

The Commission hosted more than 14,000 Aboriginal and non-Aboriginal high school students at special Education Days aimed at familiarizing them with Canada's residential school history, and allowing them to hear first-hand from Survivors. Non-Aboriginal students have been among the most vocal, and indeed, at times, outraged, in saying that someone should have taught them about all of this a long time ago. Young people have told the Commission that they want to learn the whole truth about our country—that this has helped them better understand why things are the way they are, in their homes, in their communities, on the streets of our country, and in their schools. This Commission wholeheartedly agrees with them. Better integration of Canadian history affecting Aboriginal peoples, as well as Aboriginal peoples' own perspectives, history, and languages in the public school curriculum, will assist non-Aboriginal children as well as Aboriginal children.

The Commission has received encouraging replies from ministries of education in a number of provinces, including Alberta, Manitoba, and New Brunswick, about their determination to include Aboriginal experiences in the curriculum from Kindergarten to Grade Twelve. Such curriculum changes are already in place in the territories.

In Ontario, enrolment in Aboriginal languages and Native studies programs in public schools has increased from 5,343 students in 2007 to 19,345 students in 2012 with the assistance of targeted funding.[222] Some provinces, such as Saskatchewan, have focused on education about residential schools. This is a positive development, but there is need to examine other aspects of Aboriginal history and culture—and to recognize the benefits of examining these other aspects.

## Conclusion

Residential schools failed miserably in their mission to provide Aboriginal children with a decent education. Although a few graduates of the schools went on to play leadership roles, the vast majority of students suffered from poor education and were often permanently estranged from continuing their education. This should not be surprising. The education they experienced in residential schools was a violation of their rights. It was an instrument of assimilation and limitation, and a belittlement of their personal and collective Indigenous identities, cultures, and languages.

One of the most tragic legacies of the residential schools is the significant education and income gap separating Aboriginal people from other Canadians. The Commission believes that this gap must be closed. The best way to close the gap is to monitor it accurately and to report on its standing, and to invest in the education of Aboriginal children.

The inadequate funding of First Nations schools on reserves remains a national disgrace. Those classrooms today bear a shameful resemblance to the residential schools. There must be stable and adequate funding of Aboriginal education. The funding has to be adequate to address the challenge of erasing the legacy of residential schools as well as other needs faced by Aboriginal people. In addition to fair and adequate funding, there is also a need to maximize Aboriginal control over Aboriginal education, and to facilitate instruction in Aboriginal cultures and languages.

Only with all these educational measures in place will there be a realistic prospect of reconciliation on the basis of equality and respect—principles so lacking in the residential school era.

# CHAPTER 3

# "I Lost My Talk": The erosion of language and culture

Embodied in Aboriginal languages is our unique relationship to the Creator, our attitudes, beliefs, values and the fundamental notion of what is truth ... Language is the principal means by which culture is accumulated, shared and transmitted from generation to generation. The key to identity and retention of culture is one's ancestral language.

*—Elder Eli Taylor, Sioux Valley First Nation[1]*

## Introduction

For over a hundred years, Canada's residential schools took Aboriginal children away from their parents, their families, and their communities for the purpose of destroying their connection to their traditional cultures and languages. The intent, as acknowledged by Prime Minister Stephen Harper in his historic apology on June 8, 2008, was to "kill the Indian in the child." Exercising harsh and often humiliating forms of discipline, punishment, and deprivation, those in charge of the schools repeatedly told the children that their language and their culture was worthless and evil—in the words of Canada's first prime minister, "savage."

The churches and the Canadian government believed that Aboriginal children should live their lives in Euro-Canadian cultures, speaking only English or, to a much lesser extent, French. To this end, they generally prohibited the use of Aboriginal languages both in classrooms and in the daily life of the students. Students who spoke their native language outside the classroom were often punished or ridiculed.

Indian Affairs appears to have had no other policy on the use of language in the schools beyond its requirement that English and French were to be the only two languages of instruction and the only two languages to be taught in the schools.[2] The government simply thought the languages were disappearing and would be of no interest or value to Aboriginal children in the future.

The schools were left to improvise their own policies. Those policies and their enforcement varied significantly. At the Anglican school at Moose Factory, Ontario, Billy Diamond, who went on to serve for many years as chief of the Grand Council of the Crees of Québec, recalled that in the 1950s, the punishment for speaking Cree was having one's mouth washed out with soap.[3] Jane Willis, who attended residential school in the 1940s and 1950s, recalled how the opening message from the principal at the Anglican school in Fort George, Québec, stressed that from then on, the students were to speak English in the school, since they were there to learn new ways. In practice, students refused to abide by this rule. They avoided punishment by refusing to speak Cree or English when the teachers were around, and speaking Cree among themselves.[4] When Isabelle Knockwood's mother first took her to the Shubenacadie school in Nova Scotia, they encountered a young Aboriginal girl in the school parlour. When Knockwood's mother began to speak to her in Mi'kmaq, the girl responded, shyly, in English. It was then explained to Mrs. Knockwood that it was not permitted to speak Mi'kmaq in the school.[5] According to Albert Canadien, at Fort Providence in the Northwest Territories in the 1950s, once students had learned a little English, they were forbidden to speak Slavey (Dene).[6] Raphael Ironstand wrote in his memoirs how, shortly after he entered the Pine Creek, Manitoba, school in the 1950s, a number of girls had their heads shaved: "Even though they wore scarves and toques to hide their heads, the tears were streaming down their faces. They were so embarrassed, they kept their heads bowed and eyes looking at the floor. It turned out that their crime had been speaking their native dialect to each other."[7] When James Roberts became the first Aboriginal administrator of the Prince Albert, Saskatchewan, residence in 1973, he remarked that when he had attended the school as a boy, he had not liked the fact that he and his fellow students "were not allowed to speak their own native language."[8] These examples make it clear that in schools across Canada, children were told that it violated school policy to speak their own language.

The rejection of Aboriginal languages and cultures—the belief systems, values, laws, spiritual ceremonies, and ways of life of Aboriginal people—was based on two distinct and separate principles: first, the European belief that Aboriginal people had no culture and were 'savages' living in a state of nature; and second, the belief that the distinctive Aboriginal race needed to be eliminated so that they would be no different from other Canadians.

While the children taken to the schools tried to retain as much of their languages and cultures as they could, the multigenerational battle waged against them was too hard to resist. While initially Survivors could return to communities where their languages and cultures were still alive and vibrant, with each successive generation of Survivors, there was a greater weakening of community cultural and linguistic strength. More often than not, the schools prevailed. Aboriginal students were forced to abandon their languages and cultural practices. They became alienated from their families, their communities, and ultimately from themselves. This damage was passed down through the generations, as former students found themselves unable or unwilling to teach their own children Aboriginal languages and cultural ways.

Many of the residential school Survivors who spoke to the Truth and Reconciliation Commission have stressed the pain caused to them from this loss of their very identity. It is their stories that have guided the work of the Commission. In the words of Elder Shirley Williams, "Language and culture cannot be separate from each other—if they are, the language only becomes a tool, a thing ... Our language and culture are our identity and tell us who we are, where we came from and where we are going."[9]

In this chapter, the Survivors explain how the loss of languages led to a loss of identity and ultimately brought Aboriginal people face to face with the destruction of their cultures. The loss of identity cast children into a state of confusion over what was right and good in their lives.

The chapter examines the current threats to the survival of Aboriginal languages, and looks at why the loss of Aboriginal language, identity, and culture is so important to non-Aboriginal Canadians. It will also examine the failure of the Canadian government to support the preservation of Aboriginal languages despite their protected status under the Constitution and international agreements. The final part of this chapter will address what has been done and what still needs to be done to preserve Aboriginal languages and cultures.

In our Calls to Action, the Commission will assert that a multi-pronged approach to Aboriginal language preservation—if implemented, honourably resourced, and sustained—can begin the promise of reconciliation with Survivors and their families, people who, through numerous generations, still bear the scars and the losses of the residential schools.

## Loss of language and culture

> The punishment of speaking Mi'kmaq began on our first day at school, but the punishment has continued all our lives as we try to piece together who we are and what the world means to us with a language many of us had to re-learn as adults.
>
> —*Isabelle Knockwood,*
> *Survivor of Shubenacadie Residential School*[10]

I lost my talk
The talk you took away.
When I was a little girl
At Shubenacadie School.

—*Rita Joe, Survivor of Shubenacadie Residential School,*
*"I Lost My Talk"*[11]

Thousands of children were moved into residential schools at a very young age. When Nellie Trapper went to Horden Hall in Moose Factory, Ontario, she was six years old. She recalled, "I just followed everybody around 'cause I didn't understand what they were telling me to do; just followed the crowd ... There was a lot of stuff that I got in trouble for, and I didn't know why 'cause I didn't understand what they were telling me to do, or, because I only spoke Cree."[12]

Life in residential schools was both confusing and frightening. Greg Rainville was sent to the Qu'Appelle, Saskatchewan, school. He remembered,

> I was punished because the nuns would get frustrated with you when they talk to you in French and English, and you're not knowing what they're talking about, and you're pulled around by the ear, and whatnot, and slapped on the back of the head, and stuff like that. And I didn't know what I was doing wrong. No matter what, I tried to do good, but I couldn't understand what they were saying, and they couldn't understand what I was saying, but I was punished.[13]

When the children had their languages stripped from them, they not only lost the ability to communicate with one another, they were forced to question if what they knew, and if what they had been taught since birth had any value at all. John Tootoosis, who attended the Delmas, Saskatchewan, school, said that for Aboriginal children, the residential school experience was

> like being put between two walls in a room and left hanging in the middle. On one side are all the things he learned from his people and their way of life that was being wiped out, and on the other side are the white man's ways which he could never fully understand since he never had the right amount of education and could not be part of it. There he is, hanging in the middle of two cultures and he is not a white man and he is not an Indian.[14]

According to social anthropologist Wade Davis, culture "is not decoration or artifice, the songs we sing or even the prayers we chant. It is a blanket of comfort that gives meaning to lives."[15] This section examines some of the devastating effects of taking away that "blanket of comfort" of Aboriginal cultures and languages from the children who attended residential schools, and the intergenerational effects of such deprivations.

The statements of the Survivors are our best guide to understanding what was lost, or stolen, or deemed "evil" in the residential school system. The culture that the children were forced to abandon covered everything from the basics of food and clothing and family to their essential understanding of home and history to the most sacred— their stories and their spirituality.

Mary Siemans explained the connection between language and culture:

> Our Dogrib language ... identifies us as a people in a unique culture within the land we occupy. Our language holds our culture, our perspective, our history, and our inheritance. What type of people we are, where we came from, what land we claim, and all our legends are based on the language we speak. Our culture depends on our language, because it contains the unique words that describe our way of life. It describes name places for every part of our land that our ancestors travelled on ... Rules which govern our lives bring stability to our communities, and our feast days, which bring people together, are all inter-related within our language. Losing our language will not only weaken us as a people but will diminish our way of life because it depend so much on our language.[16]

Doris Young speaking at the Commission's National Event in Saskatoon, Saskatchewan remembers the way students were forced to dress:

> They took away our clothes, and gave us clothes that, that everybody else [wore], we all looked alike, our hair was all the same, cut us into bangs, and, and straight short, straight hair up to our ears. And there was our shoes, they took away our moccasins, and gave us shoes, which I was not, I was just a baby, I had, didn't actually wear shoes; we wore moccasins.[17]

Martin Nicholas was sent to school with new, handmade clothing. A "buckskin jacket, beaded with fringes ... My mom did beautiful work, and I was really proud of my clothes." But the moccasins, pants, and jacket she made were taken from him on his first day at school and never returned. He recalled, "that was the only one time I wore them."[18]

The Survivors shared many painful memories about the way their culture was stripped away from them. Sarah McLeod spoke at the community hearing in Kamloops, British Columbia, about the residential school attack on Aboriginal spirituality:

> When I got here I was so proud of my totem pole ... and I showed it to the nun. I said, "Look what I got for my birthday. I really like my totem." She went, "Ah!" She said, "You throw that away. Throw it away right now. Put it in the garbage right now." I looked at her. I said, "But that's my birthday present." "No, that's no good. That's the devil seeing that totem pole. It's out. Devil, can't you see all the devil in there? You throw it away right now!" And she made me throw it in the garbage, and it was, I didn't know, I said to myself, "Oh, my gosh. All this time I was, I was hugging this devil?" You know I didn't know that.... I never forgot it. I still, deep

in my heart, I still think it's always something that I shouldn't have thrown away. It's just how much they, they tried to take culture away from us.[19]

Going beyond the condemnation of childhood basics like food and clothing the students were further encouraged to adopt the racist attitudes of the schools. Archie Hyacinthe recalled his time at the St. Mary's Residential School in Kenora, Ontario:

> The sad part of it was, we used to watch cowboys and Indian movies on TV, black and white TV. We would be cheering for the cowboys, you know. Here we were saying to the Indians because "they're losers," you know. See, this is what the school did to you. They taught you how to be, you know, turn against your own people, your own culture.[20]

The Commission heard time and again the wrenching memories of children who found that they couldn't even go home anymore. Mary Courchene spoke at the community hearing in Pine Creek, Manitoba, of how she felt when she returned to her parents' home after a year in residential school:

> I looked at my dad, I looked at my mom, I looked at my dad again. You know what? I hated them. I just absolutely hated my own parents. Not because I thought they abandoned me; I hated their brown faces. I hated them because they were Indians ... This is what we were told everyday; "You savage. Your ancestors are no good."[21]

Hubert Nanacowop attended Our Lady of the Snows School in Berens River, Manitoba. He recalled, "I always thought being an Indian was just like being next to a pig, and that's the way they used to call us. And I couldn't talk, talk my own language, which is Anishinaabe ... We had all kinds of troubles with that."[22]

Richard Kaiyogana, Sr., attended the Coppermine tent hostel in the Northwest Territories. He told the Commission, "Okay, why not think like a white man? Talk like a white man? Eat like a white man ... so I don't have to get strapped anymore."[23]

Agnes Mills spoke to the Commission at a sharing circle in Inuvik, Northwest Territories. She explained,

> And one of the things that residential school did for me, I really regret, is it made me ashamed of who I was ... And I wanted to be white so bad, and the worst thing I ever did was I was ashamed of my mother, that honourable woman, because she couldn't speak English, she never went to school, and they told us that we used to go home to her on Saturdays, and they told us that we couldn't talk Gwich'in to her and, and she couldn't, like couldn't communicate. And my sister was the one that had the nerve to tell her. "We can't talk Loucheux to you, they told us not to."[24]

Betsy Olson remembers how hard it was for her family to welcome her home: "Mom had to buy white man's food to feed me 'cause I couldn't eat our, our way of eating back home. I couldn't eat soup. I couldn't eat fish. I couldn't eat bannock. Couldn't eat nothing ... Mom had to get extra money to try and buy extra food just for me."[25]

Eva Lepage is an Inuk woman who attended the Churchill Vocational Centre in Manitoba. She spoke to the Commission at the Atlantic National Event:

> I was not accepted by white people because of my colour. My own people did not accept me either... I've been hurt a lot by, by white people but I also been hurt a lot by my own people because people hurting so much they hurt each other, and they don't see it. I'm not in my community either. For thirty years I live where I didn't grow up, so all my family relatives are not, never hardly are around me.[26]

Roy Thunder and his friends at the Shingwauk Residential School in Sault Ste. Marie had to, quite literally, battle for their identities. He remembered, "Reserve kids ... were making fun of us 'cause we were talking English ... There were times, too ... they wanted to fight us ... because they thought we were, you know, white kids."[27]

Sabina Hunter grew up in Goose Bay: "At eighteen I left Labrador with no intention of coming back ... When I lived outside people thought I was Oriental and so I would use that. I would take advantage of that. I didn't want to be Inuk. And during that time I drank a lot. I was not a person to be proud of."[28]

Rosemary Paul spoke to the Commission in Halifax, Nova Scotia: "They made fun of me because I couldn't speak Mi'kmaq and to this day I still try to fit in and I still, like, consider myself an outsider. I mean, I can still go to my reserve and everybody, you know, hugs and kisses me, but I still consider myself an outsider."[29]

Professor Lorena Sekwan Fontaine is from the Sagkeeng First Nation in Manitoba. She explained,

> My stepfather said he never spoke Cree to me partially because of the shame he felt. At first he never articulated the source of the shame, but a few years ago he said it was a result of his residential school experiences. He often spoke to me with a heavy heart, saying, "there are so many things I cannot express to you in English because there are only Cree words to describe what I am feeling."[30]

Henry "Curly" Ruck told the Commission that his mother attended the Elkhorn Residential School in Manitoba and consequently had a very limited understanding of Aboriginal culture:

> She phoned me one day and asked me if she could come over. It was on a Sunday morning.... But I told her I couldn't do it that Sunday because we were going to a sweat. And all she said to me was, "What?" I said, "We're going to a sweat." She says, "What's that?" And I said, "A sweat lodge. We're going to go sit in a sweat lodge." And she said, "What the hell is that?" That's why to me ... she lost everything. She lost her culture. She lost everything. That residential school took everything away from her.[31]

Listening to the voices of the Survivors, it is difficult to measure how much was lost when their languages and cultures were so systematically and savagely suppressed. Many Survivors and their descendants have a huge sense of loss and either a sense of anger or sadness about their loss. Such Survivors lead the cultural and language revitalization movements that are happening across the country. Others, who have accepted and embraced the Christian doctrines imposed on them at the schools, reject the value of the traditions and languages of their own people. These Survivors sometimes actively fight against cultural revitalization. Tension and turmoil often result between these groups when they exist in the same community. This friction too needs to be seen as one of the legacies of residential schools.

## Language, culture, and health

Culture and language are closely connected not only to a sense of self but also to physical well-being. Positive cultural identity has been linked to resilience and good mental health among minorities. Cultural loss has been recognized as a significant determinant of health in the Aboriginal community.[32]

In its 2010 review of the health of Aboriginal languages in BC, the First People's Heritage, Language and Cultures Council concluded,

> The loss of language is directly related to the troubling health issues many First Nations are facing today. Knowledge of one's language is related to physical, mental and spiritual health. It is an expression of ways of life, ways of thinking, and cultural understanding. Language revitalization plays a vital role in community growth, healing, education, development, strong families and reconnection to the past. A healthy language means healthy individuals, healthy communities, and contributing members to society.[33]

The First Nations–controlled Regional Longitudinal Health Survey has concluded that "the closer a people are to their Nation's 'roots' and their spiritual beliefs and practices, the higher the levels of health and self-esteem found within that community."[34] The attack on Aboriginal languages and cultures at residential schools was also an attack on the very health of Aboriginal students. The connection between wellness and culture will be discussed at greater length in the next chapter on health.

In the 1990 Standing Committee on Aboriginal Affairs report titled *"You Took My Talk": Aboriginal Literacy and Empowerment*, Sala Padlayat, director of the Salluit Adult Education Centre, eloquently describes the relationship between mother tongue literacy and self-esteem. She explains,

> I truly believe that my strength, my feeling of self-worth as an Inuk is in part because I had access to a form of communication, our written language, that is uniquely our own.... Not all of our young people are as fortunate to have the

support I received from my family. When alien ways are pressed on them, they cannot differentiate between what is real and what is superficial, what is essential and what in reality is trivial. They are confused, lost, bitter, because they feel abandoned.[35]

Positive cultural identity has the power to protect as well as to heal. Strikingly, researchers in BC found that significantly lower suicide rates are correlated with those bands in which a majority of members have a conversational knowledge of an Aboriginal language. Correlation does not imply causation, but the researchers concluded "that indigenous language use, as a marker of cultural persistence, is a strong predictor of health and well being in Canada's Aboriginal communities."[36] There is also evidence that the use of an Aboriginal language at home is positively associated with the success of children living off reserve at school.[37] Survivors who struggle with addictions, mental health issues, and imprisonment can benefit from greater engagement with Aboriginal languages and culture. Recognizing the connection between culture and health, the Royal Commission on Aboriginal Peoples (RCAP) observed, "it is often the most distressed and alienated Aboriginal people who find the greatest healing power in the reaffirmation (or rediscovery) of their cultures and spirituality."[38]

## Aboriginal languages at risk

In 1994, an Assembly of First Nations study of the impact of residential schools noted that "language is necessary to define and maintain a world view. For this reason, some First Nation Elders to this day will say that knowing or learning a native language is basic to any deep understanding of a First Nations way of life, to being a First Nation person. For them, a First Nation world is quite simply not possible without its own language."[39] This same report quoted Bernie Francis, a Mi'kmaq linguistic consultant, who stated, "the greatest part of our spirituality is embedded in our language. That is why it was attacked with such vigor."[40]

The Royal Commission on Aboriginal Peoples similarly noted the connection between Aboriginal languages and what it called a "distinctive world view," rooted in the stories of ancestors and the environment:

> For Aboriginal people, the threat that their languages could disappear is more than the prospect that they will have to acquire new instruments for communicating their daily needs and building a sense of community. It is a threat that their distinctive worldview, the wisdom of their ancestors and their ways of being human could be lost as well. And, as they point out, if the languages of this continent are lost, there is nowhere else they can be heard again.[41]

RCAP added that Aboriginal languages are a "tangible emblem of group identity" that can provide "the individual a sense of security and continuity with the past ...

Maintenance of the language and group identity has both a social-emotional and a spiritual purpose."[42]

The deep cultural and spiritual significance of Aboriginal languages was also reflected in some of the first principles that guided an important 2005 Task Force on Aboriginal Languages. The task force included speakers of the Michif, Secwepemc, Mohawk, Inuktitut, Cree, Plains Cree, Swampy Cree, Saulteaux, Ojibway, and Algonquin, and drew on a Circle of Experts. The task force articulated its core principles thusly:

> We believe First Nation, Inuit and Métis languages embody the past and the future. To enter into a relationship with our ancestors we must speak our languages and by doing so we honour their spirits. However, we also adapt our languages to new environments, new situations and new technologies.[43]

Aboriginal languages have survived. But only barely. Very few Aboriginal languages are in good health today. The largest and "most viable" languages are Inuktitut, Cree, and Ojibway, but all Aboriginal languages spoken in Canada are considered vulnerable to extinction.[44] In 1998, the Assembly of First Nations declared a state of emergency regarding First Nation languages, and called on Canada to act immediately to recognize, officially and legally, the First Nation languages of Canada, and to make a commitment to provide the resources necessary to reverse First Nation language loss and prevent their extinction.[45] That call was never answered. Since that time, things have become critically worse. In the 2011 census, only 14.5% of the Aboriginal population reported that their first language learned was an Aboriginal language.[46] In the previous census in 2006, 19% of those who identified as Aboriginal had reported an Aboriginal language as their first language learned, and a decade earlier, in the 1996 census, the figure was 26%. Although some of this decline may reflect the growth in the number of people now identifying as Aboriginal, especially off reserve, the rapid decline in those who learn an Aboriginal language as a first language is dramatic and significant.

In the 2006 census, 21% of those who reported an Aboriginal identity also reported the ability to conduct a conversation in an Aboriginal language; in the 2011 census, this proportion declined to 17.2%, a drop of 4% in just five years.[47] Again, some of this decline may be explained by the growth in the overall Aboriginal population, but there are plenty of consistent, disturbing signs that Aboriginal languages are in danger of disappearing completely.

There remains great diversity in language use among Canada's Aboriginal peoples. Fewer than 5% of Métis people speak an Aboriginal language, although about 50% report that keeping, learning, or relearning their language is important to them. Some of the languages spoken by Métis people, such as Cree and Ojibway, are in good health, but others, such as Michif, are spoken by fewer than one thousand people.[48]

Nearly two-thirds of Inuit speak their own language, compared to 22.4% of First Nations people. Although the Inuit have the highest percentage of Indigenous language speakers, there are signs of decline there as well. In the 2011 census, 63.3% of their population spoke an Inuit language, down from 68.8% in the 2006 census.

There are also striking regional differences, with much lower rates of language use by Inuit in urban areas as well as in the western, Inuvialuit region of the Northwest Territories, where church-run residential schooling, commercial whaling, and fur trading had more than a century-long history.[49]

## Constitutional guarantees

Canada prides itself on its official bilingualism and is admired internationally for this policy. Yet there is no comparable policy of official trilingualism to equitably honour and encompass the mother tongues of the country's third founders, the Aboriginal peoples of Canada.

The Supreme Court of Canada has interpreted section 35 of the Canadian Constitution (which recognizes Aboriginal and Treaty Rights) as protecting those Aboriginal rights that "were integral to the distinctive culture of the specific aboriginal group" prior to European contact.[50] There can be no doubt that Aboriginal languages and cultural practices fall within the scope of such constitutional protections.[51] The practice of Aboriginal languages was a pre-existing, distinctive, and continuous practice that should be recognized as an existing Aboriginal right under section 35(1) of the *Constitution Act, 1982*.[52]

In the words of Supreme Court of Canada Chief Justice Beverley McLachlin in the case *R v. Mitchell*, "European settlement did not terminate the interests of aboriginal peoples arising from their historical occupation and use of the land. To the contrary, aboriginal interests and customary laws were presumed to survive the assertion of sovereignty, and were absorbed into the common law as rights."[53] As a result, Aboriginal language rights continue to exist as part of the Aboriginal rights protected within Canada's guiding law, the Canadian Constitution. They have survived unless, as Chief Justice McLachlin wrote in *R. v. Mitchell*, "(1) they were incompatible with the Crown's assertion of sovereignty, (2) they were surrendered voluntarily via the treaty process, or (3) the government extinguished them."[54] Because Aboriginal languages do not threaten the Crown's assertion of sovereignty, and were not surrendered through Treaties, and were not extinguished by the government, the rights to these language practices, customs, and traditions continue to this day.

It can also be argued that because Treaty talks were conducted in both English and Aboriginal languages, both parties assumed that they would continue to communicate in a similar manner. Given that Aboriginal peoples owned the land by virtue of their historic use and occupancy, and exercised governance powers prior to European arrival, Treaties should be fairly understood as a grant of rights from First Nations to the Crown, leaving First Nations to still hold any and all rights not granted to the Crown, including language rights.[55] This obviously leaves broad grounds for Aboriginal language rights to be recognized and affirmed within section 35(1) of the Constitution.

The Supreme Court of Canada, in the course of interpreting French and English minority language rights under the *Canadian Charter of Rights and Freedoms*, has clearly stressed the importance of language as part of culture. The Court has written,

> Language is so intimately related to the form and content of expression that there cannot be true freedom of expression by means of language if one is prohibited from using the language of one's choice. Language is not merely a means or medium of expression; it colours the content and meaning of expression. It is a means by which a people may express its cultural identity. It is also the means by which one expresses one's personal identity and sense of individuality. [56]

Finally, section 22 of the *Canadian Charter of Rights and Freedoms* provides that the recognition of French and English language rights in the *Charter* does not take away "from any legal or customary right or privilege acquired or enjoyed either before or after the coming into force of this Charter with respect to any language that is not English or French."[57] This section of the *Charter* provides support for the idea that Aboriginal language litigation could be successful under section 35 of the *Constitution Act, 1982*.

In interpreting Aboriginal and treaty rights under section 35(1) of the *Constitution Act, 1982*, the Supreme Court of Canada has stressed the relation of those rights to the preservation of distinct Aboriginal cultures.[58] The Commission is convinced that Aboriginal languages are an integral part of Aboriginal culture, no less than English and French languages are to those cultures, in that they help define how Aboriginal peoples govern and educate themselves and relate to their environment.

13) We call upon the federal government to acknowledge that Aboriginal rights include Aboriginal language rights.

## Preserving Aboriginal languages

The residential school system was based primarily on the racist belief in the superiority of settlers and the inferiority of Aboriginal cultures. Yet, despite the frequent use of various forms of punishment, students resisted attempts to prohibit their use of Aboriginal languages in many ways. In 1887, Reverend T. Clarke of the Battleford Industrial School complained that "We have experienced a great difficulty in inducing the boys and girls to speak English among themselves in every day life."[59] In 1938, an inspector of the Sandy Bay school was still complaining that students "will only learn English by using it, and using it as continuously as possible," including in the play-grounds and at meals.[60]

Canadian anthropologist Diamond Jenness, in a 1962 lecture at Waterloo Lutheran University, lamented "that very few of our Canadian Eskimos have acquired more than the feeblest smattering of English," and he observed that they would be unable to cope in the South "unless we appoint ourselves their guardians and watch over them during the first months or year of their sojourn" while they mastered English.[61] These assimilationist views did not go unchallenged, but they remained dominant in the administration of the residential schools.[62]

## The Royal Commission on Aboriginal Peoples

In 1996, the Royal Commission on Aboriginal Peoples stressed the importance of allowing Aboriginal nations to take steps in accordance with their own conditions and priorities to preserve Aboriginal languages. RCAP also stressed that, in part because of the residential school experience, both the Government of Canada and the churches had an obligation to engage in "restorative justice." The report also stated that "Aboriginal languages have been undermined by government action ... [and] because churches have played a critical part in the destruction of languages, we consider that practical support for the restoration of the languages would be a highly appropriate reconciliatory gesture."[63] RCAP recommended the creation of an Aboriginal languages foundation that would be endowed with a total of $100 million. The foundation board would have a majority of First Nations, Inuit, and Métis members, and would "support language initiatives undertaken or endorsed by Aboriginal nations and their communities."[64]

The initial reaction to RCAP's language recommendations was positive. In *Gathering Strength*, the Government of Canada's response to the RCAP, the government commit-ted to working with Aboriginal people to establish programs to preserve, protect, and teach Aboriginal languages.[65] A new approach to language preservation was launched in 1998.[66]

## Aboriginal Languages Initiative (ALI)

The long-term goal of the program was to increase the number of Aboriginal language speakers, with an emphasis on language acquisition and retention in the home.[67] Starting in 1998, funding of $5 million per year was administered by the Assembly of First Nations, the Métis National Council, and the Inuit Tapiriit Kanatami.[68] Leaving aside the adequacy of the dollar amounts, this approach recognized that a government-controlled approach did not respect the diversity of Canada's Aboriginal peoples, especially given the diversity of Aboriginal languages. The approach also respected RCAP's view that language policy should be a key component of Aboriginal self-determination. It would mean that the Aboriginal organizations, although funded by Canada, would themselves be responsible and held accountable by their members for the ways they devoted resources to the urgent task of language preservation.

Unfortunately, Canada no longer pursues such a nation-to-nation approach. The present approach is based on federal administration of heritage subsidies. In 2006, the federal government declined to use the $160 million that had been set aside for the creation of an Aboriginal Languages and Culture Centre and a national language strategy.[69] Instead, the government committed $5 million per year "permanent funding" for the Aboriginal Languages Initiative.[70] Aboriginal language initiatives are now delivered by the Department of Canadian Heritage on a project-by-project basis. The heritage subsidy approach suggests that Aboriginal languages will, at best, be preserved with other relics of the past.

Even if one were to set aside the significant reduction in funding, it is important to understand that the Aboriginal Language Initiative made matters much worse. It is a program of government-administered subsidies. It is not based on the notion of respectful nation-to-nation relations between Canada and Aboriginal peoples; nor does it trust Aboriginal people to make decisions for themselves about how to allocate those few resources and how to administer programs. Evaluations have identified gaps in funding, especially for Métis people, urban, and non-status First Nations people, and urban Inuit.[71] These groups include many former students of residential schools and their children and grandchildren.

The Aboriginal Language Initiative budget remains $5 million per year, just as it was more than seventeen years ago in 1998 when the program was initiated. Given inflation, this funding has dramatically decreased in real terms.[72] In 2013–14, this budget was used for eighty projects, which were funded by way of "contribution agreements" with national, provincial, and regional Aboriginal organizations. ALI funding is available for programs that are designed and delivered by Aboriginal people, but only on a short-term project basis.[73] The Aboriginal Languages Initiative is financially unfit for its purpose, and structurally flawed.

Apart from the Aboriginal Languages Initiative, the only other significant programs for language preservation are the Canada–Territorial Language Accords ($4.1 million annual budget). These support territorial government-directed Aboriginal language services and community projects in Nunavut and the Northwest Territories. In Yukon, Canada provides $5 million for language revitalization and preservation projects through transfer agreements with ten of the eleven self-governing Yukon First Nations.[74] This follows RCAP's recommended approach that language policy should be included as a matter of self-government wherever possible. However, Yukon receives more money than the NWT and Nunavut combined, even though Yukon has a smaller Aboriginal population.

Thus, Canada spends roughly $14 million annually across Canada for the preservation and revitalization of Aboriginal languages, through the Aboriginal Languages Initiative, Territorial Accords, and transfer agreements. By way of comparison, the Official Languages Program for English and French spent over $350 million in 2013–14 for the promotion of linguistic duality and the development of official-language minority communities across Canada.[75]

Over the last several years, Aboriginal programming within the Department of Canadian Heritage has become smaller and less prominent. There were once fifteen different Aboriginal programs managed independently, but they were all consolidated into the Aboriginal Peoples' Program in 2005.[76] Since then a significant portion of such programs were transferred to the oversight of the Department of Aboriginal Affairs and Northern Development.[77] In April 2012, Canadian Heritage dispensed with its Aboriginal Affairs Branch altogether and moved the remaining ten Aboriginal programs (including ALI) into the Citizen Participation Branch.[78]

The profile of the Aboriginal Peoples' Program has become increasingly diminished in recent years. This is a betrayal of prior commitments, including commitments that were presented as part of Canada's response to both the residential school litigation and settlement. The preservation of Aboriginal languages should not be a part of the Canadian Department of Heritage. Such an approach does little credit to Canada's legal and moral duties towards Aboriginal peoples, and does little to make reparations for the forced assimilation of Aboriginal people in residential schools.

The Commission concludes that since the settlement of the residential school litigation in 2006, federal government policy has done little to repair the losses of Aboriginal languages and culture; in fact, the consolidations and cutbacks are a betrayal of the residential school Survivors. The consequent failure to protect increasingly fragile Aboriginal languages renders hollow Canada's 2008 apology.

The Commission concludes that the Government of Canada must abandon its tightly controlled model of program-based heritage subsidies, and instead provide sustainable resources to recognize that the Indigenous peoples of Canada have language rights tied to their protected Aboriginal rights, including their rights to self-determination.

## A federal Aboriginal Languages Act

The Truth and Reconciliation Commission believes that federal legislation is necessary for the government to recognize its constitutional obligations with respect to Aboriginal languages. The Commission is well aware that such legislation in itself will not be sufficient to revitalize Aboriginal languages, yet there is a danger that such legislation may be presented or viewed as sufficient. An Aboriginal Languages Act could takes steps to create and facilitate conditions within Aboriginal communities that would enable them to develop the types of necessary language initiatives discussed in other parts of this chapter. To ensure that such steps were taken, Parliament could create requirements enforceable in a legal forum such as a tribunal or before a commission, which would give force to these initiatives. Parliament could restrict the distribution of federal funds based on the condition that Aboriginal language initiatives are developed and supported by local communities.

There are precedents for such federal legislation. In 1990, the United States Congress enacted the *Native American Languages Act*.[79] Section 101 provided that "the status of the cultures and languages of Native Americans is unique and the United States has the responsibility to act together with Native Americans to ensure the survival of these unique cultures and languages." It also recognized that "the traditional languages of native Americans are an integral part of their cultures and identities and form the basic medium for the transmission, and thus survival, of Native American cultures, literatures, histories, religions, political institutions, and values." It recognized that the "lack of clear, comprehensive, and consistent Federal policy on treatment of Native American languages ... has often resulted in acts of suppression and extermination of Native American languages and cultures."[80]

The 1990 *Native American Languages Act* also declared in section 104 that it was "the policy of the United States to preserve, protect, and promote the rights and freedom of Native Americans to use, practice, and develop Native American languages," including placing Indigenous languages "where appropriate" in school curricula and allowing exceptions to teacher certification programs where they would "hinder the employment of qualified teachers who teach in Native American languages, and to encourage State and territorial governments to make similar exceptions."[81]

A Canadian version of this act, borrowing from Canada's *Official Languages Act*, could also establish a commissioner of Aboriginal languages. The commissioner would be appointed through a process determined in consultation with Aboriginal groups. The commissioner would have the power to report on and draw attention to the health of Canada's Aboriginal languages, to provide guidance to Aboriginal communities in the preservation of their languages, and to educate non-Aboriginal Canadians about Aboriginal languages. This is not an original concept. New Zealand's *Māori Languages*

*Act* creates a commission with such powers related to the promotion of that Indigenous language.[82]

The auditor general of Canada has written about the federal government's failure to create clarity about the service levels First Nations receive. In his 2011 status report, he wrote, "It is not always evident whether the federal government is committed to providing services on reserves of the same range and quality as those provided to other communities across Canada."[83] In fact, First Nations receive significantly fewer dollars per capita than non-Aboriginal groups when it comes to basic government services. The auditor general has also asserted that First Nations cannot effectively plan and control the delivery of their services because the federal government has not created a legislative base to hold itself accountable in dealing with Aboriginal peoples. He wrote,

> Therefore, for First Nations members living on reserves, there is no legislation supporting programs in important areas such as education, health, and drinking water. Instead, the federal government has developed programs and services for First Nations on the basis of policy. As a result, the services delivered under these programs are not always well defined and there is confusion about federal responsibility for funding them adequately.[84]

The auditor general's findings exemplify the need for the certainty of federal legislation to ensure the effectiveness of remedial and ongoing action on Aboriginal languages.

## Provincial and territorial initiatives

Some provinces and territories in Canada have made progress through legislation and other measures that focus on the official status of Aboriginal languages within their jurisdictions. First Nation and Inuit languages in the Northwest Territories[85] and Nunavut[86] have been designated as official languages. Nunavut has an *Inuit Language Protection Act* (2008) that includes a legal statement of the inherent right of the Inuit in Nunavut to use their language.[87] Since 2002, Yukon legislation has recognized the importance of Yukon Aboriginal languages and expresses a wish to take appropriate measures to "preserve, develop and enhance" those languages.[88]

British Columbia has legislation providing for a First Peoples' Language, Heritage and Culture Council, tasked with providing support and distributing funds to heritage and arts organizations.[89] An accompanying regulation recognizes thirty-four distinct First Peoples' languages.[90] Several provinces have legislation that formally recognizes First Nation languages but with no concurring obligation to protect or promote such languages. For example, the 2010 Manitoba *Aboriginal Languages Recognition Act* recognizes that the languages of Cree, Dakota, Dene, Inuktitut, Michif, Ojibway, and

Oji-Cree are "the Aboriginal languages spoken and used in Manitoba," but it does not legislate official language status or obligate the province to take steps to protect and promote these languages.[91]

In Québec, Aboriginal children are exempted from French-language educational service requirements in order to permit them to receive instruction in their own languages.[92] The preamble of the *Charter of the French Language* recognizes the rights of "Amerinds [*sic*] and the Inuit of Québec, the first inhabitants of this land, to preserve and develop their original language and culture."[93] The official languages of instruction for schools under the jurisdiction of the Cree (Cree School Board) and Inuit (Kativik School Board) are Cree and Inuktitut, respectively. In addition, "Indian reserves" are not subject to the requirements of the *Charter of the French Language*.[94] None of the other provinces have any legislation officially addressing the status of Aboriginal languages.

The Commission concludes that the Government of Canada should establish a framework for a new commitment to respecting, preserving, and strengthening Aboriginal languages by enacting an Aboriginal Languages Act that is similar to the *Native American Languages Act* enacted by the US Congress. The Act should recognize that residential schools were part of a forced policy of linguistic assimilation, and affirm both Aboriginal and Treaty rights and the *UN Declaration on the Rights of Indigenous Peoples*.

14) We call upon the federal government to enact an Aboriginal Languages Act that incorporates the following principles:

   i. Aboriginal languages are a fundamental and valued element of Canadian culture and society, and there is an urgency to preserve them.

   ii. Aboriginal language rights are reinforced by the Treaties.

   iii. The federal government has a responsibility to provide sufficient funds for Aboriginal-language revitalization and preservation.

   iv. The preservation, revitalization, and strengthening of Aboriginal languages and cultures are best managed by Aboriginal people and communities.

   v. Funding for Aboriginal language initiatives must reflect the diversity of Aboriginal languages.

15) We call upon the federal government to appoint, in consultation with Aboriginal groups, an Aboriginal Languages Commissioner. The commissioner should help promote Aboriginal languages and report on the adequacy of federal funding of Aboriginal-languages initiatives.

## Redressing the harms

Canadian governments and the churches that ran residential schools have special obligations to assist in the retention of Aboriginal languages because of their past shared policies of forced assimilation. The United Church's 1986 apology acknowledged the church's responsibility for harm caused by forced assimilation: "We imposed our civilization as a condition for accepting the gospel. We tried to make you be like us and in so doing we helped to destroy the vision that made you what you were. As a result you, and we, are poorer and the image of the Creator in us is twisted, blurred, and we are not what we are meant by God to be."[95]

The Presbyterian Church's 1994 apology sought forgiveness for the church's complicity in banning "some important spiritual practices through which Aboriginal peoples experienced the presence of the creator God" as well as for other practices that lead to "the loss of cultural identity and the loss of a secure sense of self" for former students.[96]

During a private meeting at the Vatican in 2009, Pope Benedict XVI expressed "sorrow" to a delegation from the Assembly of First Nations over the abuse and "deplorable" treatment that Aboriginal students suffered at residential schools run by the Roman Catholic Church, but he did not address the loss of language and culture.[97] No formal and public apology has been made on behalf of the Catholic Church as an organization, although some individual Catholic organizations have made apologies, such as the Missionary Oblates of Mary Immaculate, which apologized for its role in attempts to "assimilate aboriginal peoples" through residential schools.[98] In one example of a particular diocese accepting responsibility, Bishop Murray Chatlain of the Roman Catholic Diocese of Mackenzie-Fort Smith in the Northwest Territories acknowledged in 2009 that "We participated in a system that sought to strip away aboriginal language and culture."[99]

It is important that the churches that ran the residential schools recognize that the purpose of the schools was assimilation and that language and cultural loss was one of the most damaging features of residential schools, and of similar policies of assimilation pursued in other schools. At the same time, apologies can only be a meaningful prelude to reconciliation if tangible steps are taken by the churches to help repair the damage they caused. This is particularly necessary given that residential school Survivors have not succeeded in obtaining compensation for lost language and culture through the courts.

## The legal pursuit of compensation

Residential school Survivors have insisted that claims for loss of language and culture be a part of their many lawsuits against the Government of Canada and the churches. Both the government and the churches have aggressively opposed such claims. Even if the law recognized that Aboriginal language and culture loss was something that could be valued, the government and the churches argued that Survivors had waited too long to make their claims.

Claims about loss of language and culture were important for many Survivors. One former student at the Duck Lake, Saskatchewan, school alleged in a lawsuit that he was forcibly removed from his people, punished for speaking Cree, and prohibited from engaging in Aboriginal dancing, cultural, or religious activities. The Saskatchewan Court of Appeal dismissed his claim on the basis that he had not sued public authorities within one year after leaving school, and that his allegations did not amount to a breach of fiduciary duty or trust.[100]

Frederick Lee Barney sued the United Church and the Government of Canada in one early case that went to the Supreme Court of Canada. He recovered damages for being sexually assaulted but not for loss of language and culture, despite his powerful testimony, in which he explained,

> I was deprived of the love and guidance of my parents and siblings for five years. I lost my Native language and Aboriginal culture and was removed from my family roots. The enormity of the loss of both my culture and my connection with my family feels overwhelming and the effects irreversible. I lost my identity as a Native person. I live with a sense of not knowing who I am and how I should be in the world. I lost the friendship and support of my friends and community. I suffered a loss of self-esteem.... I'm angry about my loss of culture ... It's sickening. It was obvious the tremendous effect it has had on me as a person and yes, I get angry as hell.[101]

The trial judge in that case held that the federal government and the United Church did not engage in a breach of trust or a breach of fiduciary duty because they were candid and not dishonest about their plan to assimilate Aboriginal people.[102] The Canadian legal system did not hear Survivors when they said in the lawsuits that the treatment of Aboriginal languages and cultures in the schools was wrong and the language and culture that was lost was valuable.

The Common Experience Payments (CEP) arising from the Settlement Agreement provided recognition of an individual's loss of language and culture for those who could establish that they attended listed residential schools. Such payments, however, ignored the collective and intergenerational harms that have struck at the very core of Aboriginal identity. It is essential to understand, based on almost every statement the Commission received from almost seven thousand Survivors from every region of this country, that all of these losses are interconnected. These statements tell of devastating cumulative damage to Survivors, children, and grandchildren. This damage has also contributed to contemporary realities that add up to a significant financial, social, and reputational cost to Canada. It is not at all clear to this Commission why Aboriginal language and culture loss could not be recognized in Canadian courts.

The 2005 federal Task Force on Aboriginal Languages warned that the government's past policies towards Aboriginal languages, most notably the policies used in residential schools, could be viewed as a violation of Aboriginal and Treaty rights as well as the fiduciary duties that government had with respect to the children taken, and to Aboriginal people generally. The Task Force concluded,

> In our view, forcibly removing language and culture from individual First Nation, Inuit and Métis people is tantamount to a breach of Aboriginal and Treaty rights, as well as a breach of the Crown's fiduciary duty, and should therefore be compensable. It is also our view that Canada's refusal to compensate individuals who continue to suffer the devastating effects of their loss of connection to their communities and their languages, cultures and spiritual beliefs, fails to uphold the honour of the Crown. Further, this refusal has the effect of appearing to relegate First Nation, Inuit and Métis languages to the position of subjugated languages that can be forcibly removed from the memories of the people who spoke them, with impunity. Canada has taken the view that, while language is the collective right of a community or language group, compensation for loss of language will be a programmatic response to communities and language groups. We believe Canada's position to be fundamentally wrong. Government funding of First Nation, Inuit and Métis languages must be made on the basis of their constitutional status and should not be viewed as arising as part of the compensation for legitimate claims for damages that arise from wrongs committed against many individuals.[103]

The Task Force found that the revitalization and preservation of First Nations languages must be done by First Nations themselves. Canada has a duty to provide the resources necessary to restore First Nation, Inuit, and Métis languages and cultures.

The essential value of Aboriginal cultures was again emphasized in a 2014 ruling in Ontario. In *Brown v. Attorney General of Canada*, a class action has been "certified" (and thus permitted to proceed) relating to the large-scale removal of Aboriginal children by child welfare authorities between 1965 and 1984. In refusing the federal government's attempt to have the case thrown out, the Ontario Superior Court recognized that the case raises important issues about connection to culture and the harm of separation from one's Aboriginal heritage:

> Here we are not dealing with just one aspect of that culture. Here we are dealing with a person's connection to that culture as a whole. It is difficult to see a specific interest that could be of more importance to aboriginal peoples than each

person's essential connection to their aboriginal heritage. In addition, on this point, the importance of aboriginal rights cannot be disputed.[104]

## United Nations Declaration on the Rights of Indigenous Peoples

The *United Nations Declaration on the Rights of Indigenous Peoples* makes one of the most powerful and persuasive cases for governments to make reparations for forced assimilation. It recognizes Aboriginal languages as a vital part of Indigenous cultural rights. During the same time period that Canada supported and endorsed this important international declaration, it has backtracked on promises of increased funding for Aboriginal languages, and has treated Aboriginal languages as a minor part of a larger governmental portfolio devoted to all matters of Canadian heritage. Many provisions in the UN Declaration make clear that Canada has obligations to change course and to provide redress for its past policies.

Article 8 of the declaration recognizes that "Indigenous peoples and individuals have the right not to be subjected to forced assimilation or destruction of their culture." Article 8(2) then provides that "states shall provide effective mechanisms for prevention of and redress for any form of forced assimilation or integration." As suggested throughout this volume, residential schools constituted a most pernicious form of "forced assimilation." The linguistic policies pursued in the schools are among the worst forms of forced assimilation. Even if the modest payments of compensation to individuals in the form of the Common Experience Payment are seen as a form of individual reparation, Canada has not taken the kinds of steps that would be necessary to reverse the collective loss of language and culture that was the intended consequence of the residential schools. In the absence of such steps, redress has not occurred.

Article 13(1) of the UN Declaration recognizes that "Indigenous peoples have the right to revitalize, use, develop and transmit to future generations their histories, languages, oral traditions, philosophies, writing systems and literatures, and to designate and retain their own names for communities, places and persons." Article 14(1) similarly provides that "Indigenous peoples have the right to establish and control their educational systems and institutions *providing education in their own languages*, in a manner appropriate to their cultural methods of teaching and learning," and article 14(3) makes such rights real by providing that "States shall, in conjunction with indigenous peoples, take effective measures, in order for indigenous individuals, particularly children, including those living outside their communities, to have access, when possible, to an education in their own culture and provided in their own language."

Article 16 provides that Indigenous peoples "have the right to establish their own media in their own languages and to have access to all forms of non-indigenous media without discrimination" and that states "shall take effective measures to ensure that State-owned media duly reflect indigenous cultural diversity."

Article 19 is a critical provision in the declaration because it requires Canada to consult and cooperate in good faith with Indigenous peoples in order to obtain their consent prior to implementing legislative or administrative measures that may affect them. As a result, Canada cannot impose solutions upon Aboriginal peoples, but must work with Aboriginal peoples to implement its international obligations.[105]

Finally, it is difficult to reconcile the refusal of courts to acknowledge the loss of language and culture as being compensable with the very important principle that such acts could constitute acts of genocide an acknowledged crime against a racial group in breach of the *UN Convention on Genocide*.[106]

This Commission has found that the actions of the federal government in attacking and attempting to destroy Aboriginal cultures and languages, not only in residential schools but in Aboriginal communities through ceremonial prohibitions in the *Indian Act*, amounted to cultural genocide. The term *cultural genocide* is not found in the *UN Convention on Genocide*, and an analysis of the evolution of the Convention prior to its adoption by the United Nations shows that inclusion of the term was rejected. Nonetheless, while the term *genocide* generally refers to the physical destruction of members of a racialized group, the Convention contains provisions that appear to contemplate criteria other than immediate physical destruction. For example, article 2 of the Convention states,

> In the present Convention, genocide means any of the following acts committed with intent to destroy, in whole or in part, a national, ethnical, racial or religious group, as such:
>
> (a) Killing members of the group;
>
> (b) Causing serious bodily or mental harm to members of the group;
>
> (c) Deliberately inflicting on the group conditions of life calculated to bring about its physical destruction in whole or in part;
>
> (d) Imposing measures intended to prevent births within the group;
>
> (e) Forcibly transferring children of the group to another group.

Clearly, articles 2(d) and 2(e) do not require that the victims themselves be "destroyed" but that the measures taken against them be intended to result in the destruction of the "national, ethnical, racial or religious group, as such."

The forcible sterilization of women and girls for the purpose of preventing their group from repopulating itself would be an act of genocide, even though the individual female victim would be allowed to live. The forcible removal of children from their racial community in order to be indoctrinated into another racial community and thereby "destroy" their original group would likewise be an act of genocide, even though the children themselves continued to live as members of the new group.

It is the Commission's view that if Canada were to attempt to do today what it did in the nineteenth century through residential schools, it could face severe international consequences.

It seems logical to conclude that Canada's actions in forcibly transferring Aboriginal children from their racial group to another in order to eliminate or destroy their cultures and languages—and therefore their racial group—could at least amount to a legal wrong cognizable in Canadian law because of Canada's acceptance of it as a legal wrong in international law. No court has so held; nor as a Commission can we make a definitive finding on the point. The way does seem clear, however, for such legal recognition to be made at some point in the future.

The Commission concludes that the Aboriginal peoples of Canada have language rights tied to their rights under Canadian constitutional law, their rights under international law, and their legitimate claims to collective reparation for forced assimilation in the residential schools.

The Commission calls for a new approach from the Canadian government, an approach that must restore the right of Aboriginal communities to pursue the language and cultural initiatives that best reflect their own circumstances. This should be done, wherever possible, on a nation-to-nation basis, along the lines of the Yukon model where the government provides language funding to self-governing nations. A pan-Aboriginal approach is inappropriate given the diversity of Canada's Aboriginal communities, their relative access to supportive resources, and the differences in the current health of the Aboriginal languages used in Canada.

## The importance of Aboriginal languages and culture to non-Aboriginal Canadians

The neglect of Aboriginal languages affects all Canadians. It impedes the ability of non-Aboriginal Canadians to understand and to appreciate the linguistic and cultural diversity that is part of a shared history. The language and culture of all Canadians is infused with the words and the history of Aboriginal peoples. Too easily people forget that proper names such as *Québec* and *Saskatchewan* and everyday words such as *chipmunk* (Odawa) and *moose* (Ojibway) are gifts from Aboriginal people and their ancestors.

However, there is much more for non-Aboriginal Canadians in a broader appreciation of the value of Aboriginal languages. For example, the Anishinaabe word *sabawaa* is used to describe a time in the Ontario spring when cold and warm air masses intermingle and cause fine mists to rise over the earth. The snows melt and the waters start to flow at this time. The Anishinaabe word for forgiveness is a related word: *aabaweweni-maa*. It describes a process in which we loosen our thoughts towards others and let relationships flow more easily, becoming warmer towards each other.[107] Other Aboriginal languages throughout Canada hold similar examples of wisdom and beauty.

Non-Aboriginal Canadians should also care about the damage done to Aboriginal languages and cultures because their government has apologized to Aboriginal peoples on their behalf. Canada's 2008 apology for residential schools recognized explicitly that the schools were based on a "policy of assimilation" that "caused great harm, and has no place in our country." It specifically recognized that the schools "had a lasting and damaging impact on Aboriginal culture, heritage and language."[108]

There can be no real prospect for reconciliation if that apology is not seen as sincere and accompanied with a commitment to address the wrongs that prompted the apology in the first place. Those who have stolen something valuable cannot expect their apology to be believable and acceptable without the return of what was stolen, or a mutually agreeable level of compensation. In the case of residential schools, the apology is a moral commitment on the part of the Government of Canada to support the health of Aboriginal cultures and languages.

## Reclaiming names

As a result of the residential school experience, many Aboriginal people lost their language and lost touch with their culture. Many also suffered a loss of a different sort. It was common for residential school officials to give students new names. At the Aklavik Anglican school in the Northwest Territories, a young Inuit girl named Masak was called Alice—she would not hear her old name until she returned home.[109] At the Qu'Appelle school in Saskatchewan, Ochankuga'he (Path Maker) became Daniel Kennedy, named for the biblical Daniel, and Adélard Standing Buffalo was named for Adélard Langevin, the archbishop of St. Boniface.[110] Survivors and their families who have sought to reclaim the names that were taken from them in residential schools have found the process to be both expensive and time consuming. The Commission believes that measures should be put in place to reduce the burden placed on those who seek to reclaim this significant portion of their heritage.

> 17) We call upon all levels of government to enable residential school Survivors and their families to reclaim names changed by the residential school system by waiving administrative costs for a period of five years for the name-change process and the revision of official identity documents, such as birth certificates, passports, driver's licenses, health cards, status cards, and social insurance numbers.

# The way forward

## Aboriginal knowledge

Residential school Survivors do not need reports or studies to tell them that recovering their stolen cultures can assist them on their healing journey. They know this from their own experiences. Isabelle Knockwood, who attended the Shubenacadie school in Nova Scotia, writes of recovering spirituality: "Many of us have returned to a traditional path as the source of our strength ... Some of us have come to realize that we were abused not only physically but spiritually. For us, the Native Way with its Sacred Circle and respect for all living things is a means of healing that abuse."[111]

The Commission heard many stories from Survivors about their early experiences with Aboriginal language and how learning language connected them to family and to place. Paul Stanley talked about this connection at the Commission's community hearing in Deroche, British Columbia:

> When you're in bed with papa, and he tells you about your first story, and it's about how the chipmunk got his stripes, and it was so funny to me, you know that I asked him every night to say it again, you know, and, and, and these things helped, too. And if I didn't know a word, he'd let me know ... And so that's how language is taught at home, in my place ... And it's not by a desk or anything like that, which is okay, you know, other systems work anyway, but that's how we started, so that was my life, you know, like to learn the language, and maybe a bit of culture.[112]

Esther Lachinette-Diabo, echoed that sentiment in Thunder Bay, Ontario:

> I feel free to be able to speak in Ojibway, and I talk about the culture because I experienced it when I was a kid. I've seen my grandparents; I've seen my uncles; and I've seen medicine people come to our community, our trapline, and do their ceremonies. I can talk about those from first-hand experience.[113]

Matilda Lampe vividly remembers the day her younger sister first spoke to her father in Inuktitut at their home in Labrador:

> At our supper table dad, Doris said to dad, *"qanuivit?"* [How are you?] Oh my God everybody just, like we all got quiet like this; just myself and Doris and my mom and dad. My dad put his food down; he got up and oh my God that was the best ever. My dad, my dad got up off his chair and went over to Doris; me and my mom were just looking at each other like, like myself like, thinking for the worst. She's going to be hit; she's going to be smacked something.
>
> That was the best supper ever. My dad got up and went over to Doris and hugged her; first time ever and he actually took her, hugged her. He sat down and looked at Doris, *nakummiik* [thank you] ... oh my God, that was the best

ever ... Doris picked up few, few words like, not hard words but easy. My dad got comfortable with her after; took him long time, almost a year.[114]

## Case studies

The Aboriginal cultures and languages that were damaged are actually even more precious today; for as battered and broken as they are, they hold the seeds for rejuvenation. The Survivors know that the recovery of language and culture was and remains critical for their own individual healing and for the health of Aboriginal families and communities in the future. Many of the Survivors explained to the Commission how they reconnected with Aboriginal languages and cultures as the most powerful and restorative part of their very difficult healing journeys.

Many remedies to the loss of language and culture have already been tested by different Aboriginal peoples across the country. These solutions, however, need support and nourishment from governments and churches, and support has not been forthcoming.

### British Columbia

British Columbia has the greatest diversity of Aboriginal languages, having 27 of the 86 Aboriginal languages spoken in Canada, according to UNESCO. However, it accounts for only 7% of the country's Aboriginal mother-tongue population because of the small speaker population.[115] The 2011 census reported that BC is home to 30 different Aboriginal languages but that most of those languages have less than 1,000 people each.

For example, there are 925 recorded speakers of Gitksan, and 675 recorded speakers of Shuswap.[116] British Columba has some of the smallest and most endangered Aboriginal mother-tongue populations, including the Salish family (3,700), the Tsimshian family (2,400), the Wakashan family (1,200), Kutenai isolate (155), Haida isolate (130), and Tlingit (90).[117] In 2001, second-language learners accounted for over half the speakers of Tlingit, Haida, and smaller Salish languages.[118]

A 2010 study by the First Peoples' Heritage, Language and Cultures Council observed that the teaching of First Nations languages in schools in BC is "too limited to have any great effect" and has predicted that most fluent speakers of Aboriginal languages in BC may be gone by as early as 2016.[119]

The Sto:lo Nation is one of many British Columbia First Nations that is taking steps to revitalize and preserve its languages. The Sto:lo Nation spans the Fraser Valley and is comprised of eleven member First Nations: Aitchelitz, Le'qamel, Matsqui, Popkum,

Skawahlook, Skowkale, Shxwha:y, Squiala, Sumas, Tzeachten, Yakweakwioose. The total population of these First Nations is about 2,094.

Halq'eméylem is the traditional language of the territory. With fewer than five fluent speakers of the language, it is considered very close to extinction. In the face of this risk of extinction, numerous steps are being taken to preserve the language in both the short and long term. For example, Seabird Island runs a Halq'emeylem Preschool Language Nest, which is a preschool modelled after a family home where young children are immersed in their language and culture. The children learn Halq'emeylem from fluent speakers and Elders while doing daily activities. The Language Nest takes a multigenerational approach, with parents encouraged to volunteer in the preschool and then continue to use the language at home.

The Sto:lo Nation Language Program has also developed an intensive immersion program. The program runs for fifty weeks and has a goal of developing highly fluent speakers of Halq'eméylem. An extensive language archive as well as language teaching materials are available on FirstVoices.com. The Sto:lo First Nation has been working together and at great odds to preserve their language. Nonetheless, the work is far from finished and much more must be done to ensure that Halq'emeylem is not lost.[120]

## Inuit languages

As late as 1949 only 111 Inuit were receiving full-time schooling in the North. Twelve were attending a federal day school in Kuujjuaq (Fort Chimo) in Northern Québec, 8 at the Anglican residential school at Fort George, Québec, and 91 at the two residential schools in Aklavik, Northwest Territories.[121] Due to the uneven rate of development of the system, the Inuit and Inuvialuit in the Western Artic were pulled into the residential school system much earlier. Many of the communities where Inuktitut language survives are in the east (Nunavut) or above the Arctic Circle. It was not until the late 1950s, when a system of hostels and day schools was established across the North, that Inuit children began attending residential schools in significant numbers.[122] By February 1959, 1,165 Inuit children were receiving full-time schooling in the North.[123] Consequently, Inuit people were not spared the attacks on Aboriginal language and culture that characterized residential schools elsewhere. As early as 1968 social scientists were noting how Inuit children educated at residential school were forced to "play two different games"—one involving English and white ways at school, and the other in Inuktitut and involving Inuit ways at home.[124] Willy Carpenter grew up in Tuktoyuktuk, Northwest Terrorities. He remembered,

> We tried to speak our own language; we'd get scolding and punishment of
> some kind. I lost my language for a good two to three years. And I came back;
> I couldn't hardly understand my mom, when she spoke to me in Inuvialuktun.

But in time we got together speaking, I got it all back; and up to today I speak it. I could speak it really good. I got right back to it. I didn't want to forget that ... Why did they treat us the way they did? Maybe they thought we were animals or something. I can't understand that.[125]

Through the efforts of people like Willy Carpenter, Inuit languages have persisted. Inuktitut is one of the largest and most viable Aboriginal languages in Canada.[126]

Although Inuktitut remains strong, its use has declined.[127] According to the 2011 census, just over 34,000 Inuit, or 63.7% of the total, reported Inuktitut as their mother tongue, down from 68% in 1996.[128] Also of concern is the fact that the proportion is declining for Inuit who speak Inuktitut most often at home. In 2006, about 25,500 Inuit, 50% of the total, reported Inuktitut as the language most often spoken at home, down from 58% in 1996.[129] The percentage of Inuit who reported that they spoke Inuktitut well enough to carry on a conversation is also declining, down to 63.3% from 69% in 2006 and 72% in 1996.[130]

Language fluency varies across Inuit Nunangat (consisting of the four regions of the Inuit homeland). Close to 100% of Inuit living in Nunavik (Northern Québec) can converse in an Inuit language. In Nunavut, nearly 90% can do so. However, fluency is much lower in Nunatsiavut (northern coastal Labrador) (24.9%) and in the Inuvialuit region of the Northwest Territories (20.1%). Outside Inuit Nunangat, only 10% of Inuit report speaking an Inuit language well enough to conduct a conversation.[131]

The large majority of Inuit adults in each region stated that it was very or somewhat important for them to keep, learn, or relearn Inuktitut. Nine in every ten Inuit parents stated it was very or somewhat important for their children to speak and understand Inuktitut.[132] Inuit youth report a desire to increase access to learning, hearing, and using Inuktitut. Furthermore, these youth think governmental initiatives should facilitate, not replace, home and community-based efforts.[133]

Some of the health of Inuktitut can no doubt be attributed to the resources that have been devoted to its survival. Fifteen per cent of all language funding provided through Heritage Canada's Aboriginal Language Initiative is devoted to Inuktitut.[134] As well, programmers with the Canadian Broadcasting Corporation's Northern Service radio and television have worked to expand their programming in Aboriginal languages in recent years. However, those advances are also threatened by repeated funding cuts.

Inuktitut is designated an official language in Nunavut.[135] Also in Nunavut, efforts have been made to ensure that Inuktitut is integrated into political, economic, and social life. Nunavut formally recognizes by statute the inherent right of the Inuit in Nunavut to use their language. The *Inuit Language Protection Act* guarantees, among other things, the right to Inuit language instruction in Nunavut's school system and the right to work in the Inuit language in territorial government institutions. It also specifies that governments, municipalities, community organizations, and businesses can use the Inuit language in reception and customer services, on signs, posters, and advertising, for essential, household, residential, and hospitality services, and in municipal services concerning public safety and welfare.[136] Rights can be important in protecting fragile languages, but they must also be rooted in a healthy language that is used in daily life if they are not simply to be a symbolic reaffirmation of languages that may only appear to be healthy and protected.

Nunavut's *Education Act* establishes a right to a bilingual education with the Inuit language, with the goal of producing graduates who are able to use both languages competently in academic and other contexts. The *Act* provides for several different models of bilingual instruction, with the ultimate decision about which model will be used to be made with community consultation, and to be subject to review every five years. The minister of education is responsible for ensuring that the education program supports the use, development, and revitalization of the Inuit language.[137]

However, underlying this institutional support for Inuktitut is the fact that intergenerational mother-tongue language transmission continues to be the foundation for language retention in the territory.[138] In Nunavut, 83% reported an Inuktitut mother tongue.[139] Thus, many Inuit children enter school already speaking their language, which makes it easier to implement language instruction in the primary grades.[140]

Other elements of the overall strategy that have supported the maintenance of Inuktitut include

- documentation of the language and the stories of the Elders;
- Inuktitut radio and television programming;
- widespread teaching of literacy skills and use of Inuktitut in the print media;
- the training and utilization of Inuit teachers;
- production of Inuktitut language materials;
- cultural-based activities for children on the land and in school; and
- a variety of community-based projects aimed at promoting and strengthening the use of the language in the home and community.

Additionally, the Nunavut Arctic College offers a certificate program for Inuktitut interpreters; and the Bathurst Mandate (Nunavut's blueprint for Indigenous self-government) set a goal of having Inuktitut as the working language of the Nunavut government by 2020.[141] Inuktitut also has the advantage of being a vital language in several jurisdictions. Therefore, the exchange of educational materials, and collaboration in the development of them, is an important option not available to other communities.

This multi-pronged approach recognizes that languages must be supported if they are to survive and thrive. Despite the fact that Inuktitut is an official language of the territory of Nunavut, the funding available to support the language is far inferior to the funding for French-language services in Nunavut. The federal government provides support to the small minority of francophones in Nunavut in the amount of approximately $4,000 per individual annually. In contrast, funding to support Inuit language initiatives is estimated at $44 per Inuk per year.[142] Although Inuktitut is healthier than most Aboriginal languages, and language policy at the territorial level is robust, Canada could do much more to promote such languages, especially in a region that only the Inuit can claim is truly their homeland.

The Commission finds that the preservation and revitalization of Aboriginal languages is a necessary and constructive reparation for the attack on Aboriginal languages and cultures in the residential schools and in Canadian society. It also concludes that retention of Aboriginal languages could provide Canada with vital social capital to enrich our understandings of the environment, health, culture, justice, and governance.

The Commission finds that there is a willingness and ability among Aboriginal people to undertake the rewarding work of learning Aboriginal languages. The Commission recognizes that there are enormous differences in the current use of Aboriginal languages among Inuit, First Nations, and Métis, and geographically within those groups. It is clear to the Commission that a one-size-fits-all approach to language will not work.

## Community-based responses

There is a need for Canada's Aboriginal peoples to pursue their own language policies in a way that is appropriate for their own distinct situations. RCAP outlined a very practical approach to preserving and strengthening Aboriginal language, proposing an eight-stage process for language revitalization, with use of languages in government as only the seventh and eighth phases. It emphasized the importance of the communities themselves reconstructing language, mobilizing older fluent speakers, restoring intergenerational transmission through families and community.

The stories, the songs, the languages that we learn from our families as children influence how we go on to live in the world. This nurturing role in the transmission of beliefs was taken from Aboriginal parents when their children were forced into residential schools. That role must be restored and honoured. The Commission has been convinced by the testimonials from Survivors, as well as by the social science evidence, that the best way to restore Aboriginal languages and cultures is by ensuring that families and communities are the focal point for learning.

There are many possible models and no one size will fit all. As RCAP recognized, the best way to revitalize and preserve culture, including language, is to ensure that it is part of everyday life and passed on to children from a young age. As a teacher with the Secwepemc First Nation observed,

> Our children need the opportunity to hear our languages so that they can go to sleep with our language, they could hear their grandfather speaking the language, they could hear their grandmother speaking the language, they could hear and dream in the language. And I think, too, I have a belief that when we are in our sweats [sacred ceremonial lodges], if we're going to meet our ancestors wouldn't it be beautiful to be conversing in the language as the Creator has gifted us? ... Our children will be going to those levels, too, because they'll be going and meeting our ancestors and be able to understand and make sure our messages and our teachings are not lost.[143]

However, very few Aboriginal families and communities are in a position to be able to employ effective measures for language preservation. This is especially the case as fluent speakers become elderly and are not being replaced by younger generations. Loss of language will also challenge the ability of communities to impart cultural knowledge.

Yet many Aboriginal people are rising to the challenge. In the face of great odds, we are witnessing an upsurge in innovative community-based and community-controlled initiatives to revitalize and preserve culture and language. These initiatives include local development of language classes in schools; language preservation through writing and audio and video recordings; Aboriginal media on radio, TV, and the Internet; as well as cultural classes and immersion programs. These initiatives must be permitted to flourish and grow, with the choice about how to go about this important work ultimately belonging to the communities themselves. The TRC has been able to encourage and witness some of these efforts through our role in recommending funding for proposed commemoration projects.

## Language nests

'Language nests' provide one interesting model that has been used with success internationally. The nests have been adopted by a number of Aboriginal communities here in Canada. They can ensure that language and culture are part of the everyday life of children from a young age, even if their parents are not fluent speakers. There are different models but, generally, preschool children as young as six weeks of age spend their days immersed in their Aboriginal language and culture in a home-like environment. Ideally, children then transition to an immersion school available in the community.

There are a number of language nests in British Columbia and the Northwest Territories.[144] Some began simply because one or two individuals in the community took the initiative and made it happen. As one administrator from a BC language nest observed,

> People can walk in and say, "Wow, this is easy"... because all we're doing is inviting children over to grandma's house and speaking the language all day and playing with them. There's no mystery to that.... We go down to the lake and we play with logs and we put rocks on logs and we make those into canoes, we go out into the fields and we play with the flowers and we make flower wreaths and stuff ... We don't need to overcomplicate it. I think that's what people tend to do. They overcomplicate the whole thing. We forget that children need love and nurturing, they need positive reinforcement, they need acceptance, they need to be safe, they need healthy food, there's real basics that we need to do, we don't need to worry about too many other things. In a nutshell, that's what I think a language nest is.[145]

The language nests do more than simply teach language. They also ensure that children learn about their cultures, beliefs, practices, and songs. Traditional drumming and dancing are often incorporated, and one community introduced the practice of using traditional names for the children. Interviews conducted as part of a study of language nests in BC suggest that children who participated "better appreciated their history, identity, and traditions."[146]

In addition to inspiring children, language nests can also assist parents. They can learn the language from their children as they come home and talk about what they have learned. The children then become teachers themselves and valuable resources for the community. The community itself may find that connections are made, especially with Elders and others who must be fluent in the language in order to run language nests; these connections also provide social and linguistic capital that will assist the community. In one community, the first children who went through the language nest and then K–7 immersion have now graduated from high school and work at the immersion school as curriculum developers. One of the teachers reported that she has conferred with these past graduates (who are now young adults) on certain words or concepts that she does not know. She respectfully referred to them as her "little Elders."[147]

Unfortunately, the barriers and obstacles to developing such programs can seem enormous. An evaluation in the Northwest Territories identified many hurdles: a lack of administrative capacity, staffing challenges, a lack of fluent speakers, low or no wages, lack of core funding, lack of space, licensing requirements, and the lack of curriculum and materials.[148] Again, these challenges underline the importance of giving Aboriginal communities the powers and the funding they need.

## Aboriginal languages as second languages

Although Aboriginal languages are best preserved when they are learned in the home as a first language,[149] both the state of Aboriginal languages in Canada and the desire of many to reconnect with their cultures suggest that more support should be given to learning Aboriginal languages as a second language.

To begin with, many mother-tongue populations are aging beyond childbearing years; and second, for most children the ideal family and community conditions for mother-tongue transmission are becoming the exception rather than the norm. Demographic data show that the children most likely to learn an Aboriginal language as a second language are from linguistically mixed families and live in urban areas.[150] Approximately 22% of Aboriginal people who reported to the 2011 National Household Survey that they could conduct a conversation in an Aboriginal language had learned it as a second language. That proportion varied from 35.3% for Métis to 23.1% for First Nations people to 10.2% for Inuit.[151]

There is also a demand among Aboriginal people for such language training. According to the 2001 Aboriginal Peoples Survey, parents of 60% of Aboriginal children in non-reserve areas believed it was very important or somewhat important for their children to speak and understand an Aboriginal language.

The survey report also notes that in Saskatchewan, 65% of Aboriginal adults and 63% of Aboriginal youth aged fifteen to twenty-four living off-reserve considered it important to know their language; in Yukon, 78% of adults and 76% of youth considered it important.[152]

The Commission urges all parties to the Settlement Agreement to support community-based approaches to language retention as recommended by RCAP. This may require innovative approaches to the use of Elders and others as teachers and the use of language nests and immersion programs. Schools should be flexible and responsive in their attempts to encourage the teaching of Aboriginal languages.

As a way of preserving Aboriginal languages and building broader support for national reconciliation, language instruction should be extended through post-secondary institutions. This would allow Aboriginal-language speakers to develop greater proficiency while at the same time institutionalizing language instruction in an academic context.

**16)** We call upon post-secondary institutions to create university and college degree and diploma programs in Aboriginal languages.

# Conclusion

The fragile state of almost all Aboriginal languages in Canada is a damaging legacy of residential schools. Although the schools contributed greatly to the decline, so too did the federal day schools and public schools, which made no room for Aboriginal languages or cultural expression. The repressive policies used against Aboriginal languages and cultures in all schools, and in Canadian society generally, were based on the view that Aboriginal languages and cultures were primitive, savage, and inferior.

It is especially regrettable that the Canadian government did not follow through in 2006 on earlier funding commitments with respect to Aboriginal languages. Those actions are a significant barrier to reconciliation. Canada's policies on Aboriginal languages are neither fiscally nor structurally sound. Funding for Aboriginal language initiatives has not increased since 1998. Canada has pursued a paternalistic policy of heritage subsidies. These are a direct rejection of RCAP's recommendation that policies designed to preserve language respect the inherent rights of Aboriginal people.

The churches, which ran so many of the schools, simply asserted that Christianity was superior to the spirituality, values, and ceremonies of Aboriginal systems. The federal government and the churches need to make collective reparation for the damage they have done to Aboriginal languages and cultures. In particular, the Government of Canada should, as recommended by RCAP, approach the funding of Aboriginal languages on a nation-to-nation basis that recognizes that language policy is a core element of Aboriginal self-determination. Such an approach should also recognize the great diversity of Aboriginal peoples within Canada, and the different needs of different communities.

The Commission would also like to emphasize that these obligations are affirmed in the Canadian Constitution and in numerous legal precedents. Canada is also a signatory to the *UN Declaration on the Rights of Indigenous Peoples*, a document that clearly sets out obligations that the Government of Canada has to make reparations for past policies, and to address the current policy and funding failures and inadequacies.

While the Commission heard many painful stories about the direct and intergenerational harm caused by the loss of language and culture, the Commissioners were heartened by the many stories we heard of resistance, resilience, and recovery. We are convinced that reconnection with Aboriginal languages and cultures will have important healing effects. Such initiatives will also increase the social and intellectual capital of Canada by preserving Aboriginal languages.

As the 2005 Task Force on Aboriginal Languages and Cultures noted, the ultimate responsibility lies with Aboriginal people:

> Canada cannot speak our languages for us. Canada cannot restore them. And Canada cannot promote them among our peoples. We must take our rightful positions as the first and most appropriate teachers of our languages and cultures.

> We must begin by speaking our own languages to our children in our homes and communities and we must do it daily. We cannot delegate this task to our schools or leave it for the next generation.[153]

At the same time, non-Aboriginal people, as represented by the Government of Canada and the churches, have moral and legal responsibilities to help repair the linguistic and cultural damages caused by their failed attempts at forced assimilation in the schools.

The recommendations of this Commission are intended to provide a guide as to how these obligations can be discharged. We hope they honourably reflect and reaffirm what Survivors have told us about the vital importance of maintaining Aboriginal languages and cultures. As Survivor Sabrina Williams so eloquently puts it,

> All things that are attached to language: it's family connections; it's oral history; it's traditions; it's ways of being; it's ways of knowing; it's medicine; it's song; it's dance; it's memory; it's everything, including the land. Because when I listen to people speak our language I can hear where, start to hear where it might have come from. So, to me ... that's another act of reconciliation—is to be able to provide that support so we can reclaim our languages.[154]

# An attack on Aboriginal health: The marks and the memories

## Introduction

Thousands of Aboriginal children died in residential schools. They were killed by relentless waves of epidemics—tuberculosis and a host of other infectious diseases—that swept repeatedly through the institutions. Those children did not have to die. The spread of disease was fed and facilitated by crowded living conditions at the schools, along with a lethal combination of substandard sanitation, poor nutrition, and an appallingly low quality of medical care.

Health care services that might have been made available were often denied or caught in bureaucratic tangles between different levels of government and the churches. Prevailing attitudes of those ultimately responsible for the schools reflects coldness, indifference, and neglect that borders on the criminal, if it does not actually cross the line.

Not all students died of disease. Some students died from exposure when they attempted to run away from the schools. Some young children took their own lives rather than face another day in institutions where they lived in such despair. The students were also denied access to medical professionals who might have been available or willing to treat them. In one of the darkest stains on the history of Canada, documents show that the care of Aboriginal children in residential schools was deemed less necessary than that given to white children.

Students in residential schools were powerless to take any of their own healing measures. They were refused access to traditional foods and Aboriginal healers who might have helped them. Their families and communities were routinely excluded from decisions related to their care.

While many thousands of Aboriginal students took their injuries and infectious diseases back to their homes and communities, those were not the only burdens they carried. They also brought with them, as lessons from their schoolmasters and mistresses, the permanent scars of racism—lessons that taught them, in their most impressionable years, that they, and their parents and their ancestors, were subhuman. Aside from the physical and mental damage these students bore, they were the first to bear what was to become a multigenerational affliction, one that would affect the ability of Aboriginal peoples to embrace their languages, their cultures, and their trusted traditional healing practices. In this way, the residential school system was an attack on the health of generations of Aboriginal peoples, an attack first made visible by the physical scars of sickness and abuse, but also one that continues to punish Aboriginal peoples with a legacy of marginalized lives, addiction, mental health, poor housing, and suicide.

Ruby Firth shared her story with the Commission. She attended the Stringer Hall Anglican hostel, a residence for students in Inuvik, NWT. In her years there, she suffered seven different bouts of pneumonia, causing permanent damage to her respiratory system. She explained,

> I've got chronic bronchitis today. Every winter I get pneumonia like two or three times and I'm on two puffers 'cause when I was in Stringer Hall Residential School they used to put us in these little skinny red coats that weren't even warm enough for winter. And we used to have to walk across the street to go to school ... My lungs are 50%, both my lungs are 50% scarred from having pneumonia seven times in res. That's always going to be there, it's never going to go away.

Firth's medical records also show that she had numerous broken bones resulting from different instances of the physical abuse she suffered there. Today, she suffers from Post Traumatic Stress Disorder (PTSD):

> I didn't do this to myself. They did it to me, yet they still fall short of what I need. I'm still in need; I'm still in poverty; I'm still in a third world country. I still hurt and they're still standing by and not doing nothing about it ... I don't even make eye contact with no white person. No white person will ever make eye contact with me again; that's how much they hurt my nation ... If you raise a voice to me, "Ruby!" I'll cry. And so I try to avoid all that. I stay on my medication and stay with my family. If I go outside the circle much, people affect me and I don't like that so I don't go out; and that's what residential school did to me ... It was all directly put on me by the Canadian Government, through the queen who, who hired the churches to assimilate and I didn't do none of that.[1]

Ruby Firth is just one, of the many thousands of residential school Survivors who carries the marks, the memories, and the lasting effects of poor health care in the residential school system. The suffering of so many has also had a telling impact on subsequent generations, and that's the subject of this chapter.

The residential schools are closed. A number of them have been destroyed. Yet the legacy of those schools continues to infect the health of Aboriginal people today. This chapter begins by briefly reviewing the multiplicity of abuses, injuries, and diseases that residential school life inflicted on students and their families. It will then look at what is known about the health of Aboriginal people today, surveying a broad range of health indicators, including life expectancy, infant mortality, fetal alcohol spectrum disorder, HIV/AIDS, mental health, food and housing insecurity, addiction, and suicide.

The chapter then examines the failure of the federal government to fulfill its role in improving the health of Aboriginal people in general, Survivors, and intergenerational Survivors in particular. The chapter will also look at what is needed now and in the future to improve the health of Aboriginal Canadians. It will highlight programs and institutions that are working to bridge the health gap that exists between Aboriginal and non-Aboriginal people.

By tracing this "trail of death and disease"[2] back to the residential schools, the chapter will show how inequities continue today in the unconscionable political and societal acceptance of dramatically higher death, illness, suicide, and accident rates among Aboriginal peoples. It is critical that this acceptance come to an end, and soon, for it is only in good health that people will find the strength to face the truths and the opportunities for reconciliation that lie ahead.

## Aboriginal health in residential schools

The exceedingly high death rate for Aboriginal children in residential schools was never a secret. In 1906, it was publicly denounced by Dr. P. H. Bryce, then chief medical officer of the Department of Indian Affairs. He wrote in his annual report that "the Indian population of Canada has a mortality rate of more than double that of the whole population, and in some provinces more than three times."[3] His report made national headlines, and the popular *Saturday Night* magazine concluded, "Even war seldom shows as large a percentage of fatalities as does the educational system we have imposed on our Indian wards."[4]

### Infectious disease

Tuberculosis was the prevalent cause of death. Bryce described a cycle of disease in which infants and children were infected at home and sent to residential schools, where they infected other children. The children infected in the schools were "sent home when too ill to remain at school, or because of being a danger to the other scholars, and have conveyed the disease to houses previously free."[5] In 1907 Bryce published a damning report on the conditions at prairie boarding schools. In an age when fresh air was seen as being central to the successful treatment of tuberculosis, he concluded that, with only a few exceptions, the ventilation at the schools was "extremely inadequate."[6] He found the school staff and even physicians "inclined to question or minimize the dangers of infection from scrofulous or consumptive pupils [scrofula and consumption were alternate names for types of tuberculosis] and nothing less than peremptory instructions as to how to deal with cases of disease existing in the schools will eliminate this ever-present danger of infection."[7]

Dr. Bryce gave the principals a questionnaire to complete regarding the health condition of their former students. The responses from fifteen schools revealed that "of a total of 1,537 pupils reported upon nearly 25 per cent are dead, of one school with an absolutely accurate statement, 69 per cent of ex-pupils are dead, and that everywhere the almost invariable cause of death given is tuberculosis." He drew particular attention to the fate of the thirty-one students who had been discharged from the File Hills school: nine were in good health, and twenty-two were dead.[8]

Though Dr. Bryce was later removed from his position, he continued to denounce the Department of Indian Affairs' inaction as a "national crime." The senior government officials who dismissed Dr. Bryce's analysis went so far as to blame the Aboriginal students for their own high death rate, one of them noting in 1914 the "well known predisposition of Indians to tuberculosis."[9]

Aboriginal children were taken from their homes and sent to residential schools in part because of beliefs "that Aboriginal parents were negligent parents and especially that unassimilated Native women made poor mothers."[10] Yet the absurdity of this conclusion is now made clear by statistics that show it was the schools themselves where the children faced the greatest threats to their lives.

## Unsafe buildings

For Aboriginal children, the relocation to residential schools was generally no healthier than their homes had been on the reserves. In 1897, Indian Affairs official Martin Benson reported that the industrial schools in Manitoba and the North-West Territories had been "hurriedly constructed of poor materials, badly laid out, without due provision for lighting, heating or ventilation." In addition, drainage was poor, and water and fuel supplies were inadequate.[11] Conditions were not any better in the church-built boarding schools. In 1904, Indian Commissioner David Laird echoed Benson's comments when he wrote that the sites for the boarding schools on the Prairies seemed "to have been selected without proper regard for either water-supply or drainage. I need not mention any school in particular, but I have urged improvement in several cases in regard to fire-protection."[12]

Students' health depended on clean water, good sanitation, and adequate ventilation. But little was done to improve the poor living conditions that were identified at the beginning of the twentieth century. In 1940, R. A. Hoey, who had served as the Indian Affairs superintendent of welfare and training since 1936, wrote a lengthy assessment of the condition of the existing residential schools. He concluded that many schools were "in a somewhat dilapidated condition" and had "become acute fire hazards." He laid responsibility for the "condition of our schools, generally," upon their "faulty construction." This construction, he said, had failed to meet "the minimum standards in the construction of public buildings, particularly institutions for the education of children."[13] By 1940, the government had concluded that future policy should concentrate on the expansion of day schools for First Nations children. As a result, many of the existing residential school buildings were allowed to continue to deteriorate. A 1967 brief from the National Association of Principals and Administrators of Indian Residences, which included principals of both Catholic and Protestant schools, concluded, "In the years that the Churches have been involved in the administration of the schools, there has been a steady deterioration in essential services. Year after year, complaints, demands and requests for improvements have, in the main, fallen upon deaf ears."[14]

The badly built and poorly maintained schools constituted serious fire hazards. Defective firefighting equipment exacerbated the risk, and schools were fitted with inadequate and dangerous fire escapes. Lack of access to safe fire escapes led to high death tolls in fires at the Beauval and Cross Lake schools.[15]

The Truth and Reconciliation Commission of Canada has determined that at least 53 schools were destroyed by fire. There were at least 170 additional recorded fires. At least 40 students died in residential school fires.[16] The harsh discipline and jail-like nature of life in the schools meant that many students sought to run away. To prevent this, many schools deliberately ignored government instructions in relation to fire drills and fire escapes. These were not problems only of the late nineteenth or early twentieth centuries. Well into the twentieth century, recommendations for improvements went unheeded, and dangerous and forbidden practices were widespread and entrenched. In the interests of cost containment, the Canadian government placed the lives of students and staff at risk for 130 years.

The schools often lacked adequate facilities for the treatment of sick children. In 1893, Indian Affairs inspector T. P. Wadsworth reported that at the Qu'Appelle school, the "want of an infirmary is still very much felt."[17] Those infirmaries that existed were often primitive. On an 1891 visit to the Battleford school, Indian Commissioner Hayter Reed concluded that the hospital ward was in such poor shape that they had been obliged to move the children in it to the staff sitting room. According to Reed, "The noise, as well as the bad smells, come from the lavatory underneath."[18]

## Nutrition

The students often received food that was not only completely foreign to them but also lacking in the basic nutrition they needed to stay healthy. Sometimes, it was the food itself that made them sick. Paul Stanley and his brother attended residential school in Cranbrook, British Columbia. He recalled,

> My brother, who had left by the time I just got started, he was 13 years old, he found, apparently found a mouse in his soup. So, he wasn't going to eat it. And of course, who's going to eat that? And the Brother says, "You eat what's in front of you," and that kind of stuff. And they wouldn't, no, he wouldn't budge, and they went and got the principal, Father Kelly, you know, came down, and, "Come on, you eat," you know. They were gonna make him eat, just take the mouse out, and let him eat the rest kind of, and he wouldn't take it.[19]

According to Eleanor Brass, the dinners at the File Hills, Saskatchewan, school consisted "of watery soup with no flavour, and never any meat." One winter, it seemed to her that they ate fish every day.[20] In fair weather, the boys would trap gophers and squirrels, and roast them over open fires to supplement their meagre diets.[21] Mary John, who attended the Fraser Lake, British Columbia, school, recalled that the meals were dull and monotonous: a regular diet of porridge interspersed with boiled barley and beans, and bread covered with lard. Weeks might go by without any fish or meat; sugar and jam were reserved for special occasions.[22]

In 1942, the federal government issued Canada's Official Food Rules, an early version of the Canada Food Guide.[23] Inspectors quickly discovered that residential school diets did not measure up to the Food Rules.[24]

A survey of six schools from across the country conducted after the Second World War revealed significant nutritional problems in the schools, including disturbingly high incidents of low hemoglobin, rickets, vitamin deficiencies, decaying teeth, inflamed gums, low body weight, and low blood pressure.[25] In a later survey of dietary practices at thirty-eight schools, inspections found that "no school was doing a good feeding job."[26] It was not until the late 1950s that the federal government adopted a residential school food allowance calculated to provide a diet deemed "fully adequate nutritionally."[27] Even with the increase in funding, schools still had difficulty providing students with adequate meals.

The dietary regime at the residential schools was also part of the assimilation strategy. David Charleson attended the Christie residential school in British Columbia in the 1960s. He was "introduced to a diet that didn't agree to me." He contrasted the foods he ate at residential school to the "fish, seals, and all the seafood that was available right on the edge of our, I call it our, my fridge. Nothing ever went bad in my fridge. It was always fresh." However, he and the other students were not allowed to collect their own food. When they did, they were accused of stealing. For him, food at the residential school was associated with abuse. He recalled one meal in which the nuns force-fed him cabbage, a vegetable that was completely alien to him:

> They forced me to eat it, and I'd puke it up, and put it back in my mouth, and they'd hold my mouth shut, and one hold, holding my nose. And I know they used to pinch my ears really hard to make me … open up my mouth, and they'd put it back in there, and push it shut, and one holding my chin and making me chew it, and the other one holding my nose, so I would swallow. I couldn't breathe. That's the … way I ate it.[28]

David Charleson does not eat cabbage to this day.

## Physical and sexual abuse

The full extent of the abuse that occurred in the schools is only now coming to light. As of January 31, 2015, the Independent Assessment Process (IAP), established under the Indian Residential Schools Settlement Agreement (IRSSA) had received 37,951 claims for injuries resulting from physical and sexual abuse at residential schools. The IAP is a mechanism to compensate former students for sexual and physical abuse experienced at the schools and the harms that arose from the assaults. By the end of 2014, the IAP had resolved 30,939 of those claims, awarding $2.7 billion in compensation.[29] The number of claims for compensation for abuse is equivalent to approximately 48% of the number of former students who were eligible to make such claims. This number does not include those former students who died prior to May 2005.

In a survey conducted by the First Nations Centre, Survivors reported experiencing one or more of the following types of abuse in the schools: sexual abuse (32.6%), physical abuse (69.2%), and verbal or emotional abuse (79.3%). The majority (71.5%) reported that they had witnessed the abuse of others.[30]

Physical abuse and sexual abuse often were intertwined. Jean Pierre Bellemare, who attended the Amos, Québec, school, spoke for many students when he told the Commission that he had been subjected to "physical violence, verbal violence, touchings, everything that comes with it."[31] Andrew Yellowback was "sexually, physically, emotionally, and mentally abused" at the Cross Lake, Manitoba, school for eight years.[32] There was no single pattern of abuse: students of both sexes reported assaults from staff members of both the opposite sex and the same sex as themselves.[33]

First-year students, traumatized by separation from their parents and the harsh and alien regime of the school, were particularly vulnerable to abusive staff members who sought to win their trust through what initially appeared to be simple kindness. In some cases, this might involve little more than extra treats from the school canteen. This favouritism, however, was often the prelude to a sexual assault that left the student scared and confused.[34]

Many students spoke of having been raped at school.[35] These were moments of terror. Josephine Sutherland was cornered by one of the lay brothers in the Fort Albany school garage: "I couldn't call for help, I couldn't. And he did awful things to me."[36] Other students recalled being assaulted in the church confessional.[37]

The effects of sexual abuse can be long lasting, with ongoing effects of fear, anger, low self-esteem, depression, sexual difficulties, substance abuse, dissociative symptoms, and PTSD.[38] Anita Lenoir told the Commission that when she was twenty-five years old she started getting "really bad anxiety attacks … but I didn't know what they were. When I was getting them, I just thought I was going crazy. I couldn't eat for days. I got hospitalized because of dehydration." After some reading and counselling she related these attacks to sexual abuse while in residential school. Although she has overcome her anxiety attacks, the sexual abuse still affects her: "I can't be sexual. I can't be romantic. You know I just, because it just destroyed so much of me."[39]

Paul Kaludjau, who was sexually abused during his first year at residential school, stated, "it doesn't matter, their names don't matter anymore. But you live with that all of your life. You take it with you, even when you climb a few mountains sometimes, you feel good, you come crashing down again." He recalled that when he left the school, "I was like a raging bull, I was so angry, didn't know where to turn my anger except inward. I became an alcoholic. Didn't know how to raise my family." Although it took him until seventy years of age to reach this stage, he ended his comments by stating, "I'm trying really hard because I think it is important, trying to reach a stage in my life where I don't want to pass my anger on anymore."[40]

## Inadequate and punitive care

Doris Young attended the Elkhorn residential school in Manitoba. She explained,

I faced illnesses alone, like chicken pox, measles, mumps, you know. I remember sitting on a rad one evening when I could hardly swallow, and my ears were sore, and my head was sore, and I sat on this rad, and I cried on, it seemed like I cried all night. Anyway, I was by myself. I might have been in what they call an infirmary. I don't really know. But that memory remains with me. When I'm sick … I feel like I should have nobody around me, so it's hard for me to ask for help when I'm not feeling well.[41]

Shirley Waskewitch recalled a terrible experience that followed when she faked a toothache in order to escape an abusive teacher in a classroom. One of the nuns in the infirmary, who "never did anything kind," took matters into her own hands when a dentist was unavailable and pulled out a perfectly healthy tooth with a set of pliers as punishment:

She sat me down on a little stool in the infirmary, and she took out some kind of a pliers-type instrument. It looked like pliers, and said, "Where is it?" I said, "Over here, up here, my last tooth on the upper right." And so she put the pliers in there, and she proceeded to pull and twist at my neck sideways, and she twisted this way, and my jaw was cracking, and she twisted, put her hand on my head here, and pulled more, and she's just going back and forth to try and wedge it out. And I had all these noises in my ear, and my jaw was cracking ... It was for a while, took a while to get that tooth out, that she just pulled it out, and, and she's ja-ja-ja, "You go to your classroom," she said to me, and she just sent me back in the classroom. I don't remember if she put gauze, or just kind of put gauze in there, or just threw it in my mouth and just send me back to the class-room. I had to suffer like that with all the pain. I knew she did it as punishment because I lied. She wanted to show me ... that I could be scared for the rest of my life, and she did succeed in that.[42]

Doctors providing care in the residential schools were paid at a significantly lower rate than they were when caring for non-Aboriginal patients.[43] This low pay under-mined access to qualified care, at times leaving the care of sick children to untrained or incompetent individuals. Rose Marie Prosper recalled how, when she accidentally cut her head at Shubenacadie residential school in Nova Scotia, "all they did was put a cold pack on my forehead. No doctor's visit or nothing ... And today, the cut is still visible; the scar is still visible."[44]

As an excerpt from a 1934 letter to the Department of Indian Affairs Medical Branch makes clear, in some cases access to medical care depended upon the religious denomination of the school. A "field matron" was stationed at the Protestant mission at Ahousaht, British Columbia, and was expected to provide basic health care to the nearby Catholic residential school. As the letter's author Victor Rassier explained,

The fact of the matter is she has always confined her ministrations to the one school and the one reserve. It should be added furthermore that the present matron has made herself quite undesirable for work amongst the Catholic tribes because of her proselytizing propensities; an objection that very likely should always continue in the event a single matron were appointed to serve the two residential schools and the reservations.[45]

## Gender roles

Aboriginal girls were trained to perform domestic work. These enforced gender roles undermined the role of women in many Aboriginal communities and broke extended family relationships that had been central to the organization of many Aboriginal communities.

Residential schools also challenged the boys' sense of their own masculinity. Many suffered physical and sexual abuse and other forms of humiliation. The Aboriginal Healing Foundation has noted that men were less willing to participate in its healing initiatives than women, and observed that "it is often difficult for men to admit to having been sexually abused because being a victim is contrary to the widely held stereotype of manliness."[46] Charles Cardinal told the Commission how he and his brother became exceptionally close in residential school when they realized that "nobody else is gonna help us, so we'll have to stick together." He recalled how in 1992 his brother killed himself after saying "he wanted to escape." Cardinal stated that he had been told, "'you're not a man, man don't cry.' I'm crying for him right now. But I'll see him, I'll see him. And I'll be the one who's crying now. I sure do miss him."[47]

## Two-spirited people

Aboriginal people traditionally celebrated people who were gay or transgender as gifted, as being the recipients of "two-spirits." The residential schools had particular impacts upon two-spirited people, who faced numerous attacks on their identities.[48]

One two-spirited Survivor explained that few of the two-spirited students that were at the Hobbema, Alberta, school have lived to tell their stories. Some "went to the streets," and "most of them died very early," at least two to suicide. He stated, "I've heard through the years that the residential school made people homosexual ... Nothing could be further from the truth. Residential school made institutional homosexuals; true. But it did not create who we are as two-spirited people. 'Cause that— who we are—was there way before we went in." He also commented on what he saw as the particular vulnerability of two-spirited people in residential schools: "You might as well put a woman into a man's prison. You're left as a target ... For me to survive to, to be sixty-two, it's a miracle for me.... But for the first ten years after leaving that school, it was, there was a lot of things that went on, and I never went home."[49]

18) We call upon the federal, provincial, territorial, and Aboriginal governments to acknowledge that the current state of Aboriginal health in Canada is a direct result of previous Canadian government policies, including residential schools, and to recognize and implement the health-care rights of Aboriginal people as identified in international law, constitutional law, and under the Treaties.

## The health of Aboriginal people today

That the residential school system was an assault on the health of Aboriginal people is not a matter for debate. The catalogues of injury, infection, and death are a matter of public record. The Survivors present powerful evidence of the injuries to health they suffered, and the ongoing effects those injuries and illnesses had on subsequent generations. There is no question that Aboriginal Canadians live today with significant generational effects passed on by their forbearers.

A 2015 discussion paper from the Wellesley Institute titled "First Peoples, Second Class Treatment: The Role of Racism in the Health and Well-Being of Indigenous Peoples in Canada" details the research that links health and the effects of historical and systematic racism. As the publication argues, "The devastating health disparities experienced by Indigenous peoples in Canada underscore the need for comprehensive anti-racism efforts to address systemic and structural racism, as well as the development of services, programming and interventions that recognize the impacts of racism on Indigenous peoples' health and well-being and assist them in dealing with it."[50]

Ken Ward told the Commission that his and his brother's early days at the Blue Quills residential school in Alberta were "like a honeymoon for us, because we look white. Oh, we were the darlings of the res school, and, you know the nuns and the priest, you know, they welcomed us, and they thought we were white, there'll be no problem, you know." The "honeymoon" ended when he was sexually abused in the school. He recalled,

> I was hardcore. I was a hardcore kid at using drugs at thirteen, suicidal big time … Years later I found out that, you know, both parents went through the res school. My mom went through St. Albert, up by Poundmaker's Lodge there … I can't remember where my father went. But it was acknowledged that they went through it … A lot of the anger was more to me, simply because maybe I'm the one who's at fault, or maybe I, I'm bringing it on, like that blame, you know, maybe you deserve it. So, I carried a lot of guilt, a lot of shame, a lot of blame as a child.[51]

After leaving Blue Quills, Ward was placed in a series of foster and group homes. He explained, "I drank bleach, I drank Comet, I wanted, in the receiving home for the weekend, I wanted to burn out, you know, what was inside. I survived, like, I was rushed to the hospital. They pumped me out." He felt like he couldn't "compete with the world, and I just want to surrender, and go, let it go." He continued,

> So, I became a street, street person, homeless guy for, you know, a few years, in Vancouver here, Calgary, Edmonton, Saskatoon, you know, just hung around the street families, and I felt okay within. Simply, I can score my drugs easier and stuff like that…. Get me high, or get me drunk, and I'll sleep with ya, you know.

It was my way of couch surfing, but it's a place to get high and just go ahead ...
I started pumping needles in my arms ... at around the age of 22, and then my
drugs of choice were cocaine, mescaline mostly.... But the, the use of needles
was quite, was quite heavy then, and I did share it with my older sister. We used
to share it, right.... I have a sister, who went through school, and now she's HIV
positive, as well as I am, that's how I got infected. That was, for me, at the age of
32. So us older ones went through the mill, the alcohol, the abuse that's happened within themselves, but I didn't really understand where theirs were coming from, eh, until those whole about the res school, it started coming out. I'm
54 now, I knew back then that we had to talk about HIV, because being a former
user, I knew that this sickness was gonna hit our people big time, and plus we're
heavily addicted in many ways.

Ken Ward has participated in education and sharing circles about HIV prevention:
"I work in the prisons as well ... We have a lot of our own people in there, too, whether
it's safe to do this in the prison or not, but ... that's a big chunk of our lost brothers and
sister out there."[52]

## Mortality rates

One of the most significant measures of the health of a society is its infant mortality rate.[53] There are major deficiencies in the statistical information about Aboriginal
infant mortality rates, and, in particular, there is virtually no information for Métis
or non-status Aboriginal peoples.[54] However, the data that is available confirms
that First Nations and Inuit infant mortality rates range from 1.7 to over 4 times the
non-Aboriginal rate. These elevated rates are most pronounced for "post-neonatal"
children (aged 28 days to 1 year), from causes such as congenital conditions, sudden infant death syndrome, and infections. Aboriginal peoples disproportionately
experience all of these infant health issues.[55]

Increased mortality rates continue into adulthood. The mortality rate amongst
Inuit children and teenagers is extraordinarily high. From 2004 to 2008, the "age-
specific mortality rate" at ages 1 to 19 in Inuit Nunangat (the four regions comprising
the traditional Inuit homeland) was 188.0 deaths per 100,000 person-years, compared
to only 35.3 deaths per 100,000 in the rest of Canada.[56] While there have been improvements over the last several decades, the life expectancy for First Nations, Métis, and
Inuit remains well below that of the total Canadian population.[57]

Even accounting for infant mortality, Aboriginal people in Canada do not live as
long as non-Aboriginal people. A 2011 Statistics Canada study found that Canadian
women tracked from the 1991 to 2006 census could expect, at 25 years of age, to
live 57.9 more years and Canadian men could expect to live another 52.6 years. By

comparison, female registered Indians could expect to live 51.1 more years; female non-status Indians 53.3 years; and Métis women 52.5 years. For registered Indian men, the figures were 46.9 years, 48.1 years for non-status Indians, and 48.5 years for Métis men.[58] To be sure, some of the reduced life expectancy overlaps with the lower life expectancy of lower income groups, but the results are disturbing nevertheless.

## Injury rates

Serious injury rates for Aboriginal peoples are far above the Canadian average.[59] For First Nations children, there is a correlation between injury rates and whether the child's mother or father attended a residential school.[60] In Inuit Nunangat, injuries are the largest contributor to mortality of children and teenagers, accounting for 64% of deaths (as compared to 36% in the rest of Canada).[61] One study of Calgarians, for example, found that Aboriginal people suffered severe trauma at a rate of 257.2 per 100,000 compared to the non-Aboriginal rate of 68.8 per 100,000, with the leading causes of trauma being traffic accidents, assaults, and suicide.[62]

Ida Ralph attended McIntosh residential school in Ontario. She remembered that she and her sister were going to be adopted but

> that's when my sister had her accident, and she was gone for the next two, two and a half years maybe. I don't know why it took that long for her to get healed up. Today she's not with us today because she got murdered in Calgary in 1983. She was into drugs, really heavy into drugs. She left behind three children to adoption. And I never heard from niece, my two nieces and nephew.[63]

## Suicide

The overall suicide rate among First Nation communities is staggering. Forty per cent of deaths amongst young Inuit are suicides, as compared to 8% in the rest of the population.[64] Aboriginal youth between the ages of 10 and 29, who are living on reserves are 5 to 6 times more likely to die by suicide than non-Aboriginal youth. The risk decreases with age, and, after age 70, the rate among First Nations peoples drops below the rate for the general population.[65]

Many of the Survivors and their family members who spoke with the Commission drew a direct link between their residential school experience and suicide. Katherine Copenace attended the Roman Catholic school in Kenora, Ontario. She remarked,

> They used to say we were proud and spiritual people, what happened to that? What happened to that thing that proud and spiritual? ... When I got older, I had thoughts of suicide, inflicting pain on myself, which I did. I used to slash my

arms, pierce my arms, my body and I destroyed myself with alcohol, which the government introduced of course.[66]

Maurice Marceau attended the Spanish, Ontario residential school where he was physically and sexually abused. His first suicide attempt came after he watched the film *The Boys of St. Vincent* on television, which is about the abuse of children at an orphanage modelled on Mt. Cashel in Newfoundland. He explained,

> That was my first time I tried to kill myself. I overdosed on, on pills and stuff like that, and I was rushed to the hospital, and they pumped my stomach out. Apparently it took five orderlies to subdue me, so they could tie me to a table and pump my stomach out, because I wanted to die, I didn't know why, but I wanted to die, and it took five guys bigger than me to subdue me.... I ingested 40 Tylenols for supper, yeah, and then I woke up the next morning at 7 o'clock, I was puking yellow bile. It looked like egg yolk. And, and I was passing blood out of my back, back end, like my liver, or my organs were, I was bleeding, you know ... I was in a lot of pain, and from that pain, that's, that's, well God was talking to me, you know, you can't do this anymore. So after that, I went to the hospital, and I saw a psychiatrist, and I, I see a psychologist every week to, to, to deal with my emotional being, you know, and, and I'm learning, and thank God I'm learning. And I hope to progress to a point where I, I've been thinking of marriage, and I'm 62 years old, and I'm thinking of marriage again, you know.[67]

Tanya Tungilik is the daughter of Marius Tungilik, who was one of the first Survivors from Chesterfield Inlet to speak publicly about sexual and physical abuse he suffered at the school. She told the Commission about a difficult life at home:

> A lot of my cousins had committed suicide, and I find that it's almost more acceptable nowadays as a way out, to commit suicide. It's almost, yeah, it's too accepted. I had attempted three different times, because I felt hopeless, and that there was no way out. But I would think about my son, and my mom, and my dad, and how it would affect them, and I couldn't, I couldn't do it. But I remember the first time I ever thought about suicide was when I was in grade six. I was so young.... And I know a lot of the social problems today with Inuit, like alcoholism, and physical abuse, sexual abuse, discipline for children. It, it comes from the experiences at the residential school.[68]

Alcohol and drug use are frequently connected to Aboriginal suicides. One study of thirty suicides of adult Aboriginal people in Québec found that all but two individuals had a history of alcohol abuse, and twenty-three also used drugs. Seven of the suicides were incarcerated at the time of their death.[69]

However, general patterns can hide both enormous variations across communities as well as persistent problems. For example, the number of suicides increased dramatically in Nishnawbe Aski Nation communities in Northern Ontario between 1986 and 1995. At the same time, other First Nations have shown steady or even falling rates. In BC, the overall suicide rate has declined among First Nations peoples, but this decline is due to lower rates of suicide among young women; in fact, suicide rates among young First Nations men have remained high.[70] In general, though, amongst Aboriginal peoples, suicide attempts are more frequent among women than men, while the rate of "successful" attempts is higher among men than women. This gender difference, however, is not as pronounced as that seen in the general population.[71]

## Addiction

Due in large part to the residential schools, Aboriginal peoples in Canada are more likely to have experienced the types of risk factors associated with addictions. Florence Horassi attended school in Fort Providence, Northwest Territories. She told the Commission about her struggles with alcoholism:

> I was, I was caught in between two worlds, like, I'm, I'm not a white person, I'm Indian, and yet I come back home, no, you're a white person. You live like them, you act like them, you talk like them, go live with them … I learned fear, fear of the unknown … I went to treatment centre a couple of times, one for a follow-up. I must have been through about five, six, seven psychiatrists, psychologists, mental health worker, 'cause everything was a lie to me. When they say alcoholism kills, it's a disease, it's sickness, it's gonna kill you … That's when they were gonna take my kids away, 'cause I was drinking. I drank over 20 years.… My kids were going to be taken away. The police came in, the nurse came in, the Superintendent Social Services came in, they said there was help. I thought they were lying to me. I told them, "Keep them, at least they'll be better off than being with me, 'cause I drink all the time." They said there was help. "We're gonna help you." So, I went to treatment centre. So, later on, I went to training for community addictions training with Nechi Institute. I'm completing my training. Got my certificate.[72]

Although many Survivors have spoken with the Commission about their struggles with addictions, they have also provided the Commission with much information to contextualize addictions as a coping response to the way they were treated at residential school. A number of multigenerational Survivors told the Commission about turning to drugs and alcohol to cope with the scars of residential school. While this might seem to conform to negative stereotypes about Aboriginal peoples and alcohol use, it actually obscures a very complex picture. For example, the First Nations Regional Longitudinal Health Survey found that, compared to the general population, a higher percentage of Aboriginal people don't drink at all.[73]

Addictions and drug use places people at risk of multiple harms, including greater risk of violence. A recent study of young Aboriginal women who used drugs in

Vancouver and Prince George between 2003 and 2010 found that those with a parent who attended a residential school were at twice the risk of sexual assault over the study period.[74]

## Fetal Alcohol Spectrum Disorder

A tragic number of those who became dependent on alcohol have been pregnant mothers. The result has been an alarmingly high rate of fetal alcohol spectrum disorder (FASD) in Aboriginal communities, sometimes cited as another legacy of the residential schools. Permanent brain injury caused by FASD, as well as a lack of support, has created challenges for many Indigenous children, too often leading to poor performance in school, disordered lives, and conflict within families and eventually with the law. There are no known research studies that specifically examine the ways in which residential school experiences contributed to the current rates of FASD and alcohol-related birth effects (ARBE) amongst Aboriginal people. Nonetheless, researcher Caroline Tait, in a lengthy review of the literature, concludes that the residential school system contributed to high rates of alcohol abuse among those who previously attended the schools, and among significant numbers of parents and community members who had their children removed from their care because of the school system.[75] The most significant risk factors cited are the many faces of poverty, including poor housing, lack of sewage disposal and potable water, poor access to health services, and lack of adequate nutritious food.[76]

A man who attended residential school in Ontario told the Commission about his son, who was born with FASD. The man had overcome a history of abuse and alcohol use, and spoke of his belief that his son would also find a place for himself with the love and support of his family and community and his cultural traditions:

> I brought him to the Sundance, I brought him to a lot of ceremonies ... But he, he had, he hasn't been sober, and he's been living on the street, and he became a street person, and he is a street person now ... I was a victim, I'm not a victim anymore. I don't have the anger there. I don't have the thoughts about revenge.... My son's suffering now. I know it's part of that legacy. I can't explain it exactly, but I have to have faith in him, too, just like I have faith in myself. He'll succeed somehow, somehow. He's got the same spirit, same kind of spirit as you and I have, I know that. Even with the brain damage, he's gonna be all right. He's got a lot of love in, in him.[77]

Tait notes that women at risk for having a child with FASD have generally poor health and are likely to suffer from one or more alcohol-related illnesses. They are also more likely to die within a very short period of time of giving birth if they do not receive treatment for their health problems. She writes, "While a great deal of concern, which at times is expressed as outrage, has occurred in Canada over the birth of children with FAS/ARBEs, (Fetal Alcohol Spectrum/Alcohol-Related Birth Effects) there has been far less concern (and even less outrage) over young women, many of whom are Aboriginal, dying of alcohol-related illnesses or accidents. As with FAS/ARBEs, these illnesses/accidents are one-hundred per cent preventable."[78]

## HIV/AIDS

In 1992, Chief Edward John observed that the harmful legacy of residential schools was "like a disease ripping through our communities."[79] The disease metaphor was, unfortunately, prophetic. Aboriginal people are disproportionately represented among Canadians living with HIV/AIDS.[80] One study of 1,064 Aboriginal people living with HIV/AIDS, conducted between 2010 and 2012, found that 30% were residential school Survivors.[81] In another study, most of the Survivors and descendants reported that their physical and mental health had been affected by residential schools, as reflected in their problems with addictions, low self-esteem, and poor parenting skills. One respondent explained, "I can live with the disease, but the 'mental' damage from residential school is a very serious disease."[82] Other studies of HIV/AIDS have had similar results.[83] Aboriginal drug users in Vancouver have elevated HIV incidence when compared to non-Aboriginal drug users.[84]

## Mental health

Leona Bird attended the Prince Albert, Saskatchewan, school. She received a settlement for being sexually abused in residential schools but she says it did little to alleviate the long lasting effects on her and her family. She explained,

> I'm still the same. There's just barely, hardly any time that I can say that I was truly, truly happy. My wedding day was just like another day, no fun ... I can't take back what I've done in my lifetime. I was forever being charged with assault, sent to jail 18 months at a time ... Yeah, I'm suffering from depression.[85]

Physical and sexual abuse at residential schools had profound intergenerational effects. Case studies conducted by the Aboriginal Healing Foundation suggest that more than 50% of community members needed healing from the effects of residential schools.[86] Many former students told the Commission that they were denied the opportunity to learn nurturing parenting skills and they replicated the strict and uncaring discipline that they experienced at school. The lack of positive strategies for dealing with interpersonal conflict may have led to high rates of family breakdown and problems that youth carry with them into their adult lives.[87]

Anne Thomas describes herself as "third generation residential school Survivor":

> We did not belong to our families, we belonged to the government ... I faced
> a life of rejection. I faced a life of betrayal. I faced a sense of not belonging to
> my parents, to my family, to my community ... Sex, drinking, rebellion, hatred,
> anger, resentment, bitterness, hostility, chip on my shoulder were my pre-teen
> years, I had to show people they can't push me around now. 'Cause if you do, I'm
> going to flip out on you.

She has since been diagnosed with a bipolar condition, which she links directly to her years as residential school: "I started having my own little getaway in my mind."[88]

## Displacement

Angus Havioyak was sent from his home in Inuvik to Alberta for medical treatment: "I was in the hospital, 1962, I believe, 'cause I had TB, that was in Edmonton—Camsell Hospital—they used to call it. I was there for two years. At that time, I, I didn't know about my parents. I didn't know I had brothers and sisters. In our family, I had about, there's 10 of us."[89]

The hospital that Havioyak and many other Northerners were and still are sent to is more than a thousand kilometers from home, well beyond the possibility of any regular family visits, both in distance and in cost.

Mabel Brown told the Commission at Inuvik how she saw disturbing parallels between her treatment in Northern residential schools and today's lack of adequate treatment facilities close to home:

> They did away with all the treatment centres. They used to have one here called
> Delta House, and it's no longer, it's called the homeless shelter now. And they
> did away with two treatment centres in Yellowknife. Really beautiful places that
> people used to go and ... and there's just that one in Hay River, it's just always
> waiting, people waiting to get in there too; so people have to go south.

She recalled, when her grandson needed treatment,

> We didn't want to send him down south; down to another province. We want
> him to stay in our home province and not, and yeah. And they, they let me escort
> him down to Regina then I came back; he ran away. He ran to Regina. And so I,
> I told his dad and his dad just burst out crying. And we're, we're helpless; he's
> way, just like, just like what they took us away to residential schools; away from
> our own homes. Same thing.[90]

Most Inuit communities access primary health care services through nursing stations, so most Inuit patients must travel to regional centers or southern cities to consult medical specialists, have operations, and deliver babies. In general, services are delivered within a Western model of medicine.[91] In an echo of Inuit experience with southern education, many Inuit report that medical transfers to the south can be isolating and demoralizing experiences, because they are separated from their families and home communities during a time when they are most in need of support.

There are also significant service gaps, particularly in remote locations.[92] Most communities have limited availability of physical health services and virtually no specialized mental health service. Care is provided mainly by primary care clinicians (nurse practitioners) or community workers, supplemented by a rotation of occasional visiting physicians.[93]

Off-reserve Aboriginal peoples are caught in a different and difficult position. They are frequently in urban centres, far from family and home, where their access to Western medicine and doctors is limited to the emergency room at a hospital. They also face challenges in finding ways to access Aboriginal health practices. The Aboriginal Healing Foundation found that three out of ten urban Aboriginal people said it was somewhat or very difficult to access traditional healing practices.[94] Inuit, Métis, and First Nations people living off reserves were significantly less likely to have seen or talked to a family doctor, but were significantly more likely to have seen or talked to a nurse, than non-Aboriginal people. The difference was particularly marked for Inuit, where 55% of Inuit saw or talked to a doctor and 64% saw or talked to a nurse, compared to 77% and 11% of non-Aboriginal respondents, respectively.[95] The Aboriginal Healing Foundation noted that Les services parajudiciares autochtones du Québec has reported, "Our greatest challenge is the fact that clients come from afar in many cases, which means that their families also are far away. We believe very strongly in re-establishing ties with family, but geographical distances make this more difficult."[96]

## Food insecurity

In January 2013 Statistics Canada reported that "Food insecurity was more common among the three Aboriginal groups, with the highest rate among Inuit at 27%, four times the proportion of 7% for non-Aboriginal people."[97] Another recent study found that, in 2011, off-reserve Aboriginal households in Canada were about twice as likely as other Canadian households to be food insecure.[98]

A 2011 study of Aboriginal households found that those without food security "were more likely to report poor general health (36% versus 21%) and poor mental health (21% versus 10%), life dissatisfaction (28% versus 13%), a very weak sense of community belonging (20% versus 11%), high stress (43% versus 21%), and cigarette smoking (64% versus 46%)."[99] Also, First Nations people aged 45 and over had nearly twice the rate of diabetes compared with the non-Aboriginal population (19% versus 11%).[100] The Commission cites these reports simply as a reminder of the need to contextualize health indicators by explaining the circumstances behind them, and the need to avoid stereotypes that blame Aboriginal people for their own ill health.

## Link is clear

The social determinants of health are complex. It is not always possible to chart health impacts that are tied directly to the intergenerational impacts of the residential schools as opposed to other factors. However, it is indisputable that many of the recognized social determinants of health—income, education, employment, social status, working and living conditions, health practices, coping skills, and childhood development—were themselves impacted by attendance at residential school.[101] As a result, there can be no doubt that residential schools have had a lasting impact on the health of former students, their families and their communities. And whatever the cause, negative social and health conditions pose a serious obstacle to healing the wounds left by the residential schools.

The Wellesley Institute study of racism and its effect on the health of Aboriginal Canadians concludes with a sentiment that speaks to the need for change:

> We as Indigenous peoples must be the authors of our own stories. It is necessary to interrupting the racism that reduces our humanity, erases our histories, discounts our health knowledge and practices, and attributes our health disparities and social ills to individual and collective deficits instead of hundreds of years of violence, marginalization and exclusion. The stories shared here describe the ways in which racism has shaped the lives of generations of Indigenous peoples and contributed towards our contemporary health disparities. It is time for stories of change: change in how we imagine, develop, implement and evaluate health policies, services and education, change in how we talk about racism and history in this country. This is fundamental to shifting what is imagined and understood about our histories, our ways of knowing and being, our present and our future, and to ensuring the health and well-being of our peoples for this generation and generations to come.[102]

## Recent failures of government action

The Commission notes with profound regret that the Canadian government has moved backwards on issues of Aboriginal health since the settlement of the residential school litigation in 2006 and the prime minister's apology in 2008. In cutting off funding to a number of Aboriginal health organizations, the Government of Canada has acted as if all the deep wounds of residential schools have been healed, when it is clear to the Commission that they have not. This is a short-sighted approach that will increase the suffering of Aboriginal people and, in the end, will likely require more costly crisis interventions. The government's cutting of funding to Aboriginal health organizations is seen by many as mean-spirited, and a barrier to reconciliation. It suggests that there has been little change in the disrespect for both Aboriginal health and traditional medicine that was characteristic of the schools over a hundred years ago. The decision to stop funding Aboriginal healing programs is made all the more incomprehensible when compared to the lapsed funding of almost one billion dollars reported by AANDC in recent fiscal years.[103]

## The Aboriginal Healing Foundation and the Indian Residential Schools Resolution Health Support Program

The Aboriginal Healing Foundation (AHF) was an important source of knowledge and funding for the revitalization of Aboriginal healing practices designed specifically to address the legacy of the residential schools. The AHF's mandate was explicitly intergenerational, and the Foundation was "committed to addressing the legacy of abuse in all its forms and manifestations, direct, indirect and intergenerational, by building on the strengths and resilience of Aboriginal peoples."[104]

A 2009 study, commissioned by Indian and Northern Affairs Canada, found that "AHF healing programs at the community level are effective in facilitating healing at the individual level, and are beginning to show healing at the family and community level."[105] In light of the AHF's finding that it takes approximately ten years of continuous healing efforts before a community is securely established in healing from intergenerational residential school trauma and that "the healing has just begun," the evaluation results "strongly support the case for continued need for these programs, due to the complex needs and long-term nature of the healing process."[106]

The Government of Canada funded the Foundation for fourteen years, between 1998 and 2012. The last five years of funding were provided as part of the Indian Residential Schools Settlement process. However, with the conclusion of its formal settlement obligation, Canada has since refused to contribute any additional funds. As of March 31, 2010, 135 community-based healing initiatives were no longer receiving AHF support.[107] A report of the Standing Committee on Aboriginal Affairs and Northern Development recommended the continuation of the AHF for at least a further three years.[108] It was ignored. The foundation exhausted its funding. In 2012, based on repeated statements from Survivors at TRC hearings that the healing work in their communities had barely begun, the Commission's *Interim Report* recommended that there was an urgent need for the Government of Canada to meet immediately with the Aboriginal Healing Foundation to restore its funding for healing initiatives.[109]

The AHF itself has been allowed to lapse, despite the evidence of valuable work it was doing with Survivors and Aboriginal communities to address the adverse health legacies of the schools in a holistic and culturally appropriate manner. The end of the Foundation means that an important source of funding for further healing that is still clearly needed, and the knowledge about best practices for Aboriginal healing, have been lost.[110]

The Government of Canada takes the position that its Indian Residential Schools Resolution Health Support Program (IRSRHS) provides access to sufficient mental health, transportation services, and emotional support services for former Indian residential school students. Eligible clients include former students taking part in the Independent Assessment Process and their families, former students receiving Common Experience Payments (CEP) and their families, and those participating in Truth and Reconciliation and commemoration events.[111] The program administers a national twenty-four-hour toll free Indian Residential School Crisis Line and provides funding to local Aboriginal organizations for the provision of mental health services. This includes the services of Elders and/or traditional healers.[112]

A story told by a participant at the Shingwauk school reunion in Sault Ste. Marie demonstrated how frightening it can be for those reaching out for help for the first time:

> So I called that number, the crisis line. And I talked to the worker on the other crisis line and I told her about what my situation was. But she kept asking me, "Where are you? What, where, what, what location are you? What street are you calling me from?" ... So I hang up on her. I thought maybe she's going to call the cops on me or somebody; or she's going to call 911 the way she sounded like she was going to report me.

Ultimately, his experience was a positive one. When he called back a second time, he was comforted when the person on the other end of the line told him, "You're not the only one."[113]

As important as this program may be, it is completely inadequate to the task. Unlike the Aboriginal Healing Foundation, IRSRHS services are limited to former students and their immediate family members. It is only available to individuals taking part in one of the CEP or IAP compensation processes and/or Truth and Reconciliation Commission events. Unlike the AHF, the IRSRHS is not Aboriginal-operated and does not operate independently of federal government.[114]

The Standing Committee on Aboriginal Affairs found that, in contrast to the IRSRHS program, the AHF projects allowed for more holistic, culturally relevant, community-level health and wellness interventions (e.g., healing circles, traditional healing therapy, land-based and sweat lodge retreats). In testimony to the Committee, Kathy Langlois of Health Canada advised that, under the IRSRHS program, the department would not "be able to go as far as the community-based types of approaches that the Healing Foundation had." Similarly, Aideen Nabigon, a director general in the Department of

Aboriginal Affairs and Northern Development, stated that "The Aboriginal Healing Foundation provided things ... that we aren't going to be in a position to fund." Jacob Gearheard, executive director of the Ilisaqsivik Society in Clyde River, Nunavut, stated that community members on Baffin Island who had been offered a range of culturally sensitive healing programs must now call a 1-800 number in Whitehorse, Yukon, three time zones away. They are not given the name of a person to call, and there is no guarantee that they can be served in the Inuktitut language. He added, "For Clyde River members a help line in Whitehorse is almost the same as nothing."[115]

The IRSRHS cannot carry on the work of the AHF without a complete transformation of its mandate and structure. Indeed, the Standing Committee on Aboriginal Affairs review in 2010 stated categorically that the IRSRHS, while "technically proficient," is no substitute for the "real, innovative, transformational work that communities have been developing through their community projects."[116]

Jackie Fletcher's father, siblings, aunts, and uncles all attended residential school and she also did for a short time. She noted,

> Since the Aboriginal Healing Foundation got their dollars, and there was a lot of workshops being offered in different places, I, I would attend every workshop. I was just soaking them up, like, you know I just wanted to be there. I still, I'm still like that. When I hear anything like this happening, I want to be there.... Because every time I go somewhere, I learn something new every time ... And it's, it's, I've been working on this, on my own personal healing now.[117]

It must be said that throughout the work of the Truth and Reconciliation Commission, Health Canada has offered important integrated support to Survivors of residential schools and their families, often by drawing on cultural and spiritual resources and wisdom from within Aboriginal communities. High quality, integrated mental health and cultural support teams were available to support those who took part in our activities. The Commission acknowledges and honours those who have provided this health support. One of the Commission's interim recommendations was designed to ensure that such workers, particularly those specially trained and with proven performance as resolution health support workers and cultural support workers, received recognition and accreditation for their valuable work and demanding experiences.[118]

At the same time however, Health Canada's individualistic approach and its focus on providing support for Survivors who are in acute distress, rather than a strategy and commitment for longer-term continuous support for the wider community, fails to address the legacy of the residential schools. It discounts the potential for holistic community interventions that can benefit many Aboriginal people on a day-to-day basis regardless of their direct connection with residential schools.

Helen Doyle is the daughter of a residential school Survivor and works with many Survivors. She has warned that dealing with the trauma of the experience "takes a lifetime to do it. It's not something that can be done in eight weeks, 10 sessions, 12 sessions, and you know, which is how … Health Canada puts it … That's annoying too for survivors."[119]

## National Aboriginal Health Organization

In addition to allowing the important work of the Aboriginal Healing Foundation to lapse, the Government of Canada has cut the $5 million in annual funding that the National Aboriginal Health Organization (NAHO) received. As of June 30, 2012, this important organization, like the Aboriginal Healing Foundation, closed its doors.

This cut in the 2012 budget for the purpose of saving $5 million each year strikes the Commission as especially mean-spirited and unnecessary, particularly given the ongoing work at that time of the Commission and other processes established by the Settlement Agreement.

For over twelve years, NAHO has employed thirty specialists in Aboriginal health and issued over two hundred publications about Aboriginal health, including thirteen issues of the *Journal of Aboriginal Health*.[120] The available evidence suggests that there is not enough research on Aboriginal health.[121] The Commission is deeply disappointed with these cuts. It believes that they constitute serious barriers to reconciliation.

## Cuts to other Aboriginal organizations

In late March 2012, Canada abruptly terminated funding for several other key Aboriginal organizations: the First Nations Statistical Institute, Pauktuutit Inuit Women of Canada, and the National Centre for First Nations Governance. The cutting of the annual $5-million budget of the First Nations Statistical Institute is especially short-sighted given the importance of accurate data to measure progress in redressing the legacy of residential schools. The National Centre for First Nations Governance provided important capacity building for Aboriginal self-determination. The Pauktuutit Inuit Women of Canada has been working since 1984 in a broad range of health and violence matters relating to Inuit women, including human trafficking, fetal alcohol effects, and violence against women.[122] It has wide regional representation in the North and is a respected voice for Inuit women.

## The Common Experience Payment

Common Experience Payments (CEP) were the modest compensation payments given to former residential school students according to a prescribed formula based on years of attendance at schools approved by the Settlement Agreement. The whole process of claiming and receiving redress for the residential school experience has added its own new element of harm.

The daughter of one residential school Survivor described the harsh impact that the settlement process had upon her aunt:

> We went to visit her because we were out visiting my aunts and uncles here in Regina. It came up in discussion when they were first starting to negotiate the [residential school] settlement and they were wanting to put money in the healing fund. We were having this conversation and I don't know how it started but she said, "I don't want healing, I don't want any of that. They can take their money. They can't heal me. They can never give me back what they did to me." She was angry. She said, "I can't hug my kids, I couldn't be the mother to my children and I blame all of that on residential school. No amount of healing is going to fix me." It was really emotional and that was just the highlights of it. It was more of a half hour cathartic experience with my aunt and my cousin sitting there, listening to her and it was really hard knowing that there's a lot of survivors out there and they're not going to heal.[123]

The Aboriginal Healing Foundation conducted an evaluation of the effects of claiming or receiving the CEP on 281 First Nations, Inuit, and Métis residential school Survivors across Canada. Forty per cent of the respondents found the CEP process difficult or challenging; a third found that the process triggered negative emotions and flashbacks; and 20% said that the long wait caused anxiety. Although a quarter of the respondents felt that the process contributed to healing, half stated that receiving compensation made no difference to their well-being, and 20% experienced the process as a step backwards often because it left them bitter and angry. One participant commented that the application "brought up the memories ... I had a panic attack. I ended up in the hospital ... Just to realize that, yes it was true, it did really happen."[124]

## Unsafe living conditions

While issues such as poor quality housing and water are not direct legacies of residential schools, substandard community infrastructure increases the health burden, and consequently increases the challenges of addressing the legacy of the residential schools. Communities, families, and individuals that are in crisis cannot heal. For this reason, we make specific note of the shameful state of community infrastructure in many Aboriginal communities.

## Water

As part of Canada's 2014 Economic Action Plan, the federal government announced an investment of $323.4 million to be spent over two years to build and renovate water and wastewater infrastructure on reserves.[125] This money is on top of the approximately $2.5 billion it has spent since 2006 on First Nations water and wastewater infrastructure through Aboriginal Affairs and Northern Development Canada's Capital Facilities and Maintenance Program, the First Nations Water and Wastewater Action Plan, and Canada's Economic Action Plan.[126]

Sadly, even these additional funds come nowhere near what is required to ensure all First Nations have access to safe drinking water, as the government's own consultant stated in 2011. This serves as a measure not only of the urgent work that needs to be done today, but also of the extent to which services and facilities in the past have been substandard, or allowed to deteriorate without adequate maintenance. An April 2011 report on a survey of water systems in First Nations communities found that 39% are categorized as "high overall risk" with a further 34% categorized as "medium overall risk." In terms of wastewater systems, 14% are categorized as "high overall risk" with a further 51% categorized as "medium overall risk." This did not include the twelve First Nation communities (2%) with no active infrastructure. The report commissioned by the Government of Canada estimates that the cost of upgrades to meet standards is over a billion dollars (not including new service connection costs).[127] Thus, the money currently allocated is known to be utterly inadequate. As of August 31, 2013, there were 178 water systems in 122 First Nation communities under a drinking water advisory.[128]

In 2013, the Government of Canada passed the *Safe Drinking Water for First Nations Act*, a highly controversial piece of legislation that allows the government to enact regulations governing drinking water and waste treatment in First Nations communities.[129] Before it passed, the Senate Committee on Aboriginal Peoples raised serious concerns about its implications for Aboriginal and Treaty rights.[130] The Senate committee urged the Government of Canada to ensure that the development of water safety regulations be based on meaningful consultation with First Nations.[131]

A 2013 evaluation found that the First Nations Water and Wastewater Action Plan "may not address the more pervasive issues and a shift to longer-term planning is needed."[132] A serious investment in training and operational support is what is required to provide a safe drinking water supply, more so than complex equipment. It recommended, among other things, that First Nations and Health Canada develop a long-term strategy for investments in water and wastewater infrastructure and maintenance in order to address the pervasive and longstanding issues of water and infrastructure quality and maintenance and that regulations ensuing from the *Safe Drinking Water for First Nations Act* are developed with the engagement of First Nations.

## Housing

A 2007 study by the House of Commons Standing Committee on Aboriginal Affairs and Northern Development found that estimates of on-reserve housing shortages ranged between 20,000 and 87,000, with the estimated shortfall growing annually by over 2,000 units. Inuit communities, particularly in Nunavut and Nunavik, are also affected by growing shortages. Mould contamination in existing units remains a significant problem. One in five Aboriginal dwellings across Canada is in need of major repairs, compared to one in ten for Canada as a whole.[133]

The government claims that, under Canada's Economic Action Plan, "nearly 500 First Nations communities across Canada benefitted from the Government's $400 million investment to support the construction of new on-reserve housing, renovate existing social housing units and for other complementary housing activities."[134] However, part of the Government of Canada's strategy has been to fund "market-based" housing on reserves, through its First Nations Market Housing Fund, which relies on the free market to build affordable housing.[135] This could be seen as a threat to principles of communal ownership of land.

Despite these efforts, in 2014 the United Nations special rapporteur on the rights of Indigenous peoples described the housing situations in Inuit and First Nations communities as having reached a "crisis level."[136] These weaknesses in community infrastructure remain a significant obstacle to community health and wellness. The health legacy of residential schools cannot be overcome while such conditions remain too often the norm.

## Disparities in health outcomes

The Commission is concerned that too many Canadians still fail to fully understand the harmful legacy of residential schools and similar assimilation policies on Aboriginal health and wellness. In the absence of such understanding, there is a tendency to blame Aboriginal people for their poor health and lack of services. Even Statistics Canada's most recent reports on Aboriginal health focus on smoking, obesity, and drinking with little attempt to contextualize these factors.[137] There is a need for greater understanding of how the direct and intergenerational effects of residential schools have often produced trauma and self-hatred that lead too many Aboriginal people to engage in destructive behavior from suicide to smoking. Addictions in particular have contributed to the shockingly high rates of both incarceration and crime victimization.

There is a clear need to embrace a holistic approach to Aboriginal health—an approach that recognizes that health is inextricably connected with families, community, culture, language, justice, and poverty.

The persistent health gaps between Aboriginal and non-Aboriginal people in Canada can be measured by the continued and disproportionate impact of poverty and poverty-related diseases, including tuberculosis, a disease that was believed to be eradicated and that has killed so many Aboriginal people in the past, including many children.[138] In 2010, the *Globe and Mail* reported that the tuberculosis rate among status Indians was thirty-one times the rate of those of non-Aboriginal Canadians. It drew parallels with Dr. Bryce's unheeded warnings a hundred years earlier about tuberculosis epidemics in the residential schools.[139] These health outcomes would not be tolerated if they afflicted non-Aboriginal Canadians, but, more importantly, these health disparities between Aboriginal and non-Aboriginal Canadians need to be researched and explained and contextualized. Otherwise, the work of reconciliation becomes significantly more difficult.

## Statistical shortfalls

Recent restrictions on the national census and the methods of reporting used by Health Canada and Statistics Canada are making it more difficult to monitor health for Aboriginal people. Even before such restrictions, researchers were unable to properly estimate basic health indicators, such as life expectancy at birth for Canada's Inuit population, because of a lack of Aboriginal identifiers on death registrations and could only make educated guesses based on findings from areas with large Inuit populations.[140]

Much of the best information about the comparative health outcomes between Aboriginal and non-Aboriginal Canadians is incomplete and becoming outdated. It is difficult to determine whether the health gap has widened or narrowed. The lack of up-to-date information means that these issues attract less public, media, and political attention.

By contrast, the Australian government has set itself a series of health-related targets as a part of the apology issued by Australian Prime Minister Kevin Rudd in 2008. There is agreement on baseline health indicators so progress can easily be measured on health, education, and employment outcomes.[141] Australian targets include

- close the gap in life expectancy by 2031;

- halve the gap in mortality rates for Indigenous children under five by 2018. There has been a 35% decrease in the gap in child death rates since 1998, although much more will need to be done if the goal is to be met by 2018;

- halve the gap in reading, writing, and numeracy achievements for children by 2018;

- halve the gap for Indigenous students in Year 12 (or equivalent) attainment rates by 2020; and

- halve the gap in employment outcomes between Indigenous and other Australians by 2018.[142]

Setting such targets ensures that government must monitor indicators of health and is accountable for failing to meet targets. Of course, the Australian example also demonstrates that setting targets is not sufficient without committing the necessary resources to achieve them. The 2015 annual report shows that Australia has made little progress on many of its goals.

No comparable and measurable commitments were made when Prime Minister Stephen Harper delivered his 2008 apology for residential schools. In fact, the Canadian government has cut health grants to the Native Women's Association of Canada, the Métis National Council, the Congress of Aboriginal Peoples, the National Indian and Inuit Community Health Representatives Organization, and Inuit Tapiriit Kanatami.[143] These organizations have been committed to models of research in which Aboriginal communities have ownership, control, access, and possession. Their loss would significantly limit the development of accurate information about health issues and solutions for Aboriginal peoples. The cancellation of Canada's long-form census and the Aboriginal Children's Survey has further contributed to undermining access to accurate research and information.[144]

These drastic and sudden cuts have led some to conclude that the Government of Canada is "deliberately undermining capacity to generate accurate Aboriginal health data and circulating discredited health data so as to downplay the severity of the Aboriginal health crisis in Canada."[145] Dr. Janet Smylie, a professor of family medicine and research scientist, argues that the infant mortality rate on Aboriginal reserves as published by the Public Health Agency of Canada underestimates the rate by as much as 60%.[146] Organizations that could have supplied correct information have been gutted.

19) We call upon the federal government, in consultation with Aboriginal peoples, to establish measurable goals to identify and close the gaps in health outcomes between Aboriginal and non-Aboriginal communities, and to publish annual

progress reports and assess long-term trends. Such efforts would focus on indicators such as: infant mortality, maternal health, suicide, mental health, addictions, life expectancy, birth rates, infant and child health issues, chronic diseases, illness and injury incidence, and the availability of appropriate health services.

## Weaknesses in existing agreements

It may seem promising that for many years federal policy towards Aboriginal health has emphasized the language of community control. The Government of Canada permits community control over health services in three main ways: the Health Transfer Policy, the Integrated Model, and self-government agreements. However, each of these models has significant limitations.

The Health Transfer Policy, initiated in 1989, provides opportunities to individual communities and tribal councils to have increased local responsibility in the planning and delivery of community-based health services, as well as some regionally based programs.[147] However, the programs over which communities may exercise local control are those established and governed by the First Nations and Inuit Health Branch of Health Canada. In addition, most on-reserve health facilities receive funding for only a limited number of health promotion and prevention services.[148] Also, not all Aboriginal peoples are eligible. Only First Nations communities south of the sixtieth parallel and Inuit in Labrador are eligible for funding under this policy.[149]

The "integrated model," created in 1994, was designed to broaden opportunities for control to communities that were deemed "too small" to successfully manage transfers. Like the transfer policy, communities participating in the integrated model choose from a list of programs and sign a three- to five-year agreement for community administration.

Communities can also negotiate a self-government agreement. For example, the James Bay and Northern Quebec Agreement created health care structures managed by Aboriginal authorities but linked to the provincial health care system. The Nisga'a Agreement in British Columbia and the Labrador Inuit Association Agreement are tripartite agreements that include provisions for self-administration of health services. In the Yukon, the Carcross/Tagish First Nations Programs and Services Agreement Respecting the Indian and Inuit Affairs Program and the First Nations and Inuit Health Branch of the Government of Canada (2003) transfers responsibility for health and other services to the First Nation.[150] Although not a self-government agreement, the Athabasca Health Authority in Saskatchewan is another example of an Aboriginal health authority that is an extension of a provincial health care system, providing care to two First Nations and three Métis communities.[151]

The First Nations and Inuit Health Branch funds over thirty separate Aboriginal health programs, one quarter of which cannot be included in integrated, transfer or self-government agreements. An additional problem is that these programs receive "project-based funding," so community health activities survive or fail based on the availability of funds, rather than by a true reflection of community priorities.

The danger when the federal government uses the language of 'self-government' and 'community control' is that it can mask offloading of services to communities without adequate resources. Indeed, as the above descriptions suggest, Canada's vision of community control has typically entailed the transfer of administrative responsibility for existing health-related programs, thus absolving the government of responsibility for Aboriginal health. At best, Canada's policy of 'community control' has resulted in a patchwork of Aboriginal-specific legislation, policies, and provisions, with significant gaps.[152]

The latest model to emerge is the "tripartite health agreement." British Columbia is the only province to establish a framework through which agencies mandated by First Nation governments, organizations, and communities deliver health services operating under provincial jurisdiction. The Tripartite Framework Agreement on First Nation Health Governance, completed in October 2011, sets out a commitment to establish a First Nations Health Authority. Federal funding for existing federal health programs, and responsibility for First Nations health program design and delivery, will be transferred to the new Authority.[153] Ultimately, the Authority is expected to replace the Non-Insured Health Benefit Program (which covers the cost of prescription drugs, dental and vision coverage, medical equipment, and some other services) with its own program serving "Status Indians" in British Columbia, as well as potentially taking over other provincial programs.[154]

The agreement commits to a health system in which all First Nations in the province have access to quality health services comparable to those available to "other Canadians living in similar geographic locations."[155] This may seem to be a laudable goal, but it ignores the higher health needs of Aboriginal people, which are in part related to the legacy of the residential schools. There is a danger that the goal of "comparable" services may be an example of formal equality that, by failing to accommodate the higher health needs of Aboriginal people, may fail to achieve substantive equality or equal health outcomes.

The tripartite model could have the advantage of preventing jurisdictional issues from acting as a barrier to the development of Aboriginal-controlled health care. However, it is too early to tell whether the BC agreement will result in a genuine transformation of health care services under Aboriginal control.

Métis health promotion, prevention, and protection services and programs are in the very early beginning stages. Neither the federal nor the provincial governments have assumed responsibility for providing health services to Métis people, or developed a policy or strategy for addressing Métis health needs. National and provincial/territorial Métis organizations lack sustained funding for health programs, and there is little progress in the devolution of Métis health funding to Métis organizations.[156]

The only exception for Métis peoples is in the Northwest Territories, where the territory provides Métis with access to a program that is equivalent to the federal government's Non-Insured Health Benefits program.[157] However, even for Métis people in the Northwest Territories, significant gaps remain.

The federal government has been fighting for many years to stop litigation aimed at obtaining a legal ruling on federal jurisdictional obligations. In April 2014, the Federal Court of Appeal ruled in *Daniels v. Canada* that Métis are included as 'Indians' within the meaning of the *Constitution Act, 1867*, which would mean that the federal government does indeed bear responsibility for Métis peoples.[158] The Federal Court of Appeal dismissed a lower court's finding that "non-status Indians" also fall within federal jurisdiction.[159] Both sides have appealed to the Supreme Court. It is anticipated that the Supreme Court will hear the case in the fall of 2015. In the meantime, Aboriginal peoples living off reserves continue to live in a no-man's land when it comes to health services.

**20)** In order to address the jurisdictional disputes concerning Aboriginal people who do not reside on reserves, we call upon the federal government to recognize, respect, and address the distinct health needs of the Métis, Inuit, and off-reserve Aboriginal peoples.

## The way forward

Our Calls to Action for future improvements to Aboriginal health involve a two-track strategy. The first track will be to give Aboriginal communities the resources and freedom that they require to take responsibility for their own health and wellness through the development of health and wellness centres. At the same time, the Commission will also recommend that improvements be made to the existing Western-based health care system so that it can treat Aboriginal people better. This is particularly important with respect to urban Aboriginal populations.

One of the main purposes of all of the Commission's recommendations is to ensure that the harms that residential schools perpetuated on Aboriginal people are not being perpetuated again in a new form.

## Aboriginal healing practices

A belief shared among many Inuit, Métis, and First Nation people is that a sacred connection exists among people, the earth, and everything within and around it. Activities such as "on-the-land" or "bush" healing camps can allow participants to experience the healing power of the natural world. Holistic approaches to health and well-being can also include sweat lodges, cedar baths, smudging, and other spiritual ceremonies, depending upon the particular beliefs and customs of each Aboriginal community. Seasonal ceremonies, communal meals, potlatches, medicine walks, powwows, *qulliq* lighting, feasts and giveaways, Métis *réveillons*, and Inuit community celebrations are all activities that promote healing through positive relationships.[160]

There are many successful examples of Aboriginal health practices. The Sulsila Lelum Healing Centre Society in Vancouver has medicine-making workshops, a supply of remedies on hand for dispensing, a garden with natural medicinal plants, and a pond with running water. The Surrey Aboriginal Cultural Society reported that one of their best practices is on-the-land camps. The Aboriginal Health and Wellness Centre included on-the-land retreats in their men's program. Native Child and Family Services of Toronto holds a one-week healing camp in summer, and pipe ceremonies and sweats are conducted outside of the city.[161]

Aboriginal health practices and beliefs are diverse. The term *healing* has different meanings for different individuals and communities. However, a holistic approach to health is common to many Aboriginal cultures and is also more and more supported by what is referred to as Western medicine.

## Aboriginal healing centres

The Aboriginal Healing Foundation once supported twelve healing centres across the country. Many of the Survivors who participated in the work of the Truth and Reconciliation Commission acknowledged that the AHF–supported health initiatives helped them heal enough to be able to come forward and talk about their childhood school experiences and their consequences on their lives. For these centres to continue their healing and, in some cases, life-saving work, they need to find alternatives to replace the AHF funding, which has now ended.[162]

In Ontario, through its Aboriginal Healing and Wellness Strategy, the provincial government has established a network of programs, including ten Aboriginal Health Access Centres and six healing lodges.[163] These and similar programs are, however, an exception—not the norm—across the country.[164]

The Aboriginal Healing Centres involve a range of services from mainstream health care to traditional practices, all under community ownership and control. Such an approach has the power to improve the lives of all community members.

## Aboriginal approach to addiction

The experience of addiction treatments for Aboriginal people has shown that the most effective treatments are those that are grounded in the "wisdom of traditional Inuit, Métis, and First Nation teachings about a holistic approach to a healthy life."[165] These types of approaches involve "not just the mind and body of the addicted person, but his or her emotions, spirit, relationships and identity; not just the individual, but his or her family, friends and community; and not just change in the use of addictive substances, but change in fundamental patterns of living."[166] In a 2007 report prepared for the Aboriginal Healing Foundation, Deborah Chansonneuve identified the "ten characteristics of an Aboriginal approach to addictions":

1. An Aboriginal approach identifies and addresses the underlying causes of addictive behaviours unique to the historical experiences of Aboriginal people in Canada.

2. The wisdom of Aboriginal cultures and spirituality is at the very heart of healing and recovery.

3. The relationship among suffering, resilience, experiential knowledge, and spiritual growth is acknowledged and honoured.

4. The interconnectedness among individuals, families, and communities is strengthened.

5. The differing pace at which individuals, families, and communities move through the stages of healing is understood and respected.

6. Healing encompasses a range of traditional and contemporary activities with an equally valued role for everyone in the circle of care.

7. Community health and community development are inseparable.

8. Culture is healing.

9. Legacy education is healing.

10. Healing is a lifelong journey of growth and change.[167]

## Suicide prevention

A report on suicide among Aboriginal people in Canada, written for the Aboriginal Healing Foundation, concluded that the most successful suicide prevention program is one that adopts a "community wellness" promotion strategy—and thus the report's recommendations are useful beyond the goal of suicide prevention. The authors suggested the following general guidelines for a community wellness/suicide prevention strategy:

1. Programs should be locally initiated, owned and accountable, and embodying the norms and values of Aboriginal culture. Although it is crucial to develop local solutions rather than those imposed by external agencies, useful help from the latter should not be rejected when a meaningful partnership can be negotiated.

2. Suicide prevention should be the responsibility of the entire community, requiring community support and solidarity among family, religious, political, or other groups. Given the importance of community, there is a need for close collaboration among health, education, other community services, and local government ...

3. A focus on children and young people (up to their late twenties) is crucial, and this implies involvement of the family and the community.

4. The problem of suicide must be addressed from many perspectives, encompassing biological, psychological, socio-cultural, and spiritual dimensions of health and well-being.

5. Programs that are long-term in focus should be developed along with "crisis" responses. A comprehensive approach to the problem of suicide should be integrated within larger programs of health promotion, family life education, community and cultural development, and political empowerment.

6. Evaluation of the impact of prevention strategies is essential. While a program's continued existence is often taken as an indicator of its success, it is always important to examine the workings of a program and its wider impact to detect any unforeseen or harmful effects.

7. Training of community mental health workers in individual and family counselling (particularly for grief), appropriate social intervention, and community development methods is essential.[168]

Michael Chandler and Christopher Lalonde have done research in BC Aboriginal communities to identify factors that are associated with lower suicide rates there. They found that in over half the communities studied, there were no known suicides during the targeted five-year period, while the remainder of the communities experienced rates of youth suicide five hundred to eight hundred times the national average.[169]

The researchers found that "at least in the case of BC, those bands in which a majority of members reported a conversational knowledge of an Aboriginal language also experienced low to absent youth suicide rates. By contrast, those bands in which less than half of the members reported conversational knowledge suicide rates were six times greater."[170] The study's authors concluded that "Altogether these results demonstrate that indigenous language use, as a marker of cultural persistence, is a strong predictor of health and well-being in Canada's Aboriginal communities."[171]

21) We call upon the federal government to provide sustainable funding for existing and new Aboriginal healing centres to address the physical, mental, emotional, and spiritual harms caused by residential schools, and to ensure that the funding of healing centres in Nunavut and the Northwest Territories is a priority.

22) We call upon those who can effect change within the Canadian health-care system to recognize the value of Aboriginal healing practices and use them in the treatment of Aboriginal patients in collaboration with Aboriginal healers and Elders where requested by Aboriginal patients.

## Facing racism within the health care system

When looking for examples of racism towards Aboriginal peoples in the health care system, one need look no further than the shameful circumstances surrounding the death of Brian Lloyd Sinclair, the Aboriginal man who died after waiting thirty-four hours in the emergency room of the Winnipeg Health Sciences Center in September 2008. Speaking on the subject, Madeleine Keteskwew Dion Stout observed, "Shockingly, the staff said Mr. Sinclair didn't ask for help. But it just makes you think ... what do we look like to others? Do we look like a person even? Do we look like a people? Especially when both our legs are missing and we're sitting in a wheelchair, and we're vomiting all over ourselves and on the floor? Clearly we as a people aren't even looked at as human beings."[172] While an inquest report into his death did not seriously consider the role of racism in the treatment he received (or failed to receive), it noted evidence that a number of "incorrect assumptions" and stereotypes were made about Mr. Sinclair, including that he was "sleeping off his intoxication," that he was "homeless" and just "seeking shelter." Judge Timothy Preston concluded that Mr. Sinclair "did not have to die."[173] His recommendations included the use of Elders in hospitals, Aboriginal discharge planners, and ongoing cultural safety training for health care workers.[174]

The Health Council of Canada has noted that providers must be made familiar with the long history of discrimination and colonialism, and that Aboriginal people impacted by the residential school system "may have a heightened sensitivity to practices that are a routine part of hospital life."[175] For example, the institutional environment typical of hospitals can trigger traumatic childhood memories. Indeed, just the fact of having to leave home communities to obtain services reproduces harmful patterns associated with residential schools.

The Society of Obstetricians and Gynaecologists of Canada has a guide for health professionals working with Aboriginal people that sets out basic expectations about the knowledge that health professionals should have, including a basic understanding of the appropriate names for various groups, current socio-demographics, traditional geographic territories and language groups, and an understanding of the impact of colonization on the health and well-being of Aboriginal people.[176] Health professionals should recognize the need to provide health services for Aboriginal people as close to home as possible, and the need to support Aboriginal individuals and communities in the process of self-determination.[177] These guidelines were based on input from a number of Aboriginal contributors and supporting organizations, and they represent a good model for other health professionals.

## International historical and legal precedents for Aboriginal health care rights

The *United Nations Declaration on the Rights of Indigenous Peoples* recognizes that Indigenous peoples have the right to physical and mental integrity, as well as the right to equal enjoyment of the highest attainable standard of physical and mental health. In taking measures to achieve these goals, states are obligated to pay particular attention to the rights and special needs of Elders, women, youth, children, and persons with disabilities.[178] Indigenous peoples have the right to be actively involved in developing, determining, and administering health programs that affect them.[179] Indigenous peoples also have the right to their traditional medicines and to maintain their traditional health practices.[180]

The UN Declaration is but one of several international human rights documents that collectively establish a right to health, including a right to health care and a right to a culturally appropriate health care system. There are no human rights without health—and no health without human rights. In other words, the right to health in international law is a holistic concept that incorporates much more than simple access to health care. It is intimately tied to other key social, economic, and political rights: the right to food, the right to adequate housing, the right to education, the right to work and rights at work, the right to life, the right to information, the right to physical integrity, the right to be free from discrimination, and the right to self-determination.[181]

Thus, the approach to health in international law is entirely consistent with Aboriginal approaches to health.[182] It is a positive right, which requires government to take action to make the right meaningful.

The historic Treaties established additional international law obligations concerning Aboriginal health and wellness.[183] The right to medical care was enshrined in Treaties 6, 7, 8, 10, and 11.[184] Treaty 6 explicitly included provision of a "medicine chest" and relief from "pestilence."[185] However, the right to health is not limited to these Treaties. The Treaty negotiations included many references "to the protection of, and non-interference with, traditional ways of life," which encompasses Aboriginal health.[186] Health and wellness, including in some cases self-government provisions for control over health care services, have also been a component of many of the contemporary Treaties and self-government agreements signed by Inuit, Métis, and First Nation governments in many regions of the country.[187]

Finally, the honour of the Crown, with its fiduciary obligations to Inuit, Métis, and First Nations peoples, requires that the Crown ensure Aboriginal peoples enjoy the same standards of health and wellness as others.

## Self-determination and health care

Self-determination is a foundational right, without which Aboriginal peoples' rights cannot be fully realized. There is a growing body of literature tying social and health problems to a lack of "community control." As such, community control and autonomy are important protective factors in preventing ill health.[188] The Commission believes that community well-being and healing from the trauma of residential schools will only be achieved through Aboriginal self-government and self-determination.

The Inuit Tapiriit Kanatami has argued,

> Self-determination improves health outcomes since communities who control their resources and services can initiate programs that match their needs, reducing delivery gaps and creating valuable support networks for vulnerable groups. Control over fiscal resources enables communities to plan enduring, well-integrated economic, social, and health programs that spawn lasting changes. Furthermore, self-determination generates new employment opportunities associated with running institutions and programs.[189]

Research also suggests that there is a need for healing centres in cities. One study of Aboriginal women on Vancouver's Downtown Eastside found that, despite the services provided by the Vancouver Native Health Society and other organizations, many Aboriginal women wanted more holistic options. One Aboriginal woman explained, "I prefer to be around First Nations people because they're the ones who understand where we come from. When you go in there [the Clinic], a non-Native person will look at you as a client. But a First Nation's person will look at you like a friend, but will maintain her professionalism."[190]

## A place for Aboriginal people and principles

The stories that Survivors have told the Commission have convinced us that traditional healing practices and involvement in Aboriginal culture and communities are vital parts of healing the wounds that residential schools have inflicted on former students and their families and students.

The Royal Commission on Aboriginal Peoples emphasized that simply increasing resources within the current health care system would not be sufficient.[191] A fundamental reorganization was recommended based on the following four principles:

(1)  Equitable access to health services and equitable outcomes in health status

(2)  Holistic approaches to treatment and preventive services

(3)  Aboriginal control of services

(4)  Diversity of approaches that respond to cultural priorities and community needs.[192]

These remain relevant and achievable goals. Had these steps been taken at the time of the RCAP report in 1996, Aboriginal and non-Aboriginal communities would be in a much better position to truly tackle the ongoing health legacy of the residential schools. For example, RCAP found that in 1993 that only about 0.1% of physicians in Canada were Aboriginal. RCAP found similar underrepresentation in other health and social services professions such as nursing, dietetics, and dental therapy.[193] Thus, the need to develop Aboriginal health professionals is a pressing priority. This priority is, of course, closely connected to the need to transform and invest in an educational system that breaks with the residential school past. Consideration should be given to schools that will train Aboriginal doctors and nurses and facilitate research and practice that combines Western and Aboriginal approaches to health care.

In its 1996 report, RCAP challenged federal, provincial, and territorial governments to train ten thousand Aboriginal professionals over a ten-year period in health and social services, including medicine, nursing, mental health, psychology, social work, dentistry, nutrition, addictions, gerontology, public health, community development, planning, health administration, and other priority areas identified by Aboriginal people.[194]

Research based on the censuses conducted in 1996, 2001, and 2006 found that 12,965 First Nations, Inuit, and Métis people entered health careers between 1996 and 2006. The study reported that the "10,000 target" set by the Royal Commission can be interpreted as having been surpassed. However, despite these achievements, equitable representation was still not achieved, with Aboriginal people making up 3.8% of Canada's population according to the 2006 census and only representing 2.2% (or 21,815 people) of Canadian workers in health occupations. The study observed that Métis health professionals and paraprofessionals working in off-reserve areas increased from 2,895 in 1996 to 10,425 in 2006, with two-thirds of the increase coming in the 2001–06 period. First Nations representation increased from 3,745 to 7,530 between 1996 and 2006. For Inuit peoples, the increase was from approximately 325 to 430 over the same period, and for on-reserve populations, the numbers of First Nations health care providers grew from 1,435 to 2,550 over the ten-year period from 1996 to 2006.[195] Despite such progress, serious shortfalls remain.[196]

In September 2004, in part in response to several RCAP recommendations, the Government of Canada created a five-year program called the Aboriginal Health Human Resources Initiative, which has three main goals: (1) to increase the number of Aboriginal people working in health careers; (2) to adapt health care educational curricula to support the development of cultural competencies; and (3) to improve the retention of health care workers in Aboriginal communities. This program was not extended at the conclusion of its five years of funding. Rather, the development of health human resources for Aboriginal communities became part of a Pan-Canadian Health Human Resources Strategy, which subsequently became the First Nations and Inuit Health Human Resources program in 2011.[197]

A 2013 evaluation report (covering 2008–09 and 2012–13) found that there has been "progress on increasing enrolments in and graduations from health programs" through "access, bridging and support programs," bursaries, and scholarships. However, there is no "baseline information available pertaining to the number of First Nations individuals originating from reserves or Inuit communities who are enrolling in and/or graduating from post-secondary institutions from various health disciplines or on the extent to which they return to their home communities after graduation," so it is not possible to know whether representation has improved.[198]

The anticipated success of such programs is expected to be limited in light of "many barriers to enrolment in post-secondary education [that] do not fall under the purview of Health Canada, specifically gaps in education at the primary and secondary school level," which again highlights the need for a holistic approach.[199]

## Involvement of the churches

A small additional source of money and programs to promote healing has come through the churches involved in running the residential schools. Those churches involved in the Indian Residential School Settlement Agreement made commitments to fund healing initiatives, although a number had already established reconciliation and healing initiatives prior to the agreement. The Presbyterian Fund for Healing and Reconciliation, the United Church of Canada Healing Fund, and the Anglican Healing Fund were mandated under the Settlement Agreement to receive applications for initiatives or programs designed to assist with healing and reconciliation for former students and their families and communities, and to make grants or approve in-kind services.[200]

The churches fund many small but important community projects. For example, in the fall of 2013, the United Church's Healing Fund decided to fund eleven proposals at a total cost of $150,000. One project was to encourage Nuxalk language instruction; another was to allow Elders to participate in the Ekiwaamijigaadeg Inwewin Language Nest of the Chippewas of Nawash in Ontario. Another project involved anger management, grief, and loss workshops.[201]

The church-funded programs are small and project-based. They are no substitute for the Aboriginal Health Foundation. In addition, in the case of the Catholic Church, funding of healing initiatives was tied directly to the Foundation. Pursuant to the Settlement Agreement, the Catholic Church fund took applications and recommended programs to the Aboriginal Healing Foundation. If the Aboriginal Healing Foundation approved the application, the Committee would forward the funds to support the program, which was then administered by the Foundation.[202]

## The search for equal outcomes

The *Canada Health Act* requires all insured persons in Canada to have reasonable access to health services.[203] However, most Aboriginal health practices are not treated as "insured services" (and therefore are not covered by provincial or federal health programs).

Yukon is the only jurisdiction where health legislation recognizes the need to respect traditional healing practices and the importance of establishing partnerships with Aboriginal peoples. The *Yukon Health Act* provides that the minister of health "shall promote mutual understanding, knowledge, and respect between the providers of health and social services offered in the health and social service system and the providers of traditional aboriginal nutrition and healing."[204] The same section of the Act also provides that its purpose "is to secure aboriginal control over traditional aboriginal nutritional and healing practices and to protect these healing practices as a viable alternative for seekers of health and healing services."[205]

Ontario's Aboriginal Healing and Wellness Strategy funds community wellness workers, crisis intervention teams, health liaison, and health outreach as well as specialized projects such as healing lodges, treatment centres, and Aboriginal health access centres that are intended to provide culturally sensitive service through joint management with Aboriginal organizations. Traditional healing practices are encouraged.[206] These and similar programs are, however, an exception and not the norm across the country.

Integration of Indigenous knowledge and healing practices in Canada, in partnership with Inuit, Métis, and First Nations communities, continues to be fragmented and implemented on an ad hoc basis.[207] A literature review conducted in 2008 confirmed the success of community-based addictions programs as an alternative to treatment of individuals at distant residential addictions facilities. It warned that better documentation of the results of such programs was required, but that they appear to depend on long-term funding and infrastructure, and strong community leadership and engagement.[208]

To underline the importance of traditional medicine, it is worth noting here a groundbreaking ruling from an Ontario Court in November 2014 that determined that a mother from the Six Nations of the Grand River Reserve had the right to withdraw her eleven-year-old daughter from a course of chemotherapy in favour of traditional medicine. Justice Gethin Edward ruled that "the decision to pursue traditional medicine for her daughter J. J. is her aboriginal right." He went on in his judgment to say, "the point is traditional medicine continues to be practiced on Six Nations as it was prior to European contact and in this Court's view there is no question it forms an integral part of who the Six Nations are … a practice that has been rooted in their culture from its beginnings."[209] In a later "clarification" of that ruling, Justice Edward stated that "recognition and implementation of the right to use traditional medicines must remain consistent with the principle that the best interests of the child remain paramount." He elaborated,

> In law as well as in practice, then, the Haudenosaunee have both an aboriginal right to use their own traditional medicines and health practices, and the same right as other people in Ontario to use the medicines and health practices available to those people. This provides Haudenosaunee culture and knowledge with protection, but it also gives the people unique access to the best we have to offer. Facing an unrelenting enemy, such as cancer, we all hope for and need the very best, especially for our children. For the Haudenosaunee, the two sets of rights mentioned above fulfill the aspirations of the United Nations Declaration on the Rights of Indigenous Peoples, which states in article 24, that "Indigenous peoples have the right to their traditional medicines and to maintain their health

practices ... Indigenous individuals also have the right to access, without any discrimination, to all social and health services.[210]

23) We call upon all levels of government to:

  i. Increase the number of Aboriginal professionals working in the health-care field.

  ii. Ensure the retention of Aboriginal health-care providers in Aboriginal communities.

  iii. Provide cultural competency training for all health-care professionals.

24) We call upon medical and nursing schools in Canada to require all students to take a course dealing with Aboriginal health issues, including the history and legacy of residential schools, the *United Nations Declaration on the Rights of Indigenous Peoples*, Treaties and Aboriginal rights, and Indigenous teachings and practices. This will require skills-based training in intercultural competency, conflict resolution, human rights, and anti-racism.

## Conclusion

Aboriginal people in Canada suffer levels of poor health that would simply not be tolerated by other Canadians. Aboriginal people have higher mortality rates, higher rates of disease, higher rates of accidental deaths and dramatically higher rates of suicide. Many of these problems stem from the intergenerational legacy of residential schools. The destructive beliefs and behaviours of many students have been passed on to their children and grandchildren as physical and mental health issues.

Trudy King lives in Fort Resolution in the Northwest Territories. Both her father and her ex-husband attended residential school. She reflected on the need for healing in the community:

> There was a residential school here in Fort Res, and there was never ever any healing in this town. Everything is just a big hush-hush. I know there's a lot of abuse here. I learned all that when I left my ex, certain people disclosed to me. And this town needs healing, the people need healing. People in this town don't know how to open up, because every, they kept everything so secret for so many years, and it's still like that, still like that in Fort Res. And there was a residential school here, but there's no healing going on here, and it's still affecting this community. And there's just, like, a big dark cloud over here, and it's still like that. I don't know why I still live here. I used to say it's because my mom's here,

I can't leave her. My mom's been gone just about fifteen years now, and I'm still here. It's my community, and I, I don't have to run away anywhere to ... But I really believe that this town needs healing, the people need healing, the leaders, everybody. Until that happens, everything is gonna be secrets.[211]

There is a need to close the health gap that exists between Aboriginal and non-Aboriginal Canadians. Unfortunately, matters are getting worse, not better, since the residential schools settlement and the prime minister's apology. The decision to allow the Aboriginal Healing Foundation and other Aboriginal health organizations to wither and die was an alarming step backwards given the costs of crisis health interventions and the deeper causes of Aboriginal ill health, including the legacy of residential schools.

Other countries, especially Australia, offer models of reconciliatory policies that Canada could follow. Australia set specific goals for closing various gaps—including health-related gaps—between the Aboriginal and the non-Aboriginal population.

The Truth and Reconciliation Commission is concerned that Canadian governments have not made comparable, measureable commitments. Furthermore, there is a continuing erosion of funds for the Aboriginal agencies that were making the greatest progress in community-based healing efforts; and there is ongoing erosion of agencies that can provide credible data about the gaps.

The Royal Commission on Aboriginal Peoples recognized that there is a growing convergence between Western and Aboriginal understandings of health and wellness.[212] This convergence has, if anything, increased in the almost twenty years since RCAP's report was released. Today, the importance of prenatal care, early childhood development, diet, and mental health are much better recognized in Western medicine. In addition, there is increasing recognition about how environmental degradation, poor living conditions, poor education, and a lack of self-determination over one's life can manifest itself in ill health.

Although there is convergence that provides some grounds for reconciliation between Aboriginal and non-Aboriginal perspectives on health, this convergence should not be an excuse for continuing to deprive Aboriginal people of control over their health care. To ensure that the residential school experience is not being repeated in some other guise, the Government of Canada must continue to measure and compare the health indicators of Aboriginal people and non-Aboriginal Canadians. The need for equal outcomes is also supported by the fact that Aboriginal and Treaty rights and the *UN Declaration of the Rights of Indigenous Peoples* guarantee a right to equitable Aboriginal health care.

Finally, the principle of self-determination runs throughout all of our Calls to Action in this volume and is particularly important with respect to health. As RCAP noted so clearly in its report,

Whole health, in the full sense of the term, does not depend primarily on the mode of operation of health and healing services—as important as they are. Whole health depends as much or more on the design of the political and economic systems that organize relations of power and productivity in Canadian society. For Aboriginal people, those systems have been working badly. Before whole health can be achieved, they must begin to work well.[213]

Residential schools inflicted grave harms on Aboriginal peoples. Self-determination holds out the best hope for effective approaches that will begin to counter the harmful legacy of the schools. Moreover, the very act of according Aboriginal peoples the respect to conduct their own affairs will help renounce the colonial and racist views about Aboriginal inferiority that informed the failed residential schools project.

Self-determination holds the key to better Aboriginal health by allowing communities to develop programs that are suited to their own needs, and to do so in a holistic way, avoiding the jurisdictional disputes that have plagued progress in health and so many other areas where the residential schools still cast a large shadow.

# CHAPTER 5

# A denial of justice

## Introduction

Residential schools inflicted profound injustices on Aboriginal people. Children were taken far from their communities to live in imposing and frightening custodial institutions. Aboriginal parents were forced, often under threat of prosecution if they resisted, to give up their children to these schools.

Residential schools resembled prisons. Aboriginal children were often treated as if they were offenders who required rehabilitation, while the only thing they were guilty of was being Aboriginal. The regimented life and religious indoctrination and curriculum imposed on them was designed to 'rehabilitate' them by assimilating them into mainstream Canadian society. Norman Courchene was one of many Survivors who told the Commission that while he was at residential school, he "felt like an inmate."[1]

If the children disobeyed the rules, spoke their own languages, or associated with their own brothers and sisters, they were punished. If they ran away, they were tracked down and forced to return to the schools where they would be again be punished for trying to escape.

Children who attended the schools developed a variety of coping and resistance mechanisms. Some of them stole food to supplement their inadequate diets. Others adopted the bullying tactics of the school by abusing other students.

Mervin Mirasty told the Commission that both he and his brother were sexually abused at Beauval residential school: "To this day, I've, I've always wanted to go back and burn the place, and I never did." He also recalled that, "I ran away from school. I'd go out, I'd walk around town, and steal whatever I could steal ... I started stealing cars, I got caught, at 15 I ended up in jail. From, from that point of 15 years old 'til I was, the year 2000, I got sentenced to 25 years all together ... and I don't know what I was fighting, what I was trying to do."[2]

The Canadian legal system also failed the children. When it eventually began to respond to the claims of abuse in the late 1980s, it initially did so inadequately and in a way that often re-victimized the Survivors. To Survivors, the criminal and civil justice systems seemed to be tipped in favour of the school authorities and school administrators. To Survivors, the justice system was a barrier to their efforts to bring out the truth of their collective experience. The Indian Residential Schools Settlement Agreement provided them access to compensation without the trial process, but their collective need to engage in a process of public disclosure about what happened in the schools would have been denied to them without the Truth and Reconciliation Commission.

The justice system denies Aboriginal people the safety and opportunities that most Canadians take for granted. The failures of the justice system include the disproportionate imprisonment of Aboriginal people and the inadequate response to their criminal victimization. The failures of the system are perhaps most marked in the high number of Aboriginal women and girls who are missing or who have been murdered.

The first part of this chapter will review the failures of the criminal justice system in protecting residential school students and punishing those who abused them physically, sexually, and emotionally. The second part of the chapter will examine the failures of the civil litigation process to provide justice to the Survivors of the residential schools and their families. The third part of the chapter will detail the criminal legacies of the schools, the myriad harms and intergenerational damage inflicted by the government policy of removing children from their homes and forcibly separating them from their families and communities, language, and cultures, all of which have contributed to the disturbingly high overrepresentation of Aboriginal people in prison. The fourth part will look at the equally shameful overrepresentation of Aboriginal people among victims of crime, particularly women. The fifth and final part of the chapter is titled "The Way Forward," and offers suggestions and insight derived from the Commission's hearings and research.

The Commission believes that significant reform of the Canadian justice system is necessary to halt the legacy of residential schools. Resources will need to be shifted from costly and often coercive crisis intervention towards crime prevention. Aboriginal communities must also exercise their own inherent powers of self-determination, and consider designing and administering their own justice systems. By using their own traditions, Aboriginal people will be able to take a more holistic approach to offending behaviour and recognize the need to address the underlying causes of the behaviour as well.

## The failures of the criminal justice system

Attendance at residential schools was often coerced. For many Aboriginal children, their first encounter with the justice system came when an RCMP officer appeared in their community to take them to residential school. The Mounted Police, who were appointed residential school truant officers in 1927, were, along with local police, used to force parents to send or return their children to school.[3] For example, in 1914, Indian agent W. J. Dilworth reported he had sent a parent from the Blood Reserve in Alberta to jail for ten days for taking his son out of a residential school without permission.[4] Robert Keesick recalled that in 1930 "the RCMP told my grandmother that she had to take me to attend residential school at McIntosh. If she refused, she would be put in jail."[5] The RCMP also had an active involvement with the schools by investigating runaways.[6]

## Harsh punishment excused

Students had few protections from the harsh discipline imposed in the schools. In the spring of 1934, $53.44 was stolen from a locked drawer in a cabinet in the office of the mother superior of the Shubenacadie, Nova Scotia, school. Several boys were questioned: some admitted involvement in the theft; others denied it. Eight of them, including some who denied involvement, were punished that day. They were thrashed on their bare backs with a seven-thonged strap that was specially made by the school carpenter.[7] After a few more days of investigation, eleven more boys were thrashed and had their hair clipped. Most were put on a bread-and-water diet for two days.[8] A local RCMP officer was present for the initial round of punishment, and said he did not see any blood.[9]

The story was reported in the local papers. When alarmed parents showed up at the school, Principal J. P. Mackey prevented them from seeing their children because he "did not think it prudent they should see the children and talk the matter among them."[10] Sufficient public attention was devoted to the matter that the federal government appointed L. A. Audette, a retired judge of the Exchequer Court of Canada, to conduct an inquiry into the event. He held two days of hearings in June 1934, two and a half months after the boys were thrashed.

Audette defended the necessity of physical punishment and the strap not only on the basis that it was used in Britain, but because "these Indians, in terms of civilization, are children, having minds just emerging from barbarism."[11] The inquiry concluded that "far from finding fault," the principal of the school should be "commended and congratulated" for his actions in maintaining discipline in the school.[12]

## Rights denied

Just as the justice system did a poor job protecting the rights of students, it did little to uphold those of their parents. Parents would sometimes voluntarily send their children to a residential school. Sometimes in times of need, families could not provide for their children. Sometimes when a mother died, the father could not care for the children. Children sometimes wanted to go the schools to be with siblings or friends rather than spend a lonely time in their community. Unlike children who were identified and ordered to be sent to the schools by government agents, these children were not subject to a mandatory-stay determination. Legally, their voluntary enrolment should have enabled them to leave when they wished, but government policy decreed that once enrolled, all children in a school had to stay.

In some cases, Indian Affairs refused to discharge children who had been voluntarily enrolled until they turned eighteen. In 1903, when the government refused to discharge two brothers who were over fifteen, the students ran away from the Middlechurch school in Manitoba. They were apprehended and returned to the school on the basis of a warrant issued under the 1894 regulations. Their father, William Cameron, went to court and got a writ of *habeas corpus*. Normally, such a writ requires that the person under arrest be brought before a court. According to Martin Benson, Justice Richards of the Manitoba Court of Queen's Bench found on the father's behalf, and wrote, "the regulations for the detention of children until they reached the age of 18 years do not apply to children who have been voluntarily placed in the school and that as to such children the parents have a right to get them out of the school at any time they wish to demand them."[13]

In other words, the government's discharge policy for students who had been voluntarily enrolled had no legal basis. But this court victory did not change the policy. In 1907, it was still government policy that children, whether voluntarily enrolled by their parents or committed under the provisions of the *Indian Act*, could not be removed without the minister's permission.[14] In his report for the year ending March 31, 1910, Duncan Campbell Scott, then superintendent of Indian Education, wrote, "pupils of residential schools are not usually allowed to leave the institutions until they reach the age of 18."[15] Clearly, the government was willing to ignore court rulings.

One partial legal victory came in 1913 when a civil suit brought by a parent for the treatment of his daughters at the Mohawk Institute was successful. The parent, with the help of the Six Nations Council, sued the school and obtained $300 damages for "a whipping on bare back with raw hide" received by his daughter and another $100 for a daughter being kept on a water diet for three days.[16] In a pattern that would be repeated in modern residential school litigation, however, other claims relating to the cutting of the daughter's hair, confinement, and bad food were rejected by the court.

## The slow recognition of injustice in residential schools

The colonization and marginalization of Aboriginal peoples created a situation in which children were vulnerable to abuse, and civil authorities were distant, hostile, and skeptical of Aboriginal reports of abuse. As a result, there were very few prosecutions for abuse while the schools were in operation.[17] Poor pay, poor screening, limited supervision, the reassignment of perpetrators, and the normalization of abusive behaviour all increased the vulnerability of students to adult and student predators. It is also clear that abuse was often 'hushed up': people were dismissed rather than prosecuted, parents were not informed, and children were not provided with supports or counselling.[18] The police investigations that took place in the 1990s were almost invariably mounted in response to organized efforts on the part of the former students themselves.[19]

The stories of these investigations are described in greater detail in the history volumes of the Commission's Final Report: *Canada's Residential Schools: The History, Part 1, Origins to 1939*; and *Canada's Residential Schools: The History, Part 2, 1939 to 2000*. Those early convictions carry important legal weight. They demonstrate that the abuses at the residential school were recognized as criminal offences at that time, which casts doubt on officials' later assertions that they were unaware that such abuses were criminal in nature. Even if students were not the immediate victims of abuse, they were victims of collateral violence, for they often witnessed or otherwise became aware of the abuse. Memories of violence and abuse stayed with Survivors decades after they left the schools.

Doris Young recalled a child being killed in the residential school in Elkhorn, Manitoba:

> I remember was, there was all these screams, and there was blood over the, the walls. [Crying]... and we were told that if we, if we were, if we ever told, or tried to run away, we would, the same thing would happen to us. [Crying] So, it was a dangerous time for, for children, and for me at that, those days. [Crying] We never really knew who would be next to be murdered because we witnessed one already. [Crying][20]

Young struggled with this memory and "had nightmares for years." She eventually reported the incident to the police as an adult:

> The RCMP investigated, they said they couldn't find anything. They came back and told me that they found no evidence of what I was talking about, and but it was not something that I would make up. The thing about all of this violence that happened in those schools is that they had such free access to us, and there was no one there to protect us. They, they had absolute authority over all the violence they committed on, on me, and, and who, all the other children that were there as well.[21]

The RCMP reports to having investigated fifteen deaths in the schools, but no charges were laid as they concluded that all the deaths were accidental or due to illness.[22]

The often-strained relations between Aboriginal people and the police in Canada is directly connected to the history of their experience of policing at residential schools. Not only did the police coercively enforce attendance at residential school, but they also failed to protect the children from serious crimes while they were in the schools.

It has been important for the Commission to understand how the Canadian legal system responded to residential schools in order to understand the full legacy of the harms experienced by Survivors. In the next section, four separate police investigations will be highlighted: two in British Columbia, one in the Northwest Territories, and one in Ontario. Each of the following investigations points to different failures of the justice system, failures that have often led Aboriginal people to view the system with a mixture of suspicion and fear.

## The RCMP task force in British Columbia

The Nuu-chah-nulth Tribal Council (NTC), a body that coordinates political action amongst the fourteen Nuu-chah-nulth First Nations on the west coast of Vancouver Island, undertook a major study of the impact of residential schools on its members in 1992. In 1996, the NTC published *Indian Residential Schools: The Nuu-chah-nulth Experience*, a report that contains excerpts from interviews with former students, as well as several former teachers. The report states that eighty-three of the ninety-six Survivors who were interviewed reported being physically abused, and thirty reported being sexually abused.[23] The Tribal Council's report did not place primary emphasis on criminal investigations. It first called on the federal government to issue an apology, and then stated that a public inquiry was necessary because the abuse it revealed was only 'the tip of the iceberg.'

In November 1994, tribal council representatives presented their findings to members of the Port Alberni Royal Canadian Mounted Police detachment. In light of the number of potential cases that the Nuu-Chah-Nulth inquiry might give rise to, it soon became apparent to the RCMP that it needed to develop a coordinated response to the issue; it established the Native Indian Residential School Task Force. The province-wide task force was composed of officers from the central E Division Major Crime Section, as well as investigators from eight local subdivisions. The task force commenced its work in 1995 and remained in operation for over eight years. It investigated 974 allegations of criminal misconduct in British Columbia schools.

Four hundred and fifty-three people said they had been criminally victimized. Another 245 people were identified as possible victims, meaning that while there was credible evidence to believe they had been victimized, they had not contacted the police. That suggests there were nearly 700 potential victims. The task force identified 396 suspects. Complaints came from former students of 15 of the residential schools in British Columbia. There were 515 alleged sexual assaults (involving 374 victims), 435 alleged physical assaults (involving 223 victims), and 23 other alleged offences (involving 19 victims).

Yet, in its final report, the task force stated that despite "thousands of hours of investigative time and well over a million dollars in salaries and other expenses ... relatively few criminal prosecutions resulted."[24]

Its final report stated that, when the task force was formed in 1994, it

> was immediately greeted with anxiety and mistrust from the very people it sought to assist. The Aboriginal community expressed alarm at the potential impact of the investigation on their people, citing the high suicide and substance abuse rates that followed previous investigations. Their other concerns were centred around their historic mistrust of both the RCMP and the Court system. This situation was further aggravated by the RCMP's earlier role as truant officers supporting the very system that was now under criminal investigation.[25]

The Truth and Reconciliation Commission's review concluded that the task force led to the prosecution and conviction of only five men. Three of the five had already been charged and convicted of abusing residential school students before the task force was formed. The task force final report noted a further problem. It stated that "a very common situation that kept occurring over and over again" was that provincial Crown counsel refused to prosecute without corroboration in the form of physical evidence.[26] This approach was based on an unwillingness to take the complainant's own evidence as sufficient to justify a prosecution. It shows a reluctance to take the evidence of Aboriginal people as worthy of belief.

Since 1982, the legal requirement for corroboration was specifically rescinded for sexual offences and never was required for non-sexual offences.[27] The RCMP's own report acknowledged that corroboration was no longer a legal requirement, but that it was nevertheless seen as a practical prerequisite for the prosecution of these cases.[28]

There is also some evidence in the RCMP report that claims of physical assault were viewed as less serious than claims of sexual abuse. The report suggests that complaints of physical abuse "quite often ... were the result of a culture clash between the rigid 'spare the rod, spoil the child' Christian attitude, and the more permissive Native tradition of child-rearing."[29]

The RCMP's report also notes that almost every complainant told the RCMP about their loss of culture as well as the physical and sexual abuse that they suffered. This reaffirms that loss of culture and language was extremely important to many former students who looked to both the criminal and civil legal systems for justice.

Unfortunately, the Canadian legal system ignored the harms of loss of culture and language. The RCMP's E Division candidly explained, "enforced deprivation of Native culture was official Canadian government policy sanctioned by the *Indian Act*. As such, these complaints are beyond the scope of this investigation and will have to be dealt with in another forum."[30]

The RCMP, to its credit, responded to those concerns by negotiating a protocol in which the force agreed not to forward a case for prosecution without the complainant's consent. However, the RCMP eventually betrayed the trust of the Survivors when it shared files involving investigations into the Kuper Island residential school with the federal Department of Justice, which was defending the government in civil actions brought by former students. When the RCMP requested that the documents be returned, Department of Justice lawyers refused. They insisted that the RCMP documents were also the property of the federal Crown.[31] This argument ignored the constitutional principle of police independence and suggested to Survivors that the RCMP was not acting as an impartial law enforcer but as an agent of the federal government, which was actively opposing the Survivors' civil claims.

The Government of Canada stubbornly resisted RCMP demands for information. This made it necessary for the RCMP to obtain and execute multiple search warrants on the Department of Indian Affairs in Hull, Québec, in order to obtain information relevant to the criminal investigation.[32] The RCMP displayed praiseworthy independence and determination in seeking the information. Nevertheless, it is shocking to the Commission that the Department of Indian Affairs would resist cooperation with an important criminal investigation in a manner that required the RCMP to obtain search warrants to obtain material.

25) We call upon the federal government to establish a written policy which reaffirms the independence of the Royal Canadian Mounted Police to investigate crimes in which the government has its own interest as a potential or real party in civil litigation.

## Turquetil Hall, Chesterfield Inlet investigations

As was the case with the E Division Task Force, the investigation into sexual abuse at Turquetil Hall only came after Aboriginal people took the initiative to examine and reveal the abuses they suffered. In 1991, Marius Tungilik, a former student at Turquetil Hall in Chesterfield Inlet in what is now Nunavut, told a hearing of the Royal Commission on Aboriginal Peoples about being sexually abused at the school. Two years later, he and others helped organize a reunion of students, at which about forty students revealed, while participating in healing circles, that they had suffered sexual abuse.

The former students at the reunion did not stress criminal investigations as an effective remedy. They asked for an acceptable apology, resources so that Survivors, dependents, and abusers could receive therapy, and "a comprehensive independent public inquiry" to investigate sexual, physical, and emotional abuse at Turquetil Hall/ Bernier School.[33]

Bishop Reynald Rouleau of the Hudson Bay Diocese attended the 1993 reunion. He stated that he recognized "the courage of many students who accepted to reveal publicly some aspects of their personal life and of their faith ... I am very sorry for those people toward whom abuses have been committed.... According to the limited means I may have, I am willing to collaborate in the healing of those individuals who are ready to get committed in their own healing."[34] Marius Tungilik noted that nothing in the bishop's statement admitted that sexual abuse had taken place.[35]

Two RCMP officers investigated 150 allegations of physical abuse and 86 allegations of sexual abuse made by students at Joseph Bernier School in Chesterfield Inlet. The RCMP interviewed 346 former students and almost all of the living staff all over Canada. The RCMP compiled a list of 13 sexual abuse charges against 3 Roman Catholic clergy and 41 charges against a lay staff member. The RCMP expressed confidence that they could obtain convictions.[36] Of the 23 staff identified as suspects, only 4 were deceased. A report written for the government of the Northwest Territories concluded that "serious incidents of sexual assault did in fact occur at the Chesterfield Inlet school during its years of operation."[37] The allegations "of abuse include fondling of the breast areas of female students, the genital areas of female students, the genital areas of male students and inappropriate sexual exhibition. An aura of fear, confusion and silence appear to surround the students' experiences at the time ... While many students indicated that they disliked the behaviour, felt it was wrong, and were afraid of it, it is apparent that they felt on many occasions powerless to prevent repeat occurrences."[38] However, when the report was released in June 1995, it was also announced that even the charges contemplated the previous year would not go forward.[39]

In 1996, Marius Tungilik, who had served in civil service positions in both the federal and the Northwest Territories governments, accepted an apology from Bishop Rouleau. He observed at that time, "Today's a historic day in Nunavut. Today, the bishop acknowledged the pain we went through and that is very special to me." At the same time, he told the church congregation, "I felt betrayed very badly by the church for so long ... I felt betrayed, so badly, by my fellow Inuit, the church-goers who tried so hard to make us feel bad for what we did." Marius Tungilik died in 2012, at the age of fifty-five.[40] Both his wife and daughter shared with the Commission the many difficulties that he struggled with throughout his life because of the abuse he suffered in residential school and the failure of the justice system to recognize the abuse he suffered.

## St. Anne's residential school

In 1992 former students of the Fort Albany school in Northern Ontario organized a reunion that attracted about three hundred people.[41] The reunion included a special panel on physical and sexual abuse at the school. Thirty students addressed the panel. The report of the panel stated that

> Of the 19 men who gave testimony, 10 were sexually abused. Almost all of them were physically abused in other ways; spiritually abused, humiliated, strapped, hit with rulers, hair pulled and dragged by the hair, stabbed with a pencil, made to eat their vomit, etc. etc.

> Of the 11 women who gave testimony, 2 were sexually abused. Almost all of them were physically abused in a variety of ways, including strapping, being made to sit in the electric chair, being made to eat their vomit, being made to kneel on concrete floors, locked away in dark basements, being wrongly punished for things they did not do, etc. etc.[42]

The reunion report made further reference to the use of an electric chair at the school:

> Several people talked about the electric chair that was used in the girls [*sic*] playroom. It seems odd how an electric chair can find its way into a Residential School; however, it seems to have been brought to the school for fun. Nevertheless, all the people who remembered the electric chair do not remember it in fun, but with pain and horror.[43]

Like other Survivor events at the time, the reunion report did not emphasize criminal investigations and prosecutions as the appropriate remedial response. The report called for an independent inquiry of Elders and former students to be appointed to examine what happened. It also called for compensation and treatment for those who had spoken at the reunion about being abused at the school. The report noted,

> The individuals who gave testimony and disclosed physical, psychological, sexual or spiritual abuse need immediate attention. It was a profound and painful event for the victims to come forward and required much courage on their part. They must not be let down now. They must receive ongoing counselling and healing to be determined before they leave the community.[44]

The reunion included healing circles that lasted from five to eight hours to help the former students deal with the aftermath of the abuse. No one was obliged to talk in the healing circles, which were free "from destructive criticism" and provided a "safe place for the disclosure of abuse and its aftermath." In the course of the healing circle process, many Survivors disclosed "a lack of self-esteem, alcoholism, domestic violence, marriage break down and a lack of parenting skills."[45]

Following the reunion, Edmund Metatawabin, who was then the chief of the Fort Albany First Nation, asked the Ontario Provincial Police to investigate complaints of the treatment that students received at the school in the 1950s and 1960s. In 1997, seven former staff members were charged with a variety of offences.[46] None of the documents made available to the Truth and Reconciliation Commission indicate that charges were ever laid in relation to the use of the electric chair. Five former staff were convicted of assault but the sentences were generally lenient.[47] More importantly, Survivors were subject to adversarial cross-examination that suggested that they were lying simply to bolster their civil claims. The evidence available to the Commission suggests that the prosecutions were poorly managed, not a good vehicle for the discovery of the truth and re-victimized Survivors.

## Bishop Hubert O'Connor

The story of the prolonged and ultimately failed prosecution of Hubert O'Connor reveals much about the limits of the existing criminal justice system to respond to the harms of residential schools. O'Connor was the principal of the St. Joseph's residential school in Williams Lake, BC, from 1961 to 1967. He eventually became a bishop but resigned that position in 1991 after being charged with two counts of raping two Aboriginal employees and a former student of the school and having indecently assaulted two students between 1964 and 1967. He was ordered to stand trial on those charges. He was the highest-ranking Roman Catholic official charged in relation to abuses at residential schools.

O'Connor did not deny having sexual relations with the complainants but argued that they had consented, even though he was a person with authority over them. As in other prosecutions, the process of an adversarial trial was particularly hard on the complainants. It put them on trial and further victimized them.

In June 1992, Bishop O'Connor's lawyer obtained the following sweeping pretrial disclosure order:

> THIS COURT ORDERS that Crown Counsel produce names, addresses and telephone numbers of therapists, counsellors, psychologists or psychiatrists who have treated any of the complainants with respect to allegations of sexual assault or sexual abuse.

> THIS COURT FURTHER ORDERS that the complainants authorize all therapists, counsellors, psychologists and psychiatrists who have treated any of them with respect to allegations of sexual assault or sexual abuse, to produce to the Crown copies of their complete file contents and any other related material including all documents, notes, records, reports, tape recordings and videotapes, and the Crown to provide copies of all this material to counsel for the accused forthwith.

> THIS COURT FURTHER ORDERS that the complainants authorize the Crown to obtain all school and employment records while they were in attendance at St. Joseph's Mission School and that the Crown provide those records to counsel for the accused forthwith.

> THIS COURT FURTHER ORDERS that the complainants authorize the production of all medical records from the period of time when they were resident at St. Joseph's Mission School as either students or employees.[48]

These orders were obtained without hearing from the complainants and without apparent consideration of their privacy interests. It meant that, as a price of the prosecution going forward, the complainants would have to give up their privacy with respect to their medical, school, and employment records. The former students understandably refused to grant consent to such a massive and open-ended invasion of their privacy.

There was prolonged pretrial litigation with O'Connor bringing repeated motions that proceedings be stayed because of non-disclosure. The Cariboo Tribal Council wrote a letter to the trial judge to express its concerns about the possibility of the prosecution being stayed and their concern about the victimization of the community. The trial judge admonished the tribal council for inappropriately communicating with a judge about a case out of court.[49]

The judge ordered that therapeutic files be disclosed, ruling that the accused's right to disclosure trumped the privacy rights of the complainants. Further disputes arose from a failure of the Crown prosecutor to fully comply with the disclosure order. The trial judge found that a Crown prosecutor had acted improperly and allowed her personal opposition to the disclosure order to cloud her professional responsibility. O'Connor then made a fifth motion for a stay of proceedings. This time he was successful. The judge concluded,

> To allow the case to proceed would tarnish the integrity of the court. The court is left with no alternative but to order a stay of proceedings on all four counts. In doing so I recognize that the decision will not be readily acceptable to all segments of our society. It will certainly not be popular with many people. I can only encourage such people or groups to carefully consider the reasons for the decision ... Those who will be angered or saddened by the outcome of this case must strive to put themselves in the position of an accused person. They would expect the Crown to fulfill its role to the standard required by law.[50]

David Neel, a member of the Kwakiutl Nation of Fort Rupert, BC, noted that the decision revealed "two faces of justice." He wrote, "Bishop O'Connor must face charges and be found guilty or innocent in the eyes of his peers." He added that he "personally would like to have the opportunity to one day believe in the 'justice system.' For the time being, where my people are concerned, it continues to be the injustice system."

Neel also noted that, "it is not only the first nations that need to heal from this period of institutionalized oppression, but our country as well. It continues to be our national shame, as it will be until we come to grips with it."[51]

The stay of proceedings was overturned by the British Columbia Court of Appeal, which concluded that the trial judge had not found sufficient prejudice to the accused or sufficient bad intent by the prosecution to justify the drastic remedy of permanently stopping the prosecution.

The accused then appealed to the Supreme Court, which, in a six to three decision, held that the trial should proceed after all. Justice L'Heureux-Dubé stated for the majority,

> it is clear, at the end of the day, that the Crown was right in trying to protect the interests of justice. The fact that it did so in such a clumsy way should not result in a stay of proceedings, particularly so when no prejudice was demonstrated to the fairness of the accused's trial or to his ability to make full answer and defence.[52]

The Supreme Court used the case to clarify the proper approach to the production and disclosure of records in sexual assault cases. Once therapeutic records had fallen into the hands of the Crown, then the Crown's duty to disclose all relevant material to the accused would apply. Neither the privacy interests of the complainants or any privilege they might assert could be balanced against the accused's rights.

This part of the Supreme Court's decision was widely criticized. Parliament intervened and enacted new legislation that instructed judges to balance the accused's right to make full answer and defence with the complainant's right to privacy and equality before deciding whether to order the production of the record to the judge or its subsequent disclosure to the accused.[53]

As a result of the Supreme Court's ruling, a new trial was ordered for Bishop O'Connor. At the new trial, the nineteen-year-old complainant who had been O'Connor's secretary and also a member of the school's travelling pipe band had testified that she had removed her clothes because she was afraid of losing her job and her opportunity to travel with the band. In his own defence, O'Connor took the stand. He defended the two rape charges by arguing that his former students had consented to sexual intercourse. He denied the two other charges of indecent assaults.

O'Connor was convicted of one count of rape and one count of indecent assault and acquitted on the two other counts. The trial judge stressed inconsistencies between what the complainants told the police and their testimony, even though inconsistencies were in part caused by the age of the case and the prolonged nature of the preliminary battle over disclosure.

The trial judge sentenced O'Connor to two and half years imprisonment for the rape and three months for the indecent assault to be served concurrently. The judge also considered victim impact statements, including that of the victim in the rape conviction who stated that

> The effects of this trauma have had a devastating impact on my emotional well-being. As a young woman during my twenties and thirties, I had little esteem after this tragic event. I felt I could trust no one. I felt helpless and I could not tell anyone what happened. I thought they would not believe me or that they would not understand the shame I carried for years. Many times I felt vulnerable and I was an object and not a person.[54]

The three-month sentence for the indecent assault conviction seems inordinately light, given that it involved an abuse of power against a young girl who was a student at the school. However, the story didn't end there. O'Connor immediately appealed the two convictions. He sought but was denied bail. [55] He renewed the request for bail or supervised freedom in the community and was granted bail pending appeal after serving six and a half months in prison.[56]

In the end, this was the only jail time he served. The British Columbia Court of Appeal overturned both the rape and indecent assault convictions. It ordered that O'Connor face a new trial on the rape charge. The Court of Appeal also entered an acquittal on the indecent assault charge on the basis that the verdict was unreasonable given inconsistencies in the evidence.[57]

The new trial of Bishop O'Connor on the one remaining rape charge was never held. Instead, a long healing circle was held at Alkali Lake. It was attended by about seventy members of the community, O'Connor and his lawyers, prosecutors and senior justice officials, and one of the complainants. The complainant had already testified three times at court. She said she was not sure if she "had the strength or the energy to go through it all again." The complainant was frustrated that the court system had never let her express to O'Connor her feelings about the pain he had caused her. Her sister-in-law said that a circle based on trust, respect, and honesty was "one of the most painful and fearful processes O'Connor has ever had to go through," probably more so than another trial.[58]

In the healing circle, O'Connor did not admit to raping the complainant. He did, however, acknowledge that it was wrong for him as her employer and former school principal to have sex with the complainant when she was eighteen years of age. The complainant told reporters that "it was nice to get out of the control of the court system and out of the control of O'Connor himself. There was no way at Monday's Healing Circle that he got away with anything. I would say he felt some of the fear and pain that natives have felt for all these years." She recognized that O'Connor's apology was not an admission of criminal guilt, but the complainant said that "the apology to me meant a lot because it came from him personally. The important thing for me and my people is to move beyond the constant pain and to become stronger."[59]

## The denial of access to civil justice: Systemic issues

Civil law allows one person or party to take another to court, in search of financial compensation (also called damages) for a wrong that is presumed to have taken place. Having generally failed to find justice through police investigations and criminal prosecutions, residential school Survivors increasingly turned to the civil justice system. The residential schools civil litigation started in the 1990s represented the most extensive engagement between Aboriginal people and the civil justice system. The history of that development is worth considering.

Early after Confederation, the federal government had adopted, and publically communicated, the questionable legal view that Aboriginal people who were subject to the *Indian Act* were under a legal disability and were the 'wards' of the Crown. They justified this on the basis that ruthless individuals could and would take advantage of them, and therefore Aboriginal people needed to be 'protected' from such persons, and from themselves. For example, through amendments to the *Indian Act*, limitations were placed on the ability of First Nations people to market farm produce or dispose of their own personal property.[60] In her work, historian Sarah Carter points out that many Aboriginal farmers were running successful agricultural operations before and after Treaties were negotiated. Government interference with those operations after the limitations were put into place rendered those farmers into peasant farmers, able to make barely enough to feed themselves and their families.[61]

While on the face of it, the stated desire to protect Aboriginal people would be commendable, it seems more likely, based on all of the available evidence from this period, that the real purpose behind such amendments and public messaging was to allow the government to exercise greater control over the lives of First Nations peoples and their lands. The government certainly had no interest in 'protecting' Aboriginal peoples who were not governed by the *Indian Act* or once they had surrendered their status under it.

For many years, Aboriginal people were hindered in seeking legal redress in the courts of Canada because of provisions in the *Indian Act*. Provisions enacted in 1927 forbade them or anyone on their behalf from raising money to begin court action, or from beginning legal proceedings against the government, without the minister's permission.

Such limitations clearly had a chilling effect on the willingness of Aboriginal people to turn to the civil system to address their disputes with government or to assert the rights they felt they continued to have. In addition to the legislative hurdles such provisions posed, First Nation people also saw the risks inherent in challenging decisions and enactments of a government who controlled the laws, the legal administration, and the appointment of judges to the courts they would have to use.

The Aboriginal experience with the civil courts generally reinforced that view. For example, in the leading court decision from the nineteenth century of *St. Catharine's Milling v. The Queen,* the Judicial Committee of the Privy Council placed serious limitations on the nature of Aboriginal title and entrenched into law the view that Crown sovereignty held a superior and overriding position.[62] This was a case about whether the federal government had the right to issue lumber permits in surrendered territory. The Province of Ontario argued that it controlled land surrendered to the Crown by Indians through Treaty. The court held, in the absence of any Aboriginal participation, that Aboriginal title to their lands was granted to the Indians by the Royal Proclamation of 1763, and existed only at the will of the Crown. Aboriginal title the courts held was merely a "personal and usufructuary right"—meaning that it was only a right to use—and was not equivalent to legal title. Because the case was primarily about timber permits, the only parties appearing in the case were those for the federal and provincial governments and the milling company. Evidence from Aboriginal people was not present. This very narrow legal view remained the law for over eighty years.

The decision of the Supreme Court of Canada in *Calder v. The Queen* in 1973 changed everything.[63] In that decision, the court recognized the legal validity of Aboriginal title but was divided on the question of whether it still existed in British Columbia. It was a landmark case in more ways than one. It represented not only a shift in legal thinking; it also caused Aboriginal leaders and their advisers to think about the possibility that perhaps the courts, under the leadership of the Supreme Court, were prepared to rethink some of their earlier limiting legal precedents. Subsequent decisions have affirmed that confidence, but there was little reason for any confidence in the early years.

At one level, residential school litigation could be defined as a success story because it produced the largest class action and settlement in Canadian history with over $4 billion being paid out to residential school Survivors under the terms of a court-approved settlement. Despite the magnitude of the settlement, the performance of the legal system is less effective than it may seem. The residential school litigation was extremely complex, expensive, and lengthy. Even in cases where defendants decided to settle, Survivor's faced challenges and possible re-victimization in order to assert their claims. For example, Survivors sometimes had to endure insensitive questioning or adversarial cross-examination in pretrial discoveries where judges are not present to prevent the harassment of witnesses. As in the criminal justice system, the Survivors often felt they were put on trial and re-victimized by residential school litigation.

Some of the failings of the civil justice system can be seen in the case of one convicted abuser. William Starr was the administrator of the Gordon's residential school, north of Regina. A number of criminal investigations involved allegations against Starr between 1968 and his retirement in 1984. During that time, the school was administered by the Government of Canada. In 1993, Starr was sentenced to four and a half years for sexually assaulting ten boys at the school.[64]

Subsequently, hundreds of civil lawsuits were commenced by former students of the Gordon's school against Canada and against Starr. Given the criminal convictions, it might be expected that these cases would be relatively simple to conclude. However, these cases imposed further hardships on Survivors.

## Higher standards of proof

Survivors in civil litigation should only have been required to prove that they were sexually abused on a "balance of probabilities"—in other words, that it was more likely than not that they had been sexually abused. This civil standard is much lower than the "beyond a reasonable doubt" standard used in criminal trials. However, in practice, civil courts often appear to apply higher standards of proof in cases where sexual abuse is alleged.

Minor inconsistencies in Survivors' accounts led to the dismissal of many claims. A thirty-two-year-old member of the Key First Nation in Saskatchewan claimed he was sexually assaulted by William Starr at the Gordon's school in 1968.[65] By the time of this civil suit, Starr had already pleaded guilty to ten criminal charges. Yet, at the civil trial, Starr denied some of the specifics of the allegations but also "acknowledged that he cannot now remember all the children he had sexual contact with over the 16 years he was at Gordon's. He says there could have been hundreds of victims."[66] The plaintiff was subject to an adversarial pretrial discovery process in which civil litigants (through their lawyers) are allowed to ask each other questions under oath without a judge being present, but with their answers recorded for possible use in the civil trial. The plaintiff was subjected to this difficult process first in 1997, then again in 1999, and for a final time in 2000.

Because of inconsistencies in the details of his testimony at trial and in the previous discovery examinations, the trial judge found that the plaintiff was not credible. The judge reached this conclusion on the basis that the head injury and addictions suffered by the plaintiff likely contributed to the inconsistencies in his testimony. The judge said, "I am unable to accept his evidence as proof of the events described."[67] He added, "I do not find the plaintiff's evidence to be assisted in any way by Starr's failure to recall, nor by his willingness to say anything is possible."[68] This case demonstrates one of the principal difficulties that former students faced.

## Vicarious liability

In some of the William Starr cases that went to trial, Starr was held liable for sexual abuse and Canada was held "vicariously liable" for his actions. Vicarious liability means that one defendant, such as the government, is legally responsible for the fault of another defendant, such as Starr, on the basis that the second defendant acted under the direction or control of the first. Vicarious liability was the most frequent basis on which the federal government and the churches were held liable for sexual abuse in the schools, as opposed to being held directly responsible for the harms that resulted from the abuse. Residential school Survivors benefitted from judicial expansions of the vicarious liability of organizations during the time period of the litigation.[69]

In the case of William Starr, Canada generally conceded that it was vicariously liable for the actions of its federally appointed school administrator. This approach was efficient, but it avoided determining whether Canada or the churches were independently at fault for the harms that Survivors suffered at residential school. It created the impression that what happened to Aboriginal children at residential schools was the result of the government and churches making mistakes by hiring pedophiles and by giving them responsibility over the children.

The vicarious liability theory was consistent with the "bad apple" theory that focused on the criminal behaviour of a few administrators within the schools as opposed to the intrinsic harm caused by the residential schools themselves. It fed into public perceptions that the problem of residential schools was that a few pedophiles were allowed to prey on children, as opposed to recognizing and acknowledging that residential schools themselves were part of a larger genocidal attack on Aboriginal culture.

## Statutes of limitation

Limitation periods allow defendants to have cases dismissed if too much time has elapsed. Although a statute of limitation can protect a defendant from a civil lawsuit, it can also have the effect of denying a plaintiff an opportunity to have the truth of the allegation determined on its merits or to receive compensation for a wrong.

The courts do not automatically apply a statute-of-limitation defence. It has to be raised by the defendant. The Law Commission of Canada, in its 2000 report on responding to child abuse in institutions, recommended that the federal government should not rely on statute-of-limitations defences.[70] This recognized that the federal government is a unique litigant, unlike individual or even a corporate defendants, because it can use public funds derived from taxes to pay damages. It also keeps records longer than most defendants because of their historical significance and as such is in a better position to defend itself in historical litigation after the time limit in a statute of limitation has passed.

The federal government possessed many of the documents that would establish whether allegations about long ago events were accurate. This is especially true in the Aboriginal context where the Truth and Reconciliation Commission itself has discovered that the federal government has a wealth of documents about residential schools that were not always disclosed to this Commission as fully and promptly as they should have been. Nevertheless, the Government of Canada, as well as the churches, has frequently and successfully raised statute-of-limitations defences in residential school litigation. Canadian courts applied statutes of limitations to bar many claims made by residential school Survivors relating to loss of language, culture, and family relations. Some courts even applied statutes of limitations to bar claims relating to sexual abuse. For example, the Manitoba Court of Appeal concluded in a 2001 residential school case that the Oblates had "a vested right to be immune from claims 30 years after the respondents left the school." It stressed that it would be unfair for the Oblates "to have the sword of Damocles hanging over their head forever" and that it was up to the legislature to intervene "if societal standards of the past are later regarded as unacceptable or unjust in the eyes of a new generation."[71] The next year, the Manitoba legislature amended the *Limitation of Actions Act* so that it would not apply to actions based on assaults if they were of a sexual nature or other assaults if the plaintiff was dependent on one of the persons alleged to have committed the abuse.[72]

Not all legislative reforms during this era were as enlightened. Alberta enacted a ten-year ultimate limitation period that would apply regardless of when a cause of action was reasonably discoverable.[73] This forced many Survivors to rush to file residential school claims.[74] Some provinces, such as British Columbia, only provided exemptions from statutes of limitations for childhood sexual abuse, and the BC Court of Appeal refused to extend the exemption for childhood sexual abuse to other forms of abuse of children.[75]

The early civil cases involving William Starr all focused on sexual abuse even though Survivors were concerned about a much broader range of harms that they suffered at residential school. Saskatchewan's *Limitations of Actions Act* provided that no limitation periods applied to claims relating to "misconduct of a sexual nature."[76] This meant that it was easier and sometimes necessary for lawyers representing the plaintiffs to focus on sexual misconduct rather than other matters.

26) We call upon federal, provincial, and territorial governments to review and amend their respective statutes of limitations to ensure that they conform with the principle that governments and other entities cannot rely on limitation defences to defend legal actions of historical abuse brought by Aboriginal people.

## Third-party claims against Aboriginal bands

Canada employed aggressive litigation tactics in some of the cases arising from William Starr's abuse of students. In two instances, the Attorney General of Canada sought and was granted permission to make a third-party claim asserting that the plaintiff's own First Nation (the Gordon First Nation) was responsible for the abuse by sending children to the residential school and having an advisory board for the school.[77] This defence strategy not only added additional expense and delay to the litigation but sought to blame a First Nation that was itself victimized by the residential school.

## The "crumbling skull" argument

Even in cases where Canada accepted vicarious liability for sexual abuse, the Survivors faced difficulties in establishing damages. The Attorney General of Canada had considerable success with so-called "crumbling skull" arguments. These arguments assert that while the Survivors experienced difficulties in their lives, these difficulties were not sufficiently related to being sexually abused in the schools to be compensable. The argument was that Survivors were already damaged before they came to the schools. They had "crumbling skulls" and would have experienced difficulties, such as unemployment, addictions, and imprisonment, even if they had not been abused in the schools.[78]

In one William Starr case, the trial judge reduced a successful plaintiff's damages for loss of earnings by 50% on the basis that his troubled family life meant he would have made less than an average worker even if Starr had not sexually abused him. The judge stated,

> The plaintiff was raised in poverty. He was the youngest of eight children born to an alcoholic mother. He never knew his father (apparently all his siblings had different fathers). His mother was unable to care for her children and, consequently, the plaintiff was removed from her care and placed in the student residence ... He attended several different schools and was introduced to alcohol and drugs at an early age by his peers. His siblings have all had problems with drugs and/or alcohol and difficulty in holding employment. Many do not have a high school education and none have post-secondary education.[79]

The court did not appear to consider the possibility that the life and home situation upon which it relied to reduce the plaintiff's damages may have themselves, been the result of residential school experiences, or past government actions. This approach to damages essentially blamed the victim and his family for many of the problems that the victim experienced.

## Re-victimization

Several of the Starr cases that were settled still resulted in adversarial litigation about the terms of the settlement. In 1998, Canada successfully opposed paying for treatments for a number of plaintiffs even though the treatment expenses had been capped by the settlement at $15,000, and even though a therapist mutually approved by Canada and the plaintiff had proposed the treatment. The rejected treatment plans included those that would have provided money for post-secondary education, alcohol addiction treatment,[80] and a fitness club membership.[81] The rejection of these proposed treatments as luxuries unrelated to the harms also fed into media and public perceptions that the Survivors were abusing the system. The courts at times took very narrow approaches to the harms caused by residential schools by, for example, dismissing alcohol addiction treatment as not related to the admitted abuse that occurred.

Even when the courts approved treatment plans, they demonstrated distrust that the Survivors would abuse the funds that Canada had agreed to pay by specifying in detail what sort of payments would be allowed to cover travel and accommodation costs. In such cases, the Canadian legal system remained a colonial and an intrusive presence in the lives of the Survivors that frustrated reasonable healing attempts.

## Breach of fiduciary and statutory duty

Survivors brought a wide variety of different legal claims in their residential school litigation. Breach of fiduciary duty was often alleged because of the long-standing trust relationship between Aboriginal people and the Crown as well as the dependency of the children in the schools. This cause of action also had the advantage of avoiding prescription periods. The courts have recognized a distinct fiduciary duty designed to protect the relationship between the Crown and Aboriginal peoples. Claims for breach of fiduciary duty had the potential to highlight how the schools betrayed Aboriginal children, highlighting the fact that those abused in the schools were children and they were Aboriginal and that the government and the churches put their own interests in assimilation, indoctrination, and saving money before the interests of the Aboriginal children. However, the courts frequently refused to find breach of fiduciary duty. Judges noted that litigants were unable to prove there was any intentional dishonesty on the part of those who held the fiduciary duty.[82]

Another claim of liability that was frequently dismissed by the courts was that of direct or statutory duty. Lawyers for the plaintiffs claimed that Canada had a direct duty that it could not delegate or hand off to the churches with respect to the treatment of the students. The statutory duty approach would emphasize that the government was directly at fault for failing to protect the children in the schools and not simply vicariously responsible for the wrongdoing of individual wrongdoers employed in the schools. However, claims based on breach of fiduciary and statutory duty frequently failed.[83]

## Denying loss of family, language, and culture

The courts were reluctant to recognize claims that Survivors made seeking compensation for loss of family, language, and culture. Often these claims were dismissed on the basis that they had been brought too late and that statute of limitation defences applied to these claims, in a way that they did not apply to claims of sexual and sometimes serious physical abuse.

The Alberta courts dismissed such claims and the Ontario Court of Appeal found that children of Survivors of residential schools could not bring claims under the *Family Law Reform Act* because it did not apply retroactively to the schools.[84] The eventual settlement of the litigation was limited to claims made by the living Survivors of the schools. One British Columbia court specifically noted that it was "not here assessing damages for the cultural destruction suffered by native peoples."[85]

Considering that one element of the *UN Convention on Genocide* involves recognizing that the forcible removal of children from one group to another group for the purpose of wiping out the racial identity of the children is a crime, it is difficult to understand why courts have not been more willing to recognize at least intentional acts of cultural and racial destruction or deprivation as a compensable tort.

## Denying loss of Aboriginal and Treaty rights

The creation and operation of residential schools also constituted a breach of Treaty rights, which recognized that education was important for Aboriginal people but was to be provided on reserves and on the terms that Aboriginal communities desired. Treaty 1, for example, provides that, "Her Majesty agrees to maintain a school on each reserve hereby made, whenever the Indians of the reserve should desire it."[86] Treaty 3, Treaty 5, and Treaty 6 all provide that "Her Majesty agrees to maintain schools for instruction in such reserves hereby made as to her Government of her Dominion of Canada may seem advisable, whenever the Indians of the reserve shall desire it."[87]

Despite such clear language, claims relating to breach of Aboriginal and Treaty rights did not have much success in the courts. In a number of cases, the courts ruled that Aboriginal and Treaty rights could not be positively asserted by individuals.[88] This approach had the effect of eroding the power of Aboriginal and Treaty rights as constitutional rights. Other Canadians are able to assert constitutional rights in individual proceedings for damages, but by classifying Aboriginal and Treaty rights as collective rights, the courts were able to deny individual claims based on them.

## Class actions

In a class-action lawsuit one party sues as a representative of a larger 'class' of people. Such suits are seen to serve a public benefit because they reduce overall costs by eliminating the need for repetitive hearings, allow for greater access to the courts, and can modify the behaviour of actual and potential wrongdoers.[89] Changes in Canadian law in the 1990s created the opportunity for Survivors to make use of class-action lawsuits to pursue their claims for compensation. As late as 1991, such suits were permitted only in Québec.[90] Ontario adopted legislation allowing for class-action suits in 1992.[91] British Columbia's class-action legislation came into force in 1995.[92] Alberta adopted its legislation in 2003. In the following years, most other provinces adopted similar legislation.[93]

In October 1998, a group of Survivors of the Mohawk Institute in Brantford, Ontario, filed a statement of claim in the Ontario Superior Court on behalf of all students who attended the school between the years 1922 to 1969, as well as their families.[94] The plaintiffs, who were led by Marlene Cloud, claimed $2.3 billion in damages from the federal government, the General Synod of the Anglican Church, the New England Company (the missionary society that operated the school), and the local Anglican diocese, for the sustained, systematic program of physical, emotional, spiritual, and cultural abuse they suffered.[95] Cloud and the other Survivors claimed damages for a breach of fiduciary duties, breaches of the *Family Law Act*, loss of culture and language, and breach of Treaty and Aboriginal rights.[96]

In June 2000, Charles Baxter Sr., Elijah Baxter, and others filed a class-action lawsuit against the federal government in the Ontario Superior Court. The statement of claim sought damages for negligence, breach of statutory duties under the *Indian Act,* and breach of Treaty obligations.[97] Since it included claims on behalf of students who attended residential schools throughout Canada, it was often referred to as the "national class action."[98] Over time, Survivor associations and litigants from around the country joined the Baxter class-action suit.

In October 2001, Justice Roland J. Haines of the Ontario Superior Court declined to certify the *Cloud* case, saying that that the experiences of the students were too diverse to constitute a representative class, that many of the claims would be barred by statute of limitations provisions, and that the plaintiffs failed to establish that a class-action suit was the preferable procedure for their claims.[99] The decision was upheld by the Ontario Divisional Court.[100] In December 2004, however, the Ontario Court of Appeal overturned the earlier rulings and certified the *Cloud* case.[101] The Court of Appeal stressed that that class actions were preferable to individual actions because they would increase "access to justice."[102] This was a very important decision and the Supreme Court's refusal to hear an appeal of this decision played an important role in encouraging the government and the churches to settle all of the claims through a national class action settlement agreement.

## Lawyer fees

Throughout the civil litigation period, many residential school Survivors were unable to afford the legal fees required to file suit against the federal government. As a result, individual Survivors were usually required to access legal services on a contingency basis, which meant that they would not pay their lawyers unless they were successful in obtaining compensation. In most residential school litigation, the contingency fee arrangements provided that lawyers would receive at least 30% of any compensation awarded to the Survivors. Contingency fees had traditionally been prohibited in Canada because of a concern that lawyers might act unethically if they had a financial stake in the litigation. These restrictions were eased in many jurisdictions to increase access to justice. This change combined with the new availability of class actions made residential school litigation economically feasible.

The Commission acknowledges that residential school litigation would likely not have happened without the possibility of contingency fees that compensated lawyers for investing in the cases of Survivors who were unable to pay legal fees. In most cases, publicly funded legal aid or any other form of public funding for such litigation was not available. However, the payment of legal fees became one of the most difficult issues in reaching the settlement. The combination or rules governing contingency fees and class actions had provided lawyers with an incentive both before and after the settlement to represent as many Survivors as possible, thereby increasing their legal fees. In some, but by no means all, cases this resulted in Survivors not being well understood or served by their own lawyers.

There were numerous reports of aggressive, damaging, and sometimes unethical and illegal tactics employed by some lawyers in recruiting residential school Survivors as clients. Several lawyers were the subject of law society complaints and reprimands about the way they recruited and represented residential school Survivors and collected legal fees. In the end, the Indian Residential Schools Settlement Agreement provided a process under which one firm, the Merchant Law Group, would receive between $25 and $40 million in fees.[103] The Law Society of Saskatchewan, in a decision later upheld by the Court of Appeal, reprimanded Tony Merchant in connection with a misleading solicitation letter that suggested that the Survivors "had nothing to lose."

In late January 2015, the Government of Canada filed a suit against the Merchant Law Group alleging that the group claimed millions of dollars in fees that were "intentionally inflated, duplicated or simply fabricated." The suit also alleges that some individual lawyers billed for more than twenty-four hours of work in a single day.[104]

## Response of the law societies

Although many lawyers worked hard for Survivors and tried to be sensitive, some lawyers took advantage of their clients and this abuse simply added to the legacy of residential schools. It also has influenced the attitudes of Aboriginal people towards the Canadian legal system.

In August of 2000, the Canadian Bar Association recognized some of the difficulties that aggressive and culturally insensitive solicitations created for Survivors and enacted the following resolution:

> WHEREAS survivors of Aboriginal residential schools are often vulnerable and in need of healing as well as legal assistance;
>
> WHEREAS the identity of persons who attended Aboriginal residential schools is available without their consent;
>
> WHEREAS survivors of Aboriginal residential schools wanting to seek compensation from the Government of Canada and the churches involved should have legal assistance which takes into account the potential impact on their well-being when they begin to address their abuse;
>
> BE IT RESOLVED THAT:
>
> 1. The Canadian Bar Association urge each law society to adopt the following guidelines for recommended conduct for lawyers acting or seeking to act for survivors of Aboriginal residential schools, that recognizes their vulnerability and need for healing:
>
> (a) Lawyers should not initiate communications with individual survivors of Aboriginal residential schools to solicit them as clients or inquire as to whether they were sexually assaulted;
>
> (b) Lawyers should not accept retainers until they have met in person with the client, whenever reasonably possible;
>
> (c) Lawyers should recognize that survivors had control taken from their lives when they were children and therefore, as clients, should be given as much control as possible over the direction of their case;

(d) Lawyers should recognize that survivors may be seriously damaged from their experience, which may be aggravated by having to relive their childhood abuse, and that healing may be a necessary component of any real settlement for these survivors. Lawyers should therefore be aware of available counselling resources for these clients to ensure that they have opportunities for healing prior to testifying;

(e) Lawyers should recognize that damage to the survivors of Aboriginal residential schools may well include cultural damages from being cut off from their own society, and should endeavour to understand their clients' cultural roots;

(f) Lawyers should recognize that survivors are often at risk of suicide or violence towards others and should ensure appropriate instruction and training for their own employees, including available referrals in time of crisis.[105]

27) We call upon the Federation of Law Societies of Canada to ensure that lawyers receive appropriate cultural competency training, which includes the history and legacy of residential schools, the *United Nations Declaration on the Rights of Indigenous Peoples*, Treaties and Aboriginal rights, Indigenous law, and Aboriginal–Crown relations. This will require skills-based training in intercultural competency, conflict resolution, human rights, and anti-racism.

28) We call upon law schools in Canada to require all law students to take a course in Aboriginal people and the law, which includes the history and legacy of residential schools, the *United Nations Declaration on the Rights of Indigenous Peoples*, Treaties and Aboriginal rights, Indigenous law, and Aboriginal–Crown relations. This will require skills-based training in intercultural competency, conflict resolution, human rights, and anti-racism.

## Slow progress towards compensation

Despite a variety of barriers posed by the legal system, slow progress was being made to win justice for Survivors of residential schools. This progress resulted from a combination of legal and political processes and culminated in the negotiation of the Indian Residential School Settlement Agreement in 2006.

### Alternative Dispute Resolution

In 1998 and 1999, there were discussions involving Survivors, Aboriginal organizations, and representatives of the government and the churches that produced a set of principles to guide twelve different pilot initiatives, called Alternative Dispute Resolution Projects (ADR). The principles for the pilot ADR stressed the need for a sensitive and safe approach that would promote "healing, closure and reconciliation." It could include monetary compensation, but also a broad range of remedies including healing, memorialization, and prevention programs.[106] Health supports would be provided in recognition that discussing what happened in residential schools was traumatic for many Survivors.

In 2001, the federal government created Indian Residential Schools Resolution Canada as a federal department. It was designed to oversee the ADR process. Under the proposed program, the government required that those claiming injury lasting more than six weeks submit many documents related to their income, treatment, school, and correctional records. The program limited the relief available by not providing compensation for loss of culture or language. It graded injury on a point scale and provided caps on compensation of between $195,000 and $245,000 with the cost of future care being capped at $25,000. Those who claimed injury lasting less than six weeks would receive a maximum of $1,500, which could be raised by additional amounts to a maximum of $3,500 if aggravating circumstances were established.[107]

A report produced by the Assembly of First Nations (AFN), released in 2004, was highly critical of the proposed formula: "This cap ... ignores the effects of the residential schools on loss of language, culture, family life, parenting and secondary harms to spouses and descendants. There is no provision to recognize or compensate for emotional and spiritual abuse, neglect, forced labour or educational deficits, or their consequences."[108] The report advocated a more flexible process that "would be but a part of a holistic process with a truth-sharing component which would be created in consultation with survivors, survivor's families, secondary victims of residential school abuse, First Nation communities, religious entities, Canada and non-Aboriginal Canadians."[109]

The report expressed concerns that the caps on compensation were below some awards provided to non-Aboriginal people. It proposed five principles for the equitable settlement of claims:

1. Be inclusive, fair, accessible, and transparent.
2. Offer a holistic and comprehensive response recognizing and addressing all the harms committed in and resulting from residential schools.
3. Respect human dignity and equality and racial and gender equality.
4. Contribute towards reconciliation and healing.
5. Do no harm to Survivors and their families.[110]

The report drew attention to an important gap in the government's ADR program—namely, the absence of an Aboriginal perspective. The report stated that true reconciliation and healing would be possible if the AFN's recommended changes to the ADR program were followed.[111]

The AFN report recommended a "two-prong strategy." One prong would focus on compensation and the other on "truth-telling, healing and public education." The compensation part would include "a significant lump sum award" to every person who attended residential school "to compensate for the loss of language and culture," combined with another sum tied to each year or part of the year spent in residential school to "recognize emotional harms, including the loss of family life and parental guidance, neglect, depersonalization, denial of a proper education, forced labour, inferior nutrition and health care, and growing up in a climate of fear, apprehension, and ascribed inferiority. As a rule, no adjudication should be necessary for these awards to be made."[112]

The second truth-telling and healing track would include "a voluntary truth-sharing and reconciliation process designed to investigate the nature, causes, context and consequences of all the harms resulting from the residential schools legacy. This would include, but not be limited to, harms to individual Survivors, First Nations communities, Survivors' families, the future generations, culture, spirituality, language and relationships between and among all parties involved."[113] This recommendation, like those made by groups of Survivors in the early 1990s and subsequently by the Royal Commission on Aboriginal Peoples in 1996 focused on the collective harms of residential schools and collective responses to those harms—a significant contrast to the relentlessly individualistic focus of the litigation that excluded compensation for students who had died and for the children of Survivors.

The inadequacies of the ADR process were also revealed in hearings conducted in February 2005 by the House of Common's Standing Committee on Aboriginal Affairs and Northern Development. They heard from Flora Merrick, an eighty-eight-year-old Elder whose $1,500 ADR award was being appealed by the federal government. The issue was whether she should be compensated for "being strapped so severely that my arms were black and blue for several weeks" and for being "locked in a dark room for about two weeks" after she ran away from Portage la Prairie residential school. Merrick explained that she was willing

> to accept the $1,500 award, not as a fair and just settlement, but only due to my age, health, and financial situation. I wanted some closure to my residential school experience, and I could use the money, even as small as it was. I am very angry and upset that the government would be so mean-spirited as to deny me even this small amount of compensation ... I'm very upset and angry, not only for myself, but also for all residential school survivors.[114]

The Committee recognized the urgency of the matter and noted that "on average some 30 to 50 former students die each week uncompensated and bearing the grief of their experience to the grave." The Committee condemned the ADR process unanimously and in very strong terms, concluding that it "regrets the manner with which the Government has administered the Indian Residential Schools Claims program" and that the ADR process should be terminated. It recommended that "on an urgent basis, with consideration for the frailty and short life expectancy of the former students," the federal government should move to court-supervised negotiations with former students to secure a court-approved settlement.[115]

## The Settlement and its aftermath

On May 30, 2005, the federal government appointed former Supreme Court Justice Frank Iacobucci as its chief negotiator. He met with representatives from Aboriginal communities, church groups, the federal government, and various law firms. Six months later, on November 10, 2005, an agreement in principle between the parties was reached.[116] The details of the settlement were finalized and approved by the federal cabinet on May 10, 2006.[117] As a result, the thousands of legal claims made against the federal government and the churches would be settled, although individual Survivors would be able to opt out of the settlement of their class-action claims. The settlement followed the broad outline of what was recommended in 2004 in the AFN report. All Survivors would be eligible for a Common Experience Payment (CEP) based on verified attendance at one of the residential schools listed in the settlement. Claimants would receive a base payment of $10,000 for attendance, plus $3,000 for each additional year or part year of attendance.

In addition to the CEP based on attendance at a residential school, there was an Independent Assessment Process (IAP) available for those who suffered neglect, or serious sexual or physical assaults such as severe beating, whipping, and second-degree burning at the schools. This process would include compensation for assaults by other students if there was a lack of reasonable supervision. The settlement contained a points system where points were assigned both on the type and frequency of assaults. The categories used were "serious dysfunction," "some dysfunction," "continued detrimental impact," "some detrimental impact," and "modest detrimental impact." Additional points could be awarded for difficulties in obtaining and retaining employment and an inability to undertake or complete education resulting in under-employment or unemployment. Verbal abuse and racist acts, humiliation, and the witnessing of violence to others were also recognized as aggravating factors deserving of additional compensation points. The total number of points awarded to a claimant determined the amount of the claimant's award. The maximum IAP payment was $275,000, but up to an additional $250,000 could be awarded in more complex cases.

The settlement included an IAP application form. IAP adjudicators were instructed in the settlement to take an inquisitorial, truth-seeking approach in which they (and not the lawyers) questioned the witnesses. Similarly, the adjudicators (and not the lawyers) would commission expert reports. The adjudicators would be chosen not only for their legal expertise but knowledge about Aboriginal culture and history and sexual and physical abuse issues. Support persons, counselling from Health Canada, and cultural ceremonies would be provided at the hearings. It was anticipated that decisions would be speedily issued. The process would be private rather than public and it would make room for support persons and cultural ceremonies often not allowed in courts.

The settlement also had collective dimensions. In addition to compensation for individual Survivors in the form of the CEP and IAP processes, the settlement provided a $125 million endowment to the Aboriginal Healing Foundation "to support the objective of addressing the healing needs of Aboriginal People affected by the Legacy of Indian Residential Schools, including the intergenerational impacts, by supporting holistic and community-based healing to address needs of individuals, families and communities."[118] An additional $60 million of the settlement funds would also be devoted to a Truth and Reconciliation Commission "to contribute to truth, healing and reconciliation," through hearings and reports as necessary, with an objective of creating a permanent and public record of the "legacy of the residential schools."[119]

The settlement would also involve the termination of a number of class-action proceedings that the courts had authorized. Consequently, it was necessary for courts in most provinces and territories to consider whether the settlement was a fair resolution of the claims and in particular whether it adequately protected the interests of all the class members. After some modifications, court approval was eventually given in all nine jurisdictions.[120]

Survivors and other Aboriginal people were aware of some of the shortcomings in the settlement. Phil Fontaine, in his affidavit filed in support of the settlement, described how his mother, Agnes Mary Fontaine, was taken from her family when she was seven years old and forced to attend Fort Alexander residential school from 1919 to 1928. He described how his mother "suffered by being removed from the care of her parents, family, and community, and not being allowed to speak her native language, or practice traditional spiritual ways. She also suffered sexual, physical and emotional abuse, and was given inadequate food, health care and education."[121] Chief Fontaine, who acted as the executor of his mother's estate after she died in 1988, recognized that "it is tragic that so many have died during this fight to have the wrongs that were perpetuated on Aboriginal people through residential schools acknowledged."[122] He recognized that his mother, along with other deceased former students, would receive no monetary compensation in the settlement. Nevertheless, he stated that he believed that the agreement "honors the memory of those who have already died through the commemoration and truth and reconciliation initiatives" in the settlement. He concluded, "I do not believe that we could have reached an agreement that would have provided more for the deceased and that compromise was required in order to ensure that we could achieve some level of compensation for the living."[123]

## Exclusions from the Settlement

The claims of many former residential school students were excluded from the settlement agreement. Rosalie Webber told the Commission that "it was very frustrating" that schools in Newfoundland and Labrador were excluded. She also commented that even if she pursued litigation she was concerned that no money would go to her children. She explained,

> And I realized how my children have suffered because their mother was a survivor of residential school. Through no fault of their own they suffered. And their children will suffer, 'cause it will take at least generations before we come to terms with the anger that we've passed on, the negativity that we've passed on. Now that my health is failing, I want to make a documentary of this so that if my children want to do research, or my grandchildren, or maybe seven generations from now, that there might be somewhere a record of the fact that I stood up.... Our children and our children's children have to stand up and see that this not happen again. And that starts with me.[124]

Jayko Allooloo told the TRC Inuit Sub-Commission that, although he received some Common Experience Payment, he had been unable to access the IAP process with respect to sexual abuse suffered while going to school in Ottawa.

> They told me that wasn't a residential school and they can't help me ... I wrote down my story of what happened to me in Ottawa. I gave all my school records to the lawyer and he told me "The place you stayed in Ottawa was not a residential school so we can't help you."[125]

Litigation has been commenced on behalf of some students who were excluded from the Settlement Agreement. It is expected that the federal government and the churches will aggressively litigate the issues as they have in the past, even though there has been a relatively clear statement of the legal liability questions raised in the earlier class-action cases. To continue to put Survivors through an aggressive litigation process when so much has already been resolved in earlier cases seems both unnecessary and punitive. The Commission recognizes that there may be valid liability questions that need to be addressed, such as the liability related to placing children in hostels or foster homes in order to be educated in urban or other public schools in the South as opposed to residences attached to or affiliated with schools. There may also be questions about the government's liability concerning those children sent to a particular residential school managed by others but not by the government. It is noted by the Commission that, in addition to the 139 schools included in the settlement agreement, individual Survivors have asked and been denied approval for compensation for having been sent to more than one thousand other schools.

For such a large number of Survivors to be excluded from the settlement and its benefits is to make them feel excluded from the apology and from the process of reconciliation. In the long term, it is in their, and in Canada's, best interests to address this issue as quickly and as harmlessly as possible.

29) We call upon the parties and in particular, the federal government, to work collaboratively with plaintiffs not included in the Indian Residential Schools Settlement Agreement to have disputed legal issues determined expeditiously on an agreed set of facts.

## Survivor perspectives on the Settlement

It is important to appreciate Survivor perspectives on the settlement both to understand the full legacy of residential schools and to understand if there are remaining issues and grievances that may provide a barrier to reconciliation. Leona Bird attended St. Albans school in Prince Albert, Saskatchewan. She explained to the Commission how the settlement for being sexually abused in residential schools did little to alleviate the long-lasting effects on her and her family. She told the Commission that the residential school

> took away my happiness. It took everything, everything that I had known for the first four years of my life at home, love, understanding, and being taken care of, and never being hit, or anything. But ever since, ever since I learned how I was treated in school that, that really build up that anger, and I can't seem to get rid of it ... To this very day, I haven't changed. My sister prays for and I pray. That's all I can say. This is how the Indian residential school taught me how to live my life in a cruel, wicked way. I can't take back what I've done in my lifetime. I was forever being charged with assault, sent to jail 18 months at a time.[126]

Myrtle Ward stressed that no amount of money can repair the harm she suffered in residential school. She told the Commission, "They can give us all the money they want, but it's not gonna compensate for what happened to peoples' lives."[127]

Geraldine Bob attended residential school in Kamloops and later went on to become a teacher. She told the Commission at Fort Simpson that the money

> doesn't recreate society, it doesn't recreate extended family and everything it stood for. You can't recreate intergenerational knowledge that was taken from our people. You know I'll never get those stories now; yeah from my grand-

parents and my parents. They're lost, they're gone. You can't recreate a loving way; all of that was lost. And that pain and suffering will continue well into the future.[128]

## Survivor perspectives on the Independent Assessment Process

A number of Survivors have expressed concerns to the Commission that their IAP and other damage awards were considerably reduced by lawyers' fees. Joseph Martin Larocque attended the Beauval residential school. He told the Commission,

> I was mad at the government for what they do to us, so … I went through the court process. I went through the Department of Justice through the courts, and you know they, they gave me a little bit of money. They gave me a total of $33,000. What I didn't know was that the lawyer, the lawyer just to take my case got $15,000, and then he took another 11 from me, so he got about 27 and I got about 21, so, but, like, that's how it goes, yeah.[129]

Mabel Brown told the Commission her IAP payments amounted to about $25,000—an amount she observed was not enough for a house or even a vehicle and that the legal fees in the case amounted to $10,500. She recognized that the litigation process meant that Survivors had "a hard time, each one of them who went and had to make it public. That was so awful for them, I thought."[130]

Marie Brown attended Sturgeon Landing Indian residential school. She told the Commission about the inadequacy of attempts made in the IAP system to classify the degree of harm suffered by Survivors. She explained,

> There's no difference if you're psychologically abused it's the worst, worst thing ever a person can ever go through. Because my feelings, you know, about abuse, abuses, we were verbally abused … I was psychologically abused. I mean psychologically messed up in my mind…. I felt like a reject, too, from everybody, even my family … And they, they can't tell me that sexually and physically abuse are more important than, than emotion. I, I don't believe that one bit, 'cause I went through is the same kind of a hurt that as they went through. There's no difference to me.[131]

Chief Theresa Hall, who attended residential school at Fort Albany, also expressed considerable anger at the categorization of sexual abuse used in her case and other cases of sexual abuse. She remarked,

> Sexual abuse to a degree, "two." That's bullshit. Sexual abuse is sexual abuse, you know. Touching when, when you're not wanted to be touched is an abuse of the child … If I were to find out that someone was, you know, doing that to

my child, my grandchild, I'd go ballistic, you know. There's no way you could stop me, and that's the anger that, that I still have. They would have to put me in jail, you know, and that'd make headlines, a former justice of the peace goes in jail, [*laughs*] you know.[132]

The overriding concern that Survivors expressed was to question whether the system actually gave them the justice they were looking for. Amelia Thomas attended Sechelt residential school. She said,

> You can't get justice. How are you gonna get justice when the people that did this to us are gone? … Like, they have us all apply for these statements and then our abuse … Like, I've been waiting 5 years now for my appeal, and it hasn't happened yet. And it's almost time for them to stop giving the money out to us. And they opened up all our wounds for what? To turn us all down? And some people are dying…. So, so, why did they do this to us, again? They hurt us again. They shouldn't go back on their word to us. They already hurt us. Stop hurting us.[133]

Some Survivors had their IAP claims disallowed outright. Darlene Thomas told us that after a "two-part" IAP hearing, "one before Christmas and finished it in January," she was denied. Thomas explained,

> They said it, it could not be true … I haven't even got a written document. The only thing that I got was I got an email from my lawyer saying they denied me, that they didn't believe me … I went home and I gathered up all of my residential school documents and I went up to the mountain and I burned it. I said this is my story, this is what happened to me. And I don't give a shit who believes me or who doesn't.[134]

## The overrepresentation of Aboriginal people in prison

Aboriginal people in this country are imprisoned at a rate far greater than non-Aboriginal Canadians. The reasons are complex, and understanding those reasons—and their relationship to the residential school experience—is essential to moving towards reconciliation.

For example, in 2011, Aboriginal people made up 4% of the Canadian population, yet they accounted for 28% of admissions to sentenced custody.[135] As recently as 2013, Aboriginal people constituted 23.2% of the federal inmate population. And since 2005–06, there has been a 43.5% increase in the Aboriginal population in federal prisons for those serving sentences of two years or more, as compared to a rise of 9.6% for non-Aboriginal inmates. One report indicates that from 2010 to 2013 the Prairie Region of the Correctional Service of Canada (primarily the provinces of Manitoba, Saskatchewan, and Alberta) accounted for 39.1% of all new federal inmates, and that

Aboriginal offenders comprised 46.4% of the Prairie Region inmate population. This included a majority of the prisoners at the Stony Mountain Institution in Manitoba (65.3% of inmates) and the Saskatchewan Penitentiary and the Edmonton Institution (63.9% of inmates).[136]

Of those admitted into provincial and territorial custody in 2011–12, Aboriginal females accounted for 43%, compared to 27% for Aboriginal males.[137] And in the same year, 49% of girls below the age of eighteen admitted to custody were Aboriginal, compared to 36% of males.[138]

When Aboriginal people are arrested and prosecuted, they are more likely to be sentenced to prison than non-Aboriginal people. In 2011–12, only 21% of those granted probation and conditional sentences were Aboriginal, yet Aboriginal people comprised 28% of those sentenced to prison.[139]

The situation for Aboriginal youth is even worse. In 1998–99, Aboriginal youth were 24% of sentenced admissions, but by 2011–12 they constituted 39% of sentenced admissions.[140]

Prison today is for many Aboriginal people what residential schools used to be: an isolating experience that removes Aboriginal people from their families and communities. They are violent places and often result in greater criminal involvement as some Aboriginal inmates, particularly younger ones, seek gang membership as a form of protection. Today's prisons may not institutionally disparage Aboriginal cultures and languages as aggressively as residential schools did, but racism in prisons is a significant issue. In addition, prisons can fail to provide cultural safety for Aboriginal inmates through neglect or marginalization. Many damaged people emerged from the residential schools; there is no reason to believe that the same is not true of today's prisons.

David Charleson, who attended the Christie school on Vancouver Island, explained that he has

> a record in jail so bad it's unreal, but it's all abuse charges, assault. I used to be happier when I went to jail. Talking to the guards, and they'd say, "You're back." And I'd say, "Yeah," said, "I'm in a safe place." I said, "It's more safe than the fuckin' residential school," pardon my language. "You know there's a lot of bad people here ... but you can't hit me.... I feel good in here." I said, "Yeah, I feel so good the government is so stupid putting us in here. They'll look after me more than the residential [school] did."[141]

Although jail may have been a safer place for David Charleson than residential school, it held terrors for Daniel Andre, who also attended residential school. He explained that after he left school

> everywhere I went ... everything I did, all the jobs I had, all the towns I lived in, all the people I met, always brought me back to, to being in residential school,

and being humiliated, and beaten, and ridiculed, and told I was a piece of garbage, I was not good enough, I was, like, a dog.... So one of the scariest things for me being in jail is being humiliated in front of everybody, being made, laughed at, and which they do often, 'cause they're just, like, that's just the way they are. And a lot of them are, like, survival of the fittest. And, like, the, if they, if, if, if you show weakness, they'll, they'll just pick on you even more, and whatever, and then I'm gay, and, oh, fuck, it's just too many things, like, and it's almost like why am I here? ... and I had to ... I became a, a, a bad person, I became a asshole. But I survived, and learnt all those things to survive.[142]

Raymond Blake-Nukon's attended residential school, as did his parents. He explained to the Commission at the Yukon Correctional Centre that,

this year I've been in jail for I think 21 years. This past Christmas was my 18th ... year in jail ... Every time I come to jail, it's for fighting ... I just wouldn't want any of my kids to go, like, even just see any violence that, like half the violence that I've been through, yeah. Yeah, I turned out to be a pretty violent guy. Up in the penitentiary, you know, did a few stabbings in there, and on the street. I'm surprised I never killed anybody yet. I don't want to kill anybody. So want to, want to get some help, and move on with my life.[143]

## The reasons for overrepresentation

Although some Aboriginal people have been wrongfully convicted of crimes that they did not commit, most are in jail for having committed some offence. The available evidence suggests that these offences are likely to be violent and are likely to involve alcohol or other drugs. Over half of those who had been convicted had been convicted of assault or sexual offences or driving offences, 24.2% had been convicted of theft, 11.3% had been convicted of drug offences, 8.1% had been convicted of robbery, and 4.8% had been convicted of murder.[144] There are higher rates of crime on reserve than off reserve.

The Commission cannot ignore these facts, as uncomfortable as they may be. We also need to look beyond the statistics to hear from the Survivors about the reasons why they committed offences. We must understand the reasons why those affected by the intergenerational legacy of residential schools commit crimes if we are to reduce offences among Aboriginal people and the growing crisis of Aboriginal overrepresentation in prison.

Willy Carpenter was forced to attend the Roman Catholic school in Aklavik, NWT. He recalled,

The RC Mission was the roughest place that I'd ever been in my life; the hostel, you know, that school. We'd get picked on, get into a lot of fights; I was very young but I learned how to fight. I had to protect myself. As I grew up, I kept that up. I got married, and without realizing what I was doing, I've been teaching my children what I know best; hardship, rough time ... I started serving time at a very young age; started going in jail. I was not even 17 years old when I went to jail. Lots of us; I met a lot of my school mates in jail ... All my boys are in jail; two of, two of my youngest ones, right now, are in jail; waiting for court. I blame myself for that ... The thing I do best, crime. I'm not proud of it. Now my boys are in there. I've been teaching them without realizing that I was teaching them; they learned it from me. It goes on and on; probably my kids will teach their kids the same thing I taught them; I don't know, who knows? Goes on and on and on; life goes on.[145]

Ruth Chapman attended a residential school in Manitoba where she was subject to physical abuse. She recalled that by fourteen years of age she had moved "to The Pas, went on the streets. I was, I was nominated for a leader for a gang. Yeah, by that time my heart was hard. This, this is when I got out of the residence." She recalled how the experience of violence made her violent:

I've learned through that rape, I have, I've, I've learned to have power over men. Because when that guy, when that, when that situation occurred, he had a knife, and, and but somehow I got my strength, and, and I, I, I kneed his back foot, and he fell back, and I was gonna, then I somehow I managed to get that knife from him, and, and then I almost jammed it into his throat, but I stopped, something made me stop, and then he knocked the wind out of me.... I fought, and that's, that's, that's where I, I began to look at men as wimps, disrespected them. When I get mad at a male, I would cut him up. 'Cause if you punch someone, it only hurts, what, five minutes, but then you demean them with your words, 'cause that's what I learned, right, 'cause if you get someone mad in residence, man, you were cut to pieces.... And so I learned that. Even my husband, you know, he experienced some of the effects. I was charged a couple of years ago for beating him up ... I was always scared because of that anger. I knew I had the power with that anger. So, basically that, I would fight on the streets, too, with men in, in The Pas, I would, yeah.[146]

Many Canadians may fail to understand how the present crisis of Aboriginal over-representation in prison is related to residential schools when many of the remaining Survivors are over fifty years of age. The answer lies in the intergenerational effects of the residential school experience that are passed on through families and often through the child welfare systems. Diana Lariviere was hit with the strap in residential school, and she saw her daughter using the same harsh techniques; "she'll just say, 'Mom, that's how you taught us.'"[147]

While some social science research supports the connection between the residential schools and the commission of criminal offences, there is a need for more Canadian data that examines this connection. In the absence of such data, the Commission has examined examples of Aboriginal offenders. The picture that emerges through court documents is one in which Aboriginal overrepresentation in prison can be directly connected to problems experienced by Aboriginal people whose roots are deep in the intergenerational legacy of residential schools. The list of such problems reads like a social minefield. It includes, poverty, addiction, abuse, racism, family violence, mental health, child welfare involvement, loss of culture, and an absence of parenting skills. And one of the least well-understood but most insidious afflictions borne by the inheritors of the residential school legacy is fetal alcohol spectrum disorder (FASD).

## Fetal alcohol spectrum disorder

According to the 2002–03 First Nations Regional Longitudinal Health Survey conducted by the First Nations Centre of the National Aboriginal Health Organization, Aboriginal adults have a higher rate of abstinence from alcohol than the general Canadian population. Rates of alcohol consumption also were lower. For example, in 2002–03 only 65.6% of First Nations people reported consuming alcohol, compared with 79.3% of the general population. Also in that year, rates of alcohol consumption were lower among First Nations females (61.7%) than among males (69.3%), and increased with age.[148] But for many Aboriginal people, alcohol consumption has devastating consequences.

Fetal alcohol spectrum disorder is a permanent brain injury caused when a mother's consumption of alcohol affects the fetus.[149] About 1% of Canadian children are born with some form of disability related to maternal alcohol consumption, but estimates suggest that 10% to 25% of Canadian prisoners have FASD. There is a growing consensus that people with FASD more frequently come into conflict with the law. A 2004 study that involved a sample of 415 patients diagnosed with FASD found that 60% of the adults sampled had come into contact with criminal justice systems as suspects or as charged accused.[150] A 2011 Canadian study found that offenders with FASD had much higher rates of criminal involvement than those without, including more youth and adult convictions.[151]

A study done for the Aboriginal Healing Foundation drew connections between the intergenerational trauma of residential schools, alcohol addictions, and FASD and concludes that the "residential school system contributed to the central risk factor involved, substance abuse, but also to factors shown to be linked to alcohol abuse, such as child and adult physical, emotional and sexual abuse, mental health problems and family dysfunction. The impact of residential schools can also be linked to risk factors for poor pregnancy outcomes among women who abuse alcohol, such as poor overall health, low levels of education and chronic poverty."[152]

The Aboriginal Corrections Unit of Corrections Canada has also sponsored research on FASD. A 2010 workshop concluded that,

Although FASD has not been documented in the Aboriginal community to have a greater incidence rate than that of other peoples, the fact remains that alcohol abuse in Aboriginal communities is a serious issue. Furthermore, the children and youth population of Aboriginal peoples is growing at a rate that exceeds non-Aboriginal population of Canada. It is fair to make an assumption that increasing numbers of young Aboriginal people are at greater risk of being born with FASD. Without the necessary prevention and interventions, diagnosis and treatment, it is also safe to assume that the secondary characteristics of FASD will be pronounced, including involvement in the mainstream criminal justice system.[153]

The workshop report went on to observe that "currently the justice system is set up to fail FASD-affected individuals—poor memory functions results in missed court appearances resulting in fail to appear charges."[154]

One problem, especially with adult offenders, is the difficulty of obtaining an FASD diagnosis. Obtaining such a diagnosis requires a long and costly process of multi-disciplinary referrals. Even if trial judges have been educated about the symptoms of FASD, they are generally unable to take notice of FASD without evidence of a diagnosis.[155] An expert panel, using a jury-style format and chaired by retired Supreme Court Justice Ian Binnie (known as the Binnie Jury) concluded in 2013 that "the individual with FASD is in a bind. No resources. No diagnosis. No evidence. No judicial notice. Therefore no fair and appropriate FASD–related accommodation is available within the usual rigours of the legal system."[156] The Binnie Jury recommended that exemptions be made available for offenders with FASD from mandatory sentences and restrictions on conditional sentences, an important subject to which we will return.[157]

Only a small minority of the judgments of criminal courts in Canada make clear connections between residential schools, FASD, and criminal offences. One particularly dramatic case involves C. L. K., a twelve-year-old Aboriginal girl in Manitoba who pleaded guilty to committing manslaughter as part of an unprovoked and severe fatal beating of a stranger who would not give cigarettes to her group. The judgment referred to a pre-sentencing report that indicated that the girl was one of seven children of parents who are "themselves victims, having suffered from their experience in foster homes and residential schools." The parents were described as incapable of parenting and this was clearly the case. The entire family had been involved with Child and Family Services since 1987 when the children were apprehended due to abandonment and parental alcohol abuse. The report described the family as in crisis:

> Of C. L. K.'s six siblings, four are known to Correctional Services and two have had gang involvement. C. L. K. herself has gang affiliations. As an example of the total absence of parental guidance the report refers to C. L. K.'s story about how she was first introduced to crack cocaine. She apparently bought the highly

addictive drug from a friend of her brother's who came to the house selling it. When she didn't know how to use it her mother showed her how.[158]

C. L. K. was diagnosed with attention deficit hyperactive disorder (ADHD). The sentencing judge noted that "her exposure to drug and alcohol abuse, and her own drug abuse while still relatively young (particularly her use of Percocet, Restoril, and Valium), did little to help her when she was in school." When the girl was previously incarcerated at the Manitoba Youth Centre, "she was placed in the isolation cell 33 times and was involved in over 70 'incidents' which warranted documentation."[159]

In another case, *R. v. Jessie George*, an Aboriginal man received seven years for manslaughter for brutally assaulting and killing his Aboriginal friend in a dispute over a girl, after he had been drinking. Jessie George's pre-sentencing report was summarized thusly:

> Mr. George's mother was raised in residential school and foster homes and had a very difficult time. She became addicted to alcohol at a young age. Her addiction while pregnant with Mr. George affected his brain development. He has been diagnosed with alcohol related neurodevelopmental disorder which is within the class of fetal alcohol spectrum disorders. Mr. George's father is deceased … The offender's mother and his step-father separated when Mr. George was 5 years old and he bounced between both homes, always subject to the neglect and rejection born of alcoholism and drug dependency.[160]

George's subsequent life was also chaotic. His "attempts to return to school were defeated by his association with a gang that emphasized excessive drinking and drug use. He fathered a child when he was in his teens…. At 18, the offender moved back with his mother. He began selling and consuming street drugs as well as drinking heavily to escape his sadness … Life revolved around 'partying, getting drunk and going to jail.'"[161] The trial judge accepted that those with FASD "tend to be impulsive, uninhibited, and fearless. They often display poor judgment and are easily distracted…. FAS patients have difficulties linking events with their resulting consequences. These consequences include both the physical e.g. getting burned by a hot stove, and the punitive, e.g. being sent to jail for committing a crime. Because of this, it is difficult for these individuals to learn from their mistakes."[162] In delivering his seven-year sentence, the judge noted,

> Mr. George did not ask for the hand he was dealt even before his birth. He did not ask for a chaotic childhood. His mother did not ask for the hand she was dealt in her childhood. Her inability to parent compounded the prenatal effects of alcohol on Mr. George's brain. These are handicaps he will have to deal with for the rest of his life. I am sorry he has to deal with them. I hope he can overcome them. Nevertheless, the court must be concerned with the risk this young man presents to the public as a result of his impaired judgment and inability to control his impulsive behaviour.[163]

In *R. v. Charlie*, the accused was sentenced to six months and three years probation for armed robbery, failure to attend court, and breach of recognizance. In his reasons for sentencing, Judge Heino Lilles made an explicit connection between the residential schools and FASD as follows:

> Mr. Charlie is a status member of the Kaska Nation. He is from Ross River, Yukon, a remote village with a summer population of 450, of which 90 percent are of aboriginal descent. Mr. Charlie's parents were six years old when they were taken by the Indian Agents, along with other children in the community, to residential school. The parents of these children had little choice in the matter, as they were threatened with the loss of their rations if they did not cooperate. At the same time, they were offered $6 for each child that was taken to the residential school.[164]

Judge Lilles then observed,

> This history of Franklin Charlie's family is important because it identifies a direct link between the colonization of the Yukon and the government's residential school policies to the removal of children from their families into abusive environments for extended periods of time, the absence of parenting skills as a result of the residential school functioning as an inadequate parent, and their subsequent reliance on alcohol when returned to the communities. Franklin Charlie's FASD is the direct result of these policies of the Federal Government, as implemented by the local Federal Indian Agent. Ironically, it is the Federal Government who, today, is prosecuting Mr. Franklin Charlie for the offences he has committed as a victim of maternal alcohol consumption.[165]

These cases underline the link between residential schools, FASD, and offending behaviour that leads to involvement with the criminal justice system. Given the higher rate of Aboriginal involvement in the criminal justice system and the higher rates of incarceration, there is a need to take urgent measures both to prevent and better manage the harmful consequences of FASD for Aboriginal offenders.

33) We call upon the federal, provincial, and territorial governments to recognize as a high priority the need to address and prevent Fetal Alcohol Spectrum Disorder (FASD), and to develop in collaboration with Aboriginal people FASD preventative programs that can be delivered in a culturally appropriate manner.

34) We call upon the governments of Canada, the provinces, and territories to undertake reforms to the criminal justice system to better address the needs of offenders with Fetal Alcohol Spectrum Disorder (FASD), including:

i. Providing increased community resources and powers for courts to ensure that FASD is properly diagnosed, and that appropriate community supports are in place for those with FASD.

ii. Enacting statutory exemptions from mandatory minimum sentences of imprisonment for offenders affected by FASD.

iii. Providing community, correctional and parole resources to maximize the ability of people with FASD to live in the community.

iv. Adopting appropriate evaluation mechanisms to measure the effectiveness of such programs and ensure community safety.]

## Parental neglect

The connection between parenting skills and subsequent juvenile delinquency has been noted by Canadian courts. In finding an Aboriginal accused to be a dangerous offender, Justice J. E. Topolniski wrote, "For example, the negative attitudes displayed by Mr. Ominayak should be seen in light of his background as an Aboriginal man whose mother failed to learn parenting skills because her parents were products of the residential school system."[166]

In another case, an offender's father testified at his son's sentencing for sexual assault. He apologized to his son because "as a result of his own residential school experience, he did not know how to raise him properly."[167]

In *R. v. Jimmie,* the accused, a residential school Survivor, received two years plus a day for armed robbery. The Court of Appeal noted,

> Ms. Jimmie is a member of the Kluskus community which is situated in a very remote area of the Chilcotin. There are no counselling services on or near the community. Her life was described as being "full of horrors." She was raised in poverty by an alcoholic mother who often left her and her siblings alone to fend for themselves. Ms. Jimmie was sent to residential school where she was exposed to an atmosphere of violence. She has a sixth grade education. In 1985, her sister's body was found in a river; she had been badly beaten. That crime has never been solved.
>
> About eight years ago, Ms. Jimmie's children were apprehended and placed in foster care. At the time of her sentencing, her spouse was hospitalized because of a mental breakdown.[168]

## Family violence

Many studies have found that domestic violence and abuse are characteristics of dysfunctional homes that are passed along through the generations. One study based on 457 participants found that children who were exposed to domestic violence, or were themselves abused, or were exposed to both (47.5%) had higher rates of committing felony assault in comparison to those who had no exposure.[169] Research has shown that when male children witness the abuse of their mothers in the home, it significantly increases their chances of becoming intimate abusers later in life not only of their partners but also of their children. An American study, whose sample of 1,000 persons included black, white, and Latino persons found that mistreatment experienced during adolescence also increased the probability of criminal behaviour. Percentages for late adolescent criminality were 58.7% for general offending, 39% for violent offending, 30.4% for drug use, and 30% for arrest. Although such studies are rare with respect to Aboriginal people in Canada, there is support for the connections between residential school, family violence, and subsequent offending in published cases.

In *R. v. Rossi*, we see an example in which the accused was abused in residential schools and then in turn abused his own family. The sentencing judge observed, "Beverley's life is an example of the cost of the impact of residential schools, reservation life, and racism. The abuse her father suffered at the residential school at Brandon, Manitoba, resurfaced in his own relationships and he perpetuated a cycle of violence, addiction and in turn produced a broken family."[170]

In *R. v. Snake*, the judge noted that "classic background factors are present. The accused as a youth suffered alcohol-related abuse by his step-father. The step-father himself had a history with residential schools which might provide some explanation for his abusive behaviour."[171]

The Commission's point is not to suggest that family violence and related problems are valid excuses for serious offences. They do, however, help to explain them. The intergenerational legacy of residential schools is an important background and contextual factor that helps explain Aboriginal overrepresentation in prison.

## Racism

The residential school environment was deeply racist. It presumed the intellectual inferiority of the children and it demeaned Aboriginal culture, language, and parenting. The students were treated as if they were prisoners who required strict discipline simply because they were Aboriginal.

One study compared African American men who experienced racial discrimination (for example, racial slurs, racial profiling by police, having been physically attacked because of race) to subjects who had not experienced racial discrimination. Those who reported higher discrimination committed crimes of intimate-partner violence more often (28%) in comparison to those who reported lower discrimination (16%).

Another study found that black youth who personally experience racial discrimination had increased levels of general and violent delinquency.[172] As far as the Commission is aware, similar studies have not been conducted with reference to Aboriginal populations in Canada. Nonetheless, there is persuasive anecdotal evidence of Aboriginal persons experiencing racism both within and without residential schools.

In *R. v. D. M. G.*, the trial judge remarked on the troubled background of the accused saying, "D. M. G. was born in 1965 to parents who had significant substance abuse problems. Her mother was native and had attended the residential school ... suffering the effects of dislocation, loss of identity and self esteem. Her father was French Canadian and ostracized by his family because of his relationship with a native. D. M. G. felt the sting of racial intolerance at an early age."[173]

There are other cases where racial taunting and other forms of overt racial discrimination have been recognized as contributing factors to a crime committed by an Aboriginal person.[174]

## Loss of culture

Residential schools played a significant role in the loss of traditional culture and knowledge, including the loss of customary laws that could have acted as a positive mechanism of social control and restraint against criminal behaviour. This has profound consequences for contemporary Aboriginal communities. Carol La Prairie worked as the executive director of the Native Council on Justice. She wrote about the James Bay Cree:

> Residential schools, the decline of traditional activities, the emergence of the
> reserve system which binds people together in unnatural ways, and the creation
> of band government which locates power and resources in the hands of a few
> have dictated the form of reserve life across the country and have profoundly
> affected institutions such as kinship networks, families, as well as the unspoken
> rules of behaviour in traditional societies ... The lack of respect for others, and
> the absence of shame about one's bad behaviour and about harming another or
> the community were, to many Cree for example, the most troubling aspects of
> contemporary life.[175]

One 2010 Ontario study involving ninety-seven First Nations children and adolescents living in foster care found that those with more opportunities to participate in First Nations culture had significantly fewer behavioural difficulties.[176]

Many Survivors, including offenders, have told us that relearning and re-engagement with Aboriginal cultures and languages was very important in supporting them to make progress on healing so that they could live productive and law-abiding lives. Although cultural programming is available in some prisons, there aren't enough resources devoted to such programs, and Aboriginal offenders can be denied access to such programming on the basis of favoritism, punishment, or security classifications tied to an offender's past criminal history.

## Sexual abuse

The available social science evidence establishes a disturbingly strong connection between being sexually abused as a child and the later sexually abusing of others. A study of 471 participants found that a youth who was abused by a female was 3.89 times more likely to subsequently abuse a female than a youth who was not abused by a female. A youth abused by a male was 6.05 times more likely to subsequently abuse a male. A youth abused by both males and females was 1.88 times more likely to subsequently abuse both males and females.[177] Another study involving 179 pre-adolescent girls found that girls were 3.6 times more likely to experience sexual victimization if the mother was herself sexually abused as a child.[178]

In *R. v. J. O.*, the accused was sentenced to ten months jail time and eighteen months probation for sexual assault. The judge stated,

> As a child, the accused, like many other children of aboriginal communities, had to go to residential school. From the time he entered residential school until 1969, the accused was sexually assaulted by two adults in authority. The assaults included touching, masturbation, and kisses on the mouth. These events left a deep-seated scar in the accused. Mr. J. O., until his last incarceration in the mid 1990s, had never revealed the assaults he suffered. The assaults left him in a state of confusion where affection, love and sexuality are entangled. Due to these traumatic events, the accused developed an alcohol-related problem. He admits having started to drink by the end of his school years. Many of the sexual assaults committed by Mr. J. O. took place while he was under the influence of alcohol. A link must be made between the past events of the accused's life and the assaults he committed ... In the testimony given at the hearing on sentence, the accused says: "I knew it was bad. I thought that it was normal but bad."[179]

In *R. v. W. R. G.*, the accused was convicted of sexually touching his daughter. In his judgment, Justice C. Baird Ellan observed,

Mr. G was himself abused sexually in two separate incidents when he was very young, perhaps five. He also witnessed abuse at the residential school, and on the reserve before that. He once walked in on his uncle abusing one of his sisters, but she did not complain about the incident. He believed that his mother was also sexually abused, as were her sisters, but his mother herself never told anyone.[180]

Considering the effect of Mr. G's attitude to the offence, I consider that his background, in particular the sexual abuse he experienced, may have resulted in a blurring of the boundaries that would otherwise naturally prevail in a parental relationship.[181]

There is a need to help those who suffered sexual abuse to overcome that experience and not to abuse others. There is also a need for culturally appropriate forms of treatment that recognize the widespread sexual abuse that occurred in residential school and now unfortunately continues in Aboriginal families.

## Substance abuse

Substance abuse is widely recognized as a cause of offending behaviour. An analysis of thirty different studies showed that drug users were three to four times more likely to offend than non-drug users.[182] Subsequent studies have continued to confirm that drug and/or alcohol abuse significantly raise the risks of recidivism for many offences, including crimes committed while incarcerated, sexual offences, domestic violence offences, and juvenile delinquency.[183] In nearly two-thirds of non-spousal violent incidents, Aboriginal crime victims related the offence to the offender's use of alcohol or drugs. Close to 88% of Aboriginal males (and 94% of Aboriginal women) accused of homicide had consumed alcohol or drugs at the time of violent incident, compared to 64% of non-Aboriginal accused and 41% of non-Aboriginal women.[184] Aboriginal people who reported using drugs were four times as likely to be victimized by crime compared to Aboriginal people who do not use drugs.[185]

Many sentencing decisions have recognized that substance abuse was at once both a reaction to having been victimized in residential schools, and a contributor to subsequent criminal behaviour.[186] In *R. v. Craft*, the accused received a nine-month conditional sentence and three years probation for driving under the influence. Chief Judge Ruddy of the Yukon Territorial Court made very explicit connections to residential school:

His time spent in the residential school system was an extremely difficult period of time in which he, as is described in the report, suffered from extreme violence, torture and sexual abuse within the residential school system. That, in turn, led to him abusing alcohol, which in turn led to his extensive involvement with the criminal justice system between 1961 and 1986.[187]

In *R. v. M. L. W.*, in which the accused was given a two-year conditional sentence for driving under the influence, Dr. Peter Saunders, as an expert witness, connected the accused's residential school experiences to post-traumatic stress disorder, alcohol abuse, and subsequent criminal behaviour as follows:

> [M. L. W.] has been a patient of mine since May of 2001. Over the last three years I have seen him regularly on a professional basis and have come to have some understanding of the long-term effect on his health that has resulted from the abuse that he sustained while attending residential school as a child. As a result of the post-traumatic stress disorder that [M. L. W.] suffered as a young man, he experienced periods of drug and alcohol abuse.[188]

Many studies have confirmed that alcohol and drug abuse in the home environment significantly increase the chances of the cycle of substance passing on from generation to generation.[189] Judges cannot help but notice that substance abuse spans generations in Aboriginal communities.

There are cases where individuals have been both residential school Survivors and had been exposed to substance abuse in the home as a child. In one case, a judge who sentenced an Aboriginal person to four years for sexual assault noted,

> I have heard that he is a residential school survivor and I have heard that he was faced, while growing up, and surrounded by, a lot of dysfunction, and by many people who abused alcohol. There is very little doubt in my mind that Mr. G. has indeed faced systemic factors that have contributed to his difficulties with the law that probably contributed to his own unhealthy relationship with alcohol, which in turn has resulted in a fairly consistent pattern of breaking the law, going back to even before he was an adult.[190]

Intoxication by drugs or alcohol can, even in the most serious cases such as murder, be argued as a mitigating factor for criminal conduct. The courts, however, have taken a strict approach to such arguments. Even when intoxication is a factor, the accused will almost always be convicted of a less serious offence.

## Mental health issues

It is widely accepted that the criminal justice system is not well-equipped to deal with mental health problems. Although mental illness is frequently present, it does not amount to a lawful defence to a charge unless it is of such intensity that it renders an accused incapable of knowing that which actions were wrong. Nonetheless, it can be and often is, a factor in offending behaviour. The role that residential schools have played in an accused's mental health is something that the courts have to take note of.

A study done by the Aboriginal Healing Foundation looked at 127 Aboriginal persons in British Columbia who had litigated residential school claims. Ninety-three of those case files had evidence of mental health problems. They included 21.1% for major depression, 20% for other disorders related to depression, 26.3% for substance abuse disorder, and 64.2% for post-traumatic stress disorder.[191] Sixty-two of those 127 case files had criminal histories, most for sexual offences, assault, and driving offences.[192]

One recent case indicated how a man accused of murder had been held in pretrial custody for four-and-a-half years. During that time he had been unable to obtain either mental health services or Aboriginal-specific programming. This man's father had attended residential school at Chesterfield Inlet. His mother had been taken away from her parents (who had also attended residential school) and adopted into a non-Aboriginal home. The offender had been diagnosed by a forensic psychiatrist as likely to be suffering post-traumatic stress disorder, personality disorder, and FASD. The judge observed that the offender "has been 'on hold' for the last four and a half years in an environment that cannot have done much for his spiritual or psychological health" and that when he was sent to an Ontario federal penitentiary he would be "caught in a Kafkaesque situation" because of the unavailability of any Aboriginal-specific program for his alcohol and violence problems.[193] The judge went on to say that the "unavailability of Aboriginal programming in federal institutions should not become simply the latest example of how Canadian society let [him] fall through the cracks."[194]

## Poverty

Aboriginal people are more likely to live in poverty than non-Aboriginal Canadians, and when they do, the depth of their poverty is likely to be greater than that of other Canadians. They have an average income that is further below the poverty line on average than that of non-Aboriginal adults.[195] The impact of the 2008 recession was greater and persisted longer for Aboriginal workers than for the non-Aboriginal population.[196] Aboriginal people are more likely to experience unemployment and are more likely to collect employment insurance and social assistance.[197] When working, Aboriginal people have earnings well below their non-Aboriginal counterparts. The median income for Aboriginal peoples in 2010 was approximately 30% lower than the median income for non-Aboriginal workers ($20,701 vs. $30,195).[198] It is not surprising, then, that the child poverty rate for Aboriginal children is very high—40%—compared to 17% for all children in Canada.[199]

Many studies have shown a direct link between community poverty and higher crime rates.[200] This is apparently true even for the most serious of offences, including homicide.[201] Poverty and the lack of employment opportunities have also been found to be a pathway to gang membership.[202] Poverty also contributes to domestic violence. It leaves women living with violence with fewer resources to obtain independence from abusive partners.[203] A 2010 study found that residential school attendees were more likely to live in low-income households and to have experienced income insecurity. Aboriginal children who came from higher-income households were more likely to be successful in school than Aboriginal children from low-income households that were vulnerable to food insecurity.[204]

In *R. v. C. G .O.*, poverty was recognized as a strong contributing factor behind the accused being brought into court. The judge observed,

> Ms. C. O. grew up on a reserve near Regina ... Ms. C. O. has lived her life in poverty, isolation and violence. For the last ten years, if not longer, she has been disconnected from her family and traditions that are her sources of strength and support. She continues to live in poverty and violence. She is socially isolated with no one to call upon for help. Her home community still struggles with poverty, violence and offers few resources. Based on the evidence on sentencing, Ms. C. O. has had few realistic opportunities to change. In my view, the poverty, isolation and violence are precisely what brought Ms. C. O. to court.[205]

C. O. received a two years less a day conditional sentence plus three years probation for failure to provide the necessities of life and assaulting her three-and-half-year-old child.[206]

## Child welfare involvement

A child's involvement in the child welfare system has been found to increase juvenile delinquency for children, in particular male children. One study of children who were maltreated in Chicago and its Cook County suburbs found that maltreated children who were placed into care had a delinquency rate of 16%, compared to 7% for children who were not placed into care.[207] Another study of children in California's system found that children who were placed at least once in a group home were 2.5 times more likely to become delinquent in comparison to children who were placed in a foster home.[208]

Frequent changes in placement (known as placement instability) has also been found to be significantly predictive for adult criminality. A study based on 772 persons with histories of abuse or neglect prior to age twelve found that the rates of adult arrest correlated with the degree of placement instability. The rates were 35% for no child welfare placements, 45.4% for one, 60% for two, and 76.3% for three or more.[209]

*R. v. J. E. R.* presents a vivid account of how placement in the system involving one generation led to further harm for those in the next generation:

Mr. R. is the youngest of four children. He was born in Winnipeg. His parents separated just prior to his birth. Mr. R. understands that both were part of the residential school system. Mr. R. understands that his mother, V., was taken and sold as an orphan into the United States … It is believed V. and her sister were placed in adoption in the United States at V.'s age five. They were physically abused in this adoptive home. The parents divorced, and V. and her sister were again placed in foster care and at V.'s age 12, adopted a second time and over the next one-and-a-half years were exposed to emotional and mental abuse. Thereafter, V. and her sister were separated and V. lived in several group homes … in one she was sexually molested.

V. returned to her biological mom at age 16 and gave birth to Mr. R.'s brother, J., at her age 17, and moved out at age 18. Mr. R. lived with his mother initially in Winnipeg. His mother and family then moved to Calgary and then on to Vancouver. The Calgary move was when he was an infant of seven months or so. The Vancouver move in August 1994 was when Mr. R. was about age two. The father prior to separation used drugs and alcohol and abused the mother V.[210]

The reasons for the overrepresentation of Aboriginal people in the correctional system are complex and interrelated. What is clear is that governments must commit to ending this imbalance. Better monitoring and evaluation of the situation is only the first step.

30) We call upon federal, provincial, and territorial governments, to commit to eliminating the overrepresentation of Aboriginal people in custody over the next decade and to issue detailed annual reports that monitor and evaluate progress in doing so.

## Sentencing and sanctions

Over the past two decades significant advances have been made in the process of sentencing of Aboriginal offenders. However, these advances are under challenge from more recent amendments to the criminal law that expand the circumstances in which courts must impose mandatory minimum sentences.

## Section 718.2(e)

In 1996, in recognition of the fact that Canada was imprisoning more people than many other democracies, Parliament overhauled the laws relating to sentences. One key change was the introduction of "conditional sentences," which allow offenders who might otherwise be imprisoned to serve their sentences in the community. But the centrepiece of sentencing reform was section 718.2(e) of the *Criminal Code*. It instructs judges that "all available sanctions other than imprisonment that are reasonable in the circumstances should be considered for all offenders, with particular attention to the circumstances of aboriginal offenders." Then Minister of Justice Allan Rock explained that

> the reason we referred specifically there to aboriginal persons is that they are sadly overrepresented in the prison populations of Canada. I think it was the Manitoba justice inquiry that found that although aboriginal persons make up only 12% of the population of Manitoba, they comprise over 50% of the prison inmates. Nationally aboriginal persons represent about 2% of Canada's population, but they represent 10.6% of persons in prison. Obviously there's a problem here. What we're trying to do, particularly having regard to the initiatives in the aboriginal communities to achieve community justice, is to encourage courts to look at alternatives where it's consistent with the protection of the public, alternatives to jail, and not simply resort to that easy answer in every case.[211]

The 1996 reforms represented a genuine and comprehensive attempt to recognize the need for restraint in the use of imprisonment and to provide trial judges with tools to provide realistic alternatives to imprisonment.

## R. v. Gladue

*R. v. Gladue* (*Gladue*) was a landmark decision by the Supreme Court of Canada involving section 718.2(e) of the *Criminal Code*, in the case of an Aboriginal woman from British Columbia. On September 16, 1995, Jamie Tanis Gladue was celebrating her nineteenth birthday when she got into a violent disagreement with her boyfriend and stabbed him. She was eventually convicted of manslaughter. At her sentencing hearing, the judge took into account her youth, her status as a mother, and the absence of any serious criminal history. She was sentenced to three years imprisonment. When the Supreme Court dismissed her appeal of the sentence in 1999, the Court approvingly quoted a study to the effect that "the prison has become for many young native people the contemporary equivalent of what the Indian residential school represented for their parents."[212]

The Court noted that Aboriginal people constituted 12% of federal prisoners, and included the following statement in its ruling:

> The figures are stark and reflect what may fairly be termed a crisis in the Canadian criminal justice system. The drastic overrepresentation of aboriginal peoples within both the Canadian prison population and the criminal justice system reveals a sad and pressing social problem. It is reasonable to assume that

Parliament, in singling out aboriginal offenders for distinct sentencing treatment in s. 718.2(e), intended to attempt to redress this social problem to some degree. The provision may properly be seen as Parliament's direction to members of the judiciary to inquire into the causes of the problem and to endeavour to remedy it, to the extent that a remedy is possible through the sentencing process.[213]

The judgment continues: "The fact that the reference to aboriginal offenders is contained in section 718.2(e), in particular, dealing with restraint in the use of imprisonment, suggests that there is something different about aboriginal offenders which may specifically make imprisonment a less appropriate or less useful sanction."[214] *R. v. Gladue* is a much cited judgment and it has in some jurisdictions resulted in the introduction of more extensive pre-sentence or *Gladue* reports that provide the sentencing judge with contextual information on the background of Aboriginal offenders. Producing these reports has not been without difficulty and controversy. In 2012, the *Globe and Mail* reported,

> Saskatchewan, Alberta and Manitoba have barely begun to produce [*Gladue*] reports. While the number in Alberta has shot up from 14 in 2011 to 100 that are now in production, most of them are being prepared by probation officers—who are trained to assess risk factors but have no particular understanding of aboriginal culture and history. In Quebec, *Gladue* reports are almost unheard of.[215]

Many jurisdictions work with Aboriginal community groups to prepare *Gladue* reports. This is a good practice because probation officers who prepare pre-sentence reports generally do not have cultural training to work with Aboriginal offenders, families, and communities to prepare adequate *Gladue* reports prior to sentencing.

There are some concerns that defence lawyers may not always request a *Gladue* report or use it to their clients' advantage. One defence lawyer noted, "The lawyer is not compensated for the report and yet we are expected to do multiple hours of work that we are not paid for. Sometimes we are asked to review the report. That can take 3 hours. More time is spent on the *Gladue* report than other PSRs [Pre-Sentence Reports] because of the structure of the program."[216]

*Gladue* reports can often be difficult for offenders and their families. One *Gladue* report writer stated, "The interviews are very hard. They are very emotional. Especially if a person is in custody. I've had guys say, 'I can't talk about that because I can't cry in here.' Sometimes I wonder if we are re-traumatizing them."[217]

However, some judges see that they have a greater responsibility. In *R. v. Jesse Armitage,* which was heard in the first official Canadian court established to adhere to the principles expressed in *R. v. Gladue* and accordingly called a "*Gladue* court," Justice Nakatsuru wrote his entire judgment in unusually simple prose:

> In the *Gladue* court at Old City Hall, accused persons who share a proud history of the first people who lived in this nation, not only have a right to be heard, but

they also have a right to fully understand. Their voices are heard by the judges. And they must also know that we have heard them ... I know that all accused, whether they have any Aboriginal blood or not, should have this right. Judges struggle to make sure they do. However, when judges write their decisions, they are writing for different readers, different audiences. Judges write not only for the parties before them. Judges write to other readers of the law. Lawyers. Other judges. The community. In this case, I am writing for Jesse Armitage.[218]

In his ruling, Justice Nakatsuru noted that Jesse Armitage's grandmother was a residential school Survivor, and that her own children have struggled with alcoholism; and that Armitage came from a broken home. The judge went on to say,

> If I could describe Mr. Armitage as a tree, his roots remain hidden beneath the ground. I can see what he is now. I can see the trunk. I can see the leaves. But much of what he is and what has brought him before me, I cannot see. They are still buried. But I am sure that some of those roots involve his Aboriginal heritage and ancestry. They help define who he is. They have been a factor in his offending. They must be taken into account in his sentencing.[219]

### R. v. Ipeelee

The case *R. v. Ipeelee* (*Ipeelee*) involved two men—one from Yukon, the other from Nunavut, both with serious alcohol problems going back to their youth, both with long criminal records, both from broken families, and both with links to residential schools. The argument that reached the Supreme Court of Canada concerned the breach of their long-term supervision order. In its 2012 ruling, the Court reduced the sentence of one man and affirmed the other. What will be remembered from this ruling was the Supreme Court's decision to revisit and reaffirm *Gladue*. The justices noted that the problem of Aboriginal overrepresentation had gotten worse in the thirteen years since *Gladue* was decided. The Court pointed out that while Aboriginal people comprised 12% of federal inmates in 1999 when *Gladue* was decided, they constituted 17% of federal admissions in 2005. The Court then noted that

> courts must take judicial notice of such matters as the history of colonialism, displacement, and residential schools and how that history continues to translate into lower educational attainment, lower incomes, higher unemployment, higher rates of substance abuse and suicide, and of course higher levels of incarceration for Aboriginal peoples.[220]

The Supreme Court pointed out that some lower court judges had erred in their application of *Gladue* by concluding that it did not apply to serious offences or that it required an offender to demonstrate a causal connection between the commission of the crime and the legacy of residential schools or other background or contextual factors. *Gladue* mandates trial judges to consider all the background factors for Aboriginal offenders. This was clear direction from the Supreme Court's ruling that offenders need not demonstrate a direct causal relationship between the legacy of residential schools and the commission of offences.[221]

Section 718.1 of the *Criminal Code* codifies a long-standing principle of criminal justice that "a sentence must be proportionate to the gravity of the offence and the degree of responsibility of the offender." The Court in *Ipeelee* indicated that the fundamental questions of proportionality must be addressed in a different light given the reality of how Aboriginal people have been treated in Canada. The Court invited judges to revise their understanding of traditional sentencing principles, including deterrence and denunciation in light of evidence of their failure to achieve their objectives and "to meet the needs of Aboriginal offenders and communities."[222]

The *Gladue* factors require consideration of restorative principles of sentencing, including acknowledgment of harm done to victims and communities and rehabilitation of offenders in contrast to punitive principles of sentencing.

The Supreme Court's landmark decisions in *Gladue* and *Ipeelee* remind trial judges to take a different approach in applying the purposes and principles of sentencing to Aboriginal offenders, including those related to deterrence, denunciation, and retribution. These decisions recognize that the application of a uniform one-size-fits-all approach to punishment will be discriminatory and ineffective given the treatment of Aboriginal people in Canadian society, including the intergenerational legacy of residential schools. However, there is a pressing need for sufficient and stable funding to implement and evaluate community sanctions that will provide realistic alternatives to imprisonment for Aboriginal offenders and will respond to the underlying causes of offending by them. Without adequate and stable funding of community sanctions and evaluation of their success, it is likely that the overrepresentation of Aboriginal people in prison and among crime victims will continue to grow.

## *Gladue, Ipeelee*, and Aboriginal young offenders

Aboriginal youth experience the justice system in very different and more disruptive ways than other youth. They are more likely to be detained in facilities that are far from their homes, families, and communities. Having court processes hundreds of kilometres away makes it more difficult for them to have someone in court to support them or suggest alternatives to incarceration.

In an analysis of Ontario data from 2004–05 and 2005–06, Aboriginal youth were underrepresented amongst those who received non-custodial sentences available under the *Youth Criminal Justice Act* and overrepresented in more serious sentences.[223] The explanation does not lie in any differences in the types of crimes that

Aboriginal youth are charged with. In fact, Aboriginal youth receive custodial sentences at a greater rate than non-Aboriginal youth for the same offences.[224]

Sentencing decisions are one of the most obvious points in the system for reform. Courts often consider factors that may seem neutral on their face but are not. For example, a person with a good job, a good education, and wealth is likely to receive a sentence that is less disruptive to his or her lifestyle. On the other hand, as Professor Tim Quigley has observed, "the unemployed, transients, the poorly educated are all better candidates for imprisonment. When the social, political and economic aspects of our society place Aboriginal people disproportionately within the ranks of the latter, our society literally sentences more of them to jail. This is systemic discrimination."[225]

## Community sanctions

The Commission has heard testimony from Survivors about how community sanctions can work to the benefit of both offenders and the community. Gerald McLeod explained to the Commission how he developed an addiction to alcohol as a coping mechanism after being sexual abused in two residential schools in Yukon. He recalled,

> I was 16, I started getting impaireds. I ended up with 18 impaireds, 'cause of my drinking and alcoholism, and I'm not proud of it. I'm, I'm happy that I didn't kill my, nobody, or I killed myself, or one of my family members. I was blessed that way that I didn't hurt no one.

McLeod faced a ten-year jail sentence when convicted for the eighteenth time, but Justice Barry Stuart, a pioneer in community sanctions and circle sentencing, gave him an opportunity to stay out of jail. McLeod recounted,

> [I] got to treatment in Calgary, Stoney Medicine Lodge, and I sobered up for two years, and I came home to the Yukon here. The judge put me through circle court. I was the first one to go through circle court here in the community. I got cleared of this charge for two years, and blood tests for two years. So, I did that for two years, proved to them I can stay sober... and two of us did that, went to treatment, Dennis Jackson and I, and we've been sober for 19 years now. And you know when we came out of our sweat in Calgary, there was two eagles flying around, and I told Dennis that that's us up there, and then I said right on.[226]

The use of community sanctions to deal with deep traumas caused by residential schools is not a panacea, and there may be failures on the road to recovery. Gerald McLeod explained to us that despite his successful battle against alcoholism, he has been convicted and imprisoned twice for sexual assaults. He explained, "I'm marked by the government, to sign a paper saying, 'I am a sexual assault offender for the rest of my life.' ... And you know I'm marked for the rest of my life for something that I was taught as a kid, or forced on as a kid, then I go do it, and I'm marked for life for doing it." McLeod admitted his offences and said, "I'm not trying to make excuses or any-thing, but I, I can't answer it yet. I can't, you know, what was passed on to me, then am I passing it on to others? Or, you know, the only way I can answer that is go through treatment, and that's what I'm seeking right now is treatment through my counsellors, and I'm looking at residential treatment in the future."

Such treatment can be more difficult for offenders like Gerald McLeod who have served a lot of time in prison. He explained,

> It's a lot of work, and it's, it's not easy to keep opening up this can of beans to, or can of worms to spread it out ... It was all there from my childhood I was dig-ging up, fighting all my life, and then now they want me to dig it all out again, and then start over again with all this misery that I have to live with, that I've lived with. But I know it's the only answer for me is to get it out of me, and start working on a new life ... It's a lot of stuff there that you have to work on the, your spirituality, your language, your, everything that you lost, you know, you're trying to get it back so you can be in balance with yourself again a little bit. But you got so many hurdles out to overcome from the residential [school] that you're faced every day in your community, everything that you live with in your community that is, that is not right, 'cause it's a stem off from residential that we do suffer in our communities with today from our children, and from our grandchildren.[227]

All of that causes us to conclude that, for Aboriginal people, many, if not most, offences committed by them result in sentences of incarceration that fail to address the underlying causes of offending behaviour in a manner that supports their men-tal, spiritual, and cultural needs or reduces crime. The promise of the *Criminal Code* amendments of 1996 and the Supreme Court's decisions in *Gladue* and *Ipeelee* have not yet been met. More needs to be done.

31) We call upon the federal, provincial, and territorial governments to provide suf-ficient and stable funding to implement and evaluate community sanctions that will provide realistic alternatives to imprisonment for Aboriginal offenders and respond to the underlying causes of offending.

## Barriers to reducing Aboriginal overrepresentation in prison

### Bill C-10 and mandatory minimum sentences

In 2012, Parliament enacted Bill C-10. This legislation includes more mandatory minimum sentences and restrictions on conditional sentences. In announcing the Royal Assent of the Bill, several federal parliamentarians declared, "Our Government is committed to ensuring that criminals are held fully accountable for their actions and that the safety and security of law-abiding Canadians comes first in Canada's judicial system. We will continue to fight crime and protect Canadians so our communities are safe places for people to live, raise their families and do business."[228]

Mandatory minimum sentences are sentences that, if properly enacted, no judge can reduce or modify. For example, Bill C-10 introduced longer mandatory minimum sentences for several sexual offences against children, ranging from a ninety-day minimum when the Crown prosecutor proceeds by summary conviction, and a one-year minimum when the Crown prosecutor proceeds by indictment.[229] Bill C-10 also affected the mandatory minimum for various drug offences, like trafficking, exporting, and possession with intent to either traffic or export. The mandatory minimums for these offences range from one to two years depending on the nature and amount of the substance, and certain aggravating factors of which the court is obliged to consider.[230] Similarly, Bill C-10 introduced a mandatory minimum sentence of two years for the production of certain substances, or a three-year mandatory minimum where certain health and safety factors are proven.[231]

Since the enactment of Bill C-10, certain offences are also no longer eligible for a conditional sentence—a term of imprisonment to be served in the community as opposed to in a correctional facility. These include any offence that has a maximum sentence of fourteen years or life (e.g., manslaughter, aggravated assault), as well as certain offences punishable by ten years or more where the provincial Crown chooses to proceed by indictment.[232]

The legislative emphasis on whether or not a charge proceeds by way of indictment places particular importance on the role of provincial Crown prosecutors in pursuing each charge. Prosecutorial discretion, being unreviewable by the courts, can have a dramatic impact on the considerations available to the judiciary and possible opportunities for rehabilitation come sentencing. In addition, no conditional sentence is available if there is any mandatory minimum term of imprisonment even for sentences as short as thirty to ninety days.[233] The restricted sentencing options challenge courts to find appropriate sentencing, and impact the health and healing of Aboriginal people, their communities, and their families.

Joann May Cunday explained to the Commission that she became addicted to alcohol and other drugs at an early age in part because of "learned behaviour" from her mother who attended residential schools: "It's only 'till last year that I quit drinking. But the only reason I quit drinking is 'cause I was forced into it by the courts. But I feel so much better that I did and I know my kids are, I know that they're doing better because I'm, I'm not drinking."[234] She explained that the judge was able to give her a two-year "house arrest" sentence. The Crown prosecutor had initially asked that she be incarcerated for seven years, but the conditional sentence allowed her to continue her relationship with her children, attend Aboriginal ceremonies, and "to slow down" and realize the intergenerational effects of residential school on her and her children.

The conditional sentence that she received would likely not be available under the restrictions on such sentences in Bill C-10.

A number of judges have already pointed out how such restrictions are making it even more difficult for them to provide appropriate sentences for Aboriginal offenders. One judge observed,

> Legislation designed to "get tough" on crime must not lose sight of the fact that the very individuals that suffered harm, either directly or indirectly, perhaps as children of students of residential schools, may be the same individuals who are committing the crimes and who are, under such legislation, the individuals that the justice system will "get tough" on.[235]

Bill C-10 and other similar *Criminal Code* amendments have undermined the 1996 reforms that required judges to consider all reasonable alternatives to imprisonment with particular attention to the circumstances of Aboriginal offenders.

In 2015, the federal government passed a Canadian Victims Bill of Rights, which emphasizes institutional imprisonment for the sake of community safety.[236] The premise of such approaches is that imprisonment keeps communities safe; however, if that were true, Aboriginal communities should be among the safest of all Canadian communities, given the high level of incarceration of Aboriginal adults and youth. Although imprisonment prevents offenders from committing offences against the community, while the person is imprisoned, offences including violence and drugs take place in prisons just as other types of offences took place in residential schools. All but a few offenders will be released, and the prison experience, just like the residential school experience, often makes them more, rather than less, likely to reoffend. Prison also makes offenders less employable, less self-reliant, angrier, and often more violent. Far from being kept safe by mandatory sentences of imprisonment and restrictions on community sanctions, Aboriginal communities may be less safe due to the bill's movement away from alternatives to imprisonment.

The extended terms of Bill C-10's mandatory sentences and restrictions on conditional sentencing, as well as the enactment of the Canadian Victims Bill of Rights, will likely have a disproportionate impact on Aboriginal offenders who are overrepresented in the criminal justice system in part because of their poor socioeconomic circumstances and the effects of historical and systemic discrimination in Canadian society.

**32)** We call upon the federal government to amend the *Criminal Code* to allow trial judges, upon giving reasons, to depart from mandatory minimum sentences and restrictions on the use of conditional sentences.

# Changing Canada's correctional systems

Despite the disproportionate number of Aboriginal inmates, Canada's correctional systems fall short in their treatment of these prisoners.

## Provincial corrections

Provinces and territories administer facilities for those imprisoned for less than two years and awaiting trial, and they also supervise most community sanctions. Most provinces and territories, however, appear not to have made Aboriginal-focused corrections a priority. They generally underfund community sanctions that can provide an alternative to imprisonment. For example, in 2011, community supervision accounted for 37% of all admissions into provincial and territorial facilities but only 16% of expenditures.[237] Aboriginal people receive few services in provincial correctional facilities. The Manitoba Aboriginal Justice Inquiry, after visiting various correctional institutions, concluded in 1991 that "Most of the jails we visited reminded us of zoos where men and women were caged behind iron bars. For the most part, there is nothing to do as the months and years drag by."[238]

Only a few provinces, such as British Columbia, have Aboriginal justice strategies that include cultural awareness training for officials, and contracting with Aboriginal communities to provide spiritual leadership, counselling, and cultural programming.[239] Many provinces and territories have no such plans and do not provide public data on the number of Aboriginal people imprisoned in their facilities.

Judges sometimes sentence Aboriginal offenders to "federal time" of two years plus a day, or more, because the programming for Aboriginal offenders has generally been better in federal penitentiaries than in provincial correctional facilities[240] or through community sanctions.[241] This is particularly the case for the growing number of female Aboriginal offenders.

The Commission finds little evidence that most provincial and territorial correctional services are making available culturally appropriate programming for Aboriginal offenders, including those with violence and substance abuse problems relating to the intergenerational legacy of residential schools.

## Federal corrections

The 1992 *Corrections and Conditional Release Act* provides that the Correctional Service of Canada (CSC) "shall provide programs designed particularly to address the needs of aboriginal offenders."[242] Section 81 allows offenders to be transferred to an

Aboriginal community to serve their sentence where the community consents.[243] Section 83 guarantees that Aboriginal spirituality and Aboriginal spiritual leaders have the same status as those of other religions. It also requires the Correctional Service of Canada to take "all reasonable steps" to ensure that Aboriginal inmates have access to Aboriginal Elders or spiritual leaders.[244] Section 84 also provides for Aboriginal communities to be involved in an Aboriginal offender's release and integration into the community.[245]

The Correctional Service has committed itself to observing these principles. Unfortunately, the implementation of this commitment lags and compliance looks better on paper than in reality. The correctional investigator (a federal government appointee who serves as an ombudsman for federally sentenced offenders) delivered a report in 2012, that criticized the CSC for failing to live up to its statutory and policy commitments to Aboriginal inmates. This report recognized that

- Aboriginal offenders serve disproportionately more of their sentence behind bars before first release.

- Aboriginal offenders are under-represented in community supervision populations and over-represented in maximum security institutions.

- Aboriginal offenders are more likely to return to prison on revocation of parole.

- Aboriginal offenders are disproportionately involved in institutional security incidents, use of force interventions, segregation placements and self-injurious behaviour.[246]

The investigator also reported that the promise of Aboriginal healing lodges is largely illusory for most Aboriginal inmates because so few spaces are available. In any event, a prisoner has to be classified as minimum security to qualify for an Aboriginal healing lodge but 90% of Aboriginal inmates have medium or maximum security classifications.[247]

The programming for Aboriginal offenders in federal penitentiaries is deteriorating to such an extent that some judges are no longer sentencing Aboriginal offenders to "federal time." In one recent case, a judge noted that reports on federal corrections "paint a grim picture for aboriginal offenders and their access to programming," suggesting that most Aboriginal inmates are placed on waiting lists and if admitted to such programs often have their release date delayed as a result. The judge observed, "the gap between aboriginal and non-aboriginal offenders continues to widen, the situation for aboriginal people under federal sentence deteriorates, and the Service revises and updates frameworks and strategies without apparent results." The judge also cited a Standing Parliamentary Committee on Public Safety report that found the existing programs "for treating mental disorders and addiction issues constitute an inadequate response to the cultural and spiritual needs of aboriginal offenders."[248]

## Security classifications

Another barrier to accessing needed programming is that Aboriginal offenders are placed in stricter security classifications in disproportionate numbers in comparison to non-Aboriginal offenders.

Initial determination of security classification upon arrival in a federal penitentiary is mandated under to the *Corrections and Conditional Release Act,* and is made using the Custody Ratings Scale.[249] Under this scale, a score of 133.5 or higher on the security risk component qualifies an inmate for maximum security.[250] The factors to be considered in assigning a security classification are

  a. the seriousness of the offence committed by the offender;
  b. any outstanding charges against the offender;
  c. the offender's performance and behaviour while under sentence;
  d. the offender's social, criminal and, where available, young offender history;
  e. any physical or mental illness or disorder suffered by the offender;
  f. the offender's potential for violent behaviour; and
  g. the offender's continued involvement in criminal activities.[251]

The offender's prior criminal history is an important factor in the security assessment that operates to the detriment of many Aboriginal inmates.[252]

In 1990, the Task Force of Federally Sentenced Women found that Aboriginal women were much more likely to receive higher security classification than non-Aboriginal women.[253] The Native Women's Association of Canada estimated that, as of 2003, Aboriginal women comprised at least 50% of incarcerated federal women classified as maximum security.[254] A study done in 2000 found that Aboriginal inmates were classified as maximum security or medium security at rates of 27.7% and 34.7%, respectively, in comparison to rates of 20.3% and 24.1% for non-Aboriginal offenders.[255]

The Canadian Human Rights Commission describes the effects of a maximum security classification on female inmates as follows:

> Maximum security inmates, unlike their minimum and medium security counterparts, are not eligible to participate in work-release programs, community release programs or other supportive programming designed to enhance their chances of reintegration. In fact, half of all maximum security women are now being released directly from maximum security incarceration into the community after serving two-thirds of their sentence, without the benefit of preparatory programming.[256]

This is clearly detrimental to the inmate's prospects of reintegration in the community. The inmates are released without having had adequate correctional programming, as well as with a lack of resources and supports to facilitate rehabilitation.[257]

Studies have shown that Aboriginal inmates in the aggregate have criminal histories that are considered by authorities as worse than those of non-Aboriginal inmates.[258] One study for example shows that in 2003 at least 80% of Aboriginal federal inmates had previously served terms in provincial jails in comparison to approximately 70% for non-Aboriginal inmates.[259] Inuit and First Nations federal inmates were more likely to have served a previous adult community supervision sentence, at rates of 87% and 79%, respectively, in comparison to 72% for non-Aboriginal inmates.[260] Aboriginal inmates are more likely to have been convicted of serious crimes than non-Aboriginal offenders. First Nations and Métis offenders also have had greater involvement with the youth justice system.

The Correctional Service of Canada's Commissioner's Directive on Security Classification makes little reference to the unique experiences and needs of Aboriginal offenders, apart from a requirement to consider "Aboriginal social history."[261] It is a fair question to ask whether this part of the directive results or will result in any tangible benefits for Aboriginal inmates while static factors involving prior history remain a substantial component of security classification determinations. Aboriginal offenders continue to be placed more often in higher security classifications. Previous criminal history, youth history included, will represent enduring penalties for Aboriginal offenders, even during reclassification determinations. Therefore, the security classification scheme as applied to Aboriginal inmates may represent a form of systemic discrimination.

There are alternatives that may indeed be workable. The Security Reclassification Scale for Women was developed as a gender-specific method of security classification for female offenders. The nine items that are considered in this scale are as follows:

1. Correctional plan; program motivation.
2. Maintains regular positive family contact.
3. Number of convictions for serious disciplinary offences during the review period.
4. Number of recorded incidents during the review period.
5. History of escape or unlawfully at large from work release, temporary absence or community supervision.
6. Pay level during the review period.
7. Number of times the offender was placed in involuntary segregation for being a danger to others or the institution during the review period.
8. Total number of escorted temporary absences (ETAs) during the review period.
9. Custody Rating Scale incident history.[262]

What is noteworthy is the de-emphasis on static factors involving the offence, or previous criminal history, and a greater emphasis on progress and behaviour during the review period. Early field tests involving 580 files have found that the scale is reliably predictive of actual security risk.[263] Given that there is evidence that Aboriginal spiritual healing can improve offender behaviour, and improve prison conditions generally, there is no reason other than bureaucratic inertia why the Canadian correctional system could not develop an Aboriginal-specific classification scale.

## Culturally relevant prison programming

Studies based on interviews with Aboriginal inmates have confirmed that participation in Aboriginal cultural programs in prison can contribute to the healing of the inmates through increased self-esteem and positive changes in lifestyle that make release and reintegration a real possibility.[264]

Joanne Nimik's birth mother was a residential school Survivor. Nimik was adopted into a white family. She recounted,

> [I got] into the bad crowd and started partying and drinking and drugging and, I ended up having three girls that were also apprehended through CFS [Child and Family Services] ... And it wasn't until I was 28 years old that I was reunited with my birth family. Apparently my mother Rowena had been looking for me all those years that I was adopted out and we had the reunion and it was, it was really nice 'cause, you know I always wondered who my family, like my real family was, my birth family. And, there was that missing piece in my life that I'd been searching for and didn't know how to make up for it. So I was using drugs and alcohol as a coping mechanism I guess. I've had a very hard life I guess; involved with the justice system, CFS system, drugs and alcohol, the legal system. And, because of my lack of knowledge of support systems or how to ask for help, I stayed in that way of life for quite awhile. I didn't identify myself as First Nation or Aboriginal or didn't have no clue about what it meant to be Anishina-abekwe or anything.[265]

Joanne Nimik's healing journey away from crime and drug abuse started at an Aboriginal centre for addiction treatment as part of a sentence she was serving. She recounted,

> I went to treatment at Poundmakers in Alberta and that was actually the first time I've been exposed to a sweat lodge. I signed up for it, but I was too scared to go in. First time exposure to what an Elder was, to smudging, sharing circle, sweetgrass. So it, it was a real eye opener, it scared me but I was still curious to a degree ... I had, been arrested and I guess in that being arrested that was the

turning point in my life where I was able to take advantage of a program to get some help.[266]

Since she started her healing journey away from crime, Nimik has been able to help others who like her were at risk of being victimized by crime and committing crimes.

Chris Gargan spoke to the Commission from The Yellowknife Correctional Centre in the NWT. He was looking for Aboriginal guidance and not getting it:

> Right now I'm doing a program. There's a white, white woman that's treating that program, and they, and they put, they push it on us … like, I wish it was somebody like Healing Drum Society program, or something like that…. They're teaching us about anger, anger. It would be nice if our own people would come in here and teach us about life … you know, how to live. This is not the way of life for us. It's not the way for us people.[267]

The regimented and often violent life of prison has striking resemblances to life in residential schools. Judge Heino Lilles served on the Yukon Territorial Court.

> Jail has shown not to be effective for First Nation people. Every family in Kwanlin Dun [Yukon] has members who have gone to jail. *It carries no stigma and therefore is not a deterrent. Nor is it a "safe place" which encourages disclosure, openness, or healing.* The power or authority structures within the jail operate against "openness." An elder noted: "jail doesn't help anyone. A lot of our people could have been healed a long time ago if it weren't for jail. Jail hurts them more and then they come out really bitter. In jail, all they learn is 'hurt and bitter.'" (emphasis added)[268]

The Ma Mawi Wi Chi Itata program, based in the Stoney Mountain Institution in Manitoba, is a program designed for Aboriginal inmates who have been convicted of domestic violence offences. It approaches the problem through a combination of healing and spiritual ceremonies, and educational components that are designed to help inmates understand and control their violence and develop healthier relationships and parenting skills.[269] During a review of the program after its first-year pilot, many of the Aboriginal inmates who were interviewed by researchers indicated that the program was a positive experience since it provided their first exposure to their traditional cultures and helped them understand and control their violence. Correctional staff also noted positive changes, including reduced aggression in the inmates and improved relationships between staff and inmates.[270]

A study has shown that the recidivism rate for Aboriginal offenders who participated in cultural activities was 3.6% compared to 32.5% for those who did not.[271] The recidivism rate was 14.4% for those who participated in spiritual activities (for example, a sweat lodge ceremony) compared to 24.2% for those who did not.[272] The recidivism rate was 12.9% for those inmates who had contacts or meetings with an Aboriginal Elder compared to 26.8% for those who did not.[273] Authors of another survey interviewed fifty-six male and twelve female Aboriginal ex-offenders who had stayed out of trouble with the law for at least two years following their release. While other factors such as family support and steady employment were important in keeping them out of trouble, a large percentage of the respondents indicated that participation in spiritual ceremonies (71%) and cultural activities (68%) were also important in helping them avoid conflict with the law.[274]

Unfortunately, such culturally appropriate programming is not always available in Canada's prisons. In 2008, Correctional Investigator of Canada Howard Sapers indicated before the Senate Standing Committee on Legal and Constitutional Affairs that the Correctional Service of Canada had an annual budget of $1.8 billion, and yet allocated only $27 million of that for the delivery of core program services. He went on to suggest that, given these figures, it was hardly surprising that many Aboriginal inmates had no access to culturally specific programs that could help them progress towards release.[275]

Culturally relevant programming has to accommodate the diverse spiritual needs and practices of Aboriginal inmates. The Saskatchewan Commission on First Nations and Métis Peoples and Justice Reform recommended that both provincial and federal correctional authorities should ensure "that access to cultural and spiritual programming, whether traditional or religious, be made more available" to Aboriginal offenders.[276] The wisdom of this recommendation is affirmed by what the Commission has heard from Survivors about the value that traditional and other religious practices have had in their healing.

> **36)** We call upon the federal, provincial, and territorial governments to work with Aboriginal communities to provide culturally relevant services to inmates on issues such as substance abuse, family and domestic violence, and overcoming the experience of having been sexually abused.

## Aboriginal healing lodges

There are four Aboriginal healing lodges run by the Correctional Service of Canada (CSC) and four run by Aboriginal communities under section 81 of the *Correctional Services Act*. According to the Correctional Service of Canada, its lodges "provide living environments that use Aboriginal traditional healing approaches as a method of intervention. Both are rooted in the spiritual and cultural activities led by Elders, and supported by dynamic contact with the community through CSC's temporary absence program and pro-social interactions with staff members and management, many of whom are Aboriginal."[277]

A 2011 report by csc documented positive findings about Aboriginal healing lodges, including that healing lodge residents, staff members, and management interviewed during the evaluation noted improvements in offenders' attitudes and behaviours, as well as their greater understanding of, and connection to, Aboriginal culture. For example, offenders showed improvements in the areas of self-confidence, personal responsibility, motivation, and self-discipline. They demonstrated deeper understanding of their lives and criminal behaviours, greater respect, and positive attitudes towards others, and recognized the importance of seeking help and establishing support networks.[278]

Despite these positive findings, the most pressing concern about Aboriginal healing lodges is the lack of resources. At the basic level, section 81 lodges are in need of physical improvements. Furthermore, the lack of funding has affected recruitment, training, and retention of lodge staff. Recruitment is especially difficult as Aboriginal people with the required skill sets are in high demand and the lodges cannot afford to pay what the market dictates. In terms of training, most section 81 lodges do not have the funds to adequately train their staff regarding csc procedures. Programming is another area that has been affected by lack of funds. Smaller facilities do not offer structured programs, as they do not have the resources to offer programs given the small number of residents who need them.[279]

Given the positive role that healing lodges can have for those Aboriginal offenders who must serve a period of incarceration, and the proven failure of existing correctional programs not specifically aimed at supporting Aboriginal inmates, it makes considerable sense to provide more resources to healing lodges.

35) We call upon the federal government to eliminate barriers to the creation of additional Aboriginal healing lodges within the federal correctional system.

## Reintegration of Aboriginal offenders

An important factor that is considered by the National Parole Board in whether to grant or deny parole is an actuarial risk assessment of whether the offender is likely to reoffend. According to one study, the percentages of inmates who were assessed as a high-risk to reoffend were 85% for Inuit, 73% for First Nations, 67% for Métis, and 57% for non-Aboriginal inmates.[280] One problem here, as with initial security classification, is a tendency to give great weight to the static factor of criminal history. This means that Aboriginal offenders often come to the parole board with two strikes against them and there is nothing they can do to overcome their prior convictions. Some research has concluded that criminal history is a reliable risk predictor for both Aboriginal and non-Aboriginal inmates.[281] At the same time, however, prior convictions of Aboriginal offenders are frequently a response to oppressive social conditions, including the intergenerational legacy of residential school. Viewed in this light, reliance on criminal history in the parole context, as in the security context, may be a form of systemic discrimination that disadvantages Aboriginal offenders. As in the security classification context, there are strong arguments that more emphasis should be given to dynamic factors such as substance abuse that the Aboriginal offender can, to some extent, control. The John Howard Society says of dynamic factors,

> Dynamic factors have been found to predict recidivism as well as, or better than, static factors, and are also measured by several actuarial risk assessment tools. It is knowledge of dynamic factors that is necessary in order to assess changes in an offender's risk level. Through participation in rehabilitative programming, an offender may become less likely to recidivate, but corrections and parole workers would not be able to measure this change unless they assessed the offender's risk based on changeable factors.[282]

Actuarial risk assessment of Aboriginal offenders that de-emphasize static factors, and instead focus on participation in appropriate programming, including cultural and spiritual healing programming for Aboriginal inmates, along with attendant offender progress in addressing dynamic risk factors, would be just as useful and fairer to Aboriginal inmates. It would also encourage Aboriginal inmates to engage in such programs, once they know that participation would have more significant weight. Such programming and spiritual healing can affect Aboriginal inmates' behaviours so they can prepare themselves for parole and reintegration. Such an approach, however, will only achieve greater fairness for Aboriginal offenders to the extent that Aboriginal programming is made available to them.

When the National Parole Board grants parole, the delivery of correctional programming continues. The early stages of parole are often spent in a residential correctional facility—a halfway house. A halfway house, while not a prison, requires the offender to reside there and not be absent save under specific exceptions (e.g., supervised absences or employment). It is meant as a transitory phase in an offender's parole, neither full incarceration nor full freedom in the community, with the goal of gradual reintegration into the community.

There are a number of halfway houses designed specifically to provide culturally sensitive services for the reintegration of Aboriginal offenders. These include but are not limited to the Stan Daniels Centre in Edmonton, Waseskun House outside of Montréal,[283] and the Kwìkwèxwelhp Healing Village run by the Chehalis First Nation in British Columbia. The Beardy's and Okemasis First Nation in Saskatchewan began operation of a forty-bed minimum security institution called the Willow Cree Healing Lodge in 2003. In addition to core programs that address educational and life skills, the facility also provides healing circles and programs designed to raise cultural and spiritual awareness.[284]

Unfortunately, there are too few halfway houses that provide programming specifically for Aboriginal offenders. A study by Jason Brown found that Aboriginal parolees often faced a lack of adequate housing, or racial discrimination from prospective landlords. They were therefore vulnerable to residential instability, which increased their risk of reoffending. The study stressed the needs for increased community supports so that Aboriginal parolees can find adequate housing.[285] The Commission concludes that more supports are needed to address such issues.

37) We call upon the federal government to provide more supports for Aboriginal programming in halfway houses and parole services.

## Overrepresentation of Aboriginal youth in prison

Young offenders are defined as those young people who are at least twelve years of age but less than eighteen at the time of sentencing. Of the youth admitted to custody in Canada in 2011–12, 49% of young women admitted were Aboriginal, as were 36% of the young men admitted. As troubling as these statistics are, they probably understate the case, because they exclude Nova Scotia, Québec, Saskatchewan, and Nunavut, for which data was not available for the period covered.[286] Aboriginal youth accounted for only 7% of the young people aged twelve to seventeen.

Young people who commit crimes have historically been treated differently than adults. The justice system recognizes that young persons have a heightened vulnerability, less maturity, and a reduced capacity for moral judgment, standing as they do at the borderline between childhood and maturity. Canada's youth justice system has operated on the presumption that young people have a reduced degree of moral blameworthiness such that the use of incarceration should be restricted.[287]

This recognition is not only a long-standing characteristic of Canada's domestic law, but is also required by Canada's international legal commitments.[288] The *United Nations Convention on the Rights of the Child* states that children have the right to a criminal justice system that "takes into account the child's age and the desirability of promoting the child's reintegration and the child's assuming a constructive role in society."[289]

Currently, the procedures for addressing young people accused of crimes are set out in the *Youth Criminal Justice Act* (*YCJA*), which was introduced in 2002. One of the key objectives of the *YCJA* is to reserve jail for the most violent or habitual offenders. Even in such cases, one of the express goals of the youth criminal justice system is to address the circumstances underlying a young person's offending behaviour in order to rehabilitate and reintegrate young people back into society.[290] The *YCJA* recognizes that most youth come into contact with the law as a result of fairly minor and isolated incidents, or by impulsive behaviour that should not stigmatize them with a criminal record in the same way as with an adult offender. There are a number of tools to resolve youth cases in informal ways, such as "extrajudicial measures" (e.g., warnings, cautions, mediation, and family conferencing.) This emphasis on reintegration and restorative justice has much in common with Aboriginal perspectives on justice, and gives reason to hope that Aboriginal youth can expect more appropriate treatment when they come into contact with the law.

In addition, the *YCJA* requires youth courts to consider all available sanctions other than custody that are reasonable "with particular attention to the circumstances of aboriginal young persons."[291] The *YCJA* also requires that any "measures taken against young persons who commit offences should ... respond to the needs of aboriginal young persons."[292] There is nothing comparable to such a provision in the *Criminal Code of Canada* applicable to adults. In theory, this should allow Aboriginal youth to maintain access to their traditional practices and to be dealt with by the justice system in accordance with Aboriginal values.[293]

By many objective measures, the *Youth Criminal Justice Act* has been a success. Prior to the *YCJA*, Aboriginal youth had a better chance of going to jail than of graduating from high school.[294] But while there has been a steady decline in youth crime, youth court caseloads, youth supervised on a community sentence and in custody in Canada since the legislation came into effect,[295] the rate of Aboriginal youth incarceration remains high.[296]

Many of today's Aboriginal children and youth are living with the legacy of residential schools, as they struggle to deal with high rates of addiction, fetal alcohol spectrum disorder, mental health issues, family violence, the incarceration of parents, and the intrusion of child welfare authorities. All of these factors place them at greater risk of involvement with crime. In addition, the overincarceration of Aboriginal adults (also tied to the residential schools) has repercussions for their children. One study in British Columbia found that 39% of youth in custody have a parent with a criminal record and 47% have another family member with a criminal record.[297]

## Aboriginal youth crime and the child welfare system

The young person standing before a judge represents the end point of a history of colonization and marginalization that is breathtaking in its scope. The criminal justice system accomplishes little more than increasing that marginalization.

The growing overrepresentation of Aboriginal youth in custody mirrors the even more dramatic overrepresentation of Aboriginal children in child welfare care. The child welfare system plays an important role in Aboriginal youth crime. Not only do children and youth in care have poorer outcomes in education, health, and well-being than the general population,[298] some child welfare facilities are also prime recruiting grounds for Aboriginal gangs, with a large proportion of gang members reporting that they became involved with gangs after placement in either a child welfare or correctional facility.[299]

Almost three-quarters of youth in custody in British Columbia have been in government care at some point in their lives. The fact that, in 2005, 55% of children in care in British Columbia were Aboriginal, leads to the conclusion that overrepresentation within the child welfare system may be one factor contributing to higher proportions of Aboriginal youth in custody.[300] Addressing this national crisis must be a priority if we are to keep Aboriginal young people out of the criminal justice system.

Legal scholar Larry Chartrand observed that it is hard to characterize the rates of Aboriginal youth involvement in the criminal justice system as anything other than discriminatory:

> When the impact of social factors results in greater involvement in the criminal
> justice system than would otherwise be the case, and the circumstances that
> gave rise to such social factors of poverty and social marginalization are attrib-
> uted to the continuing effects of colonization, the result is systemic discrimina-
> tion of Aboriginal youth in the criminal justice system.[301]

The Commission believes that there are ways to reduce the growing overrepresentation of Aboriginal youth in custody, but that they will primarily be found outside the justice system. A recent study examined crime rates throughout Canada and found that Québec had the lowest rates of crime, including violent crime. The author of the study examined a number of possible explanations. He dismissed socioeconomic differences because Québec has lower average incomes than the Prairies, Ontario, or British Columbia, all of which have higher crime rates.[302] He related the findings to Québec's greater investment in social services, including economic supports for families, family housing, a considerable range of services against family violence, health and social services for families and children, parental educations and skills programs, child day care and parental leave systems, and related crime prevention programs.[303] Other provinces would do well to follow Québec's example.

## Barriers to reducing the number of Aboriginal youth in custody

Bill C-10 (passed by Parliament in 2012) made changes to the *Youth Criminal Justice Act*. These changes are likely to undermine attempts within the youth justice system to accommodate Aboriginal justice practices and values. The bill changed some of the most basic principles that guide the way that the justice system deals with young people.

The *YCJA* begins with a section that outlines the basic goals and aspirations of the youth criminal justice system, which include dealing with young people in a way that promotes rehabilitation and reintegration. Prior to the enactment of Bill C-10, this section used to say that the goal was to "promote the *long-term* protection of the public"[304] (emphasis added). It now says that the goal is to "protect the public."[305] This change is significant. Canada has signalled that the long-term gains that come from investing in the rehabilitation of youth are not the priority. Instead, public protection in the here and now is the focus. It may seem a subtle difference, but the consequences may signal a shift of resources away from diversion and informal resolutions and towards custodial sentences.

Under Bill C-10, the *Youth Criminal Justice Act* has been amended to increase reliance on pretrial detention and custodial sentences, in part by broadening the definition of "serious offences" to include any indictable offence for which the maximum punishment is imprisonment for five years or more. This definition of "serious offences" now captures such crimes as theft over $5,000.[306] The powers of the Crown prosecutor to apply to have youth as young as fourteen sentenced as adults have been extended.[307] Sentencing judges are now required to impose sentences that express "denunciation and deterrence" of youth crime.

Denunciation and deterrence have long been sentencing principles in the adult system. A denunciatory sentence reflects general societal disapproval of a given crime. Those convicted are meant to feel the sting of this disapproval with the severity of the sentence. Deterrence in a sentence speaks not just to the convicted, but to observers, again directing the judge to 'send a message' with a severe sentence.

The introduction of deterrence in youth sentences is based on the same questionable premise that harsh sentences will be an example to offenders and other youth, thus deterring them from committing crime. Denunciation and deterrence, however, can have a more punitive effect that can conflict with the goal of rehabilitation. Even in the adult context, there is little evidence that imposing harsh sentences has any impact in deterring crime. In criticizing the inclusion of these principles in the youth system, the Assembly of First Nations observed, "one can assume the denunciation and deterrence would be even less effective for young persons."[308] What the change does accomplish is to send a message to sentencing judges that they are expected to impose longer youth sentences.[309] There is a danger that these amendments will steer judges towards more punitive considerations and away from contextual factors such as residential schools, child welfare system, and the crisis of overrepresentation of Aboriginal people in prisons.

The *Youth Criminal Justice Act* also protects the privacy of youth by banning the publication of names and identifying information. This is an important feature of the criminal justice system designed to ensure that youthful indiscretions do not permanently mar the lives and reputations of young people, including their opportunities for employment. The underlying purpose of the publication ban is to minimize stigma and instead focus on rehabilitation of the young person.[310] The recent amendments now give youth court judges the discretion to lift publication bans whenever a youth is given a sentence for a violent offence.[311] Giving judges the discretion to lift publication bans is not necessary for public safety.

Other changes to the law will make it more likely that Aboriginal youth will find themselves in the formal court process, rather than being diverted into more informal and restorative resolutions. The *Youth Criminal Justice Act* allows police to give cautions or warnings to youth (called "extrajudicial sanctions") rather than a criminal charge. The changes to the Act now allow judges to consider these types of informal sanctions as a reason to sentence youth to a custody centre.[312] As the Canadian Bar Association has observed, these amendments undermine the purpose of extrajudicial sanctions and send a mixed message to the police that they must keep track of situations where they are lenient with a young person because the court may wish to use those statistics at a future date to impose a custodial sentence.

Overall, opportunities to find alternative and restorative means to address youth misconduct have been drastically reduced with a shift towards increased incarceration. The overrepresentation of Aboriginal youth in custody will increase under this new regime, as judges will have less discretion and less inclination to consider the particular circumstances of the young person before them.

All of this speaks to the need to recognize that Aboriginal youth incarceration rates are likely to continue to increase when the evidence shows the ongoing ineffectiveness of incarceration as a means to address Aboriginal youth criminal involvement. The emphasis in the view of the Commission should be to recognize the very clear evidence that youth crime is connected to poverty, home dysfunction, lack of proper parenting, nurturing, and parental love, inadequate child welfare involvement, community breakdown, a poor sense of personal identity and cultural connection, poor school success, youth gang involvement, substance abuse, unemployment, and systemic racism in many aspects of social involvement available to youth. In the view of the Commission, the emphasis when it comes to Aboriginal youth needs to be on how to bring about a decrease in the use of incarceration.

38) We call upon the federal, provincial, territorial, and Aboriginal governments to commit to eliminating the overrepresentation of Aboriginal youth in custody over the next decade.

# Overrepresentation of Aboriginal people among victims of crime

The justice system has historically and consistently failed Aboriginal victims of crime. Aboriginal children were victims of crime in residential schools. Close to 38,000 living Survivors have applied for compensation for sexual or serious physical abuse. Over $2.8 billion has been paid in the approximately 32,000 cases resolved so far.[313] This is the single largest recognition of criminal victimization in Canadian history. Today, the justice system continues to fail Aboriginal people who are disproportionately the victims of crime.

### Missing data

Accurate information about the rate of victimization in Aboriginal communities can be hard to come by. Statistics Canada surveys likely underreport the extent of victimization, because they are not designed to reach Aboriginal people specifically. The studies do not include people without a phone or who do not speak English or French, and do not provide the kinds of supports necessary to permit some Aboriginal victims to comfortably disclose their experience to researchers.

The most recent study by Statistics Canada indicates that the homicide victimization rate of Aboriginal people between 1997 and 2000 was seven times that of non-Aboriginal Canadians. However, that data is no longer being gathered. Statistics Canada's most recent data on homicide and family violence fails to report how many victims were Aboriginal, despite reporting many other characteristics of victims including their ages, gender, and occupations, and whether the victims consumed intoxicants.[314] It is positive that Statistics Canada has indicated that revised data on the Aboriginal identity of victims that were reported to Statistics Canada as a result of the Royal Canadian Mounted Police report on Missing and Murdered Aboriginal Women are planned for release with the 2014 Homicide Survey data.[315] However, so far Statistics Canada has not committed to collecting such information on an ongoing basis.

The Commission notes that other more recent material produced by Statistics Canada on violence against women includes data on police reports as to whether homicide victims were Aboriginal.[316] As in other areas, the Commission is concerned that our statistical knowledge about the conditions faced by Aboriginal people in Canada is getting worse and this may make these issues less visible to Canadians.

39) We call upon the federal government to develop a national plan to collect and publish data on the criminal victimization of Aboriginal people, including data related to homicide and family violence victimization.

## Women as victims of violence

> I ask that everyone here remembers a few simple words—love, kindness, respect and forgiveness ... As a survivor, I respectfully challenge you all to call for a national inquiry into missing and murdered indigenous women.[317]
>
> —*Rinelle Harper, speaking to the Assembly of First Nations*
> *December 9, 2014*

For a brief few moments in the early winter of 2014, a shy sixteen-year-old Aboriginal girl stood before the cameras at a meeting of the Assembly of First Nations in Winnipeg. She held an eagle feather and, though she spoke quietly, millions heard what she had to say. The story of the savage attack she had endured barely a month earlier had caught the attention of the country—as did the fact that she chose to make such a public appeal. Her name is Rinelle Harper. In early November, two men assaulted her, beat her, and left her for dead on the banks of the Assiniboine River in Winnipeg. That she survived the attack is a testament to her strength.

The story of Rinelle Harper is but one part of a sweeping history of Aboriginal women and girls who are victims of crime. In the past decade, there has been growing public awareness and concern about the large number of Aboriginal women and girls who have been killed or have gone missing. The recent release of data has amplified that concern and led to the widespread call for a public inquiry into the issue. It is a call that the Commission supports.

Aboriginal women are more likely than other women to experience risk factors for violence. They are disproportionately young, poor, unemployed, likely to have been involved with the child welfare system and to live in a community marked by social disorder.[318]

Statistics Canada's 2009 General Social Survey (GSS) found that 13% of Aboriginal women reported that they had experienced violence within the past year, a rate 2.5 times higher than non-Aboriginal women.[319] Most of these violent incidents were never reported to police (over three-quarters of such incidents).[320] It is likely that the GSS study itself underreports the extent of crime against Aboriginal people because of the failure to make special outreach to Aboriginal people. This makes it findings of disproportionate victimization of Aboriginal women all the more disturbing.

Extremely high rates of intimate-partner violence are one of the causes of the high victimization rate. Of those Aboriginal women with a current or former spouse who responded to the GSS, 15% reported having been a victim of spousal violence in the previous five years, as compared to 6% of non-Aboriginal women.[321] The spousal violence reported by Aboriginal women was more severe, with 59% of Aboriginal female spousal violence victims reporting injury as compared to 41% of non-Aboriginal female victims.[322] Aboriginal survivors of spousal violence were also more likely to report having been victimized multiple times in the past five years, with 59% reporting being victimized more than once as compared to 43% of non-Aboriginal victims.[323]

Tabitha Takawgak was married to a residential school Survivor. She recounted,

> I was married to him for 35 years. I couldn't take it anymore and I finally left him. I loved him and I wanted him as my husband for my lifetime. It's so hard to be married to a man who has been abused in this way. As the woman who spoke before me said, my dear children also suffered. I have many sons with my former husband and one has been in and out of jail and we lost our oldest to suicide. During those times that we were suffering I wanted to help my husband but I didn't know what to do. I loved my husband and yet he was my abuser ... I don't want people to think badly of my husband. I still love him so much but I had to make a choice to no longer be his wife today.[324]

Residential schools deprived children of access to cultural and spiritual teachings and disrupted Aboriginal women's traditional roles as "mothers, grandmothers, caregivers, nurturers, teachers, and family decision-makers."[325] Discriminatory *Indian Act* provisions that had the effect of denying Aboriginal identity to women who married non-Aboriginal men, and their children, and this contributed to the separation of Aboriginal women from their communities.

Among the many tragic cases of violence perpetrated against Aboriginal women several have become particularly well known and serve as case studies.

## Helen Betty Osborne

Early in the morning of November 13, 1971, Helen Betty Osborne, aged nineteen, was approached in The Pas, Manitoba, by four white men who wanted to pick up an Aboriginal woman for sex. She was abducted, sexually assaulted, and brutally murdered—stabbed fifty times with a screwdriver. Her skull, cheekbones, and palate were broken and her face was unrecognizable. She was left naked.

Betty Osborne attended Guy Hill residential school because there were no similar educational opportunities provided by the federal government in her home community of Norway House, a northern Cree community. In 1991 the Manitoba Aboriginal Justice Inquiry found that Betty Osborne was in The Pas because of government policy of "removing Aboriginal children from the influence of their parents and their cultures and to educate them to the 'white man's ways'" and found that "the actions of the government in doing so were clearly racist and discriminatory."[326]

It was not until sixteen years later that one of the murderers was convicted. The other three men went free. This was the conclusion of the Manitoba Aboriginal Justice Inquiry:

Helen Betty Osborne would not have been killed if she had not been Aboriginal. The four men who took her to her death from the streets of The Pas that night had gone looking for an Aboriginal girl with whom to "party." They found Betty Osborne. When she refused to party she was driven out of town and murdered. Those who abducted her showed a total lack of regard for her person or her rights as an individual. Those who stood by while the physical assault took place, while sexual advances were made and while she was being beaten to death showed their own racism, sexism and indifference. Those who knew the story and remained silent must share their guilt.[327]

One of Helen Betty Osborne's friends spoke with the Commission about life today in Norway House:

I'm glad you guys came ... There's so much drugs going on here; a lot of drinking; young kids. Not too long ago we had a murder too, a young girl got stabbed. I guess some guys went to her house, their house and beat up the dad and she jumped in to help her dad and she got stabbed and she got killed; about two weeks ago. She was only about 20 years old. I couldn't even bring myself to go to the wake, to the funeral, I just. I couldn't do it; I couldn't bring myself to come there. There's so much of that going on; holy it's bad. And I always think, "Yup, that's the schools, the residential schools" put a big hole in our lives.[328]

This statement reveals how the trauma of residential schools and disproportionate victimization by crime continue in Aboriginal communities like Norway House to this day.

## Robert Pickton's victims

Another infamous case of violence against women that is connected with the legacy of residential schools is Robert Pickton's multiple murders of women from Vancouver's Downtown Eastside. Many of Pickton's victims were Aboriginal; some were residential school Survivors. One of the first victims who went missing in 1983 was Rebecca Guno, a member of the Nisga'a Nation, who attended residential school and had been working as a sex worker. A friend told the provincial Missing Women Commission about her last meeting with Guno:

She introduced me to her son. During the course of our conversation she said "I'm a prostitute, Millie; I can't really explain why. But it's a living, we do what we have to do ... Life's not that bad. I have my baby and that's all that matters to me. His dad is really good to us, but I'm gonna keep doing what I do, his dad knows that and we are happy to be parents to our baby ... We're happy and that's what matters. I'm not ashamed of myself."[329]

Georgina Papin was from Hobbema, Alberta, and attended residential school. She was placed in foster care before she ran away at the age of twelve and began sex work in Las Vegas at the age of fourteen.[330] The police failed to investigate properly when Papin went missing. For example, they did not conduct interviews at native friendship centres she was known to attend.[331] Her remains were later found on the Pickton farm, and Robert Pickton was convicted of second-degree murder in her death.[332] Dawn Crey, another victim, was an intergenerational Survivor and was also placed in non -Aboriginal foster homes as a child.[333] When Crey was reported missing, the police apparently did nothing for six weeks and only interviewed one witness.[334]

## Marlene Bird

On June 1, 2014, police in Prince Albert, Saskatchewan, found the body of Marlene Bird. She'd been sexually assaulted, beaten with a nail-studded board, and then set on fire. Although she survived, she would later lose both her legs, and surgeons would have to reattach half her face. "What did I do so wrong to have this happen to me?" Bird asked APTN News in Prince Albert. "I do try my best to be strong."[335]

Marlene Bird comes from the small northern Saskatchewan community of Molanosa. Talking of her childhood at home with alcoholic parents she said, "I remember playing with dolls, and they'd be inside drinking. When they started getting loud that's when I knew, dad bought something again ... so I started drinking that wine, me and my little brother."[336]

She was also in the residential school system. In a graphic novel of her story, she says that she was sexually abused in the school and again later as a young adult.[337] Her daughter was also abused but refused to speak about it to the police. Bird says she blamed herself and turned to alcohol, and that's when her own children were taken away.

## Tina Fontaine

In early August 2014, fifteen-year-old Tina Fontaine, a girl from Sagkeeng First Nation, was reported missing in Winnipeg. A week later, two Winnipeg police officers stopped a car with Tina Fontaine in it. Even though she was fifteen and intoxicated, and was already listed as a missing person, they allowed the car to move on with her in it. Nine days later, her body was found wrapped in a bag in the Red River. Fontaine's great-aunt was told by the chief investigator that the officers had run her identity through the system and released her anyway. When it became known that the two officers had contact with Tina Fontaine prior to her murder, they were put on administrative leave. Several months later, the Winnipeg Police Service announced that although the officers were to be disciplined, no charges would be made against them for their conduct.[338] It is cases like this one that lead Aboriginal groups to question the willingness of the police to protect Aboriginal citizens. This lack of trust has some of its origins in the police's role in enforcing attendance at residential schools and in the less than robust performance of the police and courts in responding to wide spread violence against Aboriginal children in the residential schools.

## Missing and murdered Aboriginal women and girls

Public awareness of the issue of violence against Aboriginal women has continued to grow through the efforts of advocates and through the work of high-profile investigations, inquiries, and reports.

### Native Women's Association investigation

The Native Women's Association of Canada (NWAC), through its Sisters in Spirit project, has done groundbreaking work in discovering the truth about murdered and missing Aboriginal women and girls. This was a multi-year research, education, and policy initiative funded by Status of Women Canada, and was specifically designed to uncover the root causes, circumstances, and trends in violence against Aboriginal women in order to promote policy change to increase the personal safety and security of Aboriginal women and girls.

The Sisters in Spirit project found that, in most of the cases they identified, parents or grandparents of the missing or murdered women had attended residential school. Many grew up in families experiencing serious dysfunction, were forced into the child welfare system and adopted into non-Aboriginal families.[339] Without access to quality education and fewer employment opportunities, a high proportion of Aboriginal women and their children live in poverty and in situations of dangerous dependency and unsafe housing.[340] The devaluing of Aboriginal peoples symbolized by residential schools also contributes to the vulnerability of Aboriginal women. They are targeted for violence because they are Aboriginal, on the assumption that no one will miss them and police will not take the case seriously. Too often, this assumption proves to be true.

Sisters in Spirit also identified particular areas (and cities) in which Aboriginal women are at extremely high risk of violence, disappearance, and death. The cities include Regina, Saskatoon, Edmonton, Winnipeg, Vancouver, and communities in Northern British Columbia along Highway 16.[341] The 724 kilometres of Highway 16 that run between Prince Rupert and Prince George has been named the "Highway of Tears" because of the extraordinary number of young women who have gone missing along this stretch of road. Because of a lack of public transportation, those living in rural areas often have to resort to hitchhiking rides with strangers. Over a thirty-five-year period, some estimate that as many as forty women have been murdered or gone missing on that highway.[342] The majority of those victims were Aboriginal.[343]

In 2006, a Highway of Tears Symposium was organized by a number of affected First Nations and allied organizations. Among the recommendations that resulted from that symposium was a plan to prevent hitchhiking along Highway 16 through the establishment of a shuttle bus service. In 2012, that recommendation was adopted by the British Columbia Missing Women's Inquiry and by mayors in communities along the highway.[344] Yet, a month later, Greyhound Canada announced cuts on fifteen routes, including a 40% reduction in service along Highway 16.[345] Three years after the recommendation was accepted, it has not been implemented.

When the Sisters in Spirit project was completed, the Native Women's Association had identified 582 missing or murdered Aboriginal women and girls for the period between 1944 and 2010. Of those women, 67% were murder cases, 20% were missing persons, 4% were suspicious deaths, and 9% were simply unknown (i.e., it is unclear whether the victim was murdered, is missing, or died in suspicious circumstances).[346] Most of the cases in the database were from the previous ten years, occurring at a rate of about twenty cases per year, but the association believed that there were many unidentified older cases that were simply unrecorded and unknown.

The Sisters in Spirit final report indicated that 88% of the missing women had children or grandchildren, and it underlined the intergenerational effects of the loss of parents and parenting skills due to the residential schools experience and the Sixties Scoop (the wide-scale apprehension of Aboriginal children in the 1960s, 1970s, and 1980s). The report noted that only 13% of the women it had identified had been murdered on a reserve and only 7% had gone missing from a reserve.[347] Of the cases where location was known, 70% of the women and girls disappeared from an urban area and 60% were found murdered in an urban area. The study concluded that Aboriginal women were almost three times more likely to be murdered by a stranger than non-Aboriginal women.[348]

There were 149 cases identified where the activity of the missing women was known. About half of those women were involved in the sex trade, but the majority were not.[349] The study also found that only 53% of the cases involving homicide had resulted in a charge, a much lower rate than is typical in homicide cases.[350]

In 2010, the Government of Canada ceased funding the Sisters in Spirit project. While the Native Women's Association maintains the database as best it can, it does not have the resources that it once did.[351] The Government of Canada's refusal to continue to fund the project is part of a disturbing and recurring pattern of cuts to Aboriginal organizations that have been collecting information and knowledge about Aboriginal people. Other examples include the cuts to various Aboriginal health organizations, the long-form census, and other research conducted by Statistics Canada.

In March 2013, the Native Women's Association revised its record of cases of missing or murdered Aboriginal women and girls to 668.[352] That research was supplemented through the work of Maryanne Pearce, who completed a dissertation in 2013 at the University of Ottawa on missing and murdered women in Canada.[353] Also relying on publicly available information, Pearce's database includes 3,329 women (both Aboriginal and non-Aboriginal) who went missing or were murdered between 1946 and 2013. Ethnicity was known for only 1,595 of the women listed. Of these, 824 were identified as Aboriginal.[354]

## House of Commons Standing Committee on the Status of Women

In 2010–11 the House of Commons Standing Committee on the Status of Women heard from 150 witnesses across the country about violence against Aboriginal women. The Committee also heard about a pattern of police failing to take reports of missing and murdered Aboriginal women and of serious delays in investigations. They were told that in domestic violence situations, police do not always respond in a timely manner, and that the police sometimes dismiss claims of sexual assault by Aboriginal women who they consider to be living a 'high-risk' lifestyle.

Aboriginal women are often treated as offenders, rather than Survivors or victims, making women less likely to contact police for help. Witnesses attributed this negligent approach to violence against Aboriginal women to racism and sexism by police officers, but also to the underresourced nature of policing on reserves and in more remote communities. As with many other areas of the lives of Aboriginal peoples, their access to police services can be undermined by overlapping and unclear jurisdictional lines. In some cases, it is unclear whether the RCMP, First Nations, municipal, or provincial police forces are responsible for the investigation.[355]

## Oppal Inquiry

The Honourable Wally T. Oppal, formerly a justice of the British Columbia Court of Appeal, and later BC's attorney general, served as commissioner of the Missing Women Commission of Inquiry. In his report, released in 2012, Justice Oppal said he was

> particularly troubled by the failure of the police to employ an Aboriginal-specific investigation strategy given the disproportionate number of Aboriginal women among the missing women from the DTES [Downtown Eastside]. The First Nations Summit had brought their concerns about the large number of murdered Aboriginal women to the attention of the VPD, RCMP and PUHU [Vancouver Police Department, Royal Canadian Mounted Police, and Provincial Unsolved Homicides Unit] through its requests for action in February 1997. Independent Counsel for

Aboriginal Interests repeatedly asked police witnesses about their consideration of tailored investigative strategies involving the Aboriginal community: the responses were woefully deficient ... The police completely overlooked the Aboriginal dimensions of the missing women crisis throughout the investigations. This systemic blindness to distinctiveness and specificity of the Aboriginal communities is staggering in light of the number of Aboriginal victims.[356]

Justice Oppal also singled out the RCMP for criticism by noting,

it is particularly difficult to comprehend the RCMP's failure to prioritize the missing and murdered women investigations. The fact that it did not do so is a blatant manifestation of systemic bias. Given its long history of involvement in the colonization process, including the forced recruitment and confinement of Aboriginal children in residential schools, the RCMP has a heightened duty to protect Aboriginal people. There is no evidence that the RCMP took active steps to meet this moral obligation.[357]

## 2014 RCMP Report

In May 2014, the RCMP released *Missing and Murdered Aboriginal Women: A National Operational Overview*. The document identified 1,181 cases of Aboriginal women and girls who were murdered or still considered missing. To be more specific, that's 1,017 Aboriginal women and girls who are known to have been killed since 1980, and 164 who are missing, and suspected to have been the victims of foul play. When these RCMP statistics are compared to those of non-Aboriginal women, it reveals that Aboriginal women are four times more likely to be victims of homicide. The report notes that "In 2011, there were 718,500 Aboriginal females in Canada, representing 4.3% of the overall female population that year."[358] The report goes on to point out,

Between 1980 and 2012, there were 20,313 homicides across Canada, which averaged approximately 615 per year. Females represented 32% of homicide victims (6,551 victims) across all police jurisdictions between 1980 and 2012. Every province and territory was implicated. There were 1,017 Aboriginal female victims of homicide during this period, which represents roughly 16% of all female homicides—far greater than their representation in Canada's female population.[359]

In its review, the RCMP attempted to explain a history of confusion that had prevented the force from identifying Aboriginal victims of crime:

The use of the term "Aboriginal" as a descriptor has different definitions in the different data sources that make up this research project. For example, CPIC (Canadian Police Information Centre) captures Aboriginal as an "ethnicity" whereas Statistics Canada's official position is that "Aboriginal" is not an ethnicity but rather an origin ... Differences in police practice between agencies make it hard to create a data set that is comparable across jurisdictions. For example, in collecting data on homicides, some agencies use official Aboriginal "status" as the means to determine identity, others use officer discretion (as discussed above), and others rely on self-identification by individuals or their associations (family, friend etc.) ... Historical police service (including the RCMP) adherence to jurisdictional and organizational policies has undermined the consistent collection and sharing of information on Aboriginal identity. This has meant a high number of Homicide Survey reports where the identity of the victim (and/or the accused) remained "unknown."[360]

Because of the ambiguities in identification and data collection, many believe that the number of murdered and missing women has been underestimated. Aboriginal scholar and activist Pamela Palmater wrote, "It is logical to conclude that the RCMP grossly under-counted the actual numbers of murdered and missing Aboriginal women in Canada. This conclusion is confirmed by the RCMP's own admission that due to these methodological problems 'a high number of Homicide survey reports where the identity of the victim (and/or accused) remained unknown.'"[361]

The release of the RCMP report has intensified public calls for a public inquiry into the issue. The federal government, however, has denied there is need for an inquiry and has suggested that the causes of violence against Aboriginal women are already known. Aboriginal Affairs Minister Bernard Valcourt has said that First Nation men have a "lack of respect" for women and girls on reserve. In a March 2015 speech he told Alberta chiefs that 70% of the cases of murdered and missing Aboriginal women were the result of the actions of Aboriginal men.[362] Information subsequently released by the RCMP was interpreted as supporting the minister's assertion.[363]

Many Canadians have rejected the contention that an inquiry is unnecessary because all the contributing factors are already known and understood. Pamela Palmater writes,

> This shell game of numbers and statistics is meant to blame the victim and deflect attention away from Canada's continued inaction to address this crisis which the United Nations has called a "grave violation" of our basic human rights. The crisis of murdered and missing Indigenous women and little girls continues while Canada (through Valcourt) blames the victim and the RCMP fail to live up to their duty to serve and protect everyone in Canada.[364]

## International voices of concern

Although there are many voices calling for a national inquiry into the murdered and missing Aboriginal women and girls, the federal government has refused to establish one. That refusal has drawn international criticism. Respected international human rights organizations that often focus on disappearances in brutal dictatorships now conclude that it is necessary to examine Canada's problem of missing and murdered Aboriginal women.[365]

## United Nations

United Nations human rights treaty monitoring bodies—including those committees addressing children's rights violations, torture, discrimination against women, and civil and political rights violations—have criticized Canada for the inadequate government response to violence against Aboriginal women and girls.[366] The UN Committee for the Elimination of Discrimination Against Women expressed concern that "hundreds of cases involving aboriginal women who have gone missing or been murdered in the past two decades have neither been fully investigated nor attracted priority attention, with the perpetrators remaining unpunished."[367] The committee urged Canada to investigate the cases, to determine whether there is a racial pattern to the disappearances, and to take the necessary steps to remedy the deficiencies in the system.

The UN special rapporteur on the rights of Indigenous peoples remarked that a national inquiry "could help ensure a coordinated response and the opportunity for the loved ones of victims to be heard, and would demonstrate a responsiveness to the concerns raised by the families and communities affected by this epidemic. These and further steps are required to realize the promise of healing and a new relationship that was made in the 2008 apology."[368]

## Amnesty International

Amnesty International points out that the scale of violence faced by Aboriginal women in Canada is a human rights violation. The organization says comprehensive national response is required that "addresses the social and economic factors that place Indigenous women at heightened risk of violence; ... the police response to violence against Indigenous women; the dramatic gap in standard of living and quality of life; ... continued disruption of Indigenous societies by the high proportion of children put into state care; and the disproportionate imprisonment of Indigenous women."[369]

## Human Rights Watch

In response to the number of missing and murdered women along the Highway of Tears in Northern British Columbia, Human Rights Watch worked with the community to investigate. The organization conducted interviews with fifty Aboriginal women and girls, nineteen community service providers, and seven current and former RCMP officers.[370] The investigators found that "for many Indigenous women and girls interviewed for this report, abuses and other indignities visited on them by the police have come to define their relationship with law enforcement."[371]

Human Rights Watch was told stories of excessive use of force, racist and sexist verbal abuse, cross-gender searches, and sexual and physical abuse by police officers.

When police protection was sought in response to domestic violence, community service providers and Aboriginal women reported that police sometimes blamed the women for the abuse and shamed them for alcohol or substance use. Not surprisingly, Human Rights Watch found that "indigenous women and girls report having little faith that police forces responsible for mistreatment and abuse can offer them protection when they face violence in the wider community."[372]

For all the reasons enumerated by these organizations and many others, the Commission believes that a comprehensive inquiry must be undertaken.

41) We call upon the federal government, in consultation with Aboriginal organizations, to appoint a public inquiry into the causes of, and remedies for, the disproportionate victimization of Aboriginal women. The inquiry's mandate would include:

 i. Investigation into missing and murdered Aboriginal women and girls.

 ii. Links to the intergenerational legacy of residential schools.

In making this call to action, the Commission offers the following considerations:

1. A public inquiry will need to have two different components. It will need to be a fact-based inquiry as well as a policy inquiry, examining both individual cases as well as systemic issues.
2. In order for the inquiry to have sufficient credibility, a consultation advisory committee should be struck to make recommendations concerning its mandate. Such a committee should include professional advisors, Aboriginal women, and representatives of victims' families.
3. In examining individual cases, the inquiry must be cautious when dealing with open cases in which there may be a person of interest and where additional evidence is needed to lay a charge.
4. The inquiry should be allowed to look into the role of governments, the RCMP, and other police services, and the child welfare system.
5. An inquiry should consider using witness panels with multiple witnesses as opposed to only single witnesses testifying, when considering systemic issues.
6. Commissions would not be able to name offenders, or identify criminal wrongdoing that has not already been found through an appropriate criminal process.
7. Anyone potentially affected by an inquiry must be protected from character and reputational harm, and has the right to attend and be heard.
8. An inquiry would provide an opportunity for personal, family, and

community healing. Health supports for persons involved will need to be provided.

9. The need for families of victims to know more must be an important factor.

10. The inquiry should be mandated to study the role of police in the investigations of the cases.

11. The inquiry should gather and analyze data relating to
   • where and when incidents occurred;
   • the specific circumstances of incidents;
   • consistencies, similarities, and differences between incidents;
   • how many victims were engaged in a high-risk lifestyle; and
   • whether there been a change in the number of incidents since 2010.

12. The inquiry should examine whether there is evidence of gang involvement (e.g., street gangs, motorcycle gangs, traffickers in the sex trade with international ties).

13. Is there evidence of serial killings?

14. What did police or others know, and when did they know it?

15. What is the degree of interprovincial and national coordination in investigations?

16. Is violence against Aboriginal women and girls in Canada comparable to what is happening to Indigenous women in other countries (including the United States, Australia, New Zealand, and Africa)?

17. Is there a Great Lakes sex trade with operatives at play?

18. Since the termination of federal funding to the Native Women's Association of Canada's Sisters in Spirit project, how effective have federal initiatives to address Aboriginal female victimization been?

19. Is there evidence to support the contention that the government's tough on crime initiative is helping to reduce victimization?

20. What analysis did the federal government conduct prior to its decision to shut down further research by the Native Women's Association of Canada in 2010?

21. Has the number of missing and murdered Aboriginal women reduced in frequency since 2010?

22. Is it likely that the number of missing and murdered Aboriginal women will increase?

## Supporting Aboriginal victims of crime

Supports to victims of crime are offered by a variety of service providers. These supports may be provided by police services, community-based agencies, or by the courts. Some provide assistance in navigating the justice system; some provide residential shelter, and others focus on the victims of sexual assault, providing specialized medical care and emotional support.[373] Culturally appropriate services are needed for all Aboriginal victims of crime but particularly for Aboriginal women. A 2012 survey conducted by Statistics Canada found that only 3% of shelters exclusively serve an on-reserve population (a total of eighteen shelters).[374] At the same time, funding from Aboriginal Affairs for emergency shelters is currently available only to Aboriginal people on reserves, which excludes almost all communities in the Territories.[375] The problem is particularly severe for Inuit women living in the North, where more than 70% of the communities do not have a shelter for abused women and children. Nunavik has only three shelters to serve fourteen northern villages.[376] There is also a lack of culturally appropriate services for Aboriginal women in urban areas and a lack of any services at all in some rural and remote communities.[377]

In a Statistics Canada survey conducted in 2011 and 2012, 760 victim service providers were interviewed. Only 28% of them reported that they provide services to Aboriginal people. Twelve per cent of providers reported they could provide services in Cree, 3% in Ojibway, 1% in Inuktitut, and 11% in other Aboriginal languages. The majority of victim services said they provide protection and support for criminal justice matters: 64% offered medical related services; 59% offered shelter-related services; 56% offered assistance with compensation; and 47% offering counselling. Only 9% report providing restorative justice proceedings but 27% will provide support for crime victims in such informal processes.[378]

There is an urgent need for more study of the effectiveness of the services that are provided to Aboriginal crime victims. Some victim services are offered by the police but, given the historic strains in the relationship between Aboriginal people and the police, the police may not be the best service provider for Aboriginal crime victims. There is a danger that victim services will focus on supporting victims only in the formal criminal justice system and not on providing other supports including supports in out of court processes.

## Declaration of Basic Principles of Justice for Victims of Crime and Abuse of Power

The General Assembly of the United Nations proclaimed a *Declaration of Basic Principles of Justice for Victims of Crime and Abuse of Power* in 1985, which was co-sponsored by the Department of Justice and subsequently adopted by Canada's federal and provincial/territorial governments.[379] This declaration defines victims broadly to include both victims of crime and abuse of power by "public officials or other agents in acting in an official or quasi-official official capacity."

Article 5 of the 1985 UN Declaration contemplates that victims should receive redress through formal or informal means. Article 6 recognizes that efforts should be taken to protect the privacy of victims in the criminal process and protect them against unnecessary delay, intimidation, and retaliation. Article 7 specifically states that "Informal mechanisms for the resolution of disputes, including mediation, arbitration and customary justice or indigenous practices, should be utilized where appropriate to facilitate conciliation and redress for victims." It goes on to provide that "Indigenous individuals have the rights to life, physical and mental integrity, liberty and security of person," and article 7(2) specifically affirms that Indigenous people have "the collective right to live in freedom, peace and security as distinct peoples and shall not be subjected to any act of genocide or any other act of violence, including forcibly removing children of the group to another group."

Article 8 obliges states to both prevent and redress acts such as the operation of residential school, acts that have "the aim or effect of depriving" Indigenous people of their integrity as distinct peoples, or of their cultural values or ethnic identities. As with the 1985 United Nations Declaration, states are obligated to prevent and redress serious breaches of these rights.

Article 12 provides that "States should endeavour to provide financial compensation to:

(a) Victims who have sustained significant bodily injury or impairment of physical or mental health as a result of serious crimes;

(b) The family, in particular dependents of persons who have died or become physically or mentally incapacitated as a result of such victimization.

Article 14 of the 1985 UN Declaration recognizes the importance of Indigenous communities providing various forms of assistance for Indigenous victims of crime or abuse of state power by providing that "Victims should receive the necessary material, medical, psychological and social assistance through governmental, voluntary, community-based and indigenous means."

Article 17 also recognizes that in "providing services and assistance to victims, attention should be given to those who have special needs because of … race, colour, sex, age, language, religion, nationality, political or other opinion, cultural beliefs or practices, property, birth or family status, ethnic or social origin, and disability." This UN Declaration provides a sound basis for recognizing the distinct needs of Aboriginal crime victims and ensuring that they receive a broad range of appropriate health and economic support.

## 2007 *UN Declaration on the Rights of Indigenous Peoples*

In 2007, the UN proclaimed another declaration of particular importance for rights that are relevant to Aboriginal victims of crime or state power: the *UN Declaration on the Rights of Indigenous Peoples*. [380] The 2007 UN Declaration provides for a broad range of educational, linguistic, cultural, land, and self-government rights, and the rights not to be removed from their land and not to suffer discrimination. Although not formally framed as such, these broad rights to development and self-determination can be seen as crime prevention actions that foster strong Indigenous families, schools, communities, and health services that will allow people to live law abiding lives and to demonstrate greater resilience if crime does occur.

Article 22 of the 2007 UN Declaration also provides a right of particular relevance given the situation of missing and murdered Aboriginal women and girls in Canada by providing that "States shall take measures, in conjunction with indigenous peoples, to ensure that indigenous women and children enjoy the full protection and guarantees against all forms of violence and discrimination."

The international recognition of the need for services for the victims of crime—particularly women—has outpaced the willingness of Canadian governments to adequately respond.

**40)** We call on all levels of government, in collaboration with Aboriginal people, to create adequately funded and accessible Aboriginal-specific victim programs and services with appropriate evaluation mechanisms.

## Blurred lines between victims and offenders

One of the failings of the Canadian justice system towards Aboriginal people is its tendency to divide services between those for victims and those for offenders and ignore the overlap between the two populations. For so many in Aboriginal communities, there's no distinction between those who are the offenders and those who are the victims. The cycle of abuse that began with the residential schools has not been broken.

Michael Sillett was sexually assaulted while he was a student in a hostel in North West River, Newfoundland. He explained,

> These incidents, these incidents have had a tremendous impact in my later life outside the dorm ... I found it very hard to trust people. I didn't like to be hugged or touched. I didn't have much respect for authority figures; I had a bad attitude that stunted my full potential all my life. I have broken the law. I have

done things that I am deeply ashamed of. My greatest regret is hurting my three daughters; especially my eldest.[381]

Ron McHugh, an intergenerational Survivor told the Commission of the connection he saw between victimization and crime:

> It all stems from that one thing, that one policy, that one act—residential school. And so, today, I mean, you take a dysfunctional family of people. You know, a history of molestation over generations and generations—that's just one family. Now, you take a whole culture of people, and that kind of behaviour also goes from generation to generation.[382]

Many of the difficulties that both Aboriginal victims of crime and offenders suffer, including substance abuse and poverty, stem from the common legacy of residential schools. A related failure is the system's reluctance to appreciate that, in the Aboriginal context especially, it is often necessary to heal individuals by healing families and communities. Strategies must be directed towards community structures and dynamics as well as families. They must also recognize the tremendous diversity of cultures among Aboriginal peoples.

## The way forward: Aboriginal justice systems

The Royal Commission on Aboriginal Peoples recommended that justice systems should be central in self-government for Aboriginal communities and that such systems respond to the legacy of colonialism and forced assimilation that distinguished the circumstances of Aboriginal people from other disadvantaged groups.[383]

Article 5 of the *United Nations Declaration on the Rights of Indigenous Peoples* recognizes the right to self-determining justice systems: "Indigenous peoples have the right to maintain and strengthen their distinct political, legal, economic, social and cultural institutions, while retaining their right to participate fully, if they so choose, in the political, economic, social and cultural life of the State."[384]

Manitoba's Aboriginal Justice Inquiry concluded,

> Wherever possible, Aboriginal justice systems look toward the development of culturally appropriate rules and processes which have as their aim the establishment of a less formalistic approach to courtroom procedures so that Aboriginal litigants are able to gain a degree of comfort from the proceedings while not compromising the rights of an accused charged with a criminal offence.[385]

The Manitoba Inquiry proposed that all people within the relevant territory be subject to Aboriginal justice systems and that Aboriginal communities be entitled to enact their own criminal, civil, and family laws and to have those laws enforced by their own justice systems. If they wish, they should also have the right to adopt any federal or provincial law and to apply or enforce that as well.

Aboriginal forms of justice will be as diverse as Canada's Aboriginal peoples. Typically, they would involve community-based justice processes, employing customary law, and focusing on restoring balance to communities. This vision of Aboriginal justice would, in a manner similar to American tribal courts, allow Aboriginal courts, in some cases, to have jurisdiction over criminal, family, and civil matters involving Aboriginal people that may arise, as they frequently will, in the cities.

## Cautions

The Commission fully supports this vision but recognizes that there may be some risks in undertaking Aboriginal justice initiatives, especially in small communities that have suffered much intergenerational trauma. Aboriginal and restorative justice is slower than processing through the courts. Extra time and expense must be invested if a vulnerable victim is also included in the community justice process. Care must be taken to ensure proper supports and ceremony for both offenders and victims and their supporters.

Concerns have been raised about approaches that rely on often underfinanced and strained communities to correct offenders. If an Aboriginal offender lacks support in the community, he or she may be vulnerable to the exploitation of a power differential enjoyed by community factions who are hostile to the offender. In consensual decision-making processes such as sentencing circles, this can result in a chorus of disapproval voiced against an offender who demands especially harsh sanctions.

Joyce Dalmyn observes that such realities have tainted some sentencing circles:

> If the feather gets passed around and no-one makes any comment whatsoever, I have heard a judge state, right on the record, "Well it's clear that because nothing has been said, obviously they're not willing to say anything good about this person therefore I can only draw the conclusion that there's no sympathy for this person and I have to use the harshest penalties available to me."[386]

Ross Gordon Green is a provincial court judge in Yorkton, Saskatchewan, who has written about Aboriginal justice. He cautions, "A concern with these community sentencing and mediation approaches is that local involvement should not become a forum for the application of political pressure to the advantage of local elite and to the detriment of politically unpopular or marginalized offenders or victims."[387]

Judge Claude Fafard presided over Saskatchewan's first modern day sentencing circle. He expressed these reservations:

I guess the greater thing is that it affects so many different people in that one community, that I'm almost afraid of some political influence. Because it touches on so many people, and I just sort of felt that maybe I should be there to ensure that politics doesn't get involved, that you don't have a powerful family dictating to a weaker family, that kind of thing.[388]

Some Aboriginal scholars have expressed concerns that Elders may be idealized as participants on whom communities will depend in pursuing their visions of justice.[389] There have been times, however, when individual Elders have fallen short of conducting themselves in accordance with expectations, and with serious repercussions for justice processes.

Bruce Miller relates that abuses of power plagued the South Island Justice Education Project on Vancouver Island. Elders, often from powerful families, would try to convince female victims to acquiesce to lighter sanctions for offenders under the project rather than the usual justice system. Their tactics included the offering of various persuasions in favour of dropping the allegations, the threat of witchcraft to inflict harm, or threatening to send the abuser to use physical intimidation. Some women felt that the problem was exacerbated by the fact that some of the Elders were themselves convicted sex offenders, which left them wondering how seriously their safety and concerns would be addressed. The project ended in 1993.[390]

David Milward is a law professor, specializing in Aboriginal justice issues, and a member of the Beardy's and Okemasis Nation in Saskatchewan. He suggests that the *Canadian Charter of Rights and Freedoms* has a role in ensuring the fairness of contemporary adaptations of Aboriginal justice. One of his proposals is for Aboriginal communities to administer their own community courts. These courts would have an important role in ensuring that participants in the process behave fairly towards each other, without intimidation or coercion. The customary law of Aboriginal communities would govern the disputes and the 'sentence' without reference to Canadian sentencing law. The community court judges would intervene only when one party has tried to exploit a power differential or coerce the other party. The community court judge could, for example, suspend matters indefinitely if the process is marginalizing an accused. If it is the victim who is being coerced or harassed, the community court judge could then impose a resolution that prioritizes the victim's safety, even over the objections of the other party. A community court judge thus becomes more of an arbitrator and mediator with some judicial powers.[391]

## A prerequisite for change

Canada's legal system failed to prevent the abuses that took place in the residential schools and when it did, Survivors were often re-victimized by the adversarial and alienating nature of the justice system. Eventually, all the parties to the residential school litigation agreed that the Canadian legal system was not well-equipped to deal with the massive injustice of residential schools and designed an innovative settlement that allowed claims to be settled in a less adversarial forum. The settlement also recognized the need for collective reparations in the form of the Aboriginal Healing Foundation and this Commission. Given the failure of the Canadian legal system to stop or repair the genocidal injustice of residential schools, it is only reasonable to suggest that Aboriginal people be allowed to develop their own justice systems.

**42)** We call upon the federal, provincial, and territorial governments to commit to the recognition and implementation of Aboriginal justice systems in a manner consistent with the Treaty and Aboriginal rights of Aboriginal peoples, the *Constitution Act, 1982,* and the *United Nations Declaration on the Rights of Indigenous Peoples,* endorsed by Canada in November 2012.

## Conclusion

The justice system needs to be reformed if the crisis of Aboriginal overrepresentation is not to become worse. Aboriginal people should not continue to be imprisoned and victimized because of the legacy of residential schools. That said, the Commission is convinced that overrepresentation in the justice system will not be reduced by justice system reform alone. It will be necessary to address all of the ongoing harms of residential schools—the harms to Aboriginal family, education, language and culture, and health. A key element of that change must be a justice system, based on Aboriginal law and healing practices and under Aboriginal control. Such a system will be essential in the movement to banish the legacy of residential schools and build a new future of Canadian reconciliation.

# Calls to action

In order to redress the legacy of residential schools and advance the process of Canadian reconciliation, the Truth and Reconciliation Commission makes the following Calls to Action.

## LEGACY

### Child welfare

1) We call upon the federal, provincial, territorial, and Aboriginal governments to commit to reducing the number of Aboriginal children in care by:

    i. Monitoring and assessing neglect investigations.

    ii. Providing adequate resources to enable Aboriginal communities and child welfare organizations to keep Aboriginal families together where it is safe to do so, and to keep children in culturally appropriate environments, regardless of where they reside.

    iii. Ensuring that social workers and others who conduct child welfare investigations are properly educated and trained about the history and impacts of residential schools.

    iv. Ensuring that social workers and others who conduct child welfare investigations are properly educated and trained about the potential for Aboriginal communities and families to provide more appropriate solutions to family healing.

    v. Requiring that all child welfare decision makers consider the impact of the residential school experience on children and their caregivers.

2) We call upon the federal government, in collaboration with the provinces and territories, to prepare and publish annual reports on the number of Aboriginal children (First Nations, Inuit, and Métis) who are in care, compared with non-Aboriginal children,

as well as the reasons for apprehension, the total spending on preventive and care services by child welfare agencies, and the effectiveness of various interventions.

3) We call upon all levels of government to fully implement Jordan's Principle.

4) We call upon the federal government to enact Aboriginal child welfare legislation that establishes national standards for Aboriginal child apprehension and custody cases and includes principles that:

    i. Affirm the right of Aboriginal governments to establish and maintain their own child welfare agencies.

    ii. Require all child welfare agencies and courts to take the residential school legacy into account in their decision making.

    iii. Establish, as an important priority, a requirement that placements of Aboriginal children into temporary and permanent care be culturally appropriate.

5) We call upon the federal, provincial, territorial, and Aboriginal governments to develop culturally appropriate parenting programs for Aboriginal families.

## Education

6) We call upon the Government of Canada to repeal section 43 of the *Criminal Code of Canada*.

7) We call upon the federal government to develop with Aboriginal groups a joint strategy to eliminate educational and employment gaps between Aboriginal and non-Aboriginal Canadians.

8) We call upon the federal government to eliminate the discrepancy in federal education funding for First Nations children being educated on reserves and those First Nations children being educated off reserves.

9) We call upon the federal government to prepare and publish annual reports comparing funding for the education of First Nations children on and off reserves, as well as educational and income attainments of Aboriginal peoples in Canada compared with non-Aboriginal people.

10) We call on the federal government to draft new Aboriginal education legislation with the full participation and informed consent of Aboriginal peoples. The new legislation would include a commitment to sufficient funding and would incorporate the following principles:

    i. Providing sufficient funding to close identified educational achievement gaps within one generation.

   ii. Improving education attainment levels and success rates.

   iii. Developing culturally appropriate curricula.

   iv. Protecting the right to Aboriginal languages, including the teaching of Aboriginal languages as credit courses.

   v. Enabling parental and community responsibility, control, and accountability, similar to what parents enjoy in public school systems.

   vi. Enabling parents to fully participate in the education of their children.

   vii. Respecting and honouring Treaty relationships.

11) We call upon the federal government to provide adequate funding to end the backlog of First Nations students seeking a post-secondary education.

12) We call upon the federal, provincial, territorial, and Aboriginal governments to develop culturally appropriate early childhood education programs for Aboriginal families.

## Language and culture

13) We call upon the federal government to acknowledge that Aboriginal rights include Aboriginal language rights.

14) We call upon the federal government to enact an Aboriginal Languages Act that incorporates the following principles:

   i. Aboriginal languages are a fundamental and valued element of Canadian culture and society, and there is an urgency to preserve them.

   ii. Aboriginal language rights are reinforced by the Treaties.

   iii. The federal government has a responsibility to provide sufficient funds for Aboriginal-language revitalization and preservation.

   iv. The preservation, revitalization, and strengthening of Aboriginal languages and cultures are best managed by Aboriginal people and communities.

   v. Funding for Aboriginal language initiatives must reflect the diversity of Aboriginal languages.

15) We call upon the federal government to appoint, in consultation with Aboriginal groups, an Aboriginal Languages Commissioner. The commissioner should help promote Aboriginal languages and report on the adequacy of federal funding of Aboriginal-languages initiatives.

16) We call upon post-secondary institutions to create university and college degree and diploma programs in Aboriginal languages.

17) We call upon all levels of government to enable residential school Survivors and their families to reclaim names changed by the residential school system by waiving administrative costs for a period of five years for the name-change process and the revision of official identity documents, such as birth certificates, passports, driver's licenses, health cards, status cards, and social insurance numbers.

## Health

18) We call upon the federal, provincial, territorial, and Aboriginal governments to acknowledge that the current state of Aboriginal health in Canada is a direct result of previous Canadian government policies, including residential schools, and to recognize and implement the health-care rights of Aboriginal people as identified in international law, constitutional law, and under the Treaties.

19) We call upon the federal government, in consultation with Aboriginal peoples, to establish measurable goals to identify and close the gaps in health outcomes between Aboriginal and non-Aboriginal communities, and to publish annual progress reports and assess long-term trends. Such efforts would focus on indicators such as: infant mortality, maternal health, suicide, mental health, addictions, life expectancy, birth rates, infant and child health issues, chronic diseases, illness and injury incidence, and the availability of appropriate health services.

20) In order to address the jurisdictional disputes concerning Aboriginal people who do not reside on reserves, we call upon the federal government to recognize, respect, and address the distinct health needs of the Métis, Inuit, and off-reserve Aboriginal peoples.

21) We call upon the federal government to provide sustainable funding for existing and new Aboriginal healing centres to address the physical, mental, emotional, and spiritual harms caused by residential schools, and to ensure that the funding of healing centres in Nunavut and the Northwest Territories is a priority.

22) We call upon those who can effect change within the Canadian health-care system to recognize the value of Aboriginal healing practices and use them in the treatment of Aboriginal patients in collaboration with Aboriginal healers and Elders where requested by Aboriginal patients.

23) We call upon all levels of government to:

    i. Increase the number of Aboriginal professionals working in the health-care field.

ii. Ensure the retention of Aboriginal health-care providers in Aboriginal communities.

iii. Provide cultural competency training for all health-care professionals.

24) We call upon medical and nursing schools in Canada to require all students to take a course dealing with Aboriginal health issues, including the history and legacy of residential schools, the *United Nations Declaration on the Rights of Indigenous Peoples*, Treaties and Aboriginal rights, and Indigenous teachings and practices. This will require skills-based training in intercultural competency, conflict resolution, human rights, and anti-racism.

## Justice

25) We call upon the federal government to establish a written policy that reaffirms the independence of the Royal Canadian Mounted Police to investigate crimes in which the government has its own interest as a potential or real party in civil litigation.

26) We call upon the federal, provincial, and territorial governments to review and amend their respective statutes of limitations to ensure that they conform with the principle that governments and other entities cannot rely on limitation defences to defend legal actions of historical abuse brought by Aboriginal people.

27) We call upon the Federation of Law Societies of Canada to ensure that lawyers receive appropriate cultural competency training, which includes the history and legacy of residential schools, the *United Nations Declaration on the Rights of Indigenous Peoples*, Treaties and Aboriginal rights, Indigenous law, and Aboriginal–Crown relations. This will require skills-based training in intercultural competency, conflict resolution, human rights, and anti-racism.

28) We call upon law schools in Canada to require all law students to take a course in Aboriginal people and the law, which includes the history and legacy of residential schools, the *United Nations Declaration on the Rights of Indigenous Peoples*, Treaties and Aboriginal rights, Indigenous law, and Aboriginal–Crown relations. This will require skills-based training in intercultural competency, conflict resolution, human rights, and anti-racism.

29) We call upon the parties and, in particular, the federal government, to work collaboratively with plaintiffs not included in the Indian Residential Schools Settlement Agreement to have disputed legal issues determined expeditiously on an agreed set of facts.

30) We call upon federal, provincial, and territorial governments to commit to eliminating the overrepresentation of Aboriginal people in custody over the next decade, and to issue detailed annual reports that monitor and evaluate progress in doing so.

31) We call upon the federal, provincial, and territorial governments to provide sufficient and stable funding to implement and evaluate community sanctions that will provide realistic alternatives to imprisonment for Aboriginal offenders and respond to the underlying causes of offending.

32) We call upon the federal government to amend the *Criminal Code* to allow trial judges, upon giving reasons, to depart from mandatory minimum sentences and restrictions on the use of conditional sentences.

33) We call upon the federal, provincial, and territorial governments to recognize as a high priority the need to address and prevent Fetal Alcohol Spectrum Disorder (FASD), and to develop, in collaboration with Aboriginal people, FASD preventive programs that can be delivered in a culturally appropriate manner.

34) We call upon the governments of Canada, the provinces, and territories to undertake reforms to the criminal justice system to better address the needs of offenders with Fetal Alcohol Spectrum Disorder (FASD), including:

  i. Providing increased community resources and powers for courts to ensure that FASD is properly diagnosed, and that appropriate community supports are in place for those with FASD.

  ii. Enacting statutory exemptions from mandatory minimum sentences of imprison-ment for offenders affected by FASD.

  iii. Providing community, correctional, and parole resources to maximize the ability of people with FASD to live in the community.

  iv. Adopting appropriate evaluation mechanisms to measure the effectiveness of such programs and ensure community safety.

35) We call upon the federal government to eliminate barriers to the creation of additional Aboriginal healing lodges within the federal correctional system.

36) We call upon the federal, provincial, and territorial governments to work with Aboriginal communities to provide culturally relevant services to inmates on issues such as substance abuse, family and domestic violence, and overcoming the experi-ence of having been sexually abused.

37) We call upon the federal government to provide more supports for Aboriginal program-ming in halfway houses and parole services.

38) We call upon the federal, provincial, territorial, and Aboriginal governments to commit to eliminating the overrepresentation of Aboriginal youth in custody over the next decade.

39) We call upon the federal government to develop a national plan to collect and publish data on the criminal victimization of Aboriginal people, including data related to homicide and family violence victimization.

40) We call on all levels of government, in collaboration with Aboriginal people, to create adequately funded and accessible Aboriginal-specific victim programs and services with appropriate evaluation mechanisms.

41) We call upon the federal government, in consultation with Aboriginal organizations, to appoint a public inquiry into the causes of, and remedies for, the disproportionate victimization of Aboriginal women and girls. The inquiry's mandate would include:

   i. Investigation into missing and murdered Aboriginal women and girls.

   ii. Links to the intergenerational legacy of residential schools.

42) We call upon the federal, provincial, and territorial governments to commit to the recognition and implementation of Aboriginal justice systems in a manner consistent with the Treaty and Aboriginal rights of Aboriginal peoples, the *Constitution Act, 1982*, and the *United Nations Declaration on the Rights of Indigenous Peoples*, endorsed by Canada in November 2012.

# RECONCILIATION

## Canadian Governments and the *United Nations Declaration on the Rights of Indigenous Peoples*

43) We call upon federal, provincial, territorial, and municipal governments to fully adopt and implement the *United Nations Declaration on the Rights of Indigenous Peoples* as the framework for reconciliation.

44) We call upon the Government of Canada to develop a national action plan, strategies, and other concrete measures to achieve the goals of the *United Nations Declaration on the Rights of Indigenous Peoples*.

## Royal Proclamation and Covenant of Reconciliation

45) We call upon the Government of Canada, on behalf of all Canadians, to jointly develop with Aboriginal peoples a Royal Proclamation of Reconciliation to be issued by the Crown. The proclamation would build on the Royal Proclamation of 1763 and the Treaty of Niagara of 1764, and reaffirm the nation-to-nation relationship between Aboriginal peoples and the Crown. The proclamation would include, but not be limited to, the following commitments:

  i. Repudiate concepts used to justify European sovereignty over Indigenous lands and peoples such as the Doctrine of Discovery and *terra nullius*.

  ii. Adopt and implement the *United Nations Declaration on the Rights of Indigenous Peoples* as the framework for reconciliation.

  iii. Renew or establish Treaty relationships based on principles of mutual recognition, mutual respect, and shared responsibility for maintaining those relationships into the future.

  iv. Reconcile Aboriginal and Crown constitutional and legal orders to ensure that Aboriginal peoples are full partners in Confederation, including the recognition and integration of Indigenous laws and legal traditions in negotiation and implementation processes involving Treaties, land claims, and other constructive agreements.

46) We call upon the parties to the Indian Residential Schools Settlement Agreement to develop and sign a Covenant of Reconciliation that would identify principles for working collaboratively to advance reconciliation in Canadian society, and that would include, but not be limited to:

  i. Reaffirmation of the parties' commitment to reconciliation.

  ii. Repudiation of concepts used to justify European sovereignty over Indigenous lands and peoples, such as the Doctrine of Discovery and *terra nullius*, and the reformation of laws, governance structures, and policies within their respective institutions that continue to rely on such concepts.

  iii. Full adoption and implementation of the *United Nations Declaration on the Rights of Indigenous Peoples* as the framework for reconciliation.

  iv. Support for the renewal or establishment of Treaty relationships based on principles of mutual recognition, mutual respect, and shared responsibility for maintaining those relationships into the future.

  v. Enabling those excluded from the Settlement Agreement to sign onto the Covenant of Reconciliation.

  vi. Enabling additional parties to sign onto the Covenant of Reconciliation.

47) We call upon federal, provincial, territorial, and municipal governments to repudiate concepts used to justify European sovereignty over Indigenous peoples and lands, such as the Doctrine of Discovery and *terra nullius*, and to reform those laws, government policies, and litigation strategies that continue to rely on such concepts.

## Settlement Agreement Parties and the *United Nations Declaration on the Rights of Indigenous Peoples*

48) We call upon the church parties to the Settlement Agreement, and all other faith groups and interfaith social justice groups in Canada who have not already done so, to formally adopt and comply with the principles, norms, and standards of the *United Nations Declaration on the Rights of Indigenous Peoples* as a framework for reconciliation. This would include, but not be limited to, the following commitments:

    i. Ensuring that their institutions, policies, programs, and practices comply with the *United Nations Declaration on the Rights of Indigenous Peoples*.

    ii. Respecting Indigenous peoples' right to self-determination in spiritual matters, including the right to practise, develop, and teach their own spiritual and religious traditions, customs, and ceremonies, consistent with Article 12:1 of the *United Nations Declaration on the Rights of Indigenous Peoples*.

    iii. Engaging in ongoing public dialogue and actions to support the *United Nations Declaration on the Rights of Indigenous Peoples*.

    iv. Issuing a statement no later than March 31, 2016, from all religious denominations and faith groups, as to how they will implement the *United Nations Declaration on the Rights of Indigenous Peoples*.

49) We call upon all religious denominations and faith groups who have not already done so to repudiate concepts used to justify European sovereignty over Indigenous lands and peoples, such as the Doctrine of Discovery and *terra nullius*.

## Equity for Aboriginal People in the Legal System

50) In keeping with the *United Nations Declaration on the Rights of Indigenous Peoples*, we call upon the federal government, in collaboration with Aboriginal organizations, to fund the establishment of Indigenous law institutes for the development, use, and understanding of Indigenous laws and access to justice in accordance with the unique cultures of Aboriginal peoples in Canada.

51) We call upon the Government of Canada, as an obligation of its fiduciary responsibility, to develop a policy of transparency by publishing legal opinions it develops and upon which it acts or intends to act, in regard to the scope and extent of Aboriginal and Treaty rights.

52) We call upon the Government of Canada, provincial and territorial governments, and the courts to adopt the following legal principles:

    i. Aboriginal title claims are accepted once the Aboriginal claimant has established occupation over a particular territory at a particular point in time.

    ii. Once Aboriginal title has been established, the burden of proving any limitation on any rights arising from the existence of that title shifts to the party asserting such a limitation.

## National Council for Reconciliation

53) We call upon the Parliament of Canada, in consultation and collaboration with Aboriginal peoples, to enact legislation to establish a National Council for Reconciliation. The legislation would establish the council as an independent, national, oversight body with membership jointly appointed by the Government of Canada and national Aboriginal organizations, and consisting of Aboriginal and non-Aboriginal members. Its mandate would include, but not be limited to, the following:

    i. Monitor, evaluate, and report annually to Parliament and the people of Canada on the Government of Canada's post-apology progress on reconciliation to ensure that government accountability for reconciling the relationship between Aboriginal peoples and the Crown is maintained in the coming years.

    ii. Monitor, evaluate, and report to Parliament and the people of Canada on reconciliation progress across all levels and sectors of Canadian society, including the implementation of the Truth and Reconciliation Commission of Canada's Calls to Action.

    iii. Develop and implement a multi-year National Action Plan for Reconciliation, which includes research and policy development, public education programs, and resources.

    iv. Promote public dialogue, public/private partnerships, and public initiatives for reconciliation.

54) We call upon the Government of Canada to provide multi-year funding for the National Council for Reconciliation to ensure that it has the financial, human, and technical

resources required to conduct its work, including the endowment of a National Reconciliation Trust to advance the cause of reconciliation.

55) We call upon all levels of government to provide annual reports or any current data requested by the National Council for Reconciliation so that it can report on the progress towards reconciliation. The reports or data would include, but not be limited to:

i. The number of Aboriginal children—including Métis and Inuit children—in care, compared with non-Aboriginal children, the reasons for apprehension, and the total spending on preventive and care services by child welfare agencies.

ii. Comparative funding for the education of First Nations children on and off reserves.

iii. The educational and income attainments of Aboriginal peoples in Canada compared with non-Aboriginal people.

iv. Progress on closing the gaps between Aboriginal and non-Aboriginal communities in a number of health indicators such as: infant mortality, maternal health, suicide, mental health, addictions, life expectancy, birth rates, infant and child health issues, chronic diseases, illness and injury incidence, and the availability of appropriate health services.

v. Progress on eliminating the overrepresentation of Aboriginal children in youth custody over the next decade.

vi. Progress on reducing the rate of criminal victimization of Aboriginal people, including data related to homicide and family violence victimization and other crimes.

vii. Progress on reducing the overrepresentation of Aboriginal people in the justice and correctional systems.

56) We call upon the prime minister of Canada to formally respond to the report of the National Council for Reconciliation by issuing an annual "State of Aboriginal Peoples" report, which would outline the government's plans for advancing the cause of reconciliation.

## Professional Development and Training for Public Servants

57) We call upon federal, provincial, territorial, and municipal governments to provide education to public servants on the history of Aboriginal peoples, including the history and legacy of residential schools, the *United Nations Declaration on the Rights of Indigenous Peoples*, Treaties and Aboriginal rights, Indigenous law, and

Aboriginal–Crown relations. This will require skills-based training in intercultural competency, conflict resolution, human rights, and anti-racism.

## Church Apologies and Reconciliation

58) We call upon the Pope to issue an apology to Survivors, their families, and communities for the Roman Catholic Church's role in the spiritual, cultural, emotional, physical, and sexual abuse of First Nations, Inuit, and Métis children in Catholic-run residential schools. We call for that apology to be similar to the 2010 apology issued to Irish victims of abuse and to occur within one year of the issuing of this Report and to be delivered by the Pope in Canada.

59) We call upon church parties to the Settlement Agreement to develop ongoing education strategies to ensure that their respective congregations learn about their church's role in colonization, the history and legacy of residential schools, and why apologies to former residential school students, their families, and communities were necessary.

60) We call upon leaders of the church parties to the Settlement Agreement and all other faiths, in collaboration with Indigenous spiritual leaders, Survivors, schools of theology, seminaries, and other religious training centres, to develop and teach curriculum for all student clergy, and all clergy and staff who work in Aboriginal communities, on the need to respect Indigenous spirituality in its own right, the history and legacy of residential schools and the roles of the church parties in that system, the history and legacy of religious conflict in Aboriginal families and communities, and the responsibility that churches have to mitigate such conflicts and prevent spiritual violence.

61) We call upon church parties to the Settlement Agreement, in collaboration with Survivors and representatives of Aboriginal organizations, to establish permanent funding to Aboriginal people for:

    i. Community-controlled healing and reconciliation projects.

    ii. Community-controlled culture- and language-revitalization projects.

    iii. Community-controlled education and relationship-building projects.

    iv. Regional dialogues for Indigenous spiritual leaders and youth to discuss Indigenous spirituality, self-determination, and reconciliation.

## Education for reconciliation

62) We call upon the federal, provincial, and territorial governments, in consultation and collaboration with Survivors, Aboriginal peoples, and educators, to:

    i. Make age-appropriate curriculum on residential schools, Treaties, and Aboriginal peoples' historical and contemporary contributions to Canada a mandatory education requirement for Kindergarten to Grade Twelve students.

    ii. Provide the necessary funding to post-secondary institutions to educate teachers on how to integrate Indigenous knowledge and teaching methods into classrooms.

    iii. Provide the necessary funding to Aboriginal schools to utilize Indigenous knowledge and teaching methods in classrooms.

    iv. Establish senior-level positions in government at the assistant deputy minister level or higher dedicated to Aboriginal content in education.

63) We call upon the Council of Ministers of Education, Canada to maintain an annual commitment to Aboriginal education issues, including:

    i. Developing and implementing Kindergarten to Grade Twelve curriculum and learning resources on Aboriginal peoples in Canadian history, and the history and legacy of residential schools.

    ii. Sharing information and best practices on teaching curriculum related to residential schools and Aboriginal history.

    iii. Building student capacity for intercultural understanding, empathy, and mutual respect.

    iv. Identifying teacher-training needs relating to the above.

64) We call upon all levels of government that provide public funds to denominational schools to require such schools to provide an education on comparative religious studies, which must include a segment on Aboriginal spiritual beliefs and practices developed in collaboration with Aboriginal Elders.

65) We call upon the federal government, through the Social Sciences and Humanities Research Council, and in collaboration with Aboriginal peoples, post-secondary institutions and educators, and the National Centre for Truth and Reconciliation and its partner institutions, to establish a national research program with multi-year funding to advance understanding of reconciliation.

## Youth Programs

66) We call upon the federal government to establish multi-year funding for community-based youth organizations to deliver programs on reconciliation, and establish a national network to share information and best practices.

## Museums and Archives

67) We call upon the federal government to provide funding to the Canadian Museums Association to undertake, in collaboration with Aboriginal peoples, a national review of museum policies and best practices to determine the level of compliance with the *United Nations Declaration on the Rights of Indigenous Peoples* and to make recommendations.

68) We call upon the federal government, in collaboration with Aboriginal peoples, and the Canadian Museums Association to mark the 150th anniversary of Canadian Confederation in 2017 by establishing a dedicated national funding program for commemoration projects on the theme of reconciliation.

69) We call upon Library and Archives Canada to:

   i. Fully adopt and implement the *United Nations Declaration on the Rights of Indigenous Peoples* and the *United Nations Joinet-Orentlicher Principles*, as related to Aboriginal peoples' inalienable right to know the truth about what happened and why, with regard to human rights violations committed against them in the residential schools.

   ii. Ensure that its record holdings related to residential schools are accessible to the public.

   iii. Commit more resources to its public education materials and programming on residential schools.

70) We call upon the federal government to provide funding to the Canadian Association of Archivists to undertake, in collaboration with Aboriginal peoples, a national review of archival policies and best practices to:

   i. Determine the level of compliance with the *United Nations Declaration on the Rights of Indigenous Peoples* and the *United Nations Joinet-Orentlicher Principles*, as related to Aboriginal peoples' inalienable right to know the truth about what happened and why, with regard to human rights violations committed against them in the residential schools.

ii. Produce a report with recommendations for full implementation of these international mechanisms as a reconciliation framework for Canadian archives.

## Missing Children and Burial Information

71) We call upon all chief coroners and provincial vital statistics agencies that have not provided to the Truth and Reconciliation Commission of Canada their records on the deaths of Aboriginal children in the care of residential school authorities to make these documents available to the National Centre for Truth and Reconciliation.

72) We call upon the federal government to allocate sufficient resources to the National Centre for Truth and Reconciliation to allow it to develop and maintain the National Residential School Student Death Register established by the Truth and Reconciliation Commission of Canada.

73) We call upon the federal government to work with churches, Aboriginal communities, and former residential school students to establish and maintain an online registry of residential school cemeteries, including, where possible, plot maps showing the location of deceased residential school children.

74) We call upon the federal government to work with the churches and Aboriginal community leaders to inform the families of children who died at residential schools of the child's burial location, and to respond to families' wishes for appropriate commemoration ceremonies and markers, and reburial in home communities where requested.

75) We call upon the federal government to work with provincial, territorial, and municipal governments, churches, Aboriginal communities, former residential school students, and current landowners to develop and implement strategies and procedures for the ongoing identification, documentation, maintenance, commemoration, and protection of residential school cemeteries or other sites at which residential school children were buried. This is to include the provision of appropriate memorial ceremonies and commemorative markers to honour the deceased children.

76) We call upon the parties engaged in the work of documenting, maintaining, commemorating, and protecting residential school cemeteries to adopt strategies in accordance with the following principles:

i. The Aboriginal community most affected shall lead the development of such strategies.

ii. Information shall be sought from residential school Survivors and other Knowledge Keepers in the development of such strategies.

iii. Aboriginal protocols shall be respected before any potentially invasive technical inspection and investigation of a cemetery site.

## National Centre for Truth and Reconciliation

77) We call upon provincial, territorial, municipal, and community archives to work collaboratively with the National Centre for Truth and Reconciliation to identify and collect copies of all records relevant to the history and legacy of the residential school system, and to provide these to the National Centre for Truth and Reconciliation.

78) We call upon the Government of Canada to commit to making a funding contribution of $10 million over seven years to the National Centre for Truth and Reconciliation, plus an additional amount to assist communities to research and produce histories of their own residential school experience and their involvement in truth, healing, and reconciliation.

## Commemoration

79) We call upon the federal government, in collaboration with Survivors, Aboriginal organizations, and the arts community, to develop a reconciliation framework for Canadian heritage and commemoration. This would include, but not be limited to:

i. Amending the *Historic Sites and Monuments Act* to include First Nations, Inuit, and Métis representation on the Historic Sites and Monuments Board of Canada and its Secretariat.

ii. Revising the policies, criteria, and practices of the National Program of Historical Commemoration to integrate Indigenous history, heritage values, and memory practices into Canada's national heritage and history.

iii. Developing and implementing a national heritage plan and strategy for commemorating residential school sites, the history and legacy of residential schools, and the contributions of Aboriginal peoples to Canada's history.

80) We call upon the federal government, in collaboration with Aboriginal peoples, to establish, as a statutory holiday, a National Day for Truth and Reconciliation to honour Survivors, their families, and communities, and ensure that public commemoration of the history and legacy of residential schools remains a vital component of the reconciliation process.

81) We call upon the federal government, in collaboration with Survivors and their organizations, and other parties to the Settlement Agreement, to commission and install

a publicly accessible, highly visible, Residential Schools National Monument in the city of Ottawa to honour Survivors and all the children who were lost to their families and communities.

82) We call upon provincial and territorial governments, in collaboration with Survivors and their organizations, and other parties to the Settlement Agreement, to commission and install a publicly accessible, highly visible, Residential Schools Monument in each capital city to honour Survivors and all the children who were lost to their families and communities.

83) We call upon the Canada Council for the Arts to establish, as a funding priority, a strategy for Indigenous and non-Indigenous artists to undertake collaborative projects and produce works that contribute to the reconciliation process.

## Media and Reconciliation

84) We call upon the federal government to restore and increase funding to the CBC/ Radio-Canada, to enable Canada's national public broadcaster to support reconciliation, and be properly reflective of the diverse cultures, languages, and perspectives of Aboriginal peoples, including, but not limited to:

   i. Increasing Aboriginal programming, including Aboriginal-language speakers.

   ii. Increasing equitable access for Aboriginal peoples to jobs, leadership positions, and professional development opportunities within the organization.

   iii. Continuing to provide dedicated news coverage and online public information resources on issues of concern to Aboriginal peoples and all Canadians, including the history and legacy of residential schools and the reconciliation process.

85) We call upon the Aboriginal Peoples Television Network, as an independent non-profit broadcaster with programming by, for, and about Aboriginal peoples, to support reconciliation, including but not limited to:

   i. Continuing to provide leadership in programming and organizational culture that reflects the diverse cultures, languages, and perspectives of Aboriginal peoples.

   ii. Continuing to develop media initiatives that inform and educate the Canadian public, and connect Aboriginal and non-Aboriginal Canadians.

86) We call upon Canadian journalism programs and media schools to require education for all students on the history of Aboriginal peoples, including the history and legacy of residential schools, the *United Nations Declaration on the Rights of Indigenous Peoples*, Treaties and Aboriginal rights, Indigenous law, and Aboriginal–Crown relations.

## Sports and Reconciliation

**87)** We call upon all levels of government, in collaboration with Aboriginal peoples, sports halls of fame, and other relevant organizations, to provide public education that tells the national story of Aboriginal athletes in history.

**88)** We call upon all levels of government to take action to ensure long-term Aboriginal athlete development and growth, and continued support for the North American Indigenous Games, including funding to host the games and for provincial and territorial team preparation and travel.

**89)** We call upon the federal government to amend the *Physical Activity and Sport Act* to support reconciliation by ensuring that policies to promote physical activity as a fundamental element of health and well-being, reduce barriers to sports participation, increase the pursuit of excellence in sport, and build capacity in the Canadian sport system, are inclusive of Aboriginal peoples.

**90)** We call upon the federal government to ensure that national sports policies, programs, and initiatives are inclusive of Aboriginal peoples, including, but not limited to, establishing:

    i. In collaboration with provincial and territorial governments, stable funding for, and access to, community sports programs that reflect the diverse cultures and traditional sporting activities of Aboriginal peoples.

    ii. An elite athlete development program for Aboriginal athletes.

    iii. Programs for coaches, trainers, and sports officials that are culturally relevant for Aboriginal peoples.

    iv. Anti-racism awareness and training programs.

**91)** We call upon the officials and host countries of international sporting events such as the Olympics, Pan Am, and Commonwealth Games to ensure that Indigenous peoples' territorial protocols are respected, and local Indigenous communities are engaged in all aspects of planning and participating in such events.

## Business and Reconciliation

**92)** We call upon the corporate sector in Canada to adopt the *United Nations Declaration on the Rights of Indigenous Peoples* as a reconciliation framework and to apply its principles, norms, and standards to corporate policy and core operational activities involving Indigenous peoples and their lands and resources. This would include, but not be limited to, the following:

i. Commit to meaningful consultation, building respectful relationships, and obtaining the free, prior, and informed consent of Indigenous peoples before proceeding with economic development projects.

ii. Ensure that Aboriginal peoples have equitable access to jobs, training, and education opportunities in the corporate sector, and that Aboriginal communities gain long-term sustainable benefits from economic development projects.

iii. Provide education for management and staff on the history of Aboriginal peoples, including the history and legacy of residential schools, the *United Nations Declaration on the Rights of Indigenous Peoples*, Treaties and Aboriginal rights, Indigenous law, and Aboriginal–Crown relations. This will require skills-based training in intercultural competency, conflict resolution, human rights, and anti-racism.

## Newcomers to Canada

93) We call upon the federal government, in collaboration with the national Aboriginal organizations, to revise the information kit for newcomers to Canada and its citizenship test to reflect a more inclusive history of the diverse Aboriginal peoples of Canada, including information about the Treaties and the history of residential schools.

94) We call upon the Government of Canada to replace the Oath of Citizenship with the following:

*I swear (or affirm) that I will be faithful and bear true allegiance to Her Majesty Queen Elizabeth II, Queen of Canada, Her Heirs and Successors, and that I will faithfully observe the laws of Canada including Treaties with Indigenous Peoples, and fulfill my duties as a Canadian citizen.*

# Notes

## Introduction

1. Canadian Department of Citizenship and Immigration, *Report of Indian Affairs Branch for the Fiscal Year Ended March 31, 1954*, 88–89.
2. TRC, NRA, INAC file 6-21-1, volume 2, H. M. Jones to Deputy Minister, 13 December 1956. [NCA-001989-0001]
3. For a discussion that places both child welfare and residential schools in the context of the ongoing colonization of Aboriginal people, see McKenzie and Hudson, "Native Children."
4. Sinha and Kozlowski, "The Structure of Aboriginal Child Welfare in Canada," 1.
5. Canada, *Annual Report of the Department of Indian Affairs, 1942*, 154; Canada, *Annual Report of the Department of Indian Affairs, 1943*, 168; Canada, *Annual Report of the Department of Indian Affairs, 1944*, 177; Canada, *Annual Report of the Department of Indian Affairs, 1945*, 190; Canada, *Annual Report of the Department of Indian Affairs, 1946*, 231; Canada, *Annual Report of the Department of Indian Affairs, 1947*, 236; Canada, *Annual Report of the Department of Indian Affairs, 1948*, 234; Canada, *Annual Report of the Department of Indian Affairs, 1948*, 234; Canada, *Annual Report of the Department of Indian Affairs, 1949*, 215; Canada, *Annual Report of the Department of Indian Affairs, 1950*, 86–87; Canada, *Annual Report of the Department of Indian Affairs, 1951*, 34–35; Canada, *Annual Report of the Department of Indian Affairs, 1952*, 74–75; Canada, *Annual Report of the Department of Indian Affairs, 1953*, 82–83; Canada, *Annual Report of the Department of Indian Affairs, 1954*, 88–89; Canada, *Annual Report of the Department of Indian Affairs, 1955*, 78–79; Canada, *Annual Report of the Department of Indian Affairs, 1956*, 76–77; Canada, *Annual Report of the Department of Indian Affairs, 1956–57*, 88–89; Canada, *Annual Report of the Department of Indian Affairs, 1958*, 91; Canada, *Annual Report of the Department of Indian Affairs, 1959*, 94; Canada, *Annual Report of the Department of Indian Affairs, 1960*, 94; Canada, *Annual Report of the Department of Indian Affairs, 1961*, 102; Canada, *Annual Report of the Department of Indian Affairs, 1962*, 73; Canada, *Annual Report of the Department of Indian Affairs, 1963*, 62.
6. Canadian Human Rights Commission, *Report on Equality Rights of Aboriginal People*, 3, 12, 32.
7. Wilson and Macdonald, *The Income Gap*, 14.
8. Macdonald and Wilson, *Poverty or Prosperity*, 6.
9. Assembly of First Nations, *Breaking the Silence*, 25–26.
10. TRC, AVS, Conrad Burns, Statement to the Truth and Reconciliation Commission of Canada, Regina, Saskatchewan, 17 January 2012, Statement Number: SP036.

11. According to UNCESO, 36% of Canada's Aboriginal languages are critically endangered, 18% are severely endangered, and 16% are definitely endangered. The remaining languages are all vulnerable. Moseley and Nicolas, *UNESCO Atlas of the World's Languages in Danger*, 117.

12. Canada, Statistics Canada, *Aboriginal Peoples and Language*.

13. Library and Archives Canada, RG10, volume 3957, file 140754-1, P. H. Bryce to F. Pedley, 5 November 1909.

14. For long-term differences in the Aboriginal and non-Aboriginal tuberculosis death rates in Canada, see Wherrett, *The Miracle of the Empty Beds*, 251–253.

15. Taylor, "Grollier Meeting Emotional," *Northern News*.

16. Kirmayer et al., *Suicide among Aboriginal People*, xv, 22.

17. Canada, Indian Residential Schools Adjudication Secretariat, "Adjudication Secretariat Statistics from September 19, 2007 to January 31, 2015." By the spring of 2015, over $2.8 billion in compensation had been awarded for sexual and serious physical abuse. Canada, Indian Residential Schools Adjudication Secretariat, "Adjudication Secretariat Statistics."

18. Perreault, "Aboriginal Adults Are Overrepresented."

19. Perreault, "Aboriginal Adults Are Overrepresented."

20. Perreault, "Aboriginal Youth Are Over-Represented."

21. Canada, Public Health Agency of Canada, "Fetal Alcohol Spectrum Disorder"; Ospina and Dennett, *Systematic Review*, iii.

22. Canada, Public Safety Canada, *Fetal Alcohol Spectrum Disorder*, 5.

23. MacPherson, Chudley, and Grant, *Fetal Alcohol Spectrum Disorder*, iv.

24. A study done for the Aboriginal Healing Foundation drew links between the intergenerational trauma of residential schools, alcohol addictions, and the prevalence of FASD in Aboriginal communities. Tait, *Fetal Alcohol Syndrome*.

25. Perrerault, "Violent Victimization of Aboriginal People."

26. Brennan, "Violent Victimization of Aboriginal Women."

27. Canada, Royal Canadian Mounted Police, *Missing and Murdered Aboriginal Women*, 3.

## Child welfare: A system in crisis

1. Canadian Department of Citizenship and Immigration, *Report of Indian Affairs Branch for the Fiscal Year Ended March 31, 1954*, 88–89.

2. Hughes, *The Legacy of Phoenix Sinclair*, 2:448.

3. TRC, AVS, Kay Adams, Statement to the Truth and Reconciliation Commission of Canada, Goose Bay, Newfoundland and Labrador, 20 September 2011, Statement Number: SP025.

4. TRC, AVS, Tim McNeil, Statement to the Truth and Reconciliation Commission of Canada, Goose Bay, Newfoundland and Labrador, 20 September 2011, Statement Number: SP025.

5. The complaint of inequitable funding was brought by the Assembly of First Nations and the First Nations Child & Family Caring Society of Canada. For various documents on the prolonged litigation, see the "I Am a Witness: Canadian Human Rights Tribunal Hearing" timeline and documents at http://www.fncaringsociety.ca/i-am-witness-timeline-and-documents.

6. TRC, AVS, Daniel Big George, Statement to the Truth and Reconciliation Commission of Canada, Winnipeg, Manitoba, 17 June 2010, Statement Number: 02-MB-17JU10-059.

7. TRC, AVS, Norma Kassi, Statement to the Truth and Reconciliation Commission of Canada, Inuvik, Northwest Territories, 29 June 2011, Statement Number: NNE203.

8. Davin, *Report on Industrial Schools for Indians and Half-Breeds*, 12.

9. Canada, *Annual Report of the Department of Indian Affairs for the Year ended 31st December 1883*, 104.

10. TRC, NRA, Library and Archives Canada, RG10, volume 1347, reel C-13916, W. Lemmens to W. R. Robertson, 10 February 1915. [KUP-004240]

11. For example, in 1935, a Department of Indian Affairs official told a principal of a residential school that "Indians who come from a distance might be permitted to remain over night but not for a longer period. The Indian parents from the nearby reserves should not be given meals and not be allowed to remain on the premises over night." TRC, NRA, Library and Archives Canada, RG10, volume 6251, file 575-1, part 3, A. F. MacKenzie to E. H. Lockhart, 1 April 1935. [AEMR-010737]

12. Oreopoulos, *Canadian Compulsory School Laws*, 8.

13. TRC, NRA, Library and Archives Canada, RG10, volume 6032, file 150-40A, pt. 1, "Regulations Relating to the Education of Indian Children," Ottawa: Government Printing Bureau, 1894. [AGA-001516-0000]

14. Canada, *Annual Report of the Department of Indian Affairs for the Year Ended June 30, 1884*, xiii.

15. TRC, NRA, Library and Archives Canada, RG10, volume 6032, file 150-40A, pt. 1, "Regulations Relating to the Education of Indian Children," Ottawa: Government Printing Bureau, 1894. [AGA-001516-0000]

16. Library and Archives Canada, no. 151-711-10, Minister of Justice, "Letter and copy of warrant in reply to a request by Duncan Campbell Scott, Acting Superintendent General of Indian Affairs," 1895, 4.

17. TRC, NRA, Library and Archives Canada, RG10, volume 10410, Shannon box 36, 1918–1920, Untitled Circular, Duncan Campbell Scott, 9 November 1914. [AEMR-200902]

18. Parliament of Canada, Special Committee on Reconstruction and Re-establishment, *Minutes of Proceedings and Evidence*, no. 9, 24 May 1944, 306.

19. Canada, Special Joint Committee of the Senate and House of Commons, *Minutes of Proceedings and Evidence*, no. 1, 1947, 155, 161.

20. Sinha and Kozlowski, "The Structure of Aboriginal Child Welfare in Canada," 3, 4.

21. Sinha and Kozlowski, "The Structure of Aboriginal Child Welfare in Canada," 4.

22. Canada, Royal Commission on Aboriginal Peoples, *Report*, 3:24.

23. In 1983, Patrick Johnston used this term and wrote that "the wholesale apprehension of Native children during the Sixties Scoop appears to have been a terrible mistake. While some individual children may have benefitted, many did not. Nor did their families. And Native culture suffered one of many severe blows. Unfortunately, the damage is still being done. While attitudes may have changed to some extent since the Sixties, Native children continue to be represented in the child welfare system at a much greater rate than non-Native children." Johnston, *Native Children*, 23, 62.

24. Sinha and Kozlowski, "The Structure of Aboriginal Child Welfare in Canada," l.

25. Sinclair, "Identity Lost and Found," 65–82; Kimelman, *No Quiet Place*; Carrière, "Connectedness and Health."

26. TRC, NRA, INAC – Resolution Sector – IRS Historical Files collection – Ottawa, file 773/2901, volume 1, 12/63-10/71, DRSRO, J. R. Tully to Regional Supervisor, Alberta, 21 May 1965. [BPD-000248-0001]

27. TRC, NRA, DIAND HQ file 40-2-185, volume 1, 05/1966-02/1969, "Relationships between Church and State in Indian Education," 15. [AEMR-013448A]

28. TRC, NRA, DIAND HQ file 40-2-185, volume 1, 05/1966-02/1969, "Relationships between Church and State in Indian Education," 15. [AEMR-013448A]

29. Caldwell, *Indian Residential Schools*, 148–149.

30. Caldwell, *Indian Residential Schools*, 149.

31. Johnston, *Native Children*, 59–60.

32. Kimelman, *No Quiet Place*, 328–329.

33. Kimelman, *No Quiet Place*, 274.

34. TRC, AVS, [Name redacted], Statement to the Truth and Reconciliation Commission of Canada, Winnipeg, Manitoba; 26 May 2010, Statement Number: S-MB-101-007.

35. TRC, AVS, Tara Picard, Statement to the Truth and Reconciliation Commission of Canada, Winnipeg, Manitoba, 16 June 2010, Statement Number: 02-MB-16JU10-039.

36. TRC, AVS, Marci Shapiro, Statement to the Truth and Reconciliation Commission of Canada, Winnipeg, Manitoba, 20 November 2011, Statement Number: 2011-2501.

37. TRC, AVS, [Name redacted], Statement to the Truth and Reconciliation Commission of Canada, Winnipeg, Manitoba, 16 June 2010, Statement Number: 02-MB-16JU10-005.

38. TRC, AVS, [Name redacted], Statement to the Truth and Reconciliation Commission of Canada, St. Albert, Alberta, 12 July 2011, Statement Number: 2011-0013.

39. TRC, AVS, [Name redacted], Statement to the Truth and Reconciliation Commission of Canada, Winnipeg, Manitoba, 19 June 2010, Statement Number: 02-MB-19JU10-048.

40. TRC, AVS, Joanne Nimik, Statement to the Truth and Reconciliation Commission of Canada, Winnipeg, Manitoba, 4 January 2012, Statement Number: 2011-2662.

41. *Brown v. Canada*, 2013 ONSC 5637; *Skogamhallait v. Canada* (VLC-S-S-11366), Notice of Civil Claim; Merchant Law Group, "Indian and Metis Scoop Class Action."

42. *Brown v. Attorney General of Canada*, 2014 ONSC 6967 (CanLII) at para. 30.

43. Canada, Auditor General of Canada, "Chapter 4: First Nations and Family Services Program," 11.

44. Rae, *Inuit Child Welfare and Family Support*, 30.

45. Aboriginal Justice Inquiry of Manitoba, Aboriginal Justice Implementation Commission, *Report*, 1:520.

46. Sinha and Kozlowski, "The Structure of Aboriginal Child Welfare in Canada," 8.

47. Saskatchewan Child Welfare Review Panel, *For the Good of Our Children*, 24.

48. Canada, Standing Committee on Aboriginal Affairs and Northern Development, 15 February 2011, Evidence of Carolyn Loeppky (Assistant Deputy Minister, Child and Family Services, Government of Manitoba), 40th Parliament, 3rd Session, 1; *Child and Family Services Authorities Act*, CCSM c C90, s 4.

49. Kozlowski et al., "First Nations Child Welfare in Manitoba, 2011."

50. Manitoba, Auditor General of Manitoba, *Follow-up of Our December 2006 Report*, 8–9.

51. Sinha and Kozlowski, "The Structure of Aboriginal Child Welfare in Canada," 8.

52. Sinha and Kozlowski, "The Structure of Aboriginal Child Welfare in Canada," 8.

53. Sinha and Kozlowski, "The Structure of Aboriginal Child Welfare in Canada," 8–9.

54. Sinha et al., *Kiskisik Awasisak*, 13.

55. Sinha and Kozlowski, "The Structure of Aboriginal Child Welfare in Canada," 9.

56. Sinha and Kozlowski, "The Structure of Aboriginal Child Welfare in Canada," 9.

57. Sinha and Kozlowski, "The Structure of Aboriginal Child Welfare in Canada," 11.

58. First Nations Child & Family Caring Society of Canada, *Wen: De: We Are Coming*, 89–90.

59. First Nations Child & Family Caring Society of Canada, *Wen: De: We Are Coming*, 17, 26.

60. Sinha and Kozlowski, "The Structure of Aboriginal Child Welfare in Canada," 12. As described above, Ontario operates under the "1965 Canada-Ontario Welfare Agreement." In addition, Aboriginal Affairs also provides over $18 million annually to Ontario for enhanced prevention services provided directly to First Nations and to child welfare agencies controlled by First Nations, as well as First Nations agencies that are developing but not yet mandated. Canada, Auditor General of Canada, "Chapter 4: First Nations and Family Services Program," 20.

61. Sinha and Kozlowski, "The Structure of Aboriginal Child Welfare in Canada," 12.

62. Canada, Indian and Northern Affairs Canada, Departmental Audit and Evaluation Branch, *Evaluation of the First Nations Child and Family Services Program*, ii.

63. UN General Assembly, *Convention on the Rights of the Child*, articles 3, 5, 18, 25, and 27(3). See also United Nations Committee on the Rights of the Child, *Commentary 11*, paras. 46–48.

64. Canada, Standing Committee on Public Accounts, 19 October 2011, Evidence of Michael Wernick (Deputy Minister, DIAAD), 41st Parliament, 1st Session, no. 8, 12.

65. Government of Canada, *Government of Canada Response to the Report of the Standing Committee on Public Accounts, on Chapter 4*.

66. Canada, Auditor General of Canada, "Chapter 4: Programs for First Nations on Reserves," 24.

67. Sinha and Kozlowski, "The Structure of Aboriginal Child Welfare in Canada," 13.

68. Canada, Standing Committee on Aboriginal Affairs and Northern Development, 20 October 2009, Evidence of Mary Quinn (Director General, Social Policy and Programs Branch, Department of Indian Affairs and Northern Development), 40th Parliament, 2nd Session, 10–11; Canada, Standing Committee on Aboriginal Affairs and Northern Development, 15 February 2011, Evidence of Carolyn Loeppky (Assistant Deputy Minister, Child and Family Services, Government of Manitoba), 40th Parliament, 3rd Session, 1.

69. Canada, Standing Committee on Public Accounts, *Report of the Standing Committee on Public Accounts. Chapter 4: First Nations Child and Family Services Program*, 10.

70. Canada, Standing Committee on Public Accounts, *Report of the Standing Committee on Public Accounts. Chapter 4: First Nations Child and Family Services Program*, 10.

71. Canada, Standing Committee on Public Accounts, *Report of the Standing Committee on Public Accounts. Chapter 4: First Nations Child and Family Services Program*, 11.

72. Canada, Indian and Northern Affairs Canada, *Implementation Evaluation of the Enhanced Prevention Focused Approach in Alberta for the First Nations Child and Family Services Program*, 18–20.

73. Canada, Aboriginal Affairs and Northern Development Canada, *Final Report: Implementation Evaluation*, 21, 51.

74. Canada, Aboriginal Affairs and Northern Development Canada, *Final Report: Implementation Evaluation*, 20.

75. Canada, Auditor General of Canada, "Chapter 4: First Nations and Family Services Program," 2; British Columbia, Auditor General of British Columbia, *Management of Aboriginal Child Protective Services*, 2.

76. The First Nations Child & Family Caring Society of Canada is a non-profit organization that provides research, networking, public education, and engagement services for First Nations on children's rights issues.

77. Human Rights Commission Complaint Form, filed against Indian and Northern Affairs Canada by Regional Chief Lawrence Joseph and Cindy Blackstock.

78. Devlin, DeForrest, and Mason, "Jurisdictional Quagmire," 14.

79. *First Nations Child and Family Caring Society v. Canada*, 2011 CHRT 4 at para. 12.

80. *Canada (Human Rights Commission) v. Canada (Attorney General)*, 2012 FC 445 (CanLII).

81. *Canada (Attorney General) v. Canadian Human Rights Commission*, 2013 FCA 75.

82. *Canada (Attorney General) v. Canadian Human Rights Commission*, 2013 FCA 75 at para. 22.

83. Cradock, "Extraordinary Costs and Jurisdictional Disputes," 179.

84. Canadian Paediatric Society, *Are We Doing Enough?*, 28.

85. Aboriginal Affairs and Northern Development Canada, "Jordan's Principle."

86. *Pictou Landing Band Council v. Canada (Attorney General)*, 2013 FC 342 (CanLII) at para. 82.

87. *Pictou Landing Band Council v. Canada (Attorney General)*, 2013 FC 342 (CanLII) at para. 82.

88. Canadian Paediatric Society, *Are We Doing Enough?*

89. *Pictou Landing Band Council v. Canada (Attorney General)*, 2013 FC 342 (CanLII).

90. *Pictou Landing Band Council v. Canada (Attorney General)*, 2013 FC 342 at para. 106.

91. Canada, "First Nation Child and Family Services" (presentation), 2.

92. National Collaborating Centre for Aboriginal Health, *Child and Youth Health*, 3.

93. National Indian Child Welfare Association, "Indian Child Welfare Act of 1978."

94. BC Representative for Children and Youth, *When Talk Trumped Service*, 52.

95. First Nations Child & Family Caring Society of Canada, *Wen: De: We Are Coming to the Light of Day*, 38.

96. Canada, Public Health Agency of Canada, *Canadian Incidence Study of Reported Child Abuse and Neglect*, xiii, xxvii.

97. Canada, Public Health Agency of Canada, *Canadian Incidence Study of Reported Child Abuse and Neglect—2008: Major Findings*, 22.

98. Sinha et al., *Kiskisik Awasisak*, ix.

99. Sinha et al., *Kiskisik Awasisak*, x.

100. Sinha et al., *Kiskisik Awasisak*, 29.

101. Every region of the country was included amongst the sampled agencies, but the applicability of the findings in respect of Aboriginal child welfare is limited to the geographic jurisdiction of the sampled agencies. Sinha et al., *Kiskisik Awasisak*, xi, 29.

102. Sinha et al., *Kiskisik Awasisak*, xvi.

103. TRC, NRA, INAC File 6-21-1, volume 2, H. M. Jones to Deputy Minister, 13 December 1956. [NCA-001989-0001]

104. Canada, Statistics Canada, *Aboriginal Peoples in Canada*, 19.

105. Canada, Statistics Canada, *Aboriginal Peoples in Canada*, 19.

106. Sinha et al., *Kiskisik Awasisak*, 5.

107. UN General Assembly, *Convention on the Rights of the Child*, articles 3, 5, 18; United Nations Committee on the Rights of the Child, *Commentary 11*, para. 48.

108. UN General Assembly, *Convention on the Rights of the Child*, article 8.

109. UN General Assembly, *Convention on the Rights of the Child*, articles 3, 5, 18, 25, and 27(3). See also United Nations Committee on the Rights of the Child, *Commentary 11*, paras. 46–48.

110. UN General Assembly, *United Nations Declaration on the Rights of Indigenous Peoples*, article 7(2).
111. UN General Assembly, *United Nations Declaration on the Rights of Indigenous Peoples*, articles 11, 13, 14, 15, 16.
112. UN, Committee on Economic, Social and Cultural Rights, "Consideration of Reports," para. 24.
113. UN, Committee on Economic, Social and Cultural Rights, "Consideration of Reports," para. 56.
114. UN Committee on the Rights of the Child, "Concluding Observations," para. 55.
115. UN Committee on the Rights of the Child, "Concluding Observations," paras. 32–33.
116. UN Committee on the Rights of the Child, "Concluding Observations," para 55.
117. UN Committee on the Rights of the Child, "Concluding Observations," para. 33.d.
118. Saskatchewan Child Welfare Review, *For the Good of Our Children*, 18.
119. Sinha et al., *Kiskisik Awasisak*, 48.
120. First Nations Centre, *First Nations Regional Longitudinal Health Survey (RHS) 2002/03*, 135.
121. First Nations Centre, *First Nations Regional Longitudinal Health Survey (RHS) 2002/03*, 136.
122. From the Indian Residential Schools Adjudication Secretariat website (http://www.iap-pei.ca/us-nous/us-nous-eng.php):

    The Independent Assessment Process (IAP) is part of the Indian Residential Schools Settlement Agreement—the largest class action settlement in Canadian history. The agreement aims to bring a fair and lasting resolution to the harm caused by residential schools. It involved representatives of Aboriginal groups, churches, the government of Canada, and the legal profession. It was approved by the courts. The IAP is for former students who have a claim of sexual or serious physical abuse. It provides them with a way to settle their claim more quickly, out of court. The process is designed to be claimant-centred, but fair and neutral. It is an adjudication process. The Adjudicator resolves claims and awards compensation.

    The deadline to submit an application under the Independent Assessment Process was September 19, 2012. Consult the Indian Residential Schools Adjudication Secretariat website, "Who We Are and What We Do" pages for more information.
123. Indian Residential Schools Adjudication Secretariat, "Observations on Residential School Experience," 7.
124. Indian Residential Schools Adjudication Secretariat, "Observations on Residential School Experience,"7.
125. Indian Residential Schools Adjudication Secretariat, "Observations on Residential School Experience," 8.
126. Indian Residential Schools Adjudication Secretariat, "Observations on Residential School Experience," 9.
127. Canada, Royal Commission on Aboriginal Peoples, *Report*, 3:17.
128. TRC, AVS, Alma Scott, Statement to the Truth and Reconciliation of Canada, Winnipeg, Manitoba, 17 June 2010, Statement Number: 02-MB-16JU10-016.
129. Sinha et al., *Kiskisik Awasisak*, xi. The authors concluded that there was not enough data on Metis and Inuit children and excluded them from the study. Sinha et al., *Kiskisik Awasisak*, ix.
130. Sinha et al., *Kiskisik Awasisak*, 83–87.
131. Sinha et al., *Kiskisik Awasisak*, xviii. The study elaborates,

    The disparity in First Nations and non-Aboriginal substantiated investigation rates was smaller in the other maltreatment categories. In the population served by sampled agencies, the rate of substantiated emotional maltreatment investigations was 5.4 times greater for the First Nations population, the rate of substantiated exposure to intimate partner violence investigations involving First Nations children was 4.7 times greater than the rate for non-Aboriginal children, the rate of substantiated physical abuse investigations was 2.1 times greater for the First Nations population, and the rate of substantiated sexual abuse investigations was 2.7 times greater for the First Nations population served by sampled agencies than for the non-Aboriginal population. (Sinha et al., *Kiskisik Awasisak*, 85)

132. Sinha, Ellenbogen, and Trocmé, "Substantiating Neglect," 2083, 2088.

133. Sinha, Ellenbogen, and Trocmé, "Substantiating Neglect," 2089.

134. The authors concluded,

We found that neglect was significantly more likely to be substantiated for First Nations children than for non-Aboriginal children, and that a statistically significant difference in the odds of substantiation persisted even after controlling for investigation, child, caregiver and household characteristics. Examination of interaction effects showed that that this disproportionality in neglect substantiation of neglect is also linked to differences in the weight that workers assign to mitigating factors. Worker confirmation of caregiver substance abuse was associated with a much greater increase in the odds of neglect substantiation for First Nations than for non-Aboriginal children. The presence of a lone caregiver increased the odds of neglect substantiation for First Nations, but not non-Aboriginal children. Finally, worker identification of housing problems significantly increased the odds of neglect substantiation for non-Aboriginal children; they did not do so for First Nations children. (Sinha, Ellenbogen, and Trocmé, "Substantiating Neglect," 2088)

135. Ruiz-Casares, Trocmé, and Fallon, "Supervisory Neglect," 472.

136. Ruiz-Casares, Trocmé, and Fallon, "Supervisory Neglect," 476–477.

137. Ruiz-Casares, Trocmé, and Fallon, "Supervisory Neglect," 477.

138. Ruiz-Casares, Trocmé, and Fallon, "Supervisory Neglect," 478.

139. Sinha et al., *Kiskisik Awasisak*, xii.

140. Sinha et al., *Kiskisik Awasisak*, xiv.

141. Sinha et al., *Kiskisik Awasisak*, xiv.

142. Canada, Indian and Northern Affairs, *First Nation and Inuit Community Well-Being*, 22.

143. *Child, Youth and Family Enhancement Act*, RSA 2000, c C-12, ss 34, 58.1; *Adoption Act*, RSBC 1996, c 5, ss 3, 17(1), 37; *Adoption Act*, CCSM c A2, ss 3, 19; *Family Services Act*, SNB 1980, c F-2.2, ss 1, 8, 71(1), 78(1); Adoption Act, SNL 1999, c A-2.1, ss 3, 13; *Children and Youth Care and Protection Act*, SNL 2010, c C-12.2, ss 9, 20–21; *Child and Family Services Act*, SNWT (Nu) 1997, c 13, ss 3, 27–28, 31, 38; *Children and Family Services Act*, SNS 1990, c 5, ss 2, 22, 30, 47, 78; *Consolidation of Child and Family Services Act*, SNWT (Nu) 1997, c 13, ss 3, 7, 27, 29.1, 38; *Child and Family Services Act*, RSO 1990, c C.11, ss 1(1), 49; *Child Protection Act*, RSPEI 1988, c C-5.1, ss 2, 9, 23, 38; *Youth Protection Act*, CQLR c P-34.1, ss 3, 91, 46–48.1, 62-64, 71–72.4; *Child and Family Services Act*, SS 1989–90, c C-7.2, ss 4, 11, 16-18, 37; *Child and Family Services Act*, SY 2008, c.1, ss 2, 38, 107(1).

144. Information about ethnicity was available for 94 of the 145 children who have died in foster care since 1999. Of that number, 74 were Aboriginal. Henton, "Deaths of Aboriginal Children," *Edmonton Journal*.

145. Henton, "Deaths of Aboriginal Children," *Edmonton Journal*.

146. Henton, "Deaths of Aboriginal Children," *Edmonton Journal*.
147. Alberta Centre for Child, Family and Community Research, *A Preliminary Analysis of Mortalities*, 25.
148. BC Ministry of Health, Office of the Provincial Health Officer, and Child and Youth Officer for British Columbia, *Health and Well-Being of Children in Care*, 54, 58.
149. Ontario, Office of the Chief Coroner of Ontario, *Paediatric Death Review Committee*, 34.
150. Ontario, Office of the Chief Coroner of Ontario, *Paediatric Death Review Committee*, 42.
151. Sinha et al., *Kiskisik Awasisak*, 5.
152. Ontario, Office of the Chief Coroner of Ontario, *Paediatric Death Review Committee*, 60.
153. Hughes, *The Legacy of Phoenix Sinclair*, 1:19–20, 1:53.
154. Hughes, *The Legacy of Phoenix Sinclair*, 1:19–35.
155. Hughes, *The Legacy of Phoenix Sinclair*, 1:24.
156. Hughes, *The Legacy of Phoenix Sinclair*, 1:30.
157. Hughes, *The Legacy of Phoenix Sinclair*, 1:28; 2:148.
158. Hughes, *The Legacy of Phoenix Sinclair*, 1:28.
159. Schibler and Newton, *Honouring Their Spirits*, 6, 23.
160. Schibler and Newton, *Honouring Their Spirits*, 30, 32.
161. Schibler and Newton, *Honouring Their Spirits*, 47–49.
162. Schibler and Newton, *Honouring Their Spirits*, 57–58.
163. Schibler and Newton, *Honouring Their Spirits*, 76.
164. Canada, Statistics Canada, *Aboriginal Peoples in Canada*, 5. Issues related to Inuit history, culture, and child and family welfare discussed in this chapter focus on the Canadian context, but it is important to acknowledge that approximately 150,000 Inuit people live in the circumpolar region encompassing Canada, Alaska, Russia, and Greenland. Inuit peoples of the circumpolar region are interconnected with shared physical traits, kinships, languages, rules, concepts, myths, legends, and cultural routines. With technological and institutional progress, Inuit peoples have strengthened their connections and speak with one voice across countries on many issues of common concern, including challenges of cultural erosion and assimilation efforts directed towards them.
165. Canada, Statistics Canada, *Aboriginal Peoples in Canada*, 5, 14–17.
166. Tagalik, "Inuit *Qaujimajatuqangit*," 1, 4.
167. Inuit Qaujimajatuqanginnut (IQ) Task Force, *First Annual Report*; Bonesteel, "Use of Traditional Inuit Culture."
168. Rae, *Inuit Child Welfare and Family Support*, 10, 13–15.
169. Pauktuutit Inuit Women of Canada, *The Inuit Way*, 16.
170. Pauktuutit Inuit Women of Canada, *The Inuit Way*, 16.
171. Graburn, "Severe Child Abuse," 211–225; Pauktuutit Inuit Women of Canada, *The Inuit Way*, 2.
172. Ochalski, "Addressing Inuit Child Welfare in Canada," notes from 2012 focus group, in Blackstock et al., "Is It Over Yet?" 33.
173. Tagalik, "Inunnguiniq: Caring for Children the Inuit Way"; Roberts, *Eskimo Identification*.
174. Legacy of Hope Foundation, *Inuit and the Residential School System*, 3.
175. Bonesteel, *Canada's Relationship with Inuit*, 10, 11.
176. *Reference whether "Indians" includes "Eskimo" Inhabitants of the Province of Quebec*, [1939] SCR 104; SC 1951, c 29,4 (1), P317.
177. King, *Brief Report of the Federal Government*, 12.
178. King, *Brief Report of the Federal Government*, 7.

179. King, *Brief Report of the Federal Government*, 11, 15, 17.

180. Graburn, "Severe Child Abuse," 212.

181. Inuit Tuttarvingat, *Inuit Men Talking about Health*.

182. Inuit Tapiriit Kanatami, *Social Determinants of Inuit Health in Canada*, 38.

183. Blackstock et al., "Is It Over Yet?," 38.

184. Gough, "Northwest Territories' Child Welfare System," 1.

185. Debbie DeLancey (Deputy Minister, Department of Health and Social Services, Government of the NWT) email to Commissioner Wilson, 14 July 2015.

186. Gough, "Northwest Territories' Child Welfare System," 4.

187. Gough "Northwest Territories' Child Welfare System," 3.

188. Canada, Statistics Canada, *Aboriginal Peoples in Canada*, 9.

189. Trocmé et al., *Canadian Incidence Study of Reported Child Abuse and Neglect*, 2.

190. Gough, "Northwest Territories' Child Welfare System," 3.

191. Gough, "Nunavut's Child Welfare System," 2–3.

192. Gough, "Nunavut's Child Welfare System," 3–4.

193. Gough, "Nunavut's Child Welfare System," 2.

194. Phaneuf, Dudding, and Arreak, *Nunavut Social Service Review*, 19.

195. Blumenthal and Sinha, "Newfoundland and Labrador's Child Welfare System."

196. Gough, "Newfoundland and Labrador's Child Welfare System," 4.

197. Québec, Commission des droits de la personne et des droits de la jeunesse, *Investigation*, 11.

198. Québec, Commission des droits de la personne et des droits de la jeunesse, *Investigation*, 12.

199. Québec, Commission des droits de la personne et des droits de la jeunesse, *Investigation*, 7.

200. Québec, Commission des droits de la personne et des droits de la jeunesse, *Investigation*, 8.

201. Québec, Commission des droits de la personne et des droits de la jeunesse, *Investigation*, 58, 59.

202. Québec, Commission des droits de la personne et des droits de la jeunesse, *Investigation*, 59.

203. Québec, Commission des droits de la personne et des droits de la jeunesse, *Investigation*, 59.

204. Québec, Commission des droits de la personne et des droits de la jeunesse, *Nunavik: Follow-up Report*.

205. Rae, *Inuit Child Welfare and Family Support*, 1.

206. Canada, Auditor General of Canada, *Report of the Auditor General*, 2.

207. Arnold, *Director of Child and Family Services Annual Report 2011–2012*, 1–8.

208. Rideout, "Commission Considers Rules for Custom Adoptions," *Nunatsiaq News*.

209. Rae, *Inuit Child Welfare and Family Support*, 6.

210. Métis National Council, "Who Are the Métis?"

211. Canada, Statistics Canada, *Aboriginal Peoples in Canada, First Nations People, Métis and Inuit*; Canada, Statistics Canada, *Aboriginal Peoples and Language*.

212. Andersen, "From Nation to Population," 352.

213. Métis National Council, "Who Are the Métis?"

214. Canada, Royal Commission on Aboriginal Peoples, *Report*, 1:311.

215. Chartrand, "Métis Residential School Participation," 23.

216. Logan, "Lost Generations," 63.

217. Logan, "Lost Generations," 73, emphasis in original.

218. Métis Nation of Alberta, *Métis Memories of Residential Schools*, in Blackstock et al., "Is It Over Yet?," 49, 50.

219. Métis Nation of Alberta (2004), *Métis Memories of Residential Schools*, in Blackstock et al., "Is it Over Yet?," 50.

220. Elmer Ghostkeeper, conversation with Jeannine Carrière at Victoria, BC, 1 October 2012, in Blackstock et al., "Is It Over Yet?," 46.

221. Deborah Dyck, conversation with Sinéad Charbonneau at Victoria, BC, 20 December 2012, in Blackstock et al., "Is It Over Yet?," 46.

222. Tom McCallum, conversation with Cathy Richardson at Victoria, BC, 19 October 2012, in Blackstock et al., "Is It Over Yet?," 46.

223. Obomsawin, *Richard Cardinal*.

224. Obomsawin, *Richard Cardinal*.

225. Deborah Canada, "The Strength of the Sash," 10.

226. TRC, AVS, Robert Doucette, Statement to the Truth and Reconciliation Commission of Canada, Batoche, Saskatchewan; 20 July 2010, Statement Number: 01-SK-18-25JY10-001.

227. Carrière, "Connectedness and Health"; Richardson and Nelson, "A Change of Residence"; Richardson and Seaborn, "Working with Métis Children"; Manitoba Metis Federation, *They Are Taking Our Children*.

228. Sinha et al., *Kiskisik Awasisak*, ix.

229. British Columbia, Ministry of Children and Family Development, *Aboriginal Children in Care*, 2, 21

230. Manitoba, Auditor General of Manitoba, *Follow-up of Our December 2006 Report*, 9.

231. Gonzalez-Mena, "Cross-Cultural Infant Care," 368.

232. Carrière and Richardson, "From Longing to Belonging."

233. *Canada (Indian Affairs) v. Daniels*, 2014 FCA 101 (CanLII) at para. 159.

234. *Daniels v. Canada*, 2013 FC 6 (CanLII).

235. *Harry Daniels, et al. v. Her Majesty the Queen as represented by The Minister of Indian Affairs and Northern Development, et al.*, 2014 CanLII 68707 (SCC).

236. Manitoba Metis Federation, "Departments, Portfolios and Affiliates."

237. Gough, "Alberta's Child Welfare System," 1.

238. Canada, "The Strength of the Sash," 138, 146.

239. Métis Nation of Ontario, *Recommendations Concerning Métis-Specific Child and Family Services*, 15.

240. Chartrand, *Maskikiwenow: The Métis Right to Health*.

241. Leanne Laberge, conversation with Jeannine Carrière and Sinead Charbonneau at Victoria, BC, 18 October 2012, in Blackstock et al., "Is It Over Yet?," 46.

242. Barkwell, Dorion, and Hourie, *Métis Legacy*, vol. 2: *Michif Culture*, 56.

243. Richardson, "Métis Experiences of Social Work Practices," 120.

244. Richardson, "Métis Experiences of Social Work Practices," 123.

245. TRC, AVS, Mary Anne Clarke, Statement to the Truth and Reconciliation Commission of Canada, Winnipeg, Manitoba, 12 January 2011, Statement Number: 03-001-10-026.

246. TRC, AVS, Shirley Morris, Statement to the Truth and Reconciliation Commission of Canada, Halifax, Nova Scotia, 29 October 2011, Statement Number: 2011-2918.

247. Fletcher, "The Origins of the Indian Child Welfare Act," n.p. (1).

248. Fletcher, "The Origins of the Indian Child Welfare Act," n.p. (1).

249. Graham, "Reparations, Self-Determination," 56.

250. Graham, "Reparations, Self-Determination, 90.

251. Fletcher, "The Origins of the Indian Child Welfare Act," n.p. (4).

252. Basic, "Termination of Parental Rights," 348.
253. Basic, "Termination of Parental Rights," 348.
254. Fletcher, "The Origins of the Indian Child Welfare Act," n.p. (4).
255. Fletcher, "The Origins of the Indian Child Welfare Act," n.p. (5).
256. Cross, "Indian Family Exception Doctrine," 688–689.
257. Gajewski, "Class-Action Lawsuit," *The Humanist*, 48.
258. Atwood, "Voice of the Indian Child," 129–130.
259. Atwood, "Voice of the Indian Child," 128.
260. Blackstock et al., *Reconciliation in Child Welfare*, 4.
261. Blackstock et al., *Reconciliation in Child Welfare*, 4, 9–11.
262. Quinn and Saini, *Touchstones of Hope*.
263. Mishibinijima, *Aboriginal Child Protection*.
264. Pintarics and Sveinunggaard, "Meenoostahtan Minisiwin," 67, 74, 75.
265. Timleck quoted in Baskin, *Strong Helpers' Teachings*, 197.
266. Timleck quoted in Baskin, *Strong Helpers' Teachings*, 198–199.
267. Timleck quoted in Baskin, *Strong Helpers' Teachings*, 198.
268. Signs of Safety, *Signs of Safety*.

## The failure to educate

1. TRC, AVS, Howard Stacy Jones, Statement to the Truth and Reconciliation Commission of Canada, Victoria, British Columbia, 4 December 2010, Statement Number: 01-BC-03DE10-001.
2. Canada, *Annual Report of the Department of Indian Affairs, 1883*, 96.
3. TRC, NRA, Library and Archives Canada, RG10, volume 6323, file 658-6, part 1, Department of Indian Affairs Inspector's Report for the St. Barnabas, Indian Residential School, D. Hicks, 25 September 1928. [PAR-003233]
4. Library and Archives Canada, RG10, volume 6205, file 468-1, part 2, S. R. McVitty to Secretary, Indian Affairs, 30 January 1928.
5. Sluman and Goodwill, *John Tootoosis*, 106.
6. Bougie and Senécal, "Registered Indian Children's School Success," 26–30; Canada, Statistics Canada, *Educational Portrait of Canada, Census Year 2006*, 19; Richards, Hove, and Afolabi, "Understanding the Aboriginal/Non-Aboriginal Gap," 1.
7. UN General Assembly, *United Nations Declaration on the Rights of Indigenous Peoples*, article 14(1).
8. TRC, NRA, Library and Archives Canada, RG10, volume 6040, file 160-4, part 1, R. B. Heron to Regina Presbytery, April 1923. [AEMR-016371]
9. Canada, *Annual Report of the Department of Indian Affairs, 1941*, 189; Canada, *Annual Report of the Department of Indian Affairs, 1942*, 154; Canada, *Annual Report of the Department of Indian Affairs, 1943*, 168; Canada, *Annual Report of the Department of Indian Affairs, 1944*, 177; Canada, *Annual Report of the Department of Indian Affairs, 1945*, 190; Canada, *Annual Report of the Department of Indian Affairs, 1946*, 231; Canada, *Annual Report of the Department of Indian Affairs, 1947*, 236; Canada, *Annual Report of the Department of Indian Affairs, 1948*, 234; Canada, *Annual Report of the Department of Indian Affairs, 1949*, 215, 234; Canada, *Annual Report of the Department of Indian Affairs, 1950*, 86–87; Canada, *Annual Report of*

*the Department of Indian Affairs, 1951,* 34–35; Canada, *Annual Report of the Department of Indian Affairs, 1952,* 74–75; Canada, *Annual Report of the Department of Indian Affairs, 1953,* 82–83; Canada, *Annual Report of the Department of Indian Affairs, 1954,* 88–89; Canada, *Annual Report of the Department of Indian Affairs, 1955,* 78–79; Canada, *Annual Report of the Department of Indian Affairs, 1956,* 76–77; Canada, *Annual Report of the Department of Indian Affairs, 1956–57,* 88–89; Canada, *Annual Report of the Department of Indian Affairs, 1958,* 90–91; Canada, *Annual Report of the Department of Indian Affairs, 1959,* 94; Canada, *Annual Report of the Department of Indian Affairs, 1960,* 94; Canada, *Annual Report of the Department of Indian Affairs, 1961,* 103.

10. Canada, *Annual Report of the Department of Indian Affairs, 1942,* 154; Canada, *Annual Report of the Department of Indian Affairs, 1943,* 168; Canada, *Annual Report of the Department of Indian Affairs, 1944,* 177; Canada, *Annual Report of the Department of Indian Affairs, 1945,* 190; Canada, *Annual Report of the Department of Indian Affairs, 1946,* 231; Canada, *Annual Report of the Department of Indian Affairs, 1947,* 236; Canada, *Annual Report of the Department of Indian Affairs, 1948,* 234; Canada, *Annual Report of the Department of Indian Affairs, 1949,* 215; Canada, *Annual Report of the Department of Indian Affairs, 1950,* 86–87; Canada, *Annual Report of the Department of Indian Affairs, 1951,* 34–35; Canada, *Annual Report of the Department of Indian Affairs, 1952,* 74–75; Canada, *Annual Report of the Department of Indian Affairs, 1953,* 82–83; Canada, *Annual Report of the Department of Indian Affairs, 1954,* 88–89; Canada, *Annual Report of the Department of Indian Affairs, 1955,* 78–79; Canada, *Annual Report of the Department of Indian Affairs, 1956,* 76–77; Canada, *Annual Report of the Department of Indian Affairs, 1956–57,* 88–89; Canada, *Annual Report of the Department of Indian Affairs, 1958,* 91; Canada, *Annual Report of the Department of Indian Affairs, 1959,* 94; Canada, *Annual Report of the Department of Indian Affairs, 1960,* 94; Canada, *Annual Report of the Department of Indian Affairs, 1961,* 102; Canada, *Annual Report of the Department of Indian Affairs, 1962,* 73; Canada, *Annual Report of the Department of Indian Affairs, 1963,* 62.

11. TRC, NRA, Library and Archives Canada, RG10, volume 6342, file 750-1, part 1, Microfilm reel C-8699, J. D. McLean to Reverend E. Ruaux, 21 June 1915. [MRY-001517] For a similar report from the Battleford, Saskatchewan, school, see Canada, *Annual Report of the Department of Indian Affairs, 1909,* 349–350. For a Manitoba example, see TRC, NRA, Library and Archives Canada, RG10, volume 6267, file 580-5, part 4, Joseph Hamilton Inspection Report, not dated. [DRS-000570]

12. TRC, NRA, INAC – Resolution Sector – IRS Historical Files Collection – Ottawa, file 673/23-5-038, volume 1, H. L. Winter to Indian Affairs, 9 September 1932. [MRS-000138-0001]

13. Canada, *Annual Report of the Department of Indian Affairs, 1903,* 342–343. For other examples of the emphasis on religious training in the schools, see Canada, *Annual Report of the Department of Indian Affairs, 1887,* 27–28; Canada, *Annual Report of the Department of Indian Affairs, 1910,* 433–434; Canada, *Annual Report of the Department of Indian Affairs, 1890,* 119; Canada, *Annual Report of the Department of Indian Affairs, 1900,* 323.

14. TRC, NRA, The Presbyterian Church in Canada Archives, Toronto, Tyler Bjornson File, Presbyterian Research, "Presbyterian Indian Residential School Staff Handbook," 1. [IRC-041206]

15. TRC, NRA, Library and Archives Canada, RG10, volume 6327, file 660-1, part 1, J. D. McLean to Rev. J. Hugonard, 30 May 1911. [PLD-007442]

16. TRC, NRA, Library and Archives Canada, RG10, volume 6422, file 869-1, part 2, R. H. Cairns, inspector to J. D. McLean, 5 January 1915. [COQ-000390]

17. TRC, NRA, Library and Archives Canada, RG10, volume 6431, file 877-1, part 2, "Extract from Report of Mr. Inspector Cairns dated September 5th and 6th, 1928 on the Alberni Indian Residential School." [ABR-001591]

18. TRC, NRA, Library and Archives Canada, RG10, volume 6001, file 1-1-1, part 3, "Department of Indian Affairs, Schools Branch," 31 March 1935. [SRS-000279]

19. For a British Columbia example, see TRC, NRA, Library and Archives Canada, RG10, volume 6431, file 877-1, part 1, A. W. Neill to A. W. Vowell, 8 July 1909. [ABR-007011-0001] For a Manitoba example, see TRC, NRA, Library and Archives Canada, RG10, volume 6262, file 578-1, part 4, W. M. Graham to Secretary, Indian Affairs, 4 February 1922. [ELK-000299]

20. For example, a 1936 United Church document on First Nations education policy stated that the staff of all United Church schools should be composed of people who had a "Christian motive, or, in other words, a missionary purpose coupled with skill in some particular field to teach his specialty to the Indians." Staff members were expected to be "closely related to and actively interested in the work of the nearest United Church," and be acquainted with, and sympathetic to, "the religious education programme of the United Church." Having laid out these fairly specific requirements, the policy document added that "some minimum educational qualifications for staff members should be outlined." TRC, NRA, United Church Archives, Acc. 83.050C, box 144-21, "Statement of Policy Re Indian Residential Schools," June 1936. [UCC-050004]

21. For an example of the link between low pay and unqualified teachers, see TRC, NRA, Library and Archives Canada, RG10, volume 6039, file 160-1, part 1, Martin Benson, Memorandum, 15 July 1897, 4, 25. [100.00108]

22. TRC, NRA, Library and Archives Canada, RG10, volume 4041, file 334503, F. H. Paget to Frank Pedley, 25 November 1908, 55. [RCA-000298]

23. TRC, NRA, Library and Archives Canada, RG10, volume 6431, file 877-1, part 1, A. W. Vowell to Secretary, Indian Affairs, 14 July 1909. [ABR-007011-0000]

24. Canada, *Annual Report of the Department of Indian Affairs, 1955*, 51.

25. TRC, NRA, DIAND, file 1/25-1, volume 22, R. F. Davey to Bergevin, 15 September 1959, 3. [AEMR-019616]

26. Canada, *Annual Report of the Department of Indian Affairs, 1921*, 28.

27. TRC, NRA, Library and Archives Canada, RG10, volume 6014, file 1-1-6 MAN, part 1, Duncan Campbell Scott to Mr. Meighen, 1 June 1920. [NCA-002403]

28. Canada, Special Joint Committee, *Minutes of Evidence*, D. F. Brown Presiding, 15 April 1947, 483–484.

29. Canada, Special Joint Committee, *Minutes of Evidence*, D. F. Brown Presiding, 17 April 1947, 505.

30. TRC, NRA, National Archives of Canada, RG10, volume 8760, file 901/25-1, part 2, R. F. Davey to Director, 14 March 1956, 4. [AEMR-120651]

31. See, for example, TRC, NRA, DIAND, file 1/25-1 (E.10), "Report on Textbooks," 6–9 [AEMR-019193A]; Québec, *Rapport Parent*, para. 210; TRC, NRA, DIAND, file 1/25-1 (E.10), "Report on Textbooks," 6–9 [AEMR-019193A]; Vanderburgh, *The Canadian Indian*.

32. TRC, NRA, DIAND, file 1/25-1 (E.10), "Report on Textbooks," 1–6. [AEMR-019193A]

33. TRC, AVS, Myrna Kaminawaish, Statement to the Truth and Reconciliation Commission of Canada, Thunder Bay, Ontario, 7 January 2011, Statement Number: 01-ON-06JA11-004.

34. TRC, AVS, Paul Kaludjau, Statement to the Truth and Reconciliation Commission of Canada, Winnipeg, Manitoba, 16 June 2010, Statement Number: 02-MB-16JU10-144.

35. TRC, AVS, Walter Russell Jones, Statement to the Truth and Reconciliation Commission of Canada, Victoria, British Columbia, 14 April 2012, Statement Number: 2011-4008.

36. First Nations Centre, *First Nations Regional Longitudinal Health Survey (RHS) 2002/03*, 134.

37. Bougie, "Aboriginal Peoples Survey, 2006," 21.

38. TRC, NRA, Library and Archives Canada, RG10, volume 3920, file 116818, D. L. Clink to Indian Commissioner June 4 1895. [EDM-003380]

39. For an example from Battleford, see Library and Archives Canada, RG 10, volume 3880, file 92,499, Memorandum, Hayter Reed, undated; T. Clarke, "Report of Discharged Pupils," Sessional Papers 1894, Paper 13, 103. For an example from Brantford, see TRC, NRA, Library and Archives Canada, RG 10 (Red), volume 2771, file 154,845, part 1, J. G. Ramsden to J. D. McLean, 23 December 1907 [TAY-003542]. For an example from Kenora, see TRC, NRA, Library and Archives Canada, RG10, volume 6197, file 465-1, part 1, Minakijikok to D. C. Scott, 30 September 1924 [KNR-000804-0001]; TRC, NRA, Library and Archives Canada, RG10, volume 6197, file 465-1, part 1, Frank Edwards to Assistant Deputy and Secretary, Indian Affairs, 8 October 1924. [KNR-000803]

40. TRC, AVS, Patricia Brooks, Statement to the Truth and Reconciliation Commission of Canada, Indian Brook, Nova Scotia, 12 October 2011, Statement Number: 2011-2710.

41. Bougie and Senécal, "Registered Indian Children's School Success," 21.

42. Bougie and Senécal, "Registered Indian Children's School Success," 21.

43. Indian Residential Schools Adjudication Secretariat, "Observations."

44. Canada, Statistics Canada, *The Educational Attainment of Aboriginal Peoples in Canada*, 5.

45. Canada, Statistics Canada, *The Educational Attainment of Aboriginal Peoples in Canada*, 4, 5.

46. TRC, AVS, Violet Rupp, Statement to the Truth and Reconciliation Commission of Canada, Bloodvein, Manitoba, 25 January 2012, Statement Number: 2011-2565.

47. TRC, AVS, Esther Lachinette-Diabo, Statement to the Truth and Reconciliation Commission of Canada, Thunder Bay, Ontario, 25 November 2010, Statement Number: 01-ON-24NOV10-020.

48. TRC, AVS, Darryl Siah, Statement to the Truth and Reconciliation Commission of Canada, Mission, British Columbia, 18 May 2011, Statement Number: 2011-3473.

49. Indian Residential Schools Adjudication Secretariat, "Observations," 4.

50. Canada, Statistics Canada, *Portrait of Canada's Labour Force*, 14.

51. Bougie and Senécal, "Registered Indian Children's School Success," 3.

52. Bougie and Senécal, "Registered Indian Children's School Success," 7.

53. Bougie and Senécal, "Registered Indian Children's School Success," 28.

54. Bougie and Senécal, "Registered Indian Children's School Success," 26–30.

55. Bougie and Senécal, "Registered Indian Children's School Success," 26–29.

56. Canada, Statistics Canada, "The Education and Employment Experiences of First Nations," 1.

57. Mendelson, "Improving Education on Reserves," 2.

58. Sharpe and Lapointe, *The Labour Market and Economic Performance*, 6.

59. Canada, Auditor General of Canada, "Chapter 4: Programs for First Nations on Reserves," 13.

60. Canada, Statistics Canada, "The Education and Employment Experiences of First Nations," 2.

61. Clement, "University Attainment of the Registered Indian Population," 101; Wilk, White, and Guimond, "Métis Educational Attainment," 54.

62. Richards, Hove, and Afolabi, "Understanding the Aboriginal/Non-Aboriginal Gap," 1.

63. Clement, "University Attainment of the Registered Indian Population," 101.

64. Canadian Human Rights Commission, *Report on Equality Rights of Aboriginal People*, 3, 12, 32.

65. Canada, Statistics Canada, "Study: Aboriginal People and the Labour Market."

66. Wilson and Macdonald, *The Income Gap*, 8.

67. Canada, Statistics Canada, "The Education and Employment Experiences of First Nations," 2.

68. Wilson and Macdonald, *The Income Gap*, 4.

69. Macdonald and Wilson, *Poverty or Prosperity*, 6.

70. Wilson and Macdonald, *The Income Gap*, 14.

71. The poverty line is measured by the 2009 SLID Low-Income Measure (LIM), which is based on 50% of the median adjusted household income. Canada, Statistics Canada, "Low Income Lines, 2008–2009."

72. Canadian Human Rights Commission, *Report on Equality Rights of Aboriginal People*, 17, 18.

73. Penney, "Formal Educational Attainment of Inuit," 43.

74. Berger, *Nunavut Land Claims Agreement*, iii.

75. National Committee on Inuit Education, *First Canadians, Canadians First*, 7.

76. Canadian Human Rights Commission, *Report on Equality Rights of Aboriginal People*, 15.

77. Canadian Human Rights Commission, *Report on Equality Rights of Aboriginal People*, 18.

78. O'Donnell and Wallace, "First Nations, Métis and Inuit Women," 30.

79. Carr-Stewart, "A Treaty Right to Education," 138.

80. *Kelly v. Canada (Attorney General)*, 2013 ONSC 1220 (striking out claims based on education rights in Treaty 3 as non-justiciable); *Beattie v. Canada (Minister of Indian Affairs and Northern Development)*, 1997 CanLII 6343 (FC); *Canada (Attorney General) v. Desjarlais*, 2005 ABQB 416 (CanLII); *Ochapowace Indian Band No. 71 v. Canada (Department of Indian Affairs and Northern Development)*, 1998 CanLII 13768 (SK QB).

81. UN, Expert Mechanism on the Rights of Indigenous Peoples, "Advice No. 1," para. 91.

82. United Nations Committee on the Rights of the Child, *Commentary 11*, para. 57.

83. Wilson and Macdonald, *The Income Gap*, 17.

84. TRC, AVS, Laverne Victor, Statement to the Truth and Reconciliation Commission of Canada, Mission, British Columbia, 17 May 2011, Statement Number: 2011-3463.

85. Australia, Council of Australian Governments, *National Indigenous Reform Agreement*.

86. Australian Government, *Closing the Gap*, 10–19.

87. For a 1940 assessment of building conditions, see TRC, NRA, Library and Archives Canada, RG10, volume 6012, file 1-1-5A, part 2, R. A. Hoey to Dr. McGill, 31 May 1940. [BIR-000248]

88. Canada, Special Joint Committee, 1946, 3, 15.

89. Canada, *Annual Report of the Department of Indian Affairs, 1945*, 168, 183; Canada, *Annual Report of the Department of Indian Affairs, 1955*, 70, 76–78.

90. Canada, *Annual Report of the Department of Indian Affairs, 1949*, 199.

91. *An Act Respecting Indians*, Statutes of Canada 1951, chapter 29, section 113, reproduced in Venne, *Indian Acts*, 350.

92. Canada, *Annual Report of the Department of Indian Affairs, 1961*, 57.

93. Canada, *Annual Report of the Department of Indian Affairs, 1961*, 63.

94. See, for example, TRC, NRA, No document location, no document file source, The Canadian Catholic Conference, "A Brief to the Parliamentary Committee on Indian Affairs," May 1960, 8. [GMA-001642-0000]

95. Newman, *Indians of the Saddle Lake Reserve*, 81–87.

96. TRC, AVS, Annie Wesley, Statement to the Truth and Reconciliation Commission of Canada, Thunder Bay, Ontario, 25 November 2010, Statement Number: 01-ON-24NOV10-034.

97. TRC, AVS, Dorothy Ross, Statement to the Truth and Reconciliation Commission of Canada, Thunder Bay, Ontario, 25 November 2010, Statement Number: 01-ON-24NOV10-014.

98. TRC, AVS, Shirley Leon, Statement to the Truth and Reconciliation Commission of Canada, Deroche, British Columbia, 19 January 2010, Statement Number: 2011-5048.

99. FNEC, NAN, and FSIN, *Report on Priority Actions*, 51.

100. Haldane et al., *Nurturing the Learning Spirit*, 14.

101. Haldane et al., *Nurturing the Learning Spirit*, 14.

102. Canada, Royal Commission on Aboriginal Peoples, *Report*, 3:485.

103. Canada, Standing Senate Committee on Aboriginal Peoples, *Reforming First Nations Education*, 1.

104. Canada, Standing Senate Committee on Aboriginal Peoples, *Reforming First Nations Education*, 1.

105. Canada, Standing Senate Committee on Aboriginal Peoples, *Reforming First Nations Education*, 9.

106. Ontario, Office of the Chief Coroner of Ontario, "Schedule of Inquests."

107. Canada, "Statement of the Government of Canada on Indian Policy, 1969"; National Indian Brotherhood, *Indian Control of Indian Education*; TRC, NRA, National Capital Regional Service Centre – LAC – Ottawa, File 301/25-1, volume 9, Jean Chrétien to George Manuel, 2 February 1973. [NCA-017031-0002]

108. Canada, Standing Senate Committee on Aboriginal Peoples, *Reforming First Nations Education*, 56.

109. Paquette and Fallon, *First Nations Education Policy*, 81.

110. Nicholas, "Canada's Colonial Mission," 16, 17.

111. McCue, "First Nations 2nd and 3rd Level Education Services," 52.

112. Kirkness, "Aboriginal Education in Canada," 17.

113. First Nations Education Council, "Funding Formula for First Nation Schools," 19–22; Canada, Standing Senate Committee on Aboriginal Peoples, *Reforming First Nations Education*, 63.

114. Canada, Standing Senate Committee on Aboriginal Peoples, *Reforming First Nations Education*, 11.

115. Canada, Standing Senate Committee on Aboriginal Peoples *Reforming First Nations Education*, 31, 32.

116. Canada, Aboriginal Affairs and Northern Development Canada, *Summative Evaluation*, 32.

117. Canada, Aboriginal Affairs and Northern Development Canada, *Summative Evaluation*, 32–33.

118. *Canada (Attorney General) v. Mohawks of the Quinte First Nation*, 2012 FC 105 (CanLII) at para. 1.

119. FNEC, NAN, and FSIN, *Report on Priority Actions*, 22.

120. Haldane et al., *Nurturing the Learning Spirit*, 17.

121. Porter, "Walls Crumble," *CBC News*.

122. Rajekar and Mathilakath, *The Funding Requirement*, 51.

123. McCue, "First Nations 2nd and 3rd Level Education Services," 36.

124. FNEC, NAN, and FSIN, *Report on Priority Actions*, 60; Haldane et al., *Nurturing the Learning Spirit*, 12.

125. *Education Act for Cree, Inuit and Naskapi Native Persons*, RSQ, c I-14 at Part X.

126. Canada, Standing Senate Committee on Aboriginal Peoples, *Reforming First Nations Education*, 12.

127. *Québec c. Commission Scolaire Crie*, 2001 CanLII 20652 (QC CA) 112.

128. Canada, Standing Senate Committee on Aboriginal Peoples, *Reforming First Nations Education*, 9.

129. McCue, "An Overview," 5.

130. Canada, Standing Senate Committee on Aboriginal Peoples, *Reforming First Nations Education*, 61.

131. Canada, Standing Senate Committee on Aboriginal Peoples *Reforming First Nations Education*, 61.

132. People for Education, *First Nations, Metis and Inuit Education*, 3, 4.

133. Little Bear, "Naturalizing Indigenous Knowledge," 7.

134. Western Canadian Protocol for Collaboration in Basic Education, *Common Curriculum Framework*.

135. See Canada, Standing Senate Committee on Aboriginal Peoples, *Reforming First Nations Education*, 1–2; Canada, Task Force on Aboriginal Languages and Culture, *Towards a New Beginning*, 89.

136. Canada, Task Force on Aboriginal Languages and Culture, *Towards a New Beginning*, 88.

137. People for Education, *First Nations, Métis and Inuit Education*, 2, 9.

138. Ontario, *Ontario's New Approach*, 12, 13; Ontario, *A Solid Foundation*.

139. Ontario, Aboriginal Education Office and Ministry of Education, *Ontario First Nation, Métis, and Inuit Education Policy Framework*, 27.

140. Ontario, *A Solid Foundation*, 16.

141. Ontario, *A Solid Foundation*, 28.

142. Canada, Royal Commission on Aboriginal Peoples, *Report*, 3:421.

143. Canada, Royal Commission on Aboriginal Peoples, *Report*, 3:422–423.

144. Assembly of First Nations, "Early Childhood Education."

145. Canada, Royal Commission on Aboriginal Peoples, *Report*, 3:412.

146. Canada, Royal Commission on Aboriginal Peoples, *Report*, 3:439.

147. Canada, Royal Commission on Aboriginal Peoples, *Report*, 3:431.

148. Canada, Royal Commission on Aboriginal Peoples, *Report*, 3:435–436.

149. Canada, Health Canada, "Aboriginal Head Start on Reserve."

150. Canada, Public Health Agency of Canada, *Evaluation of the Aboriginal Head Start*.

151. Preston et al., "Aboriginal Early Childhood Education," 12–13.

152. Canada, Aboriginal Affairs and Northern Development Canada, *Summative Evaluation*, 40.

153. Mississaugas of the New Credit First Nation, "Special Education Human Rights Case."

154. *An Act Concerning Indians*, Statutes of Canada 1876, chapter 18, section 86.1, reproduced in Venne, *Indian Acts*, 47; *An Act Concerning Indians*, Statutes of Canada 1927, chapter 98, section 110, reproduced in Venne, *Indian Acts*, 285–287.

155. Canada, Statistics Canada, Table 2: "Proportion of First Nations People, Métis, and Inuit Aged 25 to 64 by Selected Levels of Educational Attainment and Sex, Canada, 2011," in *The Educational Attainment of Aboriginal People in Canada*, https://www12.statcan.gc.ca/nhs-enm/2011/as-sa/99-012-x/2011003/tbl/tbl2-eng.cfm.

156. TRC, AVS, Jennie Thomas, Statement to the Truth and Reconciliation Commission of Canada, Victoria, British Columbia, 14 April 2012, Statement Number: 2011-3992.

157. TRC, AVS, Velma Jackson, Statement to the Truth and Reconciliation Commission of Canada, St. Paul, Alberta, 6 January 2011, Statement Number: 01-AB-06JA11-003.

158. First Nations Education Council, "Paper on First Nations Education Funding," 35.

159. National Committee on Inuit Education, *First Canadians, Canadians First*, 87.

160. FNEC, NAN, and FSIN, *Report on Priority Actions*, 37.

161. Canada, Standing Senate Committee on Social Affairs, Science and Technology, *Opening the Door*, 47.

162. First Nations Education Council, "Paper on First Nations Education Funding," 37.

163. Ogwehoweh Skills and Trades Training Centre; Yellowquill College, "Programs."

164. First Nations Education Council, "Paper on First Nations Education Funding," 39.

165. Canada, Standing Senate Committee on Social Affairs, Science and Technology, *Opening the Door*, 48–49.

166. Hodgson-Smith, "The State of Métis Nation Learning," 4.

167. Hodgson-Smith, "The State of Métis Nation Learning," 17, 18.

168. Métis National Council, *Toward a Canada–Métis Nation*, 27, 28.

169. National Committee on Inuit Education, *First Canadians, Canadians First*, 7–8.

170. Canada, Statistics Canada, "The Education and Employment Experiences of First Nations," 1.

171. National Committee on Inuit Education, *First Canadians, Canadians First*, 3.

172. National Committee on Inuit Education, *First Canadians, Canadians First*, 10–14.

173. National Committee on Inuit Education, *First Canadians, Canadians First*, 80.

174. National Committee on Inuit Education, *First Canadians, Canadians First*, 69.

175. Canada, Standing Senate Committee on Aboriginal Peoples, *Reforming First Nations Education*, 3.

176. Canada, Standing Senate Committee on Aboriginal Peoples, *Reforming First Nations Education*, 56.

177. Canada, Standing Senate Committee on Aboriginal Peoples, *Reforming First Nations Education*, 62.

178. Canada, Standing Senate Committee on Aboriginal Peoples, *Reforming First Nations Education*, 64.

179. Canada, Standing Senate Committee on Aboriginal Peoples *Reforming First Nations Education*, 24.

180. Haldane et al., *Nurturing the Learning Spirit*, iv.

181. Haldane et al., *Nurturing the Learning Spirit*, vii, 40.

182. Haldane et al., *Nurturing the Learning Spirit*, 32.

183. Haldane et al., *Nurturing the Learning Spirit*, 33–38.

184. FNEC, NAN, and FSIN, *Report on Priority Actions*, 25.

185. FNEC, NAN, and FSIN, *Report on Priority Actions*, 85–86.

186. Canada, Aboriginal Affairs and Northern Development Canada, *Developing a First Nation Education Act: A Blueprint for Legislation*. For information on the consultation process see AANDC, "The Consultation Process" at https://www.aadnc-aandc.gc.ca/eng/1358799141185/1358799192535.

187. Canada, Aboriginal Affairs and Northern Development Canada, *Developing a First Nation Education Act*, 6.

188. Canada, Aboriginal Affairs and Northern Development Canada *Developing a First Nation Education Act*, 5.

189. Canada, Aboriginal Affairs and Northern Development Canada, *Working Together for First Nation Students.*

190. Canada, Aboriginal Affairs and Northern Development Canada, *Working Together for First Nation Students*, s. 23.

191. Canada, Aboriginal Affairs and Northern Development Canada, *Working Together for First Nation Students*, s. 25.

192. Canada, Aboriginal Affairs and Northern Development Canada, *Working Together for First Nation Students*, ss. 27–30.

193. Canada, Aboriginal Affairs and Northern Development Canada, *Working Together for First Nation Students*, s. 34.

194. Bernard Valcourt, Minister of Aboriginal Affairs and Northern Development, to Jean Crowder, MP, 17 April 2014.

195. Anaya, "Statement upon Conclusion of the Visit to Canada, 15 October 2013."

196. Canada, Aboriginal Affairs and Northern Development Canada, "First Nations Control of First Nations Education Act."

197. Atleo, "First Nations Control."

198. Canada, Aboriginal Affairs and Northern Development Canada, "First Nations Control of First Nations Education Act."

199. Kativik School Board, "About Kativik School Board."

200. Kativik School Board, "About Kativik School Board"; Vick-Westgate, *Nunavik*, 85.

201. *Consolidation of Inuit Language Protection Act*, SNu 2008, c 17.

202. *Education Act*, SNu 2008, c 15.

203. National Committee on Inuit Education, *First Canadians, Canadians First*, 8.

204. National Committee on Inuit Education, *First Canadians, Canadians First*, 75.

205. National Committee on Inuit Education, *First Canadians, Canadians First*, 78.

206. National Committee on Inuit Education, *First Canadians, Canadians First*, 75–90.

207. Marie Battiste quoted in Canada, Standing Senate Committee on Aboriginal Peoples, *Reforming First Nations Education*, 40.

208. Battiste, *Decolonizing Education*, 121.

209. Little Bear, "Naturalizing Indigenous Knowledge," 21.

210. Haldane et al., *Nurturing the Learning Spirit*, 11.

211. Canada and Mi'kmaq Bands in Nova Scotia, *An Agreement with respect to Mi'kmaq education in Nova Scotia*, 14 February 1997. The agreement has been formalized through the *Mi'kmaq Education Act*, SC 1998, c 24.

212. Battiste, *Decolonizing Education*, 87–94.

213. Canada, British Columbia, and First Nations Education Steering Committee, *Education Jurisdiction Framework Agreement*, 5 July 2006.

214. *First Nations Jurisdiction over Education in British Columbia Act*, SC 2006, c 10.

215. *First Nations Jurisdiction over Education in British Columbia Act*, SC 2006, c 10, ss 18–20.

216. Canada, Standing Senate Committee on Aboriginal Peoples, *Reforming First Nations Education*, 43.

217. Canada, Aboriginal Affairs and Northern Development Canada, *Government of Canada Progress Report (2006–2012)*, 5.

218. Canada, Standing Senate Committee on Aboriginal Peoples, *Reforming First Nations Education*, 43.

219. Haldane et al., *Nurturing the Learning Spirit*, 12, 13.

220. Haldane et al., *Nurturing the Learning Spirit*, 15.

221. Canada, Standing Senate Committee on Aboriginal Peoples, *Reforming First Nations Education*, 44–46.

222. People for Education, *First Nations, Métis and Inuit Education*, 11.

## "I Lost My Talk": The erosion of language and culture

1. Canada, Task Force on Aboriginal Languages and Culture, *Towards a New Beginning*, 21.

2. TRC, NRA, Library and Archives Canada, RG10, volume 7183, file 1/25-1-1-4, part 2, Panel on Indian Research – Committee on Scientific Problems of Indian Affairs. 1952–1959, Microfilm reel C-9695, FA 10-28, H. M. Jones to E. Bussiere, 13 September 1954. [AEMR-255680]

3. MacGregor, *Chief*, 23.

4. Willis, *Geniesh*, 45–46.

5. Knockwood, *Out of the Depths*, 28.

6. Canadien, *From Lishamie*, 56.

7. Dickson, *Hey, Monias!*, 84.

8. TRC, NRA, INAC – Resolution Sector – IRS Historical Files Collection – Ottawa, file E4974-2, volume 2, "Prince Albert District Chiefs Meeting on the Prince Albert Student Residence, 16 April 1973," 2. [PAR-123592-0000]

9. Canada, Task Force on Aboriginal Languages and Culture, *Towards a New Beginning*, 58.

10. Knockwood, *Out of the Depths*, 100.

11. Joe, *Song of Eskasoni*, 32.

12. TRC, AVS, Nellie Trapper, Statement to the Truth and Reconciliation Commission of Canada, Winnipeg, Manitoba, 18 June 2010, Statement Number: 02-MB-16JU10-086.

13. TRC, AVS, Greg Rainville, Statement to the Truth and Reconciliation Commission of Canada, Saskatoon, Saskatchewan, 22 June 2012, Statement Number: 2011-1752.

14. Sluman and Goodwill, *John Tootoosis*, 106.

15. Davis, *The Wayfinders*, 198.

16. Canada, Task Force on Aboriginal Languages and Culture, *Towards a New* Beginning, 21.

17. TRC, AVS, Doris Young, Statement to the Truth and Reconciliation Commission of Canada, Saskatoon, Saskatchewan, 22 June 2012, Statement Number: 2011-3517.

18. TRC, AVS, Martin Nicholas, Statement to the Truth and Reconciliation Commission of Canada, Grand Rapids, Manitoba, 24 February 2010, Statement Number: 07-MB-24FB10-001.

19. TRC, AVS, Sarah McLeod, Statement to the Truth and Reconciliation Commission of Canada, Kamloops, British Columbia, 8 August 2008, Statement Number: 2011-5009.

20. TRC, AVS, Archie Hyacinthe, Statement to the Truth and Reconciliation Commission of Canada, Kenora, Ontario, 15 March 2011, Statement Number: 2011-0279.

21. TRC, AVS, Mary Courchene, Statement to the Truth and Reconciliation Commission of Canada, Pine Creek First Nation, Manitoba, 28 November, 2011, Statement Number: 2011-2515.

22. TRC, AVS, Hubert Nanacowop, Statement to the Truth and Reconciliation Commission of Canada, Winnipeg, Manitoba, 16 June 2010, Statement Number: 02-MB-16JU10-013.

23. TRC, AVS, Richard Kaiyogana, Sr., Statement to the Truth and Reconciliation Commission of Canada, Inuvik, Northwest Territories, 30 June 2011, Statement Number: SC091.

24. TRC, AVS, Agnes Mills, Statement to the Truth and Reconciliation Commission of Canada, Inuvik, Northwest Territories, 29 June 2011, Statement Number: SC090.

25. TRC, AVS, Betsy Olson, Statement to the Truth and Reconciliation Commission of Canada, Saskatoon, Saskatchewan, 21 June 2012, Statement Number: 2011-4378.

26. TRC, AVS, Eva Lapage, Statement to the Truth and Reconciliation Commission of Canada, Halifax, Nova Scotia, 29 October 2011, Statement Number: 2011-2919.

27. TRC, AVS, Roy Thunder, Statement to the Truth and Reconciliation Commission of Canada, Winnipeg, Manitoba, 16 June, 2010, Statement Number: 02 MB-16JU10-081.

28. TRC, AVS, Sabina Hunter, Statement to the Truth and Reconciliation Commission of Canada, Goose Bay, Labrador, 20 September 2011, Statement Number: SP025.

29. TRC, AVS, Rosemary Paul, Statement to the Truth and Reconciliation Commission of Canada, Halifax, Nova Scotia, 29 October 2011, Statement Number: 2011-2933.

30. Fontaine "Re-conceptualizing and Re-imagining Canada," 314.

31. TRC, AVS, Henry Ruck, Statement to the Truth and Reconciliation Commission of Canada, Winnipeg, Manitoba, 11 February 2011, Statement Number: 03-001-10-069.

32. Kinnon, *Improving Population Health*, 10.

33. First Peoples' Heritage, Language and Culture Council, *Report on the Status of B.C. First Nations Languages, 2010*, 7.

34. First Nations Centre, *First Nations Regional Longitudinal Health Survey (RHS) 2002/03*, 147.

35. Canada, Standing Committee on Aboriginal Affairs, *"You Took My Talk,"* 31.

36. Hallet, Chandler, and Lalonde, Aboriginal Language Knowledge, 398. See also McIvor, Napoleon, and Dickie, "Language and Culture as Protective Factors for At-Risk Communities."

37. Bougie and Senécal, "Registered Indian Children's School Success,"18.

38. Canada, Royal Commission on Aboriginal Peoples, *Report*, 3:191.

39. Assembly of First Nations, *Breaking the Silence*, 25.

40. Assembly of First Nations, *Breaking the Silence*, 108.

41. Canada, Royal Commission on Aboriginal Peoples, *Report*, 3:563.

42. Canada, Royal Commission on Aboriginal Peoples, *Report*, 3:572.

43. Canada, Task Force on Aboriginal Languages and Culture, *Towards a New Beginning*, 3.

44. Moseley and Nicolas, *UNESCO Atlas*, 114; Canada, Statistics Canada, *Aboriginal Peoples in Canada in 2006*, 28.

45. Assembly of First Nations, "Language and Culture."

46. Canada, Statistics Canada, *Aboriginal Peoples and Language*.

47. Canada, Statistics Canada, *Aboriginal Peoples and Language*.

48. Canada, Statistics Canada, *Aboriginal Peoples in Canada in 2006*, 37.

49. Canada, Statistics Canada, *Aboriginal Peoples and Language*.

50. *R. v. Van der Peet*, [1996] 2 SCR 507.

51. Slattery, "Making Sense," 215, 222.

52. Leitch, "Canada's Native Languages," 107, 111.

53. *Mitchell v. M. N. R.*, 2001 SCC 33 at para. 10.

54. *Mitchell v. M. N. R.*, 2001 SCC 33 at para. 10.

55. *United States v. Winans*, 198 U.S. 371, 25 S.Ct. 662 (1905) at 381, states: "In other words, the treaty was not a grant of rights to the Indians, but a grant of rights from them a reservation of those not granted."

56. *Ford v. Quebec (Attorney General)*, [1988] 2 SCR 712.

57. *Canadian Charter of Rights and Freedoms*, s 22, Part I of the *Constitution Act, 1982*, being Schedule B to the Canada Act 1982 (UK), 1982, c 11, http://publications.gc.ca/collections/Collection/CH37-4-3-2002E.pdf.

58. *R. v. Van der Peet* [1996] 2 SCR 507.

59. Canada, *Annual Report of the Department of Indian Affairs, 1887*, 102.

60. TRC, NRA, INAC – Resolution Sector – IRS Historical Files Collection – Ottawa file 501/23-5-076, volume 1 (Ctrl #65-5). Philip Phelan to O. Chagnon, 6 June 1938. [NCA-008168]

61. Jenness, *America's Eskimos*, 14. Jenness expressed concerns that "it is only when the child begins school that he enters an atmosphere of English, and then only in relation to his teacher and the topics that are dealt with in the classroom. Moreover, as soon as school ends for the day, the door that closes behind him shuts from his mind all the English words and phrases he has been struggling to memorize; and they seldom re-enter his consciousness until the schoolbell rings again the next morning. Under such conditions progress can hardly fail to be extremely slow, and also very superficial." Jenness, "Eskimo Administration," 132–133. At the same time, Jenness was, to his credit, not blind to some of the faults of the mission school. He recalled that in 1916 he encountered a fifteen-year-old who had been "raised in a mission boarding school" from "very early childhood." He recounted that the teenager "had completely forgotten his mother tongue" but "could speak French fluently" when Jenness found him living with his family "in a primitive fishing camp at Shingle Point in the Mackenzie delta – a sad, lonely boy, unfamiliar with their way of life and unable even to converse with them except by signs." Jenness, "Eskimo Administration," 126.

62. In 1966, a R. C. Gagne challenged Jenness's stress on assimilation and argued that the language was connected with the preservation of culture and personality and that Aboriginal languages should be taught in the residential schools including by teachers in the community who would not necessarily have formal qualifications. See TRC, NRA, Library and Archives Canada – Ottawa RG85, Perm. volume 1916, file 108-4, part 8 – "Northern Conference, 1966 The Role of Eskimo culture/language/personality triplex in Northern Education," 29 March 1966. [RCN-006953]

63. Canada, Royal Commission on Aboriginal Peoples, *Report*, 3:578.

64. Canada, Royal Commission on Aboriginal Peoples, *Report*, 3:579–580.

65. Canada, Indian Affairs and Northern Development, *Gathering Strength*, 7.

66. Canada, Canadian Heritage, *Aboriginal Languages Initiative (ALI) Evaluation*. 3.

67. Canada, Canadian Heritage, *Aboriginal Languages Initiative (ALI) Evaluation Final Report*, 3.

68. Canada, Task Force on Aboriginal Languages and Culture, *Towards a New Beginning*, 102.

69. Assembly of First Nations, *Royal Commission on Aboriginal Peoples at 10 Years*, 18.

70. Canada. *House of Commons Debates*, 39th Parliament, 1st session (3 November, 2006) at 1155 (Bev Oda, Minister of Canadian Heritage and Status of Women).

71. Canada, Canadian Heritage, *Aboriginal Languages Initiative (ALI) Evaluation*, 5, 6.

72. The Bank of Canada's inflation calculator suggests that an increase of almost $4 million would be necessary to keep up with inflation. Bank of Canada, Inflation Calculator.

73. Canada, Canadian Heritage, *Aboriginal Languages Initiative (ALI) Evaluation*, 13.

74. Email from Glenn Morrison (Policy Manager of the Aboriginal Affairs Directorate in the Citizenship Participation Branch) to the Truth and Reconciliation Commission, 9 July 2012.

75. Glover, *2013–2014 Departmental Performance*, 80.

76. See the program description in Canada, Canadian Heritage, *Summative Evaluation of the Aboriginal Peoples' Program*, 1.

77. For example, Aboriginal Friendship Centres, Cultural Connections for Aboriginal Youth, and Young Canada Works for Aboriginal Urban Youth have all been transferred to the Department

of Aboriginal Affairs and Northern Development. Canada, Canadian Heritage, *Quarterly Financial Report*.

78. Canada, Canadian Heritage, *2012–2013 Report on Plans*, 21; Canada, Canadian Heritage, *Summative Evaluation*, 79; Email from Glenn Morrison (Policy Manager of the Aboriginal Affairs Directorate in the Citizenship Participation Branch) to the Truth and Reconciliation Commission, 9 July 2012.

79. Public Law 101-477, Oct. 30, 1990, 104 STAT 1153-1156.

80. Public Law 101-477, Oct. 30, 1990, 104 STAT 1153-1156.

81. Public Law 101-477, Oct. 30, 1990, 104 STAT 1153-1156.

82. *Māori Language Act*, 1987 no. 176.

83. Canada, Office of the Auditor General of Canada, *2011 June Status Report*, Chapter 4, 2.

84. Canada, Office of the Auditor General of Canada, *2011 June Status Report*, Chapter 4, 3.

85. *Official Languages Act*, RSNWT 1988, c O-1.

86. *Official Languages Act*, RSNWT (Nu) 1988, c O-1.

87. *Official Languages Act*, SNu 2008, c 10.

88. *Languages Act*, RSY 2002, c 133.

89. *First Peoples' Heritage, Language and Culture Act*, RSBC 1996, c 147, s 6.

90. *First Peoples' Heritage, Language and Culture Regulation*, BC Reg 65/2011, s 1.

91. *Aboriginal Languages Recognition Act*, CCSM c A1.5.

92. *Regulation respecting the language of instruction of children residing on Indian reserves*, RRQ, c C-11, r 8.

93. *Charter of the French Language*, RSQ, c C-11.

94. *Charter of the French Language*, RSQ, c C-11, ss 88, 97.

95. United Church of Canada, "Apology to First Nations People."

96. The Presbyterian Church, "The Confession of the Presbyterian Church."

97. Canadian Conference of Catholic Bishops, "Pope Benedict XVI."

98. Missionary Oblates of Mary Immaculate, "An Apology to the First Nations."

99. CBC News, "'I Am Sorry,' NWT Bishop Says."

100. *R. J. G. v. Canada (Attorney General)*, 2004 SKCA 102 (CanLII).

101. *Blackwater v. Plint*, 2001 BCSC 997 at paras. 436–437 (Can LII).

102. C. J. Brenner stated, "There is simply no evidence of dishonesty or intentional disloyalty on the part of Canada or the United Church towards the plaintiffs which would make it permissible or desirable to engage the law relating to fiduciary obligations. I include in this conclusion the more general complaints of the plaintiffs relating to linguistic and cultural deprivation. In my view the plaintiffs have failed to demonstrate that either Canada or the Church were acting dishonestly or were intentionally disloyal to the plaintiffs." *Blackwater v. Plint*, 2001 BCSC 997 at para. 247. He also dismissed the language and culture claims on the basis that the claims were made too late under statutes of limitations. *Blackwater v. Plint*, 2001 BCSC 997 at paras. 260–281. On appeal, the British Columbia Court of Appeal 2003 BCCA 671 at paras. 79-82 held that the language and culture loss claims were barred by statutes of limitations. *Blackwater v. Plint*, 2003 BCCA 671. The Supreme Court held that statutes of limitations would be subverted and the plaintiffs inappropriately compensated "for torts that have been alleged but not proven" if language and cultural loss was included as part of damages awarded for sexual assault that were not barred by statute of limitations. *Blackwater v. Plint*, [2005] 3 SCR 3 at para. 85.

103. Canada, Task Force on Aboriginal Languages and Culture, *Towards a New Beginning*, 80.

104. *Brown v. Attorney General of Canada*, 2014 ONSC 6967 at para. 30.

105. UN General Assembly, *United Nations Declaration on the Rights of Indigenous Peoples*, articles 8, 13, 14, 16, 19.

106. UN General Assembly, *UN Convention on the Prevention and Punishment of the Crime of Genocide*.

107. Borrows, "Residential Schools," 502n48.

108. Canada, "Statement of Apology."

109. French, *My Name Is Masak*, 19.

110. Gresko, "Everyday Life at Qu'Appelle Industrial School," 80.

111. Knockwood, *Out of the Depths*, 160.

112. TRC, AVS, Paul Stanley, Statement to the Truth and Reconciliation Commission of Canada, Deroche, British Columbia, 19 January 2010, Statement Number: 2011-5057.

113. TRC, AVS, Esther Lachinette-Diabo, Statement to the Truth and Reconciliation Commission of Canada, Thunder Bay, Ontario, 10 November 2010, Statement Number: 01-ON-24NO10-020.

114. TRC, AVS, Matilda Lampe, Statement to the Truth and Reconciliation Commission of Canada, Goose Bay, Newfoundland and Labrador, 20 September 2011, (Inuktitut words translated by Wintranslation Services, Ottawa, 2015_0244-1-1), Statement Number: 2011-4249.

115. Moseley and Nicolas, *UNESCO Atlas*, 115.

116. Canada, Statistics Canada, *Aboriginal Languages in Canada*, 2–3.

117. Moseley and Nicolas, *UNESCO Atlas*, 115.

118. Moseley and Nicolas, *UNESCO Atlas*, 119.

119. First Peoples' Heritage, Language and Cultures Council, *Report on the Status of B.C. First Nations Languages*, 4, 11. The First Peoples' Heritage, Language and Culture Council (First Peoples' Council) is a provincial Crown corporation dedicated to First Nations languages, arts, and culture. Since its formation in 1990, the First Peoples' Council has distributed over $21.5 million to communities to fund arts, language, and culture projects. The First Peoples' Council monitors the status of BC's First Nations languages, cultures, and arts, and facilitates and develops strategies that help First Nations communities recover and sustain their heritage.

120. First Peoples' Heritage, Language and Cultures Council, *Report on the Status of B.C. First Nations Languages*, 29–30.

121. For the expansion, see TRC, NRA, National Capital Regional Service Centre – Library and Archives Canada – Ottawa, volume 2, file 600-1, Locator #062-94, Education of Eskimos (1949–1957), Department of Northern Affairs and National Resources to Northern Administration and Land branch, 8 April 1958. [NCA-016925]

122. Canada, Advisory Committee on Northern Development, *Government Activities in the North – 1958*, 71.

123. For 1949 figures, see TRC, NRA, National Capital Regional Service Centre – Library and Archives Canada – Ottawa, volume 2, file 600-1, Locator #062-94, Education of Eskimos (1949–1957), Department of Northern Affairs and National Resources to Northern Administration and Land branch, 8 April 1958 [NCA-016925]. For 1959 figure, see TRC, NRA, Library and Archives Canada – Ottawa, RG85, permanent volume 1468, file 630/125-9, part 1, Govt. Hostel [R. C.] Inuvik, N.W.T 1956 – December 1959, F.A. 85-4, 1959–1960 Program, Inuvik, NWT, 10 August 1959. [RCN-008488]

124. Hobart, "Report on Canadian Arctic Eskimos," 7.

125. TRC, AVS, Willy Carpenter, Statement to the Truth and Reconciliation Commission of Canada, Tuktoyaktuk, Northwest Territories, 20 September 2011, Statement Number: 2011-0353.

126. Moseley and Nicolas, *UNESCO Atlas*, 114; Canada, Statistics Canada, *Aboriginal Peoples in Canada in 2006*, 28.
127. Canada, Statistics Canada, *Aboriginal Peoples in Canada in 2006*, 28.
128. Canada, Statistics Canada, *Aboriginal Languages and Selected Vitality Indicators*, 3, 5.
129. Canada, Statistics Canada, *Aboriginal Peoples in Canada in 2006*, 28.
130. Canada, Statistics Canada, *Aboriginal Languages and Selected Vitality Indicators*, 9; Canada, Statistics Canada, *Aboriginal Peoples in Canada in 2006*, 28.
131. Canada, Statistics Canada, *Aboriginal Languages and Selected Vitality Indicators*,. 9.
132. Canada, Statistics Canada, *Aboriginal Peoples in Canada in 2006*, 29.
133. Canada, Canadian Heritage, *Summative Evaluation*, 28.
134. Canada, Canadian Heritage, *Aboriginal Languages Initiative (ALI) Evaluation*, 13.
135. *Official Languages Act*, RSNWT (Nu) 1988, c O-1.
136. Canada, Standing Senate Committee on Legal and Constitutional Affairs, *Language Rights in Canada's North*, 13.
137. *Education Act*, SNu 2008, c 15.
138. Crosscurrent Associates, Hay River, *Languages of the Land*, 26.
139. Canada, Statistics Canada, *Aboriginal Peoples in Canada in 2006*, 29.
140. Crosscurrent Associates, Hay River, *Languages of the Land*, 26.
141. Crosscurrent Associates, Hay River, *Languages of the Land*, 26; Moseley and Nicolas, *UNESCO Atlas*, 120; Tulloch, *Preserving Inuit Dialects in Nunavut*, 10.
142. Canada, Standing Senate Committee on Legal and Constitutional Affairs, *Language Rights in Canada's North*, 19–20.
143. McIvor, *Language Nest Programs in BC*, 4. The identity of the speaker was not provided in the publication.
144. Hume, Rutman, and Hubberstey, *Language Nest Evaluation*.
145. McIvor, *Language Nest Programs in BC*, 17. The identity of the speaker was not provided in the publication.
146. McIvor, *Language Nest Programs in BC*, 22.
147. McIvor, *Language Nest Programs in BC*, 22, 23.
148. Hume, Rutman, and Hubberstey, *Language Nest Evaluation*, iv–v.
149. Norris, "Aboriginal Languages in Canada," 20.
150. Moseley and Nicolas, *UNESCO Atlas*, 119.
151. Canada, Statistics Canada, *Aboriginal Languages and Selected Vitality Indicators*, 6.
152. Norris, "Aboriginal Languages in Canada," 24.
153. Canada, Task Force on Aboriginal Languages and Culture, *Towards a New Beginning*, 28.
154. TRC, AVS, Sabrina Williams, Statement to the Truth and Reconciliation Commission of Canada, Victoria, British Columbia, 13 April 2012, Statement Number: 2011-3982.

## An attack on Aboriginal health: The marks and the memories

1. TRC, AVS, Ruby Firth, Statement to the Truth and Reconciliation Commission of Canada, Inuvik, Northwest Territories, 22 July 2011, Statement Number: 2011-0326.
2. Bryce, *National Crime*, 14.
3. Canada, Annual Report of the Department of Indian Affairs for the Year Ended June 30th, 1906, 274–275.

4. Library and Archives Canada, RG10, volume 4037, file 317,021, *Saturday Night*, untitled editorial, 23 November 1907; *Montreal Star*, "Death Rate Among Indians Abnormal," 15 November 1907; *Ottawa Citizen*, "Schools and White Plague," 16 November 1907.

5. Canada, Annual Report of the Department of Indian Affairs, 1906, 274–275.

6. Bryce, *Report on the Indian Schools*, 18.

7. Bryce, *Report on the Indian Schools*, 17.

8. Bryce, *Report on the Indian Schools*, 18.

9. Scott, "Indian Affairs 1867–1912," 615.

10. Kelm, *Colonizing Bodies*, 61.

11. TRC, NRA, Library and Archives Canada, RG10, volume 6039, file 160-1, part 1, Martin Benson, to J. D. McLean, 15 July 1897. [100.00109]

12. Canada, Annual Report of the Department of Indian Affairs, 1904, 204.

13. TRC, NRA, Library and Archives Canada, RG10, volume 6012, file 1-1-5A, part 2, R. A. Hoey to Dr. McGill, 31 May 1940 [BIR-000248]. For date of Hoey's appointment, see Manitoba Historical Society, "Memorable Manitobans: Robert Alexander Hoey (1883–1965)."

14. TRC, NRA, INAC – Resolution Sector – IRS Historical Files Collection – Ottawa, file 6-21-1, volume 4, control 25-2, The National Association of Principals and Administrators of Indian Residences Brief Presented to the Department of Indian Affairs and Northern Development as requested by Mr. E. A. Cote, Deputy Minister, prepared in 1967, presented 15 January 1968. [NCA-011495]

15. For Beauval fire, see TRC, NRA, Library and Archives Canada, RG10, volume 6300, file 650-1, part 1, Louis Mederic Adam to Indian Affairs, 22 September 1927 [BVL-000879]. For Cross Lake fire, see TRC, NRA, Library and Archives Canada, RG10, volume 6260, file 577-1, part 1, J. L. Fuller to A. MacNamara, 8 March 1930 [CLD-000933-0000]; TRC, NRA, Library and Archives Canada, RG10, volume 6260, file 577-1, part 1, William Gordon to Assistant Deputy and Secretary, Indian Affairs, 10 March 1930. [CLD-000934]

16. For deaths, see Stanley, "Alberta's Half-Breed Reserve," 96–98; Library and Archives Canada, RG10, volume 6300, file 650-1, part 1, O. Charlebois to Duncan Scott, 21 September 1927 [BVL-000874]; Louis Mederic Adam to Indian Affairs, 22 September 1927 [BVL-000879]; TRC, NRA, Library and Archives Canada, RG10, volume 6260, file 577-1, part 1, J. L. Fuller to A. McNamara, 8 March 1930 [CLD-000933-0000]; William Gordon to Assistant Deputy and Secretary, Indian Affairs, 10 March 1930 [CLD-000934]; TRC, NRA, INAC – Resolution Sector – IRS Historical Files Collection – Ottawa, file 675/6-2-018, volume 2, D. Greyeyes to Indian Affairs, 22 June 1968. [GDC-005571]

17. Canada, *Annual Report of the Department of Indian Affairs, 1893*, 173.

18. Library and Archives Canada, RG10, volume 3674, file 11422-5, H. Reed to Deputy Superintendent General of Indian Affairs, 13 May 1891.

19. TRC, AVS, Paul Stanley, Statement to the Truth and Reconciliation Commission of Canada, Deroche, British Columbia, 19 January 2010, Statement Number: 2011-5057.

20. Brass, *I Walk in Two Worlds*, 25.

21. Brass, *I Walk in Two Worlds*, 25–26.

22. Moran, *Stoney Creek Woman*, 53–54.

23. Canada, Health Canada, *Canada's Food Guides from 1942 to 1992*.

24. TRC, NRA, Library and Archives Canada, RG10, volume 6306, file 652-5, part 6, L. B. Pett to P. E. Moore, 8 December 1947. [SMD-001897-0000]

25. TRC, NRA, Library and Archives Canada, RG29, volume 973, file 388-6-1, part 2, Nutrition Division, Department of National Health and Welfare "Illness Found in Indian Residential Schools" undated. [AEMR-174244].

26. TRC, NRA, Library and Archives Canada, RG29, volume 973, file 388-6-1, part 1, L. B. Pett to P. E. Moore, 8 December 1947. [PAR-000365-0000]

27. TRC, NRA, Library and Archives Canada, RG10, volume 8796, file 1/25-13, part 4, L. B. Pett to H. M. Jones, 21 March 1958. [NPC-400776]

28. TRC, AVS, David Charleson, Statement to the Truth and Reconciliation Commission of Canada, Deroche, British Columbia, 20 January 2010, Statement Number: 2011-5043.

29. Canada, Indian Residential Schools Adjudication Secretariat, "Adjudication Secretariat Statistics."

30. First Nations Centre, *First Nations Regional Longitudinal Health Survey (RHS) 2002/03*, 135.

31. TRC, AVS, Jean Pierre Bellemare, Statement to the Truth and Reconciliation Commission of Canada, La Tuque, Québec, 5 March 2013, Statement Number: SP104.

32. TRC, AVS, Andrew Yellowback, Statement to the Truth and Reconciliation Commission of Canada, Kamloops, British Columbia, 9 August 2009, Statement Number: 2011-5015.

33. See, for example, TRC, AVS, [Name redacted], Statement to the Truth and Reconciliation Commission of Canada, Winnipeg, Manitoba, 18 June 2010, Statement Number: 02-MB-18JU10-055; TRC, AVS, Myrna Kaminawaish, Statement to the Truth and Reconciliation Commission of Canada, Thunder Bay, Ontario, 7 January 2011, Statement Number: 01-ON-06JA11-004; TRC, AVS, Percy Tuesday, Statement to the Truth and Reconciliation Commission of Canada, Winnipeg, Manitoba, 18 June 2010, Statement Number: 02-MB-18JU10-083; TRC, AVS, Isaac Daniels, Statement to the Truth and Reconciliation Commission of Canada, Saskatoon, Saskatchewan, 22 June 2012, Statement Number: 2011-1779.

34. TRC, AVS, Marlene Kayseas, Statement to the Truth and Reconciliation Commission of Canada, Regina, Saskatchewan, 16 January 2012, Statement Number: SP035. For gifts of candy, see TRC, AVS, Elaine Durocher, Statement to the Truth and Reconciliation Commission of Canada, Winnipeg, Manitoba, 16 June 2010, Statement Number: 02-MB-16JU10-059; TRC, AVS, John B. Custer, Statement to the Truth and Reconciliation Commission of Canada, Winnipeg, Manitoba, 19 June 2010, Statement Number: 02-MB-19JU10-057; TRC, AVS, Louise Large, Statement to the Truth and Reconciliation Commission of Canada, St. Paul, Alberta, 7 January 2011, Statement Number: 01-AB-06JA11-012. For field trips, see TRC, AVS, Ben Pratt, Statement to the Truth and Reconciliation Commission of Canada, Regina, Saskatchewan, 18 January 2012, Statement Number: 2011-3318.

35. See, for example, TRC, AVS, [Name redacted], Statement to the Truth and Reconciliation Commission of Canada, Winnipeg, Manitoba, 18 June 2010, Statement Number: 02-MB-18JU10-055; TRC, AVS, Leona Bird, Statement to the Truth and Reconciliation Commission of Canada, Saskatoon, Saskatchewan, 21 June 2012, Statement Number: 2011-4415; TRC, AVS, Barbara Ann Pahpasay Skead, Statement to the Truth and Reconciliation Commission of Canada, Winnipeg, Manitoba, 17 June 2010, Statement Number: 02-MB-16JU10-159.

36. TRC, AVS, Josephine Sutherland, Statement to the Truth and Reconciliation Commission of Canada, Timmins, Ontario, 8 November 2010, Statement Number: 01-ON4-6NOV10-013.

37. TRC, AVS, [Name redacted], Statement to the Truth and Reconciliation Commission of Canada, Val d'Or, Québec, 6 February 2012, Statement Number: SP101.

38. Corrado and Cohen, *Mental Health Profiles*, 19.

39. TRC, AVS, Anita Lenoir, Statement to the Truth and Reconciliation Commission of Canada, Yellowknife, Northwest Territories, 14 April 2011.Statement Number: 2011-0239.

40. TRC, AVS, Paul Kaludjau, Statement to the Truth and Reconciliation Commission of Canada, 16 June 2010, Winnipeg, Manitoba, Statement Number: SC093.

41. TRC, AVS, Doris Young, Statement to the Truth and Reconciliation Commission of Canada, Saskatoon, Saskatchewan, 22 June 2012, Statement Number: 2011-3517.

42. TRC, AVS, Shirley Waskewitch, Statement to the Truth and Reconciliation Commission of Canada, Saskatoon, Saskatchewan, 24 June 2012, Statement Number: 2011-3521.

43. TRC, NRA, Library and Archives Canada, RG29, volume 2764, file 822-1-A779, part 1, F. R. Decosse to W. L. Falconer, 17 April 1958. [NPC-601091a]

44. TRC, AVS, Rose Marie Prosper, Statement to the Truth and Reconciliation Commission of Canada, Halifax, Nova Scotia, 28 October 2011, Statement Number: 2011-2868.

45. TRC, NRA, Library and Archives Canada, RG29, volume 3404, file 823-1-A974, Victor Rassier to Department of Indian Affairs Medical Branch, 5 June 1934. [NPC-603124]

46. Archibald, *Final Report of the Aboriginal Healing Foundation*, 3:97.

47. TRC, AVS, Charles Cardinal, Statement to the Truth and Reconciliation Commission of Canada, St. Paul, Alberta, 7 January 2011, Statement Number: 01-AB-06JA11-005.

48. Meyercook and Labelle, "Namaji: Two-Spirit Organizing," 30.

49. TRC, AVS, Laurie McDonald, Statement to the Truth and Reconciliation Commission of Canada, Beausejour, Manitoba, 4 September 2010, Statement Number: 01-MB-3-6SE10-005.

50. Allan and Smylie, *First Peoples, Second Class Treatment*, 43.

51. TRC, AVS, Ken Ward, Statement to the Truth and Reconciliation Commission of Canada, Gambier Island, British Columbia, 29 July 2011, Statement Number: 2011-3279.

52. TRC, AVS, Ken Ward, Statement to the Truth and Reconciliation Commission of Canada, Gambier Island, British Columbia, 29 July 2011, Statement Number: 2011-3279.

53. Smylie, Fell, and Ohlsson, "A Review of Aboriginal Infant Mortality Rates," 143.

54. Smylie, Fell, and Ohlsson, "A Review of Aboriginal Infant Mortality Rates," 145.

55. Smylie, Fell, and Ohlsson, "A Review of Aboriginal Infant Mortality Rates," 147.

56. Oliver, Peters, and Kohen, "Mortality Rates among Children and Teenagers," 2.

57. Canada, Statistics Canada, "Life Expectancy."

58. Tjepkema and Wilkins, "Remaining Life Expectancy."

59. First Nations Centre, *First Nations Regional Longitudinal Health Survey (RHS) 2002/03*, 78.

60. First Nations Centre, *First Nations Regional Longitudinal Health Survey (RHS) 2002/03*, 274–275.

61. Oliver, Peters, and Kohen, "Mortality Rates among Children and Teenagers," 3.

62. Karmali et al., "Epidemiology of Severe Trauma," 1007.

63. TRC, AVS, Ida Ralph, Statement to the Truth and Reconciliation Commission of Canada, Thunder Bay, Ontario, 24 November 2010, Statement Number: 01-ON-24NOV10-002.

64. Oliver, Peters, and Kohen, "Mortality Rates among Children and Teenagers," 3.

65. Kirmayer et al., *Suicide among Aboriginal People in Canada*, xv, 14–15, 21–22.

66. TRC, AVS, Katherine Copenace, Statement to the Truth and Reconciliation Commission of Canada, Winnipeg, Manitoba, 16 June 2010, Statement Number: 02-MB-16JU10-129.

67. TRC, AVS, Maurice Marceau, Statement to the Truth and Reconciliation Commission of Canada, Winnipeg, Manitoba, 17 June 2010, Statement Number: 02-MB-17JU10-011.

68. TRC, AVS, Tanya Tungilik, Statement to the Truth and Reconciliation Commission of Canada, Rankin Inlet, Northwest Territories, 21 March 2011, Statement Number: 2011-0159.

69. Laliberté and Tousignant, "Alcohol and Other Contextual," 215–221.

70. Kirmayer et al., *Suicide among Aboriginal People in Canada*, 26.

71. Kirmayer et al., *Suicide among Aboriginal People in Canada*, 24.

72. TRC, AVS, Florence Horassi, Statement to the Truth and Reconciliation Commission of Canada, Tulita, Northwest Territories, 10 May 2011, Statement Number: 2011-0394.

73. First Nations Centre, *First Nations Regional Longitudinal Health Survey RHS) 2002/03*, 115.

74. Pearce, "The Cedar Project," 322.

75. Tait, *Fetal Alcohol Syndrome*, xv.

76. Tait, *Fetal Alcohol Syndrome*, 251.

77. TRC, AVS, [Name redacted] Statement to the Truth and Reconciliation Commission of Canada, Deroche, British Columbia, 19 January 2010, Statement Number: 2011-5055.

78. Tait, *Fetal Alcohol Syndrome*, xv.

79. Edward John as quoted in Milloy, *A National Crime*, 295.

80. Barlow, *Residential Schools, Prisons and HIV/AIDS*, 15–16.

81. Canada, Public Health Agency of Canada, "Chapter 8: HIV/AIDS among Aboriginal People."

82. Jackson and Reimer, *Canadian Aboriginal People Living with HIV/AIDS*, 53.

83. Ship and Norton, "HIV/AIDS and Aboriginal Women," 25–31.

84. Craib et al., "Risk Factors for Elevated HIV Incidence," 168.

85. TRC, AVS, Leona Bird, Statement to the Truth and Reconciliation Commission of Canada, Saskatoon, Saskatchewan, 21 June 2012, Statement Number: 2011-4415.

86. Canada, Indian and Northern Affairs Canada, *Evaluation of Community-Based Healing Initiatives*, 5.

87. First Nations Centre, *First Nations Regional Longitudinal Health Survey (RHS) 2002/03*, 136.

88. TRC, AVS, Anne Thomas, Statement to the Truth and Reconciliation Commission of Canada, Winnipeg, Manitoba, 17 June 2010, Statement Number: 02-MB-17JU10-058.

89. TRC, AVS, Angus Havioyak, Statement to the Truth and Reconciliation Commission of Canada, Kugluktuk, Nunavut, 13 April 2011, Statement Number: 2011-0518.

90. TRC, AVS, Mabel Brown, Statement to the Truth and Reconciliation Commission of Canada, Inuvik, Northwest Territories, 28 September 2011, Statement Number: 2011-0325.

91. Inuit Tapiriit Kanatami, "Social Determinants of Inuit Health in Canada," 17.

92. First Nations Information Governance Centre, *Regional Health Survey (RHS) Phase 2*, 19.

93. Kirmayer et al., *Suicide among Aboriginal People in Canada*, 102; Kinnon, *Improving Population Health*, 17.

94. Environics Institute, *Urban Aboriginal Peoples Study*, 116.

95. Garner et al., "The Health of First Nations," 4–5.

96. Archibald, *Final Report of the Aboriginal Healing Foundation*, 3:97.

97. Canada, Statistics Canada, "Study: Select Health Indicators."

98. Council of Canadian Academics, *Aboriginal Food Security*, xiv.

99. Willows et al., "Associations between Household Food."

100. Canada, Statistics Canada, "Study: Select Health Indicators."

101. First Nations and Inuit Regional Health Survey National Steering Committee, *Regional Health Survey*, 49.

102. Allan and Smylie, *First Peoples, Second Class Treatment*, 44.

103. Beeby, "Aboriginal Affairs Spending," *CBC News*; Staniforth, "Where Did Aboriginal Affairs?," *The Nation*.

104. Aboriginal Healing Foundation, *2009 Annual Report*, 19.

105. Canada, Indian and Northern Affairs Canada, *Evaluation of Community-Based Healing Initiatives*, 4.

106. Canada, Indian and Northern Affairs Canada, *Evaluation of Community-Based Healing Initiatives*, 4, 5.

107. Aboriginal Healing Foundation, *2014 Annual Report*, 13.

108. Canada, Standing Senate Committee on Aboriginal Affairs and Northern Development, *Study and Recommendations*, 10.

109. TRC, *Interim Report*, 10.

110. Aboriginal Healing Foundation, *2009 Annual Report*, 4.

111. Canada, Standing Senate Committee on Aboriginal Affairs and Northern Development, *Study and Recommendations*, 4, 5, 16.

112. Canada, Health Canada, "First Nations, Inuit and Aboriginal Health: Indian Residential Schools Resolution Health Support Program."

113. TRC, AVS, [Name redacted] Statement to the Truth and Reconciliation Commission of Canada, Sault Ste. Marie, Ontario, 1 July 2011, Statement Number: 2011-0306.

114. Aboriginal Healing Foundation, *2009 Annual Report*, 8.

115. Canada, Standing Senate Committee on Aboriginal Affairs and Northern Development, *Study and Recommendations*, 5–7.

116. Canada, Standing Senate Committee on Aboriginal Affairs and Northern Development, *Study and Recommendations*, 9–10.

117. TRC, AVS, Jackie Fletcher, Statement to the Truth and Reconciliation Commission of Canada, Spanish, Ontario, 12 September 2009, Statement Number: 2011-5025.

118. TRC, *Interim Report*, "Recommendation 10," 28.

119. TRC, AVS, Helen Doyle, Statement to the Truth and Reconciliation Commission of Canada, Halifax, Nova Scotia, 29 October 2011, Statement Number: 2011-2881.

120. Picard, "Harper's Disregard for Aboriginal Health," *Globe and Mail*; National Aboriginal Health Organization, "Announcement."

121. Young, "Review of Research on Aboriginal Populations," 327.

122. Murphy, "Pauktuutit Wants Action," *Nunatsiaq Online*.

123. Quoted in Stout and Peters, *kiskinohamâtôtâpânâsk*, 70.

124. Reimer et al., *The* Indian Residential Schools Settlement Agreement*'s Common Experience Payment and Healing*, xiii–xv, 37.

125. Canada, Aboriginal Affairs and Northern Development Canada, "Water"; Canada, Aboriginal Affairs and Northern Development Canada, "Backgrounder."

126. Canada, Aboriginal Affairs and Northern Development Canada, *Progress Report 2006–2012*, 12.

127. Neegan Burnside Ltd., *National Assessment of First Nations Water and Wastewater Systems*, i–iii.

128. Canada, Aboriginal Affairs and Northern Development Canada, Final Report: Evaluation of First Nations Water and Wastewater Action Plan, 18.

129. *Safe Drinking Water for First Nations Act*, SC 2013, c 21.

130. See *Safe Drinking Water for First Nations Act*, SC 2013, c 21, s. 3; Canada, Standing Senate Committee on Aboriginal Peoples, *Sixth Report: Bill S-8*.

131. Canada, Standing Senate Committee on Aboriginal Peoples, *Sixth Report: Bill S-8*.

132. Canada, Aboriginal Affairs and Northern Development Canada, *Final Report: Evaluation of First Nations Water and Wastewater Action Plan*, iii.

133. Canada, Standing Committee on Aboriginal Affairs and Northern Development, *Seventh Report.*

134. Canada, Aboriginal Affairs and Northern Development Canada, *Progress Report 2006–2012,* 12.

135. Canada, Minister of Indian and Northern Affairs, *Government Response to the Seventh Report.*

136. United Nations General Assembly, Report of the Special Rapporteur on the Rights of Indigenous Peoples, para. 24.

137. Canada, Statistics Canada, "Study: Select Health Indicators."

138. "The active TB reported incidence rate for First Nations living on-reserve in the seven regions of Health Canada's First Nations and Inuit Health Branch was 26.6 per 100,000 in 2008, which was 29.6 times higher than the Canadian-born non-Aboriginal population." Canada, Health Canada, "Summary of Epidemiology of Tuberculosis.

139. Curry, "Aboriginals in Canada," *Globe and Mail.*

140. Canada, Statistics Canada, "Study: Life Expectancy."

141. Council of Australian Governments, *National Indigenous Reform Agreement.*

142. Australian Government, *Closing the Gap,* 6–18.

143. Canadian Medical Association, "Aboriginal Health Programming," E739.

144. Canadian Medical Association, "Aboriginal Health Programming," E739.

145. Canadian Medical Association, "Aboriginal Health Programming," E739

146. Canadian Medical Association, "Aboriginal Health Programming," E739.

147. National Collaborating Centre for Aboriginal Health, *Looking for Aboriginal Health,* 24.

148. First Nations Centre, *First Nations Regional Longitudinal Health Survey (RHS) 2002/03,* 132.

149. National Collaborating Centre for Aboriginal Health, *Looking for Aboriginal Health,* 6, 24–25.

150. National Collaborating Centre for Aboriginal Health, *Looking for Aboriginal Health,* 50.

151. National Collaborating Centre for Aboriginal Health, *Looking for Aboriginal Health,* 8.

152. National Collaborating Centre for Aboriginal Health, *Looking for Aboriginal Health,* 8.

153. British Columbia and First Nations Health Society, *British Columbia Tripartite Framework Agreement on First Nation Health Governance,* s 6.3 and Schedule 3 s 1, 19, 49.

154. British Columbia and First Nations Health Society, *British Columbia Tripartite Framework Agreement on First Nation Health Governance,* Schedule 5, s 2; British Columbia, Tripartite Governance Committee, "Implementing the Vision," 10.

155. British Columbia and First Nations Health Society, *British Columbia Tripartite Framework Agreement on First Nation Health Governance,* s I.

156. Kinnon, *Improving Population Health,* 17–18.

157. National Collaborating Centre for Aboriginal Health, *Looking for Aboriginal Health,* 7.

158. *Canada (Indian Affairs) v. Daniels,* 2014 FCA 101 (CanLII) at para. 159.

159. *Daniels v. Canada,* 2013 FC 6 (CanLII); *Canada (Indian Affairs) v. Daniels,* 2014 FCA 101 (CanLII).

160. Chansonneuve, *Addictive Behaviours,* 37.

161. Archibald, *Final Report of the Aboriginal Healing Foundation,* 3:87.

162. Aboriginal Healing Foundation, List of Contacts.

163. Ontario, Ministry of Community and Social Services, "Aboriginal Health and Wellness Strategy."

164. National Aboriginal Health Organization, *An Overview of Traditional Knowledge,* 8.

165. Chansonneuve, *Addictive Behaviours,* 1.

166. Canada, Royal Commission on Aboriginal Peoples, *Report,* 3:148.

167. Chansonneuve, *Addictive Behaviours,* 60.

168. Kirmayer et al., *Suicide among Aboriginal People in Canada*, 106.

169. Chandler and Lalonde, "Cultural Continuity," 12.

170. Hallett, Chandler, and Lalonde, "Aboriginal Language Knowledge," 398

171. Hallett, Chandler, and Lalonde, "Aboriginal Language Knowledge," 398.

172. Madeleine Keteskwew Dion Stout quoted in Allan and Smylie, *First Peoples, Second Class Treatment*, 28.

173. Manitoba, Provincial Court of Manitoba, *Report under the* Fatality Inquiries Act *into the Death of Brian Lloyd Sinclair*, 66–71, 181.

174. Manitoba, Provincial Court of Manitoba, *Report under the* Fatality Inquiries Act *into the Death of Brian Lloyd Sinclair*, 186–187.

175. Health Council of Canada, *Empathy, Dignity and Respect*, 10.

176. Smylie, "A Guide for Health Professionals Working with Aboriginal Peoples," 1.

177. Smylie, "A Guide for Health Professionals Working with Aboriginal Peoples," 5.

178. UN General Assembly, *United Nations Declaration on the Rights of Indigenous Peoples*, articles 7, 21, 22, 24.

179. UN General Assembly, *United Nations Declaration on the Rights of Indigenous Peoples*, article 23.

180. UN General Assembly, *United Nations Declaration on the Rights of Indigenous Peoples*, articles 24, 31.

181. Boyer, "The International Right to Health for Indigenous Peoples," 5, 10, 11.

182. See, for example, Chartrand "*Maskikiwenow*: The Métis Right to Health," 27.

183. National Collaborating Centre for Aboriginal Health, *Looking for Aboriginal Health*, 43–50.

184. Boyer, "Aboriginal Health: A Constitutional Rights Analysis," 5, 20–21.

185. Boyer, "Aboriginal Health: A Constitutional Rights Analysis," 20–21, 23.

186. Boyer, "Aboriginal Health: A Constitutional Rights Analysis," 18, 19.

187. National Collaborating Centre for Aboriginal Health, *Looking for Aboriginal Health*, 43–50. See, for example, James Bay and Northern Quebec Agreement, Northeastern Quebec Agreement, Inuvialuit Final Agreement, Sechelt Indian Band Self-Government Act, Metis Settlements Accord, Gwich'in Comprehensive Land Claims Agreement, Carcross/Tagish First Nations Agreement, Nunavut Land Claim Agreement, Nisga'a Final Agreement, Tlicho Agreement.

188. Tait, *Fetal Alcohol Syndrome*, xix. See also Chandler and Lalonde, "Cultural Continuity"; and Kirmayer, *Suicide among Aboriginal People*.

189. Inuit Tapiriit Kanatami, "Social Determinants of Inuit Health in Canada," 21.

190. Benoit, Carroll, and Chaudhry, "In Search of a Healing Place," 821, 826.

191. Canada, Royal Commission on Aboriginal Peoples, *Report*, 3:184.

192. Canada, Royal Commission on Aboriginal Peoples, *Report*, 3:102.

193. Canada, Royal Commission on Aboriginal Peoples, *Report*, 3:240.

194. Canada, Royal Commission on Aboriginal Peoples, *Report*, 3:246.

195. Lecompte, "Aboriginal Health Human Resources," 17, 21.

196. Canada, Evaluation Directorate of Health Canada and Public Health Agency Canada, *Evaluation of the First Nations and Inuit Health*, 11.

197. Canada, Health Canada, "Aboriginal Health Human Resources Initiative"; Canada, Health Canada, *Pan-Canadian Health*; Canada, Health Canada, "First Nations and Inuit Health"; Canada, Evaluation Directorate of Health Canada and Public Health Agency Canada, *Evaluation of the First Nations and Inuit Health*.

198. Canada, Evaluation Directorate of Health Canada and Public Health Agency Canada, *Evaluation of the First Nations and Inuit Health*, iii, iv.

199. Canada, Evaluation Directorate of Health Canada and Public Health Agency Canada, *Evaluation of the First Nations and Inuit Health*, ii.

200. Indian Residential Schools Settlement Agreement, Official Court Notice, Schedules O-1, O-2, O-4; Presbyterian Church in Canada Archives, "Brief Administrative History"; Anglican Church of Canada, "Anglican Healing Fund"; United Church of Canada, "The Healing Fund."

201. United Church of Canada, "Fall 2013 Healing Fund Grants."

202. Indian Residential Schools Settlement Agreement, Schedule O-3, "Catholic Entities Church Agreement," 47.

203. *Canada Health Act*, RSC 1985, c C-6, s 3.

204. *Yukon Health Act*, SY 2002, c 106 s 5.

205. *Yukon Health Act*, SY 2002, c 106 s 5.

206. Ontario, Ministry of Community and Social Services, "Aboriginal Healing and Wellness Strategy."

207. National Aboriginal Health Organization, *An Overview of Traditional Knowledge*, 8.

208. Jiwa, Kelly, and St. Pierre-Hansen, "Healing the Community."

209. *Hamilton Health Sciences Corp. v. D. H.*, 2014 ONCJ 603 (CanLII) at paras. 79–81.

210. *Hamilton Health Sciences Corp. v. D. H.*, 2015 ONCJ 229 at paras. 83(a)–83(b).

211. TRC, AVS, Trudy King, Statement to the Truth and Reconciliation Commission of Canada, Fort Resolution, NWT, 28 April 2011, Statement Number: 2011-0381.

212. Canada, Royal Commission on Aboriginal Peoples, *Report*, 3:201.

213. Canada, Royal Commission on Aboriginal Peoples, *Report*, 3:289.

# A denial of justice

1. TRC, AVS, Norman Courchene, Statement to the Truth and Reconciliation Commission of Canada, 16 June 2010, Statement Number: 02-MB-16JU10-065.

2. TRC, AVS, Norman Mirasty, Statement to the Truth and Reconciliation Commission of Canada, Saskatoon, Saskatchewan, 21 June 2012, Statement Number: 2011-4391.

3. TRC, NRA, Library and Archives Canada, RG10, volume 6032, file 150-40A, part 1, Appointment of Truant Officers, D. C. Scott, 7 February 1927. [MRS-000045]

4. TRC, NRA, Library and Archives Canada, RG10, volume 6371, file 764-1, part 1, W. J. Dilworth to Assistant Deputy and Secretary, Indian Affairs, 8 August 1914 [PUL-000900]. For other examples of the police being used to force parents to send their children to school, see TRC, NRA, Library and Archives Canada, RG10, volume 6445, file 881-10, part 5, Agent's Report on Stuart Lake Agency for September, Robert Howe, 2 October 1940 [LEJ-002079]; TRC, NRA, Library and Archives Canada, RG10, volume 6445, file 881-10, part 6, Report of Corporal L. F. Fielder, 14 October 1943 [LEJ-001389]; TRC, NRA, Library and Archives Canada, RG10, volume 6445, file 881-10, part 7, R. Howe to Indian Affairs, 7 October 1946. [LEJ-001830]

5. TRC, AVS, Robert Keesick, Statement to the Truth and Reconciliation Commission of Canada, Winnipeg, Manitoba, 16 June 2010, Statement Number: 02-MB-16JU10-038.

6. LeBeuf, *The Role of the Canadian Mounted Police*, 75–77.

7. TRC, NRA, Report on Allegations of Flogging at Shubenacadie Indian Residential School, L. A. Audette to T. G. Murray, Superintendent General, DIAND, Ottawa, from Deschatelets Archives, Oblates of Mary Immaculate, Ottawa HR 6811.C73 R, Doc #1, Sent from J. R. Miller to I. Knockwood on Sept. 17, 1934, 4–5. [SRS-000187]

8. TRC, NRA, Report on Allegations of Flogging at Shubenacadie Indian Residential School, L. A. Audette to T. G. Murray, Superintendent General, DIAND, Ottawa, from Deschatelets Archives, Oblates of Mary Immaculate, Ottawa HR 6811.C73 R, Doc #1, Sent from J. R. Miller to I. Knockwood on Sept. 17, 1934, 6–7. [SRS-000187]

9. TRC, NRA, Report on Allegations of Flogging at Shubenacadie Indian Residential School, L. A. Audette to T. G. Murray, Superintendent General, DIAND, Ottawa, from Deschatelets Archives, Oblates of Mary Immaculate, Ottawa HR 6811.C73 R, Doc #1, Sent from J. R. Miller to I. Knockwood on Sept. 17, 1934, 8. [SRS-000187]

10. TRC, NRA, Report on Allegations of Flogging at Shubenacadie Indian Residential School, L. A. Audette to T. G. Murray, Superintendent General, DIAND, Ottawa, from Deschatelets Archives, Oblates of Mary Immaculate, Ottawa HR 6811.C73 R, Doc #1, Sent from J. R. Miller to I. Knockwood on Sept. 17, 1934, 14. [SRS-000187]

11. TRC, NRA, Report on Allegations of Flogging at Shubenacadie Indian Residential School, L. A. Audette to T. G. Murray, Superintendent General, DIAND, Ottawa, from Deschatelets Archives, Oblates of Mary Immaculate, Ottawa HR 6811.C73 R, Doc #1, Sent from J. R. Miller to I. Knockwood on Sept. 17, 1934, 16. [SRS-000187]

12. TRC, NRA, Report on Allegations of Flogging at Shubenacadie Indian Residential School, L. A. Audette to T. G. Murray, Superintendent General, DIAND, Ottawa, from Deschatelets Archives, Oblates of Mary Immaculate, Ottawa HR 6811.C73 R, Doc #1, Sent from J. R. Miller to I. Knockwood on Sept. 17, 1934, 17. [SRS-000187]

13. Canada, Department of Indian Affairs Canada, *Memorandum from William Cameron to the Deputy Superintendent of Indian Affairs,* Library and Archives Canada, RG10, volume 2552, file 112-220-1, Martin Benson to Deputy Superintendent General of Indian Affairs, Ottawa, 25 September 1903.

14. TRC, NRA, Library and Archives Canada, RG10, volume 6320, file 658-1, part 1, Microfilm reel C-9802, M. Benson to Deputy Superintendent General, Indian Affairs, 21 February 1907. [120.00284]

15. Canada, Department of Indian Affairs, *Annual Report of the Department of Indian Affairs, 1910,* 273.

16. Miller, *Shingwauk's Vision,* 357. For account of trial, see Public Archives Canada, "Damages for Plaintiff in Miller v. Ashton Case: Girls Too Severely Punished," in *Brantford Expositor,* 1 April 1914, RG10, volume 2771, file 154, 845, part 1.

17. The first successful prosecution of a staff member for the sexual abuse of a student that the Truth and Reconciliation Commission has identified took place in 1945. See TRC, NRA, Library and Archives Canada, RG10, volume 6309, file 654-1, part 3, Royal Canadian Mounted Police, Constable A. Zimmerman, 28 July 1945. [GDC-010369-0001]

18. For examples of dismissal, rather than prosecution and a failure to contact parents, see *F. S. M. v. Clarke,* 1999 CanLII 9405 (BC SC) and *R. v. Frappier* [1990] YJ No 163 (Territorial Court).

19. The inquiries described later in this chapter in British Columbia; Chesterfield Inlet; and Fort Albany, Ontario were all established in response to Aboriginal pressure.

20. TRC, AVS, Doris Young, Statement to the Truth and Reconciliation of Canada, Saskatoon, Saskatchewan, 22 June 2012, Statement Number: 2011-3517.

21. TRC, AVS, Doris Young, Statement to the Truth and Reconciliation of Canada, Saskatoon, Saskatchewan, 22 June 2012, Statement Number: 2011-3517.

22. LeBeuf, *The Role of the Canadian Mounted Police,* 91.

23. Nuu-chah-nulth Tribal Council, *Indian Residential Schools,* 201.

24. TRC, ASAGR, Royal Canadian Mounted Police, M. W. Pacholuk, *Final Report of the Native Indian Residential School Task Force*, Project E-NIRS, Royal Canadian Mounted Police, no date, 1. [RCMP-564517]

25. TRC, ASAGR, Royal Canadian Mounted Police, M. W. Pacholuk, *Final Report of the Native Indian Residential School Task Force*, Project E-NIRS, Royal Canadian Mounted Police, no date, 17. [RCMP-564517]

26. TRC, ASAGR, Royal Canadian Mounted Police, M. W. Pacholuk, *Final Report of the Native Indian Residential School Task Force*, Project E-NIRS, Royal Canadian Mounted Police, no date, 40. [RCMP-564517]

27. Section 139 of the *Criminal Code of Canada*, previously "Special Provisions" (including "Corroboration," "Marriage a defence," "Burden of Proof," and "Previous sexual intercourse with accused"), was repealed by *An Act to amend the Criminal Code in relation to sexual offences and other offences against the person and to amend certain other Acts in relation thereto or in consequence thereof*, SC 1980-81-82-83, c 125, s 5, and in 1985, the *An Act to amend the Criminal Code and the Canada Evidence Act*, RSC 1985 (3d Supp.), c 19, s 11, was introduced, which created the existing *Criminal Code of Canada*, RSC, 1985, c C-46, s 274.

28. TRC, ASAGR, Royal Canadian Mounted Police, M. W. Pacholuk, *Final Report of the Native Indian Residential School Task Force*, Project E-NIRS, Royal Canadian Mounted Police, no date, 109. [RCMP-564517]

29. TRC, ASAGR, Royal Canadian Mounted Police, M. W. Pacholuk, *Final Report of the Native Indian Residential School Task Force*, Project E-NIRS, Royal Canadian Mounted Police, no date, 45. [RCMP-564517]

30. TRC, ASAGR, Royal Canadian Mounted Police, M. W. Pacholuk, *Final Report of the Native Indian Residential School Task Force*, Project E-NIRS, Royal Canadian Mounted Police, no date, 43. [RCMP-564517]

31. Skelton and Kines, "School Abuse Queries," *Vancouver Sun*; TRC, ASAGR, Royal Canadian Mounted Police, *Affidavit of Stephen Thatcher- Investigator*, no style of cause, no court file number, no date, paras. 23–25. [RCMP-564327]

32. TRC, ASAGR, Royal Canadian Mounted Police, M. W. Pacholuk, *Final Report of the Native Indian Residential School Task Force*, Project E-NIRS, Royal Canadian Mounted Police, no date, 19, 28. [RCMP-564517]

33. TRC, ASAGR, Marius Tungilik, "A Report on the Turquetil Hall Reunion, In the Spirit of Healing: A Special Reunion, Chesterfield Inlet, NWT," 19–23 July 1993, 14. [AGCA-563571]

34. Gyorgy, "Bishop's Apology Falls Flat," *Gazette* (Montréal).

35. Gyorgy, "Bishop's Apology Falls Flat," *Gazette* (Montréal).

36. Howard, "Probes Document Abuse at NWT Church Schools," *Globe and Mail*.

37. Peterson, *Sir Joseph Bernier Federal Day School*, 7.

38. Peterson, *Sir Joseph Bernier Federal Day School*, 6–7.

39. Howard, "Probes Document Abuse at NWT Church Schools," *Globe and Mail*.

40. Gregoire, "Marius Tungilik," *Nunatsiaq Online*.

41. Moon, "Hundreds of Cree and Ojibwa Children Violated," *Globe and Mail*.

42. Canada, Aboriginal Affairs and Northern Development, *Report of the Testimonial/Panel Component*, 3.

43. TRC, ASAGR, Aboriginal Affairs and Northern Development, St. Anne's Residential School Reunion and Conference, *Report of the Testimonial/Panel Component*, Fort Albany First Nation, 20 August 1992, 3.

44. TRC, ASAGR, Aboriginal Affairs and Northern Development, St. Anne's Residential School Reunion and Conference, *Report of the Testimonial/Panel Component*, Fort Albany First Nation, 20 August 1992, 5.

45. Mary Anne Nakogee-Davis, "Summary Report–St. Anne's Residential School 1992 Reunion and Keykaywin Conference," 21 April 1994, 9. [AANDC-906125]

46. O'Grady, "School's Former Staff Face Assault Charges," *Toronto Star*.

47. Shea, *Institutional Child Abuse*, 10–15.

48. As quoted in *R. v. O'Connor* [1995] 4 SCR 411 at para. 39.

49. *R. v. O'Connor* [1992] BCJ No 2569 at paras. 19–20.

50. *R. v. O'Connor* [1992] BCJ No 2569 at paras. 66–68.

51. Neel, "Two Faces of Justice," *The Province* (Vancouver).

52. *R. v. O'Connor,* [1995] 4 SCR 411 at para. 91.

53. *Criminal Code of Canada*, s 278.3(4) as amended by SC 1997 c 30, s 1.

54. *R. v. O'Connor*, 1996 CanLII 8458 (BCSC).

55. *R. v. O'Connor*, 1996 CanLII 8393 (BCCA).

56. *R. v. O'Connor*, 1997 CanLII 4071 (BCCA).

57. *R. v. O'Connor*, 1998 CanLII 14987 (BCCA).

58. McLintock, "He Finally Confesses," *The Province* (Vancouver).

59. *Vancouver Sun*, "Bishop O'Connor Diverted."

60. Carter, *Lost Harvests*.

61. Carter, *Lost Harvests*.

62. *St. Catharine's Milling and Lumber Company v. The Queen*, [1888] UKPC 70, [1888] 14 AC 46 (12 December 1888).

63. *Calder v. Attorney General (B.C.)*, [1973] SCJ No 56 (SCC).

64. TRC, NRA, Trevor Sutter, "Starr Admits to Sexual Assaults," *The Leader-Post* (Regina), Library and Archives Canada Reel NJ FM 752, 3 February 1993, A3 [GDC-026641]; Treble and O'Hara, "Residential Church School Scandal."

65. *B. (D.) v. Canada (Attorney General)*, 2000 SKQB 574(CanLII). For another case dismissing a claim brought against Starr see *C.M. v. Canada (A.G.)*, 2004 SKQB 175(CanLII) at paras. 13–15, 32.

66. *B. (D.) v. Canada (Attorney General)*, 2000 SKQB 574(CanLII) at para. 49.

67. *B. (D.) v. Canada (Attorney General)*, 2000 SKQB 574 (CanLII) at para. 63.

68. *B. (D.) v. Canada (Attorney General)*, 2000 SKQB 574 (CanLII) at paras. 63–64.

69. Moran, "The Role of Reparative Justice," 534.

70. Law Commission of Canada, *Restoring Dignity*, 409.

71. *M.M. v. Roman Catholic Church of Canada et al.*, 2001 MBCA 148 (CanLII) at paras. 41–42, 64.

72. *Limitation of Actions Amendment Act*, SM 2002 c 5, s 2.1(2).

73. *Limitations Act*, RSA 2000 c L-2, s 3.

74. *Limitations Act*, RSA 2000 c L-2, s 13.

75. *Arishenkoff v. British Columbia*, 2004 BCCA 299 (CanLII).

76. *Limitations of Actions Act*, RSS 1978 c L-15, s 3.1 (statute repealed).

77. *P.(W.) v. Canada (Attorney General)*, 1999 SKQB 17 ; *M.A. v. Canada (Attorney General)*, [1999] SJ No 538 (SKQB).

78. Roach, "Blaming the Victim."

79. *W. (D.) v. Canada (Attorney General)*, 1999 SKQB 187 (CanLII) at para. 38.

80. *Q. (A.) v. Canada (Attorney General),* 1998 CanLII 13810 (SKQB) at paras. 62, 76. Justice Matheson concluded that "there is nothing in the treatment plan which identifies the alcohol problem as being attributable, in any manner, to the sexual assaults on Mr. [C. C.]. Thus, the claim for the cost of alcohol treatment cannot be viewed as justified."

81. In *Q.(A.) v. Canada (Attorney General),* 1998 CanLII 13810 (SKQB) at paras. 54, 57, Justice Matheson rejected the fitness club proposal stating, "No doubt many unfit individuals would feel better if they engaged in a consistent fitness program. But in what manner has it been revealed that Mr. [J. M.]'s unfitness was in any way related to the injury—sexual assault—caused to him by one of the defendants? ... The recommended expenditure for a family membership for two years at the Lawson Aquatic Centre appears to be not only a luxury but addressing a matter wholly unrelated to the injuries suffered by Mr. [J. M.]. In any event, the recommendation does not fall within the concept of 'treatment and counselling' and cannot therefore be justified."

82. *F. S. M. v. Clarke,* 1999 CanLII 9405 (BCSC) at paras. 191, 196.

83. "Fresh as Amended Statement of Claim," in court file 00-CV-192059 CP, (*Baxter v. Canada [Attorney General]*) at paras. 68, 71, 72.

84. *Re Residential Schools,* [2000] AJ No 47 (ABQB); *Bonaparte v. Canada (Attorney General),* [2003] OJ No 1046.

85. *T. W. N. A. v. Clarke,* 2001 BCSC 1177 (CanLII) at para. 305.

86. Canada, *Treaties No. 1 and No. 2.*

87. Canada, *Treaties No. 3, No. 5, No. 6.*

88. *M. C. C. v. Canada,* [2001] OJ No 4163 at para. 45, affirmed by [2003] OJ No 2698.

89. Eizenga et al., *Class Actions Law and Practice.*

90. Jones, *Theory of Class Actions,* 110.

91. *Class Proceedings Act,* 1992, SO 1992, c 6.

92. *Class Proceedings Act,* RSBC 1996, c 50.

93. Saskatchewan: *The Class Actions Act,* SS 2001, c C-12.01; Newfoundland and Labrador: *Class Actions Act,* SNL 2001, c C-18.1; Manitoba: *Class Proceedings Act,* CCSM c C130; Alberta: *Class Proceedings Act,* SA 2003, c C-16.5; New Brunswick: *Class Proceedings Act,* RSNB 2011, c 125; Nova Scotia: *Class Proceedings Act,* SNS 2007, c 28. (All statutes cited are the provincial class proceedings act in their contemporary form.)

94. "Statement of Claim" in Court File No. 29762 (*Cloud v. Canada (Attorney General).*

95. *Cloud v. Canada (Attorney General),* [2001] OJ No 4163 at para. 7.

96. "Statement of Claim" in Court File No. 29762 (*Cloud v. Canada (Attorney General).*

97. "Statement of Claim issued 13 June 2000," in Court File No. 00-CV-192059CP (*Baxter v. Canada [Attorney General]*).

98. "Joint Factum of the Plaintiffs, Motion for Settlement Approval – Returnable August 29-31 2006," in Court File No. 00-CV-192059CP (*Baxter v. Canada [Attorney General]*) at para. 256.

99. *Cloud v. Canada (Attorney General),* [2001] OJ No 4163 at paras. 63, 74, 80.

100. *Cloud v. Canada (Attorney General),* [2003] OJ No 2698 at paras. 18–36.

101. *Cloud v. Canada (Attorney General),* [2004] OJ No 4924.

102. *Cloud v. Canada (Attorney General),* 2004 CanLII 45444 (ONCA) at para. 88.

103. Gatehouse, "The Residential Schools Settlement Biggest Winner"; Government of Canada and Merchant Law Group, "Indian Residential Schools Settlement Agreement, Schedule V." See also *Fontaine v. Canada (Attorney General),* 2013 SKCA 22, outlining ongoing legal disputes over fees.

104. Kraus, "Merchant Law Group in Legal Battle of Its Own," *Global News*.

105. Canadian Bar Association, *Resolution 00-04-A*.

106. Regan, *Unsettling the Settler Within*, 121.

107. Assembly of First Nations, *Report on Canada's Dispute Resolution Plan*, 15.

108. Assembly of First Nations, *Report on Canada's Dispute Resolution Plan*, 15.

109. Assembly of First Nations, *Report on Canada's Dispute Resolution Plan*, 41.

110. Assembly of First Nations, *Report on Canada's Dispute Resolution Plan*, 2, 24.

111. Assembly of First Nations, *Report on Canada's Dispute Resolution Plan*, 107–116.

112. Assembly of First Nations, *Report on Canada's Dispute Resolution Plan*, 3.

113. Assembly of First Nations, *Report on Canada's Dispute Resolution Plan*, 5.

114. Quoted in Regan, *Unsettling the Settler Within*, 128.

115. Canada, House of Commons Standing Committee on Aboriginal Affairs and Northern Development, *Study on the Effectiveness of the Government Alternative Dispute Resolution Process*.

116. "Agreement in Principle," 1.

117. *Indian Residential Schools Settlement Agreement*.

118. *Indian Residential Schools Settlement Agreement*, Schedule M, Funding Agreement, s 3.03, 5.

119. *Indian Residential Schools Settlement Agreement*.

120. For example, *Baxter v. Canada (Attorney General)*, 2006 CanLII 41673 (ONSC).

121. "Affidavit of Phillip Fontaine," in court file 05-CV-294716CP, *Fontaine v. Canada*, 2006 at para. 17.

122. "Affidavit of Phillip Fontaine," in court file 05-CV-294716CP, *Fontaine v. Canada*, 2006 at para. 18.

123. "Affidavit of Phillip Fontaine," in court file 05-CV-294716CP, *Fontaine v. Canada*, 2006 at para. 18.

124. TRC, AVS, Rosalie Webber, Statement to the Truth and Reconciliation Commission of Canada, Halifax, Nova Scotia, 26 November 2011, Statement Number: 2011-2891.

125. Canada, Truth and Reconciliation Commission, *Internal Report of the Inuit Sub-Commission*, 11.

126. TRC, AVS, Leona Bird, Statement to the Truth and Reconciliation Commission of Canada, Saskatoon, Saskatchewan, 21 June 2012, Statement Number: 2011-4415.

127. TRC, AVS, Myrtle Ward, Statement to the Truth and Reconciliation Commission of Canada, Saskatoon, Saskatchewan, 22 June 2012, Statement Number: 2011-4162.

128. TRC, AVS, Geraldine Bob, Statement to the Truth and Reconciliation Commission of Canada, Fort Simpson, Northwest Territories, 23 November 2011, Statement Number: 2011-2685.

129. TRC, AVS, Joseph Martin Larocque, Statement to the Truth and Reconciliation Commission of Canada, Saskatoon, Saskatchewan, 21 June 2012, Statement Number: 2011-4386.

130. TRC, AVS, Mabel Brown, Statement to the Truth and Reconciliation Commission of Canada, Inuvik, Northwest Territories, 28 September 2011, Statement Number: 2011-0325.

131. TRC, AVS, Marie Brown, Statement to the Truth and Reconciliation Commission of Canada, Saskatoon, Saskatchewan, 21 June 2012, Statement Number: 2011-4421.

132. TRC, AVS, Theresa Hall, Statement to the Truth and Reconciliation Commission of Canada, Timmins, Ontario, 10 November 2010, Statement Number: 01-ON-8-10Nov10-007.

133. TRC, AVS, Amelia Thomas, Statement to the Truth and Reconciliation Commission of Canada, Victoria, British Columbia, 13 April, 2012, Statement Number: 2011-3975.

134. TRC, AVS, Darlene Thomas, Statement to the Truth and Reconciliation Commission of Canada, Vancouver, British Columbia, 19 September 2013, Statement Number: 2011-3200.

135. Perreault, "Admissions to Adult Correctional Services."

136. Canada, Office of the Correctional Investigator, "Backgrounder: Aboriginal Offenders."

137. Perreault, "Aboriginal Adults Are Overrepresented."

138. Perreault, "Aboriginal Youth Are Over-Represented."

139. Perreault, "Aboriginal Adults Are Overrepresented."

140. Canada, Statistics Canada, "Youth Custody and Community Services in Canada, 1998–99"; Perreault, "Aboriginal Youth Are Over-Represented."

141. TRC, AVS, David Charleson, Statement to the Truth and Reconciliation Commission of Canada, Deroche, British Columbia, 20 January 2010, Statement Number: 2011-5043.

142. TRC, AVS, Daniel Andre, Statement to the Truth and Reconciliation Commission of Canada, Whitehorse, Yukon, 23 May 2011, Statement Number: 2011-0202.

143. TRC, AVS, Raymond Blake-Nukon, Statement to the Truth and Reconciliation Commission of Canada, 23 May 2011, Statement Number: 2011-0201.

144. Aboriginal Healing Foundation, *Mental Health Profiles*, 47.

145. TRC, AVS, Willy Carpenter, Statement to the Truth and Reconciliation Commission of Canada, Tuktoyaktuk, Northwest Territories, 20 September 2011, Statement Number: 2011-0353.

146. TRC, AVS, Ruth Chapman, Statement to the Truth and Reconciliation Commission of Canada, Winnipeg, Manitoba, 16 June 2010, Statement Number: 02-MB-16JU10-118.

147. TRC, AVS, Diana Lariviere, Statement to the Truth and Reconciliation Commission of Canada, Little Current, Ontario, 13 May 2011, Statement Number: 2011-2011.

148. First Nations Centre, *First Nations Regional Longitudinal Health Survey (RHS) 2002/03*, 115.

149. Canada, Public Health Agency of Canada, "Fetal Alcohol Spectrum Disorder (FASD)"; Ospina and Dennett, *Systematic Review*, iii.

150. Streissguth et al., "Risk Factors for Adverse Life Outcomes," 233.

151. MacPherson, Chudley, and Grant, *Fetal Alcohol Spectrum Disorder (FASD) in a Correctional Population*.

152. Tait, *Fetal Alcohol Syndrome*, 75.

153. Canada, Public Safety Canada, *Fetal Alcohol Spectrum Disorder and the Criminal Justice System*, 2.

154. Canada, Public Safety Canada, *Fetal Alcohol Spectrum Disorder and the Criminal Justice System*, 21.

155. *R. v. Harris*, 2002 BCCA 152 at para. 26.

156. Institute of Health and Economics, *Consensus Statement on Legal Issues*, 10.

157. Institute of Health and Economics, *Consensus Statement on Legal Issues*, 22–23.

158. *R. v. C. L. K.*, 2009 MBQB 227 (CanLII) at paras. 9–11.

159. *R. v. C. L. K.*, 2009 MBQB 227 (CanLII) at para. 13.

160. *R. v. George*, 2010 ONSC 6017 at para. 7.

161. *R. v. George*, 2010 ONSC 6017 at paras. 8–9.

162. *R. v. George*, 2010 ONSC 6017 at para. 11.

163. *R. .v. George*, 2010 ONSC 6017 at paras. 52–53.

164. *R. v. Charlie*, 2012 YKTC 5 at para. 6.

165. *R. v. Charlie*, 2012 YKTC 5 at para. 9.

166. *R. v. Ominayak*, 2007 ABQB 442 at para. 150.

167. *R. v. Paulette*, 2010 NWTSC 31 (CanLII) at para. 6.

168. *R. v. Jimmie*, 2009 BCCA 215 at para. 9.

169. Sousa et al., "Longitudinal Study on the Effects of Child Abuse," 118.

170. *R. v. Rossi*, [2011] OJ No 4736 at para. 27.

171. *R. v. Snake*, [2010] OJ No 5445 at para. 17.

172. Martin et al., "The Enduring Significance of Racism," 662.

173. *R. v. G. (D. M.)*, 2006 NSPC 58 (CanLII) at para. 14.

174. *R. v. Paulin*, 2011 ONSC 5027; *R. v. Cappo*, 2005 SKCA 134; *R. v. Tymiak*, 2012 BCCA 40; *R. v. Pauchay*, 2009 SKPC 35; *R. v. Leaney*, 2002 BCCA 67; *R. v. W. R. B.*, 2010 MBQB 102; *R. v. Shawn Curtis Keepness*, 2011 SKQB 293; *R v. Renschler*, 2005 MBPC 53233; *R. v. Klymok*, 2002 ABPC 95; *R. v. R.L.*, 2012 MBPC 22; *R. v. Boisseneau*, 2006 ONSC 562; *R. v. Corbiere*, 2012 ONSC 2405; *R. v. Sharkey*, 2011 BCSC 1541; *R. v. Makela*, 2006 BCPC 320; *R. v. Loring*, 2009 BCCA 166.

175. LaPrairie, "Aboriginal Crime and Justice," 287.

176. Filbert and Flynn, "Developmental and Cultural Assets," 563.

177. Burton, "Male Adolescents."

178. McCloskey and Bailey, "The Intergenerational Transmission of Risk," 1032.

179. *R. v. J. O.*, 2007 QCCQ 716 at paras. 28–30.

180. *R. v. W. R. G.*, 2011 BCPC 330 at para. 25.

181. *R. v. W. R. G.*, 2011 BCPC 330 at para. 34.

182. Bennett, Holloway, and Farrington, "The Statistical Association between Drug Misuse and Crime," 117.

183. Phillips, "Substance Abuse and Prison Recidivism"; Looman and Abracen, "Substance Abuse among High-Risk Sexual Offenders"; Hirschel, Hutchinson, and Shaw, "The Interrelationship between Substance Abuse"; Tripodi and Bender, "Substance Abuse Treatment."

184. Canada, Statistics Canada, "Victimization and Offending among the Aboriginal population in Canada," 9.

185. Perreault, "Violent Victimization of Aboriginal People," 9.

186. *R. v. Battaja*, 2010 YKTC 145; *R. v. E.K.*, 2012 BCPC 132; *R. v. O. S.*, 2005 BCPC 727; *R. v. Simon*, 2006 ABPC 21; *R. v. McLeod*, 2006 YKTC 118; *R. v. Joe*, 2005 YKTC 21.

187. *R. v. Craft*, 2010 YKTC 127 at para. 12.

188. *R. v. M. L. W.*, 2004 SKPC 90 at para. 8.

189. Kerr et al., "Intergenerational Influences on Early Alcohol Use," 889–901; Handley and Chassin, "Intergenerational Transmission of Alcohol Expectancies"; Campbell and Oei, "A Cognitive Model for the Intergenerational Transference of Alcohol Use Behavior": Belles et al., "Parental Problem Drinking"; Thornberry, Krohn, and Freeman-Gallant, "Intergenerational Roots," 1; Dunlap et al., "Mothers and Daughters," 21.

190. *R. v. C. G.*, 2011 NWTSC 47 at para. 20.

191. Aboriginal Healing Foundation, *Mental Health Profiles*, 50, 51.

192. Aboriginal Healing Foundation, *Mental Health Profiles*, 46, 47.

193. *R. v. Land*, 2013 ONSC 6526 at paras. 65 and 69.

194. *R. v. Land*, 2013 ONSC 6526 at para. 76.

195. Canada, Canadian Human Rights Commission, *Report on Equality Rights of Aboriginal People*, 18–19.

196. Bougie, Kelly-Scott, and Arriagana, "The Education and Employment Experiences of First Nations," 24.

197. Canada, Canadian Human Rights Commission, *Report on Equality Rights of Aboriginal People*, 3, 12, 32; Anderson and Hohban, "Labour Force Characteristics of the Métis," 12.

198. Canada, Statistics Canada, Table 99-014-039, *2011 National Household Survey: Data Tables*.

199. Macdonald and Wilson, *Poverty or Prosperity*, 6.

200. Some recent studies include Hooghe et al., "Unemployment, Inequality, Poverty and Crime": Gustafson, "The Criminalization of Poverty"; Sabates, "Educational Attainment and Juvenile Crime"; Atkins, "Racial Segregation, Concentrated Disadvantage, and Violent Crime"; Case, "The Relationship of Race and Criminal Behavior."

201. Some recent studies include Eitle, D'Alessio, and Stolzenberg, "Economic Segregation, Race, and Homicide"; Pizarro and McGloin, "Explaining Gang Homicides in Newark, New Jersey"; Pridemore, "A Methodological Addition to the Cross-National Empirical Literature on Social Structure and Homicide."

202. Spano, Frielich, and Bolland, "Gang Membership, Gun Carrying, and Employment."

203. Moore "Understanding the Connection Between Domestic Violence, Crime, and Poverty," 455; Purvin, Diane, "Weaving a Tangled Safety Net."

204. Bougie and Senécal, "Registered Indian Children's School Success," 28.

205. *R. v. C. G. O.*, 2011 BCPC 145 at paras. 4, 61.

206. *R. v. C. G. O.*, 2011 BCPC 145 at paras. 62–63.

207. Ryan and Testa, "Child Maltreatment and Juvenile Delinquency."

208. Ryan et al., "Juvenile Delinquency in Child Welfare."

209. DeGue and Widom, "Does Out-Of-Home Placement," 350.

210. *R. v. J. E. R.*, 2012 BCPC 103 at paras. 30–34.

211. Allan Rock quoted in *R. v. Gladue*, [1999] 1 SCR 688; Canada, House of Commons Standing Committee on Justice and Legal Affairs, *Minutes of Proceedings and Evidence*, No. 62, 17 November 1994, 62:15.

212. *R. v. Gladue*, [1999] 1 SCR 688 at para. 60, quoting Michael Jackson "Locking Up Natives in Canada," *UBC Law Review* 23 (1988–89): 215–216.

213. *R. v. Gladue*, [1999] 1 SCR 688 at para. 64.

214. *R. v. Gladue*, [1999] 1 SCR 688 at para. 37.

215. Makin, "Aboriginal Sentencing Rules Ignored," *Globe and Mail*.

216. Legal Services Society of British Columbia, *Gladue Report Disbursement*, 61.

217. Legal Services Society of British Columbia, *Gladue Report Disbursement*, 62.

218. *R. v. Armitage*, 2015 ONCJ 64 (CanLII) at paras. 3–5.

219. *R. v. Armitage*, 2015 ONCJ 64 (CanLII) at para. 55.

220. *R. v. Ipeelee*, 2012 SCC 13 at para. 60.

221. Some legal commentators have suggested that even after *Ipeelee* some judges are insisting on a causal connection between the commission of a crime and background factors and are underestimating the intergenerational impact of residential schools. See Roach, "Blaming the Victim."

222. *R. v. Ipeelee*, 2012 SCC 13 at para. 66.

223. Rudin, "Incarceration of Aboriginal Youth in Ontario," 265.

224. Rudin, "Incarceration of Aboriginal Youth in Ontario," 268–269.

225. Tim Quigley quoted in *R. v. Ipeelee*, 2012 SCC 13 at para. 67.

226. TRC, AVS, Gerald McLeod, Statement to the Truth and Reconciliation Commission of Canada, Whitehorse, Yukon, 27 May 2011, Statement Number: 2011-1130.

227. TRC, AVS, Gerald McLeod, Statement to the Truth and Reconciliation Commission of Canada, Whitehorse, Yukon, 27 May 2011, Statement Number: 2011-1130.

228. Canada, Nicholson, Toews, Kenney, and Boisvenu, "Statement of the Government of Canada on the Royal Assent of Bill C-10," *Reuters.com*.

229. *Criminal Code of Canada*, RCS 1985 c C-46, ss 151–153.

230. Bill C-10 amended the *Controlled Drugs and Substances Act* to impose a minimum punishment of imprisonment for a term of two years if certain other aggravating factors apply, including that the offence was committed in or near a school, on or near school grounds, or in or near any other public place usually frequented by persons under the age of eighteen. As enacted: *Controlled Drugs and Substances Act*, SC 1996, c 19, s 5(3)(a).

231. *Controlled Drugs and Substances Act*, SC 1996, c 19, s 7(3)(a); Library of Parliament, Legal and Legislative Affairs Division, *Bill C-10: An Act to enact the Justice for Victims of Terrorism Act and to amend the State Immunity Act, the Criminal Code, the Controlled Drugs and Substances Act, the Corrections and Conditional Release Act, the Youth Criminal Justice Act, the Immigration and Refugee Protection Act and Other Acts*, Publication no. 41-1 C10-E, 5 October 2011, revised 17 February 2012.

232. *Criminal Code of Canada*, RCS 1985 c C-46, s 742.1(e) removes judicial discretion to grant a conditional sentence where the offence has a ten-year maximum sentence, is prosecuted by way of indictment, and either has resulted in bodily harm, involved drug import, export, trafficking, or production, or involved a weapon.

233. *Criminal Code of Canada*, RCS 1985 c C-46, s 742.1(b).

234. TRC, AVS, Joann May Cunday, Statement to the Truth and Reconciliation Commission of Canada, Winnipeg, Manitoba, 21 September 2011, Statement Number: 2011-0133.

235. *R. v. Elias*, 2009 YKTC 59 at para. 25 (quoting *R. v. Quash*, 2009 YKTC 54 at para. 56). There have been some recent cases in which courts have made decisions counter to the mandatory minimum provisions. See, for example, *R. v. Smickle*, 2012 ONSC 602.

236. Canada, House of Commons, *Bill C-32*.

237. Perreault, "Admissions to Adult Correctional Services."

238. Manitoba, Aboriginal Justice Implementation Commission, *Report of the Aboriginal Justice Inquiry of Manitoba*, 1: ch 11.

239. British Columbia, Ministry of Justice, Corrections Branch, *Strategic Plan 2012–2016*.

240. See, for example: *R. v. NB*, 2012 SKPC 99 (CanLII) at para. 24; *R. v. Alkenbrack*, 2011 BCPC 424 at para. 67.

241. See for example: *R. v. Badger*, 2013 SKQB 347.

242. *Corrections and Conditional Release Act*, SC 1992 c 20, s 80.

243. *Corrections and Conditional Release Act*, SC 1992, c 20, s 81.

244. *Corrections and Conditional Release Act*, SC 1992, c 20, s 83.

245. *Corrections and Conditional Release Act*, SC 1992, c 20, s 84.

246. Canada, Office of the Correctional Investigator, *Spirit Matters*.

247. Canada, Office of the Correctional Investigator, *Spirit Matters*.

248. *R. v. J. T.*, 2011 ONSC 7275 (CanLII) at para. 58.

249. *Corrections and Conditional Release Act*, SC1992, c 20, s 30.

250. Blanchette, Verbrugge, and Wichmann, *The Custody Rating Scale*, 35.

251. *Corrections and Conditional Release Act*, SOR/92-620, s 17.

252. Blanchette, Verbrugge, and Wichmann, *The Custody Rating Scale*, 11. Other differentiating factors between Aboriginal and non-Aboriginal women in this case included severity of current offence and "street (in)stability."

253. Canada, Task Force of Federally Sentenced Women, *Creating Choices*.

254. Elizabeth Fry Society, "Discrimination against Aboriginal Women Rampant."

255. Welsh and Ogloff, "Full Parole and the Aboriginal Experience," 469, 479.

256. Canada, Canadian Human Rights Commission, *Protecting Their Rights*, 28.

257. Walsh, "Is Corrections Correcting?," 109.

258. Holsinger, and Lowenkamp, and Lotessa, "Ethnicity, Gender, and the Level of Service," 314; Welsh and Ogloff, "Full Parole and the Aboriginal Experience," 469; Hann and Harman, *Predicting Release Risk*, 50.

259. Moore, *First Nations, Métis, Inuit and Non-Aboriginal Offenders*, 44.

260. Moore, *First Nations, Métis, Inuit and Non-Aboriginal Offenders*, 16.

261. Canada, Correctional Service Canada, *Commissioner's Directive: Security Classification and Penitentiary Placement.*

262. Blanchette and Taylor, "Development and Validation of a Security Reclassification Scale for Women," 29.

263. Blanchette and Taylor, "Development and Validation of a Security Reclassification Scale for Women," 29.

264. For a study that involved interviews with inmates in a minimum security institution designed specifically for Aboriginal inmates, see Waldram, *The Way of the Pipe*, 129–150; Heckbert and Turkington, "Turning Points"; Crutcher and Trevethan, "An Examination of Healing Lodges for Aboriginal Offenders in Canada," 52.

265. TRC, AVS, Joanne Nimik, Statement to the Truth and Reconciliation Commission of Canada, Winnipeg, Manitoba, 4 January 2012, Statement Number: 2011-2662.

266. TRC, AVS, Joanne Nimik, Statement to the Truth and Reconciliation Commission of Canada, Winnipeg, Manitoba, 4 January 2012, Statement Number: 2011-2662.

267. TRC, AVS, Chris Gargan, Statement to the Truth and Reconciliation Commission of Canada, Yellowknife, Northwest Territories, 30 October 2012, Statement Number: 2011-0430.

268. *R. v. Gingell*, [1996] YJ No 52 at para. 63.

269. Zellerer, "Culturally Competent Programs."

270. Zellerer, "Culturally Competent Programs," 183.

271. Sioui and Thibault, *The Relevance of a Cultural Adaptation*, 43.

272. Sioui and Thibault, *The Relevance of a Cultural Adaptation*, 42.

273. Sioui and Thibault, *The Relevance of a Cultural Adaptation*, 44.

274. Heckbert and Turkington, "Turning Points," 56.

275. Sapers, "Speaking Notes for Mr. Howard Sapers."

276. Saskatchewan, Commission on First Nations and Métis Peoples and Justice Reform, *Legacy of Hope*, Recommendation 6.23, 6.34.

277. Canada, Correctional Service of Canada, *Evaluation Report.*

278. Canada, Correctional Service of Canada, *Evaluation Report.*

279. Crutcher and Trevethan, "An Examination of Healing Lodges for Aboriginal Offenders in Canada," 54.

280. Moore, *First Nations, Métis, Inuit and Non-Aboriginal Offenders*, 23.

281. Bonta, "Native Inmates"; Bonta, LaPrairie, and Wallace-Capretta, "Risk Prediction and Re-offending"; Bonta, Lipinski, and Martin, "The Characteristics of Aboriginal Recidivists."

282. John Howard Society of Alberta, *Offender Risk Assessment*, 3. The studies being referred to are Gendreau, Little, and Goggin, *A Meta-Analysis of the Predictors of Adult Offender Recidivism*; Hanson and Bussière, *Predictors of Sexual Offender Recidivism.*

283. LaPrairie, *Examining Aboriginal Corrections in Canada*, 80–83.

284. Petten, "New Healing Lodge Opens for Offenders," 1.

285. Brown et al., "Housing for Aboriginal Ex-Offenders."

286. Perreault, "Admissions to Youth Correctional Services in Canada, 2011/12."

287. *R. v. D. B.*, [2008] 2 SCR 3 at paras. 1, 41, 47–59.

288. *Youth Criminal Justice Act*, SC 2002, c 1, s 3(1)(b).

289. UN General Assembly, *Convention on the Rights of the Child*, article 40.

290. *Youth Criminal Justice Act*, SC 2002, c 1, s 38(1).

291. *Youth Criminal Justice Act*, SC 2002, c 1, s 38(2)(d).

292. *Youth Criminal Justice Act*, SC 2002, c 1, s 3(1)(c)(iv).

293. Chartrand, "Aboriginal Youth and the Criminal Justice System," 326.

294. Chartrand, "Aboriginal Youth and the Criminal Justice System," 315.

295. Canada, Statistics Canada, "Youth Court Statistics 2011/2012"; Munch, "Youth Correctional Statistics in Canada, 2010/2011," 5; Canadian Bar Association, *Submission on Bill C-10*, 8. Not all provinces/territories have seen a decrease in youth in correctional services; in fact, Munch reported that, since 2004/05, rates have increased in Manitoba, Yukon, and Alberta.

296. Perreault, "Admissions to Youth Correctional Services in Canada, 2011/12." The study excluded data from Nova Scotia, Québec, Saskatchewan, and Nunavut. Overrepresentation of Aboriginal youth is evident in all provinces and territories surveyed, with the exception of Newfoundland and Labrador.

297. British Columbia, Office of the Provincial Health Officer, *Health, Crime and Doing Time*, 32.

298. BC Representative for Children and Youth, *When Talk Trumped Service*, 21.

299. Totten, "Aboriginal Youth and Violent Gang Involvement in Canada," 141.

300. British Columbia, Office of the Provincial Health Officer, *Health, Crime and Doing Time*, 32.

301. Chartrand, "Aboriginal Youth and the Criminal Justice System," 320.

302. Howe, "Children's Rights as Crime Prevention," 467.

303. Howe, "Children's Rights as Crime Prevention," 468–469.

304. Historical version of the *YCJA* is available on the CanLII website at http://www.canlii.org/en/ca/laws/stat/sc-2002-c-1/32863/sc-2002-c-1.html#history.

305. *Youth Criminal Justice Act*, SC 2002, c 1, s 3(1)(a).

306. Assembly of First Nations, *Submission: Bill C-10 Safe Streets and Communities Act*, 20.

307. Canada, House of Commons, *Bill C-10*, clauses 176–184.

308. Assembly of First Nations, *Submission: Bill C-10 Safe Streets and Communities Act*, 19.

309. Assembly of First Nations, *Submission: Bill C-10 Safe Streets and Communities Act*, 19.

310. Canadian Bar Association, *Submission on Bill C-10*, 80.

311. Canada, House of Commons, *Bill C-10*, clause 189.

312. British Columbia, Office of the Provincial Health Officer, *Health, Crime and Doing Time*, 11.

313. Canada, Indian Residential Schools Adjudication Secretariat, "Adjudication Secretariat Statistics."

314. Canada, Canadian Centre for Justice Statistics, "Family Violence in Canada"; Canada, Statistics Canada, "Homicide in Canada, 2013."

315. Canada, Statistics Canada, "Homicide in Canada, 2013."

316. Sinha, "Measuring Violence Against Women," 9, 19.

317. Kennedy, "Rinelle Harper Calls for Missing Women Inquiry," *Ottawa Citizen*.

318. Sinha, "Measuring Violence Against Women: Statistical Trends," 9, 19; Native Women's Association of Canada, *Voices of Our Sisters in Spirit*, 94–95.

319. Brennan, "Violent Victimization of Aboriginal Women in the Canadian Provinces, 2009," 7, 8. In the GSS, "Aboriginal women" refers to those persons who self-reported their sex as female and who self-identified as belonging to at least one Aboriginal group—that is, North American Indian, Métis, or Inuit.

320. Brennan, "Violent Victimization of Aboriginal Women in the Canadian Provinces, 2009," 9.

321. Brennan, "Violent Victimization of Aboriginal Women in the Canadian Provinces, 2009," 10.

322. Sinha, "Measuring Violence Against Women," 19.

323. Perreault, "Violent Victimization of Aboriginal People in the Canadian Provinces, 2009," 10.

324. Canada, Truth and Reconciliation Commission, *Internal Report of the Inuit Sub-Commission,* 9.

325. Jacobs and Williams, "Legacy of Residential Schools: Missing and Murdered Women," 127.

326. Manitoba, Aboriginal Justice Implementation Commission, *Report of the Aboriginal Justice Inquiry of Manitoba,* 2: 92.

327. Manitoba, Aboriginal Justice Implementation Commission, *Report of the Aboriginal Justice Inquiry of Manitoba,* 2: Chp. 10.

328. TRC, AVS, Eva Simpson, Statement to the Truth and Reconciliation Commission of Canada, Norway House First Nation, Manitoba, 10 May 2011, Statement Number: 2011-0290.

329. Opal, *Forsaken,* 1:52.

330. Oppal, *Forsaken,* 1:63.

331. Oppal, *Forsaken,* 2A:124.

332. Oppal, *Forsaken,* 2A:63, 124.

333. Oppal, *Forsaken,* 1:42.

334. Oppal, *Forsaken,* 2A:121.

335. Burnouf, "Marlene Bird," *APTN.*

336. *CBC News,* "Illustrations Tell Story of Marlene Bird."

337. *CBC News,* "Illustrations Tell Story of Marlene Bird."

338. Canadian Press, "Winnipeg Police Officer Suspended," *The Star* (Toronto).

339. Jacobs and Williams, "Legacy of Residential Schools: Missing and Murdered Women," 127, 132–133.

340. Jacobs and Williams, "Legacy of Residential Schools: Missing and Murdered Women," 128, 132–133.

341. Jacobs and Williams, "Legacy of Residential Schools: Missing and Murdered Women," 134.

342. Human Rights Watch, *Those Who Take Us Away,* 35.

343. Highway of Tears Symposium, *Highway of Tears Symposium Recommendations Report,* 9, 18.

344. Oppal, *Forsaken,* Recommendation 6.1; Pearce, "An Awkward Silence," 644.

345. Pearce, "An Awkward Silence," 644.

346. Native Women's Association of Canada, "Fact Sheet: Missing and Murdered Aboriginal Women and Girls," 3.

347. Native Women's Association of Canada, *What Their Stories Tell Us,* 24–27.

348. Native Women's Association of Canada, "Fact Sheet: Missing and Murdered Aboriginal Women and Girls," 3.

349. Native Women's Association of Canada, *What Their Stories Tell Us,* 31.

350. Native Women's Association of Canada, *What Their Stories Tell Us,* 27

351. Canada, House of Commons Standing Committee on the Status of Women, *Ending Violence against Aboriginal Women and Girls,* 11–12.

352. Canada, House of Commons Standing Committee on Violence Against Indigenous Women, *Invisible Women,* 13.

353. See Pearce, "An Awkward Silence."

354. Pearce, "An Awkward Silence," 18–23.

355. Canada, House of Commons Standing Committee on the Status of Women, *Interim Report – Night,* 15–18.

356. Oppal, *Forsaken*, 2B:107–108.

357. Oppal, *Forsaken*, 2B:236.

358. Royal Canadian Mounted Police, *Missing and Murdered Aboriginal Women*, 7.

359. Royal Canadian Mounted Police, *Missing and Murdered Aboriginal Women*, 9.

360. Royal Canadian Mounted Police, *Missing and Murdered Aboriginal Women*, 21.

361. Palmater, "RCMP Report on Murdered and Missing Aboriginal Women," *Rabble.ca*.

362. Barrera, "Valcourt Used Unreleased RCMP Data," *APTN*.

363. Galloway, "70 Per Cent of Murdered Aboriginal Women," *Globe and Mail*.

364. Palmater, "RCMP Report on Murdered and Missing Aboriginal Women," *Rabble.ca*.

365. Amnesty International, *No More Stolen Sisters*, 4; Human Rights Watch, *Those Who Take Us Away*, 37.

366. United Nations, High Commissioner for Human Rights, *Discrimination against Women*, para. 32; United Nations, Human Rights Committee, *Concluding Observations of the Human Rights Committee: Canada*, para. 23.

367. Committee on the Elimination of Discrimination Against Women quoted in Canadian Feminist Alliance for International Action, *No Action: No Progress*, 17.

368. Anaya, "Statement upon Conclusion of the Visit to Canada by the United Nations Special Rapporteur."

369. Amnesty International, *No More Stolen Sisters*, 4.

370. Human Rights Watch, *Those Who Take Us Away*, 18.

371. Human Rights Watch, *Those Who Take Us Away*, 8.

372. Human Rights Watch, *Those Who Take Us Away*, 8.

373. Munch, "Victim Services in Canada, 2009/2010."

374. Mazowita and Burczycka, "Shelters for Abused Women in Canada, 2012."

375. Canada, House of Commons Standing Committee on the Status of Women, *Ending Violence against Aboriginal Women and Girls*, 31.

376. Canada, House of Commons Standing Committee on Violence Against Indigenous Women, *Invisible Women*, 29–30.

377. Canada, House of Commons Standing Committee on Violence Against Indigenous Women, *Invisible Women*, 20.

378. Mulligan, "Victim Services in Canada."

379. UN General Assembly, *Declaration of Basic Principles of Justice for Victims of Crime and Abuse of Power*; Canada, Department of Justice, *Multi-Site Survey of Victims of Crime*, 15.

380. UN General Assembly, *United Nations Declaration on the Rights of Indigenous Peoples*.

381. TRC, AVS, Michael Sillett, Statement to the Truth and Reconciliation Commission of Canada, Halifax, Nova Scotia, 27 October 2011, Statement Number: 2011-2870.

382. TRC, AVS, Ron McHugh, Statement to the Truth and Reconciliation Commission of Canada, Batoche, Saskatchewan, 21 July 2010, Statement Number: 01-SK-18-25JY10-011.

383. Canada, Royal Commission on Aboriginal Peoples, *Bridging the Cultural Divide*.

384. UN General Assembly, *United Nations Declaration on the Rights of Indigenous Peoples*.

385. Manitoba, Aboriginal Justice Implementation Commission, *Report of the Aboriginal Justice Inquiry of Manitoba*, 1: Appendix 1.

386. Dalmyn quoted in Green, "Aboriginal Community Sentencing and Mediation," 113.

387. Green, "Aboriginal Community Sentencing and Mediation," 114.

388. Judge Claude Fafard interview with Ross Gordon Green (telephone), 16 December 1994, cited in Green, "Aboriginal Community Sentencing and Mediation," 111–112.

389. Turpel-Lafond and Monture-Angus, "Aboriginal Peoples and Canadian Criminal Law," 246.

390. Miller, *The Problem of Justice*, 198–199.

391. Milward, *Aboriginal Justice and the Charter*.

# Bibliography

## Primary Sources

### 1. Truth and Reconciliation Commission Databases

The endnotes of this report often commence with the abbreviation TRC, followed by one of the following abbreviations: ASAGR, AVS, CAR, IRSSA, NRA, RBS, and LAC. The documents so cited are located in the Truth and Reconciliation Commission of Canada's database, housed at the National Centre for Truth and Reconciliation. At the end of each of these endnotes, in square brackets, is the document identification number for each of these documents. The following is a brief description of each database.

**Active and Semi-Active Government Records (ASAGR ) Database**: The Active and Semi-Active Government Records database contains active and semi-active records collected from federal governmental departments that potentially intersected with the administration and management of the residential school system. Documents that were relevant to the history and/or legacy of the system were disclosed to the Truth and Reconciliation Commission of Canada (TRC) in keeping with the federal government's obligations in relation to the Indian Residential Schools Settlement Agreement (IRSSA). Some of the other federal government departments included, but were not limited to, the Department of Justice, Health Canada, the Royal Canadian Mounted Police, and National Defence. Aboriginal Affairs and Northern Development Canada undertook the responsibility of centrally collecting and producing the records from these other federal departments to the TRC.

**Audio/Video Statement (AVS) Database**: The Audio/Video Statement database contains video and audio statements provided to the TRC at community hearings and regional and national events held by the TRC, as well as at other special events attended by the TRC.

**National Research and Analysis (NRA) Database**: The National Research and Analysis database contains records collected by the National Research and Analysis Directorate, Aboriginal Affairs and Northern Development Canada, formerly Indian Residential Schools Resolution Canada (IRSRC). The records in the database were originally collected for the purpose of research into a variety of allegations, such as abuse in residential schools, and primarily resulted from court processes such as civil and criminal litigation, and later the Indian Residential Schools Settlement Agreement (IRSSA), as well as from out-of-court processes such as Alternative Dispute Resolution. A majority of the records were collected from Aboriginal Affairs and

Northern Development Canada. The collection also contains records from other federal departments and religious entities. In the case of some records in the database that were provided by outside entities, the information in the database is incomplete. In those instances, the endnotes in the report reads, "No document location, no document file source."

## 2. Indian Affairs Annual Reports, 1864–1997

Within this report, Annual Report of the Department of Indian Affairs denotes the published annual reports created by the Government of Canada, and relating to Indian Affairs over the period from 1864 to 1997.

The Department of Indian Affairs and Northern Development was created in 1966. In 2011, it was renamed Aboriginal Affairs and Northern Development. Before 1966, different departments were responsible for the portfolios of Indian Affairs and Northern Affairs. The departments responsible for Indian Affairs were (in chronological order):

- The Department of the Secretary of State of Canada (to 1869)
- The Department of the Secretary of State for the Provinces (1869–1873)
- The Department of the Interior (1873–1880)
- The Department of Indian Affairs (1880–1936)
- The Department of Mines and Resources (1936–1950)
- The Department of Citizenship and Immigration (1950–1965)
- The Department of Northern Affairs and National Resources (1966)
- The Department of Indian Affairs and Northern Development (1966–1997)

The exact titles of Indian Affairs annual reports changed over time, and were named for the department.

## 3. Library and Archives Canada

**RG10 (Indian Affairs Records Group)** The records of RG10 at Library and Archives Canada are currently part of the R216, Department of Indian Affairs and Northern Development fonds. For clarity and brevity, in endnotes throughout this report, records belonging to the RG10 record group have been identified simply with their RG10 information.

Where a copy of an RG10 document held in a TRC database was used, the TRC database holding that copy is clearly identified, along with the RG10 information connected with the original document.

## 4. Government Publications

Aboriginal Justice Inquiry of Manitoba. Aboriginal Justice Implementation Committee. *Report of the Aboriginal Justice Inquiry of Manitoba*. Vol. 1, *The Justice System and Aboriginal People*. Winnipeg: Province of Manitoba, 1999.

Anderson, Thomas, and Lori Hohban. "Labour Force Characteristics of the Métis: Findings from the 2012 Aboriginal Peoples Survey." Statistics Canada, catalogue no. 89-653-X2014004, December 2014. http://www.statcan.gc.ca/pub/89-653-x/89-653-x2014004-eng.pdf.

Arnold, Mark. *Director of Child and Family Services Annual Report, 2011–2012*. Nunavut Child and Family Services, 2013. http://cwrp.ca/sites/default/files/publications/en/NU_DCFS_Report_2011.pdf.

BC Ministry of Health. Office of the Provincial Health Officer, and Child and Youth Officer for British Columbia. *Health and Well-Being of Children in Care in British Columbia: Report 1 on Health Services Utilization and Mortality*. Joint Special Report. Vancouver: Office of the Provincial Health Officer, 2006. http://www.health.gov.bc.ca/pho/pdf/cyo/complete_joint_report.pdf.

BC Representative for Children and Youth. *When Talk Trumped Service: A Decade of Lost Opportunity for Aboriginal Children and Youth in B.C: Special Report*. Vancouver: BC Representative for Children and Youth, 2013. http://cwrp.ca/sites/default/files/publications/en/BC_RCY_AboriginalServices2013.pdf.

Berger, Thomas R. *Nunavut Land Claims Agreement Implementation Contract Negotiations for the Second Planning Period 2003–2013: Conciliator's Final Report on "The Nunavut Project."* Ottawa: Aboriginal Affairs and Northern Development, 2006. http://epub.sub.uni-hamburg.de/epub/volltexte/2010/5076/pdf/2006_03_01_Thomas_Berger_Final_Report_ENG.pdf.

Blanchette, Kelley, Paul Verbrugge, and Cherami Wichmann. *The Custody Rating Scale, Initial Security Level Placement, and Women Offenders*. Correctional Service of Canada, Research Branch, 2002. http://www.csc-scc.gc.ca/research/092/r127_e.pdf.

Bonesteel, Sarah. *Canada's Relationship with Inuit: A History of Policy and Program Development*. Ottawa: Department of Indian and Northern Affairs, 2006. http://www.aadnc-aandc.gc.ca/eng/1100100016900/1100100016908.

Bougie, Evelyne. "Aboriginal Peoples Survey, 2006: School Experiences of Off-Reserve First Nations Children Aged 6 to 14." Fact Sheet 2006, no. 3. Statistics Canada, Ottawa, 2009.

Bougie, Evelyne, Karen Kelly-Scott, and Paula Arriagana. "The Education and Employment Experiences of First Nations People Living Off Reserve, Inuit, and Metis: Selected Findings from the 2012 Aboriginal Peoples Survey." Statistics Canada Analytical Paper, catalogue no. 89-653-X–No. 001, November 2013. http://www.statcan.gc.ca/pub/89-653-x/89-653-x-2013001-eng.pdf.

Brennan, Shannon. "Violent Victimization of Aboriginal Women in the Canadian Provinces, 2009," *Juristat*, catalogue no. 85-002-X, Statistics Canada, 2011. http://www.statcan.gc.ca/pub/85-002-x/2011001/article/11439-eng.htm.

British Columbia. Auditor General of British Columbia. *Management of Aboriginal Child Protective Services*. Victoria: Office of the Auditor General of British Columbia, 2008.

British Columbia. Ministry of Children and Family Development. *Aboriginal Children in Care, October 2009 Report*. Ministry of Children and Family Development, Research, Analysis and Evaluation Branch, 2009. http://www.fndirectorsforum.ca/downloads/aboriginal-children-in-care-10-09.pdf.

British Columbia. Ministry of Justice, Corrections Branch. *Strategic Plan 2012–2016: Aboriginal Programs and Relationships.* N.d. Accessed 18 July 2015. http://www.pssg.gov.bc.ca/corrections/docs/AboriginalStratPlan.pdf.

British Columbia. Office of the Provincial Health Officer. *Health, Crime and Doing Time: Potential Impacts of the Safe Streets and Communities Act (Former Bill C-10) on the Health and Well-Being of Aboriginal People in B.C.* Vancouver: Office of the Provincial Health Officer, 2013. http://www.health.gov.bc.ca/pho/pdf/health-crime-2013.pdf.

British Columbia. Tripartite Governance Committee. "Implementing the Vision: Governance of First Nations Health Services in British Columbia." Working paper of the Tripartite Governance Committee. Tripartite First Nations Health Plan, Vancouver. Accessed 27 May 2012. http://www.hc-sc.gc.ca/fniah-spnia/pubs/services/tripartite/vision-eng.php.

Bryce, P. H. *Report on the Indian Schools of Manitoba and the North-West Territories.* Ottawa: Government Printing Bureau, 1907.

Canada. *House of Commons Debates*, 46 Victoria (9 May 1883) 14: 1107–1108.

Canada. *House of Commons Debates*, 39th Parliament, 1st session (3 November, 2006) at 1155. (Bev Oda, Minister of Canadian Heritage and Status of Women).

Canada. *Statement of Apology to Former Students of Residential Schools.* 11 June 2008. http://www.aadnc-aandc.gc.ca/eng/1100100015644/1100100015649.

Canada. "Statement of the Government of Canada on Indian Policy, 1969." Aboriginal Affairs and Northern Development Canada, 1969. https://www.aadnc-aandc.gc.ca/DAM/DAM-INTER-HQ/STAGING/texte-text/cp1969_1100100010190_eng.pdf.

Canada. *Treaties 1 and 2 between Her Majesty the Queen and the Chippewa and Cree Indians of Manitoba and Country Adjacent with Adhesions.* Ottawa: Edmond Cloutier, Queen's Printer and Controller Of Stationery Ottawa, 1957. Rpt. Aboriginal Affairs and Northern Development Canada, *Treaty Texts – Treaty No. 1 and No. 2.* https://www.aadnc-aandc.gc.ca/eng/1100100028664/1100100028665.

Canada. *Treaty 3 between Her Majesty the Queen and the Saulteaux Tribe of the Ojibbeway Indians at the Northwest Angle on the Lake of the Woods with Adhesions.* Ottawa: Roger Duhamel, Queen's Printer and Controller of Stationery, 1966. Rpt. Aboriginal Affairs and Northern Development Canada, *Treaty Texts – Treaty No. 3.* https://www.aadnc-aandc.gc.ca/eng/1100100028675/1100100028679.

Canada. *Treaty 5 between Her Majesty the Queen and the Saulteaux and Swampy Cree Tribes of Indians at Beren's River and Norway House with Adhesions.* Ottawa: The Queen's Printer, 1969. Rpt. Aboriginal Affairs and Northern Development Canada, *Treaty Texts – Treaty No. 5.* https://www.aadnc-aandc.gc.ca/eng/1100100028699/1100100028700.

Canada. *Treaty No. 6 between Her Majesty the Queen and the Plain and Wood Cree Indians and other Tribes of Indians at Fort Carlton, Fort Pitt and Battle River with Adhesions.* Ottawa: Roger Duhamel, Queen's Printer and Controller of Stationery, 1964. Rpt. Aboriginal Affairs and Northern Development Canada, *Treaty Texts – Treaty No. 6.* https://www.aadnc-aandc.gc.ca/eng/1100100028710/1100100028783.

Canada. Aboriginal Affairs and Northern Development Canada. "Backgrounder – Canada's Economic Action Plan 2012: Investing in First Nations On-Reserve Water and Wastewater." Last modified 13 January 2013. http://www.aadnc-aandc.gc.ca/eng/1358080225341/1358080569113.

Canada. Aboriginal Affairs and Northern Development Canada. *Developing a First Nation Education Act: A Blueprint for Legislation*, July 2013. Ottawa: AANDC, 2013. https://www.

aadnc-aandc.gc.ca/DAM/DAM-INTER-HQ-EDU/STAGING/texte-text/fN-Education_blue-print-ebauche_1373053903701_eng.pdf.

Canada. Aboriginal Affairs and Northern Development Canada. "Federal Funding Levels for First Nations K-12 Education." Last modified 22 May 2015. https://www.aadnc-aandc.gc.ca/eng/1349140116208/1349140158945.

Canada. Aboriginal Affairs and Northern Development Canada. *Final Report: Evaluation of First Nations Water and Wastewater Action Plan.* Ottawa: Evaluation, Performance Measurement, and Review Branch, Audit and Evaluation Sector, AANDC, 2013. http://www.aadnc-aandc.gc.ca/DAM/DAM-INTER-HQ-AEV/STAGING/texte-text/ev_wwap_1400003583366_eng.pdf.

Canada. Aboriginal Affairs and Northern Development Canada. *Final Report: Implementation Evaluation of the Enhanced Prevention Focused Approach in Saskatchewan and Nova Scotia for the First Nations Child and Family Services Program.* Ottawa: AANDC, 2013. http://www.aadnc-aandc.gc.ca/DAM/DAM-INTER-HQ-AEV/STAGING/texte-text/ev_sns_1382040083423_eng.pdf.

Canada. Aboriginal Affairs and Northern Development Canada. "First Nations Control of First Nations Education Act: The Case for Legislative Reform." 7 February 2014. https://www.aadnc-aandc.gc.ca/eng/1391788733526/1391788786996.

Canada. Aboriginal Affairs and Northern Development Canada. *Government of Canada Progress Report (2006–2012): With Strong Resolve: Advancing our Relationship with First Nations Peoples and Communities.* Ottawa: Minister of Aboriginal Affairs and Northern Development, 2012.

Canada. Aboriginal Affairs and Northern Development Canada. "Jordan's Principle." Accessed 3 January 2014. http://www.aadnc-aandc.gc.ca/eng/1334329827982/1334329861879.

Canada. Aboriginal Affairs and Northern Development Canada. *Progress Report 2006–2012: with Strong Resolve: Advancing our Relationship with First Nations Peoples and Communities.* Ottawa: AANDC, 2012.

Canada. Aboriginal Affairs and Northern Development Canada. *Report of the Testimonial/Panel Component.* St. Anne's Residential School Reunion and Conference, Fort Albany First Nation, 20 August 1992.

Canada. Aboriginal Affairs and Northern Development Canada. *Summative Evaluation of the Elementary/Secondary Education Program on Reserve.* Ottawa: Evaluation, Performance Measurement, and Review Branch Audit and Evaluation Sector, AANDC, 2012.

Canada. Aboriginal Affairs and Northern Development Canada. "Water." Last modified 3 November 2014. https://www.aadnc-aandc.gc.ca/eng/1100100034879/1100100034883.

Canada. Aboriginal Affairs and Northern Development Canada. *Working Together for First Nations Students: A Proposal for a Bill on First Nations Education, October 2013.* Gatineau, QC: Educational Branch, AANDC. http://www.aadnc-aandc.gc.ca/DAM/DAM-INTER-HQ-EDU/STAGING/texte-text/proposal_1382467600170_eng.pdf.

Canada. Advisory Committee on Northern Development. *Government Activities in the North – 1958.* Ottawa: ACND, 1959.

Canada. Auditor General of Canada. "Chapter 4: First Nations and Family Services Program: Indian and Northern Affairs Canada." In *2008 May Report of the Auditor General of Canada to the House of Commons.* Ottawa: Office of the Auditor General of Canada, 2008. http://www.oag-bvg.gc.ca/internet/docs/aud_ch_oag_200805_04_e.pdf.

Canada. Auditor General of Canada. "Chapter 4: Programs for First Nations on Reserves." In *2011 Status Report of the Auditor General of Canada to the House of Commons*. Ottawa: Office of the Auditor General of Canada, 2011. http://www.oag-bvg.gc.ca/internet/docs/parl_oag_201106_04_e.pdf.

Canada. Auditor General of Canada. *Report of the Auditor General of Canada to the Legislative Assembly of Nunavut: Children, Youth and Family Programs and Services in Nunavut*. Ottawa: Office of the Auditor General of Canada, 2011.

Canada, British Columbia, and First Nations Education Steering Committee. *Education Jurisdiction Framework Agreement*, 5 July 2006.

Canada. Canadian Centre for Justice Statistics. "Family Violence in Canada: A Statistical Profile, 2013" *Juristat*, catalogue no. 85-002-X, Statistics Canada, 2015. http://www.statcan.gc.ca/pub/85-002-x/2014001/article/14114-eng.pdf.

Canada. Canadian Heritage. *2012–2013 Report on Plans and Priorities: Supplementary Tables*. Ottawa: Canadian Heritage, 2012.

Canada. Canadian Heritage. *Aboriginal Languages Initiative (ALI) Evaluation: Final Report*. 26 February 2003. http://publications.gc.ca/collections/Collection/CH34-12-2003E.pdf.

Canada. Canadian Heritage. *Quarterly Financial Report for the Quarter Ending June 30, 2012* Ottawa: Canadian Heritage, 2012. http://www.pch.gc.ca/eng/1345648335518.

Canada. Canadian Heritage. *Summative Evaluation of the Aboriginal Peoples' Program*. Ottawa: Office of the Chief Audit and Evaluation Executive; Evaluation Services Directorate, February 2011.

Canada. Canadian Human Rights Commission. *Protecting Their Rights: A Systemic Review of Human Rights in Correctional Services for Federally Sentenced Women*. 2003. http://www.chrc-ccdp.ca/sites/default/files/fswen.pdf.

Canada. Canadian Human Rights Commission. *Report on Equality Rights of Aboriginal People*. Ottawa: Government of Canada, 2013. http://www.chrc-ccdp.gc.ca/sites/default/files/equality_aboriginal_report.pdf.

Canada. Correctional Service Canada. *Commissioner's Directive: Security Classification and Penitentiary Placement*. Last modified 24 November 2014. http://www.csc-scc.gc.ca/politiques-et-lois/705-7-cd-eng.shtml.

Canada. Correctional Service of Canada. *Evaluation Report: Strategic Plan for Aboriginal Corrections*. Correctional Service of Canada, Evaluation Branch, Policy Sector, 2011. http://www.csc-scc.gc.ca/text/pa/ev-ahl-394-2-49/healing-lodges-eng.shtml.

Canada. Department of Justice. *Multi-Site Survey of Victims of Crime and Criminal Justice Professionals across Canada*. Ottawa: Department of Justice, 2004. http://www.justice.gc.ca/eng/rp-pr/cj-jp/victim/rr05_vic1/rr05_vic1.pdf.

Canada. Evaluation Directorate of Health Canada and Public Health Agency Canada. *Evaluation of the First Nations and Inuit Health Human Resources Program 2008-09 to 2012–13*. Ottawa: Health Canada and Public Health Agency Canada, September 2013. http://www.hc-sc.gc.ca/ahc-asc/alt_formats/pdf/performance/eval/2013-fni-hr-rh-pni-eng.pdf.

Canada. Health Canada. "Aboriginal Head Start on Reserve." Last modified 15 June 2011. http://www.hc-sc.gc.ca/fniah-spnia/famil/develop/ahsor-papa_intro-eng.php.

Canada. Health Canada. "Aboriginal Health Human Resources Initiative." Last modified 19 March 2013. http://www.hc-sc.gc.ca/ahc-asc/activit/strateg/fnih-spni-eng.php.

Canada. Health Canada. *Canada's Food Guides from 1942 to 1992*. Last modified 5 February 2007. http://www.hc-sc.gc.ca/fn-an/food-guide-aliment/context/fg_history-histoire_ga-eng.php.

Canada. Health Canada. "First Nations and Inuit Health." Last modified 19 March 2012. http://www.hc-sc.gc.ca/ahc-asc/activit/strateg/fnih-spni-eng.php#ahhri-irrhs.

Canada. Health Canada. "First Nations, Inuit and Aboriginal Health: Indian Residential Schools Resolution Health Support Program." First Nations and Inuit Health. Last modified 27 May 2015. http://www.hc-sc.gc.ca/fniah-spnia/services/indiresident/irs-pi-eng.php.

Canada. Health Canada. *Pan-Canadian Health Human Resource Strategy, 2007/08 Report*. Ottawa: Health Canada, 2008. http://www.hc-sc.gc.ca/hcs-sss/alt_formats/pdf/pubs/hhrhs/2008-ar-ra-eng.pdf.

Canada. Health Canada. "Summary of Epidemiology of Tuberculosis in First Nations Living On Reserve 2000–2008." First Nations and Inuit Health. Last modified 15 May 2012. http://www.hc-sc.gc.ca/fniah-spnia/pubs/diseases-maladies/_tuberculos/tuberculos-epidemio/index-eng.php.

Canada. House of Commons Standing Committee on Aboriginal Affairs and Northern Development. *Study on the Effectiveness of the Government Alternative Dispute Resolution Process for the Resolution of Indian Residential School Claims*. 38th Parliament, 1st session, Fourth Report, 12 April 2005.

Canada. House of Commons Standing Committee on Justice and Legal Affairs. *Minutes of Proceedings and Evidence*, No. 62, 17 November 1994.

Canada. House of Commons Standing Committee on the Status of Women. *Ending Violence Against Aboriginal Women and Girls: Empowerment – A New Beginning*. December 2011, 41st Parliament, 1st Session.

Canada. House of Commons Standing Committee on the Status of Women. *Interim Report – Call into the Night: An Overview of Violence against Aboriginal Women*. March 2011, 40th Parliament, 3rd Session.

Canada. House of Commons Standing Committee on Violence Against Indigenous Women. *Invisible Women: A Call to Action. A Report on Missing and Murdered Women in Canada*. Ottawa: Queen's Printer, 2014.

Canada. Indian Affairs and Northern Development. *Gathering Strength: Canada's Aboriginal Action Plan*. Ottawa: Minister of Public Works and Government Services, 1997.

Canada. Indian and Northern Affairs Canada. *Evaluation of Community-Based Healing Initiatives Supported through the Aboriginal Healing Foundation*. Ottawa: Indian and Northern Affairs Canada, 2009.

Canada. Indian and Northern Affairs Canada. *First Nation and Inuit Community Well-Being: Describing Historical Trends (1981–2006)*. PowerPoint Presentation. Ottawa: Aboriginal Affairs and Northern Development Canada, 2010. http://www.aadnc-aandc.gc.ca/eng/1100100016600/1100100016641.

Canada. Indian and Northern Affairs Canada. *Implementation Evaluation of the Enhanced Prevention Focused Approach in Alberta for the First Nations Child and Family Services Program*. Ottawa: Evaluation, Performance Measurement, and Review Branch Audit and Evaluation Sector, 2010.

Canada. Indian and Northern Affairs Canada, Departmental Audit and Evaluation Branch. *Evaluation of the First Nations Child and Family Services Program*. Ottawa: Her Majesty the Queen in Right of Canada, 2007.

Canada. Indian Residential Schools Adjudication Secretariat. "Adjudication Secretariat Statistics, From September 19, 2007 to June 30, 2015." http://www.iap-pei.ca/information/stats-eng.php?act=.

Canada. Minister of Indian and Northern Affairs. *Government Response to the Seventh Report of the Standing Committee on Aboriginal Affairs and Northern Development; Aboriginal Housing.* Parliament of Canada, 17 October, 2007. http://www.parl.gc.ca/HousePublications/Publication.aspx?DocId=3077327&Language=E&Mode=1&Parl=39&Ses=1.

Canada. Minister of Justice. "Letter and copy of warrant in reply to a request by Duncan Campbell Scott, Acting Superintendent General of Indian Affairs," 1895. Library and Archives Canada, no. 151-711-10.

Canada. Office of the Auditor General of Canada. *2011 June Status Report of the Auditor General of Canada.* Ottawa: Office of the Auditor General, 2011.

Canada. Office of the Correctional Investigator. *Spirit Matters: Aboriginal People and the Corrections and Conditional Release Act, Final Report.* 22 October 2012. http://www.oci-bec.gc.ca/cnt/rpt/oth-aut/oth-aut20121022-eng.aspx.

Canada. Parliament of Canada. Special Committee on Reconstruction and Re-establishment. *Minutes of Proceedings and Evidence,* No. 9, 24 May 1944.

Canada. Parliament Special Joint Committee of the Senate and House of Commons. *Minutes of Proceedings and Evidence.* Ottawa: King's Printer, 1946.

Canada. Parliament Special Joint Committee of the Senate and House of Commons. *Minutes of Proceedings and Evidence.* Ottawa: King's Printer, 1947.

Canada. Public Health Agency of Canada. *Canadian Incidence Study of Reported Child Abuse and Neglect: Final Report.* Ottawa: Her Majesty the Queen in Right of Canada, 2001.

Canada. Public Health Agency of Canada. *Canadian Incidence Study of Reported Child Abuse and Neglect—2008: Major* Findings. Ottawa: Her Majesty the Queen in Right of Canada, 2010. http://cwrp.ca/sites/default/files/publications/en/CIS-2008-rprt-eng.pdf.

Canada. Public Health Agency of Canada. "Chapter 8: HIV/AIDS among Aboriginal People in Canada." *HIV/AIDS Epi Updates.* Last modified 15 May 2015. http://www.phac-aspc.gc.ca/aids-sida/publication/epi/2010/8-eng.php#a20.

Canada. Public Health Agency of Canada. *Evaluation of the Aboriginal Head Start in Urban and Northern Communities Program at the Public Health Agency of Canada.* 20 March 2012. http://www.phac-aspc.gc.ca/about_apropos/evaluation/reports-rapports/2011-2012/ah-sunc-papacun/index-eng.php#toc.

Canada. Public Health Agency of Canada. "Fetal Alcohol Spectrum Disorder (FASD)." Last modified 29 April 2014. http://www.phac-aspc.gc.ca/hp-ps/dca-dea/prog-ini/fasd-etcaf/index-eng.php.

Canada. Public Safety Canada. *Fetal Alcohol Spectrum Disorder and the Criminal Justice System.* Ottawa: Aboriginal Corrections Policy Unit, 2010. http://www.publicsafety.gc.ca/cnt/rsrcs/pblctns/ftl-lchl-spctrm/ftl-lchl-spctrm-eng.pdf.

Canada. Royal Commission on Aboriginal Peoples. *Bridging the Cultural Divide: Report on Aboriginal People and Criminal Justice in Canada.* Ottawa: Supply and Services, 1996.

Canada. Royal Commission on Aboriginal Peoples. *Report of the Royal Commission on Aboriginal Peoples.* 5 vols. Ottawa: Indian and Northern Affairs, 1996. https://qspace.library.queensu.ca/handle/1974/6874.

Canada. Special Joint Committee of the Senate and House of Commons. *Minutes of Proceedings and Evidence*, No. 1. Ottawa: Edmond Cloutier, 1947. Harriet Irving Archives, University of New Brunswick.

Canada. Standing Committee on Aboriginal Affairs. *"You Took My Talk": Aboriginal Literacy and Empowerment*. Ottawa: Standing Committee on Aboriginal Affairs, 1990.

Canada. Standing Committee on Aboriginal Affairs and Northern Development. *Seventh Report of the Standing Committee on Aboriginal Affairs and Northern Development: Aboriginal Housing*. Parliament of Canada, 2007. http://www.parl.gc.ca/HousePublications/Publication.aspx?DocId=3077327&Language=E&Mode=1&Parl=39&Ses=1.

Canada. Standing Senate Committee on Aboriginal Affairs and Northern Development. *Study and Recommendations of the Standing Senate Committee on Aboriginal Affairs and Northern Development Concerning the Aboriginal Healing Foundation*. Ottawa: Senate Committee Report, 2010.

Canada. Standing Senate Committee on Aboriginal Peoples. *Reforming First Nations Education: From Crisis to Hope*. Ottawa: Senate Committees Directorate, 2011.

Canada. Standing Senate Committee on Aboriginal Peoples. *Sixth Report: Bill S-8, An Act respecting the safety of drinking water on First Nation lands, without amendment, but with observations*. Parliament of Canada, 7 June 2012. http://www.parl.gc.ca/Content/SEN/Committee/411/appa/rep/rep06jun12-e.htm.

Canada. Standing Senate Committee on Legal and Constitutional Affairs. *Language Rights in Canada's North: Nunavut's New Official Languages Act: Final Report*. Ottawa: Senate Committees Directorate, 2009.

Canada. Standing Committee on Public Accounts. *Report of the Standing Committee on Public Accounts. Chapter 4: First Nations Child and Family Services Program—Indian and Northern Affairs Canada of the May 2008 Report of the Auditor General*. Parliament of Canada, 2009. http://www.parl.gc.ca/HousePublications/Publication.aspx?Mode=1&Parl=40&Ses=2&DocId=3731041&File=18.

Canada. Standing Senate Committee on Social Affairs, Science and Technology. *Opening the Door: Reducing Barriers to Post-Secondary Education in Canada*. Ottawa: Senate of Canada, 2011. http://www.parl.gc.ca/content/sen/committee/411/soci/rep/rep06dec11-e.pdf.

Canada. Statistics Canada. *Aboriginal Languages and Selected Vitality Indicators in 2011*. Ottawa: Ministry of Industry, 2014.

Canada. Statistics Canada. *Aboriginal Languages in Canada, Language, 2011 Census of Population*. Catalogue no. 98-314-X2011003, 2011. http://www12.statcan.gc.ca/census-recensement/2011/as-sa/98-314-x/98-314-x2011003_3-eng.pdf.

Canada. Statistics Canada. *Aboriginal Peoples in Canada, First Nations People, Métis and Inuit. National Household Survey, 2011*. Catalogue no. 99-011-X2011001. Ottawa: Minister of Industry, 2013. http://www12.statcan.gc.ca/nhs-enm/2011/as-sa/99-011-x/99-011-x-2011001-eng.pdf.

Canada. Statistics Canada. *Aboriginal Peoples in Canada in 2006: Inuit, Métis and First Nations, 2006 Census*. Ottawa: Minister of Industry, 2009.

Canada. Statistics Canada. *Aboriginal Peoples and Language. National Household Survey (NHS), 2011*. Catalogue no. 99-011-X2011003. Ottawa: Minister of Industry, 2013. http://www12.statcan.gc.ca/nhs-enm/2011/as-sa/99-011-x/99-011-x2011003_1-eng.pdf.

Canada. Statistics Canada. "The Education and Employment Experiences of First Nations People Living off Reserve, Inuit, and Métis: Selected Findings from the 2012 Aboriginal

Peoples Survey." *The Daily*, 25 November 2013. http://www.statcan.gc.ca/daily-quoti-dien/131125/dq131125b-eng.pdf.

Canada. Statistics Canada. *The Educational Attainment of Aboriginal People in Canada, National Household Survey, 2011*. Catalogue no. 99-012-X2011003. Ottawa: Ministry of Industry, 2013. https://www12.statcan.gc.ca/nhs-enm/2011/as-sa/99-012-x/99-012-x-2011003_3-eng.cfm.

Canada. Statistics Canada. *Educational Portrait of Canada, Census Year 2006*. Catalogue no. 97-560-XIE2006001. Ottawa: Ministry of Industry, 2008. http://www12.statcan.ca/cen-sus-recensement/2006/as-sa/97-560/pdf/97-560-XIE2006001.pdf.

Canada. Statistics Canada. "Homicide in Canada, 2013." *The Daily*, 1 December 2014. http://www.statcan.gc.ca/daily-quotidien/141201/dq141201a-eng.pdf.

Canada. Statistics Canada. "Life Expectancy." Last modified 21 June 2010. http://www.stat-can.gc.ca/pub/89-645-x/2010001/life-expectancy-esperance-vie-eng.htm.

Canada. Statistics Canada. "Low Income Lines, 2008–2009." Income Research Paper Series. Catalogue no. 75F0002M—No. 005. 2010. Minister of Industry, 2010. http://www.statcan.gc.ca/pub/75f0002m/75f0002m2010005-eng.pdf.

Canada. Statistics Canada. *Portrait of Canada's Labour Force: National Household Survey, 2011*. Ottawa: Statistics Canada, 2013.

Canada. Statistics Canada. "Study: Aboriginal People and the Labour Market." *The Daily*, 23 November 2011. http://www.statcan.gc.ca/daily-quotidien/111123/dq111123b-eng.htm.

Canada. Statistics Canada. "Study: Life Expectancy in the Inuit-Inhabited Areas of Canada." *The Daily*, 23 January 2008. http://www.statcan.gc.ca/daily-quotidien/080123/dq080123d-eng.htm.

Canada. Statistics Canada. "Study: Select Health Indicators of First Nations People Living off Reserve, Métis and Inuit, 2007 to 2010." *The Daily*, 29 January 2013. http://www.statcan.gc.ca/daily-quotidien/130129/dq130129b-eng.htm.

Canada. Statistics Canada. Table 99-014-039. *2011 National Household Survey: Data Tables*. Statistics Canada, 2011. http://www12.statcan.gc.ca/nhs-enm/2011/dp-pd/dt-td/Dir-eng.cfm#topic-94.

Canada. Statistics Canada. "Victimization and Offending among the Aboriginal Population in Canada." *Juristat* 26, no. 3 (2006). http://www.statcan.gc.ca/pub/85-002-x/85-002-x-2006003-eng.pdf.

Canada. Statistics Canada. "Youth Court Statistics 2011/2012." *The Daily*, 13 June 2013. http://www.statcan.gc.ca/daily-quotidien/130613/dq130613d-eng.pdf.

Canada. Statistics Canada. "Youth Custody and Community Services in Canada, 1998-99." *Juristat* 20, no. 8 (2000). http://www.statcan.gc.ca/pub/85-002-x/85-002-x2000008-eng.pdf.

Canada. Task Force of Federally Sentenced Women. *Creating Choices: Report of the Task Force of Federally Sentenced Women*. Ottawa: Correctional Service of Canada, 1990. http://www.csc-scc.gc.ca/women/toce-eng.shtml.

Canada. Task Force on Aboriginal Languages and Culture. *Towards a New Beginning: A Foundational Report for a Strategy to Revitalize First Nation, Inuit and Métis Languages and Cultures*. Ottawa: Department of Canadian Heritage, 2005.

Canada. Truth and Reconciliation Commission. *Internal Report of the Inuit Sub Commission of the Truth and Reconciliation Commission, Baffin Tour*. N.d.

Canada. Truth and Reconciliation Commission of Canada. *Truth and Reconciliation Commission of Canada: Interim Report.* Winnipeg: Truth and Reconciliation Commission of Canada, 2012.

Canadian Human Rights Commission. *Report on Equality Rights of Aboriginal People.* Ottawa: Government of Canada, 2013.

Davin, Nicholas Flood. *Report on Industrial Schools for Indians and Half-Breeds.* Ottawa: n.p., 1879.

First Nations and Inuit Regional Health Survey National Steering Committee. *First Nations and Inuit Regional Health Survey.* Ottawa: First Nations and Inuit Regional Health Survey, 1999.

Garner, Rochelle, Gisèle Carrière, Claudia Sanmartin, and the Longitudinal Health and Administrative Data Research Team. *The Health of First Nations Living Off-Reserve, Inuit, and Métis Adults in Canada: The Impact of Socio-economic Status on Inequality in Health.* Ottawa: Statistics Canada, 2010. http://www.statcan.gc.ca/pub/82-622-x/82-622-x2010004-eng.pdf.

Glover, Shelly. *2013–2014 Departmental Performance Report.* Ottawa: Canadian Heritage, 2014. http://www.pch.gc.ca/DAMAssetPub/DAM-verEval-audEval/STAGING/texte-text/dpr-rmr-2013-14_1415218344790_eng.pdf.

Government of Canada. *Government of Canada Response to the Report of the Standing Committee on Public Accounts, on Chapter 4, First Nations Child And Family Services Program – Indian And Northern Affairs Canada of the May 2008 Report of the Auditor General.* Parliament of Canada, 19 August 2009. http://www.parl.gc.ca/HousePublications/Publication.aspx?DocId=4017684&Language=E&Mode=1&Parl=40&Ses=2.

Hann, Robert, and William Harman. *Predicting Release Risk for Aboriginal Penitentiary Inmates.* Ottawa: Secretariat of the Ministry of the Solicitor General of Canada, 1993.

Hanson, R. K., and M. T. Bussière. *Predictors of Sexual Offender Recidivism: A Meta-Analysis.* Ottawa: Public Works and Government Services Canada, 1996.

Hume, Sharon, Deborah Rutman, and Carol Hubberstey. *Language Nest Evaluation Report.* Yellowknife: Department of Education, Culture, and Education, May 2006.

King, David. *A Brief Report of the Federal Government of Canada's Residential School System for Inuit.* Ottawa: Aboriginal Healing Foundation, 2006. http://www.ahf.ca/downloads/kingsummaryfweb.pdf.

Law Commission of Canada. *Restoring Dignity: Responding to Child Abuse in Canadian Institutions.* Ottawa: Supply and Services, 2000.

LeBeuf, Marcel-Eugene. *The Role of the Canadian Mounted Police during the Indian Residential School System.* Ottawa: RCMP, 2011.

MacPherson, Patricia, Albert Chudley, and Brian Grant. *Fetal Alcohol Spectrum Disorder (FASD) in a Correctional Population: Prevalence, Screening and Characteristics.* Ottawa: Correctional Service of Canada, 2011. http://www.publicsafety.gc.ca/lbrr/archives/cn21451-eng.pdf.

Manitoba. Aboriginal Justice Implementation Commission. *Report of the Aboriginal Justice Inquiry of Manitoba.* 3 vols. Winnipeg: Aboriginal Justice Implementation Commission, 1999. http://www.ajic.mb.ca/volume.html.

Manitoba. Auditor General of Manitoba. *Follow-up of Our December 2006 Report: Audit of the Child and Family Services Division Pre-Devolution Child in Care Processes and Practices.* Winnipeg: Office of the Auditor General of Manitoba, 2012.

Manitoba. Provincial Court of Manitoba. *Report under the* Fatality Inquiries Act *into the Death of Brian Lloyd Sinclair*. Provincial Court of Manitoba, 12 December 2014. http://www.manitobacourts.mb.ca/site/assets/files/1051/brian_sinclair_inquest_-_dec_14.pdf.

Mazowita, Benjamin, and Marta Burczycka. "Shelters for Abused Women in Canada, 2012." *Juristat*, catalogue no. 85-002-XWF, Statistics Canada, 2014. http://www.statcan.gc.ca/pub/85-002-x/2014001/article/11906-eng.htm.

Moore, John-Patrick. *First Nations, Métis, Inuit and Non-Aboriginal Offenders: A Comparative Profile*. Ottawa: Correctional Service of Canada, Research Branch. 2003.

Mulligan, Leah. "Victim Services in Canada: National, Provincial and Territorial Fact Sheets, 2011/2012." Statistics Canada. Last modified 24 March 2014. http://www.statcan.gc.ca/pub/85-003-x/2014001/part-partie1-eng.htm.

Munch, Christopher. "Youth Correctional Statistics in Canada, 2010/2011." *Juristat,* catalogue no. 85-002-X, Canadian Centre for Justice Statistics, Statistics Canada, 2012. http://www.statcan.gc.ca/pub/85-002-x/2012001/article/11716-eng.pdf.

Munch, Christopher. "Victim Services in Canada, 2009/2010." *Juristat*, catalogue no. 85-002-X, Statistics Canada, 2012. http://www.statcan.gc.ca/pub/85-002-x/2012001/article/11626-eng.htm.

Neegan Burnside Ltd. *National Assessment of First Nations Water and Wastewater Systems: National Roll-Up Report (Final)*. Ottawa: Department of Indian Affairs and Northern Development, April 2011.

Norris, Mary Jane. "Aboriginal Languages in Canada: Emerging Trends and Perspectives on Second Language Acquisition." Statistics Canada, catalogue no. 11-008. *Canadian Social Trends* (May 2007): 19–27.

O'Donnell, Vivian, and Susan Wallace. "First Nations, Métis and Inuit Women." In *Women in Canada: A Gender-Based Statistical Report*. Ottawa: Statistics Canada, 2011.

Oliver, Lisa N., Paul A. Peters, and Dafna E. Kohen. "Mortality Rates among Children and Teenagers Living in Inuit Nunangat, 1994 to 2008." Statistics Canada, catalogue no. 82-003-XPE. *Health Reports* 23, no. 3 (2012). http://www.statcan.gc.ca/pub/82-003-x/2012003/article/11695-eng.pdf.

Ontario. *Ontario's New Approach to Aboriginal Affairs: Prosperous and Healthy Aboriginal Communities Create a Better Future for Aboriginal Children and Youth*. Toronto: Queen's Printer for Ontario, 2005. http://docs.files.ontario.ca/documents/222/6-maa-new-approach-to-aboriginal-affairs.pdf.

Ontario. *A Solid Foundation: Second Progress Report on the Implementation of the Ontario First Nation, Metis and Inuit Education Policy Framework*. Toronto: Queen's Printer for Ontario, 2013. http://edu.gov.on.ca/eng/aboriginal/ASolidFoundation.pdf.

Ontario. Aboriginal Education Office and Ministry of Education. *Ontario First Nation, Métis, and Inuit Education Policy Framework*. Toronto: Queen's Printer for Ontario, 2007. https://www.edu.gov.on.ca/eng/aboriginal/fnmiFramework.pdf.

Ontario. Office of the Chief Coroner of Ontario. *Paediatric Death Review Committee and Deaths Under Five Committee Annual Report 2013*. Toronto: Office of the Chief Coroner of Ontario, 2013. http://www.mcscs.jus.gov.on.ca/stellent/groups/public/@mcscs/@www/@com/documents/webasset/ec163306.pdf.

Ontario. Office of the Chief Coroner of Ontario. "Schedule of Inquests: Jethro Anderson, Reggie Bushie, Robyn Harper, Kyle Morrisseau, Paul Panacheese, Curran Strang, Jordan Wabasse." Ministry of Community Safety and Correctional Services, 9 August 2013. http://

www.mcscs.jus.gov.on.ca/english/DeathInvestigations/office_coroner/ScheduleofInquests/OCC_schedule.htm.

Oppal, Wally T., Commissioner. *Forsaken: The Report of the Missing Women Commission of Inquiry.* 4 vols. Victoria: British Columbia, Missing Women Commission of Inquiry, 2012. http://www.missingwomeninquiry.ca/obtain-report/.

Oreopoulos, Philip. *Canadian Compulsory School Laws and Their Impact on Educational Attainment and Future Earnings.* Catalogue no. 11F0019, no. 251. Ottawa: Family and Labour Studies Division, Statistics Canada, 2005. http://publications.gc.ca/Collection/Statcan/11F-0019MIE/11F0019MIE2005251.pdf.

Perreault, Samuel. "Aboriginal Adults Are Overrepresented in Admissions to Correctional Services." *Admissions to Adult Correctional Services in Canada 2011/2012.* Statistics Canada. Last modified 27 March 2014. http://www.statcan.gc.ca/pub/85-002-x/2014001/article/11918-eng.htm#a5.

Perreault, Samuel. "Aboriginal Youth Are Over-Represented in the Correctional System." *Admissions to Adult Correctional Services in Canada 2011/2012.* Statistics Canada. Last modified 27 March 2014. http://www.statcan.gc.ca/pub/85-002-x/2014001/article/11917-eng.htm#a5.

Perreault, Samuel. "Admissions to Adult Correctional Services in Canada 2011–2012" *Juristat,* catalogue no. 85-002-x, Statistics Canada. Last modified 27 March 2014. http://www.statcan.gc.ca/pub/85-002-x/2014001/article/11918-eng.htm#a5.

Perreault, Samuel. "Admissions to Youth Correctional Services in Canada, 2011/12." *Juristat,* catalogue no. 85-002-x, Statistics Canada. Last modified 27 March 2014. http://www.statcan.gc.ca/pub/85-002-x/2014001/article/11917-eng.htm#a5.

Perreault, Samuel. "Violent Victimization of Aboriginal People in the Canadian Provinces, 2009." *Juristat,* catalogue no. 85-002-x, Statistics Canada, 2011. http://www.statcan.gc.ca/pub/85-002-x/2011001/article/11415-eng.pdf.

Peterson, Katherine. *Sir Joseph Bernier Federal Day School, Turquetil Hall: Investigation Report.* Yellowknife: Government of the Northwest Territories. 1994.

Québec. Commission des droits de la personne et des droits de la jeunesse. *Investigation into Child and Youth Protection Services in Ungava Bay and Hudson Bay. Nunavik: Report, Conclusions of the Investigation and Recommendations.* Montréal: Commission des droits de la personne et des droits de la jeunesse, 2007. http://www.cdpdj.qc.ca/Publications/rapport_Nunavik_anglais.pdf.

Québec. Commission des droits de la personne et des droits de la jeunesse Québec. *Nunavik: Follow-up Report on the Recommendations of the Investigation into Youth Protection Services in Ungava Bay and Hudson Bay.* Montréal: Commission des droits de la personne et des droits de la jeunesse, June 2010.

Québec. *Rapport Parent. Rapport de la Commission royale d'enquête sur l'enseignement dans la province de Québec.* Vol. 3, *L'administration de l'enseignement, part A, Diversité religieuse, culturelle, et unité de l'administration.* Chicoutimi, QC: Publications Québec, 2004. http://classiques.uqac.ca/contemporains/quebec_commission_parent/rapport_parent_4/rapport_parent_vol_4.pdf.

Rajekar, Ashutosh, and Ramnarayanan Mathilakath. *The Funding Requirement for First Nations Schools in Canada.* Ottawa: Office of the Parliamentary Budget Officer, 2009.

Roberts, Barry A. *Eskimo Identification and Disc Numbers: A Brief History.* Ottawa: Social Development Division, Department of Indian and Northern Affairs, 1975.

Royal Canadian Mounted Police. *Missing and Murdered Aboriginal Women: A National Operational Overview*. Ottawa: RCMP, 2014. http://www.rcmp-grc.gc.ca/pubs/mmaw-faap-d-eng.pdf.

Sapers, Howard. "Speaking Notes for Mr. Howard Sapers, Correctional Investigator of Canada: Appearance before the Senate Standing Committee on Legal and Constitutional Affairs," 14 February 2008. Office of the Correctional Investigator. http://www.oci-bec.gc.ca/cnt/comm/sp-all/sp-all20080214-eng.aspx.

Saskatchewan Child Welfare Review Panel. *For the Good of Our Children and Youth: A New Vision, a New Direction*. Regina: Saskatchewan Child Welfare Review Panel, 2010. http://saskchildwelfarereview.ca/CWR-panel-report.pdf.

Saskatchewan. Commission on First Nations and Métis Peoples and Justice Reform. *Legacy of Hope: An Agenda for Change. Final Report from the Commission on First Nations and Métis Peoples and Justice Reform*. Vol. 1. 2008. http://www.justice.gov.sk.ca/justicereform/volume1.shtml.

Shea, Goldie. *Institutional Child Abuse in Canada: Criminal Cases*. Ottawa: Law Commission of Canada, 1999.

Sinha, Maire, ed. "Measuring Violence against Women: Statistical Trends." *Juristat*, catalogue no. 85-002-X, Statistics Canada, 2013. http://www.statcan.gc.ca/pub/85-002-x/2013001/article/11766-eng.pdf.

Sioui, Raymond, and Jacques Thibault. *The Relevance of a Cultural Adaptation of the Reintegration Potential Reassessment Scale (RPRS)*. Ottawa: Correctional Service of Canada, Research Branch, 2001.

Tjepkema, Michael, and Russell Wilkins. "Remaining Life Expectancy at Age 25 and Probability of Survival to Age 75." Statistics Canada, catalogue no. 82-003-XPE. *Health Reports* 22, no. 4 (2011).

Trocmé, Nico, Barbara Fallon, Bruce MacLaurin, Joanne Daciuk, Caroline Felstiner, Tara Black, Lil Tonmyr, Cindy Blackstock, Ken Barter, Daniel Turcotte, and Richard Cloutier. *Canadian Incidence Study of Reported Child Abuse and Neglect—2003: Major Findings*. Ottawa: Minister of Public Works and Government Services Canada, 2005.

Tulloch, Shelley. *Preserving Inuit Dialects in Nunavut: Research Report*. Iqaluit: Office of the Languages Commissioner of Nunavut, 2005.

Western Canadian Protocol for Collaboration in Basic Education. *Common Curriculum Framework for Aboriginal Language and Culture Programs: Kindergarten to Grade 12*. Crown in Right of the Governments of Alberta, British Columbia, Manitoba, Yukon Territory, Northwest Territories, and Saskatchewan, 2000. http://education.alberta.ca/media/929730/abor.pdf.

Willows, Noreen, Paul Veugelers, Kim Raine, and Stefan Kuhle. "Associations between Household Food Insecurity and Health Outcomes in the Aboriginal Population (Excluding Reserves)." Statistics Canada, catalogue no. 82-003-X. *Health Reports* 22, no. 2 (2011). http://www.statcan.gc.ca/pub/82-003-x/2011002/article/11435-eng.htm.

# 5. Legal Sources

## Case Law

*Arishenkoff v. British Columbia*, 2004 BCCA 299 (CanLII).

*Baxter v. Canada (Attorney General)*, 2006 CanLII 41673 (ONSC).

*B(D) v. Canada (Attorney General)*, 2000 SKQB 574(CanLII).

*Beattie v. Canada (Minister of Indian Affairs and Northern Development)*, 1997 CanLII 6343 (FC).

*Bird v. Canada (Attorney General)*, 1999 CanLII 12476 (SKQB).

*Blackwater v. Plint*, 2001 BCSC 997 (Can LII).

*Brown v. Attorney General of Canada*, 2014 ONSC 6967 (CanLII).

*Brown v. Canada*, 2013 ONSC 5637.

*Calder v. Attorney General (BC)*, [1973] SCJ No 56 (SCC).

*Canada (Attorney General) v. Canadian Human Rights Commission*, 2013 FCA 75

*Canada (Attorney General) v. Desjarlais*, 2005 ABQB 416 (CanLII).

*Canada (Attorney General) v. Maracle*, 2012 FC 105 (CanLII).

*Canada (Human Rights Commission) v. Canada (Attorney General)*, 2012 FC 445 (CanLII).

*Canada (Indian Affairs) v. Daniels*, 2014 FCA 101 (CanLII).

*Cloud v. Canada (Attorney General)*, [2001] OJ No 4163.

*Cloud v. Canada (Attorney General)*, [2003] OJ No 2698.

*Cloud v. Canada (Attorney General)*, [2004] OJ No 4924.

*Cloud v. Canada (Attorney General)*, 2004 CanLII 45444 (ONCA).

*C. M. v. Canada (Attorney General)*, 2004 SKQB 175(CanLII).

*Daniels v. Canada*, 2013 FC 6 (CanLII).

*F. H. v. McDougall*, [2008] 3 SCR 41.

*First Nations Child and Family Caring Society v. Canada*, 2011 CHRT 4.

*Fisher v. Canada (Attorney General)*, 1999 CanLII 12781 (SKQB).

*Fontaine v. Canada (Attorney General)*, 2013 SKCA 22.

*Ford v. Quebec (Attorney General)* [1988] 2 SCR 712.

*F. S. M. v. Clarke*, 1999 CanLII 9405 (BCSC).

*Harry Daniels, et al. v. Her Majesty the Queen as represented by The Minister of Indian Affairs and Northern Development, et al.*, 2014 CanLII 68707 (SCC).

*Kelly v. Canada (Attorney General)*, 2013 ONSC 1220.

*M. A. v. Canada (Attorney General)*, [1999] SJ No 538 (SKQB).

*M. C. C. v. Canada*, [2001] OJ No 4163.

*Mitchell v. M. N. R.*, 2001 SCC 33.

*M. M. v. Roman Catholic Church of Canada et al.*, 2001 MBCA 148 (CanLII).

*Ochapowace Indian Band No. 71 v. Canada (Department of Indian Affairs and Northern Development)*, 1998 CanLII 13768 (SK QB).

*Pictou Landing Band Council v. Canada (Attorney General)*, 2013 FC 342 (CanLII).

*P.(W.) v. Canada (Attorney General)*, 1999 SKQB 17 (CanLII).

*Q.(A.) v. Canada (Attorney General)*, 1998 CanLII 13810 (SKQB).

*Quatell v. Attorney General of Canada*, 2006 BCSC 1840.

*Québec c. Commission Scolaire Crie*, 2001 CanLII 20652 (QC CA).

*R. v. Alkenbrack*, 2011 BCPC 424.

*R. v. Armitage,* 2015 ONCJ 64 (CanLII).

*R. v. Badger,* 2013 SKQB 347.

*R. v. Battaja,* 2010 YKTC 145.

*R. v. Boisseneau,* 2006 ONSC 562.

*R. v. Cappo,* 2005 SKCA 134.

*R. v. C. G.,* 2011 NWTSC 47.

*R. v. C. G. O.,* 2011 BCPC 145.

*R. v. Charlie,* 2012 YKTC 5.

*R. v. C. L. K.,* 2009 MBQB 227 (CanLII).

*R. v. Corbiere,* 2012 ONSC 2405.

*R. v. Craft,* 2010 YKTC 127.

*R. v. E. K.,* 2012 BCPC 132.

*R. v. Elias,* 2009 YKTC 59.

*R. v. Frappier* [1990] YJ No 163

*R. v. G(D. M.),* 2006 NSPC 58 (CanLII).

*R. v. George,* 2010 ONSC 6017.

*R. v. Gingell,* [1996] YJ No 52.

*R. v. Gladue,* [1999] 1 SCR 688.

*R. v. Harris,* 2002 BCCA 152.

*R. v. Ipeelee,* 2012 SCC 13.

*R. v. J.E.R.,* 2012 BCPC 103.

*R. v. Jimmie,* 2009 BCCA 215.

*R. v. J. O.,* 2007 QCCQ 716.

*R. v. Joe,* 2005 YKTC 21.

*R. v. J. T.,* 2011 ONSC 7275 (CanLII).

*R. v. Keepness,* 2011 SKQB 293.

*R. v. Klymok,* 2002 ABPC 95.

*R. v. Knowlton,* 2005 ABPC 29 (CanLII).

*R. v. Land,* 2013 ONSC 6526.

*R. v. Leaney,* 2002 BCCA 67.

*R. v. Loring,* 2009 BCCA 166.

*R. v. Makela,* 2006 BCPC 320.

*R. v. McLeod,* 2006 YKTC 118.

*R. v. Mitchell,* [2001] 1 SCR 911.

*R. v. M. L. W.,* 2004 SKPC 90.

*R. v. NB,* 2012 SKPC 99 (CanLII).

*R. v. O'Connor* [1992] BCJ No 2569.

*R. v. O'Connor* [1995] 4 SCR 411.

*R. v. O'Connor,* 1996 CanLII 8458 (BCSC).

*R. v. O'Connor,* 1996 CanLII 8393 (BCCA).

*R. v. O'Connor,* 1997 CanLII 4071 (BCCA).

*R. v. O'Connor,* 1998 CanLII 14987 (BCCA).

*R. v. Ominayak,* 2007 ABQB 442.

*R. v. O. S.,* 2005 BCPC 727.

*R. v. Paulette,* 2010 NWTSC 31 (CanLII).

*R. v. Pauchay,* 2009 SKPC 35.

*R. v. Paulin*, 2011 ONSC 5027.

*R. v. Quash*, 2009 YKTC 54.

*R. v. Renschler*, 2005 MBPC 53233.

*R. v. R. L.*, 2012 MBPC 22.

*R. v. Rossi*, [2011] O.J. No. 4736.

*R. v. Sharkey*, 2011 BCSC 1541.

*R. v. Simon*, 2006 ABPC 21.

*R. v. Smickle*, 2012 ONSC 602.

*R. v. Snake*, [2010] OJ No 5445.

*R. v. Sparrow*, (1990) 1. SCR 1075.

*R. v. Tymiak*, 2012 BCCA 40.

*R. v. Van der Peet*, [1996] 2 SCR 507.

*R. v. Whitehead*, 2008 SKPC 90 (CanLII).

*R. v. W.R.B.*, 2010 MBQB 102.

*R. v. W.R.G.*, 2011 BCPC 330.

*Reference whether "Indians" includes "Eskimo" Inhabitants of the Province of Quebec*, [1939] SCR 104.

*Re Residential Schools*, [2000] AJ No 47 (ABQB).

*R. J. G. v. Canada (Attorney General)*, 2004 SKCA 102 (CanLII).

*St. Catharine's Milling and Lumber Co. v. R.*, 13 SCR 577, 1887 CanLII 3 (SCC).

*T. W. N. A. v. Clarke*, 2001 BCSC 1177 (CanLII).

*United States v. Winans*, 198 U.S. 371, 25 S.Ct. 662 (1905).

*W.(D.) v. Canada (Attorney General)*, 1999 SKQB 187 (CanLII).

## Statutes

*Aboriginal Languages Recognition Act*, CCSM c A1.5.

*An Act Concerning Indians*, Statutes of Canada 1876, chapter 18, section 86.1, reproduced in Venne, *Indian Acts*, 47.

*An Act Concerning Indians*, Statutes of Canada 1927, chapter 98, section 110, reproduced in Venne, *Indian Acts*, 285–287.

*An Act Respecting Indians*, Statutes of Canada 1951, chapter 29, section 113, reproduced in Venne, *Indian Acts*, 350.

*Adoption Act*, CCSM c A2.

*Adoption Act*, RSBC 1996, c 5.

*Adoption Act*, SNL 1999, c A-2.1.

*Canada Health Act*, RSC 1985, c C-6, s 3.

*Charter of the French Language*, RSQ, c C-11, s 97.

*Child and Family Services Act*, RSO 1990, c C-11.

*Child and Family Services Act*, SNWT (Nu) 1997, c 13.

*Child and Family Services Act*, SS 1989-90, c C-7.2.

*Child and Family Services Act*, SY 2008.

*Child and Family Services Authorities Act*, CCSM c C90.

*Child Protection Act*, RSPEI 1988, c C-5.1.

*Child, Youth and Family Enhancement Act*, RSA 2000, c C-12.

*Children and Family Services Act*, SNS 1990, c 5.

*Children and Youth Care and Protection Act*, SNL 2010, c C-12.2.

*Class Actions Act*, SS 2001, c C-12.01.

*Class Actions Act*, SNL 2001, c C-18.1.

*Class Proceedings Act*, CCSM c C-130.

*Class Proceedings Act*, RSBC 1996, c 50.

*Class Proceedings Act*, RSNB 2011, c 125.

*Class Proceedings Act*, SA 2003, c C-16.5.

*Class Proceedings Act*, SNS 2007, c 28.

*Class Proceedings Act*, SO 1992, c 6.

*Consolidation of Inuit Language Protection Act*, SNu 2008, c 17.

*Controlled Drugs and Substances Act*, SC 1996, c 19.

*Corrections and Conditional Release Act*, SC 1992 c 20.

*Corrections and Conditional Release Act*, SOR/92-620.

*Criminal Code of Canada*, RCS 1985 c C-46.

*Criminal Code of Canada*, RCS 1985 c C-46 as amended by SC 1997 c 30.

*Education Act*, SNu 2008, c 15.

*Education Act for Cree, Inuit and Naskapi Native Persons*, RSQ, c I-14 at Part X.

*Family Services Act*, SNB 1980, c F-2.2.

*First Nations Jurisdiction over Education in British Columbia Act*, SC 2006, c 10.

*First Peoples' Heritage, Language and Culture Act*, RSBC 1996, c 147, s 6.

*First Peoples' Heritage, Language and Culture Regulation*, BC Reg 65/2011, s 1.

*Hamilton Health Sciences Corp. v. D. H.*, 2014 ONCJ 603 (CanLII).

*Hamilton Health Sciences Corp. v. D. H.*, 2015 ONCJ 229.

*Harry Daniels, et al. v. Her Majesty the Queen as represented by the Minister of Indian Affairs and Northern Development, et al.*, 2014 CanLII 68707 (SCC).

*Indian Act*, RSC, 1985, c 1–5.

*Indian Act (Amendment to)*, RSC 1927 c 98.

*Limitations Act*, RSA 2000 c L-2.

*Limitations of Actions Act*, RSS 1978 c L-15.

*Limitation of Actions Amendment Act*, S.M. 2002 c 5.

*Mi'kmaq Education Act*, SC 1998, c 24.

*Māori Language Act*, No. 176 of 1987.

*Official Languages Act*, RSNWT 1988, c O-1.

*Official Languages Act*, RSNWT (Nu) 1988, c O-1.

*Official Languages Act*, SNu 2008, c 10.

Public Law No. 101-477, October 30, 1990.

*Regulation respecting the language of instruction of children residing on Indian reserves*, RRQ, c C-11, r 8.

*Safe Drinking Water for First Nations Act*, SC 2013, c 21.

Statutes of Canada (57-58 Vic, cap. 32, 1895), ss. 137–139 under the 11th clause, pages 232–233.

Statutes of Canada (58-59 Vic, 1895), Orders-in-council, Canada, pages liv–lviii: o/c of 10 Nov. 1894, vide *Canada Gazette*, vol. xxviii, page 832.

*Youth Protection Act*, CQLR c P-34.1.

*Yukon Health Act*, SY 2002, c 106, s 5.

## Other

"Affidavit of Phillip Fontaine," in Court File No. 05-CV-294716CP (*Fontaine v. Canada*), 2006.

"Affidavit of Darcy Merkur, sworn July 28," in Court File No. 00-CV-192059CP (*Baxter v. Canada (Attorney General)*), 2006.

"Agreement in Principle," between Canada, the Plaintiffs, the Assembly of First Nations, and the Anglican, Presbyterian, United and Roman Catholic Entities, 10 November 2005. http://www.residentialschoolsettlement.ca/AIP.pdf.

Canada. House of Commons. *Bill C-10: An Act to Enact the Justice for Victims of Terrorism Act and to Amend the State Immunity Act, the Criminal Code, the Controlled Drugs and Substances Act, the Corrections and Conditional Release Act, the Youth Criminal Justice Act, the Immigration and Refugee Protection Act and other Acts.* 41st Parliament, 1st Session, 13 March 2012.

Canada. House of Commons. *Bill C-32: An Act to Enact the Canadian Victims Bill of Rights and to Amend Certain Acts.* 41st Parliament, 2nd Session, 23 April 2015.

British Columbia and First Nations Health Society. *British Columbia Tripartite Framework Agreement on First Nation Health Governance*, 13 October 2011. http://www.pnwbha.org/wp-content/uploads/2011/10/Tripartite-Agreement.pdf.

"Fresh as Amended Statement of Claim," in Court File No. 00-CV-192059 CP (*Baxter v. Canada (Attorney General)*), 2006.

Government of Canada and Merchant Law Group. "Indian Residential Schools Settlement Agreement, Schedule V, Agreement between the Government of Canada and the Merchant Law Group Respecting the Verification of Legal Fees," 20 November 2005. http://www.residentialschoolsettlement.ca/ScheduleV.pdf.

Indian Residential Schools Settlement Agreement, between Canada, the Plaintiffs, the Assembly of First Nations, and the Anglican, Presbyterian, United and Roman Catholic Entities, 8 May 2006. http://www.residentialschoolsettlement.ca/settlement.html.

Indian Residential Schools Settlement Agreement. Official Court Notice, 8 May 2006. http://www.residentialschoolsettlement.ca/settlement.html.

Indian Residential Schools Settlement Agreement. Schedule O-3: "Catholic Entities Church Agreement," 8 May 2006. http://www.residentialschoolsettlement.ca/Schedule_O-3.pdf.

"Joint Factum of the Plaintiffs, Motion for Settlement Approval – Returnable August 29-31 2006," in Court File No. 00-CV-192059CP (*Baxter v. Canada (Attorney General)*), 2006.

*Skogamhallait v. Canada* (VLC-S-S-11366), Notice of Civil Claim. Accessed 7 November 2013. http://www.kleinlyons.com/class/aboriginal-sixties-scoop/Aborginal-Sixties-Scoop-Notice-Civil-Claim.pdf.

"Statement of Claim," in Court File No. 29762 (*Cloud v. Canada (Attorney General)*), 1998.

"Statement of Claim issued 13 June 2000," in Court File No. 00-CV-192059CP (*Baxter v. Canada (Attorney General)*), 2000.

## 6. Other Sources

Canada. "First Nation Child and Family Services: Opportunities for Collaboration and Partnership—Presentation to the Federal, Provincial and Territorial Directors of Child Welfare Working Group." 3 October 2012.

Morrison, Glenn (Policy Manager of the Aboriginal Affairs Directorate in the Citizenship Participation Branch) email to the Truth and Reconciliation Commission. 9 July 2012.

Valcourt, Bernard (Minister of Aboriginal Affairs and Northern Development) to Jean Crowder, MP, 17 April 2014. https://www.documentcloud.org/documents/1150681-letter-to-mp-jean-crowser.html.

# Secondary Sources

## 1. Books

Barkwell, Lawrence J., Leah Dorion, and Audreen Hourie. *Métis Legacy*. Vol. 2, *Michif Culture, Heritage, and Folkways*. Saskatoon: Gabriel Dumont Institute, 2006.

Baskin, Cyndy. *Strong Helpers' Teachings: The Value of Indigenous Knowledges in the Helping Professions*. Toronto: Canadian Scholars' Press, 2011.

Battiste, Marie. *Decolonizing Education: Nourishing the Learning Spirit*. Saskatoon: Purich Publishing, 2013.

Brass, Eleanor. *I Walk in Two Worlds*. Calgary: Glenbow Museum, 1987.

Bryce, P. H. *The Story of a National Crime: An Appeal for Justice to the Indians of Canada*. Ottawa: James Hope and Sons, 1922.

Canadien, Albert. *From Lishamie*. Penticton, BC: Theytus Books, 2010.

Carter, Sarah. *Lost Harvests: Prairie Indian Reserve Farmers and Government Policy*. Montréal and Kingston: McGill-Queen's University Press, 1990.

Davis, Wade. *The Wayfinders: Why Ancient Wisdom Matters in the Modern World*. Toronto: Anansi, 2009.

Dickson, Stewart. *Hey, Monias!: The Story of Raphael Ironstand*. Vancouver: Arsenal Pulp Press, 1993.

Eizenga, Michael, et al. *Class Actions Law and Practice*. 2nd ed. Markham: Lexis Nexis, 2008.

French, Alice. *My Name Is Masak*. Winnipeg: Peguis Publishers, 1977.

Joe, Rita. *Song of Eskasoni: More Poems of Rita Joe*. Charlottetown: Ragweed Press, 1988.

Johnston, Patrick. *Native Children and the Child Welfare System*. Toronto: Lorimer, 1983.

Jones, Craig. *Theory of Class Actions*. Toronto: Irwin Law, 2003.

Kelm, Mary-Ellen. *Colonizing Bodies: Aboriginal Health and Healing in British Columbia 1900–1950*. Vancouver: University of British Columbia Press, 1998.

Knockwood, Isabelle. *Out of the Depths*. New Extended Edition. Lockport, NS: Roseway Publishing, 2001.

MacGregor, Roy. *Chief: The Fearless Vision of Billy Diamond*. Toronto: Viking, 1989.

Miller, Bruce. *The Problem of Justice: Tradition and Law in the Coast Salish World*. Lincoln: University of Nebraska Press, 2001.

Miller, J. R. *Shingwauk's Vision: A History of Native Residential Schools*. Toronto: University of Toronto Press, 1996.

Milloy, John. *A National Crime: The Canadian Government and the Residential School System, 1879 to 1986*. Winnipeg: University of Manitoba Press, 1999.

Milward, David. *Aboriginal Justice and the Charter: Realizing a Culturally Sensitive Interpretation of Legal Rights*. Vancouver: University of British Columbia Press, 2012.

Moran, Bridget. *Stoney Creek Woman: The Story of Mary John*. Vancouver: Arsenal Pulp Press, 1997.

Moseley, Christopher, ed. and Alexandre Nicolas, cart. *UNESCO Atlas of the World's Languages in Danger*. 3rd ed. Paris: UNESCO Publishing, 2010.

Newman, Morton. *Indians of the Saddle Lake Reserve*. Edmonton: Human Resources and Development Council, 1967.

Paquette, Jerry, and Gérald Fallon. *First Nations Education Policy in Canada: Progress or Gridlock?* Toronto: University of Toronto Press, 2010.

Sluman, Norma, and Jean Goodwill. *John Tootoosis: Biography of a Cree Leader*. Winnipeg: Pemmican Publications, 1984.

Vanderburgh, Rosamond M. *The Canadian Indian in Ontario's Social Studies Textbooks, Grades 1 Through 8: A Report Prepared for the University Women's Club of Port Credit, Ontario*. Toronto: Indian-Eskimo Association of Canada. 1970.

Venne, Sharon H., ed. *Indian Acts and Amendments 1868–1975, An Indexed Collection*. Saskatoon: University of Saskatchewan, Native Law Centre, 1981.

Vick-Westgate, Ann. *Nunavik: Inuit-Controlled Education in Arctic Quebec*. Calgary: University of Calgary Press, 2002.

Waldram, James. *The Way of the Pipe: Aboriginal Spirituality and Symbolic Healing in Canadian Prisons*. Peterborough, ON: Broadview Press, 1997.

Wherrett, George Jasper. *The Miracle of Empty Beds: A History of Tuberculosis in Canada*. Toronto: University of Toronto Press, 1977.

Willis, Jane. *Geniesh: An Indian girlhood*. Toronto: New Press, 1973.

## 2. Book Chapters and Journal Articles

Andersen, Chris. "From Nation to Population: The Racialisation of 'Métis' in the Canadian Census." *Nations and Nationalism* 14, no. 2 (2008): 347–368. doi:10.1111/j.1469-8129.2008.00331.x.

Atkins, Scott. "Racial Segregation, Concentrated Disadvantage, and Violent Crime" *Journal of Ethnicity in Criminal Justice* 7 (2009): 30–52.

Atwood, Barbara. "The Voice of the Indian Child: Strengthening the Indian Child Welfare Act Through Children's Participation." *Arizona Law Review* 50, no. 1 (2008): 127–156.

Basic, Christine. "Termination of Parental Rights: An Overview of the Indian Child Welfare Act of 1978." *Contemporary Legal Issues* 16 (2007): 345–349.

Belles, Stefan, et al. "Parental Problem Drinking Predicts Implicit Alcohol Expectancy in Adolescents and Young Adults." *Addictive Behaviors* 36, no. 11 (2011): 1091–1094.

Bennett, Trevor, Katie Holloway, and David Farrington. "The Statistical Association between Drug Misuse and Crime: A Meta-Analysis." *Aggression & Violent Behavior* 13 (2008): 107–118.

Benoit, Cecilia, Dena Carroll, and Munaza Chaudhry. "In Search of a Healing Place: Aboriginal Women in Vancouver's Downtown Eastside." *Social Science and Medicine* 56 (2003): 821–833.

Blackstock, Cindy. "First Nations Child and Family Services: Restoring Peace and Harmony in First Nations Communities." In *Child Welfare: Connecting Research, Policy and Practice*, edited by Kathleen Kufeldt and Brad McKenzie, 331–342. Waterloo, ON: Wilfrid Laurier Press.

Blanchette, Kelley, and Kelly Taylor. "Development and Validation of a Security Reclassification Scale for Women." *Forum on Corrections Research* 16, no. 1 (2004): 28–30.

Bonta, James. "Native Inmates: Institutional Response, Risk, and Needs." *Canadian Journal of Criminology* 31, no. 1 (1989): 49–62.

Bonta, James, Carol LaPrairie, and Suzanne Wallace-Capretta. "Risk Prediction and Re-Offending: Aboriginal and Non-Aboriginal Offenders." *Canadian Journal of Criminology* 39, no. 2 (1997): 127–144.

Bonta, James, Stan Lipinski, and Michael Martin. "The Characteristics of Aboriginal Recidivists." *Canadian Journal of Criminology* 34, nos. 3 and 4 (1992): 517–522.

Bonesteel, Sarah. "Use of Traditional Inuit Culture in the Policies and Organization of the Government of Nunavut." *Orality: Orality in the 21st Century: Inuit Discourse and Practices: Proceedings of the 15th Inuit Studies Conference*, edited by Béatrice Collignon, Michèle Therrien, and Florence Duchemin-Pelletier. Paris: INALCO-CERLOM, 2009. http://inuito-ralityconference.com/art/Bonesteel.pdf.

Borrows, John. "Residential Schools, Respect and Responsibilities for Past Harms." *University of Toronto Law Journal* 64, no. 4 (2014): 486–504.

Bougie, Evelyne, and Sacha Senécal. "Registered Indian Children's School Success and Intergenerational Effects of Residential Schooling in Canada." *International Indigenous Policy Journal* 1, no. 1 (2010): 1–41. http://ir.lib.uwo.ca/iipj/vol1/iss1/5.

Brown, Jason, et al. "Housing for Aboriginal Ex-Offenders in the Urban Core." *Qualitative Social Work* 7, no. 2 (2008): 238–253.

Burton, David. "Male Adolescents: Sexual Victimization and Subsequent Sexual Abuse." *Adolescent Social Work Journal* 20, no. 4 (2003): 277–296.

Campbell, Justine, and Tian Oei. "A Cognitive Model for the Intergenerational Transference of Alcohol Use Behavior." *Addictions Behavior* 35, no. 2 (2010): 73–83.

Canadian Medical Association. "Aboriginal Health Programming under Siege, Critics Charge." *Canadian Medical Association Journal* 184, no. 14 (2012): E739–E740.

Carrière, Jeannine, and Cathy Richardson. "From Longing to Belonging: Attachment Theory. Connectedness, and Indigenous Children in Canada." In *Passion for Action in Child and Family Services: Voices from the Prairies*, edited by Sharon McKay, Don Fuchs, and Ivan Brown, 49–68. Regina: Canadian Plains Research Centre, 2009.

Carr-Stewart, Sheila. "A Treaty Right to Education." *Canadian Journal of Education* 26, no. 2 (2001): 125–143.

Case, Patricia. "The Relationship of Race and Criminal Behavior: Challenging Cultural Explanations for a Structural Problem." *Critical Sociology* 34, no. 2 (2008): 213–238.

Chandler, Michael J., and Christopher Lalonde. "Cultural Continuity as a Hedge against Suicide in Canada's First Nations." *Transcultural Psychiatry* 35, no. 2 (1998): 191–219.

Chartrand, Larry. "Aboriginal Youth and the Criminal Justice System." In *Understanding Youth Justice in Canada*, edited by Kathryn Campbell, 313–335. Toronto: Pearson Education Canada, 2004.

Chartrand, Larry N. "Métis Residential School Participation: A Literature Review." In *Métis History and Experience and Residential Schools in Canada*, edited by Larry N. Chartrand, Tricia E. Logan, and Judy D. Daniels, 5–55. Ottawa: Aboriginal Healing Foundation, 2006.

Clement, John. "University Attainment of the Registered Indian Population, 1981–2006: A Cohort Approach." In *Aboriginal Education: Current Crisis and Future Alternatives*, edited by Jerry P. White et al., 69–106. Toronto: Thompson Educational Publishing, 2009.

Cornell, Stephen, and Joseph Kalt. "Reloading the Dice: Improving the Chances for Economic Development on American Indian Reservations." In *What Can Tribes Do? Strategies and Institutions in American Indian Economic Development*, edited by Stephen Cornell and Joseph Kalt, 1–59. Los Angeles: American Indian Studies Center, 1992.

Cradock, Gerald. "Extraordinary Costs and Jurisdictional Disputes." In *Wen: De: We Are Coming to the Light of Day*, by First Nations Child & Family Caring Society of Canada, 178–207. Ottawa: First Nations Child & Family Caring Society of Canada, 2005.

Craib, Kevin, et al. "Risk Factors for Elevated HIV Incidence among Aboriginal Injection Drug Users in Vancouver." *Canadian Medical Association Journal* 168, no. 1 (2003): 19–24.

Cross, Suzanne. "Indian Family Exception Doctrine: Still Losing Children Despite the Indian Child Welfare Act." *Child Welfare* 85, no. 4 (2006): 671–690.

Crutcher, Nicole, and Shelley Trevethan. "An Examination of Healing Lodges for Aboriginal Offenders in Canada." *Forum on Corrections Research* 14, no. 3 (2002): 52–54.

DeGue, Sarah, and Cathy Spatz Widom. "Does Out-Of-Home Placement Mediate the Relationship Between Child Maltreatment and Adult Criminality?" *Child Maltreatment* 14, no. 4 (2009): 344–355.

Dunlap, Eloise, et al. "Mothers and Daughters: The Intergenerational Reproduction of Violence and Drug Use in Home and Street Life." *Journal of Ethnicity in Substance Abuse* 3, no. 2 (2004): 1–24.

Eitle, David, Stewart D'Alessio, and Lisa Stolzenberg. "Economic Segregation, Race, and Homicide." *Social Science Quarterly* 87, no. 3 (2006): 638–657.

Filbert, Katherine, and Robert Flynn. "Developmental and Cultural Assets and Resilient Outcomes in First Nations Young People in Care: An Initial Test of an Explanatory Model." *Children and Youth Services Review* 32, no. 4 (2010): 560–564.

Fontaine, Lorena Sekwan. "Re-conceptualizing and Re-imagining Canada: Opening Doors for Aboriginal Language Rights." In *Languages, Constitutionalism and Minorities: Proceedings of a Conference Held at the University of Ottawa, Nov. 12–13, 2004*, edited by André Braën, Pierre Foucher, and Yves Le Bouthillier. Markham, ON: LexisNexis Canada Inc., 2006.

Gonzalez-Mena, Janet. "Cross-Cultural Infant Care and Issues of Equity and Social Justice." *Contemporary Issues in Early Childhood* 2, no. 3 (2001): 368–371.

Graburn, Nelson. "Severe Child Abuse among the Canadian Inuit." In *Child Survival: Anthropological Perspectives on the Treatment and Maltreatment of Children*, edited by Nancy Scheper-Hughes, 211–225. Dordrecht, Holland: D. Reidel Publishing, 1987.

Graham, Lorie M. "Reparations, Self-Determination and the Seventh Generation." In *Facing the Future: The Indian Child Welfare Act at 30*, edited by Matthew Fletcher, Wenona Singel, and Kathryn Fort, 110–126. East Lansing: Michigan State University, 2009.

Green, Ross Gordon. "Aboriginal Community Sentencing and Mediation: Within and Without the Circle." *Manitoba Law Journal* 25, no. 1 (1997–1998): 77–126.

Gresko [Kennedy], Jacqueline. "Everyday Life at Qu'Appelle Industrial School." In *Western Oblate Studies 2/Études oblates de l'ouest 2: Proceedings of the Second Symposium on the History of the Oblates in Western and Northern Canada*, edited by Raymond Huel, 71–113. Lewiston, NY: Edwin Mellen Press, 1992.

Gustafson, Kaaryn. "The Criminalization of Poverty." *Journal of Criminal Law & Criminology* 99, no. 3 (2009): 643–716.

Hallett, Darcy, Michael J. Chandler, and Christopher E. Lalonde. "Aboriginal Language Knowledge and Youth Suicide." *Cognitive Development* 22, no. 3 (2007): 392–399.

Handley, Elizabeth, and Laurie Chassin. "Intergenerational Transmission of Alcohol Expectancies in a High-Risk Sample." *Journal of Studies on Alcohol & Drugs* 70, no. 5 (2009): 675–682.

Heckbert, Doug, and Douglas Turkington. "Turning Points: Factors Related to the Successful Reintegration of Aboriginal Offenders." *Forum on Correctional Research* 14, no. 3 (2002): 55–57.

Hirschel, David, Ira Hutchinson, and Meaghan Shaw. "The Interrelationship between Substance Abuse and the Likelihood of Arrest, Conviction, and Re-Offending in Cases of Intimate Partner Violence." *Journal of Family Violence* 25, no. 1 (2010): 81–90.

Hobart, Charles. "Report on Canadian Arctic Eskimos: Some Consequences of Residential Schooling." *Journal of American Indian Education* 7, no. 2 (1968): 7–17.

Holsinger, A. M., C. T. Lowenkamp, and E. J. Lotessa. "Ethnicity, Gender, and the Level of Service Inventory – Revised." *Journal of Criminal Justice* 31, no. 4 (2003): 309–320.

Hooghe, Marc, et al. "Unemployment, Inequality, Poverty and Crime: Spatial Distribution Patterns of Criminal Acts in Belgium, 2001–06." *British Journal of Criminology* 51, no. 1 (2011): 1–20.

Howe, Brian. "Children's Rights as Crime Prevention." *International Journal of Children's Rights* 16, no. 4 (2008): 457–474.

Jackson, Michael. "Locking up Natives in Canada." *UBC Law Review* 23 (1988–89): 215–230.

Jiwa, Ashifa, Len Kelly, and Natalie St. Pierre-Hansen. "Healing the Community to Heal the Individual: Literature Review of Aboriginal Community-Based Alcohol and Substance Abuse Programs." *Canadian Family Physician* 54, no. 7 (2008): 1000.e.1–1000.e7.

Karmali, Shahzeer, et al. "Epidemiology of Severe Trauma among Status Aboriginal Canadians: A Population-Based Study." *Canadian Medical Association Journal* 172, no. 8 (2005): 1005–1011.

Kerr, David, et al. "Intergenerational Influences on Early Alcohol Use: Independence from the Problem Behavior Pathway." *Development & Psychopathology* 24, no. 3 (2012): 889–901.

Kirkness, Verna. "Aboriginal Education in Canada: A Retrospective and a Prospective." *Journal of American Indian Education* 39, no. 1 (1999): 14–30.

Laliberté, Arlene, and Michel Tousignant. "Alcohol and Other Contextual Factors of Suicide in Four Aboriginal Communities of Quebec, Canada." *Crisis: The Journal of Crisis Intervention and Suicide Prevention* 30, no. 4 (2009): 215–221.

LaPrairie, Carol. "Aboriginal Crime and Justice: Explaining the Present, Exploring the Future." *Canadian Journal of Criminology* 34 (1992): 281–298.

Lecompte, Emily. "Aboriginal Health Human Resources: A Matter of Health." *Journal of Aboriginal Health* 8, no. 2 (2012): 16–22.

Leitch, David. "Canada's Native Languages: The Right of First Nations to Educate their Children in their Own Languages." *Constitutional Forum* 15, no. 1 (2006): 107–120.

Logan, Tricia E. "Lost Generations: The Silent Métis of the Residential School System Revised Interim Report." In *Métis History and Experience and Residential Schools in Canada*, edited by Larry N. Chartrand, Tricia E. Logan, and Judy D. Daniels, 58–93. Ottawa: Aboriginal Healing Foundation, 2006.

Looman, Jan, and Jeffrey Abracen. "Substance Abuse among High-Risk Sexual Offenders: Do Measures of Lifetime History of Substance Abuse Add to the Prediction of Recidivism over Actuarial Risk Assessment Instruments?" *Journal of Interpersonal Violence* 26, no. 4 (2011): 683–700.

Martin, Monica, et al. "The Enduring Significance of Racism: Discrimination and Delinquency Among Black American Youth." *Journal of Research on Adolescence* 21, no. 3 (2010): 662–676.

McCloskey, Laura, and Jennifer Bailey. "The Intergenerational Transmission of Risk for Sexual Abuse." *Journal of Interpersonal Violence* 15, no. 10 (2000): 1019–1035.

McCue, Harvey, "An Overview of Federal and Provincial Policy Trends in First Nations Education." In *The New Agenda: A Manifesto for First Nations Education in Ontario*, edited by Chiefs in Ontario. Ontario: Chiefs in Ontario, 2004. http://www.chiefs-of-ontario.org/sites/default/files/files/An%20Overview%20of%20Federal%20and%20Provincial%20Policy%20Trends%20in%20First%20Nations%20Education.pdf.

McIvor, Onowa, Art Napoleon, and Kerissa M. Dickie. "Language and Culture as Protective Factors for At-Risk Communities." *Journal of Aboriginal Health* (November 2009): 6–25.

Meyercook, Fiona, and Diane Labelle. "Namaji: Two-Spirit Organizing in Montreal, Canada." *Journal of Gay and Lesbian Social Services* 16, no. 1 (2003): 29–51. doi:10.1300/J041v16n01_02.

Moore, Shelby. "Understanding the Connection Between Domestic Violence, Crime, and Poverty: How Welfare Reform May Keep Battered Women from Leaving Abusive Relationships." *Texas Journal of Women & Law* 12 (2003): 451–484.

Moran, Mayo. "The Role of Reparative Justice in Responding to the Legacy of Indian Residential Schools." *University of Toronto Law Journal* 64 (2014): 529–565.

Nicholas, Andrea Bear. "Canada's Colonial Mission: The Great White Bird." In *Aboriginal Education in Canada: A Study in Decolonization*, edited by K. P. Binda and Sharilyn Calliou, 9–33. Mississauga, ON: Canadian Educators' Press, 2001.

Pearce, Margo, et al. "The Cedar Project: Historical Trauma and Vulnerability to Sexual Assault Among Young Aboriginal Women who use Illicit Drugs in Two Canadian Cities." *Violence Against Women* 21, no. 3 (2015): 313–329.

Penney, Chris. "Formal Educational Attainment of Inuit in Canada, 1981–2006." In *Aboriginal Education: Current Crisis and Future Alternatives*, edited by Jerry P. White et al., 33–47. Toronto: Thompson Educational Publishing, 2009.

Petten, Cheryl. "New Healing Lodge Opens for Offenders." *Saskatchewan Sage* 7, no. 11 (2003): 1.

Phillips, Lindsay. "Substance Abuse and Prison Recidivism: Themes from Qualitative Interviews." *Journal of Addictions & Offender Counseling* 31, no. 1 (2010): 10–24.

Pintarics, Joe, and Karen Sveinunggaard. "Meenoostahtan Minisiwin: First Nations Family Justice 'Pathways to Peace.'" *The First Peoples Child and Family Review* 2, no. 1 (2005): 67–88.

Pizarro, Jesenia, and Jean Marie McGloin. "Explaining Gang Homicides in Newark, New Jersey: Collective Behavior or Social Disorganization?" *Journal of Criminal Justice* 34, no. (2006): 195–207.

Preston, Jane P., Michael Cottrell, Terrance R. Pelletier, and Joseph V. Pearce. "Aboriginal Early Childhood Education in Canada: Issues of Context." *Journal of Early Childhood Research* 10, no. 1 (2012): 3–18.

Pridemore, William Alex. "A Methodological Addition to the Cross-National Empirical Literature on Social Structure and Homicide: A First Test of the Poverty-Homicide Thesis." *Criminology* 46, no. 1 (2008): 133–154.

Purvin, Diane. "Weaving a Tangled Safety Net: The Intergenerational Legacy of Domestic Violence and Poverty." *Violence Against Women* 9, no. 10 (2003): 1263–1277.

Regan, Paulette. *Unsettling the Settler Within: Indian Schools, Truth Telling and Reconciliation in Canada.* Vancouver: University of British Columbia Press, 2010.

Richardson, Cathy. "Métis Experiences of Social Work Practices." In *Walking This Path Together: Anti Racist and Anti Oppressive Child Welfare Practice*, edited by Jeannine Carrière and Susan Strega. Winnipeg: Fernwood Publishing, 2009.

Richardson, Cathy, and Bill Nelson. "A Change of Residence: Government Schools and Foster Homes as Sites of Forced Aboriginal Assimilation—A Paper Designed to Provoke Thought and Systemic Change." *First Peoples Review* 3, no. 2 (2007): 75–83.

Richardson, Cathy, and Dana Seaborn. "Working with Métis Children and Their Families." *The BC Counsellor* 24, no. 2 (2002): 47–51.

Roach, Kent. "Blaming the Victim: Canadian Law, Causation and Residential Schools." *University of Toronto Law Journal* 64 (2014): 566–595.

Rudin, Johnathan. "Incarceration of Aboriginal Youth in Ontario 2004 to 2006: The Crisis Continues." *Criminal Law Quarterly* 53 (2007): 260–272.

Ruiz-Casares, Mónica, Nico Trocmé, and Barbara Fallon. "Supervisory Neglect and Risk of Harm: Evidence from the Canadian Child Welfare System." *Child Abuse & Neglect* 36, no. 6 (2012): 471–480.

Ryan, Joseph, and Mark Testa. "Child Maltreatment and Juvenile Delinquency: Investigating the Role of Placement and Placement Instability." *Children & Youth Services Review* 27 (2005): 227–249.

Ryan, Joseph, et al. "Juvenile Delinquency in Child Welfare: Investigating Group Home Effects" *Children & Youth Services Review* 30 (2008): 1088–1099.

Sabates, Ricardo. "Educational Attainment and Juvenile Crime: Area-Level Evidence Using Three Cohorts of Young People." *British Journal of Criminology* 48 (2008): 395–409.

Scott, Duncan Campbell. "Indian Affairs 1867–1912." In *Canada and Its Provinces: A History of the Canadian People and Their Institutions*, vol. 7, edited by A. Shortt and A. Doughty. Glasgow: Brook and Company, 1914.

Ship, Susan Judith, and Laura Norton. "HIV/AIDS and Aboriginal Women in Canada: A Case Study." *Canadian Woman Studies* 21, no. 2 (2001): 25–31.

Sinha, Vandna, and Anna Kozlowski. "The Structure of Aboriginal Child Welfare in Canada." *International Indigenous Policy Journal* 4, no. 2 (2013): 1–21. http://ir.lib.uwo.ca/iipj/vol4/iss2/2.

Sinha, Vandna, Stephen Ellenbogen, and Nico Trocmé. "Substantiating Neglect of First Nations and Non-Aboriginal Children." *Child and Youth Services Review* 35, no. 12 (2013): 2080–2090.

Slattery, Brian. "Making Sense of Aboriginal and Treaty Rights." *Canadian Bar Review* 79 (2000): 196–224.

Smylie, Janet, Deshayne Fell, and Arne Ohlsson. "A Review of Aboriginal Infant Mortality Rates in Canada: Striking and Persistent Aboriginal/Non-Aboriginal Inequities." *Canadian Journal of Public Health* 101, no. 2 (2010): 143–148.

Sousa, Cindy, et al. "Longitudinal Study on the Effects of Child Abuse and Children's Exposure to Domestic Violence, Parent-Child Attachments, and Antisocial Behavior in Adolescence." *Journal of Interpersonal Violence* 26, no. 1 (2011): 111–136.

Spano, Richard, Joshua D. Frielich, and John Bolland. "Gang Membership, Gun Carrying, and Employment: Applying Routine Activities Theory to Explain Violent Victimization among Inner City, Minority Youth Living in Extreme Poverty." *Justice Quarterly* 25, no. 2 (2008): 381–410.

Stanley, George F. G. "Alberta's Half-Breed Reserve Saint-Paul-des Métis 1896–1909." In *The Other Natives: The Metis,* vol. 2, edited by A. S. Lussier and D. B. Sealey, 75–107. Winnipeg: Manitoba Metis Federation Press, 1978.

Streissguth, Ann, Fred Bookstein, Helen Barr, Kieran O'Malley, and Julia Kogan Young. "Risk Factors for Adverse Life Outcomes in Fetal Alcohol Syndrome and Fetal Alcohol Effects." *Developmental and Behavioral Pediatrics* 25, no. 4 (2004): 228–238.

Thornberry, Terence, Marvin Krohn, and Adrienne Freeman-Gallant. "Intergenerational Roots of Early Onset Substance Abuse." *Journal of Drug Issues* 36, no. 1 (2006): 1–28.

Totten, Mark. "Aboriginal Youth and Violent Gang Involvement in Canada: Quality Prevention Strategies." *IPC Review* 3 (March 2009): 135–156. http://www.reginapolice.ca/gang/publications/IPC%20Review%203%20-%20Totten.pdf.

Tripodi, Stephen, and Kimberly Bender. "Substance Abuse Treatment for Juvenile Offenders: A Review of Quasi-Experimental and Experimental Research." *Journal of Criminal Justice* 39 (2011): 246–252.

Turpel-Lafond, Mary Ellen, and Patricia Monture-Angus. "Aboriginal Peoples and Canadian Criminal Law: Rethinking Justice." Special Edition on Aboriginal Justice. *UBC Law Review* (1992): 239–279.

Walsh, Tamara. "Is Corrections Correcting?: An Examination of Prisoner Rehabilitation Policy and Practice in Queensland." *Australian and New Zealand Journal of Criminology* 39, no. 1 (2006): 109–133.

Welsh, Andrew, and James P. Ogloff. "Full Parole and the Aboriginal Experience: Accounting for the Racial Discrepancies in the Release Rates." *Canadian Journal of Criminology* 42, no. 4 (2000): 469–491.

Wilk, Piotr, Jerry P. White, and Éric Guimond. "Métis Educational Attainment." In *Aboriginal Education: Current Crisis and Future Alternatives,* edited by Jerry P. White et al., 49–67. Toronto: Thompson Educational Publishing, 2009.

Young, T. Kue. "Review of Research on Aboriginal Populations in Canada: Relevance to Their Health Needs." *British Journal of Medicine* 327, no. 7412 (2003): 419–422.

Zellerer, Evelyn. "Culturally Competent Programs: The First Family Violence Program for Aboriginal Men in Prison." *The Prison Journal* 83, no. 2 (2003): 171–190.

## 3. Published Papers and Reports

Aboriginal Healing Foundation. *The 2009 Annual Report of the Aboriginal Healing Foundation.* Ottawa: AHF. Accessed 12 January 2012. http://www.ahf.ca/downloads/annual-report-2010.pdf.

Aboriginal Healing Foundation. *The 2014 Annual Report of the Aboriginal Healing Foundation*. Ottawa: AHF. Accessed 13 May 2015. http://www.ahf.ca/downloads/2014-annual-report-english.pdf.

Aboriginal Healing Foundation. *Mental Health Profiles for a Sample of British Columbia's Aboriginal Survivors of the Canadian Residential School System*. Ottawa: AHF, 2003.

Alberta Centre for Child, Family and Community Research. *A Preliminary Analysis of Mortalities in the Child Intervention System in Alberta*. Edmonton: Government of Alberta, 2014. http://www.humanservices.alberta.ca/documents/accfcr-analysis-mortalities.pdf.

Allan, Billie, and Janet Smylie. "First Peoples, Second Class Treatment: The Role of Racism in the Health and Well-Being of Indigenous peoples in Canada." Discussion paper. The Wellesley Institute, Toronto, 2015. http://www.wellesleyinstitute.com/wp-content/uploads/2015/02/Report-First-Peoples-Second-Class-Treatment-Feb-2015.pdf.

Amnesty International. *No More Stolen Sisters: The Need for a Comprehensive Response to Discrimination and Violence Against Indigenous Women in Canada*. London: AMI Publications, 2006.

Anaya, James (Former United Nations Special Rapporteur on the Rights of Indigenous People). "Statement upon Conclusion of the Visit to Canada, 15 October 2013." http://unsr.jamesanaya.org/statements/statement-upon-conclusion-of-the-visit-to-canada.

Archibald, Linda. *Final Report of the Aboriginal Healing Foundation*. Vol. 3, *Promising Healing Practices in Aboriginal Communities*. Ottawa: Aboriginal Healing Foundation, 2006.

Assembly of First Nations. *Breaking the Silence: An Interpretive Study of Residential School Impact and Healing as Illustrated by the Stories of First Nation Individuals*. Ottawa: Assembly of First Nations, 1994.

Assembly of First Nations. "Early Childhood Education in First Nations Communities." AFN Fact sheet. Chiefs Assembly on Education, Gatineau, QC, 1 – 3 October 2012. http://www.afn.ca/uploads/files/events/fact_sheet-ccoe-5.pdf.

Assembly of First Nations. "Language and Culture." AFN Fact sheet. Chiefs Assembly on Education, Gatineau, QC, 1 – 3 October 2012. http://www.afn.ca/uploads/files/events/fact_sheet-ccoe-10.pdf.

Assembly of First Nations. *Report on Canada's Dispute Resolution Plan to Compensate for Abuses in Indian Residential Schools*. Ottawa: Assembly of First Nations, 2004.

Assembly of First Nations. *Royal Commission on Aboriginal Peoples at 10 Years: A Report Card*. Ottawa: Assembly of First Nations, 2006. http://www.turtleisland.org/resources/afnrcap2006.pdf.

Assembly of First Nations. *Submission: Bill C-10 Safe Streets and Communities Act*. 22 November 2011. http://www.afn.ca/uploads/files/parliamentary/billc-10.pdf.

Australia. Council of Australian Governments. *National Indigenous Reform Agreement (Closing the Gap)*. Council of Australian Governments, 2012. http://www.federalfinancialrelations.gov.au/content/npa/health_indigenous/indigenous-reform/national-agreement_sept_12.pdf.

Australian Government. *Closing the Gap: Prime Minister's Report, 2015*. Commonwealth of Australia, 2015. http://www.dpmc.gov.au/sites/default/files/publications/Closing_the_Gap_2015_Report_0.pdf.

Barlow, J. Kevin. *Residential Schools, Prisons and HIV/AIDS among Aboriginal Peoples in Canada: Exploring the Connections*. Ottawa: Aboriginal Healing Foundation, 2009.

Blackstock, Cindy, Terry Cross, John George, Ivan Brown, and Jocelyn Formsma. *Reconciliation in Child Welfare: Touchstones of Hope for Indigenous children, Youth, and Families*. Ottawa: First Nations Child & Family Caring Society of Canada; Portland, OR: National Indian Child Welfare Association, 2006. http://cwrp.ca/sites/default/files/publications/en/Touchstones_of_Hope.pdf.

Blumenthal, Anne, and Vandna Sinha. "Newfoundland and Labrador's Child Welfare System." Information Sheet #130E. Canadian Child Welfare Research Portal, August 2014. http://cwrp.ca/sites/default/files/publications/en/NL_final_infosheet_0.pdf.

Boyer, Yvonne. "Aboriginal Health: A Constitutional Rights Analysis." NAHO Discussion Paper Series, no. 1, June 2003. http://www.naho.ca/documents/naho/english/publications/DP_rights.pdf.

Boyer, Yvonne. "The International Right to Health for Indigenous Peoples in Canada." NAHO Discussion Paper Series, no. 3, September 2004. http://www.naho.ca/documents/naho/english/pdf/aboriginal_health_paper3.pdf.

Caldwell, George. *Indian Residential Schools: A Research Study on the Child Care Programs of Nine Residential Schools in Saskatchewan*. Ottawa: The Canadian Welfare Council, 1967.

Canadian Bar Association. *Resolution 00-04-A*, carried as amended by the Council of the Canadian Bar Association, Annual Meeting, Halifax, NS, 19–20 August 2000. http://www.cba.org/cba/sections_abor/main/00_04_a.aspx.

Canadian Bar Association. *Submission on Bill C-10: Safe Streets and Communities Act*. Ottawa: Canadian Bar Association, 2011. http://www.cba.org/cba/submissions/PDF/11-45-eng.pdf.

Canadian Feminist Alliance for International Action. *No Action: No Progress: Canadian Feminist Alliance for International Action Report on Canada's Progress in Implementing Priority Recommendations made by the United Nations Committee on the Elimination of Discrimination against Women in 2008*. Ottawa: CFAIA, 2010. http://www2.ohchr.org/english/bodies/cedaw/docs/ngos/NoActionNoProgress_CanadaFU.pdf.

Canadian Paediatric Society. *Are We Doing Enough? A Status Report on Canadian Public Policy and Child and Youth Health*. Ottawa: Canadian Paediatric Society, 2012. http://www.cps.ca/advocacy/StatusReport2012.pdf.

Chansonneuve, Deborah. *Addictive Behaviours among Aboriginal People in Canada*. Ottawa: Aboriginal Healing Foundation, 2007.

Chartrand, Larry N. *Maskikiwenow: The Métis Right to Health under the Constitution of Canada and under Selected International Human Rights Obligations*. Ottawa: National Aboriginal Health Organization, 2010. http://www.naho.ca/documents/metiscentre/english/2011_right_to_health.pdf.

Corrado, Raymond, and Irwin Cohen. *Mental Health Profiles for a Sample of British Columbia's Aboriginal Survivors of the Canadian Residential School System*. Ottawa: Aboriginal Healing Foundation, 2003.

Council of Canadian Academics. *Aboriginal Food Security in Northern Canada: An Assessment of the State of Knowledge*. Ottawa: Council of Canadian Academics, 2014. http://www.scienceadvice.ca/uploads/eng/assessments%20and%20publications%20and%20news%20releases/food%20security/foodsecurity_execsummen.pdf.

Crosscurrent Associates, Hay River. *Languages of the Land: A Resource Manual for Aboriginal Language Activists*. Yellowknife: NWT Literacy Council, 1999.

Devlin, Christopher, Leah DeForrest, and Caitlin Mason. "Jurisdictional Quagmire: First Nations Child Welfare as a Human Right." Devlin Gailus, Victoria, 2012. http://www.dgwlaw.ca/wp-content/uploads/2014/12/Child_Welfare_Human_Rights_Paper.pdf .

Environics Institute. *Urban Aboriginal Peoples Study: Main Report.* Toronto: Environics Institute, 2010. http://www.northcentralsharedfacility.ca/docs/Urban%20Aboriginal%20Peoples%20Study-Environics%202010.pdf.

First Nations Centre. *First Nations Regional Longitudinal Health Survey (RHS) 2002/03.* Ottawa: First Nations Centre, 2005.

First Nations Child & Family Caring Society of Canada. *Wen: De: We Are Coming to the Light of Day.* Ottawa: First Nations Child & Family Caring Society of Canada, 2005.

First Nations Education Council. "Funding Formula for First Nation Schools: The Instrument of a Detrimental Policy." FNEC, 2009. http://www.cepn-fnec.com/PDF/etudes_documents/fiche_complete_eng.pdf.

First Nations Education Council. "Paper on First Nations Education Funding." Wendake, QC: FNEC, 2009.

First Nations Education Council, Nishnawbe Aski Nation, and Federation of Saskatchewan Indian Nations. *Report on Priority Actions in View of Improving First Nations Education.* FNEC, NAN, and FSIN, 2011. http://www.fsin.com/index.php/downloads-education/708-report-on-priority-actions-in-view-of-improving-first-nations-education.

First Nations Information Governance Centre. *Regional Health Survey (RHS) Phase 2 (2008/10) Preliminary Results: Adult, Youth. Child.* Rev. ed. Ottawa: First Nations Information Governance Centre, 2011.

First Peoples' Heritage, Language and Cultures Council. *Report on the Status of B.C. First Nations Languages 2010.* Brentwood Bay, BC: First Peoples' Heritage, Language and Cultures Council, 2010.

Fletcher, Matthew. "The Origins of the Indian Child Welfare Act: A Survey of the Legislative History." Indigenous Law & Policy Center Occasional Paper Series, Occasional Paper 2009-04, 10 April 2009. https://www.law.msu.edu/indigenous/papers/2009-04.pdf.

Gendreau, P., T. Little, and C. Goggin. *A Meta-Analysis of the Predictors of Adult Offender Recidivism: What Works!* Ottawa: Public Works and Government Services Canada, 1996.

Gough, Pamela. "Alberta's Child Welfare System." CECW Information Sheet #46D. Faculty of Social Work, University of Toronto, Toronto, 2006. http://cwrp.ca/sites/default/files/publications/en/Altachildwelfaresystem46E.pdf.

Gough, Pamela. "Newfoundland and Labrador's Child Welfare System." CECW Information Sheet #49E, Faculty of Social Work, University of Toronto, 2007.

Gough, Pamela. "Northwest Territories' Child Welfare System." CECW Information Sheet #53E, Faculty of Social Work, University of Toronto, Toronto, 2007.

Gough, Pamela. "Nunavut's Child Welfare System." CECW Information Sheet #55E, Faculty of Social Work, University of Toronto, Toronto, 2007.

Haldane, Scott, George Lafond, Caroline Krause, and National Panel on First Nation Elementary and Secondary Education for Students on Reserve. *Nurturing the Learning Spirit of First Nation Students: The Report of the National Panel on First Nation Elementary and Secondary Education for Students on Reserve.* Ottawa: National Panel on First Nation Elementary and Secondary Education for Students on Reserve, 2012.

Health Council of Canada. *Empathy, Dignity and Respect: Creating Cultural Safety for Aboriginal People in Urban Health Care*. Toronto: Health Council of Canada, 2012. http://www.healthcouncilcanada.ca/tree/Aboriginal_Report_EN_web_final.pdf.

Highway of Tears Symposium. *Highway of Tears Symposium Recommendations Report: A Collective Voice For Victims Who Have Been Silenced*. 16 June 2006. http://highwayoftears.org/uploads/Highway%20of%20Tears%20Symposium%20Recommendations%20Report%20-%20January%202013.pdf.

Hodgson-Smith, Kathy. "The State of Métis Nation Learning." Canadian Council on Learning, 2005. http://www.ccl-cca.ca/pdfs/AbLKC/StateOfMetisNationLearning.pdf.

Hughes, Ted. *The Legacy of Phoenix Sinclair: Achieving the Best for All Our Children*. 2 vols. Winnipeg: Commission of Inquiry into the Death of Phoenix Sinclair, 2014.

Human Rights Watch. *Those Who Take Us Away: Abusive Policing and Failures in the Protection of Indigenous Women and Girls in Northern British Columbia, Canada*. New York: Human Rights Watch, 2013.

Inuit Qaujimajatuqanginnut (IQ) Task Force. *The First Annual Report of the Inuit Qaujimajatuqanginnut (IQ) Task Force*. August 2002. http://www.inukshukmanagement.ca/IQ%20Task%20Force%20Report1.pdf.

Inuit Tapiriit Kanatami. "Social Determinants of Inuit Health in Canada: A Discussion Paper." Inuit Tapiriit Kanatami, Ottawa, 22 April 2007. http://ahrnets.ca/files/2011/02/ITK_Social_Determinants_paper_2007.pdf.

Inuit Tapiriit Kanatami. *Social Determinants of Inuit Health in Canada*. Ottawa: Inuit Tapiriit Kanatami, 2014. https://www.itk.ca/publication/comprehensive-report-social-determinants-inuit-health-national-inuit-organization.

Inuit Tuttarvingat. *Inuit Men Talking about Health*. Ottawa: National Aboriginal Health Organization, 2008. http://www.naho.ca/documents/it/2008_Mens_Health.pdf.

Jackson, Randy, and Gwen Reimer. *Canadian Aboriginal People Living with HIV/AIDS: Care, Treatment and Support Issues*. Ottawa: Canadian Aboriginal AIDS Network, 2005. http://www.aboriginalaidsawareness.com/drafts2011/research-docs/Care%20Treatment%20and%20Support%20Document1.pdf.

Jacobs, Beverly, and Andrea J. Williams. "Legacy of Residential Schools: Missing and Murdered Women." In *From Truth to Reconciliation: Transforming the Legacy of Residential Schools*, edited by Marlene Brant Castellano, Linda Archibald, and Mike DeGagné, 121–138. Ottawa: Aboriginal Healing Foundation, 2008.

Jenness, Diamond. *America's Eskimos: Can They Survive?* Waterloo, ON: Waterloo Lutheran University, 1962.

Jenness, Diamond. "Eskimo Administration: II. Canada." Arctic Institute of Canada Technical Paper no. 14, May 1964.

John Howard Society of Alberta. *Offender Risk Assessment*. Edmonton: John Howard Society of Alberta, 2000. http://www.johnhoward.ab.ca/pub/C21.htm.

Kimelman, Edwin. *No Quiet Place: Final Report to the Honourable Muriel Smith, Minister of Community Services / Review Committee on Indian and Métis Adoptions and Placements*. Winnipeg: Manitoba Department of Community Services, 1985.

Kinnon, Dianne. *Improving Population Health, Health Promotion, Disease Prevention and Health Protection Services and Programs for Aboriginal People: Recommendations for NAHO Activities*. Ottawa: National Aboriginal Health Organization, 2002. http://www.naho.ca/documents/naho/english/pdf/research_pop_health.pdf.

Kirmayer, Laurence, Gregory Brass, Tara Holton, Ken Paul, Cori Simpson, and Caroline Tait. *Suicide among Aboriginal People in Canada*. Ottawa: Aboriginal Healing Foundation, 2007.

Kozlowski, Anna, Vandna Sinha, Tara Petti, and Elsie Flette. "First Nations Child Welfare in Manitoba, 2011." CWRP Information Sheet #97E. McGill University, Centre for Research on Children and Families, Montréal, 2012.

LaPrairie, Carole. *Examining Aboriginal Corrections in Canada*. Ottawa: Aboriginal Corrections, Ministry of the Solicitor General, 1996.

Legacy of Hope Foundation. *Inuit and the Residential School System*. Ottawa: Legacy of Hope Foundation, 2013. http://www.legacyofhope.ca/downloads/inuit-and-the-rss.pdf.

Legal Services Society of British Columbia. *Gladue Report Disbursement: Evaluation*. Vancouver: Legal Services Society of British Columbia, 2013.

Little Bear, Leroy. "Naturalizing Indigenous Knowledge, Synthesis Paper." Aboriginal Education Research Centre, University of Saskatchewan, Saskatoon; First Nations and Adult Higher Education Consortium, Calgary, 2009. http://www.ccl-cca.ca/pdfs/ablkc/naturalizeIndigenous_en.pdf.

Macdonald, David, and Daniel Wilson. P*overty or Prosperity: Indigenous Children in Canada*. Ottawa: Canadian Centre for Policy Alternatives, 2013.

Manitoba Metis Federation. *They Are Taking our Children from Us: An Inside Look at How the Manitoba Child and Family Service System Deals with Métis Children and Families; A Critical Review, Analysis and Recommendations*. Winnipeg: The Federation, 1999.

McCue, Harvey. "First Nations 2nd & 3rd Level Education Services: A Discussion Paper for the Joint Working Group INAC-AFN." Harvey McCue Consulting, 2006. http://www.afn.ca/uploads/files/education/9._2006_april_harvey_mccue_first_nations_2nd_&_3rd_level_services_paper.pdf.

McIvor, Onowa. *Language Nest Programs in BC: Early Childhood Immersion Programs in two First Nation communities*. Brentwood Bay, BC: First People's Cultural Council, 2006. http://www.fpcc.ca/files/PDF/language-nest-programs_in_BC.pdf.

Mendelson, Michael. "Improving Education on Reserves: A First Nations Education Authority Act." Caledon Institute of Public Policy, Ottawa, 2008. http://www.caledoninst.org/publications/pdf/684eng.pdf.

Métis National Council. *Toward a Canada–Métis Nation Economic Development Framework*. February 2009. http://www.metisportals.ca/ecodev/wp-content/uploads/MNC_EconomicDevelopmentFramewok(2009).pdf.

Métis Nation of Alberta. *Métis Memories of Residential Schools: A Testament to the Strength of the Métis*. Edmonton: Métis Nation of Alberta, 2004.

Métis Nation of Ontario. *Recommendations Concerning Métis-Specific Child and Family Services*. Toronto: Métis Nation of Ontario, 2012. http://www.metisnation.org/media/239001/mno_cfsrpt_2012-03-30_final.pdf.

Mishibinijima, Lori. *Aboriginal Child Protection Alternative Dispute Resolution*. Toronto: Aboriginal Legal Services of Toronto, 2006.

National Aboriginal Health Organization. *An Overview of Traditional Knowledge and Medicine and Public Health in Canada*. Ottawa: National Aboriginal Health Organization, January 2008. http://www.naho.ca/documents/naho/publications/tkOverviewPublicHealth.pdf.

National Collaborating Centre for Aboriginal Health. *Looking for Aboriginal Health in Legis-lation and Policies, 1970 to 2008: The Policy Synthesis Project.* Prince George, BC: National Collaborating Centre for Aboriginal Health, 2011.

National Collaborating Centre for Aboriginal Health. *Child and Youth Health: Child Welfare Services in Canada: Aboriginal and Mainstream.* Prince George, BC: National Collaborating Centre for Aboriginal Health, 2009–2010.

National Committee on Inuit Education. *First Canadians, Canadians First: National Strategy on Inuit Education.* Ottawa: Inuit Tapiriit Kanatami, 2011. https://www.itk.ca/sites/default/files/National-Strategy-on-Inuit-Education-2011_0.pdf.

National Indian Brotherhood. *Indian Control of Indian Education: Policy Paper Presented to the Minister of Indian Affairs and Northern Development.* Ottawa: The National Indian Brotherhood, 1972.

Native Women's Association of Canada. "Fact Sheet: Missing and Murdered Aboriginal Women and Girls." Native Women's Association of Canada, Akwesasne, ON, 2010. http://www.nwac.ca/wp-content/uploads/2015/05/Fact_Sheet_Missing_and_Murdered_Aborigi-nal_Women_and_Girls.pdf.

Native Women's Association of Canada. *Voices of Our Sisters in Spirit: A Report to Fam-ilies and Communities.* 2nd ed., March 2009. http://www.nwac.ca/wp-content/up-loads/2015/05/2009_Voices_of_Our_SIS_A_Report_to_Families_and_Communities.pdf.

Native Women's Association of Canada. *What Their Stories Tell Us: Research for the Sisters in Spirit Initiative.* Ohsweken, ON: Native Women's Association of Canada, 2010. http://www.nwac.ca/wp-content/uploads/2015/07/2010-What-Their-Stories-Tell-Us-Research-Findings-SIS-Initiative.pdf.

Nuu-chah-nulth Tribal Council. *Indian Residential Schools: The Nuu-chah-nulth Experi-ence.* Port Alberni, BC: Nuu-chah-nulth Tribal Council, 1996.

Ospina, Maria, and Liz Dennett. *Systematic Review on the Prevalence of Fetal Alcohol Spec-trum Disorders.* Edmonton: Institute of Health Economics, 2013.

Pauktuutit Inuit Women of Canada. *The Inuit Way: A Guide to Inuit Culture.* N.p.: Pauktuutit Inuit Women of Canada, 2006. http://www.uqar.ca/files/boreas/inuitway_e.pdf.

People for Education. *First Nations, Metis and Inuit Education: Overcoming Gaps in Pro-vincially Funded Schools.* Toronto: People for Education, 2013. http://www.peoplefored-ucation.ca/wp-content/uploads/2013/10/First-Nations-M%C3%A9tis-and-Inuit-Educa-tion-2013.pdf.

Phaneuf, G., P. Dudding, and J. Arreak. *Nunavut Social Service Review: Final Report.* Ottawa: Child Welfare League of Canada, 2011.

Presbyterian Church in Canada Archives. "Brief Administrative History of the Residential Schools and the Presbyterian Church in Canada's Healing and Reconciliation Efforts." Sep-tember 2010. www.presbyterian.ca/?wpdmdl=94.

Quinn, Ashley, and Michael Saini. *Touchstones of Hope: Participatory Action Research to Explore Experiences of First Nation Communities in Northern British Columbia: Evaluation Report.* Toronto: Factor-Inwentash Faculty of Social Work, University of Toronto, 2012.

Rae, Lisa. *Inuit Child Welfare and Family Support: Policies, Programs and Strategies.* Ottawa: National Aboriginal Health Organization, 2011. http://www.naho.ca/documents/it/2011_Inuit_Child_Welfare_Family_Support.pdf.

Reimer, Gwen, Amy Bombay, Lena Ellsworth, Sara Fryer, and Tricia Logan. *The* Indian Residential Schools Settlement Agreement's *Common Experience Payment and Healing: A Qualitative Study Exploring Impacts on Recipients.* Ottawa: Aboriginal Healing Foundation, 2010.

Richards, John, Jennifer Hove, and Kemi Afolabi. "Understanding the Aboriginal/Non-Aboriginal Gap in Student Performance: Lessons from British Columbia." C.D. Howe Institute, Toronto, 2008. https://www.cdhowe.org/sites/default/files/attachments/research_papers/mixed/commentary_276.pdf.

Schibler, Billie, and James H. Newton. *Honouring Their Spirits: The Child Death Review: A Report to the Minister of Family Services and Housing.* Winnipeg: Office of the Children's Advocate, 2006. http://www.childrensadvocate.mb.ca/wp-content/uploads/Child-Death-Review-2006.pdf.

Sharpe, Andrew, and Simon Lapointe. *The Labour Market and Economic Performance of Canada's First Nations Reserves: The Role of Educational Attainment and Remoteness CSLS Research Report 2011-05.* Ottawa: Centre for the Study of Living Standards, 2011. http://www.csls.ca/reports/csls2011-05.pdf.

Sinha, Vandna, Nico Trocmé, Barbara Fallon, Bruce MacLaurin, Elizabeth Fast, Shelley Thomas Prokop, et al. *Kiskisik Awasisak: Remember the Children: Understanding the Over-Representation of First Nations Children in the Child Welfare System.* Ontario: Assembly of First Nations, 2011.

Smylie, Janet. "A Guide for Health Professionals Working with Aboriginal Peoples: Cross Cultural Understanding." SOGC Policy Statement, no. 100, February 2001. http://sogc.org/wp-content/uploads/2013/01/100E-PS4-February2001.pdf.

Stout, Roberta, and Sheryl Peters. *kiskinohamâtôtâpânâsk: Inter-generational Effects on Professional First Nations Women Whose Mothers Are Residential School Survivors.* Winnipeg: Prairie Women's Health Centre of Excellence, August 2011.

Tagalik, Shirley. "Inuit Qaujimajatuqangit: The Role of Indigenous Knowledge in Supporting Wellness in Inuit Communities in Nunavut." National Collaborating Centre for Aboriginal Health, Prince George, BC, 2010. http://www.nccah-ccnsa.ca/docs/fact%20sheets/child%20and%20youth/Inuit%20IQ%20EN%20web.pdf.

Tagalik, Shirley. "Inunnguiniq: Caring for Children the Inuit Way." National Collaborating Centre for Aboriginal Health, Prince George, BC, 2010. http://www.nccah-ccnsa.ca/docs/fact%20sheets/child%20and%20youth/Inuit%20caring%20EN%20web.pdf.

Tagalik, Shirley. "Inutsiaqpagutit—That Which Enables You to Have a Good Life: Supporting Inuit Early Life Health." National Collaborating Centre for Aboriginal Health, Prince George, BC, 2010. http://www.nccah-ccnsa.ca/Publications/Lists/Publications/Attachments/5/Have%20a%20Good%20Life%20-%20Supporting%20Inuit%20Early%20Life%20Health%20(English%20-%20web).pdf.

Tait, Caroline L. *Fetal Alcohol Syndrome among Aboriginal People in Canada: Review and Analysis of the Intergenerational Links to Residential Schools.* Ottawa: Aboriginal Healing Foundation, 2003.

United Nations. Committee on Economic, Social and Cultural Rights. "Consideration of Reports Submitted by States Parties under Articles 16 and 17 of the Covenant: Concluding Observations of the Committee on Economic, Social and Cultural Rights." E/C.12/CAN/CO/5, May 2006.

United Nations. Committee on the Rights of the Child. *Commentary 11: Indigenous Children and Their Rights Under the Convention.* Geneva: UN, 2009.

United Nations. Committee on the Rights of the Child. "Concluding Observations on the Combined Third And Fourth Periodic Report of Canada, Adopted by the Committee at Its Sixty-First Session (17 September – 5 October 2012)." CRC/C/CAN/CO/3-4, 2012.

United Nations. Expert Mechanism on the Rights of Indigenous Peoples. "Advice No. 1: On the Right of Indigenous Peoples to Education." Geneva: UN, 2009.

United Nations General Assembly. *Convention on the Prevention and Punishment of the Crime of Genocide.* 9 December 1948. https://treaties.un.org/doc/Publication/UNTS/Volume%2078/volume-78-I-1021-English.pdf

United Nations General Assembly. *Convention on the Rights of the Child.* 20 November 1989. United Nations, *Treaty Series*, vol. 1577, p. 3, articles 3, 5, 18, 25 and 27 (3). United Nations General Assembly. *Declaration of Basic Principles of Justice for Victims of Crime and Abuse of Power.* 29 November 1985, A/RES/40/34. http://www.refworld.org/docid/3b00f2275b.html.

United Nations General Assembly. *Report of the Special Rapporteur on the Rights of Indigenous Peoples, James Anaya, on the Situation of Indigenous Peoples in Canada.* United Nations Human Rights Council, 27th Session, A/HRC/27/52/Add.2. 4 July 2014. http://unsr.jamesanaya.org/docs/countries/2014-report-canada-a-hrc-27-52-add-2-en.pdf.

United Nations General Assembly. *United Nations Declaration on the Rights of Indigenous Peoples.* A/RES/61/295, adopted by the General Assembly 2 October 2007. http://www.un.org/esa/socdev/unpfii/documents/DRIPS_en.pdf.

United Nations. High Commissioner for Human Rights. *Discrimination against Women, Concluding Observations on Canada's 7th review*, November 2008, CEDAW/C/CAN/CO/7. http://www2.ohchr.org/english/bodies/cedaw/cedaws42.htm.

United Nations. Human Rights Committee. *Concluding Observations of the Human Rights Committee: Canada,* April 2006, CCPR/C/CAN/CO/5. http://www.refworld.org/pdfid/453777a50.pdf.

Wilson, Daniel, and David Macdonald. *The Income Gap between Aboriginal Peoples and the Rest of Canada.* Ottawa: Canadian Centre for Policy Alternatives, 2010.

# 4. Websites

Canadian Conference of Catholic Bishops. "Pope Benedict XVI Meets with Representatives of Former Indian Residential School Students and the Church in Canada." *Canadian Conference of Catholic Bishops.* Accessed 11 August 2015. http://www.cccb.ca/site/eng/church-in-canada-and-world/catholic-church-in-canada/indigenous-peoples/3203-pope-benedict-xvi-meets-with-representatives-of-former-indian-residential-school-students-and-the-church-in-canada.

First Nations Child & Family Caring Society of Canada. "I Am a Witness: Canadian Human Rights Tribunal Hearing." http://www.fncaringsociety.ca/i-am-witness-timeline-and-documents.

Indian Residential Schools Adjudication Secretariat. "Who We Are and What We Do." Accessed 9 August 2015. http://www.iap-pei.ca/us-nous/us-nous-eng.php#sthash.vkjx05c0.dpuf.

Kativik School Board. "About Kativik School Board." Accessed 10 August 2015. http://www. kativik.qc.ca/about-kativik-school-board.

Manitoba Historical Society. "Memorable Manitobans: Robert Alexander Hoey (1883–1965)." Accessed 21 December 2013. http://www.mhs.mb.ca/docs/people/hoey_ra.shtml.

Manitoba Metis Federation. "Departments, Portfolios and Affiliates: Metis Child and Family Services." Accessed 9 August 2015. http://www.mmf.mb.ca/departments_portfolios_and_affiliates_details.php?id=22.

Merchant Law Group. "Indian and Metis Scoop Class Action." Accessed 7 November 2013. https://www.merchantlaw.com/classactions/scoop.php.

Métis National Council. "Who Are the Métis: Citizenship." Accessed 4 April 2013. http://www. metisnation.ca/index.php/who-are-the-metis/citizenship.

Mississaugas of the New Credit First Nation. "Special Education Human Rights Case: About the Case." Accessed 26 October 2013. http://www.firstnationsspecialeducation.ca/about-the-case/.

National Indian Child Welfare Association. "Indian Child Welfare Act of 1978." NICWA. Accessed 8 August 2015. http://www.nicwa.org/Indian_Child_Welfare_Act/.

Ogwehoweh Skills and Trades Training Centre. OSTTC homepage. Accessed 10 August 2015. http://www.osttc.com/.

Ontario. Ministry of Community and Social Services. "Aboriginal Health and Wellness Strategy." Accessed 18 March 2012. http://www.mcss.gov.on.ca/en/mcss/programs/community/programsforaboriginalpeople.aspx/programs/hacc.html.

Signs of Safety. *Signs of Safety: Simplifying Child Protection Complexity*. Accessed 9 August 2015. http://www.signsofsafety.net/signs-of-safety/.

United Church of Canada. "The Healing Fund, Criteria for Healing Fund Projects." Accessed 12 August 2015. http://www.united-church.ca/funding/healing/grantcriteria.

Yellowquill College. "Programs." Accessed 10 August 2015. http://yellowquill.org/programs.

# 5. Newspapers and Broadcast Media

Barrera, Jorge. "Valcourt Used Unreleased RCMP Data to claim Aboriginal MEN Responsible for Majority of Murders of Aboriginal Women: Chiefs." *APTN*, 25 March 2015. http://aptn.ca/news/2015/03/25/chiefs-say-valcourt-used-unreleased-rcmp-data-claim-indigenous-men-responsible-majority-indigenous-women-murders/.

Beeby, Dean. "Aboriginal Affairs Spending Shortfall Amounts to $1B, Internal Document Says." *CBC News*, 5 June 2015. www.cbc.ca/news/politics/aboriginal-affairs-spending-shortfall-amounts-to-1b-internal-document-says-1.3100937.

Burnouf, Larissa. "Marlene Bird Talks about Being Attacked and Her Struggle Since." *APTN*, 10 October 2014. http://aptn.ca/news/2014/10/10/marlene-bird-talks-attacked-struggle-since.

Canada, Rob Nicholson, Vic Toews, Jason Kenney, and Senator Pierre-Hugues Boisvenu. "Statement of the Government of Canada on the Royal Assent of Bill C-10." *Reuters.com,* 13 March 2012.

Canadian Press. "Winnipeg Police Officer Suspended without Pay in Tina Fontaine Case." *The Star* (Toronto), 24 March 2015. http://www.thestar.com/news/canada/2015/03/24/winnipeg-police-officer-suspended-without-pay-in-tina-fontaine-case.html.

CBC News. "'I Am Sorry,' NWT Bishop Tells Dene Residential School Survivors." 28 May 2009. http://www.cbc.ca/news/canada/north/story/2009/05/28/catholic-dene-apology.html.

CBC News. "Illustrations Tell Story Of Marlene Bird, Homeless Woman Beaten and Set on Fire." 20 January 2015. http://www.cbc.ca/news/multimedia/illustrations-tell-story-of-marlene-bird-homeless-woman-beaten-and-set-on-fire-1.2919832.

CBC News. "Pope Expresses 'Sorrow' for Abuse at Residential Schools." 29 April 2009. http://www.cbc.ca/news/world/story/2009/04/29/pope-first-nations042909.html.

Curry, Bill. "Aboriginals in Canada Face 'Third World' Level Risk of Tuberculosis." *Globe and Mail*, 10 March 2010. http://www.theglobeandmail.com/news/national/aboriginals-in-canada-face-third-world-level-risk-of-tuberculosis/article4352641/.

Gajewski, Karen Ann. "A Class-Action Lawsuit Has Been Filed by South Dakota Parents and Tribes over Unlawful Separation of Children from Their Families." *The Humanist*, May–June 2013.

Galloway, Gloria. "70 Per Cent of Murdered Aboriginal Women Killed by Indigenous Men: RCMP." *Globe and Mail*, 9 April 2015. http://www.theglobeandmail.com/news/politics/70-per-cent-of-murdered-aboriginal-women-killed-by-indigenous-men-rcmp-confirms/article23868927/.

Gatehouse, Jonathan. "The Residential Schools Settlement Biggest Winner: A Profile of Tony Merchant." *Maclean's*, 11 September 2006. Rpt. *macleans.ca*, 4 April 2013. http://www2.macleans.ca/2013/04/04/white-mans-windfall-a-profile-of-tony-merchant/.

Gregoire, Lisa. "Marius Tungilik: Inuit Leader, Whistleblower and Public Servant, Dead at 55." *Nunatsiaq Online*, 22 December 2012. http://www.nunatsiaqonline.ca/stories/article/65674marius_tungilik_inuit_leader_whistleblower_and_public_servant_dead_at_.

Gyorgy, Jane. "Bishop's Apology Falls Flat: Former Students Want Public Inquiry into Abuse at Chesterfield Inlet School." *Gazette* (Montréal), 25 July 1993. E8.

Henton, Darcy. "Deaths of Aboriginal Children in Care No 'Fluke of Statistics." *Edmonton Journal*, 8 January 2014. http://www.edmontonjournal.com/life/Deaths+Alberta+aboriginal+children+care+fluke+statistics/9212384/story.html.

Howard, Ross. "Probes Document Abuse at NWT Church Schools Inuit Students Were Powerless to Stop Assaults 25 Years Ago by Clergy, Teachers." *Globe and Mail*, 28 June 1995.

Kennedy, Mark. "Rinelle Harper Calls for Missing Women Inquiry, Urges Forgiveness." *Ottawa Citizen*, 9 December 2014. http://ottawacitizen.com/news/politics/rinelle-harper-calls-for-missing-women-inquiry-urges-forgiveness.

Kraus, Sarah. "Merchant Law Group in Legal Battle of Its Own." *Global News*, 30 January 2015. http://globalnews.ca/news/1804029/merchant-law-group-in-legal-battle-of-its-own/.

Makin, Kirk. "Aboriginal Sentencing Rules Ignored Due to Lack of Funding, Interest." *Globe and Mail*, 19 November 2012. http://www.theglobeandmail.com/news/politics/aboriginal-sentencing-rules-ignored-due-to-lack-of-funding-interest/article5459491/#.

McLintock, Barbara. "He Finally Confesses: Roman Catholic Bishop Apologizes for His Sins, and a Proud Native Woman Can Start Putting The Past behind Her." *The Province* (Vancouver), 18 June 1998.

Moon, Peter. "Hundreds of Cree and Ojibwa Children Violated." *Globe and Mail*, 19 October 1996.

Murphy, David. "Pauktuutit Wants Action on Violence against Inuit Women, but Ottawa Denies Funding." *Nunatsiaq Online*, 28 February 2014. http://www.nunatsiaqonline.ca/stories/article/65674inuit_womens_organization_shut_out_of_funding_again/.

Neel, David. "Two Faces of Justice." *The Province* (Vancouver), 17 December 1992.

Palmater, Pamela. "RCMP Report on Murdered and Missing Aboriginal Women is Statistically Skewed." *Rabble.ca*, 13 April 2015. http://rabble.ca/blogs/bloggers/pamela-palmater/2015/04/rcmp-report-on-murdered-and-missing-aboriginal-women-statisti.

Picard, Andre. "Harper's Disregard for Aboriginal Health." *Globe and Mail*, 10 September 2012.

Porter, Jody. "Walls Crumble, Mould Infects First Nation School." *CBC News*, 19 April 2012. http://www.cbc.ca/news/canada/thunder-bay/story/2012/04/19/tby-mouldy-school.html.

Rideout, Denise. "Commission Considers Rules for Custom Adoptions: Nunavummiut Seek Balance Between Legal Regulations and Longstanding Tradition." *Nunatsiaq News*, 8 December 2000. http://www.nunatsiaqonline.ca/archives/nunavut001231/nvt21208_11.html.

Skelton, Chad, and Linsay Kines. "School Abuse Queries Overwhelm RCMP: The Force's Ability To Bring Suspects to Trial Is Being Impaired, a Senior Officer Argues." *Vancouver Sun*, 11 February 2000. A5.

Staniforth, Jesse B. "Where Did Aboriginal Affairs Put That Missing $1 Billion?" *The Nation* (Eeyou Istchee), 26 June 2015. www.nationnews.ca/where-did-aboriginal-affairs-put-that-missing-1-billion/.

Taylor, Glenn. "Grollier Meeting Emotional." *Northern News Services Online*, 23 January 1998. http://www.nnsl.com/frames/newspapers/1998-01/jan23_98grol.html.

Treble, Patricia, and Jane O'Hara. "Residential Church School Scandal." *Maclean's*, 26 June 2000. Rpt. in *The Canadian Encyclopedia*, 17 March 2013. http://www.thecanadianencyclopedia.ca/en/article/residential-church-school-scandal/.

*Vancouver Sun.* "Bishop O'Connor Diverted." 18 June 1998. Reproduced at *Vancouver Rape Relief and Women's Shelter*, http://www.rapereliefshelter.bc.ca/learn/news/bishop-oconnor-diverted.

## 6. Theses and Dissertations

Canada, Deborah. "The Strength of the Sash: The Métis People and the British Columbia Child Welfare System." PhD diss., University of British Columbia, Vancouver, 2012. https://circle.ubc.ca/bitstream/handle/2429/42150/ubc_2012_spring_canada_deborah.pdf?sequence=1.

Carrière, Jeannine. "Connectedness and Health for First Nation Adoptees." PhD diss., University of Alberta, Edmonton, 2005.

Pearce, Maryanne. "An Awkward Silence: Missing and Murdered Vulnerable Women and the Canadian Justice System." PhD diss., University of Ottawa, Faculty of Law, 2013.

## 7. Other

Aboriginal Healing Foundation. List of Contacts for Healing Centres. Accessed 23 March 2012. http://www.ahf.ca/downloads/updated-list-of-healing-centres.pdf.

Anglican Church of Canada. "Anglican Healing Fund, Granting Criteria." Accessed 12 August 2015. http://www.anglican.ca/healingfund/criteria/.

Atleo, Shawn. "First Nations Control of First Nations Education Announcement and Federal Budget 2014." Assembly of First Nations, Communiqué from Grand Chief Shawn Atleo, February 2014. http://www.afn.ca/uploads/files/14-02-14_nc_bulletin_fn_education_announcement_and_budget_2014_fe.pdf.

Blackstock, Cindy, Andrea Auger, Heather Ochalski, Jeannine Carrière, Sinéad Charbonneau, and Cathy Richardson. "Is It Over Yet? Residential Schools, Child Welfare and the Mass Removals of First Nations, Inuit and Métis Children from Their Families." Unpublished paper submitted to the Truth and Reconciliation Commission, April 2013.

Canada. Bank of Canada. Inflation Calculator. Accessed 15 May 2015. http://www.bankofcanada.ca/rates/related/inflation-calculator/.

Elizabeth Fry Society. "Discrimination against Aboriginal Women Rampant in Federal Prisons Claims the Native Women's Association of Canada." Press release, 14 May 2003. http://www.caefs.ca/wp-content/uploads/2013/04/nwac1.pdf.

Indian Residential Schools Adjudication Secretariat. "Observations on Residential School Experience Data Obtained from Claims Concluded under the Independent Adjudication Process (IAP)." Unpublished report, 27 March 2015.

Human Rights Commission Complaint Form, filed against Indian and Northern Affairs Canada by Regional Chief Lawrence Joseph and Cindy Blackstock. Accessed 8 August 2015. http://www.fncaringsociety.com/sites/default/files/Caring%20Society_AFN%20HR%20complaint%202007.pdf.

Missionary Oblates of Mary Immaculate. "An Apology to the First Nations of Canada by the Oblate Conference of Canada." 24 July 1991. Accessed 8 March 2015. http://www.cccb.ca/site/images/stories/pdf/oblate_apology_english.pdf.

National Aboriginal Health Organization. "Announcement." 5 April 2012. http://www.naho.ca/wp-content/uploads/2012/04/NAHO-Announcement-5-APR-12.pdf.

Obomsawin, Alanis, dir. *Richard Cardinal, Cry from a Diary of a Métis Child*. Montréal: National Film Board of Canada, 1985.

Ochalski, Heather. "Addressing Inuit Child Welfare in Canada: Traditional Inuit Parenting Methods, Impact of European Contact, and Contemporary Challenges Facing Inuit Child Welfare." Notes from 2012 focus group. In "Is It Over Yet?" by Blackstock et al.

The Presbyterian Church. "The Confession of the Presbyterian Church as Adopted by the General Assembly, June 9th, 1994." *Remembering the Children*. Last modified 8 September 2008. http://www.rememberingthechildren.ca/press/pcc-confession.htm.

United Church of Canada. "Apology to First Nations People." *United Church Social Policy Positions*. United Church of Canada, 1986. Accessed 8 March 2015. http://www.united-church.ca/beliefs/policies/1986/a651.

United Church of Canada. "Fall 2013 Healing Fund Grants." Accessed 21 May 2015. http://www.united-church.ca/files/funding/healing/grants_2013-fall.pdf.